It's All Relative

Also by J. M. Snyder

published by iUniverse.com

OPERATION STARSEED

SCARRED: FOUR NOVELLAS

POWER PLAY

published by Lulu Press

VINCE

BONES OF THE SEA

Look for them at your favorite independent gay bookstore or visit www.jmsnyder.net for purchasing information.

It's All Relative

by J.M. Snyder

Lulu Press
Morrisville

IT'S ALL RELATIVE

Lulu Press
affiliated with Lulu Enterprises

For information address:
Lulu Enterprises
3131 RDU Center Drive
Suite 210
Morrisville, NC 27560
www.lulu.com

Printed in the United States of America

For Bobbi. I miss you.

Table of Contents

Author's Note

WHILE THERE IS actually a city called Sugarcreek in Pennsylvania, I have never been there, and the town in this book by the same name is entirely fictional. As far as I know, none of the landmarks or businesses I mention in the story exist in the "real" Sugarcreek, with the possible exception of Wawa (which are spreading up and down the east coast, it seems). The other cities mentioned in the story — Franklin and Union City in Pennsylvania, Fort Myer, Fort Detrick, Fort Lee, Baltimore, and of course Washington, DC — are also real and again, fictionalized here. Just to clear the record, I realize that nobody does basic training at Fort Lee, Virginia. As I understand, it's mostly home to the quartermaster corps, but it suited the story to move that function to the more northern Fort Myer.

Though the characters in this story do not resemble anyone that I am aware of, living or dead, I must admit that the basis of this story started in 1997, when my grandmother passed away. I just knew there was a story hidden somewhere in the family drama and anxiety that surrounded the days preceding her funeral, and I must apologize to anyone I may unintentionally offend in the telling of this tale. I know it's a bit sappy in parts, a bit over the top in others, but it's a fun ride and I think — I *hope* — you'll enjoy it.

That said, I must thank my friend Billy for his role as ubiquitous beta reader (don't worry, that's not a bad thing). Also, I must thank my brother Patrick and my friend Hilary from my writers' group for their help in honing the first few chapters. They didn't get much farther than that, though, since the sex made them uneasy. Fortunately I decided to nix my brother's suggestion of removing all the sex from the story, since that's a large part of it, and what people really like to read.

Finally, I want to thank my readers for their patience in waiting for this book to be published. I mentioned it on my website over a year ago, but couldn't get it edited in time to print it that autumn. Well, your wait is over. I hope it was worth it. Thanks for reading.

J.M. Snyder, October 4th, 2004

1: Dinner

I T'S SATURDAY NIGHT, the first time I've sat down to dinner with my parents since the day after Christmas the year before, and I'm so nervous, I can't eat the food on my plate. Pot roast and boiled potatoes, green beans, cornbread stuffing, everything looks so good but I can't taste it. Dan sits to my right. Beneath the table, his knee rests against mine, a small comfort. Tonight I'll lie beside him in my childhood bed and tell him how much worse this would've been if he hadn't been there beside me. Already my hands ache to stroke over the bristles along the back of his head, and in the mirror that hangs above the credenza across from me, I admire his buzz cut, the top of his hair sheared dark. The Army keeps it that way. He looks up from something Caitlin is saying to look at my reflection and when our eyes meet, he winks at me.

Caitlin doesn't catch the gesture. My sister, sixteen going on twenty-nine, wears more makeup than most drag queens. Her hair is dyed so dark, it absorbs the light, and silver earrings run up the length of both her ears. She wears nothing but black — black jeans with a pattern of studs along the cuffs, black shirts with ripped necklines, a black jacket with silver chains draped from one pocket around her back to the other. When I walked in the front door a few hours ago, I stared at the Goth girl who had taken over my little sister's body, the pierced eyebrow, the pierced tongue that she stuck out at me from behind my mother's back as I was hugged in greeting. "It's Cat," she said, before I could even say hello. She crossed her arms and glared as if daring me to touch her, and with a jerk of her head to indicate Dan, she asked, "Who's soldier boy?"

It's the hair, I'm telling you, people see it and just know a cut that bad has to be military-enforced. He didn't wear anything overt, no *ARMY* sweatshirt, no fatigues, but he still looks every inch the soldier. It's his muscular build: nice arms, thick thighs, a tapered waist and barrel chest, tight abs and a tighter ass that his jeans frame nicely. I could see my sister checking him out, despite her disinterested act. *My lover,* I should've said then. Everyone was there, both parents, Caitlin, my older brother Raymond, who for some reason still lives at home. I could've just answered her truthfully and gotten it out of the way. *This is Daniel Biggs,* I could've said. *My boyfriend. Oh wait, you didn't know?*

Only it didn't quite come out that way — I stumbled over the word *roommate* and my sister shrugged like she didn't care. "Mom thought you were finally bringing home a girl," she remarked, then turned and left. As she trotted up the steps to her bedroom, she called back over her shoulder, "I told her not to get her hopes up."

At the time, my mother just laughed in that nervous way she has that is anything but funny. I expect I'll hear that laugh again tonight, when I finally gather up my courage and spit out the reason why I've come home. The reflection I see in the mirror behind my parents bolsters me: it shows the man Dan must see when he looks my way, intelligent eyes behind small wire-thin glasses that give me a professional appearance, blonde highlights streaked through casual, wavy hair that frame my face in a boyishly attractive way. Confident, sure. In love. I can do this.

But when I look around the table, I feel my nerve slip away. My dad is on the other side of Caitlin, *Cat,* shoveling food into his mouth and glancing past me every few minutes to the television in the other room as if I'm invisible. Twenty-five and somehow when he looks through me like that, I'm all of eight again, racking my brains for a way to get his attention, good or bad, anything to prove that I exist. When he looked up the first time, I gave him a tight grin, sure he would ask about school or the firm, but he didn't. I watch him closely, taking in his thinning salt-and-pepper hair, the deep lines on his face, his battered hands and dirty nails — he's a mechanic, self-employed since the layoffs at the plant left him without a job, and already scowling from the few beers in his system. I'm afraid of what he'll have to say when I tell him.

But to be honest, it's my mom who scares me the most. She sits beside Dad with a smile plastered to her face, and she's chattering about a girl she ran into at the grocery the other day, "Mary Margaret what's-her-face, didn't you go to school with her?" She nibbles at her food and laughs, pats her dyed orange hair like it might have somehow slipped out of place, then spears the beans on her plate with a vendetta. "She's grown up pretty, that girl, and she's un*married*, Michael. I told her you were coming in this weekend and she asked about you —"

"I wish you wouldn't do that, Mom," I mutter. From the sound of it, she has this Mary Margaret waiting in the kitchen with dessert.

"Wouldn't do what?" she asks. There's that laugh again, like she doesn't know what I could possibly be talking about. "She's a friendly girl, real pretty, works at the orthopedist's across from the deli."

The deli, meaning the tiny sandwich shop where Ray works. He's twenty-eight and a night cook — "night *manager,*" to hear him tell it, but there's only one other person there in the evenings and she's almost half his age. Whenever my classes threaten to drag me down, I think of my brother and pray to *God* that I'm never that bad. The fact that he moved out of the basement to the room above the garage this past summer is a big deal to him. "My own entrance," he said, showing off his digs earlier. "You know, like the Fonz? On my own, man. On my own." He doesn't even own a car, still rides a bicycle to work. Twenty-eight. Already balding, too, I hope I don't have that gene.

Throughout dinner he's sat beside me, an eerie imitation of Dad, elbows on the table as he leans over his plate to snarf up his food. At the mention of Mary Margaret, his ears prick up, and he narrows his eyes as he asks Mom, "Who's this again?"

From across the table, Caitlin rolls her eyes. "No one interested in you," she tells him.

Ray glares at her, suddenly twelve years old. "I didn't ask *you,*" he growls, and beneath the table, I feel a small foot kick out past my leg to connect with his shin. "Ow! Mom —"

"Caitlin, don't," my mother warns.

"It's *Cat,*" my sister replies.

With an embarrassed duck of my head, I half-turn to Dan and whisper, "Welcome to hell." I almost forgot how wonderful these family dinners could be. I knew there was a reason I didn't come home more often.

Dan raises his glass of water to hide the smirk that tugs at his lips — pretty lips, well defined, almost heart-shaped when he smiles. He rarely smiles. When we first met, I thought he was just another hard-nosed grunt, but it's shyness that makes him seem so aloof and distant. Once I dug past the hardened Army exterior, I found a soft, wonderful boy inside, and even now I can look into his dark eyes and see my lover peering out. *Tonight,* I think, after this dinner is over, after the coffee and the cake and whatever else my mother has planned for this evening. Tonight, in the darkness of my old bedroom, he'll hold me the way he does that makes everything alright again, his breath faint in my ear, his hands flat against my stomach, his legs entwined with mine.

But first, we have to get through this. When my mom starts in on the girl again — "Wasn't she in your math class?" she asks, frowning at me as if she's *sure* I'll swoon once I remember just which Mary Margaret she means. "Fourth grade, Mrs. Lingenfelter's class, sat in the last row. I'm almost sure that's her." — I clear my throat and look around, and before I can even think of how I'm going to put it, I tell them all, "I have something to say."

Mom stops in midsentence. Dad's gaze flickers from the weather report to me, then back again. Ray's still glowering at Caitlin, who glances at our parents to make sure they're not watching her before she sticks her tongue out at him, far enough so that we all get a glimpse of the thick silver ball rammed through the middle of it. But our parents don't notice it — Dad's glued to the TV and Mom's watching me, waiting. Beside me, Dan sets his silverware down, wipes his mouth neatly with a corner of his napkin, then folds the cloth into his lap. He knows what's coming — we went over it in the car all the way here. Beneath the table, his hand squeezes my thigh.

I've played it out a million different ways in my mind. I've rehearsed this moment until the words rest on the tip of my tongue like the stud that pierces my sister's. I could be witty about it, or solemn, or nonchalant. I could blow it off like it's no big deal, or get all teary-eyed and break down, or beat around the bush about the whole thing. I'm running the show here. Everyone's waiting on me.

I slip a hand beneath the table and take Dan's, my fingers folding over his for strength. I love him, he loves me. That won't change, regardless of whatever I say to my parents, whatever they have to say to me. He loves me. Taking a deep breath, I look at my brother, my sister, my dad, my lover in the mirror behind my parents, but it's my mom's face that I concentrate on, it's her eyes that I stare into — the others disappear and she's the only one I see. My throat is dry, my tongue thick, my lips chapped. "I'm …"

My voice cracks and Dan's hand tightens in mine. When I try again, I squeak like nails on a chalkboard. "Mom?" She nods, a faint ghost of a smile on her face, as if she's sure she'll love whatever news I have for her, she just knows it, so she's getting her happy face ready to put on. Only the smile never fully materializes. "I know you mean well, but I'm really not interested in … this girl. I'm —" I look at Dan, his high and tight hair dark above his eyes, and he nods at me to continue. "I already have someone. Dan."

Dad's eyes focus on me — finally, he sees *me*. He looks at me the way he looks at the TV, like any minute something interesting might happen and he doesn't want to miss it. I give him a grin that he doesn't return, and when I glance at my mother, her face has turned ashen, her eyes wide in her head. She stares at Dan as if he's just insulted her and she hasn't quite recovered from the affront.

My brother looks at me, at Dan, back at me again, then leans close and asks in a loud whisper, "So what, you like it up the ass?"

"Raymond!" my mom snaps. Her knuckles have gone white where she grips her fork, and when she attacks the food on her plate, I get the distinct impression that she wishes it were me beneath her angry hand.

Only Caitlin doesn't look impressed. "I *knew* you were a fag," she mutters, twirling one finger sardonically. "Jeez, where the hell have you people been?"

Before Mom can reply, Dad speaks up. "Caitlin," he says, still staring at me like I'm going to spout the stock reports in a minute, "go to your room."

"What'd I say?" she wants to know. She doesn't move.

In the hall, the phone rings. Mom jumps, startled, then hurries from the table to answer it. Once she's out of earshot, Ray leans across me to get a good look at Dan. "I thought they didn't let gays in the military," he says. Dan gives him a stare that terrifies new recruits, but my brother's too stupid to be afraid. "Does he have a big dick?" he wants to know. When Caitlin kicks him beneath the table, he cries, "What's the use of fucking a guy if he doesn't have a big dick?"

"It's not the size of the ship, dorkus," she tells him, rolling her eyes. "Everyone knows it's the motion of the ocean, right, Mike?" For emphasis, she wiggles in her seat, then smiles brightly at me.

My fingers have gone numb in Dan's grip. I came home to this? "Michael," I correct her, my voice wooden. I haven't been Mike in years.

From the other room comes a muffled sob, then the phone receiver drops into the cradle with a loud clatter, and when Mom comes back into the dining room, her eyes are filled with tears. "Mom," I start, *Jesus*. I didn't mean for it to go quite this way. "I'm sorry —"

With a reproachful look, she glares at me as she takes her seat. "That was Penny," she says, sniffling. She means her sister Penelope, her only sibling, who never wanted us to call her *aunt*. Call it a hunch, or gaydar, or what have you, but I always suspected my mother's sister was a lesbian. Somehow her calling right this moment, when I chose to come out to my family, seems to confirm this fact. I have a half-formed vision of her miles away, suddenly overcome with an undeniable urge to call because she knows I need support. With this family, I need all that I can get.

But it wasn't out of charity or some misplaced psychic sense that Penny phoned — that much is evident when my mom daubs her eyes with her napkin. "Mom?" I ask, concerned. "I didn't think you'd be so upset ..."

"Aunt Evie's passed," she cries, dissolving into tears. So that's the reason for the call. A hole opens in my heart. The only thing I can feel is Dan holding my hand. *Aunt Evie.*

Ray doesn't get it. "Passed what?" he asks, looking around the table. Even Caitlin can't rise to that — she's staring at the potatoes on her plate and blinking rapidly, trying unsuccessfully not to smudge her makeup. Twin black lines streak down her cheeks, like tears of a clown. To my mother, buried in her napkin, Ray asks, "Is this about those gallstones again?"

Because I'm closest to him, I kick his ankle and hiss, "She means she's dead." *Dead.* Once released, the word takes on weight and hangs between us over the table like a chandelier. My eyes feel hot and tight, my heart hurts, I want to crawl into my bed now and let my lover hold me close. *Dead.* I don't want to believe it.

Mom blows her nose noisily, then glares at me like this is somehow all *my* fault. I admit I'm gay, her worst fears realized, and Aunt Evie dies. My fault. Her gaze drifts to Dan, sitting proud and stoic beside me, his hand in mine beneath the table, lending me strength I simply don't have. "Oh God," she sighs. "What *else?*"

As if waiting for this moment, Caitlin opens her mouth and out pops her tongue. With her front teeth, she jiggles the silver rod rammed through the center of it.

The color drains from my mother's face, her hands fist in her napkin, and then she bursts into fresh tears. Without looking at either my sister or his wife, Dad takes another bite of his pot roast and says, "Caitlin, go to your room."

This time she doesn't argue.

2: Going Home

AUNT EVIE WAS my mother's mother's sister ... my Great-Aunt Evelyn, to be exact, but she was Evie to everyone and too young to be a great-aunt. To hear my mother tell it, Aunt Evie practically raised her as her own. Mom's mother Clara was barely fifteen when she became pregnant, no one knows who the father was. Family legend has it some drifter who came through Sugar Creek in the late '40's, an older boy with big hands and a roaming eye who didn't stay long after he found out about the baby on the way.

Sugar Creek used to be big back in the day, before the interstates steered traffic away from the county roads, but for as long as I've known it, it's just been a tiny little town at the crossroads of Route 1 and State Highway 650. That's where Mom grew up, raised by her teenaged mother and a gaggle of aunts she came to love as sisters — seven of them, Marjorie twenty-one the year my mother was born and the oldest of them all. They went down in age after that, a year apart: Barbara who was called Bobbie, Sarah, Wilhelmina who was Billy, Evie, Jessica, and Clara. Aunt Marge never married, spent all her days raising her sisters and tending to their ailing parents, who waited too long to have children — by the time Mom came around, they were elderly patients in a back room that she was never allowed to enter. She had to tiptoe down the hall whenever she passed their closed door. They finally died on her ninth birthday, both of them, hours apart. As the little girl who would become my mother blew out the candles on her cake, Aunt Billy went inside to get plates or something, I'm not sure just how the story goes, but when she came back, her eyes were wide and her skin pale, and she whispered something to Aunt Marge that made both of them disappear inside again. "Come on, Laura," Aunt Clara said, cutting the cake as she threw furtive glances at the house. Mom called her *aunt*, too, never *mother*. "Happy birthday, baby. Don't worry, Billy's coming right back."

A short while later, when two long black cars from the local funeral home pulled to a stop in front of the house, it was Evie who led the children to the backyard for a game of hide-and-seek to keep them out of the way. Mom said she hid under the front porch and watched through the steps as the bodies were taken out, but I think that's just something she's added to the tale down the road. Aunt Evie wouldn't have let her get away with that.

Marge died of ovarian cancer in her early forties, before I knew her. Clara had two more kids, both before she turned twenty-five years old, Mom's sister Penny and a boy who died in childbirth. No one ever named him. Clara passed at the same time — down here we say *passed* when someone dies, as if the euphemism somehow makes death less painful. The others married or moved on, all but Aunt Evie. She stayed in the house, which sits on three acres at the edge of town, and the creek runs through her backyard. I spent a week or two every summer there as a kid, for as long back as I can remember up until I was seventeen, when I graduated from high school and moved out on my own. Well, college dorms, but it was out of my parents' house, and it's farther than Ray's gone. When *he* graduated, he thought moving into the basement was newfound freedom. College never crossed his mind. Sometimes, when I look at him and Caitlin, I'm almost sure I'm adopted and no one's thought to tell me yet. Ray at the deli and Caitlin the poser-punk, and then there's me. The middle son, still in school for my second master's degree, this one in business admin, with a steady job at a big name law firm in the city and a boyfriend I'm almost ninety-nine percent sure I'm going to settle down with for the rest of my life. And suddenly I'm the bad guy for coming out to my parents over dinner.

Mom doesn't *say* she's mad at me, but it's in her snippy tone of voice, her curt answers, the way she doesn't quite look *at* me so much as *around* me. "Gay," she says, as if it's a new word and she can't get over it, she keeps muttering it to herself under her breath and saying it out loud to anyone who will listen. Clearing the plates from the table, it's all I hear. "Gay. My son." Her hands tremble and she breaks down again in the kitchen, the dishes clattering into the sink as she covers her mouth with one hand. I'm not sure if she's crying about me or Aunt Evie, and I'm too afraid to ask.

Somehow, I expected anything but this. Yelling I could deal with, I could get angry and shout back, I could storm through the house, I could get dramatic. I'm good at drama. Quiet acceptance would have been nice, though I knew better than to think things would go over *that* easy. But this crying, these tears, how do I counter that? I try a hug, coming up behind her and wrapping my arms around her waist. She seems so small and frail in my embrace. "I'm sorry," I murmur into her hair, which smells like hairspray and cigarette smoke. "I'm so sorry, Momma."

"I wanted grandkids," she sobs, but she doesn't shrug me off. Instead, she blots at her eyes with a paper towel and I look up to see Dan in the doorway, watching us. I give him a wan smile — I wish he could hold *me* right about now, but he's in shy mode, standing there halfway in the kitchen and halfway in the dining room, looking stern and disapproving. I don't know if my mother sees him or not — she's doubled over the sink, crying into her hands. "I wanted you married, Michael," she's saying, and I roll my eyes just to make Dan smile. "You'd have such beautiful children."

Yeah, I would like kids, but since I was old enough to masturbate, I knew I liked guys. Hard, lean bodies turned me on, flat stomachs, bulging muscles, thick arms and tight asses and big cocks. Dan's not body-builder material, but he's in shape, I have the Army to thank for that. He's stronger than me, too, a fact he loves to tout in bed when we're getting playful and he pins me to the mattress just to lick my nipples. And he's definitely got *nothing* to worry about in the ass and cock arena.

I don't tell my mother *that*. "There's Ray —" I start, but that makes her cry harder. Yeah, the thought of Ray having children is almost enough to make me tear up. "Caitlin?" I ask. Jeez, just saddle me with this guilt. "Mom, I'm … I don't know what to say. I'm sorry."

"Now we'll have to move him out of your room," she sniffles. "Put him on the couch, or something. We just don't have the extra *space*."

"He sleeps with me," I tell her. Slowly, I unwrap my arms from around her waist and take a step back, a dull anger starting somewhere in the back of my throat and spreading down my chest like heartburn. "I didn't drive all this way for a weekend apart, Mom. Either he stays in my room with me or we get a hotel. You said this wouldn't be a problem."

Her words, thrown back at her — a ploy I find quite useful when it suits my needs. When I called to tell her I was coming down, I mentioned I'd bring a friend along. My roommate, was how I put it. Dan has quarters on post, of course, along with a footlocker and Army issue bed sheets spread out over a narrow cot, a bunkmate who thinks I'm an just old high school friend, and a bathroom shared with a dozen other recruits. But half of my closet is filled with his clothes, and his toothbrush sits on the sink in my bathroom, and the pillow on the left side of my bed belongs to him. For the past eight months, he's lain beside me each night and woken to his alarm clock set two hours before mine. I get up while he's in the shower and stumble into the kitchen to make him coffee and eggs while he dresses. He comes up behind me while I'm at the stove, kisses the back of my neck, and smells faintly of soap and the Niagara spray starch he uses to keep the crease in his pants sharp. Once a week he stops by his barracks, but for all intents and purposes he lives with me. Sleeps with me, eats dinner in the evening after a long day on post and breakfast in the morning after a night in my bed. He's mine.

When he had a few days leave coming up, I wanted to take him home and show him off. There was no doubt in my mind he was coming with me; I wouldn't leaving without him. Maybe it was my mother's constant harping, asking "Have you found a girl yet?" the minute I answered the phone. Maybe it was Dan himself, telling me he wanted me forever after we made love the night before. Whatever the reason, I woke up Thursday morning and knew I wanted to tell my parents about him. Someone this good I had to share.

Over breakfast, I asked Dan if he had plans for his leave. "Not really," he mumbled into his eggs. He's not a big talker. Most of the time, I feel as if I'm gushing on and on, and then he'll look at me with a sparkle in his eyes and say, "I love you." Three little words, they bring me to my knees. He'll grin and kiss me speechless, my words gone. That morning, he looked across the table at me and asked, "Why? You have plans?"

"I was thinking of going home for a few days," I said.

He sort of nodded in a noncommittal way and turned back to his eggs. He had to be on base for PT in thirty minutes. I studied him as he ate, my gaze loving over his short dark hair, his thick eyelashes, his thin cheeks. Beneath his nose, his smooth upper lip curves into twin humps like the letter M. He doesn't have facial hair, even at twenty-three. Claims it's because he's part Native American, it gives him the dark hair and sultry skin. There's a little fuzz along his jaw, just below his ear, but that's about it. I like him smooth, though — no hair on his face, none on his chest, just a few scraggly bits on the soft muscle of his lower belly before you get to the shock of dark curls at his crotch. Imagining myself exploring down his stomach, down below his waist, down lower to that secret part of him I love so much, it makes me dry up with lust. At that moment, I didn't want him to leave for duty, I didn't want to go to work myself. I wanted the two of us back between the sheets for a few quick, heated moments. We could make it work.

But he would be late then, and if his CO caught him, his leave might be canceled, and I didn't want that. Five glorious days without the Army vying for his attention, I couldn't wait. I already scheduled my vacation around his free time — we'd make the most of it. "I thought you might like to meet my parents," I said cautiously. I didn't want to scare him away. I had never mentioned taking him home before.

He looked at me again, this time a small frown creasing his forehead. Toying with my eggs, I tried to keep my voice steady as I added, "If you want, babe, it's up to you. I know this is your first time off in God, I don't know how long, and if you just want to stay here, I'm cool with that. It's still not too late to get a house on the shore, if you want to do something like that —"

"Michael." The way he said my name made me stop and look at him — I was rambling. With a slight smile, he told me, "I'd love to meet your parents. That sounds great." His hand found mine beneath the table, giving my fingers a reassuring squeeze before he stood and leaned over to kiss me. "I have to run. Love you."

"Love you, too," I murmured against his mouth, and before he could pull away, I gave him another kiss. As he skirted the table, I smacked his butt, the slap of my hand on his tight ass loud in the quiet morning.

Over his shoulder, he growled at me, raising his eyebrows suggestively. "You'll apologize for that tonight," he promised.

I laughed and rose from my chair, raced through the kitchen, intent on surprising him before he could make it to the front door. But he met me in the hall, having hurried through the living room and around the foyer to catch me in his arms, and he held me close as I pretended to struggle against him. "Love you," he whispered, kissing me again. This time his lips lingered on mine as if imprinting them with the memory of my touch.

"See you tonight," I replied with another kiss. I took a step back and he followed — another, and he shuffled after me. A third, and we were outside the door to our bedroom. Straightening his tie, I sighed lustily. "If we just had five minutes, you know?"

"Tonight," he told me. That's a vow we make every day, *tonight*. That's when the rest of the world falls away and it's just me and him, our souls meld together as one. *Tonight*.

With his promise still ringing through me, I laid down on the bed and listened as he left. The front door shut quietly — he does everything quietly. Down the front stoop to the parking lot — my window was open so I heard his dress shoes on the pavement, his heels *click click click*ing to his Land Rover. The car door opened, shut, the engine started, and faint music streamed out into the day, low because he doesn't listen to it loud while he's driving. The engine revved once, the gears shifting into place — I knew each sound, I anticipated it. The Rover backed out of its spot beside my Lumina, the motor evening out as he guided it around the small parking lot to the street. Then he faded into the rest of the traffic and was gone.

I dozed for another hour, like I usually do. Woke to my alarm, showered — the bathroom held Dan's clean scent. The towel was still damp from his body, the washcloth filled with his soap. As I lathered myself, I pictured him in the shower before me, splashing these tiles, his hands on his body the way mine trailed over my own. It took all the self-control I had to will my erection away but he promised me tonight, so I dressed in a pair of khakis and a sports coat, usual office attire for me, and headed into work.

I'm a legal assistant at a fairly big law firm in the city, and while it's nothing exciting, it pays the bills and keeps us fed. Actually, it has its perks, like a timeshare in the Bahamas that I've scheduled for January, when Dan's up for a full week's leave that just happens to coincide with our one year anniversary. And it's paying my tuition — I take two courses a semester at the campus not far from where I live. I have a bachelor's in law and a master's in social work, and I'm not through yet. This term I have an internet lit class that meets in a chat room online Monday nights, and an accounting course on Tuesdays. Dan drops me off just to get in a few extra kisses in the parking lot before class starts, and he's always waiting for me when I get out.

At the law firm, my day starts at nine. On Thursday, I waited a half hour before I phoned my mother, who I knew would be home. "I'm thinking of coming down," I told her. "Just for the weekend. There's someone I want you to meet."

"A girl?" she asked, hopeful. My mother is like rice paper — you don't think you can see through it but if you hold it up to the light, everything shines right through. My getting married is a quest for her, on par with the search for the Holy Grail. "Michael, you know I think it's time you settled down."

I didn't tell her that I *am* settled. And unfortunately, I didn't tell her it *wasn't* a girl I was bringing home. Instead, I said, "We'll come down Saturday, if that's alright with you. Don't worry about an extra room, Mom. Do you still have that cot?"

"I'll set it up in your room," she told me. Then, with her not-so-funny laugh, she added, "Or should I set it up in Caitlin's instead?"

No, Dan's definitely sleeping with me. I watch her try to compose herself at the sink, but each time she manages to find a clean section of tissue to blow her nose in, she starts to cry all over again. This has to be for Aunt Evie — I'm gay, not *dead.* Jesus, it's not *that* bad. I mean, at least I'm here, right? At least I'm still alive. "Mom?"

With a loud honk, she blows her nose again. She turns her runny eyes from me to Dan and back again, then she shakes her finger at me as if I'm just a child. "He stays on that cot, do you hear me?" she asks. When I don't answer, she glares at Dan like my being gay is *his* fault — she always needs someone to blame.

From behind him, Caitlin calls out, "Move it, militia man." He turns so my sister can stalk into the kitchen, her plate in hand. My mother glares at her just for something to do. "What?"

Ignoring her, Mom's watery gaze finds me again. "I run a respectable house, Michael," she tells me. "There'll be no sex under my roof, do you hear?"

Before I can reply, Caitlin pushes between us to drop her plate in the sink. "There hasn't been in sixteen years," she mutters. I catch Dan's eye and we both stifle a laugh. "That's why you didn't have any more kids after me. I know —" She waves off whatever Mom wants to say. "To my room, yeah yeah. I'm going already."

3: In The Service

WE GO INTO the den, our retreat in times of crisis. Every single one of Ray's suspensions from high school was faced in this room, every prom, every wedding, every family trip planned right here. I should've waited until after dinner to make my announcement — this is the room where I should have told them, sitting beside Dan with his arm draped across the back of the couch, casually around my shoulders. Maybe then Aunt Evie would still be alive.

That's my mom talking, trying to guilt me into feeling like the evil son. Me, who's gainfully employed. Look at Ray, stretched out on the rug in front of the TV and laughing at an episode of *The Simpsons* that he's already seen a hundred times. Each joke, you'd think he never heard it before, the way he carries on. And I'm the disappointment here.

Dad sits in his recliner, staring at the screen, but he's not laughing and during commercials, I see him glance at me. At Dan's arm around me. What I wouldn't give to know what he's thinking. Did he even hear what I said? Maybe I should say it again, just to get a rise out of him. Mom sort of hogged the spotlight in the dining room. Now she's in the kitchen, phone in one hand as she washes up the dishes, and over the running water I can catch phrases of her conversation — she's running down the relative list in her address book, calling everyone she knows to share the bad news. Not about me, thank God. Aunt Evie. As if she might actually call someone her sister missed.

"Been sick awhile now, poor thing." Her voice rises over the water and drifts into the den where I sit on the sofa next to Dan. He's only pretending to watch TV — I can feel his gaze on my face like a hand tracing the curve of my jaw, touching my neck. With an uneasy smile I rub his knee, sure someone will say something, but as long as the TV's on, I don't exist. I learned that long ago. "Have you talked to Billy yet? Evie was so *young*." Mom dissolves into fresh tears, and Dad turns the volume on the TV up a notch.

"She was sixty something," Ray mutters from his spot on the floor. He rolls onto his side and stares at Dan's hand where it rests on my shoulder. "So how does this work, actually?" I give him a questioning look and he explains, "What goes where when you guys do it?"

I feel Dan's hand fist in the loose fabric of my shirt, and I squeeze his knee when it starts to shake in anger. "I'm not talking about my sex life with you," I say, studiously watching the TV. "You want to know about the birds and the bees, go ask Caitlin. I'm sure she knows."

"It's Cat."

I look up as my sister enters the den, dressed in a black baby-doll shirt that exposes her flat stomach and prominently displays a silver belly ring. As she passes me, I poke at her navel. "What's this?" I ask.

She swats my hand away, then sinks to the couch beside me. "Fake," she says, but the arched way she nods at our dad makes me think otherwise. Before I can argue, she kicks out, her small foot connecting with Ray's thigh. "I thought I already told you how that works," she mutters. "Guy's dick goes up the other one's ass —"

"Caitlin," Dad growls. It's the first thing he's said since dinner. Some part of me thinks maybe she talks this trash just to get him to notice her — if so, she's the only one of us who manages to draw his attention away from the damn television set. He hasn't said anything about Aunt Evie yet, or me, or Dan, or anything at all, really. After he pushed away from the table, he came straight into the den and flicked the channels until he found something to watch. Ray followed him, ever his father's son. I just came in here to get away from my mom, and Dan trailed behind me. I'd call it a night and head on to bed — I could use his arms around me right about now — but I have a feeling that Mom's not through with her hysterics yet, and no one's said anything about what we're going to do about Evie. Sugar Creek is a good eight hours' drive north of here. When's the funeral? Who's taking care of the arrangements? Who's at the house? Hopefully she's finding this out with her phone calls. This is stuff we need to know.

Dad waits until Ray turns back to the TV before he looks at Dan. Not at me, mind you, at Dan. "Army, huh?" he asks.

I told them that when I introduced him earlier. But Dan just nods and says, "Yes, sir." My dad grunts in approval — it's the *sir*, I'm almost sure of it. He eats that shit up. "Fifty-seventh Quartermaster Corps."

Dad nods, impressed. "Supply," he says, and now *I'm* impressed, I didn't think he'd know that. "Stationed where, Fort Detrick?"

That's in Maryland. We live in D.C., a good two hours north of my parents here in central Virginia. With a shake of his head, Dan corrects, "Fort Myer."

Another nod. "Where'd you do basic?" Dad wants to know. Suddenly he's Mr. Army, where the hell is this coming from?

"Fort Lee," Dan tells him.

In the kitchen my mom cries into the phone, and I think I hear her telling whoever is on the other end of the line that we'll be there tomorrow. Beside me Caitlin picks at lint on her black jeans and sighs dramatically, bored. When no one looks at her, she starts to kick at Ray, but he's watching TV again and ignoring the rest of us. "How long have you been in the service?" Dad wants to know.

I feel like a teenager again, my parents quizzing my latest date before we can get to the movies, though I never dated in high school, and if I had, I would've never brought any of the guys home. Dan's not my first boyfriend, but he's the first one I've ever wanted my parents to meet. Now I'm wondering just what possessed me to subject him to this. I'll have to tell him I'm sorry when we finally get alone.

But Dan's taking it all in stride. He's a good man, better than anyone else I've had in my life since I left home at eighteen. He has a way that makes you think you're getting to know him, even though he doesn't let you in and keeps a close guard on his heart. The night we met, I was just going to hang out at a local gay bar with a few friends from work — have a couple beers, hit on the cute boys in uniform who wandered into our midst, leave with a raging hard-on and the start of a hangover. But somewhere between my third bottle of Zima and midnight, we ended up down the street at a straight club running a drag contest. The place was flooded with soldiers from Myer, out for a night of fun. Must've been payday, it turns out the base and the boys scour D.C., looking to spend their hard-earned cash.

I'd like to say I saw Dan the moment I walked in. I'd like to think I caught his eye, but the truth is never that romantic. No, I actually didn't see him for most of the night. Not being one for drag, I hung by the bar, kept to myself, a little miffed that everyone I came with had ditched me for some aging queen with makeup pancaked on her ancient face. She was onstage doing the worse rendition of "I Will Survive" that I've *ever* heard, and even from where I sat, I could tell she was a guy in a dress and nothing more. I wasn't *that* drunk.

Two Army buddies plopped down to my right — Dan and his roommate, a kid named William Jackson who has acne scars and baby fat in his cheeks that makes him look like a chipmunk. William ordered another shot of whiskey and a barmaid, if there were any to spare, and then he laughed at his own joke, nudged Dan, nudged me. "A barmaid," he said, snorting into my drink. "Get it?"

"I get it," I told him, moving away. I looked past him and saw Dan looking back, his dark eyes like shadows in his face. The way he sort of smiled at me, like he didn't want to be the first to respond but couldn't help it, made me blush. I'd had too much to drink, I told myself. Servicemen like him don't hit on preppy boys like me.

William drank himself sick. Unfortunately he did it right there at the bar, and he stayed between Dan and me the whole time. Every now and then he said something he thought was funny, and he'd clap me on the back or nudge me with his shoulder to share the joke. Each time I looked his way, I found Dan staring back. When William finally leaned over and puked on his polished shoes, Dan stood up to go. He paid for their drinks and asked the bartender if there was a phone he could use to call a cab while William reeled sickly on his feet. "Outside," the bartender told him.

I slipped off my bar stool and followed them out.

It was January and the night was brisk, the air smelled of snow. I watched Dan start to half-carry, half-drag William down a sidewalk busy with college kids and winos despite the late hour, and before I even knew what I was doing, I grabbed his elbow. He turned to frown at me, that stern mask of his slipping easily into place. "Excuse me," I said, giving him my best disarming grin. It didn't work — he didn't smile back. Slowly, I removed my hand from his arm. "I have a car," I said. It sounded lame, but there it was. "I can give you guys a ride back to base? If you want."

"Why?" Dan asked.

I didn't know what to say. Because I thought he had pretty eyes? I liked his quiet demeanor? I thought I saw something in the way he kept glancing at me throughout the night? All that and more, but his question made me stop, made me think I might have been wrong about him. He's stronger than me, not so much taller but broader in the chest and arms, he could've easily kicked my ass if he wanted. Would he think I was propositioning him?

I dug my car keys out of my pocket, jiggled them like an enticement. "Just doing my part to help out our nation," I told him, hoping it sounded cheesy enough to make him smile.

It did. Together we managed to get William to my car, and I remember thinking that if he threw up on my floorboards, I sure as hell better get something for my troubles. I'd settle for a kiss, light petting maybe, a copped feel or a phone number, but if that drunk got sick twice, nothing less than a blowjob would salvage the night. Fortunately, William passed out before he even hit my seat, and I don't think he woke up again until the next morning.

Fort Myer wasn't too far — I took the interstate, but stayed in the right hand lane, keeping to the posted speed because I didn't want to rush through this moment. The more I talked to Dan, the more I found I liked him and his quiet manner, his soft replies, the way he called me *sir* until I told him that I couldn't be *that* much older than he was. That made him smile again, and he started to open up a bit. Told me a little about himself — twenty-two at the time, from Ohio, joined the Army straight out of high school because he needed the money. He kept looking over his shoulder into the back seat where William stretched out, snoring in long, thick bursts that threatened to rattle the windows.

He made the first move — put his hand on the back of my seat when he turned to check on his friend, then left it there like he forgot where he put it. By the time the sign for Fort Myer appeared in my headlights, that hand had found its way to my shoulder, and his fingers were brushing along the hair behind my ears. "Michael," he said when I told him my name. His hand rested on my shoulder, his fingers dangling against my collarbone — I could feel them through the thin jacket I wore. "Like the archangel."

I had to laugh. His finger touched my cheek and when I didn't jump or pull away, it traced the frame of my glasses back to my ear, circled around the outer fold of skin, then plucked at my earlobe playfully. "Why'd you give us a ride?" he whispered.

A glance in my rearview mirror showed William sound asleep. "I don't know," I admitted. I gave Dan what I hoped was a meaningful look out of the corner of my eye and told him, "I think I like you."

"You think." I nodded — I didn't want to commit to more than that.

We didn't speak again until after I was waved through the guard post onto base. Dan navigated me through the winding streets to his barracks, and when I pulled to a stop in front of the building, he said, "Maybe we can do this again sometime." With a faint smile, he added, "I think I like you, too."

I jerked a thumb at William and said, "Only if you promise not to bring him along."

That got me his number, and I called the next evening to hear Dan's quick laugh in my ear as he told me, "I was starting to wonder if I had dreamed you into existence."

"I'm not that good," I said coyly.

He laughed again. "I'd like to find out."

Since then, we've been inseparable. I know more about him than I do about myself, and I know that although he doesn't show it, he's nervous around my parents. My dad in particular, I think Dan feels he must impress him or something. I should have warned him, Dad doesn't get excited about anyone, especially not his son's boyfriend. Still, he's not screaming at us, there's that at least. He tends to leave the theatrics to my mother.

Dan answers his questions politely. Been in the military since high school, five years now. No, sir, he hasn't seen action yet. His unit was put on high alert after the attacks last September, but other than frequent security checks and bi-monthly inventory reports, he hasn't noticed much of a change in daily life around post. "Do they know you're ..." Dad waves his hand in the air almost dismissively. I wonder if he can even say the word *gay*.

"No," Dan says.

My dad nods at that and falls silent. Leaning close to my lover, I whisper, "I think you passed the test."

That earns me a smile, one I want to kiss away. But not here. So I rise from the couch and Dan stands beside me without a word. "I guess we'll head on up, then," I say to no one in particular. I'm ready to have him all to myself.

Ray winks at me like he thinks we're going to get it on the minute my door's closed, and Caitlin kicks him before I can say something. "What'd I do?" he mutters, rolling out of her reach.

Ignoring them both, I say, "Night, Dad." He brushes me off — I'm interrupting his TV time here. In the hall, I wave at my mom and mouth the words, "Good night." She's still on the phone.

She looks up at me with large, teary eyes and covers the mouthpiece with one hand. "Remember what I said," she tells me. She means the sex. I nod and roll my eyes, how old am I again? Please.

I feel Dan's arm around my waist as I lead the way upstairs. My bedroom is much smaller than I remember, and the first thing I do when Dan closes the door behind us is fold up that damn cot and set it against the door like a barricade. Everything else looks exactly the same as it always has, and suddenly I'm in high school again, it all comes rushing back.

And my Aunt Evie is dead.

The events of this evening hit me in the stomach, knocking the wind out of me — dinner, the phone call, my mother's reaction to both. Hot tears burn my eyes and I turn before Dan can see me cry. I try to keep it in but the hurt, the pain, the emotions all leak out and course down my cheeks like liquid fire burning my skin in its wake.

Dan's there — thank God for him. He takes me into his arms and I bury my head in his shoulder, hug him tight. With a tender touch, he rubs a hand along my back, rocks me gently, murmurs that he knows, he knows. I fist my hands into his shirt and cry harder. I'm not sure what's upset me most, my mother's anger or my dad's neglect. I expected something so much more than what I got tonight.

"It's okay, Michael," Dan tells me, and I let his hands and lips convince me that yes, it'll be alright. He helps me undress to my boxer briefs and white undershirt, then holds the blankets back as I slip between the covers of my bed. Stripping down to his drab olive underwear, he turns off the light, fumbles his way to the bed, crawls in beside me. Then his arms are around me again, and his lips press against the back of my neck as I cuddle up into his embrace.

4: First Night Home

WE LIE SANDWICHED together in my narrow twin bed. I've never shared it with anyone else before. I stare into the darkness of my bedroom and listen to the sounds of the house around me. The TV is loud even though it's downstairs, water runs in pipes through the walls, my mom's still on the phone. The kitchen's right beneath my bedroom and I swear I can hear her talking. I wonder if she's told anyone about me tonight. I imagine her scandalous gasp as she exclaims, "Just before Penny called, Michael told me he was gay. Jesus, Mary, and Joseph — my heart!"

Beside me, Dan nuzzles against my neck and asks, "What's on your mind?"

I blink at the ceiling and answer truthfully, "I don't know." Right now my mind is a crazy mix of disappointment and anger and sadness, and I'm not sure what I'm thinking. I replay the scene at dinner. This time it goes the way I wanted it to, but I don't know exactly what that means so I push that image away. If my dad said something, if he told me it was wrong to love another boy or if he said he's ashamed of me, or hell, even if he told me to get out of his house, at least I'd know what he thought about it. At least I'd have some clue as to how to act. But he said nothing, and I'm left feeling like a marionette two seconds after the strings are cut — I'm hovering in midair, waiting for the fall.

And then there's Aunt Evie.

My mind numbs at that. When's the last time I saw her? After high school, definitely, one summer when my being home for a few weeks just happened to coincide with our annual family vacation to Sugar Creek. I remember sitting on the front porch swing at her house, leafing *The Advocate*, which was the only half-decent magazine I could find in the last convenience store we stopped at before we got to town. I'm quite certain that no one in Sugar Creek has ever read an issue of *The Advocate*. It's just not the type of thing they sell down at Grosso's Market. As it was, I hid the magazine inside the newspaper so that none of my aunts would see it. The last thing I needed was one of them asking about the banner across the cover, *Pride Issue* written in loud, rainbow print.

I was barely twenty years old at the time and reveling in a sexual freedom I never knew could exist. A month prior I broke up with boyfriend number three, who was the first guy I ever slept with, and it's sad but since Dan, I can't even remember the kid's face. I remember his name was Matthew and he sat next to me in an economics class, but his features have blurred with everyone else in my past. When I was at Evie's that summer, though, my heart still hurt for him. Here in my bedroom, Dan's arms around me, I can't recall just why I was so torn up over the guy, but I remember the pain, the sleepless nights. Of all my relatives, only Aunt Evie noticed at the time. "You okay, Mike?" she asked, squeezing beside me on the porch swing.

I folded the newspaper quickly to keep her from seeing the magazine and nodded. I had been so busy reading an article on an upcoming pride march in D.C. that I didn't notice her step out on the porch or come over to me — I was usually more alert than that. This was back when I still wasn't comfortable with my sexuality. On campus I could hang out at the GLBSA room and take courses like Gay Lit, but I couldn't seem to bring myself to tell my parents or any of my old friends that I liked boys. It took another five years after that summer to finally come out, and I'm still not sure exactly how it went over.

To me, Aunt Evie always looked younger than she claimed to be — sixty that year, without a stitch of gray in her hair and clear, blue eyes that crinkled in the corners when she grinned. And she was a big woman, always had been. Not *fat*, mind you, just … big-boned. Well-proportioned, my mom used to say, but then she'd laugh in that less than amusing way she has that said she thought the term didn't quite fit Evie. She was tall, for one thing, almost six foot even at her age. When she stood next to me, Aunt Evie could look me in the eye, and she'd put her hands on her fleshy hips and cock her head to one side as she squinted at me as if trying to see me right, and she'd tell my mom that I needed to eat more, even though I gained the legendary "freshman fifteen" once I hit college. It still sticks to me, in my arms and ass, but Dan says he likes me meaty. More to sink his teeth into, and his eyes twinkle when he bites me playfully.

Evie was more than meaty. She was shaped like an X — big breasts, big arms, big hips and thighs, and an hourglass waist that almost seemed out of place on the rest of her. She favored baggy dresses that hid that waist, though it came out when she propped her hands on her hips. She did that often, it was someplace to rest them, I guess — in my mind I still see her at the kitchen sink, one hand on her hip and the other shaking a spatula at Ray because he got into the cake she was saving for after dinner. Evie was a great cook, worlds better than Mom, and part of me suspects that was the reason she was so big. All that food had to go somewhere, and most of the year it was just her and Penny in that house. My mom's sister lived with Aunt Evie, and the two of them rambled through the large Victorian-style home alone, except for summer vacation when everyone descended on Sugar Creek for a much needed break from the rest of the world. Up there things move slower, people linger, and time seems to trickle by like the ever-present lull of the creek behind the house.

In hushed tones I try to tell Dan exactly what that place means to me, but it's hard to put all the memories into words. Somehow they lack the luster that shines in my mind when I think of the anticipation that curled through my stomach as we rounded the last turn out of Sugar Creek and Aunt Evie's house loomed like a dream in the distance. The wooden siding painted a pale Wedgewood blue, the steepled roof dark, orange drifts of dead pine needles blown into the eaves. In the front of the house, a large bay window juts out from a turret, and the porch wraps around the corner, out of sight from the road. It's a large home, crowded inside, a jumble of rooms downstairs that are overflowing with furniture in vinyl slipcovers and wooden antiques and a staircase that runs straight up the center of the house. The second floor is like a patchwork quilt, a dozen small rooms that barely fit a bed and dresser, and above it all is an attic full of old trunks and musty clothing.

From the attic windows you can see the whole backyard — Evie's vegetable garden along one corner, row after row of tomato plants and stakes strung together with twine for her grapes, a shed were she kept yard supplies, even a small kiddie pool that I stopped playing in long ago. There's a deck, which you can't see from inside because it hems in close to the house, and between that and the garden is a large gas grill and an outdoor set, table and chairs, complete with an umbrella to keep out the sun. At the edge of it all, trees stand like sentinels, a ragged wood that we used to explore as children. It held so much adventure for us — how can I explain to Dan the trepidation I felt playing hide and seek with Ray amid the trees? How can I convey the crunch of leaves underfoot as we ran, or the magic in finding a colony of tiny snails clinging to a broken branch half-buried in water? How can I possibly express all the excitement that ran through me as I stood in a tiny room on the second floor and looked out the window, past the garden and the trees to the creek that I could just barely see twisting along in the woods?

I can't. So instead I tell him about my first kiss, right there on Aunt Evie's front porch. A girl by the name of Stephanie Robichaud, a real brute at ten, who chased Ray and me home from Grosso's, the three of us on bikes and damned if she didn't keep up. Ray threw his bike down and leaped the few steps up to the porch, raced inside, slammed the door shut just as I was kicking free of my own bike. I made it to the door but the bastard had locked it — I could hear him on the other side, giggling as he held it shut. "Open up!" I shouted, banging on the door with my small fists. "Ray! I'm gonna tell Mom if you don't open up this door right *now*!"

Stephanie was behind me — I turned just as she jumped off her bike. I swear she didn't let it stop first, and the bicycle rolled another foot or two before it realized the rider was gone and flopped to one side like a fish out of water. "Michael Timothy Knapp," she said, punctuating each word with a stomp of her foot on the porch steps. She wore black Mary Janes, I remember that clearly, and although she wore a dress, she had on shorts underneath it because she was such a tomboy. I saw those shorts once — she flashed us with them outside of Grosso's the summer before. I think I was scarred for life.

As she advanced on me, I flattened myself back against the door. Running was out of the question — even two years older than me, she was faster, I knew that already, and if I ran, then I'd get a fist in my arm for my troubles. Stephanie was Sugar Creek's number one bully back in the day. As she came closer, I squeezed my eyes shut and prayed that Ray, being the chickenshit that he is, would go and get Aunt Evie to rescue me.

The punch I was expecting never came. Instead, I felt something soft and wet touch my mouth, and my eyes flew open in surprise. Stephanie's big brown eyes were staring back, so damn close that they seemed larger than life, and her breath was hot and sour against my cheek. I had barely registered the fact that she was kissing me before she hit me in the shoulder. I shrunk away and she hit me again, twice, hard in the upper arm. "Two for flinching," she told me. Then she laughed as she raced back to her bike. "You tell anyone I kissed you, Michael, and I'll kick your butt."

Telling anyone that she even *touched* me wasn't something I planned on doing — she wasn't one of my favorite people in the world. Ironic, then, how a mere four years later it was her twin brother Stephen who gave me my first *real* kiss, this time not on the front porch but out behind Aunt Evie's gardening shed. He had the same big eyes, which his thick glasses refracted until they swam like two pools in his face, and he had a shy grin that was nothing like his sister's vicious grimace. By the time I was twelve, I knew I liked boys, and he was the first who ever looked back at me with the same telltale mix of curiosity and interest in his eyes. We were in Grosso's leafing through an issue of *Playboy*, giggling over the naked women inside while the cashier's back was turned, when we found a full-page ad for adult videos in the middle of the magazine.

It was the first time I can remember seeing two men together. Before that, I had vague dreams of letting boys touch me in places where I would touch myself, and I thought it might be nice to kiss a guy, but I had never *seen* it. And there, on the glossy pages of the magazine, were men in various sexual poses. With women, true, but one picture caught my eye, one man lying another down, the one beneath him arching in pleasure or pain, at the time I couldn't tell which. A big black swath hid their naked bodies, but I could see enough to get a pretty good idea of what they were doing, and my mind filled in the rest. Across the black bar read the words *HOT GAY SEX!!*

I knew what *gay* meant — hell, I went to public school. It meant you were a wuss who cried when someone hit you and always got picked last in P.E. class. I wasn't gay. Even when I asked Ray, in the darkness of the room we shared, what the word really meant, and he told me it was a boy who porked other boys, I didn't think it pertained to me. Mostly, I think, because I didn't really know what Ray meant by the word *porked*, and whenever I tried to ask, it set him giggling so bad that he simply couldn't tell me.

I pointed the ad out to Stephen, who I sort of suspected might like it the same way *I* liked it — call it gaydar, even at that age. There in the back aisle of Grosso's, he ran one grubby finger over the image of the men and in a harsh whisper, asked me, "Have you ever done anything like that?"

I shook my head no. He pushed his Coke-bottle glasses up the bridge of his nose and said, "Me either."

He was two years older than me, putting him at the grand age of fourteen, and he lived in Sugar Creek, of all places. Of *course* he hadn't done anything even remotely like that picture. "Have you even been kissed yet?" I asked him. I thought of his sister and her sloppy press of lips years before, and decided that if he asked me the same question, I'd say no.

But he didn't. He giggled, nervous, and looked at me in a way that said he wanted to kiss *me*. I made him chase me, though — without another word, I stuck the magazine back on the rack and ran from the store. Ran all the way down the three blocks and around the corner to Aunt Evie's house, looking over my shoulder to make sure he was right behind me. He was. Around the house, into the backyard, past Ray splashing in the kiddie pool even though he was too old to play in the thing, behind the shed. That's where I stopped to catch my breath and Stephen found me, leaning back against the wooden shed. With a breathless laugh, he touched my face, his fingers surprisingly gentle on my skin. Then he took a deep breath and inched close to me, closer, until his eyes eclipsed the world and his lips met mine.

I can still remember the way he tasted, like licorice whips and Gobstoppers, because we were eating candy at Grosso's before the girl behind the register lost interest in us and we found the *Playboy*. When we finally broke apart, Stephen looked slightly pale from holding his breath for so long, and I told him next time he might try smaller kisses to keep from passing out. "But I like it," he said. Secretly, I did, too. "I like how soft you are inside."

When I tell Dan this, he laughs into my neck. "He doesn't know just *how* soft you are," he breathes, his hands straying down my chest and stomach to cup the budding erection in my boxer briefs.

I moan as he kneads me hard. "My mother," I sigh as a reminder. She said no sex. Did I promise to that?

Dan rolls on top of me. "What a way to kill the mood," he jokes, but his dick presses into mine and I know nothing will tamp down *that*. Nothing but me, and with expert moves I hook my fingers into the waistband of his briefs, tug them down over his smooth ass, his thighs, down to his knees. As he straddles me, I hear the tiny rip of fabric, but he bends one leg and lets the briefs slip off. "Love me," he says. That's what he always says when he initiates it.

I packed condoms, of course. Heavily lubricated — they're easier to hide in my pockets than a bottle of lube, easier to explain away. What guy my age doesn't carry a condom anymore? Despite the darkness and unfamiliar bedroom, Dan manages to find the half-empty box, shoved down one side of my suitcase just in case anyone goes rooting through my stuff. I put nothing past my siblings.

Straddling me again, Dan eases my boxer briefs down over my balls, exposing my erection. Like a seasoned lover, he rolls the condom on, the lubricant cool on my heated flesh. Then he lies down over me and I guide myself into him, into the hot tight center of his being, where I love him most. We take it slow because Dan likes it that way and tonight I'm not up for much, my mind is too heavy. I'm all too eager to lose myself in him like I have so many times before, his hands holding me back to the bed, his lips on my throat. I cup his ass in both hands and pull him to me, each thrust bringing a muffled moan into my neck, my name sighed in his voice. We melt together perfectly, like we always do, and he fills the hollow ache that opened in me tonight at the dinner table. He makes me whole.

Right before I come, I get a little randy, and the bed knocks against the wall in a quiet rhythm as I drive into my lover, deeper, further, *in*. The moment my orgasm rips through me and into Dan, someone on the other side of the wall bangs back.

Caitlin. Her room is next to mine.

We giggle like schoolboys and I can finally fall asleep now, Dan's arms around me tight. In the morning, though, my little sister stares at me from the dining room table as I sit down with a bowl of cereal. Dan's still asleep, savoring his day off, and no one else seems to be awake. Caitlin waits until I put my spoon in my mouth before she says, "I have some incense, if you want it."

"What for?" I ask, innocent.

She shrugs and stirs her cereal halfheartedly. "It's good for getting rid of smells," she tells me. "You know, cum, weed, shit like that. Thought you might need some after last night. If Mom smells sex —"

"I opened the window," I say with a grin. Sixteen years old, Jesus. "Didn't mean to keep you up."

Caitlin flips her dark hair out of her black-rimmed eyes. "You didn't." Without looking at me, she adds, "Hey, if I had a guy like that in my bed? Shit on Mom, I'd fuck him, too."

Sixteen, I have to remind myself.

5: Aunt Jessie

DAN WAKES BEFORE my parents or Ray — it's the military in him. He can't sleep in even if he doesn't have to be on base before dawn. When I hear him in the kitchen, I give Caitlin a quick grin and hurry in to kiss him good morning. "Hey," I sigh, coming up behind him and wrapping my arms around his waist. He stands at the sink, pouring himself a glass of orange juice, and he looks something close to amazing in his gray ARMY t-shirt and PT shorts. They're tight around his ass and hang loose on his thighs — whoever designed those things knew just how to show off a soldier's best assets. I'm glad the t-shirt hangs low enough to hide what Dan's packing from Caitlin's young eyes and sarcastic mouth.

He half-turns in my embrace and kisses me in greeting. "Did you sleep well?" he asks. I nod in reply. With him beside me, I slept like a baby.

"I can make you breakfast," I tell him, just because that's what I do in the mornings, I cook for him. Mostly eggs, though I saw some pancake mix in the cabinet, if he's up for that. Since we're alone in the kitchen, I run my hands up beneath the bottom of his t-shirt and rub his taut stomach. Kissing his shoulder, I murmur, "I love you."

He sets the orange juice aside and turns to hug me close. His hands smooth the bangs away from my forehead, tuck the wavy hair behind my ears, but the strands fall back into place on their own accord as he cradles my chin to kiss me again. "Love *you*," he purrs, and between us I feel faint stirrings of interest at his groin. "We can head back to bed, if you want," he suggests. "Breakfast can wait."

"My eyes!" I frown at Caitlin as she stumbles into the kitchen, eyes closed, cereal bowl in one hand and the other thrown out in front of herself dramatically to feel her way. "Jeez, boys. Take it upstairs, why don't you? What will the neighbors think?"

I kick out at her as she passes, but she's quick — she dodges my foot and still manages to sock me in the arm with one small fist. I slap her shoulder and she hits me again. Damn, she has good reflexes. When I'm about to try a third time, though, Dan catches my hand and folds my arm between us as he holds me tight. "Don't," he admonishes. "No fighting."

I'm well aware that I'm suddenly Caitlin's age again, picking with her the way I am, but she doesn't seem to mind. "You're just jealous," I tell her. I stick out my tongue and marvel at how I can go from twenty-five to two in one minute flat. "I've got a hot boy to freak and you don't."

Caitlin flips her hair over her shoulder and gives me a look that simply says, *puh-leaze*. "You don't know my hot boy," she says. "I ain't jealous of yours, trust me."

Intrigued in spite of myself, I let Dan slip free and lean against the sink. "You have a boyfriend?" I ask as Dan pours himself a bowl of cereal.

"Of course," Caitlin snorts. As if she might *not*. "I'm not Ray, Michael. I *date*."

"Who?" I want to know. I realize that I don't know anyone her age here — hell, I don't know most people in this town anymore, but maybe the last name will sound familiar, maybe she's seeing someone related to someone I went to school with. This is a small place — not as backwater as Sugar Creek, but close. Not D.C., that's for damn sure.

Rolling her eyes, Caitlin takes the box of cereal from Dan and refills her bowl. "No one you know," she says.

My lover leans beside me to eat, his hip resting against mine, and I give him a wink over my shoulder. "Who?" I ask again. "I'm just curious, is all. Unless you're lying ..."

"I'm not *lying*," Caitlin sighs. "Jesus. He's the captain of the football team, okay? Shaun Donnigan. There, you happy?"

I almost don't believe it. My Goth sister dating ... "The captain of the football team?" I ask, incredulous. "You can't be serious."

With a mischievous grin, she says, "That's what his girlfriend says."

That gets a laugh out of Dan. "Hey!" I cry, turning to tickle him. He laughs again and squirms away. "That's not funny. He's seeing someone else? Caitlin —" She shrugs and returns to the dining room, leaving Dan and me alone. With a withering look, I tell him, "Don't encourage her."

The smile slips from his face. "She's cute," he says.

I'm glad they're getting along so well — Dan's an only child, but I know he always dreamed of having a large family one day. I can't imagine what it was like for him, growing up by himself. Ray might not be one of my favorite people in the world, but at least I had someone to play with when I was a kid, someone to share secrets with, someone to fight with. And every summer, there was the rest of the family at Aunt Evie's ... we easily doubled the size of Sugar Creek when we rolled into town. There are five great-aunts altogether — four, now that Evie's gone. Aunt Bobbie has two boys, both married; Aunt Sarah has two boys, two girls; Aunt Billy has three girls. Add in their children, some of whom have children of their own by now, and my head starts to spin at the thought of them all. It's going to be a madhouse over the next few days, everyone showing up at Aunt Evie's to pay their respects, where will they all stay?

At the house, of course. Evie always said there was room enough for family.

Then there's Aunt Jessie. But she won't be there.

As Dan finishes his cereal, I rest my head on his shoulder and sigh. The mere *thought* of all those people crammed into Evie's house makes my head hurt — maybe I should get a hotel when I get up there. I don't know if Dan's ready for *that* much of my family yet; I'm not even sure if *I'm* up for it. "You know," I say softly, stroking the hairs on his arm, "Mom's probably going to want to head on up to Sugar Creek today. I can drop you off at the house if you want —"

Dan looks at me sharply. "Why?" he asks.

I shrug, which settles my body closer to his. "Somehow I don't think hanging out with my wacky relatives is how you want to spend your leave."

"I want to spend it with you." He sets his empty cereal bowl in the sink and eases an arm around my waist. I don't like the way he's frowning at me, like he's suddenly not sure who I am anymore. "Don't you want me there?"

"I do," I assure him. I don't know how I would get through the next few days without him. "It'll be crowded, though. There's a lot of us."

"A lot of them, maybe," Dan says, kissing my forehead. His hand traces up the curve of my spine to rub at the back of my neck. "Only one you."

I laugh — he's so sweet sometimes, when we're alone and he doesn't have to hide himself behind his soldier's mask. I can just imagine what my aunts will say, they'll love him, how could they not? The only one I'm really worried about is Aunt Sarah, who's a little bit ultra-Christian, but last I heard, she simmered down some after her oldest son knocked up his girlfriend a few years ago. God, I can't even imagine these kids, my nieces and nephews, aunts and uncles, people *my* age who I spent my summers with horsing around at Sugar Creek, I can't imagine them grown now with children of their own. It almost makes me think *I* should be in their shoes, I should have a family underway.

But I knew long ago that I wouldn't be able to have that. I love men, I love *Dan*. I won't have children. My mom will have to learn to accept that the same way I have. Unless she's going to let it come between us ...

I think of my Aunt Jessie. That's one relative I'm quite sure won't be at Sugar Creek this week. I've only met her once, and I was just a little boy at the time, I don't remember much about her beyond long black hair and thick eyeliner that made her look like a raccoon. In my memory she wears all black, but I think I'm confusing her with Caitlin. As I recall, Jessie had a smoky, sultry voice and a lazy way of looking around the room as she talked, and there was something so overtly sexual about her that even as a child, I was drawn to her the way a moth is to a flame.

Something happened though — I don't know what, I'm not privy to the details. Despite the fact that I'm an adult myself, the fallout between Aunt Evie and Aunt Jessie is still something no one will tell me about, and I'm too afraid to ask. My mom won't even discuss it. Something happened, something so horrible that it wedged itself between Evie and Jessie and kept them apart the rest of their lives … or the rest of Evie's life, at least. I don't know whatever happened to Aunt Jessie. I don't know if she married or died or what. Family rumor has her running away to join a cult, marrying into the mob, joining the Witness Protection program, being abducted by aliens — when we gathered at Sugar Creek, the youngest of us would swap horror stories, each one worse than the last, trying to one-up each other with what *really* happened to Aunt Jessie. Truth is none of us know, and if our parents even suspected what we giggled over when the lights went out, we would've been spanked and sent to bed.

When I tell Dan what I know of my Aunt Jessie, he just raises an eyebrow and smirks. "Aliens?" he asks, amused.

I have to admit, the stories *do* sound far-fetched. "We were just kids," I tell him, but I'm almost embarrassed to admit that part of me still wants to believe something exotic happened to the dark, gypsy-esque woman in my memory. I think my lover realizes this, though, because when I duck my head, he tucks his thumb under my chin and raises my face until I look at him again. "For all I know she's not even alive anymore," I say. "And if she is, she won't be anywhere near the house, I'm sure of it. I don't know what happened between her and Evie but my mom once said Jessie wasn't welcome in any house in this family ever again."

With that smirk still in place, Dan says, "I think your mom's the type to say a lot of things when she's mad."

Silently, I agree with him. The comment had been made when I was about to graduate from high school, and I sat at the dining room table with my mom's address book and a pile of invitations in front of me. Pen in hand, I flipped through the book, looking for anyone I might even remotely know, just to send them an invite in the hopes of soliciting money from them. I started at the back of the book, because my mom's maiden name is Yates and all of the aunts are back there, married names in parentheses. That's the way Mom's mind works — put everyone under the name she knows them as, which is good because Aunt Bobbie was married four times before she finally settled on her current husband, and I'm not sure if Mom could keep up with all those name changes if she tried. Both of Bobbie's sons have a different last name, from each other and from her, but when I was still in high school she was only on husband number two. I filled out cards for her and her sons Douglas and Craig, who were both in their late 20s at the time. Then Aunt Sarah because she came next in the book, then her children, Ruth and Judith and Thomas and John, all Biblical names. Aunt Sarah scares me, to be honest. If anyone has something to say about Dan, it'll be her. I almost see my mom teaming up with her once we get to Sugar Creek, the two of them ganging up on me in an attempt to cure me from sinful living. But Tommy's girlfriend had a baby at sixteen, and I think my mom said she had a second child later on, and I know they never married, so Aunt Sarah can't say too much about my living in sin. I remember she sent me a Bible as a graduation gift. At the time I wondered if I could possibly return it to the local Christian bookstore, even without a receipt. My mom wouldn't let me.

If I had known I'd get the Bible instead of money, I might not have bothered to send her an invitation at all. But I did, and I sent Aunt Billy one, too, and her three daughters, as well, Ginger and Lenore and Sylvia. I always thought Aunt Billy should've held back on the kids and just had cats instead, naming her daughters the way she did. Aunt Marge was already gone by then, and I never met my Aunt Clara, but I had a few extra invitations left. "Can I send Aunt Jessie one?" I asked, glancing through the address book. I couldn't find her listed.

But my mom snatched the book from me and snapped it shut. "She won't be needing one," she told me. When I started to argue, she asked, "You don't really think she'd come, do you? She barely knows you're alive."

I wasn't vain enough to think that everyone I was sending an invitation to would show up to see me get a diploma. This was all about getting gifts, getting *money*. Somehow I thought my mom was missing the point. "She might send me something —"

"She won't," Mom said with a finality that scared me. "You send her something, she'll think she's welcome here and she's not. If you want to get rid of the extra cards, mail them to random names in the phone book. You'll get about the same response as you would if you sent Jessie one. Don't argue with me."

I've learned better than to do *that*. Even when it comes to Dan, I'm not going to argue with her. When she comes downstairs fully dressed, make-up already on and every hair in place, she glares at the two of us cuddling by the sink. Dan eases me away because he sees her first, and when I turn, she's already frowning. "Michael, really," she starts. "In front of the window where the neighbors —"

From the dining room, Caitlin calls out, "Did she mention the neighbors?" I laugh at the look of consternation that crosses my mother's face. "Did I call that one or what? I told them you'd bitch about the neighbors."

"Caitlin!" My mom's voice lashes out like a whip, and I cover my mouth with one hand to hide the smile I can't stifle. The look Mom gives me suggests that she thinks my kid sister has learned such language from me.

Then she busies herself with the coffeepot, and I blow Dan a kiss. He grins and starts to wash his cereal bowl — how can she not love him? But she's not watching us anymore, thank goodness, she's scooping sugar into her coffee with nervous fingers, I can hear the clatter of her spoon against the side of her mug. "I guess you'll want to bring him with you," she says.

She talks of Dan as if he's a pet and acts like he's not even in the same room with us. I touch his arm and can almost feel the anger that hums through his body at that slight. I'm not going to bother to answer her.

The side door opens by the basement and Ray comes into the kitchen, scratching the back of his head. His hair stands up in a punkish hairstyle, and he still wears the boxers and t-shirt he slept in, even though he had to walk across the driveway to get here. And Mom thinks I'm going to embarrass her in front of the neighbors? Has she looked at him lately?

He sees me, sees Dan, and with a mighty yawn, he asks, "So dude, did you guys do it last night?"

Beneath my hand, Dan's fingers curl into a fist. "Raymond," my mom warns, before I can answer him. "I've told you kids before, no sex in this house."

My clueless brother nudges me with his elbow. "You should stay in *my* room," he says, wiggling his eyebrows suggestively. "It's not *in* the house."

Caitlin can't let that one slide by. I don't know how she hears us, but from the dining room, she calls out, "Oh yeah, Ray. Like you have a harem up there, or something. You've never even been laid."

"Caitlin!" My mom's on edge, it's in her voice.

My sister hears it, too, and can't resist. Coming back into the kitchen, she pushes right in between Dan and me to drop her bowl in the sink, and in a childish voice, asks, "Mommy?"

Mom glances over at the three of us, distrustful. "What?"

With a sweet smile, Caitlin says, "Since Michael gets to bring his boyfriend to Sugar Creek, I was thinking maybe I could take —"

"No," Mom replies. When Caitlin tries to finish her sentence, Mom shakes her head. "I'm not listening, Caitlin. I don't condone this … this …"

She's searching for the right word, and I know just where she's headed.

"Go ahead and say it," I mutter, growing angry myself. "This *phase*, isn't that the word you want? Well, I have news for you, Mom. This isn't a phase. This isn't something I'm going to grow out of." Dan places a hand on my shoulder to quiet me, but I shake him off. "I'm with Dan," I tell my mother. "I love him. So you better get used to it, because I'm not going to exclude him from my life just because you don't condone this. I *love* him."

Before she can respond, I storm past her, past Ray, out of the kitchen and up the stairs. I don't have to turn to know that Dan is right behind me. He catches up to me at the door to my room, and just the touch of his hand on my arm is enough to stop me. I turn and find myself in a sudden embrace, and I cling to him desperately. "If you'd rather I not go," he begins, his voice low in the darkened hall.

"You're going," I say, clenching my fists in his shirt. "I need you with me, Dan, you know that. Don't make me face them all alone."

He rubs my back in a soothing, caring gesture. "I won't," he assures me.

6: Road Trip

M<small>Y DAD WAS</small> up before any of us, getting the car serviced. "You should get yours looked at, Michael!" Mom hollers up the stairs. "You don't want it to break down between here and Sugar Creek. They don't have a Jiffy Lube, you know."

"Close the door," I tell Dan. We're in my room, repacking everything I diligently unpacked yesterday, when I thought we would be staying for the next few days.

"Michael?" My mom comes up a few steps. "Did you hear me?"

As Dan eases the door shut, I call out, "Yeah! We're busy here, Mom. I'll be down in a minute." I toss clothes from my closet onto the bed and sigh heavily. Can I just skip to the end of the week? "God."

Dan takes the hangers from me and says, "Sit down, babe. Don't let her get to you like this."

"It's not just her," I tell him, "it's everything." But I let him guide me to the bed, where I flop back on top of the clothes and stare at the ceiling. Tonight I'll be in Sugar Creek — my stomach churns in anticipation, the way it used to when I was a little boy. I would be packed for *weeks* ahead of time, and the night before we left for vacation, I was nothing but a bundle of nerves, as if it were Christmas already and I just *knew* I was getting something good. Sugar Creek always made me feel that same breathless excitement — finally I'd see cousins I hadn't seen since the previous year, I'd go swimming in the creek again and ride bikes with Stephen Robichaud down to Grosso's. There was so much to look forward to, homemade ice cream and large cookouts and late nights spent camping out by the woods or sneaking between bedrooms to tell ghost stories. Shaved ice from the cart in front of the tackle shop, fishing and building forts and waging battles against the girls. There were so many of us at Aunt Evie's at any one time, it was like an instant play group — someone *always* wanted to do *something*. And in the evenings the kids would goof off in the backyard while the adults sat around, sipping cool drinks that made them giggly and pinked their cheeks, margaritas and piña coladas and shots of Schnapp's. When I took a break from my cousins, Aunt Evie would pull me into her massive lap and let me stick my fingers in her drink. I can still remember the icy, slightly acidic taste of the alcohol. I knew I wasn't supposed to have any, and that made me want it all the more. No drink has ever tasted quite as wonderful since.

My mom used to frown at me when I'd sip at the drinks. "Michael, no," she'd say, slapping my hand away from the salt and lime. "Run along and play. You have a drink." I had slushed Kool-Aid, which didn't tingle through my stomach and coil in my groin the way Aunt Evie's drink did.

But at Evie's house my mom was just another child, we were all the same in her eyes. "Laura, hush," she'd murmur, one large hand smoothing down my hair. "It's just a little bit. Won't harm him none." That's another reason I love Sugar Creek so much. There Evie ruled over us all, a matriarch who had the final say in anything. Punishments were lenient, rewards frequent, and if my mom rose her voice in anger, Evie was just behind her, hands on her hips and shaking her head. "Don't carry *on* so." Brushing past Mom, Evie would gather me up in her arms and tell us both, "Vases mend, Laura. Chairs can be fixed, water sopped up, the carpet vacuumed. Don't yell at the child. He didn't *mean* to do it."

My throat closes tight in sudden emotion. I'm going to miss that woman.

She would've loved Dan, I know that without a doubt. This past summer I even thought about taking him for a drive up there, just to show him off. But I wanted to tell my parents about us first — Mom would've been livid if Evie and Penny knew before she did that her son was gay. So when Dan had a week's leave, we went to Ocean City instead, took in the beach, the boardwalk, the nightlife. There was always next year, I reasoned. I could always visit Aunt Evie then.

Tears well up in my eyes and I blink them back. Dan looks at me as I turn away, I don't want him seeing me cry again. I don't *want* to cry, I hate this. Thrilled at the impending trip one minute, heart-wrenched the next.

Dan stretches out beside me on the bed and runs a hand up my arm, across my chest, over my shoulder until he's hugging me close. With a sad sigh, I tell him, "I think I'm over it, you know? I think I'm okay, I can handle this, I'll move on. Then out of nowhere it hits me again, the littlest things." My voice breaks. He kisses me as one tear slides down my cheek. "I can't imagine it without her there," I whisper, burying my face into his neck, where he smells like Tommy cologne. "Evie *was* Sugar Creek to me."

In his low voice, Dan says softly, "I understand." When he was a boy, his parents would visit his father's mother in West New York, New Jersey, a long, nauseating car ride from his hometown in central Ohio. He gets carsick in the back seat, and he tells me that he learned early on how to distinguish the rest area road signs from the others. Every one they passed, he would complain about having to pee, just to get out of the car. The minute his feet hit the tarmac, he was fine, but he dawdled at the rest areas, splashing in the sinks and hiding out in the stalls just to keep from getting back into the car. "It made me sick for days," he says, talking about the road trip. "The first night at Ma's, I couldn't eat a thing. I had to take a handful of children's aspirin and lay down in the back bedroom, the a/c on high and all the lights out while everyone talked quietly in the other room."

Ma and her second husband, whom Dan called Uncle Ernie, lived in a condo building a stone's throw from the Hudson River — from her balcony, they could look out across the stretch of water to the New York city skyline. "World Trade Center right there," he says, his voice hushed. I fist a hand in his shirt and think about all the pictures I've seen of Manhattan Island — I've never been there myself. "We ate lunch on the top of one of the towers once. Ma kept saying the whole building was shaking, she could feel it every time the wind blew. I don't even want to imagine what the view from her condo is like now that they're gone. If you leaned out just right, on clear days you could almost see the Statue of Liberty. When we went up there the week of the fourth, we would sit on the balcony to watch the fireworks. Best seat in the house."

The way Dan tells it, going to Ma's was for him how Aunt Evie's was for me. There was a pool at the condo, free for residents and their guests, and he spent his days splashing in the chlorinated water, playing water polo with the older kids, learning to dive. Sometimes they would go into "the city" — he remembers Rockefeller Center, shopping in tiny stores along the sidewalks, watching the Rockettes at Radio City Music Hall. Everything that's so stereotypically New York, he did during his summers growing up.

Uncle Ernie ran his own electrical business so he missed a lot of the trips, but Ma always tagged along. She held onto Dan's hand with a death grip, but he didn't mind. "I loved her," he tells me, unashamed. I love the way he can open up to me when we're alone. "She was short — when I was eight, I was as tall as she was, five four, five five tops. Really short, wiry hair like steel wool, always a mess of curls but close to her head, you know what I mean? Very thin, almost scrawny, with the biggest damn mouth you've *ever* heard." He grins at a memory, his tiny Ma holding him in hand and bitching out a waiter because Dan dropped his ice cream cone. She wanted another one, no charge, and she wanted it *now*. Dan mimics her in a high, eerie voice that makes me laugh. "So hot outside, it's a *shame* you give kids melted slop like that in a cone. And you have the *nerve* to call that *ice* cream? It's nothing but *milk*."

"Did you get another one?" I ask. We're still lying together on my bed, and the more he talks, the closer I draw to him. With a hand against his chest, I can feel his words rumble through my fingers, up my arm. Packing is the last thing on either of our minds.

He smoothes the hair back from my temples and kisses me quickly. "Damn straight," he murmurs against my skin. "Ma had a way of getting what she wanted, no matter what. The Pope himself wouldn't have been able to withstand her. She was like a force of nature."

Was, I hear the past tense in his voice and smile sadly. "What happened?" I ask quietly.

Quiet for a moment, Dan rubs my arm, my back, and I wait. I can feel the change in his emotion like a lull before an impending storm. "She died," he tells me, his voice almost a whisper between us. "When I was twelve. Lung cancer, I believe. She always had to have her smokes. Menthol lights. She took long drags on her cigarette and always coughed when she laughed, but I was just a kid. I didn't think anything of it." I kiss the exposed flesh of his throat and he hugs me to him like a security blanket. "She lost more weight," he sighs. "The last time I saw her, she had dark circles under her eyes and her skin was really loose, and I remember thinking she'd be in the sun too much. She was starting to look old in my eyes, you know?" I nod, yes. Though his voice is steady now, I know that it must have been something horrible for him at the time, and I know he probably kept everything inside, because that's the way he is. Or rather, was, until he met me. I know him too well to let anything fester.

"My Papaw was in the Army," he says. Ma's first husband, his father's dad. "Died in World War II, shot down in the Pacific, few days after my dad was born. I think that's part of the reason I always wanted to be in the service. I'd see his graduation picture on Ma's wall and he looked so proud in that uniform, so regal. She used to touch the frame and tell me that's your Papaw. He died to keep us free. The way she said it, it was the most noble thing he could've done. I wanted to make her that proud of me."

He never got the chance. In April of the year he turned twelve, Ma lost the battle with her cigarettes. It was the only time the Biggs family ever flew to see her, and the first time Dan rode in a plane. Being in the Army now, flying is old hat, but at the time he was terrified of crashing. "I kept asking why can't we drive?" he says, and now it's me trying to kiss away his memories, his pain. "What happens if I have to pee? I said. There's a bathroom in the back, my mom told me, but I was too nervous to go. I just knew something horrible would happen if I left my seat."

They flew into Newark, took a rental car to the condo. Uncle Ernie was there, alone. A big man with thick muscles on his arms who always reminded Dan of Brutus in the *Popeye* cartoons, he dwarfed Ma, but that day

Dan said he never thought a man could shrink the way Ernie had. "Just sort of shriveled into himself," is how he puts it. "Like he lost weight so fast, his body didn't know what to do with all the extra skin. When he looked at me and I saw he'd been crying, that's when I started to cry, too. I thought if whatever happened to Ma upset a man like him, it was okay to cry."

They stayed a week. "Mostly to help Ernie square away the bills and whatnot, and there were a ton of insurance papers that needed to be filed. I kept thinking Ma was out visiting someone down the hall and she'd be back any minute. The day of her funeral, my mother woke me up really early because we had to get to the church by nine, and I didn't ..." Dan sighs. "I wasn't thinking. I dreamed Ma was still alive. My mother was like Danny, come on. We're leaving soon. And I was so mixed up inside that I asked her if we were leaving to pick up Ma."

I stare at him for a full minute, savoring the way the early morning light that seeps through the curtains catches the highlights in his short hair and warms his face. "I love you," I whisper, because I do, and I hope that my kisses, my hands, can ease the memories of the frightened twelve-year-old boy he used to be. "I'm glad you'll be with me."

"We'll make it," he promises. "You'll get through this, Michael. I'll make sure of it."

I believe him. "I never went back there," Dan says, "after the funeral. I just couldn't. I thought I had moved on. But in September, when they kept showing the skyline on TV? It all came back. Every single moment I spent there, every word Ma ever said to me, *everything*. In such vivid detail. I closed my eyes and was back in her condo again. I could see the pictures on her walls, I could read the headlines of the newspaper she kept folded up on the kitchen table so she could do her crossword after dinner." All the years in between were gone. I know exactly what he means — I feel that way thinking of Sugar Creek.

"I'm afraid I'll forget her," I admit. Here in his arms, I can tell him anything. "I'm scared that one day something will remind me like that, but I'll have nothing to remember. It'll all be gone. I don't ... I don't want that."

His arms tighten around me. "You don't forget," he assures me. "When you love someone like that, you never forget them."

He's right, I know he is. Aunt Evie's too much a part of me to just slip away like the blurred faces of the boys I knew before I met Dan. Disregarding the clothes beneath us, I roll onto my back and pull him with me so that he straddles my waist the way he did last night. He fits perfectly, his legs alongside mine, and he leans down over me, his arms on either side of my head as his lips find my own. My hands rub his thighs, causing the light hair to stand up under my palms. My fingers slip beneath the fabric of his shorts, tickle along his upper thighs, rub against the confines of his underwear, and he grins against my mouth. "You're bad," he whispers, but he leans into my hands and I don't hear him complaining when I start to stroke across the front of his crotch —

Suddenly there's a knock on my door, and before I can extract my hands or Dan can slide away, Caitlin enters the room. "You're worse than newly-weds," she tells us, closing the door behind her. As Dan rolls off me and I sit up, Caitlin plops down on the edge of my bed and starts to pick at the clothes I laid out to pack. They're badly wrinkled now. "Oh, don't let *me* stop you," she says, sarcastic.

"Caitlin," I start.

"Cat," she corrects. I'm going to have to get used to saying that.

"*Cat*," I say, emphasizing the word. I cross my legs and frown at her — can't she see we're in the middle of something? Dan lies propped up on one elbow beside me, his body pressing against my hip so I can feel the interest hardening in his shorts. If she would just give us a few more minutes … but she doesn't look like she plans on leaving before she's told me whatever's on her mind. With a sigh, I ask, "What is it?"

She looks past me at Dan, then meets my gaze, her eyes rimmed with smudged black eyeliner, her lashes a mile long with the mascara she has caked on them. "Let me paint you a picture," she says. She wears dark lip-stick the color of crushed garnets, and even though she's still dressed in the faded shirt and boxers that she wore to bed, she already has a studded dog collar in place around her neck. The clasp hangs at the hollow of her throat like a locket. My sister, the freak. "Imagine yourself in a car," she tells me, and I nod quickly — anything to get this over with and her out of the room so I can have Dan to myself again. "Mom and Dad in the front seat, fine. Ray beside you." She lets this sink in. "For eight hours," she adds. "How many rounds of that damn license plate game do you think he can go through in eight hours?"

I have to laugh. At least it won't be *me* listening to him cry out, "I see Virginia!" every three minutes. Uncrossing my legs, I give her a slight push with my foot to get her off the bed. "Sucks to be you."

"Michael, listen!" She grabs my foot and stands, dragging me to the edge of the bed. If it wasn't for Dan's arm around my waist holding me back, I'd fall off onto the floor. "Let me ride with you guys. I'm not asking much."

"No," I tell her.

She sighs dramatically. "You're not listening to me," she says. "I've got headphones and my Gameboy and a pile of magazines, a book I'm about halfway through — don't shake your head at me. I won't say anything the whole trip, I cross my heart."

"Caitlin," I sigh. "Cat, no." The last thing I need is an audience. Eight hours in the car with Dan, that's fine. Add Caitlin to the mix and Dan won't say much, he's terribly shy. She'll think he's being standoffish, she'll pluck on our nerves, eight hours with Ray would be hell but I can't imagine Caitlin being much better, headphones or not. "I don't think it's such a good idea."

Dan tickles my stomach to get my attention. "Why not?" he asks, surprising me.

When I frown at him, she seizes the moment. "Yeah, why not?"

Ignoring her, I ask Dan, "Are you sure?" He shrugs like it's nothing to him one way or the other, but that's his way of telling me it's cool with him if she rides with us. When I raise an eyebrow in question, he nods slightly. "Okay," I concede.

Caitlin lets go of my foot and whoops in my ear as she gives me a quick hug. I push her away. "Just for this," she says, "I won't tell Mom you two got your freak on last night."

"Caitlin!" I shout, embarrassed. I swat at her but she laughs and dances out of reach. Before I can say anything else, she's through the door and gone. With a glance over my shoulder at Dan grinning at me, I point out, "Eight hours of that. I'm going to remind you that it was your call."

7: On the Road

WHEN I STAND at the foot of the stairs, my suitcase in hand, and call up to Caitlin because I'm ready to go, she comes bounding down with a bag slung over one shoulder, her pillow and a stuffed dog clutched to her chest. "Who's this?" I ask, poking at the dog's scruffy ear. She's had that thing for *years* — I know, because I gave it to her when she turned six. It's a light purple dog, well worn, with a row of safety pins holding shut the seam up its back. I'm surprised she even still has it. "You still sleep with that?"

With a meaningful look past me at Dan, she says, just loud enough for our mother in the kitchen to overhear, "I'm too young to sleep with anything else."

"Caitlin!" Dad cries, anger in his voice. He stomps out of the living room and into the foyer to glare at us — he's mad because my mom is *still* getting ready and it's almost ten in the morning. He wanted to be on the road already. To be honest, I did, too.

Caitlin shrugs like she doesn't know what she said wrong, then pushes through us out the door. "Do you believe her?" I ask Dan as he takes my suitcase. I keep my voice quiet so my dad won't answer, not that I have anything to worry about there. He barely knows I'm alive.

But somehow, miraculously, he's taken a liking to Dan. My lover heads out to the car with the suitcase and I trail behind him, one finger hooked through the belt loop on his jeans, and my dad is right behind *me*, catching the screen door when I let it slam shut and blinking in the early Sunday morning sun as we hurry down the porch steps to my car in the driveway. Caitlin leans against the side of the car, waiting for us, and my dad surprises us all by following us across the lawn. "You heading out soon?" he asks as I pop the trunk.

I look up at him and he's talking to Dan, not me. Swinging the suitcase into the trunk, Dan looks up and, seeing that my dad's waiting for him to answer, nods. "Yes, sir. Soon as we're ready to go." Then he gives me an amused glance that makes me turn away before my dad can see the smirk on my lips.

"Let me tell you how to get there, son," Dad says, calling Dan *son* like he's the one home for the weekend and I'm the errant boyfriend he's brought along to show off. With another glance my way, Dan puts on his stoic soldier's face and nods as he shuts the trunk. This is the face he wears when his CO is going on and on about something that doesn't interest Dan in the least, but the man outranks him and he knows better than to brush him off, even when I'm in the parking lot waiting. As if the back of my car's a huge map, Dad draws a line from the keyhole up towards the rear window. "Take 95 all the way up to D.C. — you ever been to Philly?"

"Yes, sir," Dan answered quickly.

Dad likes that *sir*, I just know it. Walking around behind them, I lean over Dan's shoulder and frown at the line drawn in the faint dust on my car. "Dad, he's from Ohio," I point out. Sugar Creek is in the western part of Pennsylvania, not far from the border. "He knows his way around up there."

That earns me a hateful look from my dad, as if I've just interrupted him and made him lose his train of thought. Seeing that glance, Dan reaches back to me, his fingers tickling over my stomach playfully. "Shh," he admonishes, before Dad can tell me the same thing in harsher words.

It doesn't stop him. "Do *you* know how to get there, Michael?" my dad asks, the challenge thick in his voice. He hasn't opened a beer yet — this is his usual level of meanness.

Like a chastised little boy, I reply sullenly, "I've been there often enough." True, it's been awhile, and I've never actually *driven* to Sugar Creek before, but I would swear the pathway there is carved into my heart.

We stand like two alley cats about to fight, my dad bristling and me trying hard not to pout, when Dan asks cautiously, "So you head up 95 like you're going to Philly?" It's directed at my dad but he looks at me as he speaks, and when I meet his gaze, there's a hint of a smile on his lips and a gleam in his eye that says simply, *Humor him.*

Diffused, my dad nods and I'm forgotten again. Turning back to the car, he taps the trunk like it's a map he's reading and says, "Actually, you don't go that far. Best way is to get off outside of Baltimore, 695 to 83, take that into Pennsylvania and keep to it. Past Harrisburg it turns into 322, then into 80. We're talking country roads here, boys." The front door opens and the three of us look up as my mom comes out onto the porch, enough bags in her hands to last an entire week. "If you wait a bit, you can follow us," Dad murmurs. Then, as Mom struggles with the luggage, he calls out, "We'll only be there three days, Laura. Jesus. Raymond! Help your mother. Mike —"

I don't wait to be told — I'm already halfway across the yard when my brother peers out from the door above the garage. "I've got it," I tell him. It's obvious he has his hands full with his own bag and pillow. Three days, is that all we'll be? What do these people need to *pack*?

As I take two of the bags from my mom, she gives me a tired smile. "Thanks. Do you two have pillows? You might need them."

Pillows, no. "I can stop by the house —" I start, but she shakes her head.

"It's okay," she tells me. I follow her to her small Ford Escort and wait as she unlocks the trunk. "We should be one of the first to arrive. Just grab a bedroom when you get there and don't let anyone throw you out. We might have to double up."

I toss the bags into the trunk and frown at the thought of sharing a room with one of my relatives. Doesn't matter *who* — I'm with Dan. Growing up, kids had to share rooms at Aunt Evie's — there were so many of us, the easiest thing to do was just group the girls in one room, the boys in another. The oldest usually managed to get the bed, while the rest were left with sleeping bags and blankets on the floor, like a weeklong pajama party. The only sure way to get a room of your own was to be married — Mom and Dad were afforded some privacy, along with other couples, but I remember a few summers when Aunt Bobbie was between husbands and she had to bed down with Penny. And Ginger, one of Aunt Billy's girls, always brought a boyfriend along, *always*. Once she told me it was just so she didn't have to room with anyone else.

But I'm with Dan. Not married, no, but together in the same way Ginger was with her guy friends, and she was always given a room apart. "Mom," I start, sure this is going to lead to an argument in the middle of the street — *then* what will the neighbors think? "Dan and I —"

That's as far as she lets me get. Holding up one hand, she tells me, "I don't want to hear it. It's not my house, Michael. They aren't my rules."

No, it's Evie's house, she made the rules, and I don't have to point out that she's no longer there. Which of her sisters can possibly hope to fill her shoes? Without children of her own, she was an impartial ear whenever there was an argument, judge and jury while we were guests at her home. Who would we turn to now?

Slamming the trunk shut, Mom sighs. "I guess we'll just see when we get there," she says. End of discussion.

Pissed, I brush by Ray as he comes up to the car. "Mom, my stuff," he whines because she's already closed the trunk, and just because I'm mad and he sounds so damn childish, I kick his shin as I pass. "Hey!" he cries. "What'd I do?"

At my car, I unlock the driver's side door to let Caitlin in. "Good hit," she mutters as she climbs into the back seat. "You should've gotten him right behind the knee, though. He goes down every time."

I don't bother to answer her. Instead, I trail around the back of the car, where Dad is still giving Dan directions, as if he has a photographic memory and can possibly remember all this. Holding out the car keys, I interrupt, "You want to drive?"

Dan hears the anger in my voice but doesn't comment on it. Instead, he takes the keys and gives me a small frown, one that tells me we'll talk once we're alone. Only we're *not* alone, are we? My little sister is camped out in the back seat of my car for the next eight hours, and once we get to Evie's, my mom's going to do anything she can to make sure there's someone else in the bedroom we'll share. Knowing her, she probably already thinks she can pawn Ray off on us. He'll lie awake in the dark and ask us stupid questions about gay sex and blowjobs and "Are you two going to do it when I fall asleep?" God, I can almost hear him now.

On the passenger side of the car, I pull up the handle and Caitlin reaches over to unlock the door. When I slide into the seat and slam the door shut, she asks, "Do you think Aunt Jessie will be there?"

I'm not in the mood to talk. I stare out the side mirror at Dan's reflection and tell her, "No."

She digests that for a moment as she fiddles with her Walkman. Tinny music blares through her headphones, I can hear it from here. Then she turns the volume down a little and says, "Mom told me it was heart failure." She means what killed Aunt Evie. I look at her in the rearview mirror and see tears shining in her eyes. "She seemed okay in August."

"Yeah, well," I say, my voice gruff with sudden emotion. "Sometimes things like that just happen." Caitlin studies the Walkman in her hands and nods, her chin crumpling as she struggles not to cry. Hoping to cheer her up, I add, "Aunt Evie's a big lady."

That gets a smile. "Yeah, I guess," she murmurs, wiping at her eyes. Her hand comes away streaked with black eyeliner, and she blinks quickly, dotting at her face. "Fuck, this shit stings."

There are napkins in the glove compartment, leftover from the last time Dan and I ate from a drive-thru. I hand her one and look away — I don't want to watch her cry. "Maybe you shouldn't be wearing that," I say softly. She'll just cry it all off, it's a waste of make-up.

"Maybe," she concedes as she dabs at her face.

The driver's side door opens and Dan slides in behind the wheel. I give him a bright smile that feels like plastic on my lips. "Know where we're going?" I ask.

He buckles his seat belt and starts the car. "Mostly," he tells me. With a glance at Caitlin, still rubbing her eyes, he leans across the gearshift and whispers, "Come here."

I lean closer. His lips touch my mouth in a tender kiss. When I start to pull away, he stops me with a hand on the back of my neck. He stares into my eyes until I can count the tiny black lashes along his lower eyelids. "You okay?" he wants to know.

I smile again, sad. "Fine," I assure him. "Just ..." I take a deep breath — I won't mention the room situation, not until I know for sure we won't be able to sleep alone. Then I'll tell him look, there's a Super 8 over in Franklin, we'll see everyone at the funeral. I don't want to stay anywhere else, though. To me, Sugar Creek *is* Evie's home. With a soft sigh, I say again, "I'm fine."

He doesn't believe me, but he doesn't press it, either. He knows I'll tell him when I'm ready. Putting the car into reverse, he glances at Caitlin and then smiles at me. "Are we all set?"

My stomach churns with a familiar nervousness as he backs the car out of the driveway. "You know where we're going?" I ask again.

Dan puts the car into drive and takes my hand in his. "I've got it covered," he says, giving my hand a light squeeze. He slows the car as we pass my parents. "Or do you want me to follow your dad?"

Ray is the only one in the other car — my mom is heading back into the house, my dad leans on the open driver's side door and shouts at her to hurry the hell up. "Just go," I murmur. There's no reason to wait. I'm certain I can navigate the way to Aunt Evie's in my sleep.

"Yeah, go," Caitlin pipes up. I thought she said she wouldn't be bothering us? "Maybe we'll get our pick of rooms, if we get there first," she says, talking loud over the noise in her headphones. "Mom's all about getting someone in with you guys, you know that, right? I heard her with Penny on the phone this morning. I think Doug's already at the house. He lives in what, Pittsburgh?"

I don't want to think about sleeping arrangements just yet. "We'll see when we get there," I tell her, sounding just like my mom, I hate that.

There's an exit for the interstate off the boulevard, not five miles from the house. Dan remembers the way through the convoluted streets of our subdivision without my having to guide him, and he takes the northbound lane headed towards D.C. For a crazy moment I think we're going home, and Evie's still alive, there's still next summer to bring Dan up to Sugar Creek.

But then Caitlin's arm snakes between us, reaching for the radio. She cranks up the volume, blaring George Michael's latest hit, and then she starts flipping through the stations. "Hey, do you think we can get DC101 from here?" she asks. Without waiting for an answer, she settles on something by Metallica, and the volume gets turned up another few notches. "So you think they'll stick Gordie in with you? Does he still wet the bed? Jeez, maybe you can send the kid out when you wanna get it on —"

I snap the radio off and slap her hand away. "Look," I say, growing angry again. "You said you'd leave us alone, Caitlin. *Cat.*" I correct myself before she can. "Let's get something straight here, okay? Two things. One, do *not* touch the radio. This is my car, Dan's driving. We'll listen to what we want to hear, at the volume *we* want to hear it. Understand?"

She flops back in the seat and crosses her arms defiantly. "Damn," she mutters. "Got it. Two?"

"Two," I say, turning to look at her so she knows I'm not kidding here, "no more cracks on my sex life. Not one, you here me? I'm not discussing it with you, it's none of your goddamn business. What Dan and I have is between *us*, him and me, got *that*?" She rolls her eyes and I feel a dull ire rise in me. How can my parents put up with this? "I'm sick and tired of comments from the peanut gallery, Cat. You want to pick on someone? Stick with Ray."

"Ray *has* no sex life," she says. Beside me, Dan smirks. Caitlin cries out, "He doesn't!"

Somehow I think she's missing the point. I know at sixteen, it's hard for her to believe that what I feel for Dan is more than just sex — it's the media's fault, really, they portray gay men as sex hungry fiends who fuck anything with a dick. But I'm not like that. I've only had two lovers, Matthew when I was twenty and Dan. No one in between. Not that I didn't date, but no one held my interest for very long.

Until Dan.

He tells me I'm the only one he loves. He holds me when we make love because it's not just intercourse to him — he wants as much of my body touching his while I move in him, he wants my breath on his skin, my lips, my hands on him. "I don't want sex," he told me the first time we slept together. "It has to be love or nothing at all. I want every last bit of you, Michael. If I can't have you completely, then I'll wait. You're worth waiting for."

I'm not telling Caitlin *that*. Instead I just give her what I hope is a withering look, though it doesn't seem to phase her. "Well," I say, turning back towards the front of the car again, "I'm not going to talk to you about mine."

"Fine," she huffs. "Then I won't tell you about *mine*, either."

That gets a laugh from Dan, but I don't take the bait. "Eight hours," I mutter under my breath. I know he hears me, it's in the way he squeezes my hand gently in commiseration. "Think you can get us there faster than that?" I ask, only half joking.

"I'll try," he promises. From the back seat I hear Caitlin's music, she's turned her headphones up as loud as they'll go, but I pretend I don't hear it. I wonder if I'm ready for this. I don't think eight hours will be enough time to prepare myself for facing Sugar Creek without Evie there to welcome us.

8: Rainbow Joan's

WHEN WE HIT the Capital beltway, I'm tempted to ask Dan to stop by the townhouse anyway. Grab our pillows, maybe a few more clothes — something black because I don't think I have anything to wear to the funeral — maybe call the firm and my professors, since I might not be back before my vacation's over and I know I'll miss class Tuesday night. But we're making good time, the interstate's mostly clear this early on a Sunday, and without a word, I watch the last exit into D.C. pass us by. Dan still holds onto my hand, and I've turned the radio back on so that it plays softly between us, so low that I can't make out the songs. They're like music from a dream, a tune on the tip of your tongue that you can almost remember after awakening. In the back seat Caitlin is stretched out, one foot tapping the door in time with the music in her headphones as she leafs through a tattoo magazine. She hasn't spoken to me since we got on the road.

Absently, I open Dan's hand in my lap and stroke his fingers from tip to base, each one. He has long fingers, graceful and slim, like an artist or musician. Beautiful hands that the Army hasn't managed to destroy. I can't imagine these hands holding a gun or a knife in combat — I've seen these fingers unbutton shirts, I've felt them on my flesh. I remember Aunt Evie once said that you can tell how well a man makes love just by looking at his hands. We were in Union City for the day to do some shopping, my mom and Ray and Evie and me, and we ate lunch outside of a classy Grecian restaurant. Nik's, I believe it was called. Our waiter was a young man whose flirtatious comments made Evie blush. Part of his job, I'm sure, complement the ladies for good tips. It worked, though Evie was a big tipper by nature, very easy with money. I don't know how often I heard her say, "Keep the change." That day at Nik's, she and my mom giggled over the waiter, and after he brought our food, Evie leaned across the table and lowered her voice to tell us, "Look at his hands next time, Laura. You can always tell a good lover by the shape of his hands."

If that's the case, Evie would have taken one look at Dan's large, supple hands and told me, "Michael, keep him. Only a gentle lover has hands like that." My eyes sting with tears because I can almost hear the words in her voice — I see her in my mind, one hand on her hip as she nods sagely. And she'd be right. Dan's the gentlest man I know. Quiet, soft-spoken, and so damn attentive in bed. I can't imagine ever letting him go.

I trace the love line along his palm below his fingers to where it meets his life line. I follow that down to his wrist, then trace the faint blue vein that leads to the crook of his elbow, then back again. When I work into the center of his palm, he closes his fingers around mine and I glance up to find him smiling at me. "Hey," he says. He jerks his head back to indicate Caitlin.

Turning, I find my sister asleep, her arm curled beneath her head like a pillow, the magazine fallen to the floor. The noise from her headphones has stopped. "Figures," I say, keeping my voice low. With any luck, she'll sleep the rest of the trip.

Dan laces his fingers through mine and concentrates on the road ahead. We sit in an easy silence that somehow says more than anything we could hope to convey with words alone. I love this quiet surrounding us, I love how comfortable we are together.

A little while later when we pass beneath a green road sign for Baltimore, he asks me, "Are you getting hungry?"

I shrug. "A little," I admit. Then I look at the dashboard and notice the time, almost one in the afternoon, and as if that's a catalyst, my stomach rumbles. I press the back of Dan's hand to my belly and he laughs. "I guess so," I say, grinning. "What do you have in mind?"

He gives me an amused glance from the corner of his eye and I know what he's thinking. We're coming up on Baltimore, so that means … "Rainbow Joan's?" I suggest.

"How'd you guess?" he wants to know.

It's one of his favorite places to eat, that's how. I introduced him to Joan's shortly after we started dating — back at the beginning of February, actually. Super Bowl Sunday, and he didn't want to stay in the barracks so he called me up, asked if I was doing anything special. I wasn't, but I could think of a few ways I'd like to spend the evening, and all of them included him. We had known each other for just three weeks at that point but I was already falling hard.

I told him to give me a half hour and I'd pick him up. He was waiting at the front gate when I drove onto post, barely let me stop before he was in my car. The minute Fort Myer faded in the rearview mirror, he had a hand on my knee. At the first stoplight that caught us, he leaned across the gear shaft and whispered, "Come here." Then he kissed me.

When we drove past D.C., he asked what I had in mind. "A little place I think you'll like," I told him. Rainbow Joan's is one of the only gay-owned restaurants I know of that isn't flamboyant about it. I mean, it's not a bar or club or coffee shop, and there are no drag nights or pride events — it's just a good place to eat. They have thick burgers, hoagies stacked high, specialty sandwiches and homemade lemonade, fresh baked desserts, daily specials, you name it, chances are it's on the menu at Joan's. If not, they'll try to make it. Outside there's a covered deck with a small bar and wrought-iron chairs and tables, and the booths inside have wooden tables shellacked with magazine ads, Guess and Versace and other designer names. There's a small riser by the kitchen door where local bands play on the weekends, and it's open mic Thursday nights for karaoke. At lunch time, Joan's fills up quickly, mostly with people from nearby offices. Dinnertime, though, the place is alive with college students and young people my age, mostly the gay scene in Baltimore. Joan's is *the* place to be, a jukebox in one corner, a large screen TV in the other, and the bar hopping until well after midnight.

We got to Joan's before the second quarter of the game and there was hardly any place to sit. People everywhere, laughing and calling to one another. Music from the jukebox rivaled the sounds of the TV, and outside on the deck, a college band called Black Tie Affair tried to drown out the noise with heavy guitar riffs and a steady drumbeat. I had to shout in Dan's ear just to be heard, and before a waitress came to seat us, he eased an arm around my waist to keep me close. I felt his hand fist at the small of my back. "We can go somewhere else," I yelled at him. "If you want."

He shook his head no. Joan's is far enough away from Fort Myer that he feels safe there — he won't run into anyone he knows from base. And there's no need to hide our relationship, either, not when the place is crawling with gay and lesbian couples, holding hands and sharing drinks and making out in the back booths. We're tame compared to some.

And on Super Bowl Sunday, we weren't quite the couple we are now. When the waitress asked how many, I held up two fingers, and Dan kept his hand on my waist as I followed the woman through the crowd to an empty booth near the front windows. As Dan slid into the booth across from me, he stared around with wide eyes, trying to take in everything at once. "Rainbow Joan's," he said, bemused. I could tell he liked the place.

We ate dinner, ordered drinks, watched the game, leaned across the table when we talked so we could hear each other over the surrounding din. After halftime, the crowd thinned out a bit, but when the game was over and large groups of people started to leave, our ears rang so badly that we still shouted to be heard. By his third Lynchburg Lemonade, Dan's hands were on my thighs beneath the table, and a thin blush colored his cheeks every time I made him laugh. We only left when a very tired waiter came by our table and told us everyone else was going home. "Unless you want to stay the night," he added, joking, as I helped Dan from the booth.

Outside, the night air was brisk on my heated face, and I imagined I could feel snow in my bones. Or maybe it was the alcohol, I don't know. My car was the only one in the parking lot, and Dan stumbled behind me, his hands shoved deep in the pockets of my pants as he searched for my car keys. "I can drive," he told me, his breath hot in my ear.

I felt his thick erection press against my buttocks. "You're drunk," I told him. "I'll drive."

He laughed at that, and in my pockets, his hands closed over my own dick, squeezing playfully. "What's this?" he asked.

"Not the keys," I replied. I turned in his embrace and leaned back against the side of my car, wrapped my arms around his neck and pulled him to me for a hungry kiss. "Stay with me," I sighed.

He looked at me like he wasn't sure what I was talking about. I meant that night, I meant forever. "Michael," he started, sobering up. "I don't think we're ready —"

I wasn't talking sex. We didn't make love until two months after we'd been together. I didn't want to rush anything with Dan, I wanted him too much to scare him away. So that night, out in the chilly winter air, I picked at the collar of his jacket and stared into his dark eyes, stars reflected in the inky depths like shining lights at sea. "I'm tired of looking," I told him, forcing myself to speak low. I almost couldn't hear my own words over the ringing in my ears. "I'm tired of playing the club scene, Dan. I'm tired of being alone. Remember when we met, and I told you I thought I liked you?"

He stared at me for so long, I felt my resolve begin to crumble. I was ready to tell him just forget it, I'd take him back to base, he obviously didn't feel the same and I had been wrong about him, then his brow furrowed and he whispered, "I remember."

My lower lip trembled as I kissed him tenderly. "Well," I breathed, "I think I love you now, Dan. I'm not saying we have to do anything tonight, but I want to hold you. I want to wake up and watch you sleeping beside me. I want —" He laughed and my heart stopped in my chest. "What?"

"I'm in the Army," he reminded me. "I get up at the crack of dawn, babe." I didn't get it — my mind was a fuzzy haze from the drinks, the noise, the night. "I'll watch *you* sleep," he told me. Then he kissed me, and as the neon sign above Rainbow Joan's winked out, he whispered, "I think I love you, too."

The restaurant has held a special place for us since that night. Dan takes the beltway around Baltimore, eases into sudden traffic, gets off at the

Edmondson Avenue exit. Joan's is on Orleans Street — when I see the sign, I turn around to wake up Caitlin. "Cat," I call, but she's sound asleep. Plucking off her headphones, I shake her gently. "Caitlin? Get up."

"Wha —?" She stretches into a sitting position, blinks around like she's not sure where she is. "We there already? Damn, that was fast."

I wish. "We're in Baltimore," I tell her. With a stifled yawn, she lies back down. "We're stopping for a bite to eat. Unless you're not hungry?"

"I'm hungry," she mumbles, and I have to shake her awake again when Dan pulls into Joan's parking lot. "What?" she whines. "I'm up. Jesus."

"Don't call me Jesus," I joke, climbing out of the car. I hold the door open and she stumbles out like she's drunk, staggering into me. "You want to sleep?" I ask, but she shakes her head. "We can bring you something."

She pushes away from me. "I'm fine. Awake, see?" To emphasize her point, she holds her eyes open wide and grins ghoulishly at me. "See?"

I give her a playful shove towards the restaurant. "I see," I tell her. Dan takes my hand as we step around the car, the two of us gravitating together like opposing magnets. Loudly, so Caitlin will hear, I say, "We can leave her here, you know. If she starts to act up ..."

"I hear you," she growls. She pushes through the front door of the restaurant and lets it swing back at me, but Dan grabs the handle before it hits my arm. Nodding over her shoulder at us, Caitlin tells the waitress, "I'm not with them."

Ignoring her, I say, "Three, please." As the waitress leads us to a booth, I ask my sister, "What, you paying for yourself?"

"Are you treating?" she wants to know. She slides in one side of the booth and takes the menu from the waitress.

Dan waits for me to get in across from her before he sits beside me. "I'll cover it," I say. "Long as you don't order every damn thing they have."

Caitlin gives me a sardonic look over the top of her menu. "I'm not Ray," she reminds me. "A Reuben's good enough for me." Then she folds the menu and looks around, taking in the brightly painted walls, the magazine-covered tables. Most of the booths are already filled despite the early hour, but the jukebox is off, the TV tuned to some midday movie from the late '80's whose title escapes me at the moment. One of those Jon Cusak comedies that leaves no doubt in my mind as to why the guy isn't acting anymore. "You guys come here often?" Caitlin asks. If she notices that the majority of couples around us are same-sex, she doesn't mention it.

"We like it," I tell her. Beneath the table, Dan rests a hand on my thigh, and his hip presses against mine in the seat. "The food's good, you'll see."

The waitress comes for our orders — a Reuben for my sister, two turkey and ham hoagies for myself and Dan. I want a cheesesteak but I change my mind at the last minute, because this isn't Pennsylvania yet and I swear no one south of the Mason-Dixon line can do a cheesesteak justice. I'll wait until we get to Sugar Creek for that. I'm sure one night we'll call in an order to Big Al's, the self-proclaimed Steak King. My mouth waters at the thought of one of his sandwiches. Chopped steak and melted cheese smothered in olive oil … all others pale in comparison.

While we wait for our food, I lean back in the booth and study my sister. Her eyeliner has smeared until her eyes look like bruises in her face, and her lipstick has mostly disappeared. Just the dark outline of her lips is left, making her mouth look larger than it is. Her eyelashes are clumped together into thick spikes of mascara — bedroom eyes, if I've ever seen them. She looks like she just woke up after a long night of partying. "You look frightful," I tell her.

She smiles sweetly and sips at her soda. "Thank you," she replies.

I can't tell if she's being facetious or not. Suddenly I realize I don't know much about my teenaged sister — she wasn't this Goth-girl the last time I saw her at Christmas. When did this start? Why? The whole look seems too high-maintenance for me. But she plays it off like it's nothing to her. She ignores the stares from the people around her, unaffected by the faint whispers that her appearance and black clothing seem to invite. Since the moment I came home, she's played at being impervious to anything that's said or done. My announcement at dinner didn't seem to surprise her in the least.

When Dan excuses himself and heads for the bathroom, I sit up a little and say, "Tell me something, Cat."

I use her nickname because I want to get on her good side. Unfortunately, it just makes her suspicious. She looks at me distrustfully and asks, "What?" Before I answer, she adds, "We said no talking about our sex lives, remember? I really wasn't going to tell Mom you guys did it last night."

I have to laugh. "I'm not — Caitlin, this isn't … look, I don't want to know, okay? You use condoms, right?" She nods, and I give her my most disarming smile. "Then okay. No more talk about sex, I promise." Cautiously I ask her, "I just want to know — are you cool with Dan and me?"

She shrugs. "He's alright," she says. "You could do worse. Nice ass, you know?" Then she laughs again. "Or wait, are we not mentioning that, either?"

Secretly, I agree with her — Dan has a fine ass, but she's only sixteen and I'm going to pretend she's not checking my guy out. "It's not like I'm surprised here, Mike," she tells me. The look she throws my way suggests that she's known for awhile that I like boys. Counting off on her fingers, she says, "You've never had a girlfriend, *ever*. Didn't go to prom. Didn't date in high school."

Well, I did, but no one I was serious with, no one I ever brought home. "You just figured it out on your own?" I ask, impressed. "So why can't Mom see —"

"Oh," Caitlin interrupts, flipping her hair out of her face. "And a few months ago I found some magazines in your closet that confirmed it."

I laugh. "*The Advocate*," I say. When she shakes her head, I frown and try to think what else I might have in my old room. "*Gay and Lesbian Review?*" Another shake. "*Out?* Caitlin, what?"

Dan approaches the table and she gives him a mischievous grin. "Try *Freshmen*." I feel a heated blush color my cheeks, and Dan gives me a quizzical look as my little sister reels off names of gay porn mags I totally forgot about, hidden away in my closet at my parents' house. "*Men*, something about twinks ..."

"Okay," I concede as Dan slides in beside me again, his hand drawn to my leg. "I get the point."

9: Memory Lane

AFTER WE EAT it's back on the road. Dan takes interstate 83 out of Baltimore, heading north into Pennsylvania, my hand covering his where it rests on my knee. In the back seat, Caitlin's fiddling with her Walkman again, muttering under her breath. "I think my batteries are going," she says, ripping the headphones off and throwing them to the floorboards. "Can't we stop somewhere?"

With a laugh, I ask, "Where?" The highway stretches out to the horizon and trees line both sides of the road. The signs list approaching cities that sound familiar because I've seen their names on these same green boards for as long as I can remember, but I've never stopped at any of them. I don't want to stop now, not just for batteries. One wrong turn and we could be lost for days. In the rearview mirror, I see Caitlin's ignoble pout and tell her, "We can stop in Harrisburg if you want. Isn't there a 7-11 right off the interstate?"

"I don't know," she mutters. Then she sighs dramatically and throws herself back in the seat, her arms folded across her chest, her chin tucked down so all I can see is the top of her head and the light brown roots that look almost red against the black dye in her hair. "Can't you turn up the radio a bit?" she wants to know. "It's so damn *silent* back here."

"Dan doesn't like it loud when he drives," I say.

But my lover starts to play with the radio controls. "It's okay," he tells me, turning the speakers up in the back. Glancing into the mirror, he asks, "How's that?"

One corner of Caitlin's mouth pulls up into a half-smile. "Fine, thanks." She doesn't mention the dance music, doesn't ask if we can find something heavier to listen to, and without the headphones shielding our world from hers, she feels like now it's time to talk a bit. So she leans against the back of my seat, her head right next to mine. When she speaks, she's unnaturally loud in my ear. "How much farther?" she asks.

"Couple hours," I say, looking past her to Dan. He sees the look and nods. "What, four? Five?"

"About that," he concedes. His hand squeezes my knee, and he asks, "Is any of this starting to look familiar to you, babe? Or am I off-track?"

No, he's right on track. Everything about this road brings back memories — images rise in my mind like bubbles to the surface of a pond. The years, stacked one upon the next like layers of a cake, melt and run together, until I'm not sure what happened when …

One year we stopped for fresh peaches at a stand right by that sign for the KOA campground — the cart's not there now, but I remember the heat of that day beating down on the top of my head, warming my hair until I thought it'd burst into flame. I stood there so long debating over the large, overly ripened fruit, until my mom just grabbed my hand and told the vendor to bag up five peaches. One for each of us, with one set aside for Aunt Evie. We were going to wait until after dinner to eat them, but in the backseat of the car, Ray dug into the bag when our parents weren't looking and ate his. "Go on," he said, handing me one of the softball-sized peaches. It took both hands to hold it, and when I bit into it, juice ran down my chin and throat and arms. By the time we got to Evie's, we were both so sticky and my mom so angry that she made us stand in the backyard while she hosed us down. Ray laughed the whole time, making her angrier still. We never stopped for fruit again after that.

Then one time, when I was a teenager and almost as surly as Caitlin is now, we decided to come up to Sugar Creek for the fourth of July, and to beat the holiday traffic, Dad thought it would be a good idea to leave shortly after midnight. Our headlights reflected off the silver backs of the tractor trailers that sped along the interstates at breakneck speed, until it seemed like we were surrounded by Martians in shiny metal spaceships hovering two feet in front of our car and hemming us in on either side. It was a good plan, though — the roads were clear of travelers, the only traffic being the huge semis that ran after dark. But just outside of York, we saw a car pulled over to the side of the road. A man struggled with a tire as he held an emergency light in one hand, the kind ensconced in a plastic cage that mechanics use to hang beneath the hood of a car. Inside the car, the overhead light was on, illuminating a woman and a young girl my age. Both had wide, frightened eyes.

Dad pulled over to see what the trouble was — back then, people did stuff like that. You didn't think of getting killed or calling the state police on your cell phone. Hell, we didn't *have* a cell phone. "Donald, I don't think you should —" was as far as my mom got before Dad was out of the car, the door slammed shut on her words.

Ray and I watched as he spoke with the other man, and then he was back. "Come on, boys," he said, and despite my mom's misgivings, we clambered out into the night. Just a flat tire, that was all it was, but Dad leaned on the jack and Ray rolled the old tire away when the stranger handed it to him. My job was to hold the new one in place. I was doing fine, too, until I heard a light tapping and looked up to see the girl inside the car staring at me through the window, a big smile on her face. She had just the faintest blue shadow dusted across her eyelids and pink, sparkly lip gloss. Although I was old enough to know I liked guys, this girl *was* pretty. It was the make-up, I think. Made her look otherworldly.

Dad's voice rang out in the night. "Michael! Watch what you're doing, kid!" Surprised, I let go of the tire and it fell heavily on my foot. "See?" my dad asked in righteous indignation as I yelped in pain. "You're not paying attention. Ray, get over here and help him hold that up."

My foot was swollen by the time we reached Evie's— I took my sneaker off to massage the bruised flesh and couldn't even squeeze it back on. I hobbled for almost a week after that. "One of the last times I ever looked at a girl, too," I say, telling the story to Dan and Caitlin.

My lover laughs and kisses the back of my hand. "Good thing for me," he replies.

"Was that when Ray pitched your shoe out the window?" Caitlin asks. When Dan looks at her, confused, she explains, "It's sort of a running joke at Aunt Evie's. You'll see. Everyone likes to throw their shoes at Ray because —"

"I'll tell him," I say, pushing Caitlin into the back seat to quiet her. "I was there. You weren't even born yet."

"I *know* the story," she assures me. "It was somewhere along here, right? Before Harrisburg."

Now Dan's interest is piqued and it's not even all that great of a tale. "I was just five years old," I tell him, and he grins to picture it, me a toddler. "We were goofing off in the back seat and Ray tied my shoelaces together. Double knots, I couldn't get them undone. So I kicked them off and threw them at him. Like an idiot, he pitched them out the window."

"Why?" Dan wants to know.

I shrug. Who knows why Ray does anything? "So I wouldn't throw them at him again, I guess. I don't know." I still remember the expression on my dad's face, though, when we stopped at McDonald's for a quick bite to eat and he told me to put on my shoes. "They're gone," I said, with all the aplomb of a little child. When he asked where they were, I pointed at the road. "Back there."

Ray admitted to throwing them away — he can't lie to my dad. One look into those glowering eyes and he starts to blubber like a baby. My mother was livid, refused to even *speak* to my brother until we got to Evie's. Most of the family was already there, cousins and aunts and uncles lounging on the porch in the mid-summer heat, but as my dad carried me up to the house, Mom laid into Ray. "Threw the shoes out the *window*, can you believe it? Eight years old — where's your brain?"

Even at five, I knew the answer to *that* question, though at the time I kept quiet. Everyone thought it was the funniest thing, only because Ray was old enough to know better and he so obviously didn't. One by one our cousins slipped out of their shoes, if they wore any, and as he passed, they pelted him with sneakers and sandals and flip-flops, until he was crying, "I'm sorry! I'm sorry!"

Yeah, it was mean, but children are mean creatures. From the back seat, Caitlin cackles at the image of Ray running the gauntlet of shoes. "They still do it," she laughs, hitting the back of Dan's seat to get his attention. "Hell, *I* do it and I wasn't even there at the time. It's the funniest thing. He's all like what? Like he doesn't remember."

With an enigmatic smirk, Dan replies, "He probably doesn't."

Caitlin leans forward again, this time to get a good look at Dan. He glances at her, over her head at me, then his eyes are on the road again. "What do you think of Ray?" my sister asks.

Dan shrugs, and when he looks at me a second time, I see the discomfort in his gaze. Though we haven't discussed it, I already know that he doesn't like my brother. Ray's ignorant comments last night were enough to put him on Dan's shit list. But my lover isn't one to mention it — even if I ask him outright, he'll try to play it off. He doesn't talk bad about anyone, not his hard-nosed CO, not his Army buddies, not even the sergeant at basic who ran him and dozens of other cadets into the ground. No, he'll just shrug and say nothing, like he does now, but he'll give Ray a cold shoulder whenever they have to be together. He won't initiate conversation, he won't look my brother in the eye, he won't even respond to anything Ray says if he can help it. To Dan, he won't exist. That's the way he deals with someone he can't stand but can't do anything about.

"Come on," Caitlin tries. "I won't tell him what you say."

"There's nothing *to* say," Dan tells her.

That's all she's going to manage to get out of him. When he looks at me for help, I elbow her out from between the seats and say, "It's none of your business, Caitlin. Cat. Just sit back, will you?"

"Jeez," she mutters, crossing her arms and pouting in displeasure. "It's not that hard a question." Dan doesn't answer, and her reflection glares at us in the rearview mirror. "You either like him or you don't, and if you do, then you're the first. I didn't ask for *details*."

She doesn't know when to stop. "Caitlin," I warn.. There's a dull ache starting behind my right eye and I don't feel like dealing with her anymore. "Just don't, okay?" Leaning against the window, the glass cool on my forehead, I close my eyes and murmur, "Please."

An uneasy silence fills the car, cloying and heavy like thick perfume. It makes my head hurt worse, and Dan starts to rub my thigh in long, comforting strokes. I love him. I don't care if we have to drag sleeping bags up into the dusty attic, or even pitch a tent in the backyard in the middle of October — I'm not sharing sleeping quarters with anyone else but him. I'm going to need his arms around me to get me through the next few days. I'm going to need his quiet strength, his love. I can't do this alone. Hell, I can't even deal with Caitlin for very long … how am I possibly going to survive the rest of the family?

Without Evie. She was the one who always managed to tie us all together. How will any of us stay tethered to each other without her holding on?

The lull of the road is a steady, constant rumble like a drug, dulling my senses, stretching time out like taffy around us. I remember passing Harrisburg — Caitlin isn't talking to us, so she doesn't ask to stop for batteries — and I remember the interstate narrowing down to a small, four-lane highway. I remember trees and shrubs, and blinking slowly, taking longer and longer to open my eyes. I remember faint sounds from the radio, a burst of static as we lose the station, Dan's hand leaving my leg long enough to find a strong signal and then it's back again. Sometime after that, with his hand on my thigh, the low radio, the *rumdrumdrum* of the road, I fall asleep.

I wake to a soft kiss. The car is parked and the radio off, and Dan brushes his fingers along my cheek as he kisses me again. "Michael," he sighs. I try to crawl closer to his voice but I'm still strapped in my seat.

A third kiss, my name again, his hand smoothed across my brow, and I open my eyes. Taking a deep breath, I don't bother to look around — this close, his eyes are amazing, dark as the ocean before a storm. I can see light hairs curve around his jaw, and the next time his heart-shaped lips touch mine, I don't close my eyes. He doesn't, either, and we part in breathy giggles. His hand is on the back of my neck now. "Where's Cat?" I ask. If he's kissing me so unabashedly, I know we have to be alone.

"Bathroom," he tells me. We've stopped at one of the numerous rest stops that line the interstate — we're still be on 83 then. Once we get onto the state routes, these rest areas disappear. Bathroom breaks are taken at fast food restaurants or gas stations. As I stretch awake, Dan unsnaps my seat belt. "You want to get out for a minute?"

We tumble from either side of the car, and once I'm on my feet, I stretch for the sky. It feels heavenly to be standing — my back is a bundle of knots, my arms ache, my legs tingle because they've been cramped up for too long. Coming around to the front of the car, I give Dan a sweet smile and rub a hand down his t-shirt to flatten it across his stomach. "Are you okay to drive?"

He nods as he leans back on the hood of my car. "Keeps me from getting too sick," he tells me.

He gets carsick. Concerned, I lean beside him, our arms pressed together. "You sure you're okay then?" I ask.

"Fine," he tells me, and his smile confirms it. Reaching for his wallet, he asks, "Do you think they have snacks here?"

"I'll go see," I say. When he tries to hand me some cash, I shake my head. "I've got it." With a quick kiss on his cheek — the rest area is mostly disserted, no one I know here anyway — I promise, "Be right back."

The snack machines are off to the side of the restrooms, and of course my sister is already there, juggling a bag of chips and three candy bars as she tries to force a dollar into the soda machine. "Come on, you fucker," she mumbles under her breath. Two older women edge away from her, casting furtive glances at her attire as they mutter to themselves, and in one corner, three boys a little younger than Caitlin's age sit astride bikes, grinning at her.

"Let me," I say, coming up behind her. I smooth the dollar out against the side of the machine and wonder if I have to apologize for our earlier argument. It wasn't really a fight though, was it? I shouldn't have to say I'm sorry.

Caitlin glares at me and doesn't say a word. Behind us, one of the boys says something I don't hear, but it sets his friends laughing. I wonder if they saw the kiss out by the car, or Dan waking me. I try the dollar in the machine, but it's spit back out time and again. I'm starting to feel like Caitlin must, as if the whole world is staring at me, judging me, watching, waiting, and I don't know how she can do it. I'm just about to say the hell with it and try another machine when someone behind us finds his courage and whispers, "Faggot," just loud enough for us to hear.

I'm used to it. I can ignore it, who are these kids to me? But beside me, my sister goes rigid with anger. "It's okay," I murmur, keeping my voice low. This time the machine takes her money and I sigh in relief. "What do you want here, Caitlin?"

No answer. "Cat?" I ask, turning. "What —"

She shoves her food into my arms and turns on her heel. The boys snicker amongst themselves as she approaches, her Doc Martins ringing on the concrete floor. "What the *fuck* did you just say?" she demands, propping one foot on the front wheel of the bike closest to her.

"Caitlin," I call out. Oh shit. "Really, it's —"

She points at me and tells the kids, "That's my brother, you understand? You want to talk shit about him, you say it to my face, you *understand?*" Before the boys can answer, she shoves at the bike with her foot, knocking it over. The boy astride it steps clear as it hits the floor. "I don't know who the fuck you are but I'll kick your ass."

This time she lunges at them and they scatter, dropping their bikes in her path to keep her away. "You're a freak," one of the boys says, like that's the worst name he can think to call her. His friends titter nervously.

"And you're a dumbass," Caitlin replies. The kids stagger back, out of the vending area — they look younger in the sunlight, maybe no more than ten, eleven years old. "Fucking homophobic assholes," she calls them, "all of you. You better run."

When she starts after them, I grab her shirt. "Caitlin, no," I tell her. She struggles for a moment, but the boys race off into the men's restroom where she can't follow. "It's fine, Cat. I get it a lot. You get used to it."

"You shouldn't have to put up with that shit," she says. Taking her snacks from me, she hits one of the buttons on the soda machine with a small, angry fist. "No one picks on my brothers," she mutters as a can tumbles out. "No one but me."

10: In the Car

DAN IS ALREADY coming up to the vending area as Caitlin and I head back for the car. "What's going on?" he wants to know. He heard my sister's big mouth, I'm sure. Everyone here did — the few people stopped at the rest area don't quite look at the two of us, my sister walking ahead of me with her arms full of snacks, my hand fisted in the back of her shirt to keep her from turning to hunt down those boys in the restroom. I stare ahead at the car. "Michael?" Dan asks. "What happened?"

"Get in the car," I tell Caitlin, giving her a push in that direction.

"Some kids called him —" she starts.

"Go on," I say with another shove. She almost stumbles and glares back at me over her shoulder but doesn't argue, thank God.

Dan waits until she's far enough way that she can't hear us. "Michael," he says, his hand still on my arm. When I look at him, I know he heard her words, I'm sure the concrete walls around the vending machines echoed her voice out here, that's why he came running. Finally he asks, "Are you going to tell me? Or do I have to guess?"

Behind us, I hear the bathroom door open, echoed laughter streaming out into the day, and I just want to leave. "It wasn't anything really," I tell him, but I know Dan well enough to know he doesn't buy that. I look back at the restrooms — the boys are still hiding from my sister, I don't blame them. Handing my lover one of the sodas I bought, I say, "Just some kids being mean, that's it."

"What did they say?" Dan wants to know.

I shrug and force a laugh — I'm not going to let it bother me. "Nothing, really," I insist. "Just … you heard Cat. Fucking homophobic assholes, wasn't that the term she used?"

Dan doesn't return my smile. Instead, he studies me intently and holds me back when I start to walk away. "Look," I say — I can feel his anger brewing. I want him back in the car and I want to drive away, hopefully before those boys come out. If they thought Caitlin was scary, they've never been up against an enlisted man. He might seem quiet, but Dan is *not* someone you want to anger, trust me. When he first moved in with me, we had a neighbor who used to make loud comments about our relationship from the safety of his back porch. Dan and I would spend the evening on the balcony off the bedroom, and the neighbor would be downstairs, one townhouse over, grilling on his porch and telling his wife and children and whoever else was around to hear about how disgusting it was, having to live next to flagrantly sinful men. His words, *flagrantly sinful.* As if going to church every Sunday made him so much holier than either of us.

I don't know what happened, what was said — Dan won't go into details. But one evening we sat together on the balcony, each word drifting up to us with all the hate and venom our neighbor could muster, his conversation dotted with liberal doses of *faggots* and *gays* and even a *butt-fucker* or two, in front of his children. I couldn't believe it, didn't *want* to believe it, and was just about to tell Dan that maybe it'd be nice to watch TV or something, anything to get us out of earshot, when my lover stood up and stretched. Picked up his glass of tea as if he planned on refilling it, gave me a bright grin. "Be right back," he promised.

Below me, I heard the door open and shut. I heard Dan's gentle voice, "Excuse me, sir?" Our neighbor's steady stream of hate stopped in midsentence, and I fought the urge to peer over the side of the railing to see what was going on. That would look too damn obvious, I thought ... but what was Dan doing down there? I had no clue. "Just a minute," Dan said. I could hear him clearly. "Just want to have a few words with you, that's all."

I never heard those words. They were low and whispered and kept between the two of them — Dan still won't tell me what he said. Whatever it was, though, it shut our neighbor up. We never heard him again, and when he passes Dan in the parking lot now, he always gives a courteous nod. Doesn't have anything to say to me, but I don't care. I'd rather he said nothing at all than spout bigotry and intolerance.

And I don't want Dan to go after those boys in the bathroom. They're just playing around, probably don't even *know* what a faggot is. *A bundle of sticks,* I think, and for some reason that makes me want to laugh. No, Caitlin managed to scare them enough for one day. Anything Dan might say won't compare to the scene my sister caused. So I give him my most disarming smile and assure him, "They're just kids, Dan. Just talking shit, you know how kids can be."

"And what if they weren't just talking?" he asks, but he follows me to the car, at least. "What if one of them had a gun, or a tire iron? I don't think I could've made it to you in time —"

"I'm fine," I tell him. "Jesus, Dan, they weren't going to attack me."

"You don't know that." He glares around us and actually walks me to the passenger side of the car. Holding the door for me as I slide into the seat, he says, "You're just not careful enough, babe. They could have hurt you."

Before he can move away, I grab the waistband of his jeans and tug until he ducks into the car. "But they didn't," I say, planting a quick kiss on the tip of his nose. I love him in this protective role, the soldier in him shining through like a knight coming to my rescue. "I'm fine."

"But they *might* have," he says.

When he kisses me, it's on the lips, and lingers long after he pulls away. He slams the door shut and jogs around the front of the car to the driver's side. In the back seat, Caitlin crunches on a candy bar and mutters under her breath, "Kiss kiss kiss." It's low enough that I can pretend I don't hear her.

I stare out the window as we pull away, Dan in the driver's seat and his hand on the gear shaft, his fingers stretched out to touch my leg. But the boys don't emerge from the bathroom, even though I watch the rest area until it disappears behind us in my side mirror. I'm not used to this small town mentality, this backwater country. The last time I was this far from a big city, I wasn't as comfortable with my sexuality as I am now — I sure as hell wasn't kissing on another boy where anyone could catch me. In D.C., Baltimore, the cities Dan and I live in and visit, it's not as strange a notion, two men in love, as it appears to be in the rest of the world. My mother's intolerant attitude seems to be the norm, much as I hate to admit it. If that's the case, I don't ever want to venture out of the safety of my home again.

The miles roll away beneath us. I rest my head against the window and study my reflection in the tempered glass — trees loom in my visage, pass through my eyes. The road is a gray strip that runs through my chin, and if I slide down a bit in my seat, it flows through my mouth like words I can't hold back. Maybe if my mom wasn't quite so histrionic about my announcement, or if my dad looked me in the eye just once and told me what was on his mind, or if Ray and Caitlin tried to take my relationship with Dan seriously, maybe then I wouldn't feel like the reflection looking back at me in the window. Do I even exist in the midst of everyone else? Or am I just this wispy, half-formed ghost whose presence is sensed but never seen?

The interstate dwindles down to three lanes in either direction, then two, then one long ribbon of tarmac twisting through the trees with a solid yellow line down the center. In the back seat, Caitlin's asleep again, this time curled into a tight ball at one end of the seat, her pillow shoved between her head and the door. Dan glances back at her to make sure she's out, then his hand finds mine, his fingers wrap around my own to get my attention. I give him a wan smile and he pulls my hand into his lap, presses it against his lower belly, just above the zipper that bulges at his crotch like an exaggerated erection. "Talk to me," he says. He doesn't like me brooding and mellow.

I don't blame him — I don't like this mood much, either. "It's not just those kids, is it?" he asks.

I shake my head, no. "It's ... everything," I tell him. I can't seem to narrow it down. "Evie and my family and the hateful way my mom looks at you, *everything*, hon. The kids back at the rest area were just another brick in the wall, you know? I can't ..." I sigh and turn back to the window and my own sightless reflection staring back. "I don't think I'm going to get through this," I whisper. I mean the funeral, the family. I don't see how I can possibly make it through to the end of the week.

"I'm here for you," Dan reminds me. I try for a halfhearted smile, but it comes out as a grimace and I quickly give up. Leaving my hand in his lap, Dan reaches out and touches my cheek. "Michael? Look at me." I do, but only from the corner of my eye. "What's the worse that can happen?"

My mom, I think — nothing specific comes to mind, but knowing her, she'll find some way to make my life hell at Sugar Creek. I already suspect that I'll never return when this week is over. Evie's funeral will be the last pilgrimage any of us make. Without her, it just won't be the same.

Carefully, I tell him what my mom said about the sleeping arrangements. If she has her way, Dan and I will be stuck with someone else in our room, despite Aunt Evie's steadfast rule that allowed couples some semblance of privacy. But Evie's gone — so who's to say what will happen now? Knowing my mom, she'll cry over my homosexuality with her aunts and the fact that Dan's my lover will spread like ivy. Who'll want to share a room with us then? None of my male cousins, I'm sure, and those with children won't want to let them sleep in the same room with two gay men. It's just going to be a mess, I feel it in my bones like a coming storm. Despite the fact that we're family, that we grew up together and bathed together and skinny-dipped in the creek and shared rooms when we were younger, someone is going to make this rough for me. Someone is going to equate my liking guys with my liking *every* guy, it's the way the TV depicts gays, and maybe it'll just be for the best if we drop Caitlin off at the house and get a hotel room after all.

When I suggest it to Dan, though, he squeezes my hand and says, "But you don't want to do that."

I know I don't. There's a part of me that thinks staying at Evie's house might bring me some sense of closure, some form of peace. "If we have to share a room, though," I start.

Dan laughs. "Baby," he says, and then he raises my hand to his lips, kisses my knuckles. Mirth twinkles in his dark eyes when he looks at me, a faint smile on his face. "Three days, Michael. We can hold out that long.

Jeez, how do you manage when I'm in the field?"

To be honest, I don't know. I hate that part of Dan's life, when the Army takes him from me for temporary duty. TDY, he calls it. Two weeks, sometimes four, out in the field, cut off from civilization, his survival skills put to the test. I picture him dressed in fatigues, hunkered down in a tent with another soldier, running through low grasses and ducking bullets and my heart stops in my chest whenever I hear the term *friendly fire*. The day his unit returns to base, I'm there in front of the barracks, waiting as the covered truck pulls up. He stands at attention with the rest of his men while the CO shouts out last minute orders, and when the command is given to fall out, he jogs over to me. In the car he smells of sweat and dirt and musk, manly scents that stir my groin and make me ache to hold him again, to kiss him and strip him bare and love him, to make up for our time apart. I wait until we're off post before I kiss him, but it's all I can do to hold out until we get home to take him and make him mine. I don't even let him shower — most of the time, we don't get much farther than the front door before I'm on him like an incubus, kissing and tearing at his clothes to get to the man, *my* man, underneath the soldier's guise.

The first time he left for duty, I sat by the phone the whole week, even though he told me he wouldn't be able to call. He was stationed for a few days' training at Fort A.P. Hill, and it was all I could do not to drive down to the base, which is just an hour or so from D.C. I didn't know if they'd let me on post or not, but I had grand dreams of sneaking into the fields where the men were camped, crawling on my elbows and knees like I've seen done in so many war films, slithering through the mud and grass until I found my boy. When he was scheduled back, I was at Myer two hours before his truck rolled in.

I didn't even wait until we made it home. Instead, I drove to a small park just off the beltway, a scenic spot surrounded by ancient trees that overlook the Potomac River. It's secluded there, and I drove into the underbrush and low trees until I couldn't see the road behind me, and the river filled the windshield. Turning off the car, I gave Dan a smoldering look that said everything I had kept bottled up inside myself for the past week. "What?" he asked, a faint smile on his lips. "Hon, I'm exhausted —"

My hand fumbled at his waist, unbuckling his belt, unzipping his pants, I *needed* him. "Don't you want to?" I sighed as I crawled over the gear shaft and into his lap. My mouth found his and I fell into him. When I managed to get his fly opened, his briefs down below his balls, I found he wanted me just as much as I did him. His hands clawed at my ass, tore at my shirt — his mouth was hungry on my own. At one point he found the seat release and practically dumped us both into the back of the car, giggling and half naked and hard with lust, and when I sat up to get the condoms I kept in the glove compartment for just this occasion, I leaned heavily on the car horn, startling a flock of birds roosting in the bushes nearby. "Damn," I breathed. I was starting to hurt from my desire. I needed him *now*.

Somehow we managed to get the condom out of its package. We managed to get the damn thing on Dan's hard cock, though it seemed more slippery than usual and I couldn't stop laughing. I finally had him back, I couldn't believe it. Everything else meant nothing to me — I barely noticed the gear shaft stabbing my hip, or the torn seam of my pants when I spread my legs to slide onto him, my lover, Dan. I'm usually the one in charge, the one driving into *him*, but when he tops me, I lose all control. In the car that day, I arched up to the ceiling as he pulled back, bucked against him when he thrust into me, his arms tight around my waist like he had to hold me down. I held onto the headrest behind him, gripped it so tight that my fingers throbbed the next day, but I needed that, I needed *him*. We came together in an explosive rush that threatened to tear the roof off the car and my voice from my throat when I cried out his name. I don't remember dressing, or driving home, or making him dinner while he showered — just him in me, the car rocking gently with our motions, the two of us hidden in the wildness, on the fringes of the world.

Taking his eyes off the road for a minute, Dan gives me a look that makes me think he's remembering that time, too. "You're thinking what I'm thinking," I say, my hand pressing into the V between his legs, where he's begun to stiffen.

He shrugs. "There's always the shower."

I have to laugh because I know he's playing with me now. I poke at his budding erection. "Don't try to tell me *this* is from thinking about the shower. I know you better than that."

"What?" he asks. Then, with a wicked grin, he raises an eyebrow and says, "You're thinking about the car."

"I'm *remembering* the car," I correct. His hand catches mine as I start to stroke him through his jeans. "Big difference there, babe."

He laughs at me. "So that's settled, then. We go for a drive, take a run to the store, something like that. Get it on while we're out and it won't matter who's in the room with us at night. All we'll do then is sleep. See?" he asks. "Nothing to worry about, Michael."

From behind us, my sister groans. "Tell me you guys didn't do it back here," she mutters. "God, please."

Without turning around, I reach between the seats and slap at her legs — something I learned from my dad growing up. Didn't matter who was the one causing trouble or arguing. In the back seat, all were fair game when he got angry, and he'd slap back at us while we dodged his hand.

Caitlin, though, she pushes me away. "If you guys are gonna fuck in the car," she says, kicking at my arm, "I'm riding home with the parentals."

"Is that a promise?" I want to know.

11: Behind the Wheel

ROUND FOUR IN the afternoon, we turn onto interstate 80 and it's back to three lanes rushing west, a concrete median separating us from the drivers heading the way we've come. The radio fades in and out as we pass between stations, and Caitlin starts to complain about the batteries in her Walkman again but we're so close now, I can almost *see* Aunt Evie's house from here. I don't want to stop along the way, or dawdle any longer than we have to. The sooner we get there, the sooner we can work out who's sleeping where and get the funeral arrangements over with. I'm assuming Penny has handled them, but she never struck me as the self-sufficient type. She might be waiting for someone else to get there first. My mom's sister, Penny's a little shy in person, though she'll talk your ear off over the phone. I suspect she's a lesbian but I doubt that she's out of the closet about it — even to herself. Sugar Creek isn't exactly a city teeming with pride, and with the way Mom reacted to my coming out, I just don't see Penny tripping over herself to share the spotlight. She's not the outspoken type. After living in Evie's shadow for so long, I don't know how she'll make it on her own now.

Just past the Punxsutawney exit, Dan turns off the interstate onto another two-lane back road, state route 650, which runs right through the heart of Sugar Creek. We're in mountain country now, the Alleghenies no longer towering on the horizon but rising around us, shrouded in blue haze like a half-remembered dream. This is all coming back to me — fog-draped trees that stretch to a canopy above us, creeks and runoff from the river twining through hilly land, rocks suspended up steep inclines along the road. New road signs appear between the historical markers and city signs — *Beware of Falling Rocks*, these say, and *Quiet Through Underpass*, phrases that terrified me as a child. Once or twice while I was growing up, when money was tight and my parents talked in low voices of maybe not making it to Evie's that year, I would envision this road barricaded with rocks and rubble, mountains crumbling into our path to keep us from visiting the family. That never happened, though — Evie always said that family stuck together no matter what, and it wasn't until I was older that I realized it was she who sent my mom enough money to make the trip when we didn't think we'd be able to come. One year my dad didn't go, we couldn't afford to take everyone and he told us he had to work overtime at the plant, and when we got this far, I held my breath, watched the rocks as we passed beneath them, sure that it was my steady gaze alone that held them up. If they fell, we might never get back home, but I could think of worse things than being trapped at Sugar Creek. Like not getting there in the first place, or running into Stephanie Robichaud when I went to Grosso's for a Sno-Cone.

Now those childish fears are back, and I press my face against the cold glass of the window to keep an eye on the rocks as we drive by. If I look away, they'll crash down around us in a landslide, isn't that the way it worked? Children make their own magic in the world, and in this familiar territory, I feel the years peeling back from me, one by one. I'll be eight again by the time we get to Evie's. I'll run through the yard with the other kids, giggling and shrieking — play hide and seek in the woods, swim down at the creek, race inside when Evie calls us home for cookies or ice cream …

Evie's dead.

Fresh sadness drapes over me — I have to keep reminding myself of this. Dead, as in not waiting on the porch for us to arrive, not planning to call Al's for a large order tonight, not going to sweep me up in her strong arms and hug me until my ribs threaten to crack. Dead. The one person I would have sworn was invincible is finally gone.

We pass over bridges. Tiny, wooden contraptions marked with the warning *Narrow Bridge Ahead* and large covered bridges like the kind you see in travelogues and calendars. Rotting railings hem in close to the car, keeping us on the road. Ray and I used to play silly, superstitious games — hold our breath over running water, hit the roof with one fist at the exact moment another car passed us on the bridge, I'm not sure exactly why. One year I managed to convince him that one stretch of road lined with wooden planks was actually a bridge, just for water underground, and he almost fainted from holding his breath for so long as we crossed it. I got in trouble for that one, trying to kill my brother, my mom said. I argued that it wasn't *my* fault he believed me, but the spanking was well worth his blue-tinted lips and red cheeks as he gasped for breath.

One bridge in particular I'm looking out for, and when I see it, I have to choke back sudden tears that blind me. An old metal riser stretched across a particularly narrow creek — not much to look at, corrugated copper crusted over with a greenish-blue patina like algae scum congealed in standing water. It's been that way as long as I can remember, and once we clear the bridge, we have exactly thirty minutes before we get to Aunt Evie's house. This is the last landmark before the trees thin out and houses start cropping up along the road. This is *it*, the final passage, the last outpost, before we enter Sugar Creek.

Something about the bridge catches Dan's eye, and before the car has even stopped vibrating from traveling over the bumpy span, he pulls off to one side of the road. "What's wrong?" I ask, concerned. "We're about a half hour away."

He smiles at me as he turns off the car. "I'm a little chilly," he says. With a nod at the trunk, he tells me, "I'm just going to get a sweater. You want something?"

I shake my head but the idea of getting out of the car for however brief a moment is hard to resist. I feel cramped and sore from sitting for so long — I can only imagine the tension that coils in Dan's shoulders and neck. A hot bath for him tonight, and a massage, if we manage to get a room to ourselves. That's a thorn in my side, something I can't get over. My mother and her homophobic ways.

When I get out of the car, Caitlin sticks a foot out to keep me from shutting the door, then extracts herself from the back seat like a newborn hatching from an egg. "Damn," she mutters, stomping her feet in the high grass. "Was it always this long before?"

A glance at my watch shows us actually ahead of schedule — it's barely been seven hours since we left the house this morning. "We're making good time," I tell her. "We might even get there before Mom and Dad."

"Probably not," Caitlin says. She leans against the car, her arms folded on the roof, and watches Dan fiddle with the key in the trunk. "Dad doesn't stop unless *he's* the one who has to take a piss." I swat at her playfully, but she moves out of reach. "What? It's true."

Shoving my hands into my pockets, I walk to the end of the car, where Dan is digging through the trunk for something with sleeves. It *is* getting a little nippy out — I had almost forgotten what autumn felt like this far north. We've just missed the best of the foliage, though. The leaves still clinging to their branches are dying, sodden colors, and as I walk through the grass, my feet crunch over dead leaves that look like mulch, they're so dark and worn out. A week or two earlier, and this whole world would have been on flame ... and this week, we'll miss the turning in D.C. and Virginia because we're too far north. The thought saddens me somehow. I'll miss the fall this year.

At the edge of the bridge, I stop and peer down into white-capped water that splashes over rocks to hurry away beneath the road. If I were brave, I'd slide down the short hill to the stream, plunge my hands into the icy water, wash away the trip and my parents and everything from *that* side of the bridge. If my shoes were sturdier sneakers, maybe, and not these thin loafers, and if Dan held tight to my elbow to keep me from falling in ...

Arms snake around my waist, startling me, and I give out a short gasp as I look over my shoulder at my lover. "Hey," he purrs, wrapping his arms tight around me like he's afraid I'll fall in if he lets go. His embrace is loving and strong, and I lean back into him with complete trust. He wears a black windbreaker over his t-shirt, a jacket with a snow leopard embroidered on the back — his unit's mascot. Pressing his lips to my jaw, he murmurs against my skin, "I love you."

I cover his arms with my own, lean my head back on his shoulder, savoring his touch. "No," I tell him, smiling faintly. "I love *you*."

"Are you sure?" he jokes. When I nod, he says, "Cause I was almost sure it was the other way around —"

And then Caitlin is there, her steel-tipped shoes ringing loudly off the metal bridge as she steps out to the middle of the span. "Yeah, yeah," she says, leaning down over the railing to stare into the water rushing away below. "You both love each other, we get the point. Kiss and hug and do whatever it is you have to do so we can get back in the car now, okay? We're not that far."

"My sister," I tell Dan, laughing when he ignores her and kisses me again, "the romantic."

Flipping her hair over one shoulder, Caitlin sighs dramatically. "Hey, unless you want to ride in the back and let *me* drive ..." Her eyes widen as the thought takes hold, and I'm already shaking my head when she starts. "Oh Michael, *could* I? I have my learner's —"

"No," I say. It's out of the question. I'm not teaching her to drive, no way, no how. No.

But she won't let me off so easily. "Please?" she pleads. She actually folds her hands together as if in prayer. "Come on, Mike, you *have* to let me."

I shrug out of Dan's hold and head back for the car. "I don't *have* to let you do anything," I point out. "It's my car. I'll bet you've never even *driven* before."

"Bullshit," Caitlin spits, hurrying after me. My lover catches up with us and takes my hand, but Caitlin pushes between us, stretching the link. "Dan, it's cool with you, right? I've driven before, Mike, honest. Mom let me drive around the block once —"

"Once," I echo. I'm not going for it. "No, Caitlin, okay? No." When she flusters, I ask, "Did you make it around the whole block?"

"Well, no," my sister admits. I know she didn't — Mom took me on the same route when I first got my learner's, too. The whole time, she was like,

"Watch it, Mike. You're too close on this side, move over. Watch it! Jesus, Mary, and Joseph, you almost hit that car! Just — no, just pull over here. No, just — let me drive, will you? Just stop, *stop* the car." Yeah, Mom isn't driving school material. I wonder how long Caitlin was actually behind the wheel.

At the car, I hold the passenger side door open and she pouts at me. "Get in," I say gently. She doesn't obey, just stands behind the trunk and glares at the ground. "Cat, please. I would but ..." I look at Dan beside me for help.

"But what?" he wants to know. *Damn* him. Gesturing at the road, he points out, "There's no one around, Michael. What's a few miles going to hurt?"

Pouting harder, Caitlin waits until I look at her to say, "Aunt *Evie* let me drive."

"When?" I ask, suspicious. Mom letting her drive is one thing, Evie is something else entirely. Evie's the coolest person I've ever known, relative or not, and if *she* let Caitlin drive, then why can't I do the same? "Caitlin, if you're lying —"

"I'm not!" she shouts, indignant. "Jesus, Mike, this summer, okay?" She twists her hands in her shirt and I can hear that she's close to tears as she recalls, "We came up the week of my birthday and Aunt Evie took me into Franklin for the day, just us. That's when I got this —" She sticks out her tongue to show off her piercing.

"Caitlin," I sigh, rubbing the bridge of my nose. Now I don't believe her. "I'm really sure Evie let you pierce your tongue —"

My sister nods vigorously. "She did!" she swears. "She said anything I wanted, anything, and I told her I wanted another piercing and I think she thought I meant up here," and she points at the top of her ear, where three earrings already trail down the length of cartilage. "But she gave me the money and told me to go on into the Piercing Pagoda while she went grocery shopping. And I go in and the guy goes you're not eighteen, and I'm like am too, my birthday's today, I want my tongue pierced." I can just imagine Caitlin in a dingy, back alley tattoo parlor, haggling over getting a piece of steel rammed through her tongue. I can picture the guy, too, aging, overweight, ink up both arms and a ZZ Top beard chopped off above his beer belly. Caitlin laughs. "He goes you got ID? And I said, look, just pierce my tongue, okay? So I hand him the sixty dollars Aunt Evie gave me and he looks at the money, looks at me, looks at the money again, and tells me okay, fine, but if your momma makes you pull it out, you ain't getting a refund from me."

Glancing at Dan, I ask, "What did Evie say?"

With a wicked gleam in her eyes, Caitlin says, "Don't tell Laura. That's it. Then she let me drive halfway home." Before I can question her, she tells us, "Just along 62, where it's that long, straight stretch? See, *she* let me drive."

Beside me, Dan jingles the car keys, and I sigh, defeated. "Fine," I say, sure I'm going to regret it.

As Dan tosses Caitlin the keys, she shrieks, "*Hell* yeah!"

"Ten miles," I tell her. She skirts around the car to open the door on the driver's side, and Dan climbs into the back seat behind me. "You hear me, Cat? Ten miles, and that's *only* if no one else is coming up behind us, okay? And when I tell you something, you listen to me, that *instant*, you understand?"

She crams the keys into the ignition, starts the car, then turns the keys again in her eagerness, grinding the engine. "Oops!" she giggles. "Sorry. Yeah, I understand. Get in the car, Mike. Get in."

I give Dan a distrustful look — I'm not sure I like the slight smile on his face or the glittery laugh in his eyes, but he's right, what's a few miles going to hurt? There's no one on the road — I look again just to make sure that we're alone — and I can already tell from the grin on my sister's face that I've managed to make her day. Hell, her whole week, and with all that's going on around us, it's something, at least.

So I slide into the passenger seat and tell her, "Wait until I'm in." I keep the door open to ensure that she doesn't take off before I buckle my seat belt. In the back seat, I hear Dan snapping himself in, too. Taking a deep breath, I wish I had arm rests to grip but I settle for my hands on my knees … and what do they say in cases of emergency? *Head between your legs and kiss your ass goodbye.* Maybe this wasn't such a good idea after all.

"You in?" Caitlin wants to know. She revs the engine as if we're at the start of a drag race and she plans to be first off the line.

I pull my door shut and try not to think about how many car accidents I've seen or heard about. "Ten miles," I remind her. She nods.

I take a deep breath and look at Dan in the rearview mirror but can't quite return his smile. "Okay," I sigh. "I'm in. Go slow," I caution, before her foot's even off the brake. "Check your mirror first. Caitlin, watch it —"

"Jeez," she mutters as she eases out onto the road. "You're worse than Mom."

I'm not sure if I should be offended or flattered by that.

12: Getting There

WITH CAITLIN BEHIND the wheel, we creep down the road, easily twenty miles below the posted speed limit. "You can pick it up a little bit," I tell her, resisting the urge to push her aside and step on the gas myself. At this rate, we won't get to Aunt Evie's until noon tomorrow.

In the driver's seat, my sister scowls but doesn't dare take her eyes off the road to look my way. "First it's *slow down*," she mutters, risking a glance in the rearview mirror — we're still the only ones on the road. "Now it's *speed up*. Pick one and stick with it, Mike. I'm trying to drive here."

"Is that what you call it?" I reply.

She ignores me, which is just as well. From the back seat, Dan says softly, "She's doing fine, Michael." Yeah, she hasn't wrecked yet and we're still alive, but that's about the extent of it ...

"Pull over," I say. When Caitlin looks at me, incredulous, I shake my head. "Just pull over right here, Caitlin. Cat. You're making me nervous —"

"You're making *me* nervous," she says. "I can go faster, see?" To prove her point, she leans on the gas and the car zooms ahead. "How's this?" she wants to know. The car bucks when she lets up on the gas, leaps as she steps on the pedal again. "This fast enough for you?"

I'm not playing this anymore. "Just stop." She doesn't listen, just keeps tapping the gas and lunges us up the road. "Caitlin!" I cry out, hands in front of me, arms locked tight between me and the dashboard. I don't even want to *think* about what she's doing to my engine. "You said you'd listen —"

"You said I could go ten miles!" she yells back. Every time she speaks, the car slows down again, as if she can't possibly drive and talk at the same time, and in my side mirror I can see a car in the distance behind us, gaining ground. We have to pull over, this isn't funny anymore. My car almost coasts to a stop as Caitlin fools around with the odometer. "Eight point six," she says, almost triumphant. "I've got a little ways left to go. Come on, Mike, you said ten miles. I'm almost there."

A full ten miles is an eternity away, and the car behind us races up onto my rear bumper like a demon from hell. "Caitlin," I start, but I'm cut off by the other car's horn, an angry blast that startles us all. My sister's knuckles have gone white on the steering wheel, and suddenly I see past the punk façade to the frightened little girl underneath all that black make-up and silver jewelry. Covering her hands with one of mine, I force myself to lower my voice. "Cat? Okay, how about we just pull over and let him pass, what do you say?"

Another blare of the horn — I feel Caitlin's fingers tremble beneath mine. The steering wheel practically shakes in her hands. "Okay," she whispers. She's trying so hard to impress us, to be the strong, unaffected riot-girl, but it's just a phase, it isn't *her*. With pleading eyes, she looks at me as if begging to be told what to do.

"Turn on your signal," I say. I sound much calmer than I feel. Now she's listening to me, and the steady *clik-clikclik* of the signal drowns out the low sounds of the radio. Keeping my hand on the wheel, I steer to the right, just enough to ease the car off the road. The car on our tail revs its engine impatiently. "Easy," I say gently. We're getting over, can't the fucker see that? "Ignore them, Cat. Dan's right, you're doing good." When the horn beeps a third time, I whirl around to glare at the driver —

Through the window behind Dan, my dad stares back.

Oh shit. Forget decorum, I twist the wheel hard to the right. The car bumps off the road and onto the shoulder, then into the grass. "The brake," Dan's saying, leaning past us to point at the floorboards, "Caitlin! Hit the brake. Michael, let go."

I grab Caitlin's head and force her down as my mom's Ford Escort charges by. Somehow, miraculously, my sister leans on the right pedal and the car jerks to a stop. I can't get the pissed look on my dad's face out of my mind — did he see us? Did he *recognize* us? *Please don't let him have seen Cat*, I pray, even as my sister regains her composure and starts pelting me with her fists, struggling to sit up. *Please don't, just please don't let them know it's us.* "Michael! Get the hell *off* me!"

With shaky fingers, I reach over and turn off the car. "It's Dad," I whisper. Caitlin brushes the hair from her face and I stare at the taillights on the other car, heading up the road. In the rearview mirror, I catch a glimpse of Dan's wide eyes and force myself to take a deep breath, another, anything to steady myself. "Holy *fuck*," I mutter. "That's my *parents*. Did you see ...?"

Dan nods — he saw.

As if my dad realizes the car he's just run off the road belongs to his own son, he comes to a complete stop in the middle of the road and sits there, idling. "Chinese fire drill time," Caitlin says, unstrapping her seat belt. Then she's crawling past me into the back seat of the car, the keys still in the igni-tion. "'Scuse me, Danny boy. Scoot it over." Plopping down beside my lover, she shakes the hair from her face and stares out the window at the car. "God, do you think Mom saw me? She'll have a *shit* fit if she finds out."

"I don't plan to tell her," I say. Dan climbs over the gear shaft and sinks into the driver's seat, buckles the seat belt across his waist, and gives me a tight smile that I can't seem to match. Instead, I stare out the window and run a hand down my face, trying to wipe away the emotions trembling through me. I can just hear my mom's reaction now, if she finds out I let Caitlin drive? *Oh shit.*

Dan touches my knee, a comforting gesture. "Michael?" he asks, con-cerned. "You okay, hon?"

I force a laugh at that. *Okay* would not have been to let my teenaged sis-ter coerce me into letting her behind the wheel of my car. *Okay* would not be sitting here wracked with tremors while my parents wait for us to pull back onto the road. In fact, I'm quite sure that *okay* wouldn't be anything at all like what I'm doing or feeling right now.

When I don't answer, he looks back at Caitlin, who stares out at the road and doesn't say a word. Her dark-colored lips have disappeared into a thin line drawn across her face. She knows how my mom will react — she'd be lucky if she can get her driver's license at eighteen if Mom finds out she's fooling around like this, and she'd never be able to borrow the car, *ever*. Hell, depending on my mom's mood? Caitlin might never be allowed to even *look* at a car again.

"Okay," Dan sighs, as if we've both agreed with him. He checks the road behind us, empty again, then manages to pull my car out of the tall grasses. Gravel crunches under the tires, and then we're off the shoulder and back on the road. He glances at me, at the road, then at me again. "Michael? Talk to me here."

"My mom is going to kill us," I say, my voice strangely distant to my own ears. Ahead, she's already rolled down the passenger side window and leans out to watch us approach them. Yes, she'll kill us all, Dan too, just because he's supposed to be driving and wasn't. What does she always say? *Jesus, Mary, and Joseph.*

From the back seat, Caitlin says, "She's going to kill *me*. My learner's permit is in her *purse*."

I turn to stare at her, dumbfounded. "You're not even *carrying* it? Caitlin, what the hell —"

Dan squeezes my knee almost painfully and guides the car to a stop be-hind my parents. For a long moment, we just sit there, none of us moving. "Go," I mutter as if my dad can hear me. I don't want to get into a family argument here, in the middle of a nameless street in the back roads of Pennsylvania. In front of us, the other car idles, waiting. For what, though? As if someone else might know, I ask, "What's he waiting for?"

Suddenly my dad sticks his arm out the window and waves us on. Does he want us to pass him? A solid yellow line bisects the road, we can't just *cross* it. "Dan," I start, confused, "what —"

My dad hits the horn, motions with his arm again. "Go see what he wants," Dan tells me, pulling up the parking break. That's the *last* thing I want to do, but my lover gives me a quick kiss on my cheek that imbues me with courage. "Go on," he whispers, his breath warm on my face.

Unbuckling my seat belt, I tumble from the car and out into the road. I glance around us to make sure we're still the only ones out here — we are — then I hurry around the front of my car to the driver's side of the Escort. I'm not talking to my mom, even though her window's already down. Of the two, my dad is far easier to deal with. I'd rather have him ignoring me than deal with my mother's hysterics any day. Leaning down into his window, I give him what I hope looks like a sincere smile and say, "Hey! Jeez, we didn't recognize you guys."

My mom leans past my dad. "Is everyone alright? I told you, Harry. You're going too fast, running people off the road. Slow down, will you? I don't want to show up at Evie's dead."

"We're fine, Mom," I say quickly, before my dad can reply. Anger dulls his eyes and he has an open beer can between his legs so I know he's been drinking. From the way he's looking at me, like he's not quite sure who I am or why he's sitting here talking to me, I'm pretty sure he didn't see Caitlin in the driver's seat of my car. "You just surprised us, is all. We're okay."

Now my mom's eyes narrow in suspicion, and she starts in on me. "What were you doing to veer off the road like that? Can't he drive?"

"He's Army," Dad replies, as if that's all the answer she needs. "Of *course* the kid can drive. Leave them alone, Laura."

"How did we surprise them?" she wants to know, talking to my dad and not me. "If you two were fooling around in that front seat with my *daughter* in the back —"

"Mom!" I cry, frustrated. "Damn, no! It's nothing like that." *Your daughter was in the front,* I almost say, but I bite the words back before I can set them free. "God, what do you *think* we were doing?" When she shrugs like she doesn't know but it couldn't have been anything good, I shake my head, incredulous. "Just driving, Mom. We were going a little slow and you just appeared out of nowhere. It's a no passing zone, in case you haven't noticed. We only pulled over to get you off our tail."

In the back seat, Ray sits up to hug the back of Dad's seat, a mean-spirited grin on his face. "Hey, Mike," he calls, and I don't even want to look at him but I see the gesture he makes from the corner of my eye — one hand curled in front of his mouth as if holding something, his tongue pokes out the side of his cheek in a blowjob parody. "What's it like giving head when he's trying to drive?"

"I wasn't —" I reach past my dad and smack my brother hard across the nose. Then I pinch his cheek and twist the skin as hard as I can — he howls in pain. "You're a fucking idiot," I tell him as he tries to pull away. "We were just *driving*, people."

My dad knocks my arm away. "If you're just *driving*," he tells me, his voice slurred from the drinks he's already had, "then get your ass back in the car. We're about ten minutes from Evie's." Revving the engine, he shifts gears and adds, "You two can fight there. Get back."

I level a finger at Ray and glare at him through the window. "You are so dead," I promise. I'm not putting up with his shit. It's bad enough I have to take it from everyone else — I'm not about to let him get away with it, too.

"Get back," Dad says again.

This time he doesn't wait, just gasses the car and roars ahead. I stare after him for a second, then jog back to my own car. As I slide into my seat, I sigh, disgusted. "I'm killing Ray," I announce, buckling my seat belt. Then I point at the other car and say, "Follow them."

"You have to get in line," Caitlin tells me. Dan releases the brake and we fall behind my parents, Dan easily matching my dad's speed. Gathering her things together in the back, my sister tells us, "I get him first."

"I'm older than you," I argue. My hands are fisted on my knees and one of my legs shakes in anger I can barely hold in check. "I have dibs."

"I live with him," Caitlin points out. "That gives me precedence." Noting my mood, she leans forward and jokingly asks Dan, "What about you? Don't you want in?"

Dan flashes her a troubled smile that doesn't quite reach his eyes. "Me? I'm holding him down."

I laugh, releasing some of the tension built up between us. Another few miles and we see the sign for Sugar Creek — a tall stretch of fencing by the side of the road, covered with wooden signs from civic clubs and local chapters of organizations such as the VFW and American Legion, and above them, the words *Sugar Creek* like a banner proclaiming the entrance to a legendary land. A simpler place, something like a memory to me, a safe fantasy world when I was growing up.

And it still looks the same. Weathered houses line the road like places I've seen in dreams, people outside with sweaters and rakes, a pumpkin or two already carved and lit on porches or along driveways. There's the Robichaud home — or rather, the house where the twins used to live. There's the "spook place," a house whose front porch and yard is littered with trash and half-empty boxes and discarded lawnmowers, broken appliances, a battered Chevy up on blocks in the back. We used to dare each other to run into the yard and swipe something, just to prove our courage. One time I crept up on the porch itself, the rotten floor boards creaking with each step, just to get a rag doll peeking out of an old refrigerator whose doors were long gone. I remember sounds from a TV inside the house, something like a giant's cough rumbling out a cracked window — I turned to make sure that Ray and Stephen and another boy we called Quint were still hiding in the bushes across the street, waiting for me. Then I snuck up to the fridge, intent on the doll. My plan was to grab it and run, and I was almost there ...

A face appeared in the window above the fridge, dark eyes, lank hair, lines like furrows gouged into gaunt cheeks. I screamed and ran back down the porch, empty-handed. Remembering the doll, I turned, almost twisting my ankle as I stumbled back up the steps — I heard the door unlocking, my friends calling me to hurry, get the hell *out* of there, *now*, the door opening, and I just barely managed to get the doll by the hair. Then I vaulted over the railing, landed in the scraggly azaleas that hemmed in the porch, and ran for my life, doll in hand. I don't remember what I did with the prize, toss it away? I must have — I don't have it anymore. Now as we drive pass the house, it doesn't look as scary as it used to, and my adult mind sees the monster inside as an old, lonely man, nothing more. I wonder whatever happened to him. I don't even know what his name is, or was, to ask.

We drive through the center of town. There are a few new additions — the Wawa wasn't here before, and there's a little strip mall with a Dollar Tree and Chinese restaurant where an old department store used to be. A used car dealership, those guys are everywhere, and signs for a Ukrop's coming soon, that's about it. Everything else could have come straight from my memory, it all looks the same. And there's Grosso's, on the corner of Main and 7th, the parking lot still littered with bicycles and kids. "There's Aaron," Caitlin says, pointing at one tow-headed boy with an ice cream cone. "Aunt Lennie's son, remember him?"

To be honest? No, I don't. I haven't seen my Aunt Lenore in five years, and the boy doesn't look that much older. He must've only been a toddler the last time I was up here. That makes me sad — I won't recognize any of these people I'm about to see, I don't know them. They'll hug me and kiss me and say *my, how much you've grown*, and I'll just have to smile blandly, look around for help, I won't know who they are. A hotel is starting to sound better by the minute.

But when Evie's house comes into view, all my fear and trepidation dissolves. *Home*, I think, surprising myself. The word comes unbidden to my mind and lingers long after I try to shake it away. "That's it," I whisper, awed, and Dan nods, his hand finding mine. The house looks smaller than I remember it, but there are people on the porch, cars in the yard, a bustle of activity that belies the nature of our gathering here. Anyone driving by couldn't possibly know the sadness that clings to each of us at Evie's passing — we're too happy to be together again, too many children racing around, too many adults chattering like long lost friends.

My dad pulls his car onto the shoulder of the road, where the grass has been scattered with gravel in a makeshift driveway, and Dan pulls to a stop behind him. The house looms above us and I can't shake the feeling of open arms, welcoming us.

Home.

13: A Room of Our Own

I FEEL LIKE a celebrity when I climb out of the car and find myself surrounded. My Aunt Bobbie gets to me first — a short, overweight woman in her late 60's, she has mousy, flyaway hair and a smattering of freckles across her perpetually tanned face, a symptom of her sunworshipping ways. She lives in Florida with husband number five, a Greek businessman named Sander something-or-other that I can't pronounce. I don't think she can, either, since the last I heard, she went back to using her maiden name. When she hugs me, she only comes to my shoulder, and she squeezes me so tight that I'm sure my ribs will crack. "Michael!" she cries. Before I can reply, she releases me and moves down a step, pushing me the other way as she reaches for Caitlin.

I find myself in my Aunt Billy's embrace. Unlike her sister, Billy is tall and willowy — taller than my six feet, and she favors heels that add another three inches to her height. She has a long, ski-slope nose with half-frame glasses perched on the end, and two jeweled herringbone chains hang from the glasses to drape around her neck. "Michael," she says warmly, enveloping me in her arms. Her long, billowy sleeves swirl around me like a gypsy's scarves, and she smells faintly of tea tree oil and chamomile. As we hug, I'm almost afraid to touch her, she seems so fragile in my embrace. "So tall!" she murmurs, her voice as quiet as a librarian's in my ear. "We know where you get *that* from."

Then she's gone, too, and Aunt Sarah is there, pinching my cheeks as she tells me I've grown up good. Her words. Of all her sisters, Sarah's the one who most resembles Evie, with her broad hips and round cheeks, and the infectious laugh she has that sets everyone around her to giggling. And of all my aunts, she frightens me the most, with her Bible-thumping ways and her overly zealous religion. Every meal must start with a prayer, and she's made it her own personal mission to save my soul, along with Ray's and Caitlin's. Aunt Sarah has always claimed that my mom isn't strict enough with us, and the fact that we only go to church on Christmas and Easter is a sore spot with her. In Aunt Sarah's mind, there are only two suitable futures for me — marriage or priesthood. The last time I was up here, five years ago, she slipped brochures for a seminary in Maryland into my luggage. When she finds out about Dan ...

I look over the crowd, craning my neck to find my lover. He's making his way around the car with a polite smile to the children who have hemmed us in to see the new arrivals. "Dan," I call out, nodding my head so he knows I want him here with me. He gets caught up in one of Aunt Bobbie's bear hugs — she doesn't know who he is but hey, if he's here, he's family, that's the way my aunts think — and I start to ease behind Caitlin to reach him when I'm pulled into another embrace. "Penny!"

My mom's sister wraps her arms around my neck and reels me in for a sloppy kiss on the cheek. "Michael, hey," she laughs. It's hard to look into her sad face and hear that laugh. Large dark circles hang below her eyes. I wonder how long Evie was sick before she died or if it was sudden, unexpected. Penny lives here at the house, she must have been with her at the end, and that explains the fatigue eating away at her. "Did you have a good trip? No problems?"

I shake my head as I step back to look at my aunt. She's almost the mirror image of my mother, though five years younger — they both have the same eyes, the same bone structure. Only where my mom has dyed her light brown hair an ungodly shade of auburn, Penny's long locks are a dark chestnut, and she doesn't have the bitter anger that twists my mother's mouth when she looks at me. For as long as I've known her, I've never seen Penny mad. Mom, on the other hand ... well, I tell myself that it's Ray's fault she's the way she is. After all, she did have him first, and if he were my son, I know it would've scarred me for life. I seriously think my mom's the type who should have never had kids. Look at Penny — no children, happy life. Some part of me wonders if maybe my mother isn't a little bit jealous of her sister for that.

"We made great time," I tell my aunt. "Dan drove the whole way." I turn and hold out a hand for my lover.

Penny nods because she isn't quite sure who I'm talking about, but her smile doesn't fade. "Dan?" she echoes. "I didn't know you were bringing a friend."

When Caitlin hugs Aunt Sarah, Dan tries to ease behind her to reach me, but my sister steps back before he's clear. Dan places a hand on the small of her back so she won't run into him. Unfortunately, my aunts see the gesture. "Caitlin?" Aunt Sarah asks, raising her eyebrows as she studies Dan appreciatively. She takes his hand that's reaching out for me and pumps it up and down in a quick handshake. "Laura didn't mention *him*. Your boyfriend?"

With a glance over her shoulder, Caitlin smirks at Dan, and when her gaze shifts to me, I know what she's going to say before the word escapes her mouth. "Michael's," is her flippant reply.

Dan finds my hand, his fingers closing over mine desperately, but his polite expression never changes. "Michael's," Penny echoes. For the first time I wonder if she's on anything. As if trying to grasp the concept, she looks at our hands laced together and asks, "Your friend?"

There's no use trying to pretend otherwise. "Boyfriend," I correct. I think I hear my Aunt Sarah gasp, and slowly people stop talking, one by one, to turn and look at us. At *me*. Suddenly it's last night all over again and I'm the center of attention. I don't know how Caitlin lives like this. "Look," I start, squeezing Dan's hand for comfort. "If it's going to be a problem ..."

"At least he's handsome," Aunt Billy says. Bobbie and Penny laugh, breaking the tension, until the only people still frowning at us are Sarah and my mother. Billy pushes past her sister to hug Dan again. He returns the embrace with one hand, holding onto me with the other. "Military?" my aunt asks. When Dan nods, she wants to know, "What branch?"

"Army," he says.

Penny nudges my mother, who has appeared beside me as if by magic. "Laura, you little minx," she slurs, and yes, she's definitely been taking something. Evie's death probably hit her hard enough for the doctor to prescribe a mild tranquilizer. "You didn't tell us Michael had a boy."

Mom's lips are a thin white line of anger in her closed face. "I just found out about it myself," she admits. When she speaks, she keeps her voice low, and I know she's just itching to get me alone so she can start in on how we shouldn't be advertising my homosexuality. *Take it up with Caitlin,* I think. She's the one who mentioned it, not me.

"We didn't know," Penny says as she glances around. Most of the children look openly at me and Dan, curious. Aunt Billy still has a hand on Dan's arm — she's always been the touchy-feely type — and she's whispering quietly to him about her daughter Sylvia, who's in the Navy. Penny turns around, her lips moving as she takes a quick head count. "I'm not sure we have any empty rooms," she's saying, talking almost to herself. "We didn't know there would be another couple ..."

"I'm sure they can share with the other boys," Mom says. Dan tightens his grip on my hand to keep me quiet, but when I look at him, he's nodding at something Aunt Billy's said. "It's only for a few nights. Where are the other children sleeping?"

I can't stand this. "I'm not a child," I tell her. Dan pinches my fingers but I can't take much more of my mom's righteous attitude. "I'm not sleeping alone, is that clear? I haven't in eight damn months, I'm not about to start now just because the thought of me loving another man is too much for you to stomach."

Surprisingly, it's Ray who comes to my rescue. "You and Dad get a room together," he points out. *Thank you,* I pray silently. Maybe I won't kick his ass just yet. "Couples get privacy. Isn't that the way it goes? Aunt Evie's rules —"

Mom whirls to face him, her cheeks mottled an angry red. "Evie is dead," she says. Beside me, Penny swoons like she just might faint, but Aunt Billy is there with one strong arm to hold her up. Turning to her relatives for support, Mom pleads, "They can sleep with the rest of the boys. Are you putting the kids downstairs again?" She looks at me as if she doesn't quite know who I am any more. "What's it matter if you're alone or not? If you're not …" She motions with one hand, not able to bring herself to finish the sentence. *If you're not having sex …*

Behind us, Aunt Bobbie laughs. I don't see anything amusing in this scene, nothing at all, but soon Aunt Billy's giggling, too, and Aunt Sarah lets out a sort of hiccupping guffaw that seems to startle herself more than anyone else. "Oh Laura," Bobbie chuckles. "How old are you? And you still can't say the word *sex*?"

"It's not that," Mom flusters, but now the children around us are giggling, hiding their mouths with their hands and glancing at each other from the corners of their eyes. *Sex.* We're all children here, aren't we? Me, Dan, these urchins crowding us, my mom herself. Turning to her sister, Mom implores, "Penny, a little help here would be nice."

Fortunately, whatever Penny's taking to get through the next few days has already kicked in, and she gives us all a sleepy, happy grin. "The back room," she says, clapping her hands in discovery. "I almost forgot! We didn't clean it out because Ginger said she wasn't bringing what's his face, remember?" She looks at Aunt Billy for confirmation. "There's a bed back there under all that mess. Perfect."

So it's settled. Dan opens the trunk of the car, grabs our bags, and together we follow Penny into the house. I don't look at my mom — I don't have to see the way she's glaring at me to know I won, and I can't help the smug smile that tugs at my lips and threatens to split my face in two. "Thanks," I whisper to Penny.

"My pleasure," she says with a shaky laugh. "Ray's right. Evie always said …" Her voice cracks and she clears her throat, wipes at her cheek as if wiping that thought away. "The back room's fine for you two. I'm glad you've found someone, Mike. You're a good kid."

She leads us through the foyer, filled with more luggage and bags and pillows than a college town bus station at Spring Break. There are more kids inside — how many of us *are* there? I don't recognize any of them, though I think I see my Uncle Tommy in the living room, reclining on the couch, my Uncle Craig beside him. I thought Caitlin said Doug was the only one here so far? When did everyone else arrive?

Through the kitchen, around more children. "Rec room's downstairs but everyone still hangs out up here," Penny tells us. The back room's off the kitchen — three doors line the wall behind the table and when the back door's open, the first one is hidden. That's the pantry. The next door leads to the basement, which was unfinished the last time I was here, though it sounds like they've finally converted it the way Evie always wanted. And the last door opens onto what has always been called simply "the back room."

When Penny opens the door, I feel transported in time — this cluttered storage room is exactly the way I remember it. A bed runs the length of one wall, stretching between the door and a single, circular window at the other end of the room. Old quilts are stacked up high like the mattresses in that fairy tale about the princess and the pea. Pillows pile into the corners of the bed, and there's a small table beneath the window, a bedside lamp and alarm clock among the coins and jewelry and knick-knacks scattered over its surface. Across the room is a clothes rack overstuffed with old coats, out of style shirts and slacks and prom dresses, feather boas, capes ... as kids, we used these clothes as costumes, pretending we were rich stars or singers, putting on movies and concerts in the backyard for any of the adults we could coerce into watching us. Towering boxes reach to the ceiling, a jungle gym we used to climb on when we were younger; there's a record player that still worked when I was a teenager and a case of 45s and LPs that I would listen to for hours, the Beatles and Supremes and Monkees; a bookcase bleeds encyclopedias and old issues of *National Geographic* onto the floor. This was where Evie stuck everything she couldn't fit anywhere else, a veritable treasure trove to children. Because kids were always running in and out of here, and because it was always such a mess — an eyesore, Evie used to call it — no one ever slept in this room during vacations.

That makes this hit home. This *isn't* a vacation, it's not downtime, it's not the usual family gathering that I've missed these past few years. Evie isn't with us any longer, and suddenly her absence is an open wound in my chest, an ache that I don't think will ever heal. The fact that I'm sleeping in the back room these next few days drives the point deeper into my soul. *Gone.*

"Thanks," I say again. I speak low so Penny won't hear the emotions swirling through me. When I stand aside to let Dan into the room, he touches my arm as he passes — he must sense what I'm feeling. Tired and sad and a loss so engulfing that I fear I might drown if I dwell on it, like an aggravated wound that just won't heal. I'll get through this. I'll move on.

Still, here, now? I wish to God that I had found the time to come up this past summer. Aunt Evie would've loved Dan, I just know it.

Penny busies herself cleaning off the bed, until there's just one quilt left and two pillows fluffed together at one end. "Don't mind your mom," she tells us as she works. "Laura can be ugly when things don't go her way, and she's had her mind set on grandkids for God, I don't know how long. You really threw her for a loop there, Mike."

"I'm sorry," I mumble. Setting our bag on the floor, Dan rubs at my back, then eases an arm around my waist and hugs me close.

"You must be exhausted," Penny continues. In here, away from the aunts and my mother, she seems more animated. Maybe the medication's wearing off. "Tell you guys what. You lie down for a bit, rest up, and I'll come knocking when it's time for dinner." With a bright smile, she adds, "Al's tonight. I know you've missed his hoagies."

I have to laugh. "They call them subs down south," I say.

Penny clutches her chest as if hurt. "Subs!" she cries in mock horror. "Oh, the humanity! Do they even use olive oil down there? Wait! Don't tell me. Italian dressing, right?" Now Dan's laughing as well, and Penny shakes her head in dismay. "The heathens. We'll fix you boys up with real cheesesteaks tonight, I promise."

As she turns to leave, I catch her wrist. In my hand, hers feels frail, like an intricate macramé. "Thanks again," I whisper. "How are you holding up, Penny?"

For a moment I don't think she'll answer. I'm still a child to her — she won't confide in me. But then her chin crumbles, her lower lip trembles, and she touches her hair as if checking to make sure it's still there, a habit she shares with my mom. "Fine," she whispers, forcing a brave smile. "Fine, Michael, really. I'll be fine." She gives me a tight hug. "I'll have to be, right? Thanks for coming, both of you." With a sad smile at Dan, she leaves.

And we're alone at last.

14: Alone

FOR A BREATHLESS moment, Dan and I look at each other, not daring to believe that we've managed to shuck off the rest of my family and snag a few stolen moments to ourselves. Then it sinks in — this is *our* room, that's our bed — and without a word, I lock the door to keep this sudden solitude in. As I turn towards Dan, I'm surprised to find a hungry lust shimmering beneath the exhaustion that dulls his eyes. "You're not thinking …" I let the sentence trail off as I close the distance between us.

"Why not?" Dan replies. He reaches out for me but only manages to brush a hand along my stomach before I step up behind him. My hands find his shoulders, the muscles bunched into hard knots beneath my fingers. As I rub into the tight flesh, he moans softly, leans back into my touch. "Unless you don't want to?" he murmurs.

I slip off his jacket and let it fall to the floor. "Now when do I ever not want to?" I ask coyly.

Dan's laugh turns guttural as I massage his neck. "That one time in the barracks," he starts.

Digging my thumbs into the space between his shoulder blades, I rub away the tension coiled there and growl, "I just didn't want to get you in trouble, boyfriend. Don't complain — you got some later that night." We're referring to something that happened in April, after we'd been together for a few months. Dan was already living with me, but since he's stationed on post, he keeps a room there with a footlocker and few articles of clothing, nothing important. His bunkmate knows he shares a place with me, though he thinks that we're just old friends. I don't know if he suspects we're in a relationship, and from what Dan says, he doesn't really care. Most of Jackson's downtime is spent trolling for trollops in the nation's capital — a single room means he can sneak the girls onto base, as long as he can get them out of his room and off post by first reveille.

Last spring, one of the men in Dan's troop got married, and the others managed to snag the Officer's Club for a bachelor party. Dan invited me.

"It's sort of just for Army buddies, isn't it?" I asked, unsure.

Dan shrugged. "It's for a bunch of us guys to get together one last time before Hicks gets hitched," he told me. "It's to have fun. I want you there. You'll make it fun for me."

With a laugh, I pointed out, "None of the other guys are bringing their lovers."

To which Dan wrapped his arms around me and murmured, "None of the other guys are dating someone like you." He kissed my ear. "If you don't go, I'm not going, either. A bunch of drunken Army guys isn't exactly my idea of a perfect evening, you know?"

So I went. Fortunately I wasn't the only civilian there — Hicks worked part-time at a local Wal-Mart off post and a few of his coworkers showed up, as well. There was alcohol, of course, and a couple of hired dancers, who showed up in long trench coats that hid sequined bikinis. One of them took an instant liking to me, and after every set would find some excuse to plop herself down at our table, scooting her chair close to mine. After getting a few mixed drinks into my system, I leaned over and whispered to her, "You're barking up the wrong tree. I don't ..." I didn't elaborate, but the look I gave her was enough to get my drift across.

The girl, a college student who called herself Roxie, flipped her sweaty blonde hair over one bare shoulder and laughed, a rich sound as deep as the drinks I'd been sipping all night long. "Oh honey, I *know* that," she said, dismissing me with a wave of her hand. "Why do you think I'm hanging out over here? I know I'm safe with you." At my quizzical look, she explained, "The other guys think I'm taken, right? They leave me alone. And hey, you have some cover, if you need it. Works out for both of us in the end. You'll go home with your boy tonight and I'll leave without getting groped. I'm just doing this for the money, you know? Student loans ain't shit." I bought her a drink for her honesty, and another for her continued silence.

By the end of the evening, most of the men were drunk, and they left in groups of twos and threes, some with one of the girls caught beneath the span of their arms, some just holding onto each other to make it back to the barracks in one piece. Shitfaced, the whole unit — their CO would've been proud. Roxie walked between me and Dan, both of our arms around her shoulders just to feel each other's touch. At her car, she gave me a kiss while Dan looked the other way. "You guys have fun," she purred with a wink. When Dan didn't reply, she poked his stomach playfully. "You hear me, G.I. Joe? Don't act like you don't know what I'm talking about."

Truth be told, Dan was a little plastered himself, and as platonic as it was, I think that kiss bothered him. Still, he didn't mention it. We walked back to his barracks in silence, so close together that our elbows brushed with every other step. I forget why we were stopping by his room — to pick up some clothes? Maybe, I don't remember now. I followed him into the building, past the soldier on duty, up the stairs to his room, our footsteps echoing around us in the stairwell as if a whole battalion hurried to keep up. In the hall, I waited with my hands shoved my pockets as he opened the door to his room, already unlocked. Cautiously we entered the room, Dan one step ahead of me, my hand drifting to his waist as he clicked on the light ...

Jackson was already back, passed out on his bed fully clothed and snoring heartily. With a shaky laugh, Dan clicked off the light and whispered, "Close the door." I did, plunging us into utter darkness, and I reached out to find Dan reaching back for me. Pulling me to him, he pressed his mouth against my cheek, his breath fire from the alcohol, and breathed, "Let me get my things and we'll go." I nodded, not trusting myself to speak. I didn't want to wake Jackson if I could help it.

Dan led the way to his side of the room. Like a college dorm, two large wooden wardrobes bisected the room down the center — to the right was Jackson's half and to the left, Dan's. He clicked on his lamp, tilted the shade towards the wall to keep the light diffused and indistinct, and in its glow he looked golden, like the drinks I had at the party. Intoxicating, that's what he is, no matter where or when or under what circumstances, and I couldn't stop myself from reaching out to touch his shoulder then, just to feel him. Another half hour and we'd be back at our house, in our bed. Another half hour and he'd be mine.

But he misread my touch and turned to pin me with a smoldering look. "Michael," he sighed, pressing against me. I stumbled back, surprised at his sudden ardor and half-aroused myself, but we were on an Army base, in the barracks — I had to keep that in mind. Dan wasn't making it easy, either, with his eager hands, his alcoholic kisses. He backed me up against his wardrobe, leaned into me heavily, one knee parting my legs, his hips grinding his budding erection against my own.

"We can't," I whispered, and somehow I got my hands between us, somehow I managed to push him away. He's persistent, though, and when he's been drinking, he gets horny as hell. It was so hard to resist him, his lips on my face, my neck, his hands on my chest, his knee working between my legs until I gasped in delight. It was *so* damn hard to push against him, to pull back from his kisses, his love. "Dan," I breathed, then, "Daniel, no. Listen to me." And finally, "Dan, please. This isn't — we'll get caught."

From the other side of the wardrobe, Jackson snorted in his sleep, and when Dan tried to kiss me, I turned away. I'm not sure which finally broke through to him, my reluctance or his roommate's snores, but he turned angrily from me. Staring at his back, I felt cold and alone, and I wanted to touch him again, to tell him I loved him, but I couldn't. For the first time, I felt distanced from him, closed off. I hated that. *It's for your own good*, I thought, but I couldn't find the words. *If the Army finds out about me, you're whole life in the service is in jeopardy. Please realize this, baby. Please know I could never push you away otherwise.*

The words wouldn't come.

He clung to his anger as we headed out of the room, one bag slung over his shoulder. I wanted to say something but the longer I waited, the harder it was to speak at all, and in the car we sat in silence that threatened to stifle what we had worked together to build over the past few months. All the way back to our house, *my* house, he didn't say a word, didn't touch me, didn't even look my way. I could almost hear my heart break in what he didn't do or say.

I pulled into the parking lot of our complex and turned off the car. For a moment we sat there, the clicking engine the only sound between us. I couldn't take it anymore. "Dan —" I started, and at the same exact moment, he said, "Mike —"

We looked at each other and laughed, the tension gone. "I'm sorry," he said, taking my hand. I had waited for his touch all night, and with his hand in mine, everything was right between us again. "I'm — you're right. I was an ass, okay? If Jackson heard us getting it on, I'd be in deep shit. I'm sorry."

I nodded. "It's okay," I sighed. I just wanted him, I didn't care who had to say sorry first. I was ready to apologize if I had to, anything to have him back. Rubbing his hand between both of mine, I asked, "So we're cool?"

"Come here," he said with a grin, pulling me to him for a tender kiss, then another. The third held a bit of the night's previous hunger, and we took the rest inside before we went any further than that.

Now, in the back room of Aunt Evie's house, I knead Dan's shoulders and blow along the back of his neck to make him laugh again. "You want some loving now?" I ask, trying to sound incredulous. When he shrugs, I rub into him harder and feel the muscles loosen beneath my touch. "Aren't you too tired from all that driving?"

He reaches behind me, grabs my buttocks and pulls me to him. "Not for you," he says.

Kissing the nape of his neck, I ease my hands down his back to his waist, then tug his shirt free from his pants. My hands trace the curve of his spine, his skin warm beneath my fingers. I work around to his belly, thumb his navel, move up his chest to circle his nipples, first one, then the other. He leans his head back, moans as I kiss his neck and hug him to me, his hands clenching my ass. "Michael," he sighs. "Why do you do me like this?"

I have to laugh. "Me?" I ask, the hint of a tease in my voice. I love that I can bring out the lover hidden inside the soldier. With expert hands, I pull his shirt off over his head and toss it aside. Then my hands trail down his chest again, over his stomach, to find the belt buckled at his waist. A few quick movements and I have it undone, his jeans unzipped, his erection already pressing through the open fly. I slide the jeans down, kneeling to push them to his knees, and he half-turns, his hands in my hair, to see what I'm doing. "Step up," I say, holding one leg.

He obeys, leaning on my head to steady himself while I pull his jeans off one leg, then the next. They catch on his shoes, which he kicks off, almost losing his balance while he does so, but I hold onto him and he doesn't fall. "What do you have in mind?" he wants to know.

"You'll see." Standing, I run my hands up his bare legs, over his green Army issue briefs, across his stomach again as I hug him to me. "Thank you for getting us here safely," I whisper, kissing his shoulder. His hands rub at my thighs and I cup his erection in both hands, squeeze until he gasps my name. "You're so good to me," I murmur. "What did I ever do to deserve you?"

"Get out of these pants and I'll show you," Dan replies.

With a breathy laugh, he tries to turn in my embrace but I won't let him. Instead I lead him to the bed and pull back the covers. "Lie down," I tell him. There's a part of me that secretly likes the way he jumps to do my command, like a true soldier. When he sits on the edge of the bed, I run a hand over the top of his short hair, my skin rasping against his scalp. "On your stomach."

He complies, stretching out on the mattress, his legs beneath the covers and his arms crossed beneath his cheek. He watches me as I strip down to my boxers, grins when I climb into the bed and straddle his back. My buttocks rest against his, my cock hard in the small of his back — he wiggles beneath me in an attempt to get me interested in fooling around. "Don't," I warn, gripping his shoulders as I lean down over him. "Just relax."

I start massaging his neck, picking up where I left off. The heels of my hands knead between his shoulder blades, my fingers press into his muscles, working free the exhaustion buried there. He moans beneath me, raises his hips slightly to reposition his erection that pushes into the bed, reaches back from time to time to touch my bare knee, my leg. I rub into him, his shoulders, his neck, down his arms to his elbows and up again to his biceps. On one upper arm is a tattoo, the stylized face of a growling snow leopard and the words, *57 QM — Never Say Die.* Below that are my initials in Kanji script. I have his on my chest, just under my collarbone on the left above my heart. That hurt like a bitch. It was a whim, a show of love that we talked ourselves into when we were in Ocean City this past summer, the week I should have come up here to Sugar Creek. I wonder what Caitlin will have to say when she finds out her straight-laced preppy brother has his boyfriend's initials tattooed on his body in Oriental characters. She'll probably try to talk me into taking her to get a heart on her ankle, or something. She's running out of things to pierce — she'll want to start inking herself next.

I shake my head to push the thought away. I'm not going to think of anyone on the other side of that door — just Dan, he's the only thing that exists right now. "You're tired," I tell him, and he nods as I rub his shoulders, his back. "You're so good to me, driving *all* that way." My hands caress along the sensitive skin beneath his arms, making him giggle a bit beneath me. "Giving up your leave for me. What would I do without you?"

"I don't want to know," he admits. His voice is muffled where his head rests in his arms. "I won't let you find out."

Continuing my massage, I move down his back, along his spine, easing the tension out of his body until he's completely relaxed beneath me. Then I work up to his shoulders again, down his arms — this time I stretch out over him, scooting back until I'm sitting on his thighs and my dick is hard between the cleft of his buttocks. I press my face between his shoulder blades and feel him rise beneath me with each breath he takes. His skin is warm on mine and smells faintly of soap from his shower this morning. So long ago now, another past, another lifetime it seems. When he speaks, his voice rumbles through me like thunder. "Michael —"

"Shh," I murmur, smoothing my hands along his arms, the hair standing up under my palms. I just want to lie here and feel his body against mine, each breath he takes matching my own. We fit together perfectly, my arms along his, my chest against his back, my head in the hollow where angels have wings.

15: Interruptions

WE FALL ASLEEP that way but when I wake up, I'm curled beside him with his arms and legs wrapped protectively around me. My body still feels the hum of the car, the road rolling away, and I hold my breath to listen to the sounds of the house around me. Evie's house. I almost can't believe we're here. But the room we're in is dark with early evening, the bed is musty from disuse, and beyond the closed door I can hear children laughing, the low murmur of adults talking together in the kitchen, a cool breeze rustling leaves outside. No traffic — this is Sugar Creek, not D.C., and I swear that I can hear the gurgle of the creek at the edge of the property, the water splashing away like a messenger of the gods. To tell of Aunt Evie's passing, perhaps, or to speed her soul on its way to the next life.

A chill passes through me at the thought and I cuddle closer to Dan, until his steady breath drowns out all other sound. I'm still cold, though. Sitting up, I tug at the quilt at the end of the bed, pull it up over our tangled bodies, and snuggle up to him again. His arms come up around me, holding me close. I rest my head against his chest and sigh, content. I don't want to leave this room, this bed. I don't want to let reality into this comfort zone — I don't want to have to play the adult here, I don't want to have to sit with my parents and my aunts and listen to emotionless talk of the coming funeral, arrangements to be made, people to be called, insurance policies to be cashed in … I want none of that. I want to be a child again, ignorant of the proceedings behind the curtain. I'm not even sure at this point that I'll be able to look at Evie's body during the viewing, and my mind short-circuits when I try to picture myself at her graveside — the image just isn't there. I can't do it, any of this. I don't want to do it.

At least I have Dan to see me through.

My lover's hand smoothes down my hair and I look up to find him staring at me. He kisses my forehead and, his lips damp on my skin, murmurs, "How are you doing, babe?"

"Fine," I lie. If Penny can do it, it can't be that hard — I'll keep telling myself that I'm fine and sooner or later.

I don't know if Dan believes me or not, but he kisses me again and doesn't press the issue. His lips are soft on my face, his breath a whisper as he kisses the tender flesh under my eyes, below my nose. "Love me," he sighs, one hand straying between us to rub at the front of my boxers.

I don't need further prompting. My mouth finds his and I ease him back against the pillow, crawling on top of him beneath the quilt until I'm straddling him again, but this time we're facing each other and my hands are on his chest, not his back. I caress his neck, his chin, trail kisses around his jaw and down his throat. He gasps my name when my lips close over one nipple, and as I tongue the hard bud, he fists his hands in my hair, holds me against him. When he sobs and arches up against me, his erection straining at his briefs, I move to the other nipple, swirl my tongue around it until it's as hard and sore as the first. Dan practically cries with want of me. I do this to him, bring this soldier to his knees with lust. Me. It's a heady thought, and it turns me on more than I like to admit.

Down his chest, further, down to the waistband of his briefs and the thickness that swells in his underwear. I lick the material, tasting fabric and a hint of cum because he's already that hard. My mouth closes over his dick, tracing its outline through his briefs, and his legs open for me, his knees rise on either side of my head and his hands touch my face, my hair as I go lower. With my nose, I rub over his balls, then lick them through the material, my tongue flicking beneath the elastic band to lick heated flesh. All I hear is my lover's fevered breath, my name in his hitched sighs. I spread one hand out over his crotch, lick my own fingers, my palm, and then ease into the leg band of his briefs to rub my saliva over his skin, down below his balls, down to where he aches for me.

My other hand follows, sliding between him and the mattress to part his buttocks. I sit up as I rim around his secret flesh — the front of my boxers tents obscenely, and as one finger slips into him, he reaches for my erection, unsnapping my fly to stroke at my thick shaft. I push into him further, spreading him wide, and he rises to meet my hand, his breath in short gasps that tell me he's ready, he wants me, he's almost there and I'm close to coming myself —

A knock on the door interrupts us.

We freeze, locked in position, and stare at each other in the darkness. "Who …?" I start, but Dan is beyond words right now. When the knock isn't repeated, he tugs at my dick, pulling me to him, driving my fingers deeper into him as he bucks into the thrust —

On the other side of the door, Caitlin calls out my name. "Dinner time, kids," she says, knocking again.

"Fuck," I mutter, but I don't extract myself from my lover's body. Instead, I push into him slowly, my hand hot inside him, and his eyes close in pleasure with my ministrations, his hands grasp at me, working me towards release. "Go away, Cat," I call out, even as I thrust into Dan's palms. "We'll be right out."

She doesn't answer. Maybe she's left, a few minutes, that's all we need. Dan's briefs are stained a dark color where he's begun to weep pre-cum and I want to feel his tight ass around my erection before either of us lose this moment. Moving his underwear aside, I guide my dick to the heat in my hand and lean down over him. "I love you," I sigh. Whatever he says in return is lost when I thrust and he pulls me in.

Another knock, this one hard enough to rattle the door. "Are you guys doing it in there or something?" Caitlin cries. "Your damn hoagies are getting cold."

Dan laughs as he holds me to him, his arms tight around my waist because he's not letting me go until we've finished what we started. "Tell her to go away," he whispers as we find a steady rhythm.

"You tell her," I laugh, breathless. I move in him, above him, and fortunately this bed is a little sturdier than the one I have back at my parents' house because it doesn't hit the wall with each thrust.

Dan's fingers dig into my buttocks. "Cat, go away," he calls out, surprising me into giggles. "What?" he asks with a grin.

"Shh," I say, kissing him quiet.

Against my mouth, he murmurs, "I don't want to rush through this."

As if to prove his point, he slows the pace, squeezing me when I'm deep inside of him so I don't want to pull out, and when I do draw back, the elastic in his underwear bites into my balls and shaft. I'm close, *damn* close, another couple of minutes and this will all be over, no matter how much he wants to make it last …

The door knob rattles. "Caitlin!" I cry out, pissed. Of all the people in this family, I would've thought she'd be the first to leave us the hell alone at a time like this.

But it isn't her voice that answers me, it's Ray. *Of course.* "Mike, we got dinner —"

"We'll be right out!" I am *not* carrying on a conversation with my brother while I'm making love to Dan, it's just not happening. Much as I don't want to rush through it, either, I find myself thrusting harder, deeper, pouring my anger out into my lover. He takes me in completely, pulls me closer, lets me drive into him until I come. And then it's over, finished, but I feel unsatisfied and bitter. I'm not letting Ray get away with ruining the first moment

I've had alone with my boy all goddamn *day*.

I'm not the only angry one — Dan rips off his briefs, soiled with his juices, and tosses them to the floor. Naked, he climbs out of the bed and heads for the suitcase. Pops it open, fishes through our clothes for another pair of briefs, pulls them on roughly to cover his smooth ass. "I'm going to hurt him," he swears, stepping into his jeans. I'm still kneeling on the bed, surprised at the sudden change in Dan's mood. When he looks over his shoulder at me, I see him as others must, closed and forbearing, a soldier to the core. "Get dressed," he tells me.

I don't question him, just start snapping up my boxers before sliding off the edge of the bed to grab my pants from the floor. "Dan," I begin, fumbling with my shirt. His hands brush across my chest to pull the shirt down over my head. "Dan, babe, wait."

He doesn't look at me, just tugs on his own shirt, tucks it into his jeans, buckles his belt. When I catch his arm, he tries to shrug me off, but I don't let go. "I'm sick of his shit," he mutters. I can feel his muscles bunched beneath my hand. "I know he's your brother but I'm going to hurt him, Michael. I promise you."

I rub at his arm, trying to work the muscle loose, but he hates being interrupted during sex. During *love* — it's not just sex to him. When we make love, he wants to hold as much of my body against his as possible, he wants the foreplay, the licking, the kisses, the quiet sweet talk after it's all over. The few times that we've made it quick, just to have a piece of each other before one of us had to rush out the door, he was grumpy and irritable for the rest of the day, until I could get him alone in bed that night and kiss him, hug him, cuddle with him to make it right. I have a feeling he's going to be like that until we get together again tonight.

Fortunately for Ray, he's not waiting on the other side of our door. He's not in the kitchen at all — a few kids are, one or two adults who are probably my cousins but I don't recognize them, I don't know their names. They're crowded around the kitchen table and barely glance at us as we step out among them. I feel as if they all know I just had sex, but no one says anything about it, they're too busy shouting to each other, who ordered mushrooms? Who got the one with no mayo? Where are the hot peppers? Turning to Dan, who keeps one hand on my waist like he's afraid of losing me in the midst of all these people, I laugh and ask, "Didn't you always say you wanted a large family?"

He gives me a wan smile — he looks afraid. I don't blame him. Pushing my way to the table, I snag a large cheesesteak wrapped in white deli paper. "This mine?" I call out, asking no one in particular.

Penny is on the other side of the table, trying to divvy up the sandwiches.

"Take it," she tells me. As I back away, she points at the sink. "Drinks are in there, Mike. We're all outside."

Actually, it looks to me like we're all crammed in here. "Drinks," I tell Dan, who's already heading over in that direction. He pulls two canned sodas from the ice in the sink and follows me through the screen door out back. A low bench runs the length of the deck, a new addition since last I've been here, but there's no room to sit. Kids run everywhere, dripping soda and sandwiches and calling to each other. A few women huddle together around two or three strollers, cooing over babies and passing the children back and forth like boys trading baseball cards. I see my dad over by the shed, hoagie in one hand, surrounded by men his own age, my uncles and the men my aunts have married. They have a game of horseshoes set up out there, though most of the guys seem to be eating more than playing at this point. In the middle of the yard, my mom sits at a picnic table with Aunt Sarah and Aunt Billy, and around them other relatives sit at patio tables, huddling four or five people beneath one umbrella. I see people I vaguely remember — Doug and Ginger and Ruth, Judith's sons, Aunt Bobbie, a few cousins I recognize from my childhood. Kenny and Jerry and Autumn and Marie, Caitlin followed by a gaggle of little girls, Uncle Tommy with Ray in a viselike neck grip as they wrestle to the cheers of some of the boys — my head swims to take them all in. There are easily thirty adults, maybe more, and twice that number of kids. This isn't a funeral, it's a damn circus.

Dan leads the way down the deck steps to a recently vacated table, and I sink into the wicker chair gratefully. "Jesus," I mutter, unwrapping the hoagie. Dan scoots his chair close to mine and takes half of the sandwich I offer him. "I didn't know there were this *many* of us. Where are they all staying?"

"All over the place." I turn as Aunt Bobbie maneuvers her broad hips around my chair. "Mind if I join you boys?"

"No, ma'am," Dan replies.

Before Bobbie can answer, he stands to pull a chair out for her, then slides back into the seat next to mine only after she's seated. *Two points,* I think. He's already won her heart, I can see that when she smiles warmly at him. "Michael," she says, unwrapping her own sandwich, "keep this one, you hear me?"

I laugh and nudge Dan with my elbow. "Yeah," I say, teasing. "I think I will. I've grown used to him."

Embarrassed, Dan ducks his head and bites into his sandwich. "Keep talking," he mumbles. "I'll get you back, just you wait."

My Aunt Bobbie laughs. "That sounds like a promise to me."

Trying to ease away from the impending subject of my love life, I ask my aunt, "So everyone's staying at the house?" When she nods, I look around and ask the inevitable, "Where?"

"Whole downstairs is refinished," she tells us. "You have to check it out. Evie put in a pool table and Jacuzzi down there, you'll love it." With a wink, she adds, "See if you two can slip into that spa alone sometime. Damn, last time Sander and I were here, you couldn't get us *out* of that thing."

"Sander's her husband," I tell Dan, to clarify things. He nods dutifully.

"A good man, too," Aunt Bobbie says. "He's overseas on business or he'd be here himself. Asked me if I wanted him to come anyway, when I called him with the news of Evie's passing, but I told him no sense in it. It's the thought that counts."

A little girl no more than four or five runs up to our table, a late-blooming mum in one hand that she's plucked from Evie's garden. "For you," she says, holding the flower out to me. Before I can take it, she's climbing up into my lap, and she taps my sandwich with the petals. "Mine?"

I have to laugh. "Who's this?" I ask. I tear off the end of my cheesesteak and hand it to the girl.

"Crystal!" My cousin Theresa runs over to our table, another little girl in her arms. She's ... right now, I don't remember how she's related to me, to be honest. One of Aunt Sarah's children's children, John's I think. She's my age — we grew up together. Now she takes Crystal's arm and deftly removes the child from my lap. "That's Uncle Mike's sandwich," she admonishes. Crystal doesn't care, just sticks the end of the hoagie into her mouth and stares up at us with wide eyes. When it's obvious the girl isn't giving it up, Theresa shakes her arm and asks, "Well? What do you say?"

Around a mouthful of food comes the muffled, "Thank you."

"Mike," Theresa sighs. "I'm sorry —" Then she sees Dan, and a smile breaks across her tired face. "This must be the boyfriend everyone's talking about. He *is* cute. Theresa," she says, introducing herself, and nodding at her children, "Crystal and Sam. And you are?"

"Dan," I tell her. She shakes my lover's offered hand and giggles like a schoolgirl when he gives her his gentleman's smile. "Who told you we were together?"

Rolling her eyes, Theresa asks, "Who didn't? A family like this, news travels fast. Everyone knows, Mike. It's cool, really. We always sort of ... I don't know, I don't want to say we knew because we didn't but it's not a surprise, you know what I mean?" As I search for an answer to that, Theresa shakes Crystal's arm to get the child's attention. "Tell Uncle Mike bye, baby," she says.

Instead, the girl says, "I gave him a flower." She's still sucking on the sandwich as her mother leads her away.

We watch them disappear into the crowd. "Kids all stay downstairs now," Aunt Bobbie tells us, picking up the conversation right where she left off. "From Crystal's age on up to Caitlin's, I guess. We clear out the main room down there, cover the floor with blankets and pillows and say go at it. Then we're putting all the singles in the living room and den. Ginger grumbled a bit but hey, she didn't bring anyone so it won't hurt her to sleep on the rollout again. God knows she's done it before." She waves her hoagie as she speaks. It's a habit most of my aunts have, talking with their hands. I suspect if you tie them down, they would be rendered speechless, at a loss for words. "Kenny brought a girlfriend — real pretty, you have to see her to believe it." When I laugh, she gives me a serious look. "You know? He's not much of a catch himself, if you ask me. Like your brother. Lord knows when he'll settle down."

Dan shifts beneath the table, his leg bumping mine. "Ray's a special case," I say carefully.

"Ray ain't all there," Aunt Bobbie says in a matter-of-fact tone of voice that leaves no room for argument. "Never has been. Don't you go telling him I said that, though, you hear? If I were your mom, I might've stopped there and given up all hope."

My lover snickers into his hoagie.

16: By the Creek

W HEN WE'RE FINISHED eating, I ask Dan if he wants to take a walk. It's grown dark out, but there are citronella candles lit at the tables and a large spotlight shines down over the backyard like the one my parents have glaring behind their house. There's a feeling of suspended animation in all that bright light with the night tucked into the trees and around the corners of the house, and kids running around the edges where dusk begins.

Too many people still for my tastes, and every last one of them seems to recognize me. What did Theresa say? *Everybody knows.* And so far my mom and Aunt Sarah are the only ones upset by Dan. Everyone else, even the smallest children, seem cool with it. My dad called out to us, asked if we wanted in on a game of horseshoes — he didn't ask Ray, and I suspect that he wouldn't have asked me, either, if Dan wasn't with me. My lover declined, of course, with his usual graciousness that already has half my cousins swooning after him. It's the way he excuses himself when we stand, the way he takes charge and cleans up after me, the way he touches my back as we walk to the trash cans Penny has set up along the garden shed. Most of the girls giggle when he looks at them, and the few who find the courage to approach us just stare or sigh. "You're so lucky," my Aunt Lennie says, cornering us near the shed. She's in her thirties and doesn't bother to keep her voice down, which makes Dan duck his head and look away. I take his hand, hold it against my thigh in some small measurement of comfort as she winks at us. "I had me a soldier boy once. Let me tell you —"

Fortunately, a handful of kids push between us, laughing as they fight to reach the trash cans first. "I'll talk to you later, Lennie," I say, letting the kids widen the gap between us and my aunt. Before she can reply, Dan pulls me into the darkness behind the shed, leafless branches scratching out at us as we pass. "I'm sorry," I murmur as I lead him through low tangles of ivy that cling to our feet. "At least they all like you. That's a good thing, right?"

In the muted light that finds its way back to where we are, I can see the amused gleam in his eye. With a slight tug of his hand, I stumble into the span of his arm. It comes up around my back to drape over my shoulders and keep me close. "If you say so," he whispers, kissing the hair above my ear. His breath is warm in the cool autumn night. Out here where the light doesn't quite reach, I wrap an arm around his waist, hug him close for a quick kiss that tastes like cheesesteak and Coke. "You said you wanted to go for a walk?"

With a laugh, I slip out of his embrace and catch his hands in both of mine. "This way," I tell him, leading him further into the darkness, away from the house.

I find the worn path easily enough, despite the fact that I haven't been here in years — other children have kept it open, a short run that leads to Sugar Creek. I can hear it in the night, gurgling away over rocks and roots, liquid memories of all the times I ever visited Aunt Evie. I knew about the path before I was old enough to navigate it myself — it's always been here, for as long as I can remember, and I know it was here when my mom was a little girl, too. It's a part of the forest, as much as the sarsaparilla trees and poison oak and tent caterpillars in the spring. A broad path cut through the trees, leading right to the edge of the creek. Even it the darkness, it's easy to find my way — no roots grow up through the dirt here, and the earth is packed hard from generations of wear. I imagine Evie as a young, bubbly girl, racing down this same strip of land with her sisters in tow, the seven of them dressed in the cumbersome bathing suits women wore back in the 1940's.

Dan lets me lead the way. He walks surefooted behind me, trusting me completely. I know where I'm going — I grew up in these woods, by this creek. These are the trees where I built forts with Stephen Robichaud and Ray, staging mock battles and camping out under the stars. These are the waters where my cousins and I would come to swim, trying to dunk each other beneath the surface of the creek or snagging hold of someone's shorts and ripping them away, tossing them on shore while the girls laughed at our antics. I remember catching the brunt of that joke one year — Ray tore my shorts off under the water, held them high like some sort of prize before throwing them away. *Away* — the fool didn't even toss them to the shore, to make me climb out naked to retrieve them. No, Ray had to let them go downstream, and I watched helplessly as they drifted away. Everyone laughed as the shorts billowed full of water, rising over rocks and stumps, but once they were out of sight, the giggles dried up one by one. "Um," Ray started, then he laughed nervously and wiped the water from his face with one hand. He must've been about eleven or twelve that year. "Oh shit."

"Go get them," I told him. The water was cold on my nude flesh, a pleasing sensation, but I wasn't getting out until I had my shorts back. I wasn't about to walk to the house naked.

Only they were gone — the boys climbed out of the creek and combed both shores while I swam near the old log that still serves as a bridge across the creek. The bark was rough against my bare shoulders when I leaned back on it. "Go get me another pair," I told Ray. He looked scared — I didn't blame him. I was already planning to tell Mom what had happened. I wanted to make sure I was there for the punishment.

But I didn't get to see it. Ray ran back to the house but it was Stephen who brought me a new pair of shorts. "Where's Ray?" I asked. I looked around to make sure we were alone before climbing out of the creek. The last thing I needed was one of my girl cousins to see me in the nude. I'd never have lived it down.

Stephen held the shorts open as I stepped into them. "Your mom caught us going in," he explained. In a high voice, he mimicked her. "Get out of this house! Soaking wet, what the hell has gotten into you boys?" I laughed, tugging the shorts on completely to hide my nakedness. Stephen pushed his glasses up on his nose and grinned. "Ray goes Mike lost his shorts and we all sort of laughed, you know? And she wants to know how. I dunno, Ray says. And she gave him this look —" He glared at me the way my mom must have glared at Ray, and I had to laugh, I knew *that* look all too well. "And then she dragged him inside. I could hear him bawling but I didn't see him. Your mom told me to bring you the shorts."

When I tell Dan that story, he laughs and says, "I think I've seen that look myself." Kneeling at the edge of the creek, he picks at the stones by his feet, then sits down, crossing his legs, and tells me, "Come here."

I sink into his lap, his arms around me to ward off the chill. When he kisses my neck, I bury my face in the soft bristles of hair on top of his head. "I love this place," I sigh. His hands fist in my shirt and I kiss his forehead, the bridge of his nose. "So much has happened here. So much of me is still in this landscape. You just don't know."

"Tell me then," he whispers. His words are mere breath that tickles beneath the collar of my shirt to coil around my body, warming me. "I love it, too, because it's made you who you are, Michael, and I love that person. So tell me how he came to be the man I'm holding now."

With a soft laugh, I say, "My cousins are jealous." He grins — I can feel the shape his lips make against my skin. "They are! I'm going to have to keep a close eye on you."

"I'm not going anywhere," he assures me. I know he isn't, but the quiet sound of the creek trickling over the rocks behind me, the gentle soughing of the breeze through the trees, it makes me playful. Dan spreads his hands open on my back and I lean against them, their strength exciting me. "You just tell those girls I'm not interested," he says.

"You're not?" I ask, feigning surprise.

He sighs into the hollow of my throat. "You're all I need. Talk to me."

I tell him about the creek, keeping my voice low so it doesn't drift far. He kisses my throat as I speak, his lips on my Adam's apple, his tongue along my collarbone. He finds a spot just below my ear that he likes and he pulls me closer, sucks at my neck, his tongue warm and soft, his lips gentle. It's hard to concentrate with his mouth on me, but he wants me to talk, so I tell him about the time a terrible storm came through and the creek swelled past its banks — you could see it from the house, tumbling through the trees, a rush of dirty water filled with toys and broken branches and shrubbery. When the waters finally receded, we were out there in galoshes, trooping through mud to clean up the debris.

I talk about the few winters we spent Christmas here, and how the ice crisps along the shoreline in the cold weather. One time Ray tried to step out over it, just to prove he could, and the fool fell right into the freezing water below. Fortunately the creek isn't too deep, and his coat was so big that he didn't slip under the ice. My dad was with us —he hauled Ray out of the creek, sopping wet and crying, and my mom really laid into him after *that*. Me, I had nightmares for weeks of falling into the swirling waters. I always heard the same sickening crack of the ice, I could see the break, but I couldn't manage to get to the shore fast enough, I always went down. I think sometimes I still have those dreams, though I don't remember them — but I'll wake shivering in the darkness, an irrational fear clawing at my throat, I can't breathe ... and I have to burrow into Dan's arms, snuggle up against him in our bed until the feeling passes and I can sleep again.

While I speak, Dan plants kisses along my neck, my shoulder, my ear. He takes my earlobe between his teeth, bites down just enough to make me shiver in delight. I cup my hands around the back of his neck, shift into a more comfortable position on his lap, one that presses my crotch against his hard stomach, my knees on either side of his hips. His hands have worked their way beneath my shirt to rub at my back, his fingers cool on my warm skin, and I fight the urge to lay him back to the ground, straddle him like I did earlier, love him out here beyond the light where no one can see us, nothing but the creek keeping us company.

I could do it, too — I know a spot just upstream, not two yards from where we sit. A thicket hidden in the bushes, the perfect place for a stolen moment between lovers. I got my first blowjob in that thicket at fourteen, years ago but when I close my eyes that day comes back like it happened just this morning. I wanted a soda — Grosso's keeps them near frozen in the summer, so cold that there are actual chunks of ice in the can when you first open it. I had fifty cents in my pocket, a gift from Aunt Evie. My plan was to walk down the street to the market for a soda, then hurry over to Stephen's for … well, I wasn't sure what for, but he was two years older than me and that first kiss behind the shed sure as hell wasn't the last, and I was at an age where I couldn't think of much more I'd rather do than lie on Stephen's bed and let him pet me through the thin shorts I wore, until I ached so bad. I wasn't in love with him, I knew that much, but he was the only guy I knew who wanted to touch and kiss me, and I thought maybe by the end of that summer, if he asked me to be his? I thought at the time that I might say yes.

Outside of Grosso's stood a boy that I had never seen before, older than me, with wavy black hair, dark eyes, dark skin — he had some Native American in him, possibly Asian, I wasn't sure which, and I couldn't stop staring. He wore tight jeans that left nothing to the imagination, I could see every curve of his cock, already half-hard, and his ass was encased in smooth denim. He had a white mesh crop-top, which Dan laughs at when I tell him but this was the 80's, Duran Duran was all the rage, these shirts were the style. I could see a flat stomach, ink around his navel that probably wasn't a real tattoo, and black Converse hi-tops completed the outfit. When I passed him and entered the store, I told myself he wanted me. As I bought the soda, I knew I'd think of him later, when Stephen put his hand on my dick.

Back outside again, he really *was* looking at me, and he pushed away from the wall as I walked by, falling into step behind me. *Change of plans,* I thought, veering back the way I had come, towards Evie's house. It wasn't fear that coursed through me as he stayed a few feet back, and I kept looking over my shoulder to make sure he was following. I didn't know what would happen — I was heading home, it wouldn't be anything *bad,* I reasoned. If he tried to hurt me, I'd scream and a dozen cousins, aunts, and uncles would come running. This emotion roiling my blood? When I glanced back and saw his hand rub across the front of his jeans, I could've come from my excitement alone.

I skirted the house, found the path through the trees, followed it down to the creek, him behind me every step of the way. No one was in the water — we were alone, just him and me and neither of us had said anything yet. At the edge of the creek, I stopped. I had this thought that I'd turn and face him, maybe ask his name, maybe get to know him a bit, and if all went well, get a kiss or two in the bargain.

Only I turned to find him right up on me, suddenly so close that I couldn't move, I'd fall into the creek if I stepped back. This close he didn't look that much older — eighteen maybe, at the most. "Kid," he breathed.

He smelled of cloves and reminded me of going to the dentist for some reason. His hands twitched at his sides, brushed across the erection that strained his jeans, then dared to reach out to touch mine. I almost jumped from the sensation. "You want to make a buck?" he asked. He spoke in low whispers, as if afraid of being overheard. "Let me do you, real quick. What do you say?"

I didn't know what he meant. "A buck?" I asked.

"Make it five," he told me. He must've seen the confusion on my face because he explained, "Easy money, kid. Let me blow you and get off on it, I'll give you five bucks. How can you say no to that?"

I didn't think I could. *A blowjob* — my mind went numb, I had never had one before. With my heart beating in my throat, I led the way to the thicket upstream, a place I discovered earlier in the week. I came out there to jerk off, just because I liked the sun on my bare genitals, and it was so hard to find privacy in the house. The guy followed me, crawling into the space between the bushes and pushing me down as I sat up. "Lie back," he said, his hands pulling down the front of my shorts and briefs in one motion. "Five dollars, kid. Easiest damn money you'll every make."

Expert hands encircled my shaft and I leaned back on the grass, gasping at the sensation. No one else had ever touched me *there*, not without the cover of clothing. Then a hot, wet mouth closed over me, oh *Jesus* I couldn't breath, I couldn't think, I couldn't even *moan* to release the tumult of emotions building in me. Soft cheeks sucked at me, a tongue rasped down my length, saliva dripped onto my balls and I came with such force that I was sure I'd shoot out the back of this kid's head. Two minutes, tops, that's all it had to be, but he continued to suck at me long after I was finished, swallowing every last drop. I started to get hard again and thought maybe for five bucks I could at least give him another few minutes, but I heard Ray's braying laughter and that scared the guy away. When he sat up, I saw the front of his jeans were stained dark where he had gotten off on it himself. "Maybe we can later," I started, sure that we could do this again.

But he shook his head, his hair sticking to his face in sweaty strands. "Thanks," he said, pulling a five dollar bill from his pocket. He wrapped it around my still-wet member, then tucked me back into my shorts before backing out of the thicket. The money felt like plastic crammed in my pants. "Thanks," he said again, a grin on his damp lips, and then he was gone.

"How romantic," Dan tells me now, and the nameless boy dissolves into the past, just another flickering memory that holds nothing to the flame of desire that Dan sets in me. He kisses me like he's marking territory, tiny pecks around my neck, up my jaw, until his lips press to mine and he claims me completely. I moan into him, try to ease him to the ground, I want him all over again — "Shh," he sighs.

His hands grasp my head to keep me still. "What?" I whisper. I can't hear anything but the creek and the wind in the trees and our staggered breaths, our hearts beating in the night.

He puts his lips to my ear, and I feel his words more than hear them. "In the bushes," he says. "Someone's watching us."

I try to stare into the darkness but see nothing. Dan covers my eyes with one hand and *now* I hear them, faint giggles, someone telling someone else to move over, she can't see, the snap of a twig beneath sneakered feet. My cousins or their kids, sneaking to spy on us. I don't know whether to laugh or chase them off.

"Keep kissing me," Dan says. "Like they're not there."

I do as he says, though it's hard to pretend I can't hear them, now that I know what to listen for. Still, I lose myself in his kisses, his hands, and the bolder children push to the front of the bushes for a better view. I lie Dan back and he rolls onto me, pinning me to the ground. I'm just about to suggest we take this inside when suddenly he leaps up from me and runs towards the trees, a ferocious roar escaping his throat.

Children squeal and race away, tripping over each other in their haste. Laughing, I push myself up from the ground and find Dan there to help me, his hands brushing the dirt from my pants and back. "You're as bad as they are," I say.

"I can be much worse," he promises with a tender kiss.

17: Among Adults

DAN CHASES THE children back to the house, suddenly a child again himself. He holds tight to my hand and pulls me along after him, both of us laughing as we race into the safe circle of light. The tables are empty now, the game of horseshoes over, most of the kids inside at this hour. Only a few adults linger on the deck, smokers and some of the older teenagers, Caitlin among them. I don't see my parents or Ray, but as we follow the kids up to the house, Aunt Billy catches my arm to stop us. "We're moving into the living room," she says, snubbing out her slim cigarette on the deck railing. "Give everyone a few minutes to get the children settled before we get started, what do you say?"

The living room is the gathering place in Evie's house. For as far back as I can remember, the adults always retired there at the end of the day, pulling the French doors shut on their muffled talk and muted laughter, which stretched well into the night. When I was little, I would sneak out on the landing upstairs with my cousins, stick my legs through the railing, rest my head against the cool banister as I watched the closed doors, shafts of faint light shining between the slats, and wondered what went on in the living room after the children were sent to bed. Sometimes I could hear the TV — explosions from action films too violent for us to see, or a sappy romantic soundtrack when it was just the aunts in there. Once I asked my mom what they talked about that was so important they had to close the doors to keep the words inside. "Nothing *important*, Michael," she told me, brushing off the question. "Just grown up stuff. Nothing you'd be interested in."

But still, curiosity ate at me, and I would find any excuse to slip downstairs and knock on the doors, to interrupt them and see if maybe I would be invited to stay. "Mom, Ray's kicking me," I said one time, standing in the doorway and biting on the end of my thumb as I stared into the room. It was one of the few times I saw my dad's arm around my mom's shoulders. A few of my uncles sprawled on the floor like little boys. Penny sat on the couch between Billy and Sarah, and Aunt Evie was lying across the loveseat, her head resting in Bobbie's lap as they watched a movie that I couldn't see from where I stood. I heard kissing, though, so I knew it was probably something I didn't *want* to see. Kissing wasn't yet on my list of fun things to do at that age, and I was years away from meeting Dan. When my mom looked at me, her eyes flashed with anger or drink, I wasn't sure which. "Under the covers," I elaborated. It wasn't quite a lie — Ray *had* been kicking me earlier, but I didn't dare sneak downstairs until after he fell asleep, or he'd want to come, too. "He won't stop."

"Tell him I said to cut it out," my mom sighed, exasperated.

"He won't," I started.

"Michael," she warned. I could tell from her tone of voice that I was pushing it. Beside her, my dad added, "Get to bed, buddy."

I didn't move. Aunt Evie sat up and, pushing herself off the loveseat, admonished, "Leave him be, Harry." With wide eyes, I watched her cross the room, until she loomed above me, and I let her take my hand. "Come on, Mikey. A glass of warm milk should set you right."

"Ray —" I tried, peering around Evie into the living room.

Deftly she closed the door on the others and led me into the kitchen. "I'll give him a talk," she promised, her large hand easily enveloping mine. "If he keeps it up, I'll just have to move him in with the girls. I don't think he'll like that much, do you?"

I always hoped that one day I'd be old enough to join my aunts in the living room — join *Evie*, with her quick wit and quiet humor, the way she had of talking that made you think everything was right in the world for that one moment in time, how she managed to see the good in everything around her, everyone. *Should've come this summer,* I think, struggling against the tears that fill my eyes. For the rest of my life, I'm going to think that, I just know it. If nothing else, it will be the one thing I'll always regret. I came back to Sugar Creek too late.

It's different in the house without Evie — despite the children running through the halls, the adults milling around, the endless chatter, the noisy prattle, the food set out on the kitchen table and countertops like a smorgasbord, there's something missing, a hole in the midst of it all where Aunt Evie belongs. Here, with us. I'd give anything to see her smile again, to hear her laugh, to feel her generous hugs. I can almost feel her here, a ghost drifting through these crowded rooms. If I close my eyes, I can believe she's just in the other room, she'll call out to me, give me a bright smile, clap Dan on the back and tell me I picked out a keeper.

Sensing a sudden change in my mood, Dan eases an arm around my waist and asks, "Michael?" I blink away the emotions clawing at me, the pain in my heart, the sadness filling me, and try to grin. I don't think I succeed —

my lover frowns at my lame attempt and tells me, "If you're not up for being social tonight, babe, I'm sure they'll understand."

"No, I'm fine." I lean against him, thankful for his strong arms, his sure hands. Forcing a laugh, I admit, "I've been waiting years to get in on that room. I'm not giving up my chance, you know?"

He laughs and we shuffle along after the kids, heading inside the house. At the door, though, Caitlin sticks a foot out in our path to stop me. "Hey," she says. In the fierce white light, I can tell she's been crying.

"You okay?" I ask. I touch her cheek but she turns away. A number of young girls crowd around her as if she's the most popular girl in school and they all want to stand right beside her. The oldest can't be more than ten, my Uncle Tommy's daughter Emily, who elbows her cousins aside to get up next to Caitlin. Nodding at the girls, I say, "You have a fan club."

Caitlin rolls her eyes, and I can't tell if that's supposed to be good or bad. "Tell me about it," she mutters. When one of the other girls tries to shove Emily aside, Caitlin pushes them all away like an angry mother bird trying to force her chicks out of the nest and into flight. "Keep off me," she growls, and though the girls widen the space between them, they still hover like annoying mosquitoes. "Jesus. Don't fucking crowd me."

The girls giggle at the cuss word. Nudging Caitlin, I joke, "You're the coolest thing they've probably seen in years, Cat. With your Goth-girl routine and my being gay, we're the talk of this town, you know that, right?"

"I'm about to beat them down," Caitlin threatens, and the girls back off another step or two. When Dan and I laugh, my sister asks, "You guys heading for the living room?" I nod. "I'll be there as soon as I ditch the groupies."

A twinge of jealousy stabs through me. "I never got in when I was your age," I mutter.

"Like you're so damn old," she says, amid another flutter of giggles. Glaring at the girls, she asks, "Will you guys shut up? Not everything I say is a riot." More giggles — she's quite the hit among the preteen crowd. With a sigh, she shakes her head. "Were we adopted?" she asks suddenly. I laugh and she says, "No, seriously. You and I are the only half-sensible ones here."

"We're okay," I tell her. "It's everyone else."

She nods. "I know!"

Around us the deck has cleared, most everyone inside now — just Caitlin and her little entourage, me and Dan, Aunt Billy and one or two others are left, cigarettes winking like fireflies in the night. I start for the door again, intent on getting to the living room for a good spot on one of the sofas before the room fills up completely, when Caitlin steps on my foot to get my attention. When I look up at her, she shrugs and tells me, "Just wanted to say thanks. For covering for me this afternoon. In the car?"

She means when my parents drove past us. "No problem," I say, but I feel my face heat up and my mouth can't stop trying to pull into a self-depreciating grin. Suddenly I want to be the favorite brother, I want my little sister to like *me* best, no matter how bad that sounds. Then again, look at my competition. I could never say two words to her and I'd win over Ray hands down.

Dan pokes at my cheek. "You've made him blush," he says, and that just deepens the color that burns my skin. My lover plants a quick peck in the spot below my eye where my jaw connects — that sets the girls to giggling again. He whispers into my ear, "You're cute."

"Damn," Caitlin laughs. "You're red as hell."

I push past her into the house. "Hey everyone, it's let's pick on Michael night," I mutter.

Dan holds onto my hand, trailing behind me as I shove my way through the people gathered in the kitchen. "Baby, wait," he says. I don't slow down, don't stop. I can still hear those girls laughing at that kiss, I can see Caitlin's smirk burning behind my eyes. *Try to be nice,* I think, *and this is what you get.* "Michael, hold up. Mike —"

And Dan stops in the middle of the hallway. I take another step only to find myself tugged back to him because he's holding me tight. "She's just playing," he tells me, touching my face. Kids elbow around us and he pulls me to one side, out of the flow of traffic. Concern laces my lover's face as he studies me. "Are you sure you're up for this tonight? We can beg off if you want. Maybe you just need some rest."

"I'm …" I run a hand down my face and sigh. "I'm fine," I tell him. I am. Just … I don't know. One minute I'm on top of the world, laughing and joking and everything's fine, and then the next minute something stops me, some reminder that we're here for Evie's funeral, and it all comes crashing down around me again. "I'll be okay," I promise, leaning into Dan's touch. I love his hand on my face, curved around my jaw, his fingers in my hair. "I'm fine."

He stares at me like he's not sure if he should believe me, but before I can assure him again, he nods. "Just let me know if you need to get away," he says. "You hear me, Michael? If it's too much for you, tell me and we'll leave, I don't care what anyone else thinks. I'm here for you, got it?"

With a sad smile, I nod. "Got it," I whisper, and I kiss his thumb before he pulls away. Then I take his hand and pull him through the open French doors into the living room.

It's like a party in here, people sitting on the sofas, the floor, leaning on the arms of chairs, draped over each other like guests waiting on their host.

Some hold glasses of whiskey, bourbon, or beer, and the quiet chink of ice in the drinks lends to my surreal sense of being at a business dinner, moving among clients, Dan at my side like a dutiful spouse. I spy an empty loveseat and guide him to it, sinking to the cushions gratefully. He sits beside me, an arm across my shoulders to keep me close. *I'm* intimidated here — I can only begin to imagine how he must feel, among people he doesn't know.

My aunts move through the crowd like salesmen working the floor, refilling drinks, pointing out places to sit, ushering the children out of the room and down the hall to the basement stairs. I catch a glimpse of my mom on the far side of the room but I ignore the looks she throws my way, angry little stares that make me cuddle closer to Dan. My dad isn't here, but I don't expect him to be — chances are he's in the den with a few of my uncles, watching TV. But Billy's here, and Bobbie, Sarah, Doug and Tommy and Ginger, she waves at me as she goes by, her long curls almost platinum in the soft lamplight. My cousin Kenny sees me, crosses the room, a pretty Muslim woman beside him dressed from head to foot in a traditional habib. "Man, you saved my ass," he says, perching on the edge of the seat beside me. He's my Aunt Ruth's son, about my age, and Bobbie's right, he's never been all there. One year he took a handful of Aunt Evie's heart pills just because Ray told him they were candy. After a bottle of Ipecac and my dad holding him upside down over the kitchen sink to shake the pills loose, he ended up in the emergency room with an IV in his arm to flush his system. Not all there, no, but he's always been nice to me.

Holding out a hand, he introduces himself to Dan. "I thought I was gonna get chewed out for bringing Neeshi along," he tells us. "If I hear one more thing about finding myself a good Catholic girl ..." He shakes his head and laughs. "But then you one-up me, Mike. Aunt Sarah's all over me about dating a terrorist and here you are with a *boy*. Jesus Christ." At the look Dan gives him, he quickly amends, "No offense, man, really. It's cool. You can't help who you love, right?"

That's one way of looking at it. I smile past him at his girl — Neeshi, he called her, and she's very pretty, just like Aunt Bobbie said she was. Beneath the hood of her outfit, she has skin like milk-laced coffee, and her eyes are dark beads set in her face. I introduce myself and Dan, and when she smiles, I nod at Kenny and ask, "What are you doing with a lug like this?"

"Hey!" Kenny cries, wounded. "I could ask your boy the same thing."

I like the way that sounds, *your boy*. Ruffling my hair, Dan asks, "How did you put it? You can't help who you love?"

Kenny laughs. "I'm just glad you guys are here." He elbows me, trying for playful but he's always been a big guy, burly like a football player, and his arm rams mine harder than he intended. Dan's hand drifts down to rub at the spot, almost as if he felt the nudge himself. "Get them off my ass for awhile, right? Already Momma's like at least you're not into guys."

Yeah, sounds like Ruth. Sarah's daughter to the core, definitely, and I can't think of anything to say in reply so I don't bother to say anything at all. Losing interest in us, Kenny lets his gaze roam around the room until it settles on Theresa, who looks less harried without the kids dragging at her. "Terry!" he calls out. She cringes — she's always hated that nickname, but Kenny doesn't notice. Instead, he takes his girlfriend by the arm and leads her to the other sofa to introduce her to Theresa. "You meet Neeshi yet?"

Dan says softly, "I'm not sure if I should be offended or not."

With a laugh, I take his hand in both of mine and lace our fingers together in my lap. "That's Kenny," I tell him, as if that's all the explanation he needs for my cousin's behavior. "You get used to him. He's less annoying than Ray, but only by a notch or two. Idiocy must run in the family."

"I'm glad it skipped over you," he murmurs, rubbing my arm where Kenny socked me. "Speaking of idiots ..."

I look up as Ray enters the room. He has a beer in one hand, ever his father's son, and laughs a little too loudly when my mom tells him to sit down. Caitlin comes up behind him and without breaking her stride, lashes out with one small fist to punch him in the arm. When he turns to glare at her, she hits him again. "Mom," he whines — I can hear him from over here, twenty-eight and can't even defend himself against his little sister. Out of spite, Caitlin hits him a third time. Ray tries to hit back but she's quick — she moves out of reach and then slaps him again. "Mom! Tell Caitlin —"

Mom doesn't even look at them. "Caitlin, stop it," she says.

Caitlin sinks into the seat beside her before Ray can, and hits him once more. The look on Ray's face is priceless, and Dan's snickering into his hand now, I'm giggling stupidly. There's no sport in it really, like shooting fish in a barrel, but Caitlin keeps it up and Ray can't seem to grasp the concept of trying to get away. "Mom —"

"Raymond, move," Mom says, suddenly angry. "Go sit somewhere else and leave her alone."

He stands there a moment longer and frowns around the room. When he sees the seat next to me, Dan groans. "Ray, no —" I say as my brother squeezes down next to me. "It fits two people, not three, moron. It's a loveseat, not a *ménage à trois* seat."

Pouting, Ray asks, "What's that mean?"

"It means get up," I tell him, giving him a shove.

He doesn't budge. "You get up," he mutters into his beer. Dan rubs my arm, hugging me closer, then slyly moves his hand to the back of the couch, his arm spread out behind me. When Ray takes a sip from his mug, Dan smacks the back of his head, hard enough to splash beer up into my brother's face. "Hey!" he cries, glaring at me.

I can't stop laughing. "I didn't do it!" I tell him, but I'm the one giggling here, not Dan, who sits like a statue beside me, innocent. Ray punches my arm, already sore from Kenny's friendly nudge, and I hit him back, causing more beer to splatter onto his pants. "I didn't — don't start with me, Ray. I'll kick your ass and you know it."

"Bullshit." Ray hits me again.

This time Dan catches his wrist. He gives my brother a look that can terrify new recruits and squeezes his hand until I can see muscles stand out like cords in his arm. Tears fill Ray's eyes, his face goes red, and across the room I hear Caitlin laugh. "Dan," I caution. My brother gasps in pain, tries to twist away. "Dan, please …"

He lets go. Ray clutches his injured hand to his chest and glares into his beer as he pretends we're no longer here.

18: End of a Long Day

WHEN THE COUCHES and chairs are filled, people sit on the floor, and when there's no room left to walk through the living room, those standing congregate in the doorways and spill out into the hall. We're all here — the great-aunts, my own aunts and uncles, my adult cousins. We talk quietly among ourselves, telling each other of our trip to Sugar Creek, where we were or what we were doing when the phone rang Saturday night. Like survivors of a terrible disaster, come together to reminisce, to prove to ourselves and each other that we made it, we're still alive, we'll get through this if we only stick together.

Only it's not over — this ordeal has barely begun. Dan stays at my side, his arm draped behind me, his body a comfort where it presses against mine. I keep a hand on his knee as if to assure myself he's still here. Ray dozes into his beer at the end of the loveseat, curled into himself in an effort to get as far away from us as possible, and across the room, Caitlin rests her head on Mom's shoulder, though I don't know if it's because she's tired or upset — her hair hides her face, and Mom keeps rubbing her arm in a soothing gesture, like she's six again and has just lost her best friend. On Mom's other side is Penny, her arms wrapped around herself as she rocks gently, her eyes glazed and staring. Aunt Bobbie sits with her, talking low, and every now and again, Penny will nod at something that's said, though I get the impression that she doesn't understand the words, simply hears them. Maybe at this stage, that's enough.

As if by some unspoken signal, we grow quiet, each of us pensive, lost in our own thoughts, almost moody from the late hour and the alcohol. Somehow a small tumbler of spiced rum has appeared in my hand, a gift from Sarah when she last walked by the loveseat, and I sip at the tepid liquid. It was cold but the ice has long since melted. I offer some to Dan, who takes a quick swallow the first time, then shakes his head when I hold it out to him again. He rests his nose against my hair and whispers to me, "I'm fine, Michael." Every time he speaks to me, he does that, leans in real close so no one else will overhear.

Finally we start to look around like lost children — Aunt Bobbie rubs Penny's shoulders, trying to persuade her to talk to us, tell us what has happened, what's going on, what next. Aunt Sarah and Aunt Billy sit on the floor by their feet, one on either side like sphinxes, impenetrable, waiting. We're all waiting. "Heart failure," Penny says softly. The rest of the room is silent, and even those out in the hall can hear her clearly. Her slow, halting speech makes me suspect she's had another Valium.

With an encouraging nod, Aunt Bobbie prompts, "That's what the doctor said?"

"Yeah," Penny murmurs. "Evie was a big lady, you know." A low sigh runs through us, and I smile into my drink as I remember Aunt Evie. Even now I can't think of her as *fat*, because that word has such negative connotations in our society. *Fat* means slovenly, unhealthy, overweight. Evie's body was merely an outward portrayal of the size of her heart, her arms enveloping you in her generosity, her hips wide as if she was mother of us all. My vision blurs and I take a deep breath, inhaling the heady vapors of the rum. I should've come this summer.

Dan massages my neck, puts his lips to my ear. "Are you going to be okay?" he wants to know. I nod, yes, but can't seem to find the words to reply.

Across the room, Penny sighs, a desolate sound like wind through trees. "Her doctor told her to slow down," she says, "but you know Evie. Always on the go, doing for others and never thinking of herself. Said she'd have plenty of time to rest when she was dead. And now … and now …" She dissolves into fresh tears that come sudden and intense like a spring shower. Those tears scare me. They hint that, for all her earlier laughter, her composure, she's really not holding up well at all. They make me think that maybe my own calm is nothing more than a thin veneer over the grief that swells inside of me, and I'm afraid that it won't be long before it overflows as well, consuming me.

Aunt Bobbie clucks soothingly. "It's okay, Pen," she murmurs, holding Penny as she cries. I feel like crying now, too, and around the room people shuffle their feet, shift in their seats, uncomfortable. Caitlin buries her face in Mom's shirt, and beside me Ray sniffles into his beer. Aunt Bobbie's soft voice speaks to us all. "You're doing beautifully, hon. Few more days, we'll get through this."

No one dares to ask what will happen after that — I don't think any of us can even plan that far ahead. From the hallway, Aunt Lennie asks the one thing that's on everyone's mind. "What do we do now?"

On the floor, Aunt Sarah answers, "We need to go through the house, for starters." She looks at Bobbie, who nods. "It needs a good cleaning —"

"I'm sorry," Penny says, wiping her eyes. "God, I haven't had a chance to get things together here. It's been a rough week."

Aunt Billy pats Penny's knee. "We know, dear. We'll take care of it."

"And the …" Penny gropes for the words. "The casket, and the service, all that …" She trails off, uncertain.

My hand tightens around Dan's knee. I don't want to hear this. "We'll handle it," Aunt Sarah assures her — she's stronger than I am. I don't even want to think about this right now, picking out a casket and buying a burial plot and getting a priest for the service — *no*. I drown the rest of my rum, the alcohol searing a path down my throat to coil in my stomach like dragon's breath. I'm going to need more if I have to sit through this.

But Penny simply nods and fortunately my aunts don't elaborate on the details of the arrangements. Let someone else handle it, please. "Wednesday," Penny whispers. Another low murmur rises through the room. *Wednesday.* If we can make it that far, then we're going to be fine.

Looking around the room as if seeing us for the first time, she asks suddenly, "Is everyone here? I'm not — are we still missing a few folks? Everyone needs to be here for this."

"Sylvia's coming in tomorrow night," Aunt Billy says, meaning her daughter in the Navy. "Don't worry, dear. We'll all make it. Craig, what about Molly?" My Uncle Craig rouses himself where he sits on the sofa between Kenny's girlfriend and his own son, Marshall. "Is she going to be able to make it?"

Last I heard of Molly, she was an intern at a geological facility out in the wilds of Alaska. "She should," Craig says. "I wired her the money for a flight last night." Though dry-eyed, my uncle looks like he'd rather be anywhere else but here. *Me too*, I think. I stare into my empty glass and wonder how bad it'll look if I get up now to get more drink.

And then … "What about Jessie?" someone asks. I'm not sure who.

Suddenly the room drops ten degrees. I scoot closer to Dan, uneasy. *Aunt Jessie* … when I glance around at my relatives, none of them meet my gaze. Only my sister looks back. Leave it to her to be the only one who dares to ask, "Does she even know?"

Aunt Sarah's reply is quick and caustic. "I don't care if she knows or not," she says bitterly. "She hasn't been welcome in this house in almost twenty years. No need to change that now."

"Why not?" I ask, surprising myself as much as anyone else with the question.

The look Aunt Sarah gives me could curdle milk, it's that sour. Before she can snap back, though, Aunt Billy is on her feet, a plastic grin on her face. "Refills?" she asks, a ploy to change the subject. "Michael? Theresa? Anyone up for another drink?"

I need one. Holding out my glass, I tell her, "Sure." She plucks it from my fingers, gathers a few others before hurrying from the room. I should follow her, I think. I don't want to be here, this quiet time in the evening among the grown-ups is nothing I thought it would be. I'm still a child, I want to say. I don't belong here.

But Dan's arm is heavy where it rests across my shoulders and I can't move. "Someone could at least *call* her," Caitlin mutters.

"She's not invited," Mom says. She sounds like a petulant child, and when I open my mouth to ask again, she covers her eyes with one trembling hand. "Michael," she warns. "Now is not the time."

Dan squeezes my arm and I keep quiet. When Billy returns, filled glasses in her hands, I take my rum and drink from it greedily, stare at the ground between my feet so I don't have to look at my mom. How can someone not be invited to a funeral? Not welcome at the house, I can see. Not invited to a wake, sure. But the funeral is the last time Aunt Jessie will be able to make any kind of peace with Evie — the other sisters can't deny either of them that. Can they?

As if thinking similar thoughts, Kenny clears his throat and asks, "What if she comes anyway?"

"She won't come here," Aunt Sarah replies, but there's a tremor in her voice that suggests she doesn't quite believe that herself. Behind her, Penny starts to cry again, silent tears that trail down her cheeks to drip from her jaw and stain her jeans in dark tiny circles. "I'll talk with Jay. If she has the *audacity* to show up, they'll see to it she doesn't make a scene. I knew that boy's father. They're good at what they do."

She's talking of Jay Morrison, not anyone I would call a *boy* by any stretch of the imagination — he was old when I was a kid, a tall, spindly man with a shock of white hair that sticks up from his head like a mad scientist's. The mortician — Morrison's is the only funeral home in Sugar Creek, of course we'd use them. Softly, almost as if she's talking to herself and we're not supposed to overhear, Penny murmurs, "He's so efficient. Came right when I called, praise the Lord. I was in Union City all day, just doing the weekly shopping, you know? Evie wasn't feeling well and begged off. I came home and she didn't come down so I thought she was just taking a nap. She liked to lie down in the early evenings."

I don't want to hear this. But I can't get up and leave, I can't be that rude, I have to be strong. It's what Evie would want, I tell myself, if she were still here. My rum has disappeared — did I drink it already? Aunt Billy must have filled the glass only halfway. My throat burns and I feel parched, as dry as dust, as bone. I can't breathe. "Dan," I sigh, finding my lover's hand. I pull it into my lap and frown at his fingers, wrapped around mine but I can't feel them.

Penny sounds far away, like she's moved into another room and is still talking to me. I try to focus on her words but I can't seem to concentrate. I'm too thirsty. "I made dinner," she says, and I have to strain to hear her speak. "Set it out and called up to her. No answer. Went halfway upstairs, called again. Nothing."

Something warm sighs into my ear, and then I hear my lover's voice fill the world around me. "Michael?" he asks, concerned. I give him a sleepy smile but when I reach up to brush my fingers over his hair, he catches my hand and squeezes it tightly. "Are you okay?"

"So cold," Penny's saying. I'm fine. "I didn't know — I called Dr. Hartsell, first thing. She was so cold. I couldn't get her warm, I used all the blankets. She wouldn't wake up and she was so damn *cold*."

Dan touches my face, his fingers warm. My chest is heavy and I can't breathe, I can't seem to draw in air and it's making me sleepy. I can't breathe … the world fades around the edges of my vision, people and things rubbed away, erased from my sight. My head is so heavy, I can't keep it up. I'm still incredibly thirsty. Handing Dan my glass, I whisper, "I think I need some more."

He takes my glass away. "I don't think so." Then he's on his feet and helping me up, his hands made of steel, his arms iron bars that I lean against for support. "If no one minds," he says softly, "I think we'll be heading on to bed now."

A dozen people turn towards us, two dozen, three — everyone's staring at me again, I feel their gazes like lead weights dragging me down, my mom's worst of all. But Dan doesn't buckle under the pressure. Instead, he helps me from the room and my relatives move aside as we pass, close again behind us as if we were never there at all. A few whisper to us, "Good night. Nice meeting you. See you guys in the morning." I wave at them halfheartedly. It's all I can do to raise my hand.

The hallway is dark. As we leave, others push into the living room, vying for the loveseat we just vacated. I feel Dan against me, his hands on my hips, his chest on my back as he guides me to the kitchen. The liquor bar is in the den, though. "I thought we wanted more drink," I say, pointing back towards the stairs. The den is that way.

Dan doesn't let me turn around. "We're fine," he tells me. "Aren't you tired, babe?"

"A little," I admit. In the kitchen, I stare at the refrigerator longingly, my throat still raw. "Aren't we thirsty?"

"Are we?" Dan asks. I nod and he stops at the sink to pour me a glass of water. It's cold and sharp as ice, and he holds the glass for me while I drink, pulling it back before I can choke and then letting me have more, just small sips that I swallow greedily. When the glass is empty, he sets it in the sink but I want more. "Come on, Michael," he sighs. "Why don't we get to bed?"

I try to think of a reason, but nothing comes to mind. "I don't know," I murmur honestly. My words slur together. Aren't we supposed to be in the living room now?

Gently, oh so gently, Dan takes hold of my elbow and leads me to our room. Once inside, he closes the door behind us and turns on the lamp, dispelling the shadows. Then his hands are on my body, tugging at my shirt, fumbling with my pants. The air is cool on my nude flesh, raising bumps on my arms that I try to rub away. "Cold," I breathe, I'm freezing, and I move closer to Dan just to feel the warmth of his body against mine. "Hold me."

"In a minute, Michael," he tells me, but his arms come up around my bare back in a quick hug. Then he's stripping his own clothes away, dropping them to the floor, until we both stand in our underwear in the chilly room. Pulling back the covers on the bed, Dan says, "Lie down."

I slip between the sheets and back up against the wall to make enough room for him to join me. He does, pulling the blanket halfway over my head. I cuddle up against him and *now* he holds me, his arms strong, his lips tender on my face. Vaguely I remember this afternoon, how Ray interrupted us, how Dan probably wants to get back those few moments we normally share after making love, the snuggling, the sweet talk, the kisses. But I can't seem to keep my eyes open, the pillow is so soft, and he holds me so close, all I breathe in is him. I love him.

I don't know if I say the words out loud or if he replies. But I hear his voice inside me, I see his eyes behind mine — even the bed disappears beneath me, leaving just his touch, his strength, his love.

19: Wake Up Call

S OFT HANDS CARESS my face. A gentle thumb curves over one eye-brow, smoothing it down, then follows along my cheekbone, down to my chin. Tender fingers brush across my forehead, trail down the slope of my nose, over the tip and into the dimple above my upper lip. I feel the touch in half-formed dreams, someone out of sight stroking me, petting me, comforting. Even though I hear no voice and see no one, I recognize the sensation of hands on me, it's a touch I know intimately. *Dan.*

When I open my eyes, he's beside me, sitting on the edge of the bed and looking down at me with such love that it makes me dizzy and weak. Or maybe it's the alcohol — how much did I drink last night? I'm not usually that bad. Then again, the extent of my drinking repertoire is beer when we eat out, wine at classier restaurants, mixed drinks at business parties or clubs. Straight up rum? Never. No wonder I feel woozy and sick. "Hey," Dan murmurs.

I kiss his thumb as it traces my lips. He's dressed in his PT shorts and a white t-shirt, his company mascot emblazoned on the front — a snow leop-ard growling at me. Despite the slight headache that pokes behind my eye, I extract a hand from beneath the covers and, rubbing at the downy hair on his thigh, ask coyly, "Who said you could get out of this bed?"

His smile falters as behind him someone says, "Morning, Michael."

It's Aunt Billy. Now that I realize she's there, I can hear her, rummaging through papers as if searching for something. Slowly, so I don't aggravate my headache, I raise up on my elbows and look past Dan at my aunt, who squats in front of a small file cabinet partially hidden in one corner of the room. "Billy, hey," I say, chagrined. Here I am trying to get frisky with my boy and there's someone else in the room. *Welcome to Evie's,* I think, lying back down. *No such thing as privacy among family.*

I stare at Dan and he at me, his smile back again. "You're bad," he whis-pers. His hand rests in the center of my chest — I can feel the beat of my heart where it lays.

"I thought we were alone," I reply.

Aunt Billy laughs. "Don't mind me, guys. I'll just be a minute."

"Take your time," Dan tells her, ever polite. He laughs at the look I give him. "What?" he wants to know.

I just shake my head. When I close my eyes, he touches my face again and I sigh into his hand. "What are you looking for, Aunt Billy?" I ask. Whatever it is, I wish she'd just find it already and get out. Close the door behind her, leave us alone. The mornings are my time with Dan — from the moment his alarm goes off to when he kisses me before he leaves, all that time belongs to me. I'm the one who wakes to his lips, his touch. I'm the one who makes him breakfast, I'm the one he talks to while he eats, I'm the one who lies on the bed and watches as he gets dressed. Me. And sure, we're off from work, we're in Sugar Creek and our daily schedule has been interrupted, but I still want our time. It's still early. I'm not ready to let the rest of my family in just yet.

As if sensing this, Aunt Billy tosses her hair over one shoulder the way Caitlin does and asks with a laugh, "Am I busting up your groove, as my grandkids say?"

Rubbing Dan's leg, I admit, "Well, now that you mention it ..."

Dan slaps my arm playfully. Now it's my turn to feign ignorance, though I can't keep the grin from my face. "What?"

"He's just kidding," Aunt Billy says. When I don't reply, she glances back at me, her eyebrows arched high over the frame of her glasses. "You *are* kidding, Michael, aren't you?"

I give her a wink that makes her smile and turn away. Taking Dan's wrist, I press the back of his hand to my lips. As he watches me, I open my mouth and lick out at his flesh, soft and slightly salty, a wonderful taste. The feel of my tongue on his skin makes him grin, almost embarrassed because we're not alone. "So what," I ask him, "she just came knocking this morning? Woke you up and forced her way in? Did my mom put you up to this?"

The last statement is directed to Aunt Billy, who shakes her head. "You've figured it out, Mike," she says. Dan laughs and I kiss the damp spot I've made on his hand. "Laura caught me in the kitchen and was like, make up something, Billy, any reason to get into that room. My son will *not* be happy as long as *I* have anything to say about it."

I laugh so hard that my headache flares to life and I have to press a hand against the side of my head to keep it from splitting open wide. Concern flickers across Dan's face. "Are you —"

"Fine," I assure him between giggles. "Hung over a little, that's it. Damn, how much did I drink last night?"

"Just like your mom," Aunt Billy says — I thought she said she'd just be a minute? What's the hold up here? "Laura never could hold her liquor. Beer, yes. Wine, a little. But give her the hard stuff and she keels right over."

Dan smoothes the hair back from my brow, his fingers riffling through my bangs. "Aren't you done yet?" I ask, impatient. Some time alone with my boy before the day rushes in, is that too much to ask?

"I'm looking for insurance papers," she tells us, leafing through files in the cabinet. "Evie used to keep them here but jeez, Louise, I can't figure her system out. She could've at least kept them all together, you know?"

I frown and close my eyes, my headache blooming again. I don't know how she does it, where this strength of hers comes from. "Michael?" Dan asks softly. I roll away from him, fist the blankets up to my face, hiding from the rest of the world.

Dan strums my back with long, loving strokes. "Lie down with me," I whisper. If Aunt Billy overhears me, she doesn't say anything this time. I need the comfort of my lover's body against mine. I need his arms right now, his warmth, his strength.

I know he's thinking about my aunt in the room, because he likes to keep our relationship between just the two of us — we don't show off in public, mostly from fear of him losing his position in the military if anyone found out about me. But he knows me well enough to realize that if I ask him to hold me or kiss me or touch me in front of others, it's not an idle or vain request. He knows there's more to it than that. So he stretches out on his back beside me, on top of the covers, his arm pressed between my shoulder blades, his hand trailing down my spine. The blankets are all that separate us.

Aunt Billy continues through the cabinet, the rustle of papers the only sound in the room. Every now and then, Dan shifts beside me, settling his body closer into mine, and I scoot back until I'm right up against him. He's looking at me, I know it, because I can feel his breath tickle like a feather over the back of my neck, and he keeps a hand on my arm, rubbing a smooth place in my skin with his thumb, over and over again, a circle just above my elbow. It's a barely-there touch and I find myself drifting back to sleep, my headache ebbing away like the sea at low tide.

The noise of the file drawer rattling shut wakes me. "Michael," Dan murmurs, sitting up.

I blink my drowsiness away as I roll over to find Aunt Billy on the edge of the bed. She shuffles the papers in her hands and smiles at us. Beside me, Dan sits cross-legged, his knee on my arm — some part of him touching me at all times, because he knows this is our time, he knows what it means to me. With a sigh, Aunt Billy says, "Mike, honey, I was only kidding, what I said about your mom earlier. I'm not here to spy on you two."

Giving her a quick smile, I assure her, "Oh I know. I didn't mean —"

She pats my leg through the blanket to quiet me. "Your momma means well," she says. I nod but don't quite believe that. "She's just worried for you, Mike, that's all. When you have kids of your own ..."

She trails off, as if remembering that I'm with Dan, I probably *won't* have kids of my own, and that's part of my mom's issue with my being gay. Her mouth twists into a tight half-smile. "She'll get over it," she tells me. Her hand drifts to Dan's knee, and suddenly she looks old to me, older than her sixty-some odd years, ancient with her soft words, a wise woman who knows all, sees all. I can still feel her touch burning through the blankets to sear my leg. "You've got a good boy here, Michael. Don't let your mom or Harry or any of us drag you down or tear you apart, you hear me? I want a front seat at your wedding."

I feel my cheeks heat up and I curl onto my side, pressing my face into Dan's hip so she won't see my blush. "Aunt *Billy* —"

Ruffling my hair, Dan laughs. "We're not quite *that* far yet," he admits, but his hand lingers on the back of my neck, as if she has him thinking now.

"I just want to make it through today," I tell her, resting my head on Dan's thigh. His shorts feel impossibly thin against my face, and his hand still toys with the ends of my hair. "And tomorrow, and the next day. Once this is all over with, we'll see what we can do about the rest of our lives."

I don't mention the funeral, but Aunt Billy knows that's what I mean. "Michael," she says carefully, her hand returning to the insurance papers in her lap. "Penny's not ... I don't know if you remember what all she said last night? But she was the one who found Evie —"

"I know," I interrupt. I don't want to hear it all over again. Can't we just move on without rehashing what happened? "I wasn't *that* drunk — I remember."

She gives me an arched look. "You just about staggered out," she says. "If Dan hadn't been there ..."

"He would've fallen out on the couch," Dan finishes.

"Hey!" I cry, smacking his knee. "Who's side are you on here anyway?"

My lover laughs and catches my hand when I try to smack him again. In a dramatic whisper, he tells Aunt Billy, "He would've fallen out."

She whispers back, like I'm not supposed to hear their conversation. "I know."

"I don't like you two," I mutter, childishly hiding my face in Dan's shorts. Aunt Billy says my name, but I burrow deeper into my lover's leg. "I'm not listening."

But when she says my name a second time, the tease is gone from her voice. "Listen, Mike. Penny's not handling this whole situation well, you know?" She rubs my shoulder to get my attention — I'm listening, but I don't look at her, I don't want her to see that maybe I'm not handling things very well myself, either. "Bobbie and I are going to Morrison's today. We'll make all the arrangements, and Sarah will call the insurance companies now that I've found the paperwork. Laura said she'll take care of getting everyone else organized. There's so much that needs to be done, so much to go through. Just ... don't bother Penny with the details, if you can help it, okay? Don't mention the funeral around her." She talks to me like I'm a brave little boy, trying to imbue me with a sense of purpose to help *me* get through this, too. "Can you do that for me?"

I nod into Dan's thigh, but she can't see the gesture. "Michael?" she prompts.

"Yeah," I mutter, sure, fine, whatever. *Just leave,* I add silently.

As if she hears the thought, Aunt Billy pats my leg and leans heavily on it to push herself up from the bed. "Help out around here," she tells us, finally heading for the door. "Evie always said family helps family out, you heard it often enough growing up. When you boys get dressed, there's a lot of stuff to do. The rooms upstairs need emptying out, the yard needs to be spruced up, get the leaves up and pull out the veggies, plenty to do. Sarah's making pancakes to get us all started." She pauses and I look up — she has one hand on the knob and the hint of a smile on her face. "I'll give you two fifteen minutes until I send the kids in here to drag you out of bed, deal?"

Dan laughs. "We don't really need —" he starts.

Sitting up, I cover his mouth with one hand and grin at my aunt. "You're eating into our time."

"I'm gone," she laughs. When she opens the door, noise from the kitchen that had been muted before rises to a crescendo, spilling into the room. A dozen different voices shouting and laughing and talk talk talking, the clank of silverware, someone opening the fridge and someone else telling them to close that door, they're letting all the cold air out. Drinks poured into glasses, the sizzle of food cooking in a pan, and through it all threads the smell of pancakes and warm maple syrup, butter, sausages, I'm *starving.*

And then Aunt Billy really *is* gone, the door closed behind her, leaving the din of my relatives and the heavenly scents of breakfast outside. Now we're alone at last, but Dan's hand still rests on my cheek, and it's a comforting touch, it makes me lay my head down on his leg again. I wrap my arms around his waist, try to hug him close, but I only succeed in pulling myself into his lap. With a laugh, Dan runs his fingers through my hair and I nuzzle into his crotch, nipping playfully when he hardens beneath me. "Why did you let her in?" I want to know. I close my lips over the erection starting to poke at me through his shorts.

Slipping a hand beneath my chin, Dan raises me up and I go willingly, climbing over him until our lips meet in a tender kiss, the first of the morning. "She knocked," he murmurs, kissing me again. "What was I supposed to do, tell her to go away?"

Yeah, like *that* would've worked. "You could've tried," I say. But knowing my aunt, she probably knocked *while* opening the door, and by the time Dan was out of bed, she was already in the room, excusing herself with a whispered, "I'll just be a minute, dear." And knowing my lover, he would have never turned her away. When we made love yesterday and he told Caitlin to leave? That was rare for him, a sign that he's accepted her as someone it's okay to let in past his defenses. It means a lot to me, that he can feel comfortable with my family, or at least my sister ... my dad I'm not too sure about yet, my mom is out of the question, and Ray? Let's not even *go* there.

We could go back and forth for the next fifteen minutes, Dan defending his position and me trying to wear him down, until he concedes that yeah, he should've kept the door shut. Then I would win — sometimes I think he lets me win just to shut me up, and he'll kiss me hungrily, his lust driving all talk from my mind. I can't think when he touches me, I can't breathe when we kiss, I don't know how I manage to survive him, he's so good to me, it makes me ache with a sweet pain. I love him.

But we don't have much time so I just skip the flirtatious talk — we'll get to that part later, after breakfast when we're alone in one of the rooms upstairs, cleaning and boxing things up. I'll talk and he'll listen, and if I say too much, he'll catch me in a quick embrace amid all that dust and kiss me quiet. There are a lot of rooms to go through. If we get one by ourselves, maybe we can take a little break now and then to fool around ...

I'm looking forward to it already. Now, though, I lean him back against the wall at the head of the bed, press my mouth to his, moan into him when his hands come up around my waist, over my back, down to cup my ass. He pulls me into his lap, our kiss deepening, and I caress his cheeks and brow, rub my nose along his, breathe his name as I sit down on his thighs, the hardness in his shorts pushing up between my legs. "Was she serious about sending the kids in here?" he murmurs between kisses.

"Them or Ray," I tell him.

I kiss away his grimace. "I'll have to really hurt him then," Dan growls.

Who's the talkative one now? "Thirteen minutes and counting," I remind him. More kisses, his hands on me, his breath on my face, and this time it's me who silences *him*.

20: Getting on My Nerves

AUNT BILLY STAYS true to her word — fifteen minutes after she leaves, on the *dot*, someone knocks on the door. Good thing, too. Dan has both hands down the back of my boxers, his fingers curved between my buttocks, pressing into me and rubbing in maddening circles that make me rise up into his palms, and my erection tents through the fly of the shorts to rub against his stomach where his shirt's pulled up to expose his navel. Without that knock, someone would've walked right in on *this*, even though we know we don't really have the time right now to live out this passion. Whoever it is outside knocks again, a small sound made by a small fist, and Dan extracts his hands from my shorts. Reluctantly, I snap up the fly, tucking myself back into the confines of the boxers, and I kiss him one final time, long and lingering.

The knock doesn't come again. Instead, someone turns the knob and the door swings open to reveal a little boy with big glasses that eclipse his face — no more than three or four with a shock of dirty blonde hair. I lie down on top of Dan and smile brightly at the boy. "Who are you?" I ask.

His big blue eyes widen in terror. Obviously someone else put him up to this, and from the kitchen I hear Caitlin's voice. "Tell them what I told you, Trevor."

Trevor takes a deep breath as if screwing up his courage, then squeezes his eyes shut and shouts at the top of his lungs, "It's time to get your horny asses out of bed!"

The force of the announcement sets Dan laughing, and Trevor opens his eyes, blinks at us for a second, then slams the door shut. I hear tiny feet running across the kitchen floor, and I can almost picture him barreling into Caitlin's legs, terrified. Between giggles, I tell my lover, "I think you scared him away."

"Oh?" Dan asks, wrapping his arms around my waist in a tight hug. "What gives you that impression?"

Before I can answer, another knock interrupts us. With a quick kiss on the tip of Dan's nose, I call out, "Come in."

The door opens cautiously and Caitlin is there, peeking in at us. "What did you say to Trevor?" she wants to know.

Dan laughs. "Nothing!" I cry, but the look she gives me suggests she isn't buying that. "Honest. Dan, tell her …"

"You should've heard him," my lover says, surprising me. "Said the most *awful* things —"

"Hey!" I sit up and try to glare at him, but it's hard when I see the mirth shining in his eyes. Pulling away from him, I kick the blankets off my legs and climb out of the bed. "You're pushing it, mister."

He catches me around the waist, his hands closing over the erection still straining the front of my boxers, and despite my sister watching us, he drags me back onto the bed, crawls onto me to keep me with him, the both of us laughing like children. "Dan!" I push against his chest, my arms ineffectual against his strength. "We've got an audience, babe."

"Oh don't mind me," Caitlin says. Dan nips at my neck, nuzzling into me, as if she's not even there. But she is — and while my lover licks behind my ear, she comes into the room to plop down at the foot of the bed, just above my head. "Did you guys get the *don't disturb Penny* talk?"

This time when I push at Dan, he lets me roll him onto his side next to me. When I try to sit up, though, a hand on my chest keeps me beside him. Craning my neck to look at my sister, I ask, "So everyone got that? Here I thought she was just telling me."

"Like we don't *know* Penny's taking it hard," Caitlin says. She picks at the blankets with one hand, frowns at the fabric as it falls from her fingers. "I mean, jeez. Like we're going to run to her and start blabbing on and on about the funeral, you know? We're not *that* heartless."

I don't answer. Personally? I don't want to talk about it, either, but I'm the older brother here, I'm not going to let Caitlin suspect I'm weak. If I do, I'll never live it down. "Bobbie and Billy are going to the funeral home," she says, her voice soft — I don't want to hear this. But she doesn't get my drift when I turn away and I don't know how to ask her to stop. As she speaks, her lower lip trembles like she's close to crying, and I *really* don't want her to do that. Then I'll have to comfort her somehow, and what comfort can I give when I'm feeling the same way inside? "I asked if maybe I could go, too," she tells us. "I don't know. It's almost like it's not real yet, you know? Like any minute I'll hear Aunt Evie and she'll tell us all this was just a cruel joke. And we'll laugh and have a cookout and all go home. It's like —"

I can't take it any longer. "Caitlin, okay."

"What?" she asks, confused.

I push Dan's arm away and sit up. "Just …" *Just stop,* I want to say, but I can't, the words won't come. So I get out of bed, snag a t-shirt from the floor and tug it down over my thin boxers as far as it'll go, and start digging through our suitcase, open on the floor where we left it last night. "We have to get dressed," I say — it's a lame excuse but it's the only one that comes to mind. "Can we talk about this later? After we get something to eat maybe?" *Or never, that would work for me.* I'm well aware of the peevish tone in my voice but I can't help it. Penny's not the only one who doesn't want details. "Just go, Caitlin. Cat. We'll be out in a few minutes."

I don't have to look at my sister to know she's glaring at me now, but tough shit. "Michael," she starts.

Holding up one hand to ward off whatever she has to say, I shake my head. "I said go," I snap at her.

With that little *eh* noise from the back of her throat that only teenaged girls seem to do well, the one that manages to perfectly convey her irritation at me, she pushes herself up from the bed and storms past me for the door. "You tell your *boyfriend* to check his attitude on his way out," she mutters to Dan, "because I'm not putting up with his shit today."

Then she slams the door shut. I sigh — I don't need *her* shit, either. Suddenly I'm the one with the problem? What the hell is up with that? I tug at a pair of dark jeans from the bottom of the suitcase, beneath everything else and probably wrinkled as all get out, I'll have to iron them now, I can't get them out from under the other clothes, I pull and pull and the damn things are going to *rip* before I'm through, and you know what? *Fuck* her for making me feel like this. So I don't want to listen to her go on and on about Evie not being here — I know how it is, I'm in this, too. Talking isn't going to bring her back. It's just picking at the wound, she has nothing to say that I haven't thought myself, nothing that I haven't heard since Saturday night, nothing at all ...

Tears blind me and I tell myself I'm not crying, I'm *not*. Behind me the bed shifts, and then Dan says gently, "Come here."

One final tug and the pants pull free. "I'm getting dressed," I tell him, as if he might not see that. The jeans get thrown on the floor and I start rooting for a pair of underwear but all I find are drab Army green, nothing that's mine. Where the hell *is* all my stuff? "We did pack some of my clothes in here, didn't we?" I ask bitterly.

"It wasn't really a request," Dan says.

Anger flares in me — what, first Billy, then Caitlin, and now him? Is *everyone* against me today? "I'm not one of your Army buddies," I mutter. Mercifully I spy a pair of white briefs wrapped up in his shorts and yank them out. "I don't jump when you bark, Dan. You can't order me the fuck around."

My words hang suspended like gunshots between us, each one potentially deadly, the aftershock reverberating around the room. I'm shaking now, so badly that I almost drop a handful of shirts while picking out one to wear, and I know I should apologize but I can't. Somehow I think this is all Caitlin's fault. If she hadn't pissed me off, I wouldn't bite at him, I wouldn't have to say I'm sorry.

For a moment I think he's going to walk out like she did, just up and leave me. I deserve it. Shit, the way I'm feeling right now, I'd walk out on me, too.

But Dan's not me, and before I can think around words of apology, his hands are on my waist, his touch still tender, still loving. "Where's this coming from?" he asks, his voice so soft that it reopens the ache in my heart and I turn to find myself caught up in a tight embrace. "Michael?" he asks, his hands soothing over my back. "Do you want to tell me what's going on?"

I bury my face into his shoulder and sob, "I'm sorry." My voice is muffled against his shirt and once the words escape, I can't rein them in. "I'm so sorry, Dan. Oh God, I'm sorry. I didn't mean to take it out on you, or Caitlin, or anybody. I'm just … I'm — I don't know." It scares me to admit it, but I don't. In barely a whisper, I say it again. "I just don't know."

"It's okay," he murmurs, stroking my hair, and with his arms around me, I can almost believe that. His lips brush my ear, his words sigh into me. "I think you don't want to talk about it much, either." Tears close up my throat and I nod because I don't trust myself to speak. He knows me so well.

"I'm sorry," I breathe again. "Dan —"

"It's okay," he assures me. "I know, baby, trust me, I do. I've been there myself. Just don't push me away, please. I'm here for you, you know that."

I nod against his shoulder, his body so warm against my cheek. "I know."

"So don't push me away," he says again. I fist my hands in the back of his shirt and hug him close. No, I can't do that, I need him too much to let him go now. With the hint of a smile, he tells me, "Anyone else, that's fine, but not me, you hear?" I grin and kiss his neck. "And probably not Caitlin," he adds. "I have a feeling you don't want to be on her bad side."

That makes me laugh. "Somehow I don't think that would be a good thing," I agree. Now I'm going to have to apologize to her, too. Maybe I can just blow it off, act as if nothing ever happened, but I have a hunch that Caitlin doesn't play that way.

With things smoothed over between us, we dress — to show how much I'm sorry, I wear a gray t-shirt that I once bought as a joke at the commissary on post, the words *Military Wife* written across the front in government-issue letters that look stenciled on. I packed it specifically this weekend just to piss my mother off, and I'm not about to miss that opportunity, not after the cold shoulder she's given Dan. The smile it brings to my lover's face more than makes up for whatever my mom will have to say about the shirt.

Out in the kitchen, Aunt Sarah stands over the stove, cooking pancakes, and every chair at the table is filled. Kenny's there, and Aunt Billy, too. Caitlin sits at the head like a guest of honor, Trevor on one side, our cousin Emily on the other. The little boy looks up when our door opens, his eyes like small moons in his face, but Emily doesn't bother with us — she's too busy talking at top speed about how her mom says she's too young to wear makeup yet. "Just *lip* gloss," she sighs, her voice scandalous. She speaks without looking at Caitlin or Trevor or anyone at all, and she has a way of shaking her hair back from her face that reminds me of a prom queen. "I mean, *really*. Just a little and she's all like *no*. How old were you when Aunt Laura let you start wearing makeup, Cat?"

Caitlin's eyes have glazed over, as if she's grown bored with this endless prattle. She looks up and stares through us, through me at least, if that's possible, and that alone tells me that she's still mad. "She doesn't let me," she replies in a lifeless voice.

Confusion crosses Emily's young face. "But —"

"This isn't eyeliner," my sister says, deadpan. Her eyes are rimmed with kohl, twin dark circles that resemble Trevor's glasses. "These are tattoos."

Emily gasps, impressed. "Don't tell that child such lies," I say, grinning at Caitlin. She ignores me — I don't blame her. Taking her cue from Caitlin, Emily ducks away from my hand when I reach out to ruffle her hair. Only Trevor watches me, his eyes large and devouring in his face. He unnerves me. "Those aren't tattoos."

Cocking her head to one side, Emily asks, "Did you hear something?"

Caitlin turns her head slowly to stare at our cousin. "Don't do that shit," she says, and Emily recoils as if slapped. "It's childish and fucking stupid."

"Caitlin! Don't talk like that," Aunt Sarah admonishes. She offers me a cheek when I come up to the stove, and I give her a quick kiss. "Does your mother put up with such language?" she asks.

"I don't know," I admit, opening the fridge. I find a half-gallon of milk that's almost empty, but it'll do. "I don't live at home."

Dan has two tall glasses ready when I turn around. I pour him a full glass, then empty the rest of the milk out into my own. It only fills about a third of the way up. Before I can stop him, Dan dumps half of his own milk into my glass, evening them out, then he hands it to me. "You're wonderful," I tell him. Aunt Sarah scrapes loudly at the pan — I can almost feel her bristling, and I wonder if she got a good look at my shirt yet. Aunt Billy has, I see her smile as she reads over the insurance papers that she's spread out across the table in front of her. I'm sure Sarah will have something to say to my mother about *that.* "Your children ..." she'll mutter, and shake her head as if *her* kids never did anything that wasn't sanctioned by God above Himself.

With a wink that no one else sees, Dan says, "I'm not the only one." He sips his milk, which leaves a moustache beaded above his upper lip, and even though we're not alone, I can't stop myself from kissing it away. The milk tastes cool against his warm skin, and while I'm still close, he whispers, "Why don't you apologize to her?"

Because she's my sister, I think. I shouldn't have to say I'm sorry. Still, he gives me a slight nudge in her direction, and when I move past him, he slaps my ass playfully. Yes, I definitely *can't* wait to get him alone again, in one of the upstairs bedrooms maybe, or the attic where Aunt Evie stores slip-covered furniture. Just the two of us, the door locked on the rest of the family, and I'll show him just how contrite I can be. I'm looking forward to it already.

"Caitlin," I sigh, leaning over the back of her chair. Emily stops in mid-sentence and frowns at me, fuming at the interruption. Caitlin doesn't even stop eating — she simply holds up one hand the same way I did earlier, like she doesn't want to hear whatever it is I have to say. "Look," I tell her, "I'm sorry. I got frustrated —"

Without turning to look at me, she mutters, "Bit my goddamn head off, is more like it."

"Caitlin," Aunt Sarah warns. "What did I tell you about —"

"No cussing," my sister says, "I heard you."

She hunkers down over her plate a moment longer, almost unwilling to let her anger go. Beside her, Emily sighs lustily. "As I was *saying,*" she starts.

"Just shut up already, will you?" Caitlin snaps. Now she turns towards me, and I have to stifle a laugh at the way she rolls her eyes. "Je-*sus* but these kids are annoying the fuck out of me. I know, I know," she adds quickly, before Aunt Sarah can say anything else. "Wash my mouth out with soap, why don't you? So my mom raised horrible kids. A queer boy and a punk chick."

Trevor stares at Caitlin and Emily pouts into her plate as if she might cry. That enigmatic smile still haunts Aunt Billy's face, and Kenny ... well, he's ignoring us all, too intent on his food to bother with us. "And Ray," I add, grinning. Behind me, Dan chortles into his milk. "A queer, a punk, and Ray."

"She should've drowned us all," Caitlin says. "Is that what you would've done, Aunt Sarah? Put us out of our misery? Send our souls straight to heaven before we could fuck them up?"

"Heathens," Sarah announces, and Caitlin and I both snicker at the venom in her voice. "The lot of you. Don't think I'm not telling Laura how impertinent you are, young lady."

I stand as Caitlin pushes her chair back. "Don't bother," she says, leaving the room. "I'll tell her myself."

21: Change of Plans

AUNT SARAH PILES pancakes onto two plates that I hold out to her — one for Dan, the other for me. "Have a seat," my lover says, holding Caitlin's vacated chair out for me.

"No, you." When he starts to protest, I shake my head. "Sit, baby. The food's getting cold."

Without further argument, Dan slides into the chair and I set one plate down in front of him. I look around but there really isn't room left — people keep strolling through the kitchen, making it almost impossible to sit on the floor, and no one else at the table seems willing to part with their seats yet. "Sit here," Dan tells me, pushing his chair out and patting his knee. There's a gleam in his eye that makes me think of our bed in the other room. When I don't answer immediately, he tugs at the leg of my jeans like a little kid. "Michael?"

Somehow, I don't think that'll go over well. Frowning down at Emily, who has finished eating and now sits in front of an empty plate, I ask, "Aren't you done yet?"

But she's mad that Caitlin brushed her off, and I'm sure in her pre-teen mind, she blames that on me. So she flicks her hair back in that infuriating way she has that suggests she's so much better than anyone else here and doesn't look at me as she says, "No. Sit somewhere else."

"Here," Dan says again. I glance back at Aunt Sarah by the stove, but she's busy dishing out more pancakes to whoever holds up a plate, and what do I care what she says or thinks, anyway? Before I can change my mind, I plop down on Dan's leg. He moves his plate over so I can put mine beside it, and his arm comes up around my waist protectively, as if he's afraid I'll fall off his knee. He's become more open around my family, and I like that — it must be because there's no threat of running into someone he knows from Fort Myers way out here, and he can be himself, just a boy in love with me and not a soldier in the Army. His hand splays flat across my stomach, his fingers ticklish through my t-shirt, and his chin brushes against my shoulder every time he leans forward to take a bite. If anyone minds, no one says so, and by the time Emily finally decides to relinquish her chair, I'm too comfortable — and too busy eating — to switch seats.

Dan finishes before I do, as usual. I'm always the last to finish a meal, and if it wasn't for our dishwasher, I have a feeling that I'd be washing the plates every night because Dan doesn't wait for me to be done before he cleans up after himself. On one of our first dates, I took him to a classy steakhouse just to impress him a bit. "Are you usually like this?" he asked, watching me eat.

Confused, I wanted to know, "Like what?"

Dan shrugged — at the time we weren't where we are today, this comfortable with each other, and that whole evening was spent on edge, both of us afraid to say or do something to chase the other away. But even then there was something between us, some magic that transcends our corporeal beings and allows our souls to touch. We were old friends from lives before, come together again in *this* world, to find in each other a love that is deeper, older, more real than any other I've ever known. There, in that steakhouse, I stared across the table at him, his short cropped hair, his glistening eyes, the cut of his jaw and the slightest smile on his lips, which might have been nothing more than a shadow cast by the dim lighting. "Like what?" I asked again.

"Like this," he replied, motioning at my plate. We'd been at the restaurant for about an hour already and I still seemed to have more food left than I had eaten. "Are you always such a slow eater?"

With a wink, I grinned at him and purred, "You wouldn't complain if it wasn't this steak I was going down on."

That earned me a smile, not a figment of my imagination or a trick of the lighting but a genuine smile, and later that night, I could've sworn his kisses held more ardor than before, more passion. There was no denying the hand that snuck between my legs to rest against my crotch when I drove him back to the barracks, either. And after the first time I *did* go down on him, twenty long minutes of my tongue around his shaft, my lips working him, sucking and licking until he couldn't possibly hold it in any longer and he came in a sweet, explosive rush that I drank down like honey ... after *that*, he never complained that I took too long to eat again.

And I'm still eating when my mom joins us in the kitchen. Finished, Dan rests his head on my back, both arms now around my waist, waiting patiently. I look up from my perch on his knee to give her a bright smile. "Hey, Mom," I say between bites.

Her eyes narrow into thin slits, and when she speaks, her words are chipped in ice. "Hello, Mike, Dan."

My lover's voice rumbles through me as he says, "Morning, Mrs. Knapp." He's so polite — how can she not fall for that the way everyone else has?

But her face is like stone, her eyes obsidian beads, I have to turn away from the hurt I see in their depths. So I lean over my dish and shovel food into my mouth, hurrying now. I don't like the way she looks at us, at Dan but particularly at me, as if I've driven a knife into her very heart and every word of love spoken twists the blade deeper, every touch, every smile. Already I'm thinking that if she's going to be like this next month, we'll visit Dan's parents out in Ohio for Thanksgiving instead of coming to the house. His dad doesn't know we're lovers so we'll have to tone it down while we're there, but his mom has no problem with who I am to her son.

"Do you have to sit there?" Mom asks, frowning at us. "How old are you, Michael? There's a perfectly good chair right here ..." She pulls out Emily's chair, now empty, and indicates it with a sweep of her hand. "Why don't you sit here?"

"She just left," I explain, making no move to follow her suggestion. "I'm fine, Mom. Dan doesn't mind —"

"No," he agrees. He holds me closer, if that's even possible. "Not at all. You're fine."

I smile sweetly at her and she plops into the chair herself with a disgusted little sigh. "Billy," she starts.

My aunt doesn't look up from her insurance papers. "Hmm?" When Mom doesn't answer, Billy glances over at us and says, "Oh Laura, hush. They're fine, really. You get all worked up over the silliest things."

"I don't think this is silly," Mom announces. Her voice rises in sudden anger. "My son being *gay* is not *silly*."

Quietly, Aunt Billy points out, "And it's not something you can change or control, either. Admit it, that's what has you so upset."

Mom shakes her head, indignant. "I'm *upset* because it's wrong," she says, and I have to clench my fork to keep from throwing it at her. *Wrong* — how can what I feel for Dan be wrong? She's too damn blind to see what a good man he is, how much he loves me. When she surges to her feet and levels a finger at Aunt Billy, Dan holds me tight to keep me from jumping up, as well. "Don't you dare get on me about this, Billy," she threatens. "He's *my* son, not yours. The way he's living isn't natural and you know it. It's not *right* and if he can't respect me enough not to flaunt it —"

"He's right here," I cry out — I *hate* her doing this, talking as if I'm not standing right in front of her or I'm a child incapable of understanding what she says. Tossing my fork onto my plate, I slide off Dan's knee and stand beside her, my hands curled into fists at my sides to keep them from shaking. "I'm right here, Mom. Don't talk about me like I don't know what the fuck is going on."

"Michael," she sighs. "This is between me and Billy —"

"And it's about me," I point out. I feel my lover stand behind me, his hand tentative on the back of my waist, and I reach out for him blindly, clutch at his arm to keep myself steady. Around us, the kitchen falls silent, and I find myself once again the unwilling center of attention. Everyone's watching us, *everyone* ... "You don't approve of my relationship? Fine, I didn't ask you to. I'm not your little boy anymore, in case you haven't figured that one out yet, and I don't live under your roof any longer. If you're going to treat us like shit when we visit, I can guarantee you we won't make the mistake of coming down again."

Before she can reply, I turn away and storm from the room. A few older kids clog the doorway, curious what's going on, but I shove through them and they shrink back to let me pass. Dan keeps his hand on my waist and follows so close behind me that he almost treads on my heels with each step. "Fuck," I mutter under my breath. I don't need this, not today.

In the hallway, Penny stops me with a light hand on my arm. "Michael?" she asks, unsure. She still sounds drugged, and her gaze wavers between me and Dan but can't seem to focus on either of us before flittering away again. "What happened? Who's arguing?" At the closed look on my face, she adds, "What's Laura said now?"

"Nothing," I mutter, pulling away. I don't need her concern, I don't *want* it. Right this second, my mind is too clouded to keep my voice civil, I don't care who I lash out at while I'm like this. I should've never woken up this morning. No, I should've never gotten out of bed. Everything was fine when it was just the two of us beneath the sheets — I should've locked the door on the rest of the family and maybe I wouldn't be in this mood from hell.

Penny's eyes widen, and a hand flutters to cover her mouth. "Michael," she sighs. "I'm not the one you're fighting with here. Keep that in mind."

Her gentle tone of voice diffuses me, and my ire is gone as quickly as it sprung up. "I'm sorry," I murmur, taking her arm. When I rub her wrist, she nods in forgiveness. "Penny, I'm sorry. It's just — she's so *wrong* about me."

With a wan smile, Penny admits, "She's just stubborn, honey. Where do you think you get it from?"

"I'm not stubborn," I mutter. Penny raises a questioning eyebrow that makes me grin sheepishly. "I'm not," I say again, this time crossing my arms in front of my chest to prove my point.

Dan massages the bunched muscles in my upper arms and winks at Penny. "Excuse me?" he asks, teasing me. "Did you just say what I think you said?"

I try to shrug him off but he doesn't let go. Instead, he plants a kiss above my ear and murmurs, "I'm playing, babe. I love you just the way you are." His arms come around me, hold me back against him, and he presses his cheek to mine. "Even if you *are* ornery," he adds.

"Hey!" I cry out. He makes it hard to stay angry for long, and it takes all the strength I have to keep the frown on my face. Penny laughing at us doesn't help any, either. *I'm mad,* I tell myself, but without my mom right in front of me, I can gloss over her self-righteous attitude and forget what just happened in the kitchen. This is a big house, there's a lot to do before we leave, and there are so many other people here, I can easily stay out of her way while we're here.

"Don't pout," Dan tells me, and that just makes the corners of my lips pull down harder. "Michael," he warns. I struggle to hold the expression, but he's giving me that look now, the one where I can see everything I am reflected in his eyes, and I can't even help it, I turn away so he won't notice my shy smile. With a soft kiss in the corner of my mouth, he purrs, "There you go."

I could lose myself in him. But Penny touches my arm, bringing me back to the chaos that is Aunt Evie's. "Just give your mother some time," she says. I nod grudgingly — time, yeah, sure, but how long? It's just been two days and already I'm sick of the way she acts around me now, as if with Dan, I'm not the same son she's known for the last twenty-five years. Patting my arm, Penny asks, "Can you do that, Michael? Just give her some time. She'll come around, you'll see."

"Thanks," I whisper. Her words are meant to be comforting, even if they don't quite work.

She gives us a tight smile. "Go on up with the others," she says, nodding at the stairs. "Evie once told me when she passed ..." Her eyes cloud over, her lips tremble, and her smile is more forced than ever. She has to take a deep breath to steady herself before she can continue. "She said that this place belongs to you kids," she says softly. Tears bead in her eyes but she blinks them away. "She once told me that she wanted you guys to pick out whatever means Sugar Creek to you and take it, keep it, make it yours. Evie told me she would rest easier knowing that you all had something to look at and remember her by."

"Penny," I sigh, covering her hand with my own. I'd like to say something more but I can't, there are no words left that could possibly explain everything inside me right this second. *Pick out whatever means Sugar Creek to you* ... God, just one thing? Every corner of this house holds memories for me — every knick-knack means something, every picture on the wall, every piece of furniture, every room. How can I possibly choose just one thing that would remind me of everything I've ever done here? I have toys packed away in the attic, and I bought that vase by the credenza for Evie at a yard sale one year for Christmas, and there's a spoon in the kitchen drawer that I found one day while digging at the creek with Stephen. If only I could capture everything at once, shrink the house and its surrounding land and the creek until it's no larger than a dollhouse or even smaller, something I can hold in my hand, and I'd gaze into the windows whenever I want to relive the moments trapped inside.

"Go on up," she tells me. "There's a ton of stuff to go through, Michael. I can't keep it all. Take what means the most to you, okay?"

I nod. Another pat on my arm, then she extracts her hand from beneath mine and heads for the kitchen. To calm my mom down, I hope. Turning to Dan, I suggest, "Let's see if we can find a private room."

We're halfway up the stairs when the front door bangs open and my dad calls out, "Mike? Hold up."

I stop and behind me, Dan stops too, his hands on my hips. Leaning on the banister, I look down into my dad's upturned face, his cheeks windblown and red. "Yeah?"

He's been drinking already, I can tell that from the way his gaze wavers, as if he's trying to see something behind me and I'm in the way. "You ever change a lock?" he asks.

"A what?" I don't know what he's talking about.

With an impatient sigh, he says, "A lock. On a door. Ever change one?"

"I have," Dan offers. When I look at him, he shrugs. "Busy work on post, changing knobs, replacing locks, whatever they can find for us to do. It's not that hard."

"Then come on," my dad says. "We've got a few we need to get up —"

I shake my head. "No, wait. We're cleaning out the upstairs —"

My dad gives me a hard look that dares me to argue. "You can't clean without him?"

Yes, there's definitely an edge to his voice that beer puts there. "It won't take long," Dan murmurs.

"Why do you need to change the locks?" I want to know. "Dad —"

He wears a baseball cap with the Phillies' *P* embroidered on the front, and he takes that off now to scratch at the top of his head. His salted hair stands up in the back from the cap. Smoothing it down, he mutters, "Your aunts think Jessie might come by or something, I don't know. The sooner we get these locks changed, the sooner they'll stop pestering me about that damn woman."

"Jessie?" I ask, dubious.

"God *dammit*, Mike!" my dad cries. I cringe at his outburst. "We're wasting time." To Dan, he asks, "Are you coming or what?"

My lover gives me a helpless look — what can he say, no? Not when my dad's the only one other than Caitlin who seems to like Dan. "Go," I tell him.

"You okay with this?" he asks. I take a step up, another, and he tugs at the belt loop on my pants to make me look at him again. "Michael?"

"Fine," I lie, hating the fact that I'm *not* okay with this, I'm pissed. There goes my whole day — he won't be done anytime soon, I know my dad, he'll find a hundred other things for Dan to do and I won't be able to kiss him or hold him or joke with him while I work through the rooms upstairs, I won't have him as a buffer to help keep my emotions at bay. Because I can see he doesn't believe me, I turn away and hurry up the steps. "Go on, Dan. It's cool. Find me when you're through."

If you're finished sometime today, I add silently. I hear footsteps descending the stairs and don't look back when the door shuts between us.

22: A Visitor

I'M NOT MAD at Dan. I have to keep telling myself this, it's not his fault my dad wanted his help ... what could he do? He doesn't have it in him to say no, and that wouldn't have gone over well at *all*. You don't say no to my dad. I've never done it, and Ray's not that stupid nor Caitlin that brave. It's just something you don't do.

So this irritation that spreads through me like an infection, it's not directed towards my lover. Even when the minutes turn into hours and I stop looking up every time I hear footsteps out in the hall because I know it's not going to be him, even then it's not his fault. It's my dad's for snagging Dan away from me. It's Penny's for keeping us in the hall so long. It's my mom's for the argument in the kitchen that sent me storming out. Hell, for all I know it might even be *my* fault, but it's not Dan's. He said he'd just be a few minutes, and any second now ...

But I don't see him all morning. When I get upstairs, I pick the first room I come upon to work in, one of the guest bedrooms that Evie used to reserve for the children when we came to visit. The only furniture in it is a daybed along one wall and a couple of low dressers with enough small drawers for each of us. We used to sleep in this room, sleeping bags spread out to cover the middle of the floor, pillows and blankets tossed every which way — the makeshift beds are still here but they're neat now, folded against the walls and out of the way. Already my aunt Ginger reclines on the daybed, flipping through an old photo album, and my cousin Theresa sits in front of the closet, folding clothes into a black garbage bag. She looks up as I enter the room, a tired smile on her face. "Michael, hey."

Ginger glances at me and turns back to the album. "Where's your boy?"

"My dad stole him away," I joke, trying to pretend I don't want him right here with me.

Ginger sighs. "Don't you hate when that happens? My daddy was always stealing my guys."

Across the room, Theresa laughs. Then she pats the floor beside her and says, "Sit with me, Mike."

To be honest, going through old clothes isn't what I had in mind when I came up here. I was thinking more of a continuation of what Dan and I started this morning, and I don't like that he's not here with me. I should've went with them — how hard can it be to change a lock? "What are we doing this for anyway?" I want to know.

"Because Penny can't," Theresa tells me. She shoves more clothes into the bag as she talks — it's already swollen like a full sponge and I'm almost sure I see the plastic stretch thin in places. "This is old stuff. I'm talking ancient — most of the clothing I've found so far belonged to Aunt Evie's parents, if you'll believe it. I don't think anyone ever got rid of anything in this house."

Interested in spite of myself, I hunker down beside Theresa and pick up a polyester blazer from the top of the pile of clothes folded into her lap. It's a light powder blue, maybe bright once upon a time but now faded to an almost colorless shade and definitely several decades out of date. I try to picture the man who wore this back in the day, but I can't put the image I have of my great-grandfather into this fashionable jacket — the man I see in my mind is old and weathered and thin, a memory gathered from years of looking at old photo albums like the one Ginger's leafing through now. Handing the jacket back to my cousin, I stand and finger another suit that hangs in the closet, a gray so light that it might be an aged white, dingy with time. Each room up here is probably filled with similar clothing. "They're getting rid of everything?" I ask, incredulous.

"Everything we don't take with us when we leave," Ginger says. She doesn't look up from the pictures again and her voice is dreamy, as if trapped in the past when those photos were taken. "You see something you want, Mike, grab it up now. There's no real will — everything was left to Penny — but Evie wanted us each to have something. I guess she figured it'd mean more if we picked it out ourselves, you know?" With a laugh, she adds, "I'd consider doing that but I think the only thing any of my children or ex-husbands will want after I'm gone is my money. And Lord knows there ain't enough of that to go around."

Ginger's like Aunt Bobbie, married more times than anyone cares to remember, and I've lost count of the boyfriends in between. She's currently separated, not legally divorced yet, but I think someone mentioned a lover or two in the wings. Penny said Ginger arrived alone, and that surprises me. For as long as I've known her, she's always had someone with her here at Sugar Creek. Secretly, though, I'm glad she doesn't this time, because it leaves the back room for me and Dan, who still isn't back yet ...

I help Theresa clean out the closet. There's nothing I want to save —

this is the first time I've even seen most of the clothing, and it's all so old, I'm thinking we could sell it online and probably make a fortune. But Ginger quenches that notion real quick. "Momma's taking everything to the Goodwill. She'd have a fit if she heard you wanted to put it on the internet. Jeez, Mike, I never pegged you as a gold digger."

"I'm not!" I laugh from my spot inside the closet. It's dark in here, plastic dry cleaner's bags draped around me like ghosts, boxes hemming me in, clothes on the rod above me blocking out the light. "Is Dan out there yet? I'm sick of being picked on."

"We're not picking on you," Theresa assures me. She peeks into the closet as she slings a bag of clothes over her shoulder. "Not much, anyway. You're fun to tease."

With another laugh, I pull down a shirt from the hangers above me, ball it up and chuck it at her. She swats it aside easily. "Seriously, is he out there?" I ask. How long has it been now? "What time is it?"

"Almost noon," Ginger calls out. Even though I can't see her from where I am inside the closet, I'm fairly sure she's still stretched out on the daybed. "Going through the pictures," she explained when I asked what she was doing to help out. "Someone needs to do it. Why not me?"

Because it gets you out of honest work, I should've said. Ginger's the type to watch others do something and then claim she helped out all along. "I am helping," she likes to say. "I'm supervising. Not everyone can be worker bees, Michael, and not everyone can be the queen."

But there's something in the way she says it that makes you want to thank her for just watching, while you do all the work, and just to tease her, I ask, "You still sitting on your lazy ass, Ginger?"

"You bet I am," she replies. "And no, your boy's not here yet. Send Caitlin after him."

Caitlin? Out in the room I hear my sister's voice. "I'm not tracking him down," she grumbles. "Where's Mike?"

"In the closet," Theresa says with a huff. "Cat, can you get that other bag? I'm just putting them out in the hall."

I wonder what Caitlin's doing here. If it's noon, maybe it's time to eat already. Surely someone's whipping up lunch, one of our aunts or Penny, sandwiches or soup or something to feed all of us. And if I go downstairs, everyone else will be there, Dan included, and I'll get to steal him back. I'll give him my sad-eyes look that I know he can't resist, and I'll corner him when no one else is watching, and I'll give him a long, lingering kiss. "I miss you," I'll whisper, in that low voice I know does terrible things to him. With one finger I'll trail down his throat, down his chest, circle around his navel through his shirt and then hook onto his jeans, right behind his belt buckle, and I know he won't be able to resist that. "Come play with me now, baby," I'll say. And I guarantee neither of us will get much more work done today.

Just thinking of him makes my heart race and my palms sweat. "Is Dan with you?" I ask as I climb out of the closet. Over precariously stacked boxes, overstuffed bags, through the plastic that rustles and clings to me … when I finally break free, I find my sister sitting on the edge of the daybed, peering over Ginger's shoulder as she flips through the photos. "Caitlin?" I ask, but neither of them look up at me. Brushing dust from my jeans, I want to know, "Have you seen Dan? Cat —"

"Out back," comes the terse reply. For a second I think she's still mad at me from this morning, but then she points at a picture in the album before Ginger can turn the page, and I realize she's been sucked into the past just as readily as our aunt has. What is it with women and old photographs? They look at a picture and suddenly the memories seem to rush back like a tide, engulfing them, drowning out the present for the past. With a quick laugh, Caitlin cries, "Michael, look! It's you and Ray and oh my God, is that Kenny? Was he ever really that small?"

Just what we need, two people not doing any work. When Theresa comes back into the room, I roll my eyes to make her giggle. To my sister, I ask, "Did you want something? Or did you just come here to hang out?"

"You have a visitor," she tells me. Tucking her hair behind one ear, she points at another picture and gasps. "That's not me! Jesus, what the hell am I wearing?"

"A visitor?" I can't imagine who — I glance at Theresa but she simply shrugs. "Caitlin, who is it?"

My sister looks at me with something akin to contempt. "Your one o'clock appointment," she says, and before I can answer, she adds, "I don't know, Mike, I didn't ask. I'm not your secretary."

"Smart ass," I mutter, brushing at my jeans again. Gray dust has settled into long streaks where the black denim was folded as I squatted in the closet, and my shirt's pulled out of the waistband in the back — I tuck it in self-consciously, wondering what my hair looks like. A visitor? I can't even begin to imagine who it might be. I don't know anyone in Sugar Creek anymore — all the kids I played with growing up are gone now, moved to Pittsburgh or York, all except for …

Stephen Robichaud.

I comb down my hair quickly. "Is it Stephen?" I ask. My skin tingles but I don't know why. I haven't seen him in what, five years? Has it been that long? The last time I was down here, and he stopped by one day, said he saw my mom in Grosso's and hoped I was here, too. The two of us went for a walk by the creek — I remember telling him about Matthew and how hurt I was at the time because we just broke up and he was the first guy I ever slept with. It was strange how easily we slipped into our friendship again, almost like pulling on a bodysuit that's been washed a few times — tight at first, a little uncomfortable, but the more you move around, the more the fabric stretches, until it fits you like a second skin. There on the banks of the creek, a few yards upstream so none of my family would see or hear us, he kissed me again and his lips were so familiar to me, he tasted exactly the same as he had the first time we kissed. The grass was lush, a carpet I laid him back on, our bodies rubbing together, our erections aching beneath our shorts, our lips hungry on each other once again. We made out until his glasses fogged up, and I think I promised to call or write or something. I think I said I'd come back the next year, the way I used to visit when I was younger.

But there were no letters, no calls, and no further visits. I don't know if he expected that? Or if he waited to hear from me? Is he mad now? I don't know what he thinks about me, what he's doing here, what he wants from me now, after all this time … I don't even know what it is thinking of him has done to me, why it feels as if pins prick my skin and needles course through my veins. My stomach churns nervously — where's Dan? I don't want to see Stephen again.

I have no choice. With one last look at the album, Caitlin jumps up from the bed and steers me out the open door and into the hall. "Come on," she tells me, leading the way downstairs. "You can introduce me. It's Cat, remember."

He's in the living room, frowning at a flurry of school portraits framed above the TV. Same mousy hair parted on one side and kept short, comb marks gouged into the thin strands. Same thick glasses — no fashionable wire frames for Stephen Robichaud, his prescription is too strong for anything less than chunky black glasses that Dan calls BCDs, birth control devices, standard issue on post. Same big eyes, same wide mouth, same lanky frame and large Adam's apple and thin chest — he hasn't aged a bit. This is the same boy I kissed at fourteen, the same one I fooled around with my teenaged years, the same one I rubbed against five years ago when I needed someone's hands and lips to convince me that I was still desirable after Matthew left. And when he turns around and sees me, his smile says that he thinks I'm still the same, too. "Hey, Michael."

His voice is soft and a little high, just the way I remember it. "Stephen," I say, and because I hear the awkwardness in my own voice, I laugh to cover my discomfort. Is he thinking of the last time we were together? The way I touched him, how we kissed? Does he remember what I taste like? I don't want to know. I hold out a hand which he takes before he pulls me into a quick hug. I keep my eyes open, my mind blank, and pretend I don't feel the warmth of his body next to mine. "How have you been, guy?" I ask, step-ping back to get out of his embrace. "Damn, where's the time go, you know?"

He laughs because he's supposed to, but his smile doesn't reach his eyes. "Mike," he sighs, "believe me, I wish it was anything else to bring you back here — anything other than this." He means Evie's passing, but he can't say the words and I don't offer them myself, I don't want to hear them aloud. Holding a hand out to me as if he wants me to take it again, he says gently, "I'm sorry."

"Yeah," I whisper. "Me too." Don't tell me how much you loved her, I pray. I don't want to hear someone else's reminisces, I don't want to have to share mine. I want to keep them all inside because I'm afraid that the more I talk about it, the sooner I'll forget. Already I can't quite recall Aunt Evie's features, and that scares me. I'll go upstairs when Stephen leaves, go through the photo albums with Ginger, until Evie's face is burned behind my eyes. I can't forget her.

Not one to be left out, Caitlin nudges the back of my leg with one knee. My own knee buckles but I catch myself and tell Stephen, "You know my sister. Caitlin?"

Stephen nods but doesn't offer her a hand to shake, which is good. She's the type to leave him hanging. "This is Stephen," I tell her. "You remember him — he was always over here. God, I've known him forever." Lowering my voice, I wink and add, "My first kiss, even."

That makes him blush, thin pink color rising in his pale cheeks, and he ducks his head, scuffs his feet on the carpet. "Mike," he warns, but there's laughter in his eyes and a hint of something more in his voice, and all of a sudden I'm glad Caitlin's here with us. I have a funny feeling he didn't just come over to say he's sorry that Evie's gone.

She looks at him, her face expressionless as she works through who he is in her mind, who he must be to me. No one, I want to assure her, but how awkward would that be? I can't just out and say it — he's done nothing to make me think he expects this visit to revive what we used to feel together; he's said nothing to suggest that he wants me. Years ago, when I was in high school and he already in college, he told me that he didn't think he could ever love someone he didn't know his whole life. We were lying together on his bed, both of us naked, me still hard and him already spent, the flavor of him lingering in my mouth, and we didn't look at each other but at the ceil-ing. It was safer that way. "I just don't think I could do it," he whispered then as we watched late afternoon shadows play across the lazy blades of his ceiling fan. "I mean, stay with one person forever? Promise to love them until I die?"

"It can't be that hard," I replied. I was still a long way from Dan, but I knew there was someone out there for me, there had to be, and I already knew Stephen wasn't it. "People fall in and out of love all the time."

"I don't," Stephen told me. His hand drifted across the covers to brush mine, then pulled away quickly, as if the touch were anathema to him. "Maybe if I knew him long enough, though. How long do you think that would have to be?"

I didn't know — I still don't. I wonder if there's anyone else in his life now, if he's happy, or if he's here hoping for … I just don't know. If Caitlin weren't here, maybe we could talk freely, he could tell me what he wants or expects and I could tell him how it is, but she keeps this silence between us. "Stephen," she says, and he nods, I nod, Stephen.

Hope shines in his eyes as he asks, "I was thinking maybe we could go for a walk?"

He remembers the last time then, the two of us by the creek. Dread curls in my stomach. But before I can reply, Caitlin gives us a sweet smile. "Oh hey, did you meet Dan yet? Let me go get him."

"Dan?" Stephen asks, frowning slightly.

"Mike's boyfriend," Caitlin replies sweetly. She flips her hair back over one shoulder and spins on her heel. "He's just out back helping Dad. I'll get him for you."

And she's gone. The look Stephen gives me says that everything he was looking forward to today, everything he hoped to find in me, is gone. "Boyfriend?" he asks, his voice softer than I've ever heard it before.
Now it's my turn to duck my head and stare at my feet as I mumble, "I'm sorry."

23: Stephen Robichaud

WITHOUT CAITLIN, THERE is nothing between us, nothing hindering our speech, nothing keeping us apart. I can't quite meet Stephen's steady gaze, though, and when he takes a step closer to me, I shift uncomfortably but don't move back. We've been too much to each other over the years — best friends, summer buddies, daresay lovers? At such young ages, it was more curiosity than love to me, more feeling good and getting off than anything else, and since we used to be so close, I thought nothing of being that open with him. It was only friendship, nothing more, not to me.

Still, I can see the pain in his face — it hurts too much to see how Caitlin's careless words have wounded him. My fault. I should've known she do something like this, mention Dan just to stir up shit. She doesn't know the meaning of the word *tact*. "I'm sorry," I say again. From the corner of my eye, I see Stephen shrug helplessly. With a forced laugh, I tell him, "You know how sisters are."

That makes him smile. His own twin sister, Stephanie, was the terror of Sugar Creek when we were kids. Chasing us around on her bike, beating us up, even that kiss she gave me was brutal. Last time I was here, Stephen told me she was in law school, of all places. I still can't wrap my mind around that one. I'm about to ask how she's doing when he wants to know, "What's he like?"

He means Dan. "Wonderful," I say simply. That's it in a nutshell. But Stephen stares at me and I feel like he's waiting for more. "He's good to me," I tell him. "Funny and thoughtful and sweet. Quiet — he lets me talk." Stephen grins at that. I've always been a rambler, filling the silence with whatever comes to mind until someone interrupts. I've never been at a loss for words until this weekend. Until now. "Um ..." I try to think of something else to say, something to describe everything I feel about Dan, everything he means to me, but I don't want to hurt Stephen more. After all we've been through, all we meant, I don't want to rub it in. "He's in the

Army," I offer.

Stephen nods. "Hence the shirt."

"Yeah." I give a weak laugh and cross my arms in front of my chest, hiding the words written there, *Military Wife*. Somehow it's not quite so funny anymore.

If Stephen notices my not so subtle gesture, he doesn't say anything. Instead, he shoves his hands down deep into his pockets and rocks back on his heels. What is there to say? Maybe nothing anymore. I stare at his denim-clad legs and remember dark hair curled over pale skin, soft flesh that used to tremble beneath my touch. His hands fist in his pockets, pushing against the front of his pants like an exaggerated erection. I wonder what he's trying to hide. I tell myself I don't want to know. Where is Dan?

"An Army brat," Stephen says, his voice quiet. He shakes his head. "I never pegged you as that type." When I shrug, he asks, "How long has it been for you guys?"

"Ten months." It feels like forever, though. I try for a smile, but Stephen just stares at me, his eyes twin facets of pain in his face. Why is this so damn hard? We weren't ever *serious*. "How about you?" I ask, hoping to lighten the mood. "Anyone swept you off your feet yet?"

He studies me for a silent moment. I think I know what he's going to say. *Don't*, I pray. I don't want to hear it, not now, not ever. I don't want to know ... "Someone already did that a long time ago," he says quietly.

I close my eyes, try to swallow past the emotion that rises unbidden in my throat. "Stephen," I sigh.

He takes a step closer — I don't hear it so much as feel it, a sudden nearness, an intimacy I put behind me long ago. He always liked me more than I did him. That first kiss was *his* doing, the first time his hand cupped my dick beneath the waters of the creek, the first time he ever licked my navel and then drifted lower, his lips closing over me ... his suggestions, all of them. To me, it was feeling good, fooling around. It was two friends exploring, growing up, learning together. It never meant anything more.

At least, not to *me*.

Another step and he touches me. His fingers slip between my arm and chest, his thumb rubs my wrist in a slow, soothing gesture. This was how he touched me the summer we started ... a few days after that first kiss, which neither of us mentioned again. We were goofing off down by the creek, wasting away the summer afternoon in the cool water, me and Stephen and a handful of others — Ray and Kenny and Stephen's cousin Brent, a few boys whose names I don't remember anymore. The smell of charcoal permeated the air, hot dogs and burgers on the grill, one of Aunt Evie's cookouts. Easiest way to feed a crowd, she always said, and no one was ever turned away. I swear half of Sugar Creek came over when she fired up the grill. One by one the boys drifted away from the creek, lured back to the house at the prospect of food, until it was just me and Stephen in the water. I didn't even realize we were alone at first — I climbed up on the log that spanned the creek and leaped in, splashing water everywhere, and when I came up for air, Stephen was right *there*, so close that I had to back into the wooden bridge. "Stephen," I sighed, wiping water from my face. I glanced around and that's when I noticed that everyone else was gone.

Without his glasses on, Stephen's eyes were huge and slightly out of focus — he stared at me with a smoldering look that I had never seen in him before, a lust that stirred my groin and made me think of that unmentionable kiss. He drifted closer, his leg brushing mine beneath the water, his hand tentative on my stomach before floating away. "Stephen? What ..." I wiped at my face again just to break his steady gaze. "Where are the others?"

"Left," he breathed. Suddenly I was cold, all too aware of my own near nakedness. Goose bumps pimpled my skin. Trying to look unperturbed, I crossed my arms in front of my chest and pressed back against the log as far as I could go — I was young, I didn't know what that look in his eyes meant, I couldn't begin to imagine what he might want from me. I had just recently discovered the pleasures of my own hand — I couldn't think of anyone else touching me the same way.

But his hand curved over my wrist, his fingers rubbing over one nipple as they eased beneath my arm. One knee parted my legs, eased up into my crotch, where I was already aching from a tension I didn't quite understand. "Kiss me again," he sighed, leaning against me. His body was warm in the cool water, his skin slippery on mine, and I let him open my arms, I let him in closer, I couldn't help it. I was drowning in those eyes and I couldn't breathe, he stood too close ... this time when our lips met, one hand drifted from my arm, down my belly, down further. I almost came from just his fingers fumbling into my shorts, his kiss, it was that intense. I'm afraid to look in his face now, I'm afraid to look at him after all these years and still see that same lust, that same need, looking back.

I'm not twelve anymore, I remind myself. I'm twenty-five, I'm not some boy willing to settle for any touch at all. I have a lover. I can't just slip back into who I was before — I've changed, even if nothing else in this tiny little town has.

"I hoped maybe ..." Stephen starts, but he doesn't finish the thought. I keep my eyes down, stare at the hair on the back of his hand, and tell myself I don't feel anything at his skin against mine. I have Dan ... where is he?

But I don't like the sentence hanging between us, a loaded gun waiting to discharge. I shrug, hoping to shake his hand loose, but it doesn't work.

"Maybe what?" I ask.

When I dare to look at him, his eyes are just as large as I remembered this close. "Maybe you'd ..." He sighs, and his breath is soft on my face, slightly minty like a promise. "This is going to sound bad."

"What is?" I ask, hoping I sound as if I don't know exactly what he's trying to say, what he's feeling and thinking and wanting right now.

His hand drifts up my chest, is he still touching me? His fingers play across the hollow of my throat, remembering the feel of forgotten flesh. "I was sort of hoping you'd want me," he whispers. "Like last time? I thought you'd want me to hold you again, Michael. I came here hoping you needed that." When I don't answer immediately, his thumb hovers above my lips and he gives me a sad smile. "See? Told you it'd sound bad."

He came here to comfort me. Like last time, after Matthew, when I needed someone to hold me and kiss me and tell me the guy was a fool to let me go. Only now ... I have Dan, I think, turning before Stephen's thumb touches me. "I'm sorry," I tell him. What else can I possibly say?

And where the hell is Dan? Didn't Caitlin say she'd get him? I need him. Stephen's touch is too familiar, it's too easy to slip back into the past, I want my lover here with me.

Somehow I find the strength to take a step away from my friend. "I'm sorry," I say again. I am, God so damn sorry. "I can't. I mean, I'm with —"

"I know," Stephen concedes. He lets me move another step back without following, thank the Lord. But when he sighs, it's such a lonely, desolate sound that I almost stumble. "It's stupid, I know, but remember when you used to say you wanted to move up here? You wanted to live in Sugar Creek forever — do you remember that?"

I do. Childish words from a child. I'm grown now, I have a life in DC, I have a lover and a job and a home, I can't just pull up roots and relocate to the summer home of my youth. "I was just talking smack," I say, trying to keep my tone light. Smack, a word we used as kids, when we were too young to say shit. "I was playing, Steve."

His eyes are serious, his mouth a sad line drawn on his face. "I wasn't," he murmurs. "I never played around with you, Mike. It was always something more than that to me."

"I'm sorry," I say again. I can't stop apologizing.

He shrugs as if it's too late now. "I used to dream up these convoluted scenarios, you just don't know. Even when I was just a little kid, I wanted you here all the time. From the moment you left in August until the day your mom's car pulled into town the next year, I played out these fantasies in my mind. Something would happen and you'd have to come live here with Evie. Or you'd sign up for an exchange program at my school and stay in my room with me. Or hell, I'd go to college in Virginia, I don't know, anything to be near you."

I had no idea these thoughts lived in his head. I thought we were friends, nothing more. The times we spent finding pleasure in each other's bodies had been nice, true, but I never thought of him as more than a friend. A close friend, yes, but not a boyfriend, sure as hell not a lover. "Stephen —"

He continues as if I didn't interrupt. "I was so sure it would just be a matter of time, Michael, before you looked at me the same way I look at you. Every guy I ever dated at State had eyes like yours, hair the same shade, the same style. But there was never anything there, nothing like what we had, all those summers spent together, all those adventures we shared."

I blink back tears that blur my vision and think of the years I've known him. I see them fanned out like a deck of cards, each one as vivid and as bright as if they happened yesterday. The day he fell off his bike and cut his knee, and he rode on my handlebars while I hurried him home. The time I stepped in a snake hole in the woods, twisted my ankle, and he half-dragged, half-carried me to Aunt Evie's. The first time we ever met, me in the back yard digging up the grapes and him a lanky eight year old watching me from the shadows by the shed. I saw him, the sun winking off his glasses, thick even back then, and I picked up one of my shovels, held it out to him like an invitation. When he didn't move, I set the shovel down, handle turned towards him, just in case he wanted to play, and went back to my dirt. A few minutes later, I looked up as he sank to his knees beside me, shovel already in hand. "Here," I told him, pointing at the hole I was working so diligently on. "I'm trying to get to the other side."

"You can't," he told me, but that didn't stop us. We dug until water bubbled into our hands, and our laughter made my dad come over to see what we were up to. He saw the hole, the piles of dirt, the exposed roots of Aunt Evie's grapes, and his face turned the same purple shade as the ripening fruit. He made us fill the hole back in, which was messy work, the water turning the soft soil to mud, and by the time we were finished, it was dark and we were both so filthy that my mom wouldn't let us into the house until after we rinsed off in the creek. From that moment on, we were inseparable.

And now this.

"I used to come home from college every summer just to see you," Stephen tells me — doesn't he know when to stop? Can't he see my tears, the way his words are hurting me? "Even after you stopped coming, I kept hoping … I'd walk over here the first night, sit on the porch with your mom and Ray, ask them all about how you were and what you were doing. Any little part of you I could have, Michael. I clung to that. I thrived on it."

A tear courses down my cheek and I wipe at it brusquely. "Stephen, please," I sigh. "I didn't know. I'm sorry."

He touches the hand on my face, his fingers folding over mine to rest against my cheek. So soft, that touch. So tender. I remember those same fingers on other parts of my body, stroking me, grasping me, bringing me to release. He's close again, so near to me that I imagine I feel his aura press against mine, sadness and blatant desire and unashamed need. I hate this — we were such good friends once ... his words fan my face. "Do you love him?" he wants to know.

I nod. Completely and utterly, I love Dan. I'm about to apologize when Stephen's fingers trace the curve of my jaw. "Remember when I told you I didn't think I could love one person forever?" he whispers.

I nod again — we were lying on his bed, the scene stands out so vivid in my mind. I can almost smell the musky scent of sex hanging over us, I can still recall the taste of him on my lips. "Stephen," I whisper. "Don't —"

"I lied," he tells me. I squeeze my eyes shut, I don't want to hear this. His fingers brush over my brow, and before I can pull away, his lips touch the corner of my mouth in a tiny kiss, barely there. "I've always loved you, Michael. I know it's too late to tell you now, but I think I always will."

God. I choke back more tears, sob his name. "I should go," he says. I press my hand to my mouth and nod, yes, he should. "I hope he makes you happy."

I keep my eyes closed. I don't want to see him leave. His face is already etched into my memory, that sadness in his eyes writing over the memories I have of him, until all I see is the lonely boy who just said he'll always love me. Though I have Dan, though I wouldn't give what I have with him up for the world, right this second I wish fervently that there was some way I could make Stephen happy. Something I could say, or do, for the sake of the friendship we once shared, and I would say it without hesitation, I would do it without a second thought, anything to take away the hurt I've caused him, the pain. Anything at all ...

But nothing comes to mind, and I hear his footsteps quiet on the carpet, in the hall, I hear the front door open. I can almost see him in my mind looking back at me one last time, and then the door shuts, and he's gone.

I tear blindly from the living room, down the hall into the kitchen, pushing past relatives in my stumbling haste to get out, get away, put him behind me and move on. If I never loved him the way he loves me, why does it feel as if my heart is tearing in two? Why am I crying if he never meant anything to me?

Dan's at the sink rinsing his hands, Caitlin leaning on the counter beside him. "Nothing to worry about," she's saying as I pass by. "I mean it, Dan. He's got nothing on you, trust me on this."

My lover sees my tears and his smile disappears from his face. "Michael?" he asks, concerned. "What happened? Where's your friend?"

"Gone," I mumble. I don't want to talk about it. I don't want to think about it, about Stephen or anything we ever did together, but I can't get his words out of my head. Over and over again I hear him. I've always loved you ... like a wave crashing down around me, threatening to sweep me under. I think I always will.

Dan reaches for me but I dodge his grasp, stagger through the kitchen into the back room. I hear my name again but I slam the door shut and lock it for good measure. On the other side my lover knocks, calls out to me, rattles the knob. "Go away," I sob. "Please."

When I shut my eyes Stephen's are behind mine, lonely and so damn sad. I throw myself down on the bed and bury my head in the pillow, which turns hot and damp. Even though I haven't seen him in years, haven't talked to him, don't really know the person he's become, I can't help but feel like I've just lost my best friend.

24: Alone Again

ALL THE TIMES we laughed together, gone. All the fun, all the tears, all the adventures and camp outs, all the forts we built, everything is gone. I never had a friend like Stephen back home — he was my summer buddy, a forever friend, someone I thought would always be there for me, up here in Sugar Creek, away from the madness and uncertainty of my "real" life. All year long I used to look forward to the trip to Aunt Evie's — freedom, excitement, Stephen there every single day, knocking on the door first thing in the morning, not heading home until well after dusk. A summer of friendship, a lifetime of summers. And now it's gone.

Any other time and it wouldn't be hard to patch this rift between us. It's not like we haven't had arguments before — boys fight, and Stephen and I were no exception growing up. Stupid shit, though, like who got the last Mr. Goodbar at Grosso's and who called dibs on the prize in the Cracker Jacks box. We fought over who ran the fastest and whose dad was the strongest and where we wanted to live when we were older — I'd say New York and Stephen would say no, *he* was living there, not me, and that would start a shouting match that made my mom yell at us to keep it down. And our angry words would dissolve into giggles, he'd hide his face in my shoulder and whisper, "You can live there with me, Mike. I was just teasing."

Then came the kiss, which led to more kisses, and touching, and soft lips, grasping hands, probing tongues on smooth flesh ... why couldn't I see how he felt for me? Why couldn't I feel it in his hands, his lips? And why the hell couldn't I have felt the same?

We were friends, nothing more. I should've put a stop to anything that might have misled him but to be honest, I loved the attention, I loved the feel of another's body against mine. I didn't know many other boys, one or two in high school but those encounters were brief and skittish, both of us too nervous to do more than make out in an unlit parking lot. Hot hands on an aching dick, hot breath against my face, mutual masturbation and it didn't matter to me if I ever saw the guy again. There was nothing special about the boys I knew in back home, nothing out of this world, nothing phenomenal.

True, I didn't find that until Dan, but with Stephen there was at least a little bit of understanding between us, an affection so deep from the time we shared that, while not *love*, filled that need easily enough. I liked his kisses, his hands, his lips and tongue and the way he always touched me, tentative and almost unsure, as if I were a fragile dream that he didn't want to shatter. Why couldn't I feel that same trepidation, that same awe?

If only you told me last time, I think. I lie on my back on the bed, stare at the ceiling and pretend these aren't tears that trickle down the sides of my face. Dan's still on the other side of the door — every now and then he jiggles the knob but he doesn't say my name, he knows I'm not going to answer. "Go away," I've told him, but he doesn't listen. I really don't expect him to.

Five years ago, the last time I was here, after Matthew? I would have killed to hear Stephen, *anyone*, say he loved me, and if he told me then, I might have listened. I know I don't feel the way he does for me, I don't feel for him the way I do for Dan, but at that time, if he told me? I might have given him a chance. If he had only said something then ... we've shared too much together over the years. There is *some* feeling there. I could have made it love.

So now it's his fault.

It's easier to think that, to blame him. If he had only said something a few years ago, given me some indication of what went through his mind when we were together ... *then what?* I ask myself. *You would've left that summer and promised to keep in touch, the way you always did, but you were in school, Michael, you wouldn't have stayed here. This town is too small for you, it always has been and for all the daydreams you've had of moving up here one day, you know you could never stay in a place like this. You'd stifle. You'd die. You need the large city to lose yourself in. Sure, if Stephen said he loved you then, you might have tried your hand at a long distance relationship. But you need a man strong enough to hold onto you, you need physical reassurance, you need tangible love. You need Dan* — "Michael?"

My lover's voice is muffled through the closed door. I can't help it if Stephen didn't tell me how he felt sooner — I can't keep apologizing simply because I don't feel the same.

I need Dan.

When he calls my name again, I push myself out of the bed and unlock the door. The next time he jiggles the knob, it turns easily in his hand and as he steps inside, I have to look away from the concern and love I see in his wounded eyes. "Do you want to tell me what's going on?" he asks, closing the door behind him on the rest of the world.

To be honest, I don't want to talk about it. "Nothing," I mumble. I sit on the edge of the bed, my head in my hands, and tell myself I have a headache.

Only it's not my heart that hurts this bad. I don't want to believe that I just lost my oldest friend.

"Michael," Dan starts.

I'm not up for it. "Not now," I snap.

My fingers dig into my cheeks — I don't need to look up to know that now I've hurt *him*, too. I should really go back to bed, start this day all over again, maybe it'll go right this time. Or hell, redo last night while I'm at it, keep away from that rum and stay out of the living room and damn, never leave the side of the creek or the safety of my lover's arms. I want him now, I want him holding me, I want his kisses and his hands to tell me everything's going to be alright. Why can't someone tell me everything's going to be alright?

But he stands there like a sentinel, watching me, and I can't take back what I've just said, I can't erase the tone of my voice that still echoes in my ears. "I'm sorry," I whisper, face in my hands. "God, Dan, I'm — I didn't mean ..." I trail off with the hope that he'll say it's okay.

He doesn't. "Please," I sigh. I look up at him through splayed fingers and have to look away again, I can't bear the pain I see in his face, pain *I've* put there. "Baby —"

"What's your problem today?" he wants to know.

It's a simple question, asked without malice, without reproach. But it's the words themselves, *your problem*, that set me on edge. "My problem," I say softly. Anger bubbles up in me, *my* problem. Is that all my emotions are to him? I lash out without thinking of what I'm going to say — the words surprise me. "Well, you know Dan, maybe if you had decided to come in and meet Stephen yourself, you'd know what the hell my problem is now."

A muscle in his jaw twitches. "I was on my way," he tells me, the tension between us palpable when he speaks. "I had to wash up first —"

I interrupt him with a quick laugh that startles us both. "Maybe it's just me," I mutter, "but if you had an old boyfriend show up out of the blue? I'd be right there the whole damn time."

"I didn't know he was a boyfriend," Dan says. I hear the anger growing in his own words. "Shit, Michael. I didn't think I had anything to worry about. If you just waited a few more minutes —"

"It doesn't matter anyway." I glare at a spot on the floor by his shoes and tell myself it doesn't matter at all, a few minutes one way or the other. The fact is that Dan didn't meet him. He was too damn busy doing something else much more important and I don't care if he met Stephen or not. *Though if he were there*, my mind whispers, *would Stephen have said he loved you? Would you feel this shitty now if Dan had been in the room, too?*

So what, now it's *his* fault? Jesus.

He waits for me to say something else but I'm not apologizing again — I pick at the pleat ironed into my jeans and wait for *him* to speak, I'm not the only one here who has to say he's sorry. Dan props his hands up on his hips and watches me, his gaze unwavering. Finally he asks, "Well? Are you going to tell me what he said or do I have to guess?"

Guess, I almost say — I'd like to hear what his reply would be but I bite the word back before I let it go. *He said he always loved me ...* I can still hear Stephen's voice in my head, I can see his eyes when I close mine. *He said he probably always will. Tell me what I'm supposed to say to that, Dan. Tell me how I'm supposed to feel now.*

With a defeated sigh, Dan asks, "Michael? Baby, talk to me."

It's the *baby* that gets to me. "Why didn't you at least stop in to say hi?" I want to know. Tears clog my throat but I swallow them down, hide them away. I'm through with crying, I'm sick of it — emotion chokes me as I tamp it down, and I imagine my stomach roiling beneath the sadness, as sour and bitter as terrible medicine. I'm sick of this emptiness inside of me, this hole in my chest that opened up Saturday night and still hasn't completely closed yet. I feel like my heart has been ripped out, and the leaves that fall from the trees outside now fill the hollow space in my soul, my bones, dead leaves like those littering the ground. They rustle in me when I walk, they crinkle together like torn paper when I move. I want to rake them up into a large pile, tie them up into bags and set them on the curb, let someone come and take them away. I don't need their insidious whispers, their dying breath. I don't need their pain, their ache. Take away the autumn in me, someone *please*, and let the winter come, let the snow cover my hurt, a silent shroud to hide behind until I thaw again.

If Dan hears the crisp rustle of the leaves, he doesn't say anything. He doesn't come over to me, doesn't wrap his arms around my shoulders, doesn't pull me into a strong embrace. He just stands there, waiting. For what, me to come to him? I need him now, can't he see that? I need him to love me, I need his words to drown out Stephen's, his lips to erase the thin press of my friend's mouth still caught in the corner of mine. I'm not strong, he *knows* this. I need him to tell me I didn't just throw away the last bit of Sugar Creek that meant anything to me. First Aunt Evie, then Stephen. After the funeral on Wednesday, I have no reason to come back here ever again.

So who do I blame for that?

"I was in the middle of something," he says softly. I look up and take in the set of his chin, the thin line his lips make, the hard glint to his eyes. Like he's mad at me. Like he has *reason* to be. "I was on my way, babe. I had to finish up —"

"What?" I want to know. I can't keep my voice from rising dangerously, until it fills the room and threatens to crush us both. "What's so goddamned important that you can't take two minutes to come meet an old friend of mine?"

Dan's reply is steady and even, calm in the face of my anger. He enunciates clearly, as though I might miss something if he speaks too quickly, and he wants me to catch every word. "I was helping your father."

My dad, of course. "It takes you that long to change a fucking lock?" I ask, pissed.

Confusion crosses his face. "What are you talking about?"

"This morning," I remind him. I can't believe he's forgotten about that already. "What, four hours ago? I'll be right up, isn't that what you said?" He frowns at me, scuffs his shoe on the carpet, looks away. Yeah, he knows exactly what I'm talking about. "If you were upstairs with me," I point out bitterly, "like you were *supposed* to be, then Caitlin wouldn't have had to hunt you down, would she? And you wouldn't be standing here wondering what the hell was said because you would've been right there beside me the whole damn time."

I'm pushing him too far, I can see it in his eyes — there's only so much he can take from me, and this is just about it. His face reddens, his cheeks flush, his mouth disappears into a white line of anger that will take the rest of the night to smooth away, if we stop now. But my mind whirls with emotions, my thoughts are torn to shreds in the storm, I'm not quite finished here yet. "You're not his son, Dan!" I yell, surging to my feet. Dimly I'm aware of the door opening behind my lover and faces pressed into the crack, Aunt Bobbie and Caitlin and little Trevor, all watching us, listening to us fight. I don't care. "You're here for me, *babe*, in case you forgot that little fact, and sure, it's nice that you want to help out but Dad can change his *own* goddamn locks, he has an army of uncles at his command. You're not one of his soldiers here, Dan." Fresh tears fill my eyes but I blink them away, I will *not* cry, I won't *let* this get to me. Lowering my voice, I turn away from him and mumble again, "You're supposed to be here for *me*."

If he touches me now, I'd fall into him gratefully. I'd lock the door and apologize the only way I know how, with hands and lips, me in him and him beneath me, I'd show him how sorry I am with each touch, each kiss. But he stands his ground and I don't go to him, I tell myself I can be stronger than that, if just this once. I pretend that I can be strong without him.

Softly, so low that I almost don't believe I've heard him at first, he asks, "What did he *say* to you?"

So we're back to that. "I told you, nothing," I growl, wiping at my eyes.

"Nothing," he echoes.

"Nothing important," I amend with a sigh. I've had enough of this. I want to lie down and sleep everything away. Maybe when I wake up, things will be back to normal. I'll have a tighter rein on my emotions, I'll have some semblance of control over this whole situation, if I can just lie down for a half hour, that's all I'm asking for here. Thirty minutes to myself, is that too much? "Just ... just leave me alone, will you? Please?"

Now he touches me, but I shrug his hand off my arm and that angers him, I can feel his ire rise from him like deadly radiation. I *never* turn him away. "Michael," he tries. When I cross my arms in front of my chest and refuse to meet his gaze, he pinches my elbow, hard, trying to get some reaction out of me. I've pushed him too damn far. "Michael," he says again.

I still don't answer. With a jerk of his hand, I stumble into him and he grabs my arms, both of them, squeezes until I'm forced to look at him, to *see* him, and the anger in his face, the pain I've put there. He's close to tears himself — I can see myself faceted in those stormy eyes. When he speaks, his voice breaks. "Talk to me," he pleads. "What did he say, Michael? And don't you *dare* say nothing."

"Let go of me," I snarl. I try to twist out of his grip and can't. "Dan —"

"What the hell did he do to you?" he wants to know. He peers at me through angry tears and demands, "What's happened to my Michael?"

This time when I pull away, he lets me go. "I'm right here," I grumble.

He narrows his eyes in disbelief. "The man I love talks to me," he says, rubbing at my wrist, trying to open me up to him. I don't respond. "The Michael *I* know tells me what's wrong and lets me make it right. He doesn't keep me out. He doesn't make me fucking *guess* what the problem is."

"I don't feel like talking about it," I say. "Is that such a hard concept to grasp here, Dan? Just leave me the hell alone."

Taking a step towards me, until we're so close that his shirt tickles the hair on the back of my arms, Dan gets in my face like I'm one of the cadets at boot camp and he's a drill sergeant out to whip me into shape. I can't move, can't breathe, can't do anything but stare up into his livid eyes and wonder how things got this far. "I'm going outside," he whispers, his words as gentle as fingers on my face. "I've got work to do. Whenever you're ready to let me back in, you let me know. I'm not fighting with you over this, Michael. I'm not going to let you fight with me."

He holds my gaze a moment longer, then turns on one heel with a fluid precision that would make even the Commander-in-Chief proud. *Oh no, you're not leaving me,* I think, incredulous, as I watch him do just that.

When he yanks the door open and pushes out into the kitchen, my sister tumbles into the room and glares at me. *He did NOT just walk out in the middle of this.* The thought paralyzes me. "Smooth move, Ex-Lax," Caitlin mutters.

"Get the fuck out," is my only reply.

25: It's All Been Done Before

I N MIDDLE SCHOOL, I had a friend named Joey Kneesi, pronounced *ka-nee-see*. I thought it was a wicked cool name at the time, and to be completely honest, that was one of the main reasons we *were* friends — just so I could holler down the halls between classes, "Ka-*nee*-see!" It made people stop and heads turn, and kids moved out of my way as I barreled towards his locker, right next to mine. Knapp, Kneesi ... we were destined to be best friends throughout the rest of the school year.

His dad was in the Air Force, just transferred from Watertown, New York, and Joey didn't know a soul in Colonial City, Virginia. As a seventh grader at the middle school, I didn't know many of my new classmates, either — the last six years were spent in a small elementary school, and the junior high was the first time I met kids from other parts of the city. I felt lost and alone and afraid, though I tried not to show it. I figured that if Ray could make it through the living hell of junior high a few years ahead of me, then it couldn't be *too* hard for me to survive.

I met Joey the first week of classes. He wore baggy jeans that were all the rage up north but hadn't quite found their way down to our part of the country yet, and I could hear whispers of the other kids preceding him down the hall. When I turned and saw him for the first time — jeans hanging down his hips, oversized jersey, bandanna wrapped around his head gangsta-style — I almost laughed. But one look at his face and I could see that he heard the stifled giggles, the low whispers. Each one was a barb that stuck to him, an arrow that pierced his tough exterior and wounded him. He kept his head up, his face expressionless, but I could see the pain behind his eyes and I knew that look of impassive, stony defiance all too well. This *was* middle school, and I was already hearing rumors about the way my gaze lingered a little too long on some of the other boys when we changed out for PE. I ignored those comments the same stoic way Joey ignored the murmurs about his clothes.

He stopped at the locker next to mine and looked at me, and in that instant we recognized each other as fellow outcasts. I gave him a half-smile that he didn't quite return, and with a nod at his jeans, told him, "I saw a pair like that I wanted this summer in Philly."

Now he grinned. He had a large mouth, olive skin, dark hair cut into spiky bangs that stood up in a spray above his forehead, gravity-defying strands dyed a bright blonde that I envied, and he spoke like an Italian from New York *should*, saying *yous guys* and *pop* instead of *soda*, ordering a *pie* when he wanted a pizza. In the months that followed we became fast friends, and I have to admit that I had it bad for that boy, one of the worst crushes I've ever had on a straight guy — I was so far gone that I'd even listen to him ramble on about girls he knew back home, anything to watch the way his mouth worked as he talked in that forced Brooklyn accent of his. On weekends we'd hang out at the mall and I'd watch him flirt with the high schoolers who worked at the clothing stores. At night I dreamed that I worked in those stores and he came in just to flirt with *me*.

But he never knew I liked him like *that* — I wasn't so sure of myself back then. I didn't have the guts to actually come out and tell him, what would I say? That just thinking about him was enough to get me hard? That I moaned his name when I jerked off in the shower? I'd die if he even *guessed* what his touch did to me, how I lived for the casual arm draped around my shoulders, the smiles he saved for me, the way his eyes sparkled when he laughed at something I said. No, I'd rather have any little part of him that I could get than tell him I wanted more and risk losing him completely.

But we only had one year of friendship that burned as bright and fleeting as a candle caught in a draft. At the end of the school year, his dad got orders to ship out. This was just temporary duty for him, one stop before the family flew overseas for an extended tour in Korea. One of the hazards of living so close to a military base — every year there were new faces in the classrooms, and familiar friends simply disappeared over the summer, never to be heard from or seen again. When Joey told me he was leaving at the end of May, my young heart broke for the first time, and the fact that he didn't even know how I felt for him made it hurt worse.

He promised to write. And he did, for a little while, but over time his letters grew shorter and shorter, and reading about all the pretty girls he was meeting didn't have quite the same appeal as watching him flirt or listening to his stories, and somewhere along the way, we drifted apart. The time between letters grew longer — he forgot to write as frequently, maybe, or I forgot to write back so fast, and I moved onto other boys, I grew up and went to college, I met Dan. I don't know what ever became of Joey, to be honest, and I'm sure he never even thinks of me. We were friends for one precious year, that was it, though at the time I was convinced it would simply be a matter of time before he opened his eyes and saw in me the look of love staring back.

After he moved, my smile was forced, my laughter strained. I couldn't call Joey up the way I did during the school year, both of us sitting in separate living rooms with the televisions tuned to the same channels, giggling over the same programs as if we were watching them together. Korea was too far away for a phone call like that. But the day before we left for our annual trip to Sugar Creek, I got his first letter — a few sheets of air mail stationary folded into an envelope with red and white lines around the edges, Joey's block writing so dark that I could hold the envelope up to the light and read his words right through the thin paper. But it was a *letter*, it was proof to me that we were still friends, and I couldn't stop talking about it. All the way up to Sugar Creek, I thought of a million different things I would tell him when I finally sat down to reply. When we got to Aunt Evie's, I told everyone about him, my friend in Korea, which at that time sounded exotic and faraway. Among my cousins, I pulled out the letter and grinned as everyone *ooh*ed over the postmark but I wouldn't let them touch the envelope. It was *mine*. He wrote it to *me*.

Later that first day, I met Stephen at the elementary school playground. It was halfway between my house and his, and he was on the swings waiting for me when I walked up. Sitting in the swing beside his, I pulled out the letter but didn't get quite the breathless response that I anticipated. "What's that?" he asked, dubious.

"Joey wrote to me," I replied. "He's in Korea now. His dad —"

Stephen pushed his glasses up on his nose and frowned at the envelope in my hand. "Joey who?"

None of my cousins had thought to ask me that. "Kneesi," I said. "He went to my school."

Stephen's frown deepened. "Why did he write you a letter?" he asked.

"He moved," I explained, sure that it was just a matter of minutes before Stephen clued into what this meant to me and grew impressed.

But Stephen wasn't reading from the same script. He glared at the letter with sudden jealousy and wanted to know, "Is he your boyfriend?"

This was the summer after our first kiss, so he knew I liked boys, and I had a letter in my hand from a boy I knew back home, of *course* Stephen would put two and two together and assume we were going steady. And I'll admit, the thought was heady, and with Joey so far away, who could call my bluff? So I shrugged a little, fingered the edge of the envelope and, with a shy grin, told him, "I wouldn't call him *that*." There was just enough embarrassment in my voice to suggest that, despite my words, Joey and I *were* dating, and this wasn't just a letter in my hands but a *love* letter, which I clung to desperately and wore tucked in the waistband of my shorts so I wouldn't lose it. "He's sort of just a friend."

Stephen didn't buy that. "The way we're friends?" he asked.

That right there should've told me that he considered us something more. But I nodded, yeah, friends like us. Two guys who hung out together, spent the night over each other's house, talked on the phone and went to the store for candy and rode bikes through the woods, friends like *that*. "He's like my best friend," I told Stephen. I saw the wounded look in his large eyes and amended, "Back home, anyway. You're my best friend here."

"He's your friend the same way I am?" Stephen pressed. When I nodded, he asked, "He kisses you?"

No, I thought, but because I *wanted* him to and he wasn't there to defend his honor, I just shrugged again. *Don't hate me,* I prayed silently. *Please Joey, I didn't SAY it, you know? But if that's what he THINKS ...* what was so wrong with that?

Apparently everything, because Stephen didn't speak again. Instead he pushed his swing slowly, almost thoughtfully, and watched me. Uncomfortable under the scrutiny of his gaze, I turned Joey's letter over in my hands and told him, "He's from New York. Joey Kneesi. It's spelled like knees but you say it *ka-nee*, the way it looks. He's in Korea now —"

"So you said," Stephen interrupted.

I didn't hear the warning in his voice. With a laugh, I describe the way he was dressed the first time we met. "Like he was right out of the city," I said, calling Manhattan *the city* as if I were native. I always liked to pretend that I was more of a northerner than I really was. "I swear his hair never stays down, *ever*. He spends more time on it than any girl does, honest. One time we went swimming at the pool and he refused to get into the water because it'd wash out all his mousse."

Softly, Stephen said, "I don't care."

I thought he meant about Joey's hair, so I tried to think of something else to talk about. "He loves those baggy pants," I said. "You know, the ones yous guys have up here? He says that all the time, *yous guys*. You'd think he was from Philly or something."

"Michael," Stephen sighed. At my quizzical look, he asked, "Is he the only thing you're going to talk about? 'Cause if so, I can leave now. I truly don't want to hear about him."

"Okay," I murmured, chastised.

We sat in silence for a few moments, me lost in thoughts of Joey and what he was doing now on the other side of the world and Stephen staring at the designs his sneakers were making in the dirt beneath his feet. *Something else to talk about,* I thought, though nothing came to mind. Finally Stephen asked, "How'd you do in school this year?"

"Mostly okay," I told him. "I had a D in pre-Algebra but Joey helped me bring it up to a B. He's amazing in that class. All those Xs and Ys, he picks it up like that." I snapped my fingers and gave Stephen a grin he didn't return. "My mom even paid him like five dollars to tutor me, but we really didn't study much."

Stephen jumped up from his swing. "Joey Joey Joey," he cried. "You know what, Michael? I didn't come out here to listen to you go on and on about some boy I don't even know."

The sudden outburst startled me. "Stephen?" I asked. I reached for him but he was already storming across the blacktop, heading for his bike. "Steve, wait. It's not like that —"

He shook my bike off his. "I don't care what it's like," he told me as he straddled his bike and started to pedal away. "Call me if you think of something else to talk about."

Angry tears burned my eyes. I told myself he was jealous, which he probably was — jealous of me with my letter from Korea, jealous of what I had with Joey ... *which is nothing*, my mind whispered, but I didn't listen. I didn't need Stephen Robichaud. Aunt Evie had a whole damn *house* full of kids my age, I didn't need anyone else.

That lasted three days. The first night, I watched a movie with Ray and wished Stephen was there to watch it, too, because *Star Wars* was his favorite. The second day I picked up the phone to call him before I remembered we weren't speaking to each other, and that night I couldn't sleep for wondering if my friend thought of me. By the third day, Joey's letter had become crumpled, its appeal worn thin. Before noon, I dialed Stephen's number and didn't let myself think — when the ringing stopped, I took a breath deep enough to let everything I had to say ramble out. "Stephen, I'm sorry, I didn't mean what you thought I meant, he wasn't my friend the way you are, I promise, I never did anything with him and I want you to come over here now, I put the letter away, please come over and I said I'm sorry so can we just forget about it now? Because I was just kidding, we weren't like *that* —"

Only it was Stephanie's voice that filled my ear, not Stephen's. "Like what, Michael?" she asked. My blood froze in my veins and I almost dropped the phone. With a malicious giggle, she said, "Oh please, don't stop now, it's just getting good."

I slammed the phone down, my hand trembling. *Oh shit, what did I say?* I couldn't remember, my mind was blank. Did I mention the kisses? The way Stephen touched me sometimes? My God, did she *know?*

When the phone rang, I jumped. It was her, I just *knew* it, calling to tease me, I'd never live that down. It rang again, a third time, a fourth before Aunt

Evie came into the hall, wiping her hands on a washcloth and frowning at me. "Michael?" she asked. "You just going to watch it ring, honey?"

I picked the receiver up, put it to my ear, listened for ... "Michael?" Stephen's voice this time. "Stephanie, are you sure it was him? What did he say? Mike, are you there?"

"I'm sorry," I whispered, well aware of Aunt Evie hovering nearby. "For everything, Stephen. Just come over here, okay? I won't — I'm not ... just come over. Please."

His reply? "I'm on my way."

It was that easy to mend our friendship after Joey Kneesi. But now? Could I call him up and apologize, would that make everything better between us? I have a feeling I could say I was sorry until my dying breath, and still nothing would change. There was too much hurt in Stephen's eyes when Caitlin mentioned Dan, too much sorrow in the way he pressed his lips to mine. How can I possibly put those emotions into words to explain to my lover what I'm feeling now? The pain in my old friend's face, pain *I* put there, how can Dan understand that without seeing it for himself?

Why didn't he come sooner?

I didn't think I had anything to worry about, isn't that what he said? And that wasn't the issue at *all*. I simply needed someone there with me, I needed *Dan*, and he didn't come. He was too damn busy helping my father that he couldn't spare a thought for me.

I don't feel like going back upstairs, so I close the door to the back room and lock it for good measure, then sit down on the floor. I'll clean this room and stay away from everyone else for a little while, just until this feeling of quiet desperation disappears. Maybe I *could* apologize to Stephen, try to get back the innocent friendship we had before the first kiss ...

But I don't remember his phone number. For some reason, that makes me sad, it brings everything home. He's gone to me now. I might see him at the funeral but after that, there will be nothing more. I can't call him because I've lost his number over the years, I can't just pick up the phone and dial it from memory anymore. It's gone.

And Dan doesn't understand, because he wasn't there, he doesn't know how we were together, he didn't realize that there might have been something between us that I didn't want brought up today. If he had been a few minutes sooner, that's all, then Stephen would have never said he loved me and I wouldn't be sitting here now, remembering each kiss, each word, each touch. If he had come just a little bit quicker, then maybe the three of us would have gone out for a drive, we'd be laughing together now, we wouldn't each be alone with our separate hurts, our individual pain. Any other time I call him, he comes running, except when I need him the most.

He's outside now, waiting for me to come to him. *Well*, I think, *you know what? You're just going to have to wait.* Furiously I start on the closet, tearing through boxes and bags, sorting through old clothes and records and books, anything to keep me busy and occupy my mind.

26: Just Trying to Help

THE AFTERNOON PASSES in a blur. I work hard to keep my mind blank, my heart empty — I concentrate on filling boxes with old books and trinkets and clothes, I pile up bags with broken toys and scratched records and torn magazines that should have been thrown away years ago. If there's anything I want to take home to remind me of Aunt Evie and all the times I spent at Sugar Creek, I'm quite sure it will be in this back room, not in one of the overflowing bedrooms upstairs. This is the room where as a child I came to find something to play with on rainy days, the room full of costumes we could wear year round, a place full of books and music and magazines, coloring books and sketch pads, toys and knick-knacks and everything under the sun, it all wound up back here. And I go through it all, focusing on each item, flipping through each magazine, sur-rounded by memories as warm as summer on my skin ...

A little stuffed cat that I bought one year at Grosso's, spending my whole allowance on it as a gift for Penny. A large hole gaps in one seam now, and the whiskers have been trimmed short — Ray did that, took a pair of scis-sors to half of the stuffed animals in here, and when my mom found out, she spanked him so hard with a yardstick that the wood snapped right in half. I remember him laughing, and eighteen inches of thin plywood went *smack!*, right across his mouth. He had a welt on his cheek for days.

A stack of horror paperbacks that Evie bought for me from a garage sale, back when I was younger and would read anything even remotely scary. I went through these books in one summer, devoured them, sometimes read-ing two in one day. They're quick, nothing spectacular, just a bunch of fluff tucked between the covers, stories about vampires and werewolves and a few true crime serial killers. I only remember a handful of the storylines — as I pick up the books one by one, the plots and characters whirl together in my mind, the equivalent of those outrageous B movies from the fifties. They go back into their paper bag, and the bag goes by the door.

A box full of shot glasses, a collection of Evie's I never understood.

Each tiny glass is wrapped in tissue paper with a date and name written on a strip of masking tape — *08-23-92*, one reads, and below that, *Kenny. 12-25-89, Ray. 01-28-90, Michael.* I open that one, carefully pulling back the tape so I don't tear the tissue paper. Inside is a clear small glass with the state of Virginia etched onto one side, a cardinal and a dogwood tree blossom on the other. I don't remember buying this, or packaging it, or mailing it to Aunt Evie, but the weight feels familiar in my hand, and I can imagine the hug I received as thanks for the gift. Here in the back room, amid the dust I've stirred up, the memories, I choke back a sob as I feel warm arms envelope me. I swear I smell gardenia, Evie's favorite scent. My heart threatens to burst in my chest.

I have to get out.

Out into the kitchen, where Aunt Lennie stands in front of the sink, shirt sleeves pushed up to her elbows and hands plunged into thick, soupy water that stinks of bleach. She looks at me through frazzled bangs and, without a word, goes back to scrubbing what looks like the glass housing of the porch light. A thin black scum crusts the water, dead bugs and flies, I presume. Better her than me. I would've hosed the thing off and called it done.

Boxes and bags line the wall beside the door to the back room, things I've put there just to get them out of my way. The bags are trash — I lug them two at a time outside, where the sun slants low across the yard now, dusk approaching. By the shed, the trash cans are overflowing and the garden is bare now, the dead plants pulled up and bagged, the leaves that once littered the ground raked up or swept away. I make one trip, two, and the third time I start across the yard, a bag in either hand, I feel someone's gaze on me. I turn to see Dan watching through the railing of the porch, hammer in one hand and a mouthful of nails. I almost stumble at the look in his eyes, unreadable even after our ten months together.

I throw the bags with the others by the shed, then head back for the house, my head down, though I can't keep from stealing glances at my lover as I approach. I could say I'm sorry now and things would be mended between us — it'd be that easy. I could lean over the railing and plant a quick kiss on the top of his head, feel the stubble of his crew cut tickle my nose, tell him I love him and everything would be alright. I *do* love him. Just because I'm a little ticked that he didn't drop everything and come running to meet Stephen doesn't mean it's over between us. I just need some time to get past it, that's all.

So I don't stop, I don't smile, I don't even meet his eyes — every time he looks at me, I look away. The screen door slaps shut behind me and if I had more trash to take out, I'd leave it for now, I don't want to go back outside and feel him watching me, an almost silent plea to open up to him. One more trip and I probably *would* apologize, drop the bags at the shed and race around the porch steps to where he stands, wrap my arms around his waist, hug him close to me and rest my head between his shoulder blades, feel each breath he takes as intimately as if it's one of my own. But not yet. I'm not quite ready to let go of this anger yet.

Anger directed towards him, though he did nothing. *Because* he did nothing, maybe. Anger at Stephen for taking my heart in his hands and squeezing, the same way I must have twisted his own all these years. Anger at myself because I was too damn blind to think that we were never more than friends, and hell, for somehow blaming Dan for all that.

No, I'm not ready to forgive yet. But not Dan — myself.

The boxes I've filled are still by the door to the back room. One by one I carry them through the kitchen and down the hall, out onto the front porch where other boxes have been stacked into pyramids waiting to be hauled away. Oversized bags full of old clothes and bedding hem in the piles like sandbags to hold back a rising tide, and kids crawl over everything, scavengers digging for treasure in all this trash. Most of them are my cousins but a few I'm not so sure about — Sugar Creek is small enough that the news of Aunt Evie's passing has spread like wildfire, and some of the children going through the boxes of books and toys are definitely no relation to us. I have half a mind to shoo them away, but I suspect they'll just run out of reach, hover around like gulls until I disappear inside, then circle back again for more. The only thing that keeps me quiet is the thought that Evie would have let them stay.

But by the time I'm down to my last box, the others have been torn open by over-eager kids, paperbacks and magazines passed around like artifacts from a lost era. I'm sick of this. "Get out of there," I say, swatting at a little girl rummaging indiscriminately through Evie's shot glasses. I drop the box in my arms onto the floor and snatch an unwrapped glass from another kid, a mean-looking boy who glares at me with Stephanie Robichaud's angry eyes. "Do you belong here?" I ask him. He doesn't reply, just gives me that sullen look and has the audacity to stick his hand in the box for a second glass. "Hello?" I slap his hand away and give the kid a shove for good measure. He looks too much like his mother, like *Stephen*, and right now I don't need to be faced with him. "What are you, deaf? Get the hell out of here."

From behind me, someone whistles low. I turn to find my sister standing there, arms crossed, face hardened in her perpetual pout. "Picking on the little kids now, Michael?" she asks, venom in her voice. Our cousin Trevor clings to her jeans and stares up at me with those wide eyes. "Jeez, you're out to piss off everyone today, aren't you?"

"Shut up," I growl. When the little Robichaud brat makes another move for the box, I kick him in the shin. "Damn, you're as relentless as your momma." His scowl deepens but I don't care. "Go on," I taunt. "Tell her I said that. You tell her Michael Knapp called her a —"

Caitlin smacks the back of my head before I say anything I might regret. "You know what your problem is?" she tells me, pushing her way between me and the kid. "Go on, Adam. Go play somewhere else, will you? Just until Mr. Dumbass here gets his shit together and leaves."

The boy stares balefully at me and I know he's going to echo her words when he opens his mouth, so I pinch his cheeks with one hand to keep him quiet. "Don't you dare," I tell him. His expression doesn't change and I squeeze harder, until his lips pucker like a fish and his skin turns white beneath my fingers.

"Let him go, Mike." My sister claws the back of my hand, fingernails scratching into my skin. "Michael, let go. If you don't …"

With a slight shove, I release Adam and he steps back, away from me. He looks at Caitlin with eyes I swear I've seen before, eyes like Stephen's, and I hate that. "Go on," she tells him, and as he stumbles away, she mutters to me, "Just because you broke his uncle's heart doesn't mean you have to hurt him, too."

"Shut the hell up," I tell her. I don't need her to remind me of the pain I saw in my friend's eyes before he left.

But Caitlin doesn't know when to stop. As I wrap the shot glass up again in the torn tissue paper, she nudges me with her shoulder and asks, "So have you patched things up with Dan yet?"

"That's none of your business," I say, and it isn't. I busy myself with straightening the glasses in the box, counting them to keep from looking at my sister and the reproach I don't want to see in her eyes. What's it to her if Dan and I aren't quite back to normal yet?

Apparently everything. Not taking the hint, she plops down on a nearby bag with a rush of air from the plastic and reclines back on the boxes. Trevor stands at her side like a servant, watching me. Jesus, but that kid's *always* watching me anymore. "You know what your problem is?" my sister asks. I'm sure I don't want to know what she thinks my problem is, but she's going to tell me anyway. She picks at the tissue paper even as I smooth it down, and I have to swat her hand away as if she's just another one of the kids looking through all this old stuff. "You," she tells me, pointing at my chest, "need to get laid. A mind-blowing fuck, it'll straighten you right out. So just march around the house and tell that hot boy of yours that you're sorry so he can freak you silly —"

"I'm going to tell Mom you said that," I threaten. The last thing I need is love advice from my little sister — sixteen! — of all people. When another urchin reaches into the box of shot glasses, I lift the whole thing up out of reach and start for my car. That's it — I've decided I'm taking these home.

Unfortunately Caitlin follows me, Trevor trailing behind her like a lost puppy. "You ain't gonna tell her," she says, the hint of a challenge in her voice. Then, raising her voice to mimic mine, she squeals, "Momma, Caitlin said a bad word!"

With a lusty sigh, I juggle the box in one hand as I dig into my pocket for my keys. "Don't you have someone else to bother?"

"Nope," she answers brightly. "Today's your lucky day."

I can't think of anything to say to that, so I don't. Instead, I ignore her as I open the trunk of my car and set the box inside, careful not to jostle the glasses. I'm thinking I'll take the records, too — who else will want them? And the turntable, though there were no needles when I checked, so I can't actually *listen* to the records, but at least I'll have them. Though Dan might ask me why I bothered to take them at all, and I don't have an answer for that … "Michael," Caitlin says, interrupting my thoughts. She leans down into the trunk before I can close it and move on. Her eyes are serious, almost severe rimmed in that black eyeliner she favors. "Listen. Okay, so I'm not Dear Abby, but you're being a real jerk, not to put too fine a point on it, and I really think you should just —"

"Don't you ever let up?" I ask, incredulous. Before she can reply, I nod at Trevor and ask, "Where's the rest of your posse?"

She frowns at me. "Emily is Trevor's older sister," she explains, "and she's at that age where she can't stand him. As long as he's around, she's not, so he's my new best friend. Don't try to change the subject. You're not listening to me."

I take her arm and pull her gently away from the car. "I *am* listening," I assure her, slamming the trunk shut. "Emily doesn't like Trevor so you're using the kid to keep her away. Human pest repellent."

"I'm not talking about *that*," she cries, exasperated, as she twists out of my grip. "Michael, you're an ass and you need to apologize for it."

"Your bitching won't goad me into action," I say. I start across the yard, heading for the house and the other boxes. Maybe I'll take the records. Evie said what matters most to us, right? I can't even begin to count the hours I sat in that back room, listening to the scratchy music on those albums. Maybe that's what I need to remind me of this place when I'm gone …

"Michael," Caitlin tries again. "Dammit the hell! Turn around and *listen*!"

Without warning, I do just that, pivot on one heel to face her, and she smacks right into my chest, she's following that close. "Caitlin," I sigh. Then, because I want her to listen to *me*, I amend, "Cat. Look, I appreciate your concern but what Dan and I argue about isn't any of your business. I'll talk to him when I'm good and ready to, not because you're hounding me to death about it. *Capeche?"*

Her full lower lip starts to pucker out and her chin crumbles in an effort to fight back sudden tears. "I'm just trying to help," she murmurs.

I don't know if I've pissed her off so bad that now she's going to cry about it, or if I've scared her, or what. I'm just not up for this today. *Is it too late to go back to bed?* I think, but one look around at the fading sunlight assures me that there isn't much time left in this day. I can make it a few more hours. I'll be better tomorrow, I tell myself. I have to be.

"Cat," I whisper, looking over my shoulder at the house to make sure no one's watching us. I can just hear my mother now, or my aunts — twenty-five years old and still making my sister cry. The black lines along the bottom rim of her eyes have begun to soften, and when she tries to wipe at them, she gets smudges like coal on her fingers, and black stains the reddened whites of her eyes like ink. "Don't ..." I frown at the makeup and sigh. "Damn, girl, don't cry. It's not a pretty sight."

"Shut up," she mutters. She runs a finger beneath each eye, smearing eyeliner out to her hair. Cat eyes. The thought makes me grin, which only makes her pout harder. "I'm *not* crying."

Yeah, right. "Look," I start, reaching out to touch her arm.

She shrugs my hand away. "You want to ruin the one good thing you've ever had?" she asks me — what, suddenly she knows everything about me, knows Dan's the best man I've ever known? *He is,* my mind whispers. "You think you can just play the diva and that boy out back will wait around until the final act is over? Grow the fuck up already, Michael. I don't know what's crawled up your ass today because you were bitchy before your old friend even stopped by, and I don't know what he said after I left but the way he was looking at you when I *was* there gives me a damn good idea of what got you all worked up." Now one small fist strikes my chest, and Caitlin tries to push me away but she's not strong enough, and her eyes overflow with more tears. "But he's *gone*, Michael," she tells me, "don't you get it? Whatever crap he said to you, he turned around and hauled ass out that door and who's still here? Who came running to comfort you even though you wouldn't let him? Who wanted to talk about it even though you pushed him the hell away?"

Dan. She's right. Stephen said he loved me, true, said he always had, probably always will, but he left. When I needed someone the most, when my emotions threatened to swallow me, when I couldn't see from the pain in my heart and the tears in my eyes, Stephen left. *It was too much for him,* I think. *He was hurting more than I ever could over losing each other and the friendship we once shared. He couldn't stay. To touch me again, to meet Dan, to see the way he knows we must be together, that would have been too much for his heart.*

So he left. And Dan came to me, wanted to hold me, wanted to comfort me and I wouldn't let him. I pushed him away, held him at arm's length, told him to leave me alone. *Just leave me alone ...*

And it took a sixteen year old girl to point it out to me.

I pat her arm and this time she doesn't shrug away. "We'll be alright," I assure her. We will be, this isn't the end. "We'll get through this, Caitlin. *Cat.*" Hoping to make her laugh, I wink and ask, "Whatever doesn't kill you only makes you stronger, right?"

Her eyes narrow into thin raccoon slits. "He's fucking awesome," she grumbles. "If you lose him because you're moping about that geek you used to freak back in the day, hell, *I'll* kill you."

I have to stifle a grin. "Didn't I say it wasn't any of your business?" I ask.

Caitlin glares at me and shoves me away. I stumble back to the house, giggling and giddy for the first time since my dad stole Dan from me this morning.

27: Never Go to Bed Angry

I COULD MAKE it easy on us both and apologize now. Sidle up behind Dan, ease my arms around his waist, rest my chin on his shoulder and blow gently on his neck, my breath cooling his sweat. "I'm sorry, baby," I could say. It would be that simple. He'd turn in my arms and kiss me, and everything would be right again.

Only it *isn't* that simple. From the kitchen door I look out into the back yard, thinking that if Dan is still working on the porch, I'll see him from here, give him a smile, maybe call him inside with a slight nod. That's the plan, at least, but he isn't by the porch any longer, I've waited too long. Now he's at the garden shed with my Uncle Doug, the two of them hefting the full garbage cans into the bed of someone's pickup truck. I could still call to him — he would know what I want. Given my earlier mood, he would probably even take a quick break, fifteen minutes, could Doug wait that long? Long enough for me to pull him into the back room, close the door, let my lips and my hands show him just how sorry I am. If I called out to him, he'd let me start something that I could promise to finish later tonight. He wouldn't leave me hanging.

I step out onto the porch, let the screen door slam shut behind me, lean over the railing and watch my lover. His t-shirt has grown damp, a dark V-shaped stain that spreads from his shoulders to taper down into a point at the small of his back. His pants pull taut across his round ass and along his thighs when he squats by the next trashcan. Muscles stand out in his arms and neck as he lifts the can up onto the tailgate of the truck, and Doug takes it from there. Dan moves to the next can, and the next — there are easily a dozen already in the truck, and twice that amount left to go. I can't interrupt him now.

Before he can notice me on the porch, I go back inside. This time I don't let the screen door slam behind me. I go into our room alone, close the door softly, lock it for good measure. This is all my fault, isn't it? I've alienated everyone today. Lucky me.

Boxes litter the floor of the tiny room, things I haven't finished going through yet, or odd items I didn't know what to do with so I just left them here. A bag half-filled with torn magazines and crumpled paper sits in one corner like a deflated balloon. Old costumes and out of date clothes are strewn across the bed, tossed there as I cleaned out the closet just to get them out of my way. The thought of straightening this room up exhausts me — I just want to lie down on top of all those musty clothes and sleep until tomorrow. I want to feel Dan's arms around me right this second. I want to be anywhere but here, amid the chaos of this house, this family. Is that too much to ask?

Kicking off my shoes, I shove the clothes to the foot of the bed and curl up at the other end, my pillow crammed under my head. *A few minutes,* I tell myself. I'll close my eyes for a few scant minutes, that's all. Then I'll be ready to face the onerous task of putting this room back together again. Dust rises from the clothes when I shift into a more comfortable position and I bury my face in the blankets to keep from choking on the stale odor. Hidden deep in the quilt, I find a small spot that still smells like my lover, warm and sexy, his scent first thing in the morning after a long night wrapped up with me. With a deep breath, I draw him in, hold him in me, only releasing him when my lungs start to ache for air, then take another breath, until I swear all the smell is gone, it's in me now, it's mine. Another deep breath, again, and somewhere between one breath and the next, I fall asleep enveloped by his musky warmth.

Low knocking wakes me up sometime later. It's dark now, the room draped in shade, the boxes phantoms that loom around me. The clock beside the bed reads a little after six, but it's late in the year, it gets dark early. There's a slight chill to the air that raises tiny pimples on my bare arms, and I burrow beneath the blanket, trying to snuggle into the warmth I felt earlier. My head is foggy, unclear.

The knock comes again, and this time the door knob jiggles against the lock. Still groggy with sleep, I reach out with one leg and try to twist the knob with my toes. It doesn't work. "Michael?" a voice comes from the other side of the door. It's Dan.

I sit up, unlock the door, and lie back down as my lover enters the room. The heavenly smell of melted cheese wafts in with him — he carries a pizza box in one hand, two cans of soda in the other, and he doesn't turn on the light as he eases the door shut behind him. In the darkness, I watch him approach the bed, just another shadow. Softly, as if I'm still sleeping, he whispers, "Did I wake you up?"

I shake my head, though he can't see the gesture. Curling the blanket into my fists, I cuddle into it as I scoot back to make room for him to sit beside me. "What's this?" I ask when he sets the pizza box down on the bed. It's hot where it touches my knee.

"Dinner," he explains. He opens the box and heat pours around my legs like dry ice. "They ordered pizzas for everybody. Are you hungry?"

Sitting up, I click on the lamp beside the table and a sudden golden glow surrounds us. The pizza looks amazing in this light, a meal fit for a king, and my stomach growls in anticipation — I haven't eaten all day. "I'm famished," I tell Dan as he digs into the pie. It's covered with gooey cheese and pineapples, my favorite, and I feel like a little kid beside himself with excitement, waiting as he pulls apart the first piece. Because I'm the only one I know in my whole family who likes pineapples on my pizza, I ask, "They ordered this just for me?"

"I did." He tears one piece off and hands it to me, cheese and grease dripping from the tip. "Lean over, baby," he says as I take the slice from him. "You'll get it all over the bed."

"No, I won't," I promise. The first bite is ambrosia, and grease runnels down my chin. I moan at the next bite, a guttural sound that makes my lover grin. "Amazing," I sigh.

We eat in silence. Between the two of us, the pizza is gone in mere minutes, and when we're finished, I move the empty box to the floor. "This room's a mess," Dan says, still speaking low. Neither of us has dared to talk much — I get the feeling that he thinks I'm still angry with him, which I'm not. If I'm mad at anyone, it's myself. But he doesn't ask and how can I just come out and tell him that?

The room, though, that's a safe topic. I stretch cat-like across the bed and land in his lap, my arms crossed over his legs, my head resting on his thigh. "I'm cleaning it up," I assure him. *Don't speak,* I pray, cuddling up against him. *Just keep quiet a little while, baby, let us have this moment without words.*

Dan runs a hand through my hair, his fingers feathering over my ear, down my neck. So soft, that touch, so gentle. I close my eyes again, savoring his hands on me, his warmth beneath my cheek, the sharp scent of his sweat in the dark. "Do you need some help?" he wants to know.

"I've got it," I say. I do, I'm working on this room, he's been outside all day. When he starts to say something else, I cut him off. "Dan, baby, I'll get it straight, I promise. Just let it go."

His hand curls over the ends of my hair — did that sound bad? I didn't mean for it to come off that way, but before I can say anything else, Dan smoothes his fingers down my neck, stroking my skin, relaxing me. I melt beneath his touch. "Your aunts are home," he murmurs — he must mean Billy and Bobbie, back from Morrison's. "I know you probably don't want to talk about that ..."

"I don't," I whisper. My hands fist in his jeans, my fingers dangerously close to his crotch as I dig in. Mentally, I make a list of things I don't want to discuss. The funeral, Aunt Evie's death, Stephen ... I don't want to have to enumerate them or say them out loud. He's my lover, the man I sleep with every night, the man I wake up beside in the morning — some part of me thinks he should already know what things are off limits. He should be able to read into my silences and clue in to what I don't say.

Maybe he does, because he doesn't mention the funeral home again. Instead, his hand rubs the base of my neck, slipping into my shirt between my shoulder blades, his skin warm on mine. "Your sister mentioned another powwow tonight," he says.

"Powwow?" I ask. I get the idea he's simply trying to make conversation and that saddens me. Why can't we just be quiet together? Is our relationship that strained right now, that he feels the need to fill the silence around us with idle chatter?

"In the living room?" Ah yes, one of *those*, and for all the times I spent wanting to join in while growing up, I'm not up for it again, not after last night. I needed the rum to get through Penny's story of how she found Evie ... in a low whisper, Dan tells me, "I don't really think you should go. Unless you want to?"

I press my face against his thigh and shake my head. "I've got to clean up in here," I say — it's as good an excuse as any. "You go, babe."

"Do you want me to?" he asks.

I shrug. "If you want." I realize that's not quite the answer he's looking for, but what can I say? *Don't go, stay here with me* ... how needy would that seem?

I feel his stare and roll onto my back to look up at him, his expression hidden in shadows cast by the lamp. His fingers drift to my face, brush my cheek like cobwebs. "What do *you* want, Michael?" he asks.

I kiss his thumb and sigh. *Stay with me,* I think, but I don't say the words. The room has grown darker, it seems, the lamp absorbing light instead of shining on us, is this just me? What's happening between us? "You can go, Dan," I say. I touch his hand, press it to my face, then turn away. "Don't let me stop you. I have to get this place back together again, that's all."

When he doesn't answer, I sit up and swing my legs over the side of the bed. His touch trails away. I stand, step on the pizza box and stumble over it, almost knock over the canned drinks before I catch myself. "Jesus," I mutter, flicking on the overhead light. Suddenly the shadows are pushed back, tucked into the corners as neatly as folded laundry. "You want to schmooze with the rest of my family?" I ask brusquely. "That's fine with me, Dan, I don't care. We've just spent the whole damn day apart, what's another few hours? Hell, why are you even in here at all?"

Hot tears burn my eyes — what's *wrong* with me? I bend to pick up the smashed box. I don't want him to see me like this. "You can go," I sigh.

"Michael," he starts. He touches my back, *God.*

I hide my face in the crook of my arm and stifle a sob. "Please," I murmur. "Just go."

He takes the empty pizza box from me, one of the soda cans. "I don't like you like this," he announces. I fold my arms around my knees and hunker into myself. I don't like me like this much, either, but I don't tell him that. I don't say anything at all, and he must mistake my silence for apathy because he's pissed now, I can feel his anger. He opens the door and stops — he's watching me, I feel his gaze on my back, a weight pinning me down. "How long is this shit going to last?" he wants to know. "Because I'm getting sick of it. What the hell am I doing here if you won't talk to me, babe? Why won't you let me in?"

"I don't know," I whisper. I don't.

"Figure it out," he says, closing the door softly as he leaves.

I don't want to figure it out just yet. I don't know what's wrong with me, why I can't open up to him, why I can't tell him what I feel inside. What *do* I feel? I don't even know that. My mind is a jumble of emotions and memories, a painting left out in the rain and the colors have run together now, everything is sordid shades of gray. How can I put it all into words to explain it to him when I don't even know what I'm looking at myself? What I'm feeling, or why, or what I'm thinking of anymore? I want a fresh canvas, I want to start anew.

For a few minutes, I stay squatting on the floor, I wait — I'm sure he's coming right back. But he doesn't, and when my legs go numb, I stand and shake the feeling into them again. I need to clean this place up. It'll keep me occupied. As long as I'm busy, I don't have to think, and if I don't think, I don't have to feel.

Though it took me most of the day to make the mess, I manage to get the room put back together again in a couple hours. The boxes I stack together along one wall, the bags propped in front of them — I'll pick up where I left off in the morning. At least now we can walk in the room, and our suitcase isn't buried beneath a ton of crap, the bed isn't hidden under armloads of clothes. When I'm finished, I undress slowly, taking my time just in case Dan is on his way back. I pull off my shirt, my jeans, my socks, turn down the sheets and sit on the edge of the bed, waiting ...

At some point, I turn off the light and crawl beneath the sheets. I leave the lamp beside the bed on for him. I don't want to fall asleep without him, I don't like this. I should have said I was sorry earlier, when he brought me dinner. Why didn't I say anything? Why did I send him away again?

I face the wall, the light at my back, and close my eyes but I'm not really tired. I lie awake and listen to the sounds of the house around me, water in the pipes, a shutter creaking in the wind, low murmurs from beyond my door. Through the wall I can hear talking — the living room is right on the other side — but I can't make out words. Every now and then I hear a loud donkey laugh, *Ray*. I wonder how Dan is faring against my brother. I wonder if he's sitting on the loveseat alone or with Caitlin, thinking of me and wishing I were there, the same way I'm lying here and wishing he were with me.

An eternity later, I hear soft footsteps cross the kitchen floor — the tile by the sink is warped, it squeals when stepped on. A hand on my door, no knock this time, just the gentle twist of the knob and I hold my breath, stare at the wall, don't think. It's Dan, it has to be. No one in this family is as quiet as him.

The door shuts without a sound — the only way I know it's closed is the slight noise of the lock sliding home. A large shadow eclipses the light on my wall, Dan's hand as he turns the lampshade towards him, away from the bed. He thinks I'm asleep.

I hear his clothes hit the floor, and when he rummages through the open suitcase, I glance over my shoulder to catch a glimpse of his bare ass as he steps into a pair of my boxers. His skin is smooth by the lamplight, golden and almost glowing in the close shadows. *So beautiful,* I think, sculpted muscle and flawless flesh, a statue of a young god or an angel. I turn away before he sees me looking.

Getting into the bed, he turns out the light. Then he slides in beside me, his leg brushing mine before pulling away. I should apologize now, bring him into my arms and make love to him, show him just how desperately sorry I am for being … how did my sister put it? For being such an ass today. But it's easier to stay quiet, he thinks I'm asleep, and the longer I wait, the more awkward it is to untie my tongue. Soon I'm afraid I won't have anything left to say to him at all, and then what? Where will we be if I can never talk to him again?

He doesn't touch me and I lie on my side in the darkness, listening to him breathe. I should say something, even just sigh, just to let him know I'm awake. It should be easy now, shouldn't it? Under cover of night, we don't have to look at each other, I don't have to see the hurt or pain in his eyes.

Finally, he sniffles and a tender hand touches my hip beneath the sheets. "Michael?" Dan asks, his voice barely audible over the wind outside. "You awake?"

"Yeah," I whisper. I feel like I did years ago as a child, upstairs with Stephen spending the night, and the two of us would talk quietly beneath the covers long after we were supposed to be asleep. Thinking of him now threatens to tear down the wall I've spent all day building against those memories. I push them away.

My lover's breath tickles the back of my neck as he asks softly, "Are you still mad?"

I think about that. "Yeah," I say again. There's so much tearing me up inside and I don't know if it's anger or not, but it's there. I can't deny it.

"At me?" Dan wants to know.

I shake my head. Because he can't see the gesture, I turn my face into my pillow and mumble, "No."

I don't know if he hears it or not. He's silent for a little while, long enough that I begin to suspect that he's fallen asleep, when he shifts beside me and whispers, "Can I hold you?"

Can I ... the fact that he has to ask hurts my soul. "Please," I choke, and before he can respond, I'm backing up into him, his arms finding their way around my waist with familiar ease. He buries his face into my hair, sighs my name, presses his body tight against mine until we're like two spoons in a drawer, curved together as one. My voice is almost nonexistent as I cover my face with my hands and murmur, "I'm sorry."

"Shh," he replies, nuzzling my neck. He kisses my jaw and with his next kiss, I turn my head so his lips meet mine. When I try to say it again, my words dissolve in his mouth, and I can't seem to find the will to resist his hands on my stomach, my face.

28: Promise of a New Day

A T SOME POINT I wake to kisses, but it's too early and I don't want to get out of bed, so I snuggle into my lover's arms, murmur something incoherent, breathe deep his warm scent. *Just a few more minutes,* I think, unsure if I actually speak the words out loud or not. My arms tighten around his waist, trying to hold him close, keep him with me.

I don't succeed — somewhere between those early morning dream-like kisses and the time I become aware of being fully awake, Dan gets out of bed. I lie curled into blankets that hold his scent and keep my eyes shut as I listen to the house around me, listening for his voice. I still don't want to get up just yet. Maybe if I wait long enough, he'll come back from the bathroom or the kitchen, or wherever it is he's gone off to, and he'll crawl in beside me again, he'll wrap his arms around me, he'll whisper silly nonsense in my ear until I just can't keep my eyes closed any longer and I wake up to more kisses, breathless giggles, my name in his voice. In my mind I hear him ask again, "Can I hold you?" And this time I'm not so tired or worn out, this time I let his kisses lead to something more. Beneath the covers, I trail my fingers up my own stiffening cock as I think of his body next to mine, him in me, his skin as supple and pliant as my own beneath my hands.

I grow hard thinking of his touch. Encircling my shaft, I thrust into my palm and stifle a moan in my pillow. "Dan," I sigh. I need him now. I need him to hold me, I need his hands on mine, his fingers strumming below my balls, slipping inside of me as he kisses me quiet. When's the last time we made love? Not the heated rush when we first arrived in Sugar Creek, not the half-clothed tryst at my parents' house, but a long, luxurious moment just to ourselves, a time when he was the only thing on my mind and I was his only concern. I can't recall the last time we allowed ourselves to simply be *us* — how long has it been? Since I held him for hours at a time, since we cuddled in the bed naked? Not just sex, not just fulfillment or release, but *love*, where nothing else mattered but the man beside us, where the rest of the world disappeared?

God, I don't remember. It's been awhile since we've had that time to ourselves. During the week, we both lead lives too hectic to simply take a moment to enjoy each other. True, we have the evenings together, and Dan's an attentive lover — when he wants me, he knows just how to tell me without a word, and the look he gives me is enough to make me come from anticipation alone. He'll take my hand, lead me to the bedroom, undress me and kiss me and ease down onto me. He'll whisper he loves me, only me, forever me. We fall asleep in each other's arms, we wake together, we *are* love. We're perfect.

Aren't we?

If what we have is so undying, why are we at odds right now? *Because of Stephen*, I think, but that can't be right. He's not a part of our relationship, past lovers have *never* been an issue until now. How can Stephen be at fault here when Dan didn't even meet the guy?

Maybe it's me.

The thought freezes my hand in mid-stroke, numbs my fingers where they're curled around my dick. Maybe it *is* me, this sudden uncertainty between us, this animosity I feel toward no one in particular. It isn't Dan's fault that my oldest friend has always had a crush on me, it isn't *his* fault I probably encouraged those feelings. So why can't I just accept that and move on? I can't live my life and worry about living everyone else's, too. I can't change the fact that Stephen loves me, the same way I can't change the fact that I don't love him in return.

Under the blankets I squeeze myself again, trying to find a slow rhythm, hoping to erase that thought, but I'm not interested in getting off anymore. If Dan came in now, maybe he could slip between the sheets and kiss away my insecurities — I'd tell him exactly what Stephen said and let him convince me that I have no reason to tear myself up over this. If he came in now, maybe he could make everything right again. He could touch me in the same places I'm touching myself, he could keep me aroused, he could take care of this, of *me*. If he came in right now.

But he doesn't appear just because I think he should. I hear his voice, though, a low sound that barely carries in from the kitchen — he must have left the door to our room ajar when he left. He says something I can't make out, then Caitlin laughs, I hear the faint *chink* of silverware on porcelain, *breakfast*. Part of me wonders why he didn't wake me up to eat, but I smother the thought. Dan is just letting me sleep. After my mood yesterday, it's no wonder he doesn't want to disturb me unless absolutely necessary.

So I wait. My hand keeps up its halfhearted motions, a thoughtful kneading, a steady rubbing, just something to do as my mind drifts. I fall back into a sort of waking slumber, a dream-like state where I imagine him coming in,

I feel his hands on my lower belly, my balls. His breath on my face, his lips on my cheek, his fingers ease into me, *my* fingers, I'm doing this myself and dreaming it's him. Above me, laying me back, whispering he loves me even as I lick the words from his lips.

It seems so real that when I open my eyes, I expect Dan to be loving me, kissing my neck and moving within me — that's what my mind sees, what my body feels. I'm disappointed to find myself still alone, my dick throbbing in my hand, my balls aching and sore. For a selfish moment I toy with the idea of calling out to him — he's right in the kitchen, I can hear his voice. Ask him to come here a minute and kick back the covers to expose my thick erection poking through the fly of my boxers. He'll open the door, my name on the tip of his tongue before his throat closes with lust. Will he even be able to find the words to tell Caitlin he'll be right back as he closes the door behind him, locks it to keep the two of us in this tiny room, this small bed?

I decide not to find out. With a few quick thrusts, the deed is finished, my hand covered in my own juices, which I wipe off onto my t-shirt as I climb out of bed. The shirt gets fisted into a tight, embarrassed wad and shoved deep into the bottom of the pillowcase that serves as our laundry bag. The boxers are stripped off, damp with sweat and cum — they join the shirt. I nudge the door shut completely with one foot, lock it for spite, because I know that whoever's out in the kitchen now knows that I'm awake, and if Dan wants to come see me, he's going to have to wait until I'm dressed. *Until I'm good and up,* I think, tugging on a clean pair of underwear, tight and unstretched. Khakis and a thick sweater, socks, shoes, a comb through my hair and a fumbled search for deodorant, a spritz of Dan's cologne because it's right at the top of our suitcase and I like the way he smells on me, and *now* I'm ready to face the world. I'm ready for anything ...

Except Stephen, I amend silently, opening the door. Dan sits at the table with Caitlin, Trevor, my cousin Kenny's Muslim girlfriend. My lover looks up from a plate of scrambled eggs as I step out into the kitchen. *Please, God,* I pray, pushing thoughts of my old friend out of my head, *don't throw something like THAT at me again. I'll make it through the funeral because I have to, but just let Stephen Robichaud keep his distance. The same goes for any other blast from my past You might have hiding up Your sleeve. I'm not here to play a round of "This is Your Life."*

Dan gives me a sunny grin that almost stops my heart, it's so damn beautiful, and the memory of Stephen's sad eyes burns away like fog in the heat of the afternoon. "Hey, baby," my lover says, scraping his chair along the floor as he pushes it back to stand. He takes my hand and gives me a quick peck on the lips which everyone in the kitchen pretends to ignore. Well, everyone except my sister, who watches with arched brows, a cocky look on her face that screams, *I told you so.* I don't meet her smug gaze — I won't give her the satisfaction of thinking she's right.

A squeeze of my hand brings my attention back to Dan. "How are you feeling today?" he wants to know, concern etched into his face like lines of worry or age. "Are you doing better?"

"I'm fine," I assure him.

He frowns, unsure if he should believe me or not. So I say it again, trying on a sincere smile this time, and I lean close enough to catch a brief whiff of his spicy scent, though I'm not sure if that's him or me I smell. "Fine, hon," I say with a kiss in the corner of his mouth. "Honest."

Before I can elaborate, Caitlin pipes up. "What'd I tell you, Mike?" she asks, pushing her eggs around on her plate. "You just needed to get laid to loosen up."

Dull anger hums through me at her careless words. "Don't," I warn as I pull out the chair beside Dan's. Sinking into the seat, I take a piece of toast from my lover's plate to nibble on — suddenly I'm starving.

But Caitlin isn't listening to me. "I'm serious," she says, with a wink at Kenny's girlfriend. To her credit, Neeshi simply stares at my sister, then looks at me, her face a mask of neutrality. Scooping up a forkful of eggs, Caitlin points them at me and says, "A good fuck cures almost everything, I'm telling you. I mean, shit, so what if you guys went at it last night? It's not like anyone can hear you knocking boots all the way down here."

"Shut up," I growl. Dan sits down beside me, his hand finding my knee beneath the table, and it's his strong touch that keeps me from just getting up and walking out of here. I don't want to listen to this. When Caitlin opens her mouth to say something else, I turn to my lover and ask loudly, "Didn't I have this conversation already? The one entitled *I'm not going to talk to my little sister about my sex life*? Because I distinctly remember —"

Under the table, a small foot connects with my shin. Glaring at me, my sister mutters, "Okay, so I was wrong, you didn't get any ass last night. Doesn't mean you have to be one today."

Frowning at Dan, I ask, "Am I being an ass to you?"

For a moment, fear flickers across his face — I'm forcing him to choose sides, something he hates to do. But much as he likes Caitlin, there shouldn't be any question here. He's with me. He's *my* lover. Lives with me, sleeps with *me*. He can be nice to my sister, he can think she's cool and laugh with her and get along great, I don't care, but when push comes to shove and she's trying to make me look like a jerk, he needs to stand behind me.

But he's in rare form this morning, having grown comfortable around my family, and there's an impish gleam in his eye when he gives me a smile so sweet, my teeth hurt to see it. "Not to *me*," he says.

Across the table, Caitlin snickers into her plate. "Just in general," I amend. "Am I an ass today?"

"Not today," he replies. This time Neeshi giggles, and beside Caitlin, Trevor looks around the table, a silly, uncomprehending grin on his face. He doesn't know what we're going on about, I'm sure, but hell, everyone *else* is laughing at me, why shouldn't he?

"Dan," I sigh. "I'm talking about —"

He squeezes my knee to let me know he's just teasing as he says, "I thought we weren't talking about your ass in front of your sister."

I feel an ignoble pout tug at my lips, which I try to hide by stuffing the rest of his buttered toast into my mouth as they laugh at me. "I'm not talking about my ass," I mutter. I *hate* being picked on, and by my lover, of all people! In front of my sister, too. I'll never live this down.

A melodic voice speaks up from the head of the table — Neeshi, surprisingly. "It's alright, Michael," she says.

I pout harder. At least there's someone here on my side. "Thank you —"

"You have quite a nice ass," she interrupts, and Caitlin, Dan, even Trevor erupt in fresh giggles.

In her soft voice, the word sounds almost decadent, *ass*, and with all of them laughing, it takes every ounce of strength I have to keep the frown on my face. "I'm telling Kenny you said that," I threaten. "What's he going to say when he knows you're checking out my ass?"

"Who's talking about your ass?" Ray asks as he stumbles into the kitchen, still half-asleep.

I look up at my brother, dressed in a t-shirt and boxers so thin, they're almost obscene. Neeshi and Caitlin exchange a glance, then cover their mouths with their hands and giggle like schoolgirls, but I'm not sure if the laughter is directed at me or Ray. Either way doesn't seem to care — he opens the refrigerator, bends over to lean inside, his shorts threatening to split across his scrawny ass. In the fridge, he yawns with a leonine roar that sets the girls off again. If I were closer, I'd slap his butt, hard enough to make him jump, and then I'd be in on the laughs, too. I even push my chair back, I could stretch behind Dan and still get in a good smack, but before I can reach out Ray stands, milk carton in one hand. When he sees me I play it off, stretching my arm around my lover's shoulders and smiling at the distrust on my brother's face. "What?" I want to know.

He looks from me to my sister, then back at me again, but I think it's the smirk on Dan's face that makes him uneasy. "Who's talking about your ass?" he asks. As we laugh, he glares at me like I'm the one who started it. *Actually,* I think, *as long as they aren't laughing at me anymore ...* Ray opens the carton and frowns in at the milk. "You know," he starts, but that's as far as he gets because he can't think of anything witty or quick to say, and that makes us laugh harder. "You guys suck."

Actually, I know how he feels, but I'm glad they've moved away from teasing me and are onto him now. In a rare burst of sympathy, I tell my brother, "You know we're just playing around. If we didn't like you, we wouldn't bust on you so bad."

"Yeah we would," Caitlin says.

Ray glares at me as if *that's* my fault, too. "What?" I ask, standing. "I didn't say it. How much milk is left?"

"You didn't *have* to say it," Ray mutters, and before I can say anything else, he tips his head back and guzzles down what's left in the carton.

Milk courses down the corners of his mouth like cum, trickles down his chin, down his throat. He's watching me stare at him, and I swear the corners of his lips are pulled into a faint smile, he's *enjoying* this. "There better be another carton in there," I tell him, pissed. "Hell, Ray, I was being *nice*."

"All gone," he says, wiping his arm across his mouth. He *is* grinning, the fucker.

A dozen scenes flit through my mind, me pinning him to the fridge, cramming that damn carton down his throat ... my hands curl into fists just picturing the pain I could cause him. "That was damn rude," I growl.

With a shrug, my brother crumples the carton up in his hands, splattering milk on his shirt, his legs, the floor. I jump back to keep from getting sprayed. "Ray! You fucking slob!" I punch him in the shoulder, hard. When he tries to hit back, I pull a Caitlin and pop him again. "Clean this shit up."

"Shut up," he mutters, but he knows I'm right — if one of our aunts comes in here, or our mom? And finds the floor sticky in front of the fridge, they'll look for someone to blame, and there are enough witnesses here that no matter what excuse Ray tries to come up with, it won't work. Hell, Caitlin's likely to send Trevor running to tattle just to be mean. Grabbing a hand towel from the counter, Ray snaps it in my direction. "Leave me alone."

"You drank all the milk," I point out. I cross my arms defiantly in front of my chest and look down at him as he wipes at the floor in quick, ineffectual strokes. From this position I can see the beginnings of a bald spot on the top of his head — I wonder if he knows about that? Receding in the front, falling out in the back ... if that happens to me, I'm shaving my head, even though Dan likes my hair. He loves to tug at my bangs during sex, loves to brush the blonde strands from my face and tuck them behind my ear. He might not go for the Telly Savales look, though if I start balding like Ray ... "I should make you walk your lazy ass over to Grosso's," I grumble. "Drink all the goddamned milk."

"It's just up the street," Ray huffs. "You want milk that bad, go get it yourself."

"Good idea." Turning to my sister, I tell her, "Take note of that, Caitlin. Ray had a good idea. We need to mark the calendar or something."

A damp towel flicks my pants leg and I kick my brother in the hip. "You leaving?" Dan asks. When I nod, he starts to rise, shoveling food from his plate into his mouth as fast as he can. "You want me to come?"

That would be nice, the two of us alone for a few minutes, but he's eating and I don't want to rush him. "I'll just be a few minutes," I tell him, and my kiss eases him back into the chair.

29: Grosso's Market

GROSSO'S USED TO be a five minute bike ride from Aunt Evie's, in the summer when time stretched out across the day like a cat sleeping in the sun, and the distance was nothing to a little boy anxious for Gobstoppers and frozen Cokes. But the middle of October in western Pennsylvania is *nothing* like August — a slight wind blows through me and sends dried leaves scuttling over my shoes, skittering across the street with a sound that reminds me of caught crabs scurrying over the deck of a ship to get away. It's a cold sound, empty and alone. Around me the houses are silent, the trees foreboding guardians that watch me pass, and there are just enough clouds in the sky to suck any warmth out of the morning sunlight. It looks like rain, actually, the clouds low and bruised, threatening that sort of drizzle which seeps through the skin into your bones. A good day for a funeral, actually — too bad we have to wait for Sylvia to show up. Or did she come in last night? I feel out of the loop now, I don't even know if she's here. *Serves you right*, a voice in my head whispers, *playing the bitch last night. You're lucky your boy even slept in the same room with you, after the snit you threw.*

Yeah, well, that's over with, isn't it? Dan and I are cool again, right? He even asked if I wanted him to come to Grosso's, there's nothing wrong between us. I won't let there be. Because if there *is*, then who's to say that I'm happier with him? Who's to say that I was a fool for turning Stephen away?

I can't think like that. I love Dan, I do, I *know* I do. What I feel for him is worlds stronger than whatever friendship tied me to Stephen. I won't doubt our relationship, I won't doubt *myself*, I can't. I could spend my whole life regretting the choice, if I'm not careful.

So I lose myself in the walk. I let the brisk air hollow out my mind and blow through me as if I'm nothing more than a bent reed. I focus on the trees, the pavement, the clouds. I've never seen Sugar Creek draped in autumn hues before, the leaves falling like tears from bare branches, stark and naked against the sky. Summer is a bustle of activity — kids everywhere, flowers in bloom, the woods full with foliage. Winter is silent, enshrouded in snow, the town itself barren as everyone huddles inside to stay warm. But this, now? There's an almost uneasy sense of anticipation that surrounds me, a not quite pleasant feeling of baited breath. I feel caught, hung in suspended animation, waiting for a punch line that I'm not sure I'll like when it finally comes. I won't return here again, not after the funeral tomorrow, I know it. And what saddens me isn't so much the fact that I'm not coming back but that this will be my final memory of this place. The Sugar Creek of my youth is gone, much the same way that my memories of Stephen are gone, replaced with his sad, haunted eyes. In my dreams and thoughts of summers past, there will always be these dying leaves that I trample on as I walk, this chill wind that bites through to my soul.

A little further and I swear the wind has grown colder. It slips beneath my sweater, tickles along my skin. I should've let Dan come with me. He could hold my hand right about now, or drape an arm around my shoulders and hug me to him, keep me warm. Five minutes, my ass. I haven't been out here half that yet and I'm ready to turn back. I'd get my car and drive to Grosso's but that's something my mom would do, a waste of gas, and with all those vehicles parked in front of Evie's house, I'll be lucky if I can even maneuver out of the front yard. It's like a used car lot back there and if I *do* manage to get out, what happens when I can't pull in again?

No, I'll walk. I'm already halfway there, the house out of sight behind me or I really *would* turn back, for Dan or the car or both. What the hell am I doing out here anyway? For milk ... damn, like I can't live without it for one day. Though, truthfully? I think I just needed to get out for a bit, out by myself, away from my family and my lover and the ghost of my great-aunt that I feel in every room of that house, in the yard, by the creek. Evie is still here, despite the fact that her body lies in a cold steel vault down at Morrison's. She was too large in life to just disappear.

The road curves away and I follow it around, out of the leaves if I can help it. Out of the shade that falls from the trees, too, and when I *have* to walk beneath the overhanging branches, I hug myself to ward off the chill. It's still early, no one's out, and if it weren't for the whistle of the wind through the leaves, I could almost believe that I'm not really here. Maybe I'm still in bed, and Dan left the covers up when he slipped out, that's why I'm so cold. Maybe this is still part of the dream I had when I fell back asleep, the one where Dan's kissing me awake, making love to me while I'm only half-aware.

That thought exhausts me. It would mean that I'd have to do this morning all over again, the whole sitting at the kitchen table thing, bickering with Ray and being the butt of Caitlin's jokes — I don't think I could handle a second round. No, this is real, I'm here, and I scuffle my feet through leaves that have drifted into a pile along the curb just to prove it. I keep to the edge of the road, around an empty wooded lot, pass a weathered and faded *For Sale* sign that I swear has always been there for as long as I've been coming, and Grosso's is up ahead. A squat building with walls of white stucco brick that are the same sordid shade of dingy gray that they were the very first time I laid eyes on them. Small — the place is small, with metal bars on the windows that make it look like a prison, a neon sign in one of them that flickers *Open* at all hours of the day and night, even though the place closes at nine. No parking to speak of, just gravel strewn over the lot to tamp down the grass, and two antique gas pumps in front of the door, beneath a sagging awning. Grosso's doesn't sell gasoline — never has, and as far as I know, those pumps don't work. Just decoration, I guess, or ambiance, like the weeds growing around the steps that lead into the store, or the shingles crumbling off the roof, or the tires stacked beside the dumpster out back. This isn't 7-11, but it passes as such in Sugar Creek. You need eggs? Run out to Grosso's. Milk, candy for the kids, an iced drink to combat the summer heat? Grosso's has the coldest freezer in town. Condoms? Sold individually, for those special occasions. Cigarettes? For an astronomical price — tobacco isn't native here, these aren't Virginia smokes they sell. Beer and lottery tickets and fresh bait, sliced meats wrapped in white deli paper and pickles the size of your arm in a barrel by the door, deodorant and shampoo and razors if you forgot to pack them, flip-flops and nudie magazines and a squealing rack of paperback books like the ones I used to read. Grosso's. Every city in America has a place like this, if you look hard enough down the back alleys and side streets. The kind of store you don't want your kids to go into alone, but just the place that children adore.

There are two cars in front of the store — one an aging rust-colored pickup that I remember from my youth, the owner's car. The other is a newer model Saturn in a light mauve, polished to reflect the meager sunlight the way fog throws back the glare of oncoming headlights. New York plates, that stops me. Someone passing through, or a relative of mine? I don't remember seeing the car in front of Aunt Evie's, but that doesn't mean anything. My mind has been spun out in a million different directions since the phone call Saturday night — I'm not the most coherent person right at this moment. I could've parked behind this car when I first got here, I wouldn't know it. Maybe it's Sylvia, just getting into town, and she stopped at Grosso's first before heading to the house.

It's not my aunt, though. It's not anyone I know — when I enter the store, there's a woman by the magazines dressed in a gunmetal silk blouse tucked into black pants that flow around her legs like a skirt, a flamboyant hat on her head with dotted Swiss lace pulled over her face, large gold earrings that I can see from here and dark hair pulled into a severe bun beneath the hat. That's not Sylvia. My aunt is almost impish, short and petite and sort of butch, now that I think of it, with hair cut close to her scalp. The type to wear combat boots, not high-heels, and I've never known her to wear a hat, *ever*, not even the white cap that's standard issue in the Navy. I should've known it wouldn't be her, actually. She's probably driving a rental car, something sporty, not that purple-pink Saturn outside.

As the door closes behind me, the woman glances over her shoulder then looks away before our eyes can meet. My half-smile dies on my face. An out-of-towner, definitely. Any local would've made a beeline for me, already apologizing for Aunt Evie's passing as if her heart giving out was somehow *their* fault. Thank God she doesn't know me.

Inside the store, it's cool and dark — Grosso's has always reminded me of a secretive back room, one of those illegal betting houses maybe, or the front parlor of a brothel. The walls are covers in ads, most of them old enough to be worth something to collectors, Pepsi signs for 5¢ a bottle, Coca-Cola girls from the '50's, Salem cigarettes and the Marlboro camel and even Spuds Mackenzie. Behind the counter, black and white glossies line up beneath a Miller's Light sign, promotional photographs signed by celebrities passing through, people like Dirk Benedict or Linda Evans, people no one remembers anymore. There's one photo of Mr. T even, in an angry, mud-sucker pose, ready to fight — my gaze finds it instantly, in the same place it's always been. When I was little, I used to dream of getting my hands on that picture somehow. Thwart a robbery maybe, and Mr. Grosso himself would hand it to me as if it were a key to the city, and I'd accept it with due gravity, something like *that*. Mr. T. I wonder how much I could offer the old man to part with that picture. I'm surprised I still want it after all this time.

Speaking of Mr. Grosso, I don't see him behind the register. It's just me and the woman flipping through *Family Circle* down at the end of the aisle, and we're both ignoring each other. I pass by a wire display of greeting cards on my way to the cooler, turning the stand so it squeals in the quiet store — the woman glances at me again and quickly returns to her magazine. I wonder if they still carry that porno rag I looked at all those years ago with Stephen. Those magazines have migrated to the top of the stand, I notice, out of the reach of little kids, and there's a sign that hangs over that corner of the store, *15 Minutes Browsing Only, No Exceptions*. That's new. Back in the day, young girls would crowd around the magazines, giggle over pinups of Rob Lowe and Simon Le Bon from Duran Duran, and the nudies were on the lowest shelf, not hidden behind cardboard racks or wrapped in plastic like they are now. *Back in the day* — that makes me feel impossibly old.

When I open the cooler door, cold air curls around me, easily twenty

degrees lower than the wind outside. I grab the first carton of milk I see —
if my mom were here, she'd tell me to take one from the back, but it's too
cold to stand here trying to find the one dated furthest into the future. Shit,
with all those people at the house, I'm sure the milk will be gone tomorrow.
I've already decided Ray isn't getting any. I'll drink it all myself if I have to.
Let him come out here to get his own damn milk.

I let the door go and the seal sucks shut. I look around for something to
buy Dan, just a little knick-knack or candy bar or something, but other than
coin-shaped condoms, I don't see anything he might like. Nothing he needs,
at any rate. By the counter, I pick over bubblegum, cigarette lighters, CD
singles for pop songs I don't know, energy pills ... there's a small display of
tiny vials, the size of golf pencils, short and thin. The kind of plastic tube
that I've seen pocket tool kits come in, or eyeglass repair kits, something like
that. Only this vial has a tiny rose inside, silk of course, and the letters on the
tube read, *In Case of Emergency, Break Glass.* Definitely something you buy at
the last minute for your anniversary or Mother's Day, and very girly, yes, but
... what the hell. Without a second thought, I grab one of the vials, set it
down beside the milk. What am I doing? He'll look at that and ask, "What
the fuck?"

But it'll make him smile. That alone is worth the five dollars. It costs
more than the milk, Dan *better* like it.

A door behind the counter opens and Mr. Grosso shuffles out from the
back room, just as old and hunched over as I remember him. I swear he
hasn't changed a bit since I saw him last, same tufts of white hair sticking
out over his ears, same gnarled hands, same hooked nose with the same
John Lennon glasses perched on the bulbous tip. He doesn't remember me,
I'm sure, but he knows I'm not a local and he pushes his glasses up as he
studies me. "You're one of Evie's kids, ain't 'cha, son?" he asks.

Evie's kids, I like that. "Yes, sir," I say, pushing the milk and rose closer to
show I'm ready to be rung up.

Mr. Grosso shakes his head and clucks softly. "It's a shame," he murmurs, though to me it seems as if he's shouting, his voice fills up the whole
store. I glance behind me at the woman by the magazines and am not the
least bit surprised to find her looking back. "A fine woman," Mr. Grosso is
saying — my attention snaps back to him. He turns the milk over in his
hands, looking for a price or UPC, or something. *Just hurry up,* I pray. *Don't
tell me how great she was, please. I already know that.* "A real shame. Sudden, too."

He looks up at me and I nod just because I think he expects it. "Yes, sir,"
I say again. "Real sudden." *Ring up the milk, is that asking too much?*

Finally he pushes the glasses up on his nose as he peers at the carton in
his hand and types the UPC number into the register hunt-and-peck style.

Thank God I'm not buying a shitload of stuff — it'd take me *years* to get out of here. In the middle of the number, he stops and looks at me over the top of his glasses. "So which one are you?" he wants to know.

"Laura's son," I say. When his expression doesn't change, I elaborate. "Clara's daughter?"

"Ah yes." He nods again, goes back to typing in the product code on the milk. "Used to hang out with the Robichaud boy, didn't you?"

"Used to," I agree softly. Can't I get away from that? *Not here,* my mind whispers.

Mr. Grosso looks at me again, gauging me. "You ain't the one that got his hand caught up in my fountain one year, are you?"

Despite my reluctance to make small talk, I have to laugh at *that* memory — "That was my brother," I tell him. The summer I was ten, Grosso's soda fountain didn't work all the time. You'd pay for a drink and then not get any ice, or the cola would be too thick, or the Sprite came out pink like the lemonade. After a few days, Ray thought he knew how to fix it, being all of thirteen, and he managed to get his hand halfway up the ice dispenser before it got stuck. I remember flashing lights and fire trucks blocking off the road outside, and my dumbass brother crying as all three police officers on the Sugar Creek force stared at him in disbelief. They finally had to cut him out. "Ray," I tell Mr. Grosso now — heaven forbid he confuse me with *him*. "He's older than me."

"Always thought that one was a little touched," the grocer says, and I laugh again. "Always told the wife how good your momma was for taking in a retarded boy. We all have our crosses to bear."

I'm about to tell him that's just the way my brother is when someone brushes against me in passing and I turn to catch a glimpse of the woman from the magazines as she swirls by on her way out. When she opens the door, it looks too bright outside, and I can't see her face but I know she's looking back at me. Then the door closes behind her, and it's just me and Mr. Grosso in the store. He picks up my rose in the vial, turns it over in his hands, and grins toothlessly. "You hoping to get lucky tonight?" he asks me.

God. I shrug, well aware of the blush that heats my cheeks. He places the milk in a brown paper bag, hands the rose to me, and then hands me one of the coin-shaped condoms, as well. "On the house," he says with a wheeze. "Just in case you *do* get lucky, kid. You tell your Aunt Billy to stop by here tomorrow before the service. I got a half dozen lilies in the back I want her to take to the viewing for me."

"Yes sir," I say, pocketing the rose and the condom. I take the bag with the milk in it, feeling like a wino when I tuck it under my arm, but I just want to get out of here. Jesus, a condom and a rose. Dan will *really* get a kick out of that.

"A shame," Mr. Grosso mumbles again. He's not looking at me, though, and I think that I'm already gone to him, he's staring off into the past where I'm just a little kid again and Aunt Evie is still alive.

I duck outside quickly, hoping to put as much distance between myself and the store as I can. I skirt around the gas pumps, my shoes kicking gravel ahead of me, but as I'm about to cross the street, a car revs out of the parking lot and skids to a stop in front of me. The Saturn. Dread fills me as the passenger side window glides down.

Inside, the woman from Grosso's leans over the seats to smile at me. Her hat is gone now, tossed in the back seat, and she's looking at me with a face identical to Evie's, if my aunt had been fifty pounds lighter. "Michael?" she asks, her smile widening. "Damn boy, is that you?"

I stare back, incredulous. There's only one person I can think of that she could be. "Aunt Jessie?" I ask.

The door swings out towards me. "Get in," she says. I'm too stunned to refuse.

30: Aunt Jessie, In the Flesh

THE RESEMBLANCE BETWEEN the woman in the driver's seat beside me and my dead aunt is so uncanny that I can't look at Jessie straight on. Instead I stick with glimpses from the corner of my eye, little peeks at her hair, her earrings, the collar of her shirt — never her face, or her hands on the steering wheel, I can't bring myself to really *see* that part of her. She's not much younger than any of my other aunts but like Evie, her skin is unlined and pliant despite her age, she has the same wide mouth, the same pouty lips. Eyes, too — it's like looking back through the years and peering into every memory I have of my great-aunt. Jessie is thinner than Evie was, but she has the same hips, the same height, the same *hair*, for Christ's sake. My fingers crumple the top of the paper bag rammed between my knees. I can't handle this.

She pulls out of the parking lot and turns right, away from the house. "Why are you here?" I ask suddenly, sure that if anyone's going to break the silence, it'll have to be me.

The silk of her blouse rolls over her shoulders like the tide as she shrugs. "Same reason you are," she says. She even talks like Evie, though the hearty voice is thicker, as if laced with smoke.

I feel like a child again, self-conscious and unsure. "You know?" I ask, before I can think better of it. Of *course* she knows — she's here, isn't she? At her slight frown, I stare out the window at the quiet houses of Sugar Creek that pass us by and fumble through my thoughts. "I mean, how'd you find out? Who told you?"

"No one *told* me," she replies. With one hand on the steering wheel, she reaches between the seats for a newspaper behind her — Monday's copy of the *Sugar Creek Gazette*. The page is folded open to the obituaries, and there's a picture of my aunt in the center of them all, large as life. The photograph is recent, I don't remember ever seeing it before, and there's a hint of hair in the corner that has been cropped out, one of the kids sitting on Evie's lap for the pose. My aunt is laughing in the picture, her cheeks dark and shiny like apples, her eyes gleaming even in black and white newsprint. She was a beautiful woman, I've always thought that. Everything inside of her heart shone through on her face when she smiled or laughed, all the goodness and amusement and joy she held, it all poured out as refreshing as a summer rain. I blink back hot tears and set the paper back on the seat behind me, out of sight.

Jessie glances into the rearview mirror as if to make sure the paper's safe and says again, softly, "No one told me, Mike. It *is* Michael, right? Laura's boy?" When I nod, she asks, "How's she doing, anyway?"

I force a laugh. "You picked the wrong son to kidnap if you want the inside scoop on my mom," I tell her.

"I didn't kidnap you," she points out. I can feel her looking at me so I keep my face turned studiously away, my gaze on the houses we drive by. "You got in the car willingly enough. I'm just giving you a ride back to the house, that's all. Nothing to get excited about."

"I'm not excited," I lie, but my hands are sweaty and my heart thuds in my chest. Part of me *is* excited, very much so, and when I get back, I'm going to rub this into Caitlin's face, guess who *I* ran into at Grosso's, you'll never believe it. God, my mom will shit, and when word gets out that Jessie's in town and she gave me a ride home from the store, I'm going to be the center of attention. My aunts will be pissed, I'm sure, but my cousins? They'll be climbing over themselves with envy. If Evie was the favorite aunt, Jessie is definitely the most notorious, and I have a feeling that I'll be retelling every second of this car ride tonight to a room full of breathless, jealous kids.

I fist my hands tight around the bag holding the milk so Jessie won't see them tremble. "You don't get on with your mom?" she asks. Yeah, definitely related to me — everyone in my family is open and frank when it comes to being nosy. To them, if you're blood, your life is instantly a topic for discussion, whether or not you want to talk about it. You can't grow up staying at a house as crowded as Evie's and retain any semblance of privacy. "What," Jessie laughs, "are you the bad seed or something? Welcome to my world."

"I don't do it on *purpose*," I assure her. "That's my sister."

"You have a sister?" she asks. "I'm out of the loop. How old?"

She wouldn't know about Caitlin, would she? "Sixteen," I say. The last time I saw Aunt Jessie, Mom wasn't even pregnant yet, it was just me and Ray. "I have a brother, too —"

Dismissing him with a wave of her hand, she wants to know, "So what have you guys told her about me? I'm sure she knows."

I try to sound nonchalant and fail miserably. "No one really mentions you ..."

"Bullshit," Jessie says, surprising me. I see her reflection on the glass beside mine, watching me, and I meet her furious gaze in the safety of the window. I don't dare turn around. "When I drove by yesterday, they were out there changing the locks, Michael. Don't tell me they did that just for shits and giggles."

"I mean normally," I correct. With a halfhearted smirk, I add, "You're sort of off limits, I guess. One sure way to get someone in trouble. Mom, Ray's talking about Aunt Jessie again."

She smiles in spite of herself. "That easy, huh?"

I give her a sideways glance — her eyes have softened, the anger gone from her face, and with that grin she looks so much like Evie that my heart hurts in my chest. "Ray's never been mistaken for an honor student," I say. "All I had to do was ask him something like what's our aunt's name? The one Evie doesn't like? And he'd blurt it out, Jessie, just like that, and I'd go running for Mom."

Her smile widens. "And you're *sure* you're not the bad seed?" she jokes.

"I'm gay," I tell her. If it bothers or surprises her, she doesn't let it show. She simply nods, almost encouraging me to continue, so I do. It's nice to be able to say it out loud — up at the house no one's really asked about it. Dan's my boyfriend, they all know that, but it's almost a novelty that they don't want to discuss, as if it's not *real*. "It's nothing new to me," I say, trying to keep Evie's smile on her face, "and hell, Caitlin knew, but apparently my mom's gaydar is broken, or something, and she never figured it out. So I come home this weekend with my boyfriend to share the good news, right? I mean, I'm twenty-five, it's about time she knows. And not two seconds after I come out at the dinner table Saturday night, Penny calls about Evie."

Jessie whistles low. "Talk about bad timing," she says.

"Tell me about it," I mutter. "I'm not exactly her favorite right now, as you can imagine." We drive past the houses heading out of town and I ask, "Where are we going again?"

"Taking the long way home," Jessie replies. "Don't worry, I'm not snatching you away. So he's here with you? Your boyfriend?"

I nod. "That's another sore spot with her."

"Yeah, it would be." Jessie falls silent as we drive out of town. Between my legs, the paper bag has grown damp from the carton, and I wonder if the milk will sour. A five minute run down the street and now look at me, riding shotgun with a woman I almost thought didn't exist. There's a little voice inside my head that whispers I should put an end to this now, just tell her to stop the car and get out, I can walk back to Evie's from here. But I squelch that voice, I don't want to hear it. I'm already in deep with my mom as it is — anything she might say or do when she discovers I hung out with the elusive Jessie will be nothing compared to the shit she's been given me since learning about Dan. I'm even going to enjoy it, I think. The look on her face will easily be worth anything she'll dish out at me for this.

About a mile outside of Sugar Creek, Jessie slows the car down, does a three point turn in the middle of the street, and heads back. Thoughtful, her voice barely audible over the slight hiss of the heater, she asks, "Evie hated me?"

Did I say that? "I don't know," I whisper. "I wouldn't put it *that* way."

Jessie's laugh is quick and bitter. "How would you put it, then?" she asks, clenching the steering wheel so hard that I swear I can feel the car shake in the grip of her emotions. When I don't answer immediately, she prompts, "Michael?"

"Evie never mentioned you," I say, thinking about it. Rumors of Aunt Jessie were relegated to the bedroom, whispered beneath the covers like ghost stories told in the dark to frighten each other. The few times someone managed to work up the bravado — or, in Ray's case, the stupidity — to blurt out her name around adults, it was met with instant punishment, you were yelled at or slapped across the mouth or sent from the room. My mom was one for the proverbial washing your mouth out with soap, something I was never a victim of but Ray ... she'd squeeze his cheeks together until his lips popped apart, no matter how tight he was trying to hold them shut, and squirt dishwashing liquid into his mouth. "Raymond Thomas Knapp," she'd mutter — somehow it always made things worse, when she added that middle name. "How many times have I *told* you about bringing her up in this household? Don't play dumb with me, open up. You knew it was coming — open your mouth right this *instant.*"

Come to think of it, she's probably the worst. Aunt Sarah's pretty bad, too, and Bobbie ... even Billy's usually placid voice will harden in warning if Jessie's name comes up. The only one who *didn't* get all bent out of shape was Evie. Once, a year or two after Jessie's single visit, I sat at the kitchen table with Evie and Stephen — he's in every one of my damn memories of this place. We ate bologna sandwiches and homemade potato chips, which I stuck on my sandwich. Penny stood at the sink, cutting flowers from the garden to put into a vase. I remember the sound of the water running as she held each stem under the spigot, snipped the end at an angle, tucked the flower carefully into the vase with the others before moving onto the next. When Aunt Bobbie came into the kitchen, she stopped to bury her nose in the blooms. "So gorgeous," she sighed — even from where I sat, I could smell a cacophony of scents, gardenia and rose and mimosa, a dozen other flowers I had no names for. Fluffing the petals gently, Bobbie joked, "We should have a dinner party or something. Put these out in the middle of the table so everyone can see how beautiful they are. Who could we invite?"

"Aunt Jessie," I said without thinking. Why not? She stopped by a few years ago, right? I opened my sandwich and placed a few chips on the bologna, covered them with the bread, pressed down with my palm to flatten them out. When I realized no one answered me, I looked up, surprised. Penny glared at me, Bobbie stared hatefully, and Evie ...

Her face drained of color, white like the sundress she wore, her eyes as dark as the deep blue wooden fish on her necklace and so impossibly *sad*. She pressed her lips together, dropped her gaze, obviously upset. "I'm sorry," I whispered, suddenly terrified. I had never see my aunt like this before, laughing and joking one minute, almost ready to cry the next. Reaching across the table, I covered her large hand with my small fingers and murmured, "Aunt Evie? I'm sorry, really, I didn't mean —"

Penny dropped her scissors into the sink, the metal blades clattering against the steel finish. "Michael, go upstairs," she said, curt, as she dried her hands on a dish towel. When I tried to protest, she shook her head. "Go on. You and Stephen both. Take your lunch up there."

"She was here before," I pointed out, but I slid out of my chair, gathered my napkin full of chips in one hand, my sandwich in the other. "I didn't think —"

"She's not welcome here anymore," Aunt Bobbie told me. Her voice was brisk and cutting like a winter wind. "I don't want to hear you talk about her again, do you hear me? Not one *word*."

With a slight pout in my voice, I mumbled, "I said I was sorry." I looked to Evie for reassurance, a warm smile, *something*, but she just fiddled with the edge of the tablecloth, her lower lip trembling as if she were struggling not to cry. "I'm sorry," I said before slipping upstairs, and when I came down, I said it again, coming up behind Evie and wrapping my arms around her wide waist, pressing my face into her back to dry tears that threatened to fall. "I didn't mean what I said earlier. I didn't mean to make you so sad."

She turned and caught me in a massive embrace, her hands soothing on my hair, my neck. "It's okay, Michael," she sighed. "Just ... please don't ..."

She couldn't seem to finish the thought, but I knew what she meant. *Don't talk of Jessie.* "I won't," I promised, and for all the times I spoke of her in hushed whispers among my cousins, all the times I provoked Ray into saying her name just to get him in trouble, all the times I made up horror stories for Caitlin about our infamous aunt, I never once mentioned her again in front of Evie. I didn't like the person she became when her thoughts turned to her sister, melancholy and almost depressed, not at all *my* Evie, the happy woman for whom I would give the world just to keep her that way. There was something between her and Jessie, something that drove a thorn so deep into Evie's heart that she could never, ever pull it free. She couldn't forgive, couldn't move on, couldn't get past whatever it was that kept the two of them apart. Just thinking of Jessie was enough to plunge her into a mood as black and depthless as the undertow at sea. It threatened to drag her down, to drown her in a past she couldn't forget.

No, hate wasn't something she felt for Jessie. A love so tattered and torn that it ached in her chest like a wound that wouldn't heal, maybe, but not hate. "She didn't hate you," I tell my aunt. "She ... I think she loved you too much, maybe? It hurt to think of you, or hear your name, and the others ... well, I guess they just thought it'd be best not to bring it up, you know? Nothing to remind her about ..." I shrug, helpless. "I don't know about what, Aunt Jessie. No one ever talks about whatever it was that happened."

She looks at me from the corner of her eye. We're halfway through town now — there's the Robichaud place, can we just stop driving by it already? Isn't there another way to Evie's? I wonder if Stephen's inside ... "You don't know?" Jessie asks, incredulous. "No one ever told you?"

I shake my head and she falls silent again, stares at the road ahead, lost in thought. When she does speak, she lowers her gaze to her hands on the steering wheel, watching them as if they belong to someone else. "Clara was young," she tells me, "when your momma came along. You know that." I nod, yes, I know the story. Fifteen at the time, twenty when she had Penny, twenty-five when her unborn son took her life. "Margie never had kids, never had time, what with Ma and Dad like they were. You know *that*, too." I nod again. "Some time after Clara passed, the others married off, Bobbie and Billy and Sarah, leaving the three of us at the house. Evie has always loved kids —"

I laugh. That's the understatement of the year — to my aunt, there was nothing more wonderful in all the world than a child, who could do no wrong in her eyes. How could you not love a woman like that? Who spoke to you at eight with an uncanny ease that most adults seem to lack, with respect and dignity that didn't condescend? To a child, that's a priceless gift. "She was great with kids." I hate talking of her in the past.

Jessie smiles sadly. "She couldn't have her own," she murmurs. "A childhood illness — she knew she wouldn't be a mother. I think that's why she took to Laura so well, and Penny. She practically raised them as her own, and you and Ray, your sister too, she loved you like her own, you know?"

I never thought of it that way, but pride swells my chest, closes my throat. *Like her own* ... not nieces and nephews. Somehow that means more.

We pass Grosso's. Another few minutes, that's all we have together before we reach the house and she'll be gone. "So what happened between you guys?" I ask.

"I was young," Jessie explains. "Not married, not really looking. Evie cared for the kids, Marge had our parents, and me?" With a wry grin, she says, "Hell, Mike, look at your sister. Youngest kid, striving to break out on her own, you know what I'm talking about here."

I think of Caitlin and her Goth girl phase. I know *exactly* what she means. "There was this boy over in Union City," she tells me. "I thought it was love. I liked the attention, you know? And Evie didn't like him, so that was fuel to the fire, I *had* to have him. One thing led to another ..." She trails off and gives me a knowing look. "Three guesses."

"You got pregnant," I offer. It's the only thing I can think of.

She nods. "Bingo." We round the last curve — the house is up ahead. I feel like I've been gone for years. "I didn't want a baby," she says. "Didn't want that responsibility — I saw what Evie went through with Clara's kids. So I went to her. Told her look, this is how it is. She wanted me to keep it."

"But you didn't," I whisper. It's not a question.

"I couldn't," she replies. A tear courses down her cheek which she doesn't bother to brush away. "She gave me the money for an abortion because I couldn't afford it, and she told me never to come back when it was done."

31: Forgiveness

JESSIE'S VOICE IS as distant as the past she speaks of. "I was young," she tells me, as if she feels the need to explain herself to me. "I didn't want a kid, you know? I didn't want to get married or settle down — and if you got knocked up, that's what you did back then. I just couldn't see myself as a wife, a mother, not at that age."

"How old are we talking?" I ask softly. I'm guessing somewhere around my own age, and I can't imagine a child of my own, not at this point in my life, no matter what my mom wants for me.

"Twenty-six." With a sad smile, Jessie reminds me, "Clara passed not five months before I missed my first period. Five months. Can you imagine what that does to someone? Seeing your little sister die giving birth? I didn't want that to happen to me."

I nod — that makes sense. "So Evie loaned you the money —"

"*Gave* me," she corrects. "She didn't want it back. Hell, she didn't want *me* back, let alone the money. Blood money, she called it. I want you to know what this is doing to me, she said as she counted out every single twenty dollar bill. Crisp, too, because she went to the bank and got them out just for me." Jessie grimaces at the memory. "I can still hear the sound they made as she pulled them through her fingers, I'll never forget it. Fifteen of them, three hundred dollars in all. She counted them out and told me that each one was a knife in her heart. You remember this, Jessie, she said, when you're on the table and the doctor does whatever horrors it is they do to kill the unborn. You think of me then, because I'm going to die with that baby you carry."

I whistle low. "Damn." I can't imagine Evie, *my* Evie, saying something like that. "Talk about a guilt trip."

Nodding, my aunt gives me a knowing glance. "Tell me about it."

Curious, I ask, "So what did you do?"

Jessie shrugs. "What *could* I do? I took the money. Packed as much of my stuff as I could fit in an old suitcase and left. The guy I was with picked me up and I stayed with him for awhile, until he lost interest and just never came home from work one night." Forcing an insincere laugh, she tells me, "Jesus, Mike, what do you think I did? I got by. Isn't that what you do when there's nothing left? You get by."

We're still about a block from the house but Jessie slows the car down, pulls over to the side of the road. I can see the front porch through the bare branches of the trees. I wonder how long it's been since I left for Grosso's. I can't imagine the depth of Evie's love for her sister if she actually paid for an abortion — Evie, of all people, a woman who valued children more than anything else in the world. Of course thinking of her sister would bury her in sorrow — she'd remember the infant she helped abort, and she would die all over again. Not just once but every single day, a new sunrise that child would never see, a new pain in her heart. Thinking back to the year that Jessie did visit, I remember Evie stayed in her room most of the time, sick with a migraine or stomach flu, something like that. The memory made her ill, I'm sure, festering in her soul until she couldn't bear the sight of her sister. No wonder she surrounded herself every year with as many children as she could, all her nieces and nephews, great-nieces, great-nephews, her sisters and their kids and their kids' kids, their friends, everyone. Maybe she hoped our laughter and tears would drown out the cries of Jessie's baby that she surely heard reverberate in her soul.

My other aunts must have known what happened. Jessie's pregnancy, Evie's help in the abortion, how a part of her died in that doctor's office with the baby. Of course they wouldn't want to speak of Jessie around her — she was the family matriarch, she meant too much to everyone and with Jessie gone it was easier to pretend she never existed. I don't remember ever hearing her name before she simply showed up that summer, all those years back. I have a feeling that if she hadn't stopped by, I might have never known of her at all.

But Evie is dead. "Why don't you come in with me?" I ask. When she shakes her head, I point out, "It sounds to me like Aunt Evie was the only one keeping you away, Aunt Jessie. Now that she's not here —"

"Michael," Jessie sighs. The car idles beneath us, a steady purr like a contented cat, and when the wind blows outside, I can feel a faint puff along my arm where it rests by the window. My aunt closes her eyes, leans her head back against the headrest. "Michael," she says again. "Michael. It's not that simple, honey. You can't erase forty years just like that. Too much has happened to me, without me, I can't ..." She shakes her head, her mouth a tight, sad frown. "Just because Evie's gone doesn't mean I'm instantly absolved, Mike. God might forgive but relatives never forget."

I laugh. "Especially ours," I kid. I already know that I'll never, ever live this weekend down with my mom. For as long as she draws breath, I know she's going to find some way to blame me, as if my coming out at dinner Saturday was what did Evie in, not her weight or her heart. "My mother alone —"

Jessie holds up a hand and grins. "No need to say it. I lived with her growing up, lest you forget. That woman invented grudges, I'm telling you."

"I know." My smile lingers as we both grow quiet, lost in our own thoughts. Suddenly I'm all too aware of a cold dampness between my legs, the milk sweating through the paper bag. I should go. I open and close the bag, nervous. "So you're coming tomorrow?" I ask softly. To the funeral.

She shrugs. "I don't know," she whispers. "I don't want to cause a scene and between Sarah and your mother ..." She trails off, rubs at her eyes, pinches the bridge of her nose in quiet desperation. "I just don't know, Michael. I was hoping to feel you out and sort of test the waters, but they changed the *locks*, you know? How sad is that?"

"Yeah," I agree, "I know." Who am I kidding? It wasn't just Evie, it's all of them. Through the years, they stood behind Evie for so long that they barricaded Jessie out, and she's right, there's no way in. They've been closed off to her for so long that it would be almost impossible to open up now. As long as Evie was alive, there was some hope of reconciliation, however slim, but now ... "But you're here," I remind her. "You drove all this way. From New York, right? For what? Just to turn around and head back with no closure at all?"

"I just got in," she tells me. "I'm thinking I'll head on over to the funeral home — Morrison's?" I nod and she laughs. "Who else, right? Sugar Creek's too small for more. I'll stop by and see what they suggest. Maybe I can still see her one last time before the funeral, or they can warn the others that I'm here, just to keep things from getting messy. I mean, this is what they do. Families have these types of issues all the time, Michael, you know that."

Sure, but *our* family doesn't. I can only imagine what will happen if Jessie walks in at the viewing. Aunt Sarah will faint dead away, my mom will go off ... I don't even want to think about it. I'm tempted to beg Jessie *not* to show up, I don't think *I'll* be able to handle it if she does. I have a tenuous grip on everything at this moment as it is — I feel like a little boy lost at a carnival, a handful of helium balloons in one hand and a cone of sticky cotton candy in the other. I'm looking around, wide eyed and scared, trying not to give into the panic that eats away inside of me, and my stomach churns with the sugary sweetness I've been gorging on while my arm is tugged up up up by the balloons. Every step I take, my feet threaten to leave the ground, and I'm so sure that before I find where I'm supposed to be, I'll just be pulled into the air to float away over the crowds. That thought *terrifies* me. I have to find something to hold me down or release the balloons but I can't, they're tied to my wrist, I can't let go.

I don't know what to say so I bite my lower lip and wait. Through the trees ahead, the house looks foreign to me, the home of a stranger, a woman I didn't know. I try to picture Evie in her twenties, counting out money into her younger sister's open palm, her face a mask against whatever turmoil tore her up inside, but I can't do it. The Evie I knew and loved never had a bad word to say to anyone, never raised her voice in anger ... what had it taken for her to banish her sister from her heart forever? I don't know.

Finally Jessie sighs and, reaching across the gap between the seats, she pats my knee almost as if she's the one comforting me, when it should be the other way around. "Thank you," she says.

When I look up at her, she forces a smile for my sake. "For what?" I want to know.

"For talking to me," she explains. With a laugh, she adds, "For not running screaming from the car when I stopped you outside of Grosso's. Even though you knew who I was —"

Now it's my turn to laugh. "Shit, Aunt Jessie," I say, grinning. "I grew up thinking of you as some kind of bogeyman or something. Just saying your name was enough to get me grounded for life. Of *course* I'd jump at the chance to meet you after all this time. I mean, really. You're so damn notorious, who wouldn't?"

Her smile widens. "And you're the good one, right?"

"You should really meet Caitlin," I say with a wink. "She's trying to rival you as the black sheep. If you're at the viewing, I can introduce you —"

"I might not come," Jessie sighs. Her smile fades and she looks out the windshield at the house, her eyes glazing over with memories. "I don't want it to be ugly, Michael. Evie was a wonderful person — I know, I kept up with her through the years." She gestures behind us at the newspaper on the back seat, the *Gazette*. "She deserves a quiet ending. What would the others say if I showed up?"

"Who cares?" I counter. "You've come to apologize, right? You've come to say goodbye. Not to any of *them* — to Evie. She's the only person you have to think about right now, Aunt Jessie. You're doing this for her." I let my words sink in before I add, "And for yourself." She doesn't answer. "If you don't see her one last time," I say, "then you'll regret it for the rest of your life."

Quietly, Jessie murmurs, "Maybe I can see her today. I don't have to go to the viewing. At the cemetery I can watch from the road."

"Will that be enough for you?" I ask. Why can't I shut up? Just nod and say *yeah, you can do that* and let the matter drop? She doesn't want to face her sisters, fine. I don't know if I want her to, either. But part of me thinks that maybe if she *does* show up at the funeral, maybe I'll find some strength in her to help me get through it, myself.

I can tell that she's wavering. "Maybe it'll have to be," she whispers. "I just don't know, Michael, okay?"

"Okay," I concede. I grip the top of my bag in my hand, the crinkling noise a signal that I'm ready to leave. "I better go."

She leans over and gives me a motherly kiss on the cheek. "Thanks," she whispers again. I dig into my wallet for one of my business cards and hand it to her without a word — anything I say might make this more awkward than it should be, but when she looks at the card and smiles at me, I know that she gets my drift. *Keep in touch.* She nods as if I said it out loud and slips the card into her purse. "Take care," is her reply.

As I climb out of the car, I say, "See you tomorrow."

"Maybe," she corrects. I'll be looking for her, though, craning my neck to see the people lining the back of the funeral parlor, turning every now and then at the graveside to look at the road. I'm going to expect to see her — I'll be disappointed if she doesn't show. I close the door on her final words. "Bye, Mike."

Taking a step back from the car, I raise one hand in farewell, the other holding the soggy bag of tepid milk against my chest. Silently the silvery mauve Saturn pulls away from the curb, slips down the street, past the house and around another bend and out of Sugar Creek altogether. I watch the brake lights through the trees until I can't see them anymore. *Aunt Jessie.* I almost can't believe it now that it's over and she's gone. Was she even here? Will I ever see her again?

The conversation we had in the car turns over slowly in my mind, like a rotisserie chicken on a spit, turning over an open flame. I was hoping for something ... I don't know, sensational? A torrid love story maybe, Evie and Jessie fighting over a man who drove them apart. Or a secret so terrifying that neither of them wanted to see the other and remember it, like poisoning their parents or something. As children, we used to make up shit like that, reasons why Aunt Jessie wasn't welcome at Sugar Creek. A murder or bank robbery and she was on the run. A mobster marriage turned sour, and now she was in the Witness Protection Program. An alien abduction, and she hasn't been seen since. We had a million answers, as many as our imaginations could conceive.

But if there's one thing I've learned growing up, it's that the truth is never that glamorous. It was nothing that reeked with drama and angst, nothing spectacular, nothing out of a Steven Spielberg film. Two women, that's all, one with child and one who would never be able to bear her own.

One who simply saw a way out of a bad situation, the other who would do anything for her sister, anything at all, even if it ripped them asunder. The others caught in the middle, torn between two loyalties and in the end choosing the easiest, choosing Evie's side simply because Jessie was gone. And Aunt Jessie is right — Evie's death isn't going to change that overnight. If anything, it's managed to solidify the rift dividing this family, because Evie was the one who opened it, only she could have built a bridge to cross over and welcome her sister home.

And she can't.

Absently, I kick at small stones in the road as I head for the house. Nothing I can say will be enough to open the hearts of my aunts and uncles, nothing I do will make them see the Jessie I just met and welcome her at Morrison's. So I won't mention it. I won't brag about meeting her, I won't recite what we said, I won't tell a soul. Well, maybe Dan, but only when we're alone, and only after he's sworn to secrecy. I always thought it would be exciting if I ever met up with her, an epic tale worthy of endless repeating, but there was too much pain in her eyes, too much hurt in her words — I can't revel in that. I won't.

I take the porch steps slowly, one at a time, listening to my sneakers shuffle over the wood. Halfway up the stairs, I hear heavy footsteps inside the house, angry thuds that make me stop where I am and look up as the door swings open. "Just down the street," Caitlin is saying, though it's my lover I see first — he's shrugging into his jacket, a scowl on his face. One of his hands snags in the sleeve and I resist the urge to rush up there to help him straighten it out. When he steps out onto the porch, my sister is right behind him. "Not even five minutes, Dan. You round the corner that way and you see it —"

She stops when she sees me. Dan struggles with the jacket for a few more seconds before he realizes she's not talking anymore and then he looks up, sees me, too. His scowl grows deeper. "Where the hell have you been?" he wants to know.

His voice is hard, his eyes stonier. The distracted way he settles into the jacket tells me that he's waiting for an answer. Everything about him is mad and suddenly I'm on the defense — what have I done wrong? Nothing, not a damn thing. I feel my own mouth pull down into an angry frown as I mutter, "Well, hello to you, too."

With his hands on his hips, Dan gives me that knee-buckling stare he's perfected, the one that floors even the strongest of men, but it doesn't work on me. I've seen the kitten behind the lion's roar, I know he's mad but not *savage*. Before he can ask again, I raise a hand to ward off the argument. "Don't, okay? Just don't. I went to the store —"

"An *hour* ago!" Dan cries. Now I see the concern beneath his anger, the fear he's trying so hard to hide. "Five minutes down the street and you disappear. What the hell am I supposed to think, Michael?"

"I ran into someone," I tell him. My gaze flicks over my sister — if she weren't here, I would tell him about Jessie, he'd know exactly what happened and he wouldn't be so pissed, but I won't say a word with her around. She'll tell everyone, I know her too well.

But that's not enough for Dan. "Who?" he wants to know. When I shrug and look away, he spits, "That boy you used to fuck around with? The one who came over yesterday? Did you meet *him*?"

"What?" I ask, surprised. He means Stephen. "Dan, no. I didn't ... Jesus, you can't think ..." But I can see it in his eyes, that's *exactly* what he thinks, that maybe I ran into Stephen at Grosso's and we got it on, picked up where we left off all those years ago — the distrust I see shining back at me from my lover's eyes makes me livid with rage. "You know me better than that, Dan."

"I thought I did," he mutters in reply.

Indignation wells within me but I tamp it down. Pushing past him for the door, I say, "You know what? We'll talk later. Without the audience —"

With surprising speed, Dan plucks the bag from my arms and shoves it at my sister, who fumbles to hold onto it when he lets go. "We'll talk now," he tells me, and before I can argue, he threads an arm through mine, pulls me back down the porch steps and across the yard to our car.

32: We Need to Talk

D AN," I PROTEST, digging my heels into the hard ground as he drags me towards the car. His anger scares me, the set of his shoulders, the grip of his fingers on my wrist. In all our ten months, I've never seen him like this, not towards *me*. Even that one time back at the barracks, after the bachelor party? He wasn't *this* pissed. Then he had been sullen, drunk and silent, but now I feel his emotions hum just beneath his skin like an electric current powering his anger. "I went to the *store*," I try again. He doesn't stop, doesn't turn around. Because we're far enough away from the house now that Caitlin and whoever else has gathered on the porch to witness this little spectacle can't hear what I say, I tell him, "I ran into my *aunt*, Dan."

The announcement doesn't phase him.

I try to wrest my hand from his but he's too strong and we're already at the car, he holds on tighter as if afraid I'll run away. Without a word, he pulls my keys from his pocket, unlocks the door, holds it open and gives me that look of his that defies argument. "Get in," he tells me.

His face is a mask of anger — the lips I love to kiss set in a harsh frown, the eyes I could drown in storm-tossed. "Dan," I whisper. Did I do this to him? When did I let things get this bad between us? I had no clue ... tentatively I touch his cheek, the skin taut beneath my fingers. "Baby, what —"

He closes his eyes, hiding from me the sparkle of unshed tears. His jaw clenches, his teeth grind together. "Please," he sighs. "If you love me, Michael, please just get in the car."

There's only one response to that. I do as he says, buckling my seat belt as he shuts the door behind me. Looking back at the house, I can see Caitlin, Trevor hugging her legs, Ray and Neeshi and Aunt Billy ... I feel chastised, a child sent home for playing too rough, this car a prison around me. *What have I done?* I want to ask. They all stare back at me as if they already know.

Know what?

When Dan slides into the driver's seat and starts the car, I ask, "What's this all about?"

"Just don't," he warns. He pops the car into reverse, backs out of the yard. Then he slams the car into gear and tears down the street, tires squealing beneath us. What happened to the quiet, courteous driver my lover used to be? Where the hell is *this* coming from? I grip the belt across my chest as Dan says, "Don't talk, Mike. Let me work this out first, please. I don't want to say or do anything that I won't be able to apologize for later."

"Are you mad at me?" I ask, even though the answer is obvious — it's in the way he stands on the gas as he drives, the way his hands fist around the steering wheel, the way the world rockets by.

He shakes his head as if he's surprised that I dare to speak. "Michael," he starts, and then he sighs, but he doesn't look at me. His gaze is on the road ahead, leading out of town. "I love you," he tells me. "Just ... please, okay?"

In a tiny voice I whisper, "Okay." *I love you.* That doesn't answer my question.

We follow the same road Jessie and I just took, past Grosso's, past the neighborhood where I played growing up, past the city limits sign. For a crazy moment I think we're heading home, Dan's that fed up. He packed our things while I was at the store, the suitcase is already in the trunk, he's had enough. But that can't be right. The funeral's tomorrow, we have to stay for that. Besides, if we leave now, like this? There won't *be* a home to go back to, not if we don't find some way to overcome whatever it is threatening to tear us apart. *Me*, I think, staring out the window at the autumn forests blazing by. *I'm the problem here, it's me and I don't know why, I don't know how to change it. I just know that I'm not the way I used to be, I'm not the same man I was when we left our place Saturday morning and headed to my mother's. And I don't know how to fix it, either. I don't know what Dan's thinking anymore, I don't know what he wants from me.* But there's a sinking feeling in the pit of my stomach, a steadfast belief that tells me if I don't find out soon, then he might be thinking that he needs to pack up the rest of his stuff and move back into the barracks once we get home. I'll do whatever I have to, say anything he wants to hear, do anything he wants to keep that from happening.

So he wants quiet — I stay quiet. I bite the inside of my cheek to keep from apologizing for ... whatever it is he's angry about. Taking too long at the store this morning, not telling him what Stephen said, keeping him away these past few days. *I miss you*, I want to say, but I don't — he doesn't want to hear it just yet. He's mad as hell, I can feel his irritation like a barricade between us but he still loves me, he said that much. He loves me enough to not want to say anything that he might regret, so I'll keep my mouth shut and let him think. I'll let his anger ride itself out. Then we'll talk.

With Sugar Creek behind us, the road seems to open up, the sky stretches away like a blanket draped over the tops of the trees, clouds hover above as if eavesdropping on us. Too bad there's nothing to overhear — even the radio is turned down low, I can barely hear it. I feel confined, claustrophobic despite the open fields that line the road. The trees keep back behind tall grasses, empty stretches of land, but I feel them closing the distance between us, I feel them nearing the road. I can't fight this feeling of helplessness that clings to me. I just know that we won't get far enough away from Sugar Creek to talk things out between us, up ahead the trees will form a barricade across the road, keeping us in, keeping us *here*, and we'll never work things out. I'm scared we'll never be as good as we were, we'll never be more than we are at this exact moment in time, we'll never be *love* again.

That thought terrifies me. We have to get out.

I want to tell Dan to go faster, drive harder — maybe we'll zoom through the trees then, put my family and my past behind us, move on into the future together. But I'm being quiet, he wants me silent and I am, I couldn't speak now if I wanted to, and I don't say a word. Instead, I stare at the trees and swear they glare balefully back, their naked limbs shaking at us as we pass. They're closing in on us, I just *know* it.

The car starts to slow to a normal speed even as my heart skips faster in my chest. *The trees*, I think, panic rising in my throat, but a warm hand covers mine where it's clenched around my knee and I relax. "Dan," I sigh, rubbing my eyes as his fingers curve into mine. Beneath me the car veers to one side of the road, slowing as we trade tarmac for gravel, the crunch of grass under our tires. I imagine the sound is the trees creeping closer, moving through the tall grass, reaching out with skeletal limbs for the car, for *us* ...

I open my eyes and the trees are where they belong, back away from the road. Dan cuts off the car and we sit in silence, holding hands while the engine winds down. I want to say I'm sorry but I don't know if that's what he wants to hear, so I sit still and say nothing at all. I'll wait for his lead.

With a final squeeze of my hand, he climbs out of the car, slams the door shut behind him. Confused, I watch him skirt around the hood and then he's at my side, taking my arm, helping me out. As he closes the door, I look back the way we came — the road is empty. I can't even see the sign for Sugar Creek, we've come that far. Ahead of us, the highway is a single ribbon that winds through the land like a promise. There's no one else in sight. Finally, for the first time all weekend, we're alone.

Alone.

"Dan," I start, but he shakes his head, he's not ready to talk yet. Taking my hand in his, he leads me away from the road and into the grass, tall for this time of the year. It brushes along my knees, leaving little triangle-shaped burrs stuck to my jeans. I pick at them, toss them away, but more take their place. Even though I can't get rid of them fast enough, I concentrate on them anyway, they give me something to do. Beside me, Dan keeps a fast pace, crossing through the grass quickly in wide steps that I struggle to match. I want to ask if he knows where he's going, but I know he doesn't. Far away from everyone else, that's what he must have in mind. Someplace where we can just be us. Maybe we haven't drifted *too* far apart if I can still read something of his thoughts.

Another dozen yards or so and the trees loom ahead now, almost shadowing us. Between their branches the sky looks puffy and swollen, strained. It's going to rain and we'll be caught out in the storm. Maybe this isn't such a good idea after all …

Before I can object, Dan plunges into the woods, pulling me along behind him. "Baby," I sigh as I tug on his hand, but he keeps going, through fallen leaves, around stumps and rotting logs, tramping down branches and shrubs and anything else in his way. "Dan, wait. Where …"

He stops suddenly. I take another step or two past him before I realize it and turn to find him frowning at me, concern brightening his eyes. "Not much farther," he tells me. "Are you doing alright?"

I take a deep breath and nod. Sweat sheathes my back, my arms, making my sweater stick to me, and my hair is damp along my forehead, my lungs burn from his quick steps, my thighs quiver slightly. But the way he's watching me now is damn close to the way I'm *used* to seeing him look at me, so we can't be that far from where we need to be. *I need to be with him,* I tell myself. Everything else is just details.

He's waiting for an answer. "Fine," I say, and I flash him a bright smile because I *am* fine, I'm doing better than I have all weekend from that look in his eyes alone. Glancing around at the trees drenching us in their shade, I ask, "Do you know where we're going?"

With a laugh, he admits, "I have no idea. You said we needed to talk —"

"So we head for the hills?" I joke. When he shrugs, a little embarrassed, I pull him to me and he comes willingly enough, thank God. His arms find their way around my waist on their own, he hugs me to *him*, buries his face into my neck, his breath warm on my skin. I hold him in my arms, rest my head on his shoulder, it feels so *good* to be here again, to be with him. When I breathe in I can smell him, fresh and musky, his cologne enflaming my blood, filling my mind with images of me and him and a hundred different positions, a million different ways to show him my love. "I love you," I sigh as I hold him tight. "Dan, I'm sorry, so sorry, you just don't know."

"I want to know," he murmurs. His words are soft like his breath along my neck. "Don't push me away, Michael. I'm sick of it. Don't tell me you're fine when I know you're not. Tell me what you're going through here. Talk to me, please."

Will that be enough to set things right between us? At this point, I'm willing to try anything. The anger I saw in his face earlier scared me, anger directed my way, and the thought that I might make him mad enough to move out once we get home? That *terrifies* me. Fisting my hands in his jacket, I tell him, "I don't know where to start."

His arms tighten around me, keeping me close. "How about telling me why it took you an hour to run down the street for milk?" he asks softly.

Okay, I can do that. Gingerly I extract myself from his embrace, take a step back so I can look into his eyes. The concern is still there, and love — the shadows can't hide that. "I ran into my aunt," I tell him. "Jessie? The one everybody is afraid will show up tomorrow and ruin the service?"

Dan whistles, surprised. "She's *here*?" he wants to know. I nod and he asks, "What did she want? You talked to her? Mike —"

"Walk with me," I interrupt. I take his hand again and move around him, back the way we came, out of the woods. I don't like these trees that hem us in, listening. They tower over us like guards. I want to be in the open, the sky endless above us, the earth stretching out for miles around.

My lover's frown returns, his mood darting to distrust in an instant. "I thought you said we'd talk," he cautions. When I tug at his hand this time, he stands his ground.

"I don't like it here," I admit. I look around at the trees, I feel like they're swaying above us, too close, too damn close. Mindless panic threatens to choke me despite the comforting hand in mine, my lover's body beside me. It's too quiet here, still and unmoving like a grave, like death. "Dan, I don't …" I trail off, unable to put my fears into words. *I don't like it here, baby,* I think — the only coherent thought that makes it through the swirl of madness in my head. That's the best I can do. *Please.*

He must see something of that in my troubled face because he starts off again, deeper into the woods, but he's walking slowly now, I can keep up with him well enough. "You act like you have someplace in mind," I say cautiously, lacing both hands through one of his. I don't want to point out that I don't know where we are, and I don't want to tell him that I'm afraid we're going to get lost. At least we're together. That's the only thing I'm banking on here.

With a nonchalant shrug, Dan keeps walking. The forest floor is an obstacle course of deadwood and foliage, the ground mushy like a thick carpet beneath our feet. Sunlight filters down through evergreens, illuminating small patches of land where a sapling struggles to grow or a single plant rises from the undergrowth. I clutch his hand in mine for some comfort, no matter how small, and I walk so close beside him that our shoulders brush with every other step. The car is miles behind us it seems, and there's no one around, no one at all. In his low voice, Dan prompts, "I thought you were going to tell me about your aunt?"

"Jessie," I say. When he nods, I swallow back my fear and focus on what happened this morning. I tell him about Grosso's, warm and dark and so much the way it always was that I felt transported back in time, a boy again. I imagine my words a steady stream that trickles from my lips to paint the landscape — the description of my aunt left on the tender branches of a young sarsaparilla sprout, Mr. Grosso's condolences tumbling over a moss-covered log, the bright sunlight as I stepped out of the store shining on leaves of late season poison sumac. I glance behind us, almost convinced that I've left a trail of words leading back to safety — we just have to follow the story to where we entered the woods, a literary Hansel and Gretel, my words proverbial breadcrumbs leading us home.

But there is no path behind us, just trees and swatches of sunlight, and maybe a glimmer through the branches that might be our car. Dread rises in me again but I talk it away, telling Dan of how Aunt Jessie pulled to a stop in front of me, told me to get in the car. How she took the long way home, right out of town and then turning around, heading back. What she's doing here, what she hopes for, why she came and what she has to apologize for, even if it's too late to say she's sorry in person. "An abortion?" he asks, unsure. "They hate her because she had an abortion?"

"This is my family," I remind him. Around us the trees are starting to thin, and I swear I hear the trickle of running water up ahead. "They don't really need a good reason to hate someone."

Besides, I can see where Evie was coming from, all those years ago. Back then, the stigma of an abortion would have been an almost unbearable cross for the family, particularly a handful of young sisters living together in a house with two children and no parents or husbands. In a small town such as Sugar Creek, that might have been enough right there to send Jessie away. People did those things back then, sent young girls who were "in a bad way" to live with relatives in another city or another state, where their "condition" might not raise as many eyebrows. And then there were Evie's own convictions, her love of children mirrored with her inability to have one of her own. Of course she would resent Jessie, who saw the life within her womb as an inconvenience and seemed ready to kill it without a second thought. A giving person by nature, Evie probably felt obligated to help her sister but in turn must have hated her part in the affair every single day of her life.

Finally the woods break away, revealing a small stream that splashes away, sparkling water over smooth river stones and the gnarled knuckles of exposed roots. The trees stand back as if in awe. Moss grows along the banks, a beach of lichen that disappears beneath the clear surface, gives the rushing water a dark green tinge that reminds me of spring. Tiny silver fish flicker through the fecund water like flashes of sunlight captured in the rocks, winking at us then hurrying away. There's a faint breeze, it stirs the wild oats that shoot up here, and the few cattails that have started to go to seed. A magical place, I feel it in the very center of my soul, a small section of heaven set down here on earth and untouched for centuries, waiting for someone to come along and savor its solitude. Waiting for *us* — the water didn't run before we came, the fish didn't swim, the grasses didn't rustle amongst themselves like whispering children. "You knew about this?" I ask with an incredulous laugh, folding my lover's hand to my chest.

"The creek behind the house runs out this way," Dan explains. He leads me to the edge of the stream and sinks down, pulling me with him. I've never felt anything as soft as this damp moss — it's all I can do not to lie back on it. "I was thinking that it meant so much to you," he says, watching me with the hint of a smile in his eyes. "But it was too tied up with everyone else in your life. I wanted to find a place that would be just ours. A place where we could make our *own* memories."

"This is perfect," I tell him, and it is.

33: Making It Right

I T'S THE MIDDLE of October, true. Chilly beneath a sky that threatens rain. But there's enough down home country boy left in this city slicker to make me kick off my sneakers and shed my socks before plunging my bare feet into the rushing stream. "Jesus!" I gasp as Dan laughs at me. Water like ice swirls around my ankles and numbs my toes.

"Cold?" my lover asks with a grin. He sits cross-legged on the ground beside me, his knee barely resting against my thigh.

I punch his leg playfully. "Just slightly," I admit, but to be honest, it feels absolutely wonderful. Leaning over, I roll up my pant legs, the left one first, then the right. A fine spray mists my fingers, incredible and so amazingly *cold*, I just love it. "Come on, baby," I cajole. "It's not that bad. Take off your ..."

My words trail off when I turn and see the lust in Dan's eyes, the insatiable way he's staring at me, like he's famished and I'm just what he's has in mind. "Take off my what?" he asks softly, his meaning worlds different from what I had started to say.

A flirty shyness descends over me and suddenly I feel like I did when we first started dating, when everything between us was still new, we were both explorers in uncharted lands, and the slightest touch was enough to set me grinning like a fool for weeks on end. "I love you," I say simply. My heart swells with the emotion and in this instant, I fall for him all over again. I love him completely. There's no doubt in my mind that I do.

He moves closer. One arm eases around behind me, one hand on the ground by my hip as he leans against me, his chin on my shoulder. His breath flutters over my neck as he whispers, "What do you want me to take off, Michael?" His chest is so warm against my back, and on my arm he traces the pattern of my sweater. My body thrills to his touch.

Clearing my throat, I hope I sound coy and unaffected when I tease, "I thought we just came out here to talk."

His arms come up around my waist to hug me back against him. "We are talking," he tells me. "I'm afraid I'm going to lose you."

"You won't," I promise. I half-turn in his embrace so he can see the truth in my eyes — I'm not going anywhere without him.

He studies me for a long time before he asks, "So what do you want to talk about?"

I don't know. Despite our comfortable position — me in his arms, right where I belong — I still sense a barrier in me, keeping us apart. I imagine him on one side, yelling and kicking and trying his hardest to tear through the obstacle that stands between us while I wait on the other side, my arms folded around myself, pleading silently for help. For *him*. I want him in, why did I ever push him out? What made me close the door to my heart on him? And how can I possibly find the strength to open it again?

"Michael." My name purred into the hollow of my throat, tickling away beneath my sweater. Arms tight around me, keeping me close. I'm not getting out of this so easily. Gentle fingers slip beneath the hem of my sweater, play across my stomach, as quick as the light that refracts off the water at my feet. "You're not talking."

"What do you want me to say?" I murmur. I give into the embrace, lay back against my lover's body, my head on his shoulder, my legs stretching out. I feel like a cat asleep in the sun, an owner's hand stroking my chest, lower, over my belly where I'm ticklish, *lower*. Dan fingers the fly of my jeans, flicks open the button, eases the zipper down and rubs until I moan softly. Does he really want to talk? *Now?* He's got to be kidding me.

But he's not. "Yesterday," he whispers. I nod as if it's a question, *yesterday, yes. Anything you want*, I should tell him. *Yesterday, tomorrow, next week, last year. Anything you want, it's yours, just don't stop touching me like this, please.* "Talk to me about what you were going through yesterday."

Stephen. Is that what he means? He wants me to talk of my old friend at a time like this? I can barely *think* at this moment, let alone remember.

His hands, warm and strong, burrow into my open jeans to cup my budding erection. I'm expecting more — his fingers sliding lower maybe, moving my briefs aside, slipping inside me and making me arch against him in desire, but he does nothing like that. He just waits. The sweet pressure at my crotch is a promise waiting to be fulfilled. *Talk to me*, his hands say, his fingers, his arms. *Tell me what I want to know, Michael, tell me what's wrong, let me in, and I'll fill you completely, I'll make you whole. If you'll just talk to me ...*

I say simply, "Stephen loves me."

Dan doesn't reply at first and I don't say anything else, I let him digest that. *Loves me.* Not *loved*, not past tense, because it's not an emotion relegated to the past. *Loves*, as in he came over yesterday hoping to get with me. *Loves*, as in his heart shattered like a dropped mirror when I told him about Dan, when Caitlin told him. *Loves*, as in right this minute, wherever he is, he's probably thinking about me.

In his soft voice, Dan echoes, "Loves." I nod and swallow against the lump rising in my throat. "He told you this?"

"Yesterday," I whisper, nodding again. "After Caitlin left to get you, and he was like you have a boyfriend? And God, I knew it then, Dan. I could *see* it, his whole face just collapsed. I felt like shit."

"It's not your fault," Dan tells me. He squeezes my cock in tender hands and kisses my neck. "Baby, you can't control something like that —"

I shake my head — he doesn't understand. "I didn't have to encourage him," I scowl, growing mad at myself for not realizing it at the time. Could I have prevented any of this if I had only had the strength to keep him at bay? I don't know. "I didn't have to kiss him, Dan, every damn time we came up here. I didn't have to fool around with him, I didn't have to let him blow me, I didn't have to fondle him and stick my fingers up his —"

"You don't need to go into detail," Dan snaps. As I sit up, he pulls away, and a cold so poignant, a loneliness so sharp, settles into my bones. The look on my lover's face has solidified into something I can't quite discern, but it scares me. I don't like what I see — disgust? Jealousy? "I didn't know you two were like *that*," he mutters. "You said you were friends."

"We were," I say, and catching the past tense, I correct, "*are*. It never meant anything more to me, baby, and it was *way* before you came along. Don't get all indignant about it now. I know you messed around before me. Hell, you told me all about the shit that went down after hours at boot camp. Stephen and I stopped *years* ago."

Dan narrows his eyes and challenges, "When?"

With a sigh, I pull my feet from the water and start to stand. "Don't do this to me," I grumble. I'm not in the mood, this is a stupid idea, talking about it is just inviting trouble and I have enough of *that* as it is.

But as I try to stand, Dan won't let me go. He holds me to him, keeps me down, and the most I can manage is to turn my body until I'm facing him, his hands still on my waist, anger or tears shining in his eyes. "When?" he asks again. "When's the last time you got with him?"

If it was all those years ago, why am I afraid to admit it? "Last time I came up here," I tell him, my gaze sliding away from his. "After I broke up with that kid Matthew, remember *him*? I told you all this, Dan." I did, too — before we ever slept together, we sat down at my kitchen table one afternoon and talked all this out. My previous lover, all of our old boyfriends, the senior cadet at boot camp who took a liking to Dan and came to his barracks night after night, once the lights were out, just to lick his dick. I was Dan's first *real* lover and he knew about Matthew, how the boy used to be at one time my whole world but I was over him, I *am*. I haven't thought of him — or any other guy I've ever known — in the entire ten months that we've been together, not *once*. Least of all Stephen Robichaud and whatever it was we played around at growing up.

It occurs to me that I never told Dan exactly what that was, either.

"I never thought of him like that," I admit. I've begun to shiver and I want to ask Dan to hold me, but that will sound needy. I don't want to have to *ask* for his touch, I want him to simply look at me and not be able to keep his hands off. But he's watching me, weighing my words, and I pull my knees up to my chest, curl my hands over my icy toes to warm them. I'll talk through this. He loves to hear me talk, right? So I'll talk until he loves me again. Until he holds me … "I was never like oh Stephen, my *boyfriend*, you know?" I glance up at Dan's closed face and find in it the encouragement to continue. "It was just that we were friends, and when I had something I was curious about, I went to him. I wanted to know what a boy kissed like, he kissed me, stuff like that. It was all experimentation to me, Dan, I swear it. I mean, sure, I stayed up some nights and wanted him with me, but only because I was lonely or horny or … something like that. It was never Stephen, I *love* him."

Dan stays silent. I figured he would — he doesn't like to interrupt when I speak. He knows me too well. If I don't want to talk about something, I'll jump on the first thing someone says, anything to change the subject, and he hates that. If something needs to be said, he sits down and wants to talk about it until he's satisfied that the matter is settled. Me, I'm all too willing to steer the conversation away, anything to lighten the mood and get us laughing and happy together again. Somehow, though, I don't think I'll be able to do that today. I have a feeling that if I *don't* see this through, then there will be no more laughter, no more happiness, not with him, and I don't want that. I'll talk about anything, anything at all, to keep from losing him.

"I've never loved anybody but you," I say. That's the truth. Even Matthew, who I thought I was in love with, never made me feel the way Dan does. Hugging my knees tight, I set my cheek on them and stare at him, trying to see past the mask he's hidden behind, trying to see my lover inside the man. "You know that, baby. I love you."

Softly, Dan wants to know, "Why were you so upset then? If you don't feel the same …"

"Because he's still my friend," I tell him. I still feel for Stephen, even if it isn't love. When I sigh, tears prick my own eyes, and try as I might, I can't seem to blink them away. "Because you didn't come meet him," I say, sniffling. I feel as if I might start to blubber at any minute, and I rub the back of my hand across my nose, I don't want *that*. "I know Caitlin went to get you just to stir up trouble, that's the kind of girl she is and she didn't need me to tell her how it was between us, she could see it well enough when he looked at me. So she went to track you down and I was like I can do this, at least until you show up, and you never did."

I'm crying now, when did that happen? Hot tears spill over the corners of my eyes to dry in the cool air. I wipe my face on my knees, the denim rough against my face. "Maybe if you were there, Dan, he wouldn't have said shit. He wouldn't have told me he always loved me, or that he probably always will, and he sure as hell wouldn't have kissed me right here —" I point at the corner of my mouth where I swear I can still feel Stephen's lips, the ghost of our friendship and what we used to be together. "If you showed up, none of *that* would've happened."

Dan reaches for me but I shrug his hand away. "My being there wouldn't have changed the way he feels about you," he tells me — *damn* him. I don't want to hear this, I bury my head in my arms and struggle against tears that continue to course down my face. "Just because I showed up doesn't mean he wouldn't love you."

"But I wouldn't have to know!" I cry as sobs rack my body. "I wouldn't have heard his heart break, Dan. I might have seen it in his eyes but I would never have to hear the words out loud. What would it have hurt? Five minutes of your time, that's *it*, and I wouldn't see his broken eyes every time I close my own, I wouldn't hear he loves me every time I'm alone."

A comforting hand smoothes along my shoulders, across my back, and quietly, my lover asks, "So that's my fault?"

My anger dissolves in an instant. "No," I whisper — how can he *do* this? In the face of an argument, he remains a rock that the sea of my emotions rages against, and like stone, he simply waits the storm out. When the tears come, he knows the end is in sight, and with one touch, one word, he can take the wind from my sails and calm the waters again. Like now, he scoots closer, pulls me to him, presses my head against his chest so I can hear the beating of his heart as he strokes my hair, my brow. I cling to him desperately, my arms wrapped around one of his, my face burrowed into his jacket where the sweet scent of him lingers. "No," I sigh again, a thousand times, *no*. It's my fault, I'm the one who let it get this far. I knew it last time, who am I kidding? I knew what Stephen felt for me even if I never let myself admit it. He came by yesterday to comfort me because in the past, I let him. It's not Dan's fault that I held no regard for my friend's feelings, it's not *his* fault that I used Stephen when it felt good and didn't care what it might mean to the boy. It's mine, my fault, I shouldn't have done it but I did, and maybe Stephen and I weren't as good of friends as I thought we were, if I let my own pleasure come before him.

In a small voice, I admit it aloud. "My fault," I say. There's no weight lifted from my heart, the pain in my chest isn't dulled in the least, and the admission brings with it fresh tears. But they're softer this time, a gentle, cleansing rain, washing away the lump in my throat that formed when I saw in Stephen's large eyes his hopes and dreams shatter the instant he realized I didn't love him back. So I say it again, "My fault," and Dan holds onto me as I cry it out, my fault. Not Dan's, not Stephen's, *mine.*

At some point I start telling him about Stephen because I think I have to, but my voice is strained. He wants to hear this, right? Even though it's gone to me, it means nothing anymore, Dan told me to talk ... "Michael," he interrupts, kissing me quiet. I look up at him and there is no anger or judgment staring back — only love. Just the man I've always seen when I look at him. "This is our place," he tells me. "Not Stephen's. Unless you really want to talk about him ..."

"No," I breathe. He's so close to me, every heart beat fills my head, an echo of my own. "It's over, Dan. *I'm* over it, honest. I just thought you wanted me to go on."

His reply is another kiss. With gentle hands, he lies me back to the ground, the moss impossibly soft beneath me, the grasses tall around my head. He covers my body with his own, pins me down, moves above me until I'm hard between us, my jeans still unzipped and his crotch rubbing into mine. My lips ache from his kisses, my body throbs for him, his name is a litany I sigh over and over again.

He trails kisses over my chin, down my throat, his arms as thick as the trucks of trees on either side of my head. I move against him, thrusting up as my hands slip into the back pockets of his jeans and pull him down to me. Our moans drown out the water's gurgle, the rustling grass, the distant rumble of thunder when it rolls across the sky. Somehow he manages to get my jeans down to my knees, my briefs, without breaking the hunger of his kisses, and when he sits back to unzip his own pants, I fumble in my pocket, looking for ... my fingers find a small vial — the rose — and then the coin-shaped condom. When I pull it free, Dan laughs. "Where'd you get that?" he wants to know.

"Grosso's," I reply. With a wink, I add, "Always prepared, you know?" He takes the condom from me and slides down his pants, his erection standing up from a patch of dark hair where his legs intersect. *So beautiful,* I think as I run my fingers through the kinked hair, watch it curl around my nails. *And mine. Thank you, Lord, all mine.*

He lays me down again, pulls the condom on, then lies over me, his strong arms corded muscle as he holds his body above mine. There's a sharp pain, I'm not accustomed to this position, but it's gone the instant he pushes completely in, filling me, making me whole. I dig my fingers into the soft grass, into the ground — I lean my head back and gasp out his name, cry it to the trees, scream it as he drives into me, I don't care who hears. Faster, harder, deeper, until he's in every crevice, every hollow, he's filled my head and my senses, he's in the whole of me, from my fingers up my arms and down my legs to my toes — he's half of my soul. I want it, I want this, I want him forever and when I come, it's an orgasmic rush that rips from my throat and cock, a bellow of intense love that leaves me weak and trembling and utterly satiated in his arms.

Small kisses on my throat, my face, as soft as the grasses that dance around me. A warm tongue licks away my tears, tender lips cover mine. Every breath he expels, I take in. "Love you," I murmur, hoarse, my throat raw from my lusty cries.

With a grin, Dan whispers, "Reason number one why we don't do *that* when we're staying with relatives. You're so loud when I top you." I laugh, breathless, and snuggle up to him. Despite the sweater I wear and his jacket, I still feel as if I'm naked against his skin, he's that much a part of me, so deep inside that there's no telling where I end and he begins. We're just one, we're *love*, and that's all we need to be. "I love you," he sighs as he kisses me again. He moves within me and is mine.

34: What's Really Wrong

I CRY WHEN it's over, like I did the first time he ever entered me. Then I had felt empty, used, the moment he pulled free — Matthew was the first guy I ever had sex with but Dan was the first to make love to *me*, and the wild, uncontrollable lust that consumed my body when he was inside terrified me to tears when we were finished. They scared him too, my tears, because it was the first time he ever saw me cry. In my bed, *our* bed, we were sharing it by then, he held onto me until the storm passed, his legs entangled in mine, his arms around my shoulders, his face buried deep into my hair. "Shh," he murmured, over and over again. "It's okay, Michael, shh, I love you, it's okay."

I love you, as if that alone made everything better. But it worked, my tears tapered off and later that evening, I took up my usual position, thrusting into him with long, slow motions, the words repeating in my mind like the pounding surf. *I love you.*

He whispers it now, here beside the bubbly creek, amid the tall grasses and tall trees, and it's still enough to dry up my tears. We lie together on the ground, his body covering mine, his arms cradling my head and his hands clasped together in my hair, his kisses sweet and tender and soft on my face, my neck, my lips. He's still inside of me — I swear I can feel his heart pounding in my groin. Every now and then he shifts above me, small movements that cause his wilting member to flare to life briefly, a thickening throb deep in the very center of my being. I don't want to lose this moment, I don't want to lose *him*, and the tears that fill my eyes and course down the sides of my face leave me shaky with relief. *Mine*, he tells me in a gentle voice that barely rises above the rustling leaves. "I'm yours, Michael. Forever and you know it. Don't block me out, baby, please. Don't turn me away."

"I won't," I swear. "I won't, Dan, ever again. I'm so sorry." He kisses the apology away.

Some time later, when the sun begins to slant through the trees with the golden glow of early afternoon, he extracts himself from me and I let him go. From my position in the grass I watch him stand, a glorious shape of a man blocking the sky and eclipsing the sun, the trees. He fills my whole world. "How are you feeling, hon?" he asks, nudging my leg with one foot as he tucks himself into his jeans and zips them up.

"I'm okay," I tell him, and I am, mostly. I still feel this lingering sadness in the back of my throat that might dissolve into fresh tears if I let it, but it's not the same cloying helplessness that I felt before. Once he's put himself together again, Dan offers me a hand and pulls me to my feet, my jeans dropping to my ankles as I stand beside him. Almost instantly, his hand is on my bare ass, wiping away dirt and grass and whatever else I've picked up from the ground. With a laugh, I tease, "Copping a feel?"

As I lean against him to pull up my pants, his hand eases between my legs, rubbing over hidden flesh tender after sex. One finger slips inside of me up to the knuckle, his palm open across my buttocks, and I clutch at his arm, push back against the sensation. "God," I moan, guttural. His other arm comes up around me, holds me steady, while he shoves further inside. Between my legs, I've grown hard again, and I wish I had picked up more than one condom at Grosso's, because I know we just made love but with his hands on me like this, all of a sudden I'm ready for a second round. "Again?" I ask, arching into his hand.

Dan laughs and tells me, "I like you like this." His finger slides out of me, rims around quivering flesh, trails over sensitive skin that yearns for more.

Somehow I manage to let go of his arm, and I'm surprised that my weakened knees hold my weight as I stand. His hand falls away. "I like me like this, too," I say with a shaky smile. As I tug up my briefs, my jeans, I give him a wink and ask, "Tonight?"

"You promise?" he replies. He leans closer for a sweet kiss, his hands covering mine at my waist. I drop my arms at my sides and let him straighten out my clothes like an overprotective mother — gently he cups my erection and folds it into my underwear, then he jiggles my jeans up over my ass, hefts them once, twice, to settle them on me comfortably while his kiss deepens, his breath soft on my cheek, his tongue licking into my mouth. I don't feel the rose from Grosso's slip free — he does this to me, makes me blind to everything else — but he brushes the tiny vial with the back of his hand as it works itself out of my pocket and looks down to see the glass tube as it falls by our feet. "What's this?" he asks, bending to retrieve it.

"Just something I picked up at the store," I say, taking the vial from him. "It came with the condom." He laughs and I have to assure him, "No, really. It did. I bought it for you."

He holds a hand out but I turn it over between my fingers, studying it. Inside the glass, the silk rose is undamaged, trapped. Its stem is straight, unbent, the petals folded perfectly, the ribbon around it unfrayed and whole. My gaze finds the legend etched into the tube — *In Case of Emergency, Break Glass*. I almost don't want to because then what? The rose will get crushed, the red will fade, the stem will snap and break off and the ribbon will be lost somewhere along the way. *That's not damage*, I think, and it's not the rose on my mind now, it's me, it's my own heart trapped inside these walls I've erected to shield myself from the world. *That's love that dulls the edges, dilutes the colors, smoothes it all together and makes it right.* I imagine Dan's strong hands on my chest, reaching inside me, *in case of emergency* ...

Break glass.

Without further thought, I snap the vial in half. "Mike!" Dan laughs, surprised. "If you bought it for me, why'd you break it?"

I grin and toss the two halves of the tube into the creek. They'll float away downstream to that mythical netherworld where everything winds up eventually, every lost object, every broken toy, even my swimming trunks that Ray stripped off and threw away in the creek behind Aunt Evie's house all those summers ago. The rose is fragile in my clumsy fingers, so damn delicate that I'm sure *I'll* be the one to break it, before Dan even takes it from me. But his hand covers mine, his touch is warm, and the rose fits snugly into the palm of his hand. I can feel that same warmth on my soul, cradling me, loving me. "I thought you might like it," I whisper.

"I do," he tells me.

For a moment, I'm afraid I'll start up again. I can feel that unmistakable swelling in my throat, the one that creeps up on me when I'm listening to a sappy song or watching a chick flick. I'll start to cry, I just know it, and Dan will hold me, I feel so damn pathetic like this. With a sniffle to keep back the tears this time, I hope I sound nonchalant when I shrug and say, "If I had known about the free condom up front, I would've bought you a whole damn bouquet."

That earns me another kiss and I duck my head, chagrined at the sudden attention he's giving me over a silly gift. "It's just paper," I mumble. "I'm sure it'll get messed up in no time."

He gives me a strange look, one of those unreadable expressions that have become all too common for him this weekend, and I realize that despite the progress we've made this morning, we still have a long way to go before we're perfect again. "I'll keep it safe," he says, twining the stem around his finger. The rose looks like the stone of a ring. "Thank you."

"You're welcome," I whisper. I shove my hands down deep into my pockets and rock back on my heels, staring at his hand and that rosy ring and wondering what else I can possibly say. I feel like I'm out of words.

Dan kisses my cheek, a tender press of lips, and murmurs, "Can we take a walk maybe? If you want?"

"Sure." Hurriedly I put my socks back on, my shoes — I straighten my sweater, smooth it down over my stomach, run a hand through my hair to set it right. When I'm ready, Dan takes my hand in his and starts for the trees. He pulls me to him, then slips his arm around my shoulders, hugs me against his side and my own arm encircles his waist — I feel like one half of a couple in a postcard walking along the beach at sunset, the words *Wish You Were Here* scrawled above us somewhere to the left in a flowing script. The image is so bright in my mind that I actually glance up, but all I see are dark branches written out in runes against bruised clouds in the sky.

A lone raindrop lands on my wrist as we enter the safety of the trees. *Just in time,* I think when we're beneath the shelter of the forest, but now that we're on the path back to the car, I don't want to go home. At Aunt Evie's, Caitlin will hound me about what we talked about, though it's none of her business. Ray will want to bitch about the milk being too warm — I know that bastard drank some of it, he's too damn lazy to hike his ass to Grosso's for his own carton. There will be all those kids running around and vying for my time, and there's still so much to do in that house before tomorrow, so many rooms to go through, so many knickknacks and closets full of clothing and boxes in the attic, has anyone even touched those yet? And then there's my father, who will see that we're back and snatch Dan away from me again under the pretense of fixing this or moving that. Ugh. Without realizing it, I start to walk slower, forcing Dan to shorten his strides to keep beside me. I don't want to go back now. Dan and I are just getting to where we need to be. I don't want to let all of *them* in, as well.

Sensing the change in my mood, Dan kisses my temple and wants to know, "Something wrong?"

I shrug, the word *nothing* on the tip of my tongue, but that will make him angry, it would suggest that this little getaway hasn't improved things in the least, and more than anything else right this second, I want us to be okay. Even if nothing else is right out there, as long as we're fine, together, then I'll be fine, I just know it. Still, I don't want to sound petulant or jealous. "I don't want this to end," I admit softly.

With an indulgent smile, Dan's arm tightens around me. "It won't," he swears to me. "And you already promised me later."

I laugh at the eagerness I hear in his voice. "I mean I don't want to have to share you just yet," I explain, nuzzling into his shoulder. "We get back to Evie's and everyone will want a piece of our time. Out here it's just us. You're all mine."

Now it's Dan who slows the pace, until we're standing still, ringed by trees that surround us like curious onlookers. What leaves remain on their branches whisper together like rumors, the steady fall of light rain that we can't feel an insidious hiss like discontent in a crowd. "Is this about your father?" Dan wants to know.

The way he stares at me, a mix of love and something else, something darker, in his gaze, I can't look away, and I can't not answer him. "Not just my father," I say, feeling around what's going on inside my mind. "I mean, don't get me wrong, hon, I think it's great that he likes you. Or he acts like he does. Maybe he's just not as disgusted with the whole thing as my mom is, I don't know."

"Michael," Dan warns. I grin sheepishly and he touches my face, his fingers wandering over my cheek to curve around my jaw. "Are you trying to change the subject?"

Maybe not *change* it completely, but I know I'm drifting away from it, I don't want to think about my family or the bright thorn of jealousy that digs into my heart every time my dad calls out Dan's name or Caitlin makes him smile. "I don't know," I murmur. Any way I say what I feel is going to sound bad. "I'm just … it's like I don't exist when we're both with them, you know what I mean? There's Cat, the girl, the punk. There's Ray, the oldest, the village idiot. Then there's me. I'm in the middle, sort of lost in the whole scheme of things. I've just always been overlooked somehow."

Growing up, I was never the one in trouble — that was my brother. I got good grades in school, nothing outstanding but they passed me to the next level year after year, they got me into college. I kept away from a bad crowd, went for my degree — *several* of them, maybe I keep going back for more on the off-chance that the next one I get will be the one to make them notice me. I moved out on my own as soon as I could afford it, have a steady job that pays well, drive a nice car and somehow it's still not enough for my parents. They still don't *see* me. I was never into the things my dad likes, sports and fishing and drinking, those are Ray's pastimes. And I was never rebellious like Caitlin, I was a good kid. I'm witty and a good conversationalist, I read the books on the *New York Times* best-seller list, I take in all the new movies, go to the theater, I have plenty to talk about, but put us all in a room together and I'm the one who disappears into the wallpaper. I'm the one no one notices. Around my family, I simply vanish.

Part of me wonders if maybe I didn't bring Dan home in the hopes of stirring shit up with my family. I'm gay, of *course* that would get my mom's attention, the woman's been trying to marry me off since I was old enough to masturbate. But I expected more of a reaction from the others, not Caitlin's *so what?* attitude or my dad's silent acceptance. I bring home a boy and the first thing he does is try to bond with him, like he's the son, not me. I feel like I'm the boyfriend here, awkward around a family not my own. I feel like I think *Dan* should feel, and I hate that. I force a laugh that isn't humorous in the least and say, "Hell, even *you* get more attention than I do, you know?"

"And what, you think that's my fault?" Dan asks softly. He holds me in the middle of the forest, his arms around my shoulders, his lips against my hair. I've never felt so safe in my life — at this exact moment in time, *nothing* is his fault. It's all mine.

But he doesn't agree with that, either. "You can't blame yourself, Michael," he tells me, though that's what I'm doing, it's what I've always done. I was a good kid with a good childhood but nothing outstanding. Nothing to make my parents glow with pride, nothing to differentiate me from thousands of other kids out there, and now that I've grown, I still feel the need to please my mom, to strive for my dad's approval even though I know that's one thing I will probably never get.

I cling to Dan and, my face hidden against him like a shy child's, I can admit that I'm sorry. "I've disappointed my mom," I whisper. "I didn't ... I didn't think she'd take it this bad, you know? She's acting as if I'm gay just to spite her."

"It's going to take time," Dan murmurs, his hands soothing on my back. "You can't just expect her to be okay with it, Mike. It's taken you twenty-five years to get to the point where you're comfortable enough to tell her. You have to give her awhile to get comfortable with it, too."

"I know, but still ..." Actually, I hadn't thought of it like that. I guess I just assumed that I would come home, make the announcement, and ... I don't know, everyone would be okay with it? There might be tears at first, of course, but we'd talk past that, I was sure we could move on. Only we didn't get a chance to talk, did we? Not two seconds after the hardest moment of my life, the phone rings and Evie's dead. *Passed.* As much as I hate myself for it, I can't help thinking she somehow ruined the whole thing.

Maybe if my mom had had a chance to digest my words first — horrible as it is, that's what this all boils down to, isn't it? If I could've had that one night to myself, was that too much to ask? One unadulterated evening where I fielded whatever questions my family might have, when we talked out all we thought or felt instead of each of us keeping those emotions hidden away inside, one communal moment and we might not be living these different hells, my dad might be more open, my mom more forgiving, and Dan wouldn't have had to drag me out to the middle of nowhere just to get me to open up to him. One night that was just *me*, I've never had my family to myself before, they've never known the *real* me. I'm so much more than the middle child, the shadow son. One night to prove it ... that's all I really wanted from this weekend. It's the one thing I didn't get.

"I'm sorry," I whisper. My voice is muffled in Dan's shirt — I don't know if I'm apologizing to him or Evie. I feel so damn selfish for even entertaining these thoughts, I just want to curl into a tight ball right here in my lover's arms and disappear. "God, Dan, I'm so sorry, I feel awful for thinking this. My aunt *died* and here I am acting like it's all a big inconvenience to me, like she did it on *purpose*. What kind of evil ingrate does that make me? Aunt Evie was the one refuge I had as a kid, Sugar Creek was the only place I could be *me* without reprimand, and now I've fucked it all up just because things didn't go the way I hoped over dinner."

"You didn't —" Dan starts.

But I insist, "I did, Dan. I almost ruined *us* because ..." I sigh, close to tears again. Will I ever stop crying? "Because I'm an ass, okay? I'm sorry. It's hateful what's been going through my mind these past few days but I can't help the way I think. I'll never see Evie again, I'll probably never come up here for the rest of my life, and now all my memories are tainted with thinking that maybe if Penny could've waited until Sunday to call, or maybe if Evie could've held out a little while longer, things might be okay." Tears trail down my cheeks and I rub my face in his shirt to brush them away. "I should've come up here over the summer and I didn't. I didn't."

He kisses me, his lips a brand on my skin. "You can't change that now," he murmurs. "It's too late. Stop thinking it's your fault, or Penny's, or Evie's. Maybe it's no one's fault, it's just the way things happened, and you're just going to have to live with that."

35: The Way Home

W E'RE ALMOST TO the car when the skies open up. Rain beats down around us so hard, the grass is flattened, and the drops sting my skin, my face. It's freezing but so damn refreshing and ferocious that I can't help it, I start to laugh in child-like wonder, the way I laughed when I was eight and everything was right in my world. Dan looks at me with a goofy grin on his face, surprised at my lifted spirits maybe, or concerned at the sudden change in my mood. "Race you!" I call out, and before he can respond, I take his hand in mine and pull him towards the car, leaping and running over the grass.

A mist rises around the car where the rain hits it and bounces up. I bump into the passenger side, the rainwater seeping through the front of my sweater, my jeans, in an instant, leaving me deliciously cold. Dan's right behind me and I roll away, still laughing, so he can unlock the door. "Hurry!" I tell him between giggles. "I'm all wet."

The look he throws my way grabs me below the belt and squeezes until I'm hard and aching all over again. "I thought you wanted to wait until tonight," he jokes, opening the door. I have no answer for that, but fortunately he stands aside as he holds the door so I can slide into my seat.

Inside the car is dry and cool and dark from the clouds outside. Rain pounds the steel body like whips, lashing at the windows, the roof. Water runnels down the glass, streaking the world outside, the too-green grasses, the overly-brown trees. Everything out there has intensified, all the colors bleeding like too much oil on a canvas, wet and beginning to seep together around the edges. I swear I can see the bruised sky running into the black branches, into the battered land.

Dan runs around the front of the car, fumbles with the key in the lock and the rain comes down harder as he struggles with the door. Then it's open, and icy air curls around my damp legs, my heavy sweater as he gets in. "Whew," he sighs, almost breathless with another laugh. "Chance of rain, isn't that what they said this morning?"

I don't know, but I laugh with him. The sound of the rain hammering around us is almost deafening in the closed car. He puts the keys in the ignition but doesn't turn the engine over yet, just sits there and waits, staring out the windshield at the downpour. The way it's coming down now, we could float home. "Maybe we should wait for it to ease up," I say, my voice hushed. A glance at the dashboard clock tells me it's still early enough to be considered morning, but the clouds have erased the sun from the sky and inside the car it feels like late afternoon, it's that shady. Almost unconsciously, my hand snakes between the seats to find Dan's. His fingers closing over mine are a warm comfort. "We might not make it home in this," I worry.

"We'll be fine," he assures me with a squeeze of my hand. He turns the key and the car comes alive around us with a quiet hum. As if in competition, the rain seems to pick up a bit, flinging down with a fierceness that's almost beautiful. My lover puts the car into gear and eases back onto the road, which *I* can't see through the rain so I have no clue how he thinks he's okay to drive on it. It's not blacktop, it's a swirling river now. Remembering his wipers, he turns them on full speed but they do little to clear our vision — water pours down our windshield in buckets and the wipers just cut right through it, clearing a swath across the glass for a brief second before its filled again with more water, more rain. What's so bad with waiting this storm out? Just cuddling up in the back seat, watching the world rage around us while we keep each other warm?

But Dan has a mission — he is *going* to get us home. I can almost hear his thoughts, we're back to where we used to be, thank God, he's thinking that he needs to get me back to Evie's, he has to keep me safe. His hand clenches mine like he's holding on for dear life, he won't let go, won't let me drift away again. With one hand on the steering wheel, he turns the car around in the middle of the road, driving all of five miles an hour, cursing beneath his breath because the heat has begun to fog up the bottom of the windshield. "Just head back the way we came," he mutters, leaning close over the wheel and squinting out at the rain. I don't mention that if someone is barreling down the road, they'll hit us broadside, they won't even see us in this mess. "We can't get lost if we just go back the same way we got here, right?"

It's a rhetorical question so I don't reply. Instead I kick on the defrost and, watching Dan from the corner of my eye to make sure he doesn't see me, I check my seat belt to make sure it's secure. Beneath us, the road feels as slick as ice or oil and if we start to hydroplane, the *last* thing I want is to go flying from the damn car because my seat belt comes undone.

Halfway through the turn, we *do* start to skid and I let go of Dan's hand the same instant that he shakes free to grip the wheel. "Baby," I caution, my heart in my throat. The world dips away dangerously and I clutch the door, my seat, anything to hold onto while the car threatens to pull out from under us. "Maybe this isn't a good idea —"

Dan's reply is caustic. "Michael, please," he snaps. I purse my lips in a frightened grimace but stay silent. *He knows what he's doing,* I tell myself. *He won't hurt me, he'll keep me safe.* Though I can't help but wonder why we can't just sit this out on the side of the road, would that be too much to ask?

He turns into the skid and for a few heart-stopping moments, I don't think we're going to make it, we'll go out in a spin and get all turned around and end up in the grass on the side of the road, alive if we're lucky and if we're not … but Dan bullies the car into straightening out, the black river of highway fills the windshield and the grasses stay on either side where they belong. I don't dare breathe yet, though. It's not over. I have a feeling I won't draw air into my lungs again until we pull onto the lawn at Aunt Evie's where we belong. With a long, shuddery breath, Dan relaxes slightly, his shoulders loosen, he sits back from the wheel a little and sighs. "Okay, there. See? We're good to go." He looks away from the road long enough to give me a wink. "Not a problem —"

The car fishtails and he overcorrects, sending us dangerously close to the muddy shoulder. "Watch the road," I tell him.

"I am," he answers. He's leaning close to the windshield again, as if he can see through the shit pouring down out there if he just squints hard enough. "I've got it."

You're going to get us killed, I think, but I press my lips together and keep the words inside where he can't hear them and I don't have to apologize for them. He's so tight, hunched over the wheel like that, he's going to be a bundle of hurt when we get back to the house. My hand trails up his arm, over bunched muscles, around his shoulder and up the back of his neck. Raindrops stand out like dew in his close-cropped hair — they dissolve beneath my palm when I brush over them gently. My fingers rub through the tight bristles and come away flecked with water. His hair is that short, so close to his scalp that it's almost a pelt when it gets wet like this, it lies down in tiny little waves like a dark sea. It's a fine, light brown when he lets it grow out — I know not because I've ever seen it long but because I've seen the *rest* of his body, and the hair that curls at his crotch and trails down his legs is a fuzzy tan color that's darker than mine. Though mine's dyed, at least on top, bleached to a shade that makes me look like I spend my days bumming down the shore. But it's naturally that dirty blonde shade that on children seems to darken as they grow. I wonder if mine never did that because I never *have* grown up. I've never put the past behind me, I've never considered myself an adult until this weekend. Until now, actually. Now Stephen is behind me, Dan is my future, and my family ... well, I'll just deal with them as I have to, that's all. *We'll* deal with them, together. And that makes me feel okay about it, I know I'll handle anything my parents or my aunts might throw at me, simply because I know Dan will be right beside me the whole time.

I'll make it through the funeral tomorrow, I know I will. Because of this man beside me. Because of Dan.

He relaxes at my touch. His breathing evens, he leans back into my hand, he smiles, though this time he keeps his eyes on the road. "That feels nice," he murmurs. "If I wasn't driving ..."

"I told you to pull over," I laugh as my hand finds the top of his ear and I trace the curved flesh, pinch the cartilage playfully. "We don't *have* to rush back, you know. Just park somewhere on the side of the road to wait it out."

"And do what?" he challenges. He shivers when my fingers slip behind his ear — he's tender there, almost ticklish, and I know for a fact that it turns him on something horrible when I play like this. When I want him hard in a hurry, all I have to do is blow in his ear a little bit, or bite his ear-lobe, or lick the sensitive skin at the top of his ear and he melts in my arms. Sometimes in the middle of making love, I'll thrust deep into him, as far as I can go, and hold it there while I nuzzle his ear — I've brought him to tears that way before, I've made him *beg* for release. Now he squirms away and warns, "Michael, I'm trying to drive."

"If you listened to me," I tease, "then we wouldn't be on the road in this mess. We'd be snuggled up in the back seat and out of these wet clothes —"

Dan laughs. "Why didn't you bring this up before?" he asks. "I was open to suggestions."

A spot of color has appeared high up on his cheek, just below his eye, where the skin is starting to pink with excitement. Me playing with his ear, that's what it's from. "You seemed so gung-ho to get home," I counter. "I thought you had a hot date, or something."

"You and me in that back room," he says. "That's the only thing I'm rid-ing on here. You know what you're doing to me, don't you?"

I'm well aware of the effect I have on him — I can see his arousal begin-ning to tent the front of his jeans, I'm thinking the back room, too, and the sheets wrapped around our legs, the two of us beneath the covers in the dark, the only light whatever sun filters in through the single window, rain like tears tracing watery patterns down the glass. But the storm is easing up a bit — the roar outside has abated somewhat and when the wipers cross the windshield, the path they clear doesn't seem to fill in as fast as it did before. "Picture this," I say, and I pause for so long that he dares to look away from the road and at me again, a quizzical expression on his face. "Didn't Aunt

Bobbie say something about a hot tub downstairs?"

His lips pull into a slow grin. *"Someone* mentioned it," he says, turning back to the road. Up ahead the Sugar Creek town sign materializes from the fog and rain like a lighthouse on the edge of rough seas. My heart swells inside my chest and there's a sense of homecoming so strong that it threatens to choke me. *This is where I belong,* I think suddenly, the thought simple and pure and true. *Right here, Dan beside me. I can live anywhere else but this is where I'll always be. This is home.* As if he can hear my thoughts, my lover rubs his cheek against my wrist, still on his shoulder, and says softly, "Almost there."

The torrents trickle off to a light rain and the world looms up around us from the wet landscape, houses drenched and darkened, yards verdant, shrubbery overripe. Leaves drift like tiny boats in rivulets of rainwater, sailing to clog in gutters and drains, those already raked into piles now soggy and clumped together. Here and there a few children splash in puddles or run along with a stick caught in the current, follow the leaves down to wherever it is they're off to now. These kids wear bright raincoats, yellows and reds and oranges, Day-Glo colors too vibrant to be real. I almost think that I could roll down my window, stick my hand out into that damp world, brush my fingers along the coats, the grass, the sky, and come away slick with fresh paint.

On our left, Grosso's slides by, *almost there.* Maybe if I'm lucky, we can sneak inside without anyone knowing that we've returned, we can slip into the back room without being seen, I won't have to share him with anyone else just yet. It looks like I might get my wish after all, because when we round the bend and the house comes into view, the porch is empty, there's no one outside. I let out a breath I didn't realize I was holding — I guess there was some part of me that almost expected to see Caitlin out on the swing, or my dad ready to put Dan to work, or even Ray with that damn bag of warm milk still in his arms. But we're still alone. It's just the two of us against the world, thank the Lord. As Dan glides the car into the spot we vacated hours before, I tweak his ear and am only half joking when I suggest, "Maybe we can wait *here* for the rain to let up."

"It's not so bad," he starts, cutting the engine, but then he turns and sees the look of lust I know shines in my eyes. Before I can laugh and break the moment, he rolls into my arms, crawling onto me, pushing me back to my seat as his lips find mine. "Right here," he murmurs, and my hands grasp at his back, his neck, his ears because I know he's worked up and it's all my fault. Gloriously, *this* is my fault, and I'm all too willing to admit it this time. "We're still alone," he sighs between kisses, his hands already beneath my sweater and plucking at my hardened nipples, sending shivers of delight through me. I moan beneath him and he shifts above me, trying to find a more comfortable position — it's hard in these bucket seats. I know, I've been in his position before, I've been the one kneeling over *him* and it's hard on the legs, we really should head inside …

Fuck that, I think, and the thought makes me giggle. "What?" Dan wants to know — I can feel him grin against my neck. "What's so funny?"

"You," I whisper. I get one hand between us and work his zipper down. Instantly his erection pokes out at me, straining at his boxers, he's ready to go. Wrapping my hand around his shaft, I start working him harder, squeezing at him, kneading until he hisses against my neck and thrusts at me. My fingers get into the fly of his briefs, I feel warm flesh, kinked hair, the tip of his cock already damp in my palm. My hand encircles him, slides down to the base, the heel against his soft balls, my thumb rubbing at the magical spot in between that makes him whimper with need. "You like that?" I purr — I know he does, he doesn't have to nod against my throat where he sucks at me, he's close to coming, I can *feel* it.

Suddenly the seat falls out beneath me as Dan finds the release and lays me down. I start giggling again and tug at him harder, faster, like I'm trying to jerk him into the back seat with me to do that cuddling thing I was thinking about earlier. With each squeeze he thrusts into my hand, and with each thrust, he growls deep in the back of his throat. He's not kneeling over me anymore, he's stretched out like the sky above me, a blanket that covers me completely, a protective lover. I want him now. I don't want to wait until we get inside, I don't want to wait for the hot tub or our bed, and I sure as hell don't want to wait until we find the condoms packed away in our suitcase. I want to enter him, I want to possess him, I want to feel his dick against my stomach as I take him again. He's had me today — now it's my turn. "Baby," I moan as his lips find a tender spot on my throat. Between us my hand is moist with sweat and pre-cum, and the musty scent of sex fills the car. I've got less than a minute to get my own throbbing erection out of the confines of my pants and into his before he comes and the moment is lost.

A thin tapping on the window startles us. "Fuck," I sigh as Dan sits back.

My sister stares in at us, her hands cupped to the glass. "You guys aren't getting it on, are you?" she hollers, her voice muffled through the window.

"We were *hoping* to," my lover mutters. He starts to sit up, then remembers that he's hanging out below and instead buries his face in my neck as if hiding away. "Tell her to leave us alone," he whispers. "I'm *this* close."

I know — tell me about it, I *know*, I have him in hand and practically quivering with release. "Caitlin," I shout. When she just grins, I pound the window with an angry fist. "Go away."

She steps back but doesn't leave. "Looks like you guys are busy getting your fuck on in there," she laughs.

At least she's not right up on us anymore, she can't see anything when Dan sits up enough to jam himself back into his pants. "I'm getting sick of this," he mutters, zipping up his jeans, which look as if they've shrunk two sizes in the rain. That *has* to hurt.

"The minute we're inside, those are coming off," I tell him.

Outside my sister kicks at the car. "You two coming out or what?"

"Oh no, she did *not* just kick my car." I try to sit up, the splayed-out seat hindering me, but Dan pops the door open and grabs my hands, tumbling both of us out into the wet grass. Glaring up at my sister, I threaten, "You are *so* dead."

She has the audacity to laugh. "So I take it things are cool with you guys again. Did you get laid? Because you needed it, Mike, I'm telling you —"

"Dead," I promise, scrambling to my feet. She turns and races for the house, her laughter streaming out behind her, enticing us to give chase.

36: Interrupted

I REACH HER first, a few yards from the front porch. The rain has stopped for the most part but there's still a fine mist hanging in the air, though I can't tell if it's something falling or something kicked up as Caitlin runs ahead of me. Every few feet she looks over her shoulder and, seeing me right behind her, starts to laugh again. "You guys are so *slow*," she calls out, and damned if she doesn't spur on ahead faster, how does she *do* that? *She's sixteen*, I remind myself, racing to catch up. *This is nothing for her. Another nine years and she'll be out here wheezing like me.* As if I'm *that* old.

With a burst of speed that surprises me, I close the distance between us and reach for her. I get a handful of her t-shirt before the black material slips free of my grip and I go down, the grass slick beneath my feet. As I land on one knee, bright pain shoots up my thigh like a bolt of lightning and somewhere behind me, Dan calls out my name, alarm sharp in his voice.

Caitlin slows, starts to turn, and that's all the time I need. I launch myself at her legs in a halfhearted tackle and manage to bring her down. "Michael!" she shrieks, laughing in spite of her anger. She claws at the ground, digging deep, dark gouges in the damp grass, her legs kick against my arms and chest but she's lost, I won, I *caught* her — I whoop loudly in victory even as she struggles beneath me. "Let me go," she mutters bitterly, then she laughs when my hands find her waist and I turn her over ... *ticklish*, I think, *how fun.* "Michael, get *off* me! Let me *go!*"

"Who's slow now?" I ask, tickling her. She giggles uncontrollably, swats at my hands but I can't help it, her bare midriff practically *begs* for the torture. "Who said you could interrupt us like that? While we were getting our groove on, huh?"

"I'm s-s-s-s-*sorry*," she sobs, her laughter mixed with tears. My nails rake her stomach, her sides, and try as she might, she can't squirm away. Her legs kick out ineffectually above my thighs, she's laughing too hard to peg me with a good shot, and her arms batter mine with all the strength of a kitten's paws. "Let me up, Mike," she gasps, breathless.

Strumming a hand across her stomach, I tease, "You're ticklish as hell."

"I am *not*," she cries, but my fingers pinch around her navel and she dissolves into fresh giggles. "I'm not, get off, let me up. I didn't know you guys were getting it on in there, okay? I said I was sorry."

"Sorry doesn't cut it," I tell her with a glance over my shoulder at Dan, who makes his way towards us with a noticeable limp from the equally noticeable erection that's crammed down the front of his jeans. He's even pulled the hem of his shirt out of his pants in some effort to cover it, poor guy. "See what you've done to my baby?" I ask my sister. I stop tickling her long enough for her to sit up and get a good look at him, walking like a soldier wounded on the battlefield, and what she sees sets her to laughing again. "A few more minutes and I could've taken care of that for him."

Caitlin flops back to the ground, hands over her ears. "I'm not hearing this," she says loudly as she tries to wiggle away from me. "We said no talk about sex, remember? I don't want to know —"

"*You're* the one who crashed our party." I catch her by the waist and she squeals in delight. "You're getting to be as bad as Ray."

Her laughter dries up instantly, and this time when she kicks out, her foot connects with my upper thigh, dangerously close to the family jewels, which are still a little hard themselves from playing with Dan. Lucky for me, she's wearing a small pair of Mary Janes instead of her usual Doc Martens, or that foot would've sent me clawing at the sky in agony. "Jesus *Christ*, Caitlin!" I twist away from her next shot, blocking her foot with my leg so she can't get any closer to hitting home. "Watch it, kid."

She kicks at me again, her foot glancing off my hip to connect with my elbow, and pain flares up my arm like wildfire. "You take that back," she growls, all playfulness gone.

I laugh in shock, surprised at her sudden change of mood. "No," I tell her. "It's true."

Fisting her hands into the grass, she grimaces as she tries for another shot, this time with both feet — they land in the center of my stomach and she knocks me back to the ground. "Fuck you, then," she mutters. Her face scrunches up, is she about to cry? I can't believe it but when I reach for her, she flails out and pushes me away. "Leave me alone."

I shrug her off as Dan comes up behind me. "What?" I ask, confused. "All I said was —"

"Shut up!" My sister kicks at me a final time before heaving herself up on her feet, and then she pounds me with one small fist, hard on the shoulder. "Shut up, Mike. I'm not talking to you anymore."

With that, she turns and storms up the stairs to the porch, the thin wooden soles of her shoes *clap clap clapping* with each step. There's an anxious moment where she struggles with the screen door — the latch is caught and won't open for her, it's ruining her big dramatic exit and I could run up there now and apologize, she might still laugh this off — but she finally gets it to work and disappears inside, slamming the door shut behind her. "What did you say?" Dan wants to know.

"I told her she's as bad as Ray," I say.

I expect a laugh — it *is* a funny thing to say, I can't be the only one who finds the humor in it. But Dan just shakes his head and sighs my name. "What?" I ask. Am I the only one here who doesn't get it? "It's true. We get a little frisky and poof! She shows up out of nowhere. You said it yourself, it's getting old."

He shrugs. "But as bad as *Ray?*" he presses. "Michael, that's ... damn, that's low."

Now it's my turn to sigh, and when I hold a hand up, he helps me to my feet. "This means I'm going to have to say I'm sorry, doesn't it?" I ask. He just shrugs again. If it's not one person mad at me, it's another. *Gotta piss somebody off,* I think sourly. I'm almost not in the mood to pick up where Dan and I left off before we were so rudely interrupted ... and she thinks I'm not going to comment on that? So she's pissed, so what? What about me and my lover's jilted libido? "Fine," I mumble. "Make me the bad guy."

"I'm not." Dan's arms come up around me and he hugs me to him, his erection poking into my buttocks like a steel rod shoved down the front of his pants. Kissing my ear, he murmurs, "I'm on your side here, Michael. Don't get pissy with me, we just fixed all this."

"I know," I admit. I lean back against him, defeated. I just can't win with Caitlin, can I? "There goes our good time —"

"Why do you say that?" Dan wants to know. I turn in his arms and frown at him — surely he's not still up for fooling around ... but he is, painfully so, he's pressed into me like a loaded gun under a shirt during a hold-up and when I look into his eyes, he gives me a slow, sly grin. "Unless you're not up for it anymore ..."

Oh no, I'm *up*. Slipping his hand into mine, I lead the way inside, fumbling with the lock for a few seconds the same way Caitlin did, the damn thing doesn't want to open, but it comes free in my hands and then we're inside. Aunt Billy is in the hallway, taking down framed pictures and stacking them carefully on the floor — she looks down her nose to peer over the tops of her glasses at use when we enter. As Dan closes the door, she gives us a warm smile. "If you're looking for your sister, she's upstairs," she says by way of hello. "You two having a fight?"

I laugh and kiss my aunt's papery cheek. "How can you tell?" I ask.

Aunt Billy shuffles a few feet down the hall to the next set of pictures.

"Women's intuition," she says. With another look down her nose, eyes twinkling, she adds, "Or maybe Caitlin's *I freaking hate him sometimes* was a clue, you think?"

I doubt my sister said *freaking*, but this is Billy. I laugh as we edge around her, Dan up on me so that every step bumps the hardness at his crotch against my hip, and tell her, "She'll get over it, I'm sure."

My aunt's smile is infectious. "I'm sure," she says, her voice warm as she watches us shuffle around behind her. "What are you boys up to?"

"What do you mean?" I counter. I feel like I did when I was younger and Stephen came over for some fun, and the two of us were trying hard not to let our excitement show on our faces until we managed to get alone. I'm sure Billy knows what's on my mind, I'm sure she practically *sees* me salivating for Dan, one look at my face and she sees my sordid thoughts written out in my eyes, she *knows* ... but she just smiles and shakes her head, a sort of *boys will be boys* gesture that makes my heart want to burst with sudden love for her. "We're just going to slip into the back room for a few minutes," I say, giving her a wink as I steer Dan down the hall. I put a finger to my lips as if it's a secret that I don't want her to share. "You didn't see us, if anyone asks."

"You boys are bad," she teases.

With a laugh, I correct her, "This boy is bad." For emphasis, I slap Dan's ass and hurry him into the kitchen.

Over his shoulder, my lover murmurs, "Like I'm the only one."

My hands on his back propel him around the table to our closed door. "I didn't say *that*," I tease.

Inside our room, the door once again shut on the rest of the family, Dan plops on the edge of the bed and unzips his jeans with a huge sigh of relief. "Damn," he breathes, lying back. His erection stands up from his open fly like the short, hard tail of a small dog. How does the saying go? *Snips and snails and puppy-dog tails* ... the thought makes me grin like a fool, and Dan closes one eye as he watches me from where he lies on the bed. "What are you thinking about?"

"You," I tell him. It's the truth. Locking the door, I cross the room and stand between his legs to stare down at him. He crosses his arms behind his head and smiles at me, his shirt pulled up slightly to expose a sliver of pale flesh along his stomach, his Army green briefs tented above his hard cock. Carefully I poke at the tip of his dick and he laughs but he doesn't move. "We need to finish cleaning up this room," I tell him, *poke*. His member stiffens beneath my fingers, *poke poke*, and the look he gives me suggests that getting this place in order is the last thing on his mind. "Unless you're going to work with my dad again today?"

Like a cat, he watches me toy with him, my forefinger painting the outline of the spongy tip of his dick through his briefs. The material is darker beneath my finger where he started to cum in the car before Caitlin interrupted us — it's still damp and warms to my touch. "I wasn't planning on it," he purrs, watching me, waiting, the way a cat watches a string drawn before it across the floor, waiting for just the right moment to pounce. "Unless you want me to?"

I shake my head. "Let him find his own soldier boy," I say with a giggle. Around and around my finger goes, smoothing the fabric out that keeps us apart, I'm mesmerized by the patterns I'm making ...

Suddenly Dan clamps a hand around my wrist, startling me. "Gotcha," he laughs, his fingers strong on me. With a gentle tug, he says, "Come here."

I let him pull me down but at the last minute I prop myself up above him, a hand on the bed on either side of him, and I hold his gaze as I slide down between his legs. "Let me take care of this first," I tell him, easing his briefs down to expose his hard length. His grin widens as he watches me — I start at the base, where the sharp scent of sex clings to him. My eyes never leave his as I lick around the bottom of his shaft, in that tender area just above his balls where he's most vulnerable. I work my way up, my tongue wetting him, up to the inverted V on the underside of his tip. When my lips close over him, take him in, my tongue finds that little spot and rubs at it in short, quick licks that send him thrusting up into me. I can taste him, salty and eager and so damn *close*, I don't know how he managed to hold it in from the car to here. I know I wouldn't have been able to do it.

My arms slip beneath his thighs and my hands grip the bed sheets as he arches into me and I take him down, as far as he goes, until I feel him tickle the back of my throat and still further, until tiny curls fill my nose. My tongue swirls down his length, I work him hard, harder, one of his hands is fisted in my hair and pushing me down *further* as he shoves into me, seeking release. His other hand finds mine beneath him and he laces our fingers together, my name escaping his throat like a sacred mantra, over and over again with each suck, each thrust, each time his ass leaves the bed and my tongue works over that little nub at the base of his shaft. And I watch him, the whole time, I never look away from his face, his slack cheeks, his eyes squeezed shut in pleasure, his mouth a perfect O of desire. "Yes," he sighs, like it's the only word he knows. "Yes, Michael, *yes*."

He comes in an explosive rush that I swear I feel in the back of my head, as furious as a jackhammer pounding the sidewalk, it rattles my teeth and fills my throat and I drink him down, sucking long after he's started to wilt. "Michael," he gasps, his hand clenched so tight in my hair that my scalp tingles, and in his other hand, my fingers have gone numb. "Oh *God*, Michael."

"He had little to do with it," I joke, letting him slip free. He shudders on the bed as I crawl over him again, I love this, I love him. This morning I thought we were okay but I was wrong — that camaraderie at the kitchen table over breakfast was *nothing* compared to this, his soul bared for me, his lips trembling against mine, the taste of him still in my mouth. "I love you," I tell him, I do.

There's a knock on the door ... *of course*, I think with a groan. "If it's Caitlin," I start.

Dan rolls his eyes. "If it's her," he agrees, "then you're right, she *is* as bad as Ray. If not worse."

"I'll tell her you said that," I laugh.

When I try to push myself up off the bed, though, he holds me down. "Don't you dare," he warns. I laugh again and kiss the stern look from his face. "Michael, don't —"

"I'm playing," I assure him. But I keep it in mind, ammunition if she doesn't learn to cut this shit out quick. As long as she's around, I'm going to have the worst case of blue balls ever, and she thinks I'm an ass when I'm not getting any? She hasn't seen me frustrated yet.

It *is* her at the door, no surprise there. "Caitlin," I sigh, leaning against the half-opened door to block her view of Dan. My lover still lies on the bed, his pants undone, his shirt pulled up to his navel, his lower belly a glorious pale stretch in the darkened room. His briefs are still tucked beneath his balls — she *so* doesn't need to see that. "Look, can't we talk about this later? We're sort of picking up where we were before ..."

My sister holds up one hand in that annoying way she has that seems to say, *what the fuck ever*. "I'm not talking to you," she announces. The angry set of her jaw and the way she studiously avoids actually *looking* at me makes me laugh, which pisses her off more. "Shut up."

Over my shoulder, Dan grins when I start, "I thought you said —"

"I forgot to tell you *why* I came looking for your sorry ass," Caitlin says, talking over me as if she doesn't want to hear anything I might have to say. "Dad wants you to help him out in the shed today." There's a wicked gleam in her eye that I don't care for, and now she looks at me, a faint smirk on her lips. "Oh, no wait. He doesn't want *you*. He wants Dan."

A familiar dull ire rises in me. "Tell him I said —"

Caitlin turns away. "Tell him yourself," she calls out as she walks away. "I'm not talking to you, remember?"

I slam the door shut — a childish act but it releases some of my irritation. For added measure, I kick it, too, much good it does. My dad wants Dan out there to help him, no asking this time, he just *assumes* that I won't care. Fuck that. I gave my boy up yesterday — I'll be damned if I let him usurp my lover again today.

When I turn, Dan's already struggling to sit up. "I'll go talk to him," he tells me.

I straighten my hair where Dan had worked his hands in it while I sucked him off. "No," I say, "I'll tell him. He'll just have to do without you today, that's all. He's got plenty of other guys out there to help him — I want you here with me." With a worried glance, I add, "Unless you want ..."

Dan shakes his head. "After yesterday?" he asks, giving me an easy wink. "I'm not leaving your side today."

Embarrassed, I my head and mumble, "I wasn't *that* bad." The look Dan gives me says otherwise, but it bolsters my courage — I'll talk to my dad, tell him look, this is how it is. Dan is mine, he's with me, he came to Sugar Creek to help me through this, not to play handyman. "He'll live without you," I say, sounding bolder than I feel. "I won't." Dan laughs and I promise him, "I'll be right back. I don't think we're done here yet."

37: In The Kitchen

I T TAKES EVERYTHING I have to leave Dan spread out on the bed like that, stomach and cock exposed, a bemused look in his eyes that tells me he knows just how difficult this is for me and he thinks it's funny, damn him, because he knows I'm going to race right back. If I survive my dad. I've told him off plenty of times in my mind, I used to shout at him behind the closed door to my bedroom when I knew he couldn't hear me, I talk a real good game but when it comes right down to it? I'm scared. Plain and simple, the man terrifies me, he always has. That's part of the power he has over me, I think, the knowledge that he can just give me that mean-ass look of his and my arguments dry up like so much dust. He's never raised a hand against me — in our family, my mom doles out the punishments, swift and uncompromising like the black Queen in a game of Hearts. I was rarely the victim, that was Ray. Having a brother like him was enough to keep me out of trouble, just because he was always *in* it, no one had time for me.

Like my dad — we never did those father/son things, camping trips, fishing, hunting. The extent of Henry Knapp's night out was a trip down the street to the bar, where they had the game on a big screen TV, and that was never for me. I wonder if that's what makes me a disappointment to him, that I never fell into the suburban ideal of manhood, feet kicked up in front of the television, beer in hand. Again, that's Ray. And somehow it seems like no matter how hard I try, I can never please my father, *never*. Part of me says just fuck it, I'm old enough not to worry about him anymore, I'm an adult living out my life the way I want to, I don't *need* his approval. But there's another, deeper, childish part that wants him to look at me just once, to *see* me and accept me and I don't know, just tell me that I'm not the biggest fuck-up in his life, is that asking too much? If he would've gotten angry over dinner the other night, at least I'd know what he's thinking, I'd have some sense of where I stand with him. But that's my mom's role, she plays it willingly enough. She's sharp with her disappointment while he just sits there and simmers. No use trying to talk to him about it, he won't respond. I don't even know what I hope to say to him now. *Hands off my boy* seems a little ridiculous, even though that's exactly how I feel.

Out in the kitchen, Ray sits at the table, eating a bowl of cereal in what I know for a fact has to be *my* milk. "Did you go to Grosso's, too?" I ask, my voice tight as I close the door to the back room behind me. At my brother's blank look, I tell him, "Because if you didn't, then that's my milk."

"Caitlin gave it to me," Ray mumbles around a mouth full of food. For emphasis, he points at our sister, who leans against the counter and studiously ignores me. Beside her, Aunt Bobbie leans over a large, round pumpkin that fills the entire sink, one of the gourds from Evie's garden, no doubt. Her sleeves are rolled up to her elbows and her hands are orange with stringy seeds — as I watch, she holds her arms out so Caitlin can scrape the messy innards off into the sink. "She said —"

"I didn't say drink it," she says with a grimace. Bobbie gives me an exhausted smile and digs into the pumpkin again, scooping out more slop. "Hold up," Caitlin mutters, picking white seeds out from the goop already in the sink. "I'm still on this batch."

The room smells overripe and Aunt Bobbie sighs as she scrapes more seeds into the pile my sister's going through. "This is nasty, Caitlin."

"Cat," my sister corrects absently. She picks at the seeds with the tips of her fingers, like she knows it's nasty and she'll be damned if she gets it all over her. Each seed is placed in the cup of her hand, and when she gets a few saved up, she dumps them on a cookie sheet set out next to the sink. After the pumpkin's been carved into a jack o' lantern, they'll roast the seeds in the oven. From the corner of her eye, Caitlin looks up, her gaze not quite finding me — she's clearly annoyed. "Tell your brother I didn't give you the damn milk."

Your brother ... so she's still playing like that. Crossing the room, I peer over Aunt Bobbie's shoulder down into the hollowed-out pumpkin and point out, "I'm right here, Caitlin. You don't have to talk about me in the third person."

In an eerie imitation of our cousin Emily yesterday morning, Caitlin cocks her head to one side and asks no one in particular, "Do you hear something?"

I curl my hands into useless fists to keep from hitting her. "How did you put it?" I ask, my words curt. "That's childish and fucking stupid?"

"Mike," Aunt Bobbie warns. "Please don't —"

"Say fuck," I say, grinning at the frustration that crosses my aunt's face. "I know, I'm sorry."

"If you were sorry," Bobbie points out, "then you wouldn't have said it again."

A strand of hair slips from behind my aunt's ear to curl in her face. Tucking it back into place, I tell her, "It's true, though. She *is* being childish."

Aunt Bobbie shakes her head, but her lips curve in the ghost of a grin and she plunges her hands into the pumpkin again, scrapping the inside of the gourd to clean it out. "She's not the only one," my aunt says, nudging me with her hip.

On the other side of her, Caitlin snorts with stifled laughter. "Shut up," I mutter, and in an unexpected move, I reach around Bobbie and smack the back of my sister's head playfully.

The look she gives me is pure fury. Before I can say I was only teasing, she lashes out, one foot kicking my ankle despite my aunt between us. "Hey!" I cry, indignant. "Stop it with the kicking already, will you? First you kick my car —"

"Because you were being mean to me," Caitlin retorts.

"Oh, now you're talking to me again?" She rolls her eyes and shakes her head but doesn't answer. As Aunt Bobbie pulls out another handful of pumpkin guts, I pick a few of the seeds out myself and peg them at my sister. "I wasn't *mean* to you."

Caitlin swats away one of the seeds before it can hit her in the face, but the others fall harmlessly to the floor. "You were, too," she mumbles. The next seed she picks out, she aims at me, and she's a better shot than I am, it hits right below my eye and sticks. As I wipe it away, she falls back into her ignoring me routine. "He said ugly things about me, Aunt Bobbie. Called me ugly names."

With an exasperated sigh, I protest, "I did *not* —"

"Michael?" my aunt asks in mock surprise, but I can hear the amusement in her voice, she thinks this is funny. "What kind of names?"

"She kicked my car *first*," I stress. This is an important factor in our fight, I don't think Caitlin realizes it. I'm not the villain here. "Dan and I were minding our own business —"

My sister raises her voice to talk over me. "They were getting *dirty*."

"We were having a little bit of *fun*," I correct, "of the horizontal variety, when she comes busting in on us and kicks my goddamn car!" At Aunt Bobbie's reproachful glance, I add hastily, "I'm sorry."

Behind us, Ray frowns into his cereal and asks, "What were you doing?" Apparently that *horizontal* comment confused him. I didn't think he would get it.

"We were getting it on," I explain. And because he's my brother and I know him all too well, I fist my hand and pump it a few times in a jerk-off action just so he gets my drift. "You know ...?"

He does. He laughs so hard that he almost chokes, and milk sprays from his nose as if he's sneezed. That sets Caitlin giggling — Ray's the only adult I know who prides himself on being as disgusting now as he was twenty years ago. "In the *car?*" he asks, like he's never heard of sex in the front seat before. The thought bugs his eyes out wide, and he stares at me with something akin to God-fearing awe. Then he turns to Caitlin. "You *saw* them?"

"No, stupid." She throws a seed at him — it pings off his forehead and he rubs at the spot with a tiny *ow*. She would probably throw another one but Aunt Bobbie stops her by plopping another heaping mess into the sink. Remembering that she's been wronged, Caitlin picks at these fresh seeds and mutters, "Despite what he thinks, I'm not as bad as you. He actually told me that, Aunt Bobbie, can you *believe* it? He said I'm as bad as Ray." Worried, she frowns up at the older woman and asks, "Am I?"

"As bad as me?" Ray starts to laugh that long, braying donkey laugh of his — he shakes his head like this is all just *too* funny for him, and then it hits him, it was an insult, he's laughing at his own expense. I have to grin as it dawns on him. His eyes go blank, his face freezes, he obviously can't laugh and think at the same time. Then his brows draw together, somehow we're picking on *him* and that's not funny, not one bit. "Hey," he cries. "Wait a minute. I'm not that bad." He tries to think of something more but can't, so he pouts into his cereal and glares at us, Caitlin and I giggling by the sink and even Aunt Bobbie smiling now. "*I'm* not the one getting a piece of ass in the car," he mutters, like this is the worse insult he can come up with.

"You're not getting a piece of ass, period," Caitlin tells him. Before Bobbie can scold her, I add, "I'm not getting any either, standing here shooting the shit with you guys."

"Such language!" my aunt exclaims, even though she's getting a kick out of our bickering, I can tell. "From the mouths of babes."

With a nonchalant shrug, I tell her, "We try."

But Caitlin is through playing. She remembers that she's mad at me and that she's not supposed to be talking to me, and she turns back to her seeds with a vengeance. "He started it," she says. It's still all my fault, isn't it? "That *bad as Ray* comment hurt, Mike."

My brother gives a sort of little half-laugh that ends with him choking on the food in his mouth. "You think?" he asks.

"Do you?" I counter, but I know the answer to *that* question already. For a few tense moments, no one speaks, we're drifting away from easy banter and drifting towards something darker, something mean. I wouldn't say I started it, but I realize that I'm keeping it up, just because of the thought that looms foremost in my mind — the reason I came out here, to go talk to my dad. The longer I fool around here, the more I manage to put off *that* impending conversation. Or maybe I'm trying to build up my anger, get Caitlin and Ray pissed at me enough to steel myself for the coming confrontation with my dad.

Whatever the case, it needs to stop. I'm sick of this fighting — even if it *is* the norm around here. Dan and I are alright again, I don't want anything my family might say or do to interfere with that. Why can't I just put an end to all of this madness? What would it take, what could I say, to make my family like the families you see on TV, where no one gets offended or hurt by off-color remarks, where the drama is wrapped up in a half hour, where they're all friends in the end?

Or hell, like Dan's family, maybe — he's an only child, there is no fighting when we go to visit his parents. His mom is the stereotypical June Cleaver type of woman, always cooking or sewing or running off to Bingo on Tuesday nights. She knows that I'm Dan's lover and she's okay with that, unlike my own mother. The first time he brought me home, for his parents' anniversary in June, he told her straight up, here's how it is. It seemed so *easy* for him, too. The three of us sat at a picnic table under a canopy outside of the American Legion, where his dad was helping with a weekend cookout. His mom made some comment about meeting any nice girls yet and Dan just shrugged. "I'm not looking," he told her, taking a bite of his cheeseburger. I remember thick juices running down the side of his hand, that instant is frozen in my mind, the reddish brown drop coursing beneath his pinky in a bumpy pattern and I could see myself leaning over right there on that warm spring day, right there among the veterans, leaning over and licking that drop away. I could almost taste it, and the image glowed in my mind as brightly as a white shirt on a stage bathed in black light. What would Mrs. Biggs have said then? When the boy she just met, the one her son introduced as his roommate, leaned over and licked Dan like a dog?

From across the picnic table she frowned at us, at Dan and then at me. She swatted an annoying fly away and her eyes narrowed, as if she were processing what Dan just said, running it through the circuits in her mind, matching it up with what she saw in front of her eyes, me and Dan sitting a little too close together on a narrow bench ... it hit her the same way an abstract thought or complicated sentence will hit Ray, suddenly and without warning, a rush that tears through the mind like a train through the night. Her eyes held my gaze, I couldn't look away. "Michael," she said softly. She always speaks softly, his dad does, too — it must be where Dan gets it from. I've never met people who can talk as low as his family does and still command a presence wherever they go.

I ducked my head, ashamed of the sordid thoughts I was sure she could read written out in my eyes. Beneath the table, Dan's hand covered my knee, much the same way it would months later when I finally came out to my own parents and needed all the strength I could muster to face them. I wonder if it would have made any difference in the way things turned out if Evie hadn't passed away, if Penny hadn't called, if we hadn't overstayed our welcome and could have just gone home at the start of the week instead of up here to Sugar Creek, where my mom is forced to watch the two of us together and see how we feel for each other. But has she even really seen that yet? Has she seen what he means to me? If she did, how could she possibly find anything wrong with our love?

Maybe I should have shirked the responsibility and let Dan tell my parents for me — he did a good job with his mom. As she stared at me, trying to pin me in her mind as her son's boyfriend and not just a guy he knew off-base, Dan told her simply, "We're in love, Mom. He means everything to me. I'm just not interested in anyone else."

For a full minute, she said nothing. Just watched, thinking. I would have given anything to hear those thoughts. Perhaps they were much like my own mom's at the time, I don't know. When she finally spoke, it was with a slight nod that didn't seem to condone our relationship so much as accept it — this is how it's going to be, she knew she could do nothing to change that. "You're happy," she said. It wasn't a question, more like a statement of fact, she could see what I did to her son and it was enough for her to know that he was loved. Dan nodded, though, and she glanced past us to the large grill several feet away, where her husband stood in oven mitts and an apron, turning hot dogs for the kids. "Were you planning to tell your father?"

I knew that Dan was hoping to come out to *both* of his parents, and on the long drive from D.C. to Ohio we talked over different scenarios, ways to get them both together, ways to just come out and say it, we're a couple. Together, in much the same way they are, though we haven't gotten quite *that* far in our relationship yet. I'm hoping, and I know Dan's thinking it, we've pretty much decided that we're both in it for the long haul and prior to this weekend, we had just reached the point where he made a comment about marriage and I didn't feel a cold hand seize my heart in my chest. But his mother asked about girls and that sort of hurried things up a bit, and a quick look at my lover told me that he thought maybe springing it on his dad at this point would seem as if we were all ganging up on him. It would be unfair. Still, he's the quiet type, doesn't like to appear to be directing the show, so he shrugged again and asked his mom, "What do you think we should do?"

We, including her into the secret circle, making her feel involved. "I think maybe now isn't a good time," she replied, and Dan nodded, I nodded, yes, there might be a good time somewhere down the road but now was probably not it. "Let me feel him out, honey. I'll tell you when."

Four months later and *when* hasn't rolled around yet. But Dan's okay with it. "As long as Mom knows," he says, and the quiet assurance that gave him made me think that telling my own parents wouldn't be so bad. But standing here in the kitchen with my brother and sister both glaring at me, I wonder what the hell was going through my mind to make me think that telling my parents anything wouldn't be so bad.

At the table, Ray shoots me a hateful look that I meet with a steady gaze, until he's the one to turn away. I need to go talk with my dad, tell him Dan's not coming to his beck and call. I've wasted too much time arguing here — by the time I return, Dan won't even be in the mood anymore. Heading for the back door, I call out bitterly, "I'm sorry, okay?" I'm talking to Caitlin but she's not looking at me, she's probably not even listening. "Just stop fucking interrupting us."

"Stop interrupting you fucking," she corrects. Her slight smile tells me we're cool again.

"Caitlin!" Aunt Bobbie warns. I make my escape, the sounds of my sister's quick laughter following me outside.

38: My Dad

THE GRIN SLIPS from my face as I step out onto the porch. The screen door slaps shut behind me with all the finality of a coffin lid — what the hell am I doing? I feel like a father who has to tell his son's friends sorry, he can't come out today, only it's *my* dad I'm going to see, to tell him that he can't play with Dan, the boy is mine. And what will he do, yell at me? Laugh? Or slip into his silent treatment and not talk to me, not acknowledge my presence — he's better at that than Caitlin is, *worlds* better. When Henry Knapp is mad with you, you damn well know it. You cease to exist for him. Some days I don't even need to make him angry to feel like I've already disappeared.

Outside, the sky is a deep denim blue, and dark, wispy clouds scurry away above the trees. The wind is colder now than it was this morning — there's an edge to it that cuts through my sweater to bite at my chest and arms. In the distance I can hear the tell-tale buzz of power tools, a drill or saw or something like that, reverberating with a hollow echo inside the garden shed on the other side of the yard. That's where he is, where I'm headed. Beneath the noise comes the steady rush of water from the creek, an ever-present sound out here. Shoving my hands into the pockets of my jeans, I cross the porch and take the steps quickly, it's too chilly to linger. I think of Dan, half naked among the bed sheets, *that* spurs me on. The thought of him in a warm bed, it's enough to get me hard all over again, and a fierce heat burns at my groin, spreads through my legs like melted butter, churns my stomach into giddy knots.

I start across the back yard, my shoes rustling in the wet grass, the cuffs of my pants growing damp. Once I'm out in the open, the wind picks up like an overeager puppy happy to see me — it snuffles over my back, my sleeves, nips at my face, tousles my hair. I bow down before it, my face turned studiously away, my lips pressed together to keep from getting chapped. *This* is winter, this wind, a harbinger of what's to come. For the first time since we arrived in Sugar Creek, I have to admit that I'm glad I'm going back home before the rest of this weather comes through. *Going home for good*, I think, and I nod even though I didn't say that out loud. I just know. I'm not coming back here again.

The wind catches my sweater, pulls it out in front of me like an insistent playmate. *Run*, it tells me. *Take flight with me and make a memory. Make this moment count, make it stand out in your mind, make it forever.* "I did that already," I say quietly, my words whipped away in the short, quick gusts that rail around me. Before the rain, back in the woods, that part of Sugar Creek that I shared with Dan will always stay with me, more than all the summers I spent here in childhood or the winters I came and played in the snow, all the times I tasted Stephen Robichaud and held him and Jesus knows, all the times I let him taste and hold me. Most important of all, that time with my lover cancels out the wounded look in Stephen's eyes that has haunted me since yesterday, when he kissed me goodbye.

Goodbye.

It's cold out here, colder than I thought it would be, and Dan's waiting. I pick up the pace, weave through the tables with their folded umbrellas and their chairs tucked in to keep them from blowing around. Up ahead I see Kenny and my Uncle Doug putting a coat of weatherproofing on what looks like a freshly constructed bench propped up against the garden shed. My dad built that, I'm sure, probably as a place to set the trash cans, to keep them out of reach of raccoons or whatever other woodland animals will come up from the creek for food. As I approach, the sound of my shoes swishing through the grass makes my cousin look up at me, and he smiles as he squints into the noon sun. "Mike, hey," he says, waving the paintbrush at me. "Heard you were back. Things okay?"

"Fine," I tell him. *Heard you were back* ... in this family, gossip spreads like poison ivy, you can't control it. So I'm sure he and Doug know about the scene on the porch this morning, they must have a pretty good idea of what happened between Dan and me on our little drive, and from the way they're grinning, I know they heard about us getting frisky in the car out front. I don't even feel disgusted at that anymore — it's just a fact of life. I'm part of this family, my life is an open book to them. There's no such thing as *privacy* at Aunt Evie's.

Uncle Doug looks past me at the house, then turns back to the bench to wipe up excess proofing before it can drip. "Where's Dan?" he asks. "Your dad's looking for him."

"I know, well —" I take a deep breath, let it out slowly, and with a smug wink, I tell them, "He's somewhat ... *preoccupied* at the moment. You know how it is."

Kenny whoops loudly — he's not as dense as Ray can be. "That boy is whipped," he says. I shrug, embarrassed, but I like the awe shining in their wide eyes, their wicked grins. Jerking a thumb at me, he tells Doug, "Color me impressed. He's got a soldier in his room just *begging* for it."

"I didn't say *that*," I start.

But it's too late. They like the idea of me laying down the law for my Army boyfriend. Maybe it makes me stronger in their minds somehow, it takes away the stigma of me being gay, the implied femininity of one boy in love with another. Whatever the case, suddenly I'm one of the guys again, I'm cool, okay to hang with — Doug nudges me and says, "Hey, nothing wrong with being whipped. Ask Kenny. His girl isn't even putting out and he's wrapped around her finger." Turning to my cousin, he wants to know, "Hasn't she lifted those skirts just a *little* bit for you yet?"

"Hey, hey!" Kenny cries. His brow creases and he glares at us, all jest gone. "We're not talking about Neeshi here, got that?"

Before Doug can reply, I add, "We're not talking about Dan, either. Jeez, why is it that suddenly everyone wants to know all about my damn sex life? I should sell tickets or something."

Doug laughs. "I hear you're giving free previews out in the front lawn."

"Okay, I can explain that," I say, and they both laugh this time, Kenny too. Hurriedly changing the subject, I ask, "Where is my dad anyway?"

Kenny motions at the shed with the paintbrush, and proofing flecks in a spray across the painted boards. "Ken, dammit!" Doug cries, wiping at the splatter with the bottom of his shirt. "Shit, he'll make us do that next if you mess it up."

"It's too wet out here to paint," I say. I look up at the sky like it might start to rain again any minute now. "He's inside?"

With a backhand swing, Kenny flings his brush at Doug, misting his cheek and neck with the proofing. I laugh at the look of horror that crosses my uncle's face — then he dips his own brush back into the can and runs his thumb across the bristles. Proofing sprays Kenny like mace, his cheeks, his nose, his lips, his *hair* ... "Okay, you know what?" he asks, dipping his brush in the can with all the solemnity of a soldier reloading ammo. "You're dead."

Before he can retaliate, I laugh and duck behind him, heading for the front of the shed. "I'm not getting in the middle of this," I tell them.

Doug turns a half second before Kenny attacks. Most of the proofing this time winds up in his hair, beading like rain. "What," he asks, slapping the back of my cousin's wrist with his brush, "can't get messy? You have a hot date lined up?"

"Something like that," I say. His next hit goes wide, misses Kenny completely to splash the side of the shed — so much for keeping it clean. I feel tiny droplets seep through my sleeve and I brush at the dampness on my sweater, indignant. "Hey! I'm not in this fight, remember?"

They look at me with such pure mischief that I step back, my hands up in warding gesture. "Don't," I warn, and even though it makes me sound childish and petty, I add, "I'll tell my dad you two are fucking around." I take another step back — I'm in front of the shed door now, I can see the bright light thrown from the bare bulb that hangs from the ceiling, I can see my dad's back as he stands on a small stepladder to straighten the shelves that he's putting in. If I raise my voice, he'll hear me, and from the way Kenny and Doug lower their paintbrushes, I figure the *last* thing they need is my dad riding their asses. Getting me a little messy wouldn't justify the punishment, I'm sure.

With a pout that rivals Caitlin's — if there's anything this family does well, it's argue and pout — Kenny holds his loaded brush at his side, aimed at the ground in defeat. Large drops of proofing drip onto the toes of his black Converse hi-tops, the kind I used to wear as a kid ... they still *make* those? "You're no fun," he grumbles. Like a child trying to get in the last hit, Doug flecks his brush at him, and Kenny winces as fresh proofing splatters the side of his face.

"I'm plenty fun," I assure them. "Just ask Dan."

I turn away from their laughter, grinning myself. On my way into the shed, I swear I feel a few drops land on the back of my neck, but it's a scant sensation, it could be anything, proofing or rainwater dripping from the eaves above the door, anything at all. So I just ignore it — mentioning it would be an open invite to include me in their horseplay, and I've got things to see and people to do, as they say.

Inside the shed, I feel trapped — it's a small building, I could hold my arms out at my sides and the fingertips on either hand would brush against the walls. The ceiling is corrugated tin, which I know from my childhood makes the shed sound like the inside of a tribal drum when it rains. The cacophony is deafening, I don't know how my dad worked through it. Beneath my feet, the floor is concrete, but there's river sand and sawdust scattered across it and each step I take leaves behind a thin footprint. A window on either side of the shed lets in muted sunlight, refracted through the trees, and the bare bulb above illuminates everything with a stark clarity, like the negative of a photograph. My dad's tools, fanned over the work table. Gardening supplies stacked in one corner. Long wooden shelves leaning against the wall, waiting to be hung. My dad on the stepladder, righting one such shelf across two metal brackets. "Hey Dad," I say, my hands once again in my pockets simply because I don't know what else to do with them. My stomach churns nervously, and all of my cocky playfulness is gone.

"Is this straight?" my father asks by way of hello. I stop where I am in the middle of the shed and frown at the shelf he's trying to hang. With an exasperated glance over his shoulder, he asks, "Well? Straight or not?"

"Looks straight to me," I tell him. If it were anyone else up there, I might add a comment about just how reliable am *I* when it comes to straight, Caitlin would get a laugh out of something like that, but it's not her, it's my dad, and I learned early on in life that he has no real sense of humor.

Like now. *Looks straight* isn't good enough for him — he grumbles as he climbs down the stepladder, moving slowly like an old man. "Goddamn shed is build on a slant," he mutters beneath his breath. He drops his drill on the table with the other tools and stands slightly in front of me, his hands on his hips. "Level don't work if the whole damn thing is crooked."

I don't know what to say. After a moment, he nods. "Yeah, it'll work." Over his shoulder, he asks, "Where's that friend of yours?"

I'm almost glad he's in front of me, because that gives me a clear shot at the door if I have to run. Clearing my throat, I tell him, "He's not coming."

My dad's back stiffens as if I've just insulted him. Slowly he turns, his jaw clenched, his brow furrowed. "Why the hell not?" he wants to know. "He's got things to finish today."

Somehow I meet that terrible gaze — I even manage a shrug, as if my heart isn't racing in my chest. "I want him to work with me today," I say. My voice is quiet, I'm going to try to keep it that way. The guys outside don't need to hear this and, quiet always works for Dan. Maybe this time it'll work for me. "He's my boyfriend, Dad. I shouldn't have to explain this to you. I want him with me."

For a moment I think I've said too much. His eyes cloud over with anger, his hands fist at his hips. "He helped you out yesterday," I hurry on — what happened to quiet? I should just shut up but I can't, my dad's silence goads me on, I have to fill the emptiness between us. "Changing those locks? I thought that was all you wanted him to do but then you kept him all day long, doing this, fixing that … I barely saw him at all. There are plenty of people here, you know. Get someone else to help you out today. Dan's staying in with me."

"He said this?" my dad asks.

I can hear the anger in his voice. This isn't going the way I anticipated — he's not mad at me, he's getting mad with Dan, and that's the last person he needs to be pissed at. It's my fault Dan's not coming today, doesn't he see that? I'm the one out here telling him all this. He still doesn't see *me.*

"No, Dad," I say, growing angry myself. "I did."

With great difficulty, he focuses on me, standing right in front of him. For the first time since I can remember, he looks in my eyes, not through them, not *at* them, but *in* — he studies my face, the smooth skin, the blondish eyebrows, the slanted nose that looks like his own did twenty years ago, before long nights of alcohol ruddied it. He looks me over like I've suddenly become a complete stranger to him, someone he doesn't know, and there's a wariness in his eyes that I like, a look that says he's not quite sure what to do now. The fact that it was *my* words that put that confusion there, that strengthens me, it makes me stand taller, my shoulders back and proud. *Now* he sees me, *me*, not his son but a man before him, a man with dreams he might not know about, a man with a life beyond his own, a man to be reckoned with. Me.

That wary look in his eyes gives me the courage to tell him, "I know you have things to get done. We all do. But when you take him like that, without even bothering with me? It's like I'm not ... I don't know, Dad, it's like you don't think I'm man enough, you know? Like I'm still a little boy and I'm not." He doesn't answer, just stares at me, *say something*, I pray. *Anything at this point. Let me know you're hearing this.*

The lines across his forehead deepen. "I know you're not," he says gruffly. This is new to him, this talking things out. "I didn't say you couldn't come along. He'd just done it before." As an afterthought, he adds, "You could've come, too."

I sigh. That's beside the point — I didn't go and I can't turn back time now. "You know, Dad," I try, feeling my way around the words gingerly. This is hard for us both, I realize that. "When you do stuff like that? It makes me think that you're using him as some kind of ... I don't know, substitute son, or something. I mean, since I've been home this time? It's like I'm not really here to you. There's Dan instead. He's the one you speak to, he's the one you want to do things with, not me. And that's not fair." His frown almost turns to a scowl, almost, but I hurry on, "Not to me, because I *am* your son, and not to him because it puts him in a very awkward position, almost like you're trying to play us off one another. That's just not going to work, I'm sorry."

I've said too much, I know it — it's in the way he glares at me again, it's in the set of his jaw, the thin line of his lips pressed together. I'm about to say I'm sorry again, I've gotten good at apologizing these past few days, but my dad sighs and looks away. Without his gaze pinning me in place, my knees feel trembly and weak. His voice is husky when he talks, like the words hurt him to say aloud. "Caitlin brings a boy home," he tells me, "and I know what to expect. It's twenty questions while he squirms on the couch and the riot act before they leave. Don't touch my daughter, don't even *look* at her if you can help it, that whole thing. I know what he expects of *me*, so I can play the part of the overbearing father while he's in the house, I keep my daughter safe."

So she'd have you believe, I think, but I keep silent. Emotions flicker across my dad's face like sunlight playing over the rippling waters of the creek — his anger has faded, replaced with a sadness I don't think I quite like. "Ray brings his buddies over," he continues, still not looking at me, "and I joke with them a bit, offer them beers, we sit and watch TV and eat chips, guy things. I know how to handle that." He turns towards me again slowly. "Then there's you, Mike. You come down here and tell us what, you like boys? You even bring one along for show. Out of the blue, though I told your mother plenty of times over the years, I thought you might be a little funny." He seesaws his hand in that way people have when they don't want to out and *say* that someone's queer. "And what am I supposed to do about it? You're not my daughter, I'm not going to run him through the gauntlet. But he's more than just one of my son's friends."

He looks at me, and this isn't the father I've always known, this is the man beneath that, the man the world sees. I notice the gray that silvers the hair by his temple, when did he get old? Lines rim his eyes, his mouth, and tiny dark spots have cropped up like stubble on his cheeks. An old, sad man. "So tell me, son," he says softly. "Tell me just how you want me to react to this."

39: Just One of the Guys

I'M STUNNED. THAT has to be the most my father has said to me at one time, *ever*. Even the "facts of life" talk we had when I was what, ten? About two years after the kiss Stephanie Robichaud gave me — I've always suspected that Ray finally ratted on me about it and that's the only reason my dad came into my room one day, a look on his face that clearly read, *I'd rather be anywhere but here*. Sitting on the edge of my bed, he patted the mattress beside him and waited until I sat down as well before he spoke. I could smell the alcohol on his breath, a tart scent mingled with the cologne he only wore to church, a Sunday smell that in my mind I'll always associate with the heavy pall of flowers and the bitter taste of wine. "You know when you jerk off, Mikey?" he asked then. "Don't play dumb with me, son, I know you do it — boys have been doing it forever. That's what makes babies."

The thought horrified me. Touching myself under the covers at night, jerking off in the shower, that was just fooling around. Ray told me babies came from girls, I knew that much, you stick it in and get off in *there* and you have a kid. But this was Ray we're talking about — maybe he had it wrong. I mean, my father knew what he was saying, right? He already had two kids, he should know.

Still, I had to clarify things. "By yourself?" I asked, trepidatious. All I could picture was me naked in the shower, the steady beat of hot water heavenly on my back and thighs, my legs apart and one hand pumping my hard dick while the other gripped the towel rack to hold my balance. My hand on my balls, squeezing, kneading, working them together like dice in my palm. My finger easing below them, back, until it found a tender spot and with a sharp pain slipped inside. Instant tightness sucking me in, the sting of soap, a wonderful sensation I had never felt before and knew without a doubt that I would want to find again and again. Just thinking of it make me want to shoo my dad out now and take care of the growing heaviness at my groin. I stared at the floor so he wouldn't see the color rise in my cheeks or the hunger in my eyes. I could almost taste the release, it lingered sweet in the back of my throat ... but if that's the way babies were made, if everyone had it wrong and licking my hand when I was done to savor every drop was a sure way to get *pregnant*, I was going to have to reevaluate this new past-time of mine.

My dad laughed then, an uncomfortable titter that was more my mom than him. "Not by yourself," he said, and he laughed again, a real laugh this time. Running a hand down his face, he sighed. "Jesus. You know, maybe this isn't a good idea."

I couldn't imagine what he was talking about. In an effort to help, I told him, "Ray says you need to get with a girl."

"For once, Ray is right." He looked around the room, studiously avoiding me, and I looked at my feet on the floor, my legs, the budding bulge in the front of my jeans. I willed my father to leave. I had things I wanted to take care of now that he had brought the subject up.

As if hearing my thoughts, he rose to his feet. "You get with a girl," he said, raising his voice a little the way people do when they're on the phone and ready to hang up. "You need a girl to have babies, Mikey, keep that in mind. You keep her panties on and you won't have to worry about none of that shit, you hear me?" I nodded, though to be honest, getting into a girl's panties was the last thing on my mind. When I got off, it was to thoughts of boys doing the exact same thing I was doing, rubbing and fingering themselves. It was still a few years before I started to think of two boys together, and long before Stephen's first kiss, when I would think of another boy doing that stuff to me. *What about boys?* I almost asked, but my dad was heading for the door and I didn't want to delay him. Besides, I was curious, not *stupid.* There was a part of me that knew even then that keeping my thoughts to myself on *that* subject might be a good idea. "Your mom knows more about this stuff than I do," my dad said on his way out. "Go ask her if you have any questions."

Then his voice had been just as gruff as it is now, standing here in Aunt Evie's shed and staring at each other like complete strangers. This time he knows my thoughts, though, I've told him where my desires lay, and he wants me to tell him what to do about it. What am I supposed to say? This is just as new to me as it is to him.

Choosing my words carefully, I tell him, "Maybe it'd be good to know where you stand on this ... I mean, how you feel about ... about me, first." I look at him with questioning eyes but see no answers written on his face. "Before we go any further."

As if changing the subject, my dad asks, "How old are you again?"

I don't see what that matters. "Twenty-five," I say. "I guess what I'm asking here is —"

He nods and waves the rest of my sentence away, distracted. "Twenty-five is damn near old enough to start living your own life," he tells me, "and stop wondering what the hell everyone else is going to say about it. I had a wife and baby by the time I was your age. I had a good paying job, a car, my first mortgage. I didn't care that my momma didn't like Laura or wouldn't be bothered with my son. And I wasn't about to lose any sleep at night thinking if so-and-so at the plant thought I was doing the right thing. Right or not, it was *mine*."

I know about the animosity between my mother and her in-laws. From the start, my father's parents didn't like her much, mostly because Dad's an only child like Dan is, and believe it or not, he was always a momma's boy. His father suffered with polio as a child and could only walk with the help of two metal canes that latched to his arms, so when something broke around the house or something needed to be done, Henry was the one his mother looked to for help. Before he was married, he lived down the street from his parents and hurried home whenever they called.

Then came Laura. She attended college in Philadelphia, where they met while my father was working on a construction crew putting in new dorms. It was love at first sight, or so my mom would have you believe, though to hear my dad tell it, he got shitfaced at a frat party one night and a week later when she called, she had missed her period. The "sort of dating" relation-ship suddenly accelerated to "engaged to be married," no questions asked, do not pass Go, do not collect two hundred dollars. One of the only times I remember visiting Ma Knapp was shortly after my fifteen birthday, when we stopped through to say hi before heading out west to Sugar Creek. Her hus-band Earl had given up the ghost years before, and his wife was an elderly woman, so damn bitter that my mom found any excuse to leave the house while we were there, leaving me and my brother with my dad and his dying mother. With a claw-like hand, Ma gripped my wrist and held me tight, squeezed until I felt my bones grind together. "She trapped him, Mikey," she hissed at me, her face a mask of wrinkles and lines etched so deep into her skin, they looked like folds in cloth. "She trapped him into marrying her, oldest trick in the book, stole my son away from me and look where he's at. Saddled with you kids, that's where. Trapped him."

She stared at me with bird's eyes, beady and hard. The whites were yel-low with age, and there was a smell that rose from her whenever she shifted, a dry, dusty scent of lilac that made me want to sneeze. There was so much hate staring at me, *saddled with you kids*. Her fingers strangled my wrist, *this* was the old hag in the fairy tales I had read about as a little kid, *this* was the wicked witch, the evil stepmother, *this* ... trying to twist free from her hold, I grimaced and fought the urge to kick out, knock her down, get her away from me. I didn't like her, not one bit, that bitter, hateful woman. *Look where he's at* — the words echoed in my head. *Saddled with you kids.* "Well, it's better than with *you*," I muttered. And I wonder where Caitlin gets it from. "Dried up old crone. Let me go, I'll tell my mom. Let me *go*."

Oh yes, she hated my mother, up until the day she died, she hated my mother. I was in high school when she passed, and my dad drove up alone — I remember sitting in the living room, all of us, shocked into silence because he just told us Ma was gone. Well, quiet except for my sister, who asked, "Gone where?" And when no one answered, she leaned against my mother and whispered loudly, "Mom? Gone where? Where did she go?" Six years old, the concept of death was beyond her. Hell, I'm having trouble coping with it myself, here, now. We stayed home for that funeral — Dad went up alone, and though Mom cried when we heard the news, I've always suspected they had been tears of relief that the woman who loathed her so much, loathed her own *son* for daring to live on his own, *that* woman was finally gone.

"Tell me, Michael," my dad says, snapping me back to the present, "what you want from me. What you want me to feel about all this."

"I don't know," I admit softly. I try for a smile but it feels weak on my lips. "I thought you might be upset. Yell and scream, you know, the whole bit. Banish me from the house, maybe, or disown me." *Anything but this silence*, I add to myself. *I can handle anything but that.*

He laughs, a short, quick bark that seems to surprise him. "Your momma's the one for drama in this family," he says, making me laugh, too. "I leave that up to her."

"So ..." *You're okay with it?* I'm almost afraid to ask, that would pin the question down, force him to answer yes or no, commit him to one side or the other. I can't seem to get the words out, I don't want to lose this bizarre intimacy we've finally managed to find. With an almost helpless shrug, I mumble, "I don't know. Maybe if I knew where you stood exactly, what *you* were thinking ..."

He lets me trail off, expecting more. There *isn't* more, nothing else I'm comfortable enough to say. "Mike," he starts, but when I look at him, he loses that thought and frowns at me, I can almost hear the gears shift in his mind. "I'm not *proud* of ..." Here comes the hand gesture again, rolling this time, indicating whatever it is we're talking about, my being gay, he can't come out and actually *say* the words. That's okay. It's enough that we're on the same page, in my book. I never dreamed we'd come this far. His voice is gruff with uneasiness, and he can't meet my gaze as he says, "Whatever it is you do in your bedroom, in your *house*, is your own business, you know that. I don't advertise the fact that your mother and I still sometimes ..." Is that a thin blush rising to his cheeks? A reddening of the flesh that hints at embarrassment? It makes him human, it makes him *real*.

"Oh God," I say, stifling giggles that threaten to ruin this moment. I hold up one hand — "Dad, I so don't need to hear this." I don't even want to *think* about what he's suggesting. Sure, they had to have done it before, they have three kids, but the image of my *parents* ... I just can't picture it. I don't *want* to. "I get your drift, honest. Say no more." Almost pleading, I add, "Please."

He doesn't need to be told twice, it's a subject he'd rather not touch. "All I'm saying is as long as you keep it quiet, there's nothing much I can do about it even if I wanted to. Like I said, it's your life, son."

My life ... something loosens in my chest, a weight that breaks free from my soul, buoys my heart, I hear his words again, *all I'm saying*. And it's not what he's said, it's what remains unspoken between us, it's what he's hinted at that pulls my lips into a foolishly happy grin — he's okay with this, with *me*. "So you're cool with it?" I ask, just to see if maybe he could be pushed into something a little more definite. But already this is the closest he's ever come to telling me that I'm not a disappointment to him, and because it's my father, because I know he'd never in a million years out and *say* the words, I can be satisfied with this.

That color is back, twin spots like a fever burning just below the outer corners of his eyes, and he turns away so I won't see it. He straightens the power tools on the bench just to busy himself, and I fight the urge to ask again. I wait. I have all day, if need be — I want to hear his answer.

But when he starts to pick through the shelving brackets, it becomes obvious that he's avoiding me. "Dad —"

"I'm not saying I condone it," he scowls, like I've come here to ask for money and he wants to make me work for anything I get. "I'm not saying you have my blessing, Mike, if that's what you're asking." To punctuate this, he presses the trigger on his drill, and an electric buzz fills the shed.

I can feel that whine in my teeth, but I don't say anything, just wait until he tires of the noise. He releases the trigger and the buzz winds down to a few choppy clicks, and then only the dull memory remains. "I'm not asking that," I say, keeping my voice low. He has to keep the drill off to hear me — I see his finger hover over the trigger again, I'm sure he'll press it in again and drown me out, he's been known to do shit like that, and when he doesn't, I think it surprises him. He wants to hear me out. "What I guess I want to know is if this is going to be a problem. Dan coming down —"

"Might want to take that up with your mother," he tells me. "She's the one you have to watch out for and you know it."

"But you're okay with Dan?" I insist. "With us visiting?" Not that his staying behind while I come down is an option.

Dad's finger flecks over the trigger and the drill flares to life briefly before winding down like an outboard motor. "He's a nice boy," he says, almost grudgingly. He's not looking at me again but stares at the tip of the drill, the bit still turning in a lazy circle. "You could do worse, you know. In the Army, good job, serving the country, specially at time like this. Now if you came home with some flaming *homo*, things might be a little different, but he's okay."

The corner of his mouth flickers in a stifled smile — is that his attempt at a joke? Does he think he's being *funny*? I honestly don't know, I've never heard him take a stab at humor before. *Failed miserably*, I think. I wonder if I should point out that the term *homo* is a slur, but maybe he's trying to tell me something, not just about Dan, but about me. Maybe he's trying to say if *I* were flamboyant or effeminate, he might take my mom's stand on this whole issue. As long as I *look* normal enough ... I wonder if I should even bother being offended. What's the use if he doesn't realize the insult?

"He's okay," I echo. Dad shrugs, he might have said that, maybe. All these half-truths with him, all these shades of grey. He can't just commit to his feelings, he can't be open with me, I have to take what I can get. He thinks Dan's okay, fine. He says he's cool with us being together, great. "So you don't mind if we come down sometimes?" I press. Some things I want to make sure I have absolutely clear. He shrugs again, we could come or not, it's all the same to him. "I just want to make sure, Dad, because if Mom's going to get strident and want us to sleep apart, I'm not having it. He's my boyfriend, my lover, definitely my longest relationship to date and sure as hell my most serious, and I'd like to think he might be the one I want to stay with for the rest of my life, so if it means that every single time we troop down to visit, we have to stay in separate rooms —"

"Jesus Christ," he mutters, slamming the drill down. His face is clouded with anger again, the father I've always known, the man I fear. "Sleep with him or not, I don't care. Just don't be loud about it, don't make a damn *scene*, and your mother will never know. You don't have to make an announcement whenever you want to ... do whatever it is you do." Now it's his turn to hold up a hand, in eerie imitation of my previous gesture. "I don't want to know."

I laugh, relieved. "Don't worry, I won't share," I promise.

For long minutes we stand there, not quite looking at each other, neither willing to believe it was that easy or it's over now. I shove my hands deep into my pockets, and when my fingers brush against my dick through the thin material, I think of Dan. Back in our room, waiting for me. How long have I been gone? The familiar swirl of anticipation fizzles through me. "I should go," I say simply.

Dad nods. He runs a hand over the shelves stacked against the wall, feeling the smooth wood like he's looking for cracks. "You're sure you guys can't help me out?" he wants to know.

I shake my head. "We've got a few things to take care of," I tell him, though what I'm thinking of now has nothing to do with cleaning up that back room or any other part of the house. "You can probably get Ray —"

That earns me a laugh. "If I ever needed a surrogate son," he starts, but then he shakes his head as if to clear the thought. When he speaks again, his voice is so quiet that I have to strain to hear it. "I didn't ... I just didn't know what you wanted from me, kid. I didn't know how you expected me to treat him. I guess I went a little overboard." Another laugh, this one distracted, almost a sigh. "I just thought you didn't need more shit thrown at you, is all. That's your momma's department, not mine."

One side of my mouth tries to pull up but the other doesn't follow suit and I don't quite manage to smile. "It's okay," I murmur, and oddly enough, it is. "Just — I guess just don't leave me out. Be good to him, please, but invite me next time, too."

"I never said you couldn't come along," is his reply.

40: Sibling Rivalry

I DON'T REMEMBER the walk back to the house — I'm fairly certain I floated the whole way, my feet never touching the ground. I have no memory of swishing through the damp grass or clomping up the porch steps, or even opening the screen door to duck inside. It's just not there. I was in the shed with my dad, my heart swollen with a fierce love I had begun to think I would never feel for the man, my mind bound out in a whirl of emotions, his words echoing in me, his quiet acceptance of me for who I am and his nonjudgmental stance such a refreshing contrast to the bigotry I've found in my mom, and then I walked through the kitchen door. There was no in-between.

Aunt Bobbie is still at the sink, rinsing her hands, but the pumpkin is now in the middle of the table on a bed of newspaper. Caitlin leans over it dangerously, knife in hand like a surgeon about to operate. "They let you have sharp objects?" I joke, closing the door behind me. I have to hold onto the knob to keep from drifting up to the ceiling, I'm still flying that high because my dad's okay with me. I can't get over that, he's cool with this whole thing, he likes Dan, thank God.

"Only on days that end in Y," my sister replies blithely. The blade of her knife hovers over the black lines of a jack-o-lantern smile that's been drawn on the face of the pumpkin with a thick magic marker. *Just dig in*, I think, but it's obvious she's hesitating because she doesn't want to mess it up. Our cousin Trevor sits on his knees in the chair beside her, leaning onto the table and watching her with large eyes behind his owl-like glasses.

At the end of the table, Ray is still eating, but he's watching her, too, and when he tries to shovel another spoonful of cereal into his mouth, he misses, spilling milk and Frosted Flakes into his lap. "Shit," he mutters.

As he pushes back his chair, his elbow bumps the bowl and it follows the spoon into his lap, splashing milk onto his crotch, his legs, the floor. "Aunt Bobbie," Trevor calls out, dead serious. "Ray said shit." Like Caitlin hasn't said worse.

Wiping at his boxers, Ray shakes his head childishly. "I did not."

I have to laugh as I lean against the counter. "We all heard you, dipwad."

"I said shoot," Ray mutters. Now Caitlin laughs, and Trevor starts in — Ray's cheeks flush the color of ripened apples. "I said shoot," he cries, half-turning to our aunt as if in appeal. Her hands are full of pumpkin innards, picked clean of seeds and ready to be worked into a pie, and though she's turned from him, there's no mistaking her indulgent grin. "Aunt Bobbie, I did *not* say shit."

"You just said it again," I point out.

My brother purples, whether in anger or embarrassment, I don't know. We're beginning to gather an audience now — a few younger cousins stand in the doorway to the hall, huddled together and giggling into their hands. More push against them from behind, trying to see. They laugh when Ray stands, milk staining the front of his shorts like the drying remnants of a wet dream, and I'm surprised that I feel an unexpected sympathy for him. He wipes at his damp crotch ineffectually and growls at the kids behind him, "Get out."

More giggles, more children — this is fun for them. Someone calls out, "Hey, come on! You gotta see this," and someone else squeals in delight. Amid the snickers, Ray's cheeks darken, his brow pulls down almost completely over his eyes in a Neanderthal scowl. This isn't embarrassed, this is downright *humiliated*, and I can almost see his anger building with each laugh, each catcall, each playful whistle. Like storm clouds lowering on the horizon, coming in fast and ready to break. Milk seeps into his boxers, his shirt, I know that has to be uncomfortable, clammy and cold and with everyone watching, too. Where the material is glued to his skin, it's almost transparent —plastered to his dick, outlining it obscenely, painting the crack in his ass, hugging his balls which have shrunk to the size of walnuts from the cold milk As he picks it away, I don't even think humiliation does this justice — I believe the phrase I want here is utter mortification.

"Get out!" he cries again, and this time he whirls around, arms waving, hands slapping at those who have ventured closest to him. Children scatter away like flies. "You think this is funny? Get the hell out of here, get *out!*"

Footsteps race down the hall, thunder up the stairs, laughter lingering in their wake. "Jeez, calm down," I say. Caitlin gives me an arched look but I shake my head, we've pushed him too far. With some difficulty, the smile slips from her face. Crossing the room, I start, "Ray, really —"

But when I reach out to touch his arm, he jerks away. "Fuck you," he snaps, and whatever compassion I feel for him dissipates like smoke torn apart by the wind. White droplets runnel down his thigh like cum or that android blood in the *Alien* movies and he goes for a napkin only to knock it and the spoon onto the floor. "Dammit the hell," he mutters as he bends to retrieve them. Halfway down he changes his mind and shouts out, "Shit! There, you guys happy? I said it, okay? Shit shit shit."

At the sink, Aunt Bobbie turns on the faucet to clean her hands, and the sound of running water is loud in the silence that follows Ray's outburst. Somewhere far away I hear laughter, and above us the floorboards creak under tiny feet. "Raymond, honey," Bobbie starts, but there's a smile aching to curl at her lips, I just know it. He looks stupid, bending over with his ass up in the air and boxers like a pair of eyeglasses, you can see right through them, and it takes every last ounce of strength I have to keep from smacking him right across his fleshy buttocks. I can almost *hear* the satisfying crack, my palm tingles with the anticipated sting. And it would be worth it, God, *so* worth whatever retaliation he might plan, just to kick at him now that he's about as low as he can get. Finally, I'm not the one having a bad day, it's someone else's turn, and damn but I'm savoring it.

Fortunately, Bobbie saves me — she eases between us and the moment when I could've played it off and gotten a laugh from the others is gone. It would just be downright mean if I slapped him now. When *she* touches his arm, Ray tries to shrug her off but it doesn't work. Our aunts are nothing if not tenacious. "Raymond," she murmurs. He stands and she kneels to pick up the napkin and spoon. "It's okay, honey. Let me help you."

"This is all *your* fault," he pouts. I'm watching Bobbie and don't realize at first that he's talking to me. "Everyone laugh at Ray."

"You're easy to laugh at," I admit. I keep my voice light and hope he sees I'm just kidding, but no, he's in a mood — there's no teasing when he gets like this. With a dramatic sigh, I run my hands through my hair to push the bangs from my face and tell him, "I'm only picking at you, damn. Lighten the hell up."

Without warning, he lunges at me. If Aunt Bobbie wasn't down on the floor between us, he could've knocked me down, maybe run me into the counter, he caught me that off guard. Instead, he only manages to shove at me, the palms of his hands leaving painful imprints on my shoulders. Taking a step or two back, I glare at him and want to know, "What's your problem today?"

He doesn't answer. That's no surprise — he probably doesn't *know* what he's mad about, he just knows that he's pissed. Angry myself, I level a finger at him and say, "You know, Ray, I'm not going to put up with your shit. Nothing I said or did made you drop your damn cereal in your lap, okay? So don't take it out on me. It's not *my* fault you're a clumsy ass."

"Shut up," he snarls again. His eyes are downcast as he watches Bobbie use his napkin to clean up the milk that's spilled on the floor and he doesn't look at me, which is fine. "Just leave me the hell alone, Mike."

From the other side of the table, little Trevor speaks up. "Aunt Bobbie," he calls out in a sing-song voice, "Ray said —"

My brother lashes out, one hand curled into a tight fist. He stretches across the pumpkin, aiming for our cousin, but Caitlin whacks his wrist with the flat of the knife blade. I wince at the sound, the dull slap of metal on skin, and he snatches his arm back, eyes wide. "Watch it," she growls. "I'll cut your fucking hand off."

Staring at Trevor, Ray points out, "She cusses like a sailor. Why don't you tell Aunt Bobbie on *her*?"

"Because he doesn't like you," Caitlin says simply. She turns back to the pumpkin, Ray dismissed. "He likes me. You look like you wet your pants."

When I laugh at that, my brother turns his hateful gaze to me again. "Shut up," he says, like that's his only reply. "Don't you have shit to do?"

"Aunt Bobbie —" Trevor starts.

Rising to her feet, Bobbie nods. "I know, honey," she says, distracted. "It's fine. Why don't you run along and play?"

"I'm watching Caitlin," he answers. At the withering look Ray shoots him, he sticks his tongue out and hides behind my sister.

Aunt Bobbie dabs at Ray's stomach, a good five inches above where the milk drenched his shorts. "Here," she says, shoving the napkin into his hand. "Maybe you should get cleaned up, Ray. It's after noon already, too late to be lounging around in your PJ's anyway. I'm sure you have something else you need to do ..."

She trails off, hopeful, but Ray shakes his head as he wipes at the front of his shorts. Trying to help, I tell him, "Dad's out in the shed. He could use a hand —"

"That's your job, isn't it?" Ray asks bitterly. "Or wait, just your boy-friend's. He didn't want you out there."

"We straightened all that out," I say. My anger is back, choking whatever banter I was hoping for between us. What, is he *trying* to piss me off? "Not that it's any of your business. Is that okay with you?"

He doesn't answer, just wipes his shorts in quick, fast strokes. I watch him for one full minute, giving him ample opportunity to reply, but he doesn't. He's ignoring me. From the other side of the table, Caitlin stares at me, willing me to look her way, but I don't. I'm not taking this any further. I'm not going to argue just because Ray's in the mood for a fight.

I turn away and take a step towards the closed door of the back room and the promise of Dan on the other side when Ray mutters, "Goddamn faggot."

My blood freezes in my veins and I'm not even aware that I've turned towards him until my hands fist in the collar of his raggedy t-shirt. "What the *hell* did you just call me?" I snarl.

His face drains of color and his lips tremble as if he's mumbling beneath his breath. "I didn't," he starts, but he loses the rest of that sentence and just shakes his head. "Mike, it wasn't … I didn't mean it like that."

I let his fingers scramble at mine for a few seconds, until his nails bite into the back of my hands, and then I let him go. "How'd you mean it?" I ask. "As a complement?" He glares at the floor and can't even meet my gaze. I tell him, "Just because you're my brother, Ray, doesn't mean I have to take this from you. I *won't*. If you have a problem with me, let me know."

That gets a laugh. "And then what?" he asks. "We sit down and talk it out and everything's hunky dory? I don't *want* to talk about it."

I look at him, confused. "Ray —"

He shakes his head, he's not going to hear me out. "You know, I'm glad," he says, and laughs again. With another halfhearted swipe at the front of his shorts, he folds the napkin up into a tiny square and presses it to his mouth as if he's going to be sick. When he speaks, his voice is muffled until he moves the napkin away. "You know why? Because it just goes to show that you're not perfect."

Hell, I could've told him that if he just asked. I'm a far cry from perfect, believe you me. Dan might be — when we're loving each other, we're just a stone's throw from heaven, and most days he's up there with the saints in my book. Me, I'm just a pilgrim on this journey, a sinner seeking salvation, and God knows I've found it in my lover. The curve of his buttocks, the firm weight of his cock in my hand, my mouth … his kisses, the tender way he touches me in the morning, the feel of his body against mine while we sleep, *that's* perfection. Without him, I don't even come close.

I didn't think I had to point out that I'm not perfect, especially not to Ray of all people. But there's a wild relief in his eyes that scares me, and before I can say anything, he hurries on. "All my life, it's been, why can't you be like Michael? Why can't you get the grades he gets? Why can't you go on to college? Why can't you get a job like his, or drive a flashy car like he does, or move out on your own? And now this."

This being my homosexuality, I assume — I don't correct him or mention that for the first three years of his life, I wasn't even around. "Ray, I didn't know," I murmur, I *didn't*. My parents hold us up against each other like that? Not my dad, I'm sure, he's not one to hound you into what he wants you to be, he'd leave that to … "Mom says this crap?"

Behind me Caitlin laughs. "You have no idea," she says. "Til Saturday you could do no wrong in her eyes."

I turn, surprised to find her still here. And Aunt Bobbie wiping down the table, a sad look on her face. And Trevor watching me with his Sphinx-like eyes. And Dan leaning in the doorway to the back room, when did he show up? His t-shirt hangs down over his open fly, the zipper wide on either side of the hem, his drab green Army-issue briefs hidden from view. He's watching us, too, arms crossed, one foot over his ankle, but there's nothing easy about his stance — it's an alert pose, a ready position. Ray makes the wrong move, says the wrong thing, and my lover will cross the room in three, maybe five steps, he'll come to my side. If he has to.

"You know what she told me on the way up here?" Ray laughs, a strangled sound that he cuts off before it can run away from him. "She actually said thank God you're not gay like Michael is. Like Michael. That's all I ever hear — like Michael."

"I'm sorry," I tell him. I am. What else can I say? Grudgingly Ray rubs at his nose and sniffles, which is the closest he ever comes to crying. For the first time I can remember, I feel a deep ache in my chest, I feel *sorry* for him, and I touch his shoulder in a comforting gesture, which isn't much but is all I can think to do. I can't take away my mother's hateful nature. I can't take away the years of hearing her compare him to me. As if I'm all that to begin with, I'm not. He said it himself, I'm *not*. "Ray —"

He shrugs my hand away. "Leave me alone," he mutters, and picks at the front of his shorts absently. In a tiny voice, he whispers, "I didn't mean to call you that."

It's okay, I almost say, an automatic response. The words are on the tip of my tongue but at the last second I bite my lip, keeping them inside. It's *not* okay. What did he say, *goddamn faggot?* That's a bit more than sibling rivalry, if you ask me. That hurt.

He glances at Caitlin and then past me at Dan, who I know has stepped out of the doorway now, it's in my brother's calculating gaze, as if he's measuring the distance between my lover and himself. I hear bare feet pad on the floor behind me — *you called me a fag*, I could say, and Dan would close the gap between us in double time, he'd grab my brother by the collar same as I did but this time it wouldn't be just milk wetting his shorts. He'd piss himself scared if Dan came at him and I think he knows it, I see that fear in his eyes, ready to erupt. "I didn't mean it," he whispers again, and before I can reply, he adds, "Call him off me, Mikey. I said it without thinking. You know how I am, I do that shit all the time."

I reach behind me without turning and my hand flattens across Dan's stomach, he's that close. "It's okay," I say, talking to Dan. To my brother, I add, "It's not my fault she does that crap and you know it. I'm not the favorite one, trust me."

With a bitter snort, he concedes, "Not now."

"Not before now either," I assure him. "I got the best grades and went off to college just so she'd finally pay some attention to me." He rolls his eyes, he's not buying it. "Honest. You're the one she was always on about, Ray. You're the one who was always in trouble. I didn't think Mom would know I was alive if I didn't compete with that somehow."

"Yeah right." He wipes his nose again, picks at the front of his shorts, then balls up the hem of his shirt between both hands. "It's not the same, Mike. You moved out years ago and it's like you're still living with us. It's Mike's doing this, Mike said that. Almost like you never left. It's not the same at all." When I start to apologize again, he raises his hand, he doesn't want to hear it. "Just forget it, okay? If you can. Forget I said anything. Forget I was even here."

And he storms from the kitchen, down the hall, up the stairs. I hear tinny laughter, distant like a fuzzy radio signal. Ray yells at someone to shut up, just shut the fuck *up* —

Whatever else he says is cut off by a door slamming shut, and when Dan touches my waist, I almost fall into his arms. *Goddamn faggot.* I don't know how I can ever forget *that.*

41: Dan On Alert

NO ONE SAYS anything at first — there's nothing really *to* say. I lean back into Dan's touch and frown at the floor, resisting the urge to meet anyone's eye, particularly Caitlin's. I can feel her gaze on me, weighing me down, willing me to look at her and I won't. Because if I do, I'll see the laughter bubbling within her, I'll smile myself, she'll giggle, and all hell will break loose. Ray calling me a faggot is nothing to laugh about. There's nothing funny with my mom comparing him to me in everything he says and does. But the image of his jiggling ass through those thin boxers as he stormed out of here, *that's* worth a laugh or two, and his damp front where he spilled the milk, and the way Trevor kept picking on him, *Trevor* of all people, barely five years old and already every inch one of us. Ray slamming the door shut upstairs, add that to the list. And if I look at Caitlin, I just know I'll bust out, she'll start in, Dan too. What's my brother going to think if he hears us down here laughing at him?

So I keep my head down and say nothing. But Dan — who came in late on Ray's little snit, he missed the best part, *goddamn faggot* my ass — he presses his lips to the back of my neck in a gentle kiss and wants to know, "What was that all about?"

The question is a catalyst that sets everyone else into action. "You really shouldn't pick on him," Aunt Bobbie starts, and right over top of her, Caitlin cries out, indignant, "I can't believe he had the *nerve* to call you that!"

"Caitlin," I warn with a shake of my head.

Too late. "Call you what?" Dan asks. When I don't answer immediately, he turns me around in his arms so we're face to face, and he asks again, "Call you what, Michael?"

With a weary sigh, I start, "Nothing —"

But Caitlin pipes up. "He said —"

"Caitlin!" I snap at her. "He didn't ask you."

My lover grasps my shoulders, his strong hands insistent until I raise my eyes to his. "I thought we talked about this," he says softly. His voice is always like this, so damnably soft, how can I take offense at it? "This morning? About letting me in?"

"We did," I agree. But I don't want to get into it here, with Caitlin just waiting for her chance to jump in and fan the flames. *He called me a fag*, I'd say, and I have a feeling that I wouldn't be able to hold Dan back — my lover would race up the stairs two at a time like a one-man SWAT team, kick in the door Ray slammed behind him, and tear my brother apart for that comment alone, family or not.

Or worse, he'd calmly bide his time, he'd wait, the silence in him coiled and deadly like a snake choosing the right moment to strike. Sometime when he can get Ray alone, he'll sidle up beside him, take his arm, pinch that tender spot just above the elbow that makes you want to claw at the ceiling in pain. "I'd like a word with you," he'd say in that same soft voice, and my unsuspecting brother would nod, sure, a word, he could do that, anything to loosen the grip on his arm. Dan knows just how to squeeze *that* nerve, and by the time he's finished talking, Ray would probably never even *look* at me again.

Dan's waiting, watching me, an air of silent alertness about him like the quiet that descends over a hunter in the bush, gun ready, listening for his prey. "Not now," I tell him. When he starts to object, I shake my head. "Not here. When we're alone, okay, baby?"

At first I think he'll protest — he wants to know *now*. But it's the *baby* that stops him and he sees the promise in my eyes, I'll tell him later, he knows I will. He has ways of getting it out of me, ways that include his tongue on hidden flesh, his lips over secret skin, his hands on my body, in me, he knows just where to touch to bring me out. "Later," he says, almost asking. I nod, yes.

"You should tell him now," Caitlin says, a pout in her voice.

"You should mind your own business," I reply.

Caitlin doesn't let up. "It was an evil thing to say. If I were you, *I'd* tell him."

Frowning, Dan asks, "Was it that bad?"

She's making this worse, can't she see that? Getting him worked up like this over nothing. "Caitlin, shut *up*."

"Do I have to kick some ass?" Dan asks, only half-joking. I glare at my sister but she's back to her pumpkin, impervious to my irritation. With one gentle hand, Dan turns my face towards his and prompts, "Michael?"

My gaze holds his for a moment then trails down, over the firm muscles bunched beneath his taut shirt, his biceps, his pects, down lower over his hard, flat stomach, down *lower* ... "Look at you," I admonish lightly, slipping my hands beneath his shirt to tug his open jeans closed. "Hanging out all over the place."

His lips are hot and damp as he nuzzles my ear. "I was under the impression that we were going to pick up where we left off," he teases. I laugh at his warm breath, ticklish along my neck. Nimbly, I thumb the button on his fly shut and try to ignore the eager hardness that responds to my touch when I zip him up. "Did you talk to your dad?" he wants to know.

Another issue I don't want to share with my nosy sister present. From the corner of my eye I can see her leaning intently over the pumpkin in concentration, fixated on her carving, but the knife doesn't move, she's too busy hanging on my every word. "Dan," I sigh. He makes a small, annoyed sound in the back of his throat and his hands bunch in my shirt — he hates being put off. "Yeah," I admit. "We talked."

Pulling back slightly, he frowns at me and asks, expectant, "And?"

Caitlin gives up all pretense now — she's watching us openly, the knife stuck into the side of the pumpkin like an afterthought. With a nod in her direction, I tell him, "And I'll tell you about it later." I tuck his shirt into his pants, my fingers brisk like a mother getting her child ready for school. But my blood rushes at the feel of his stomach through the thin material, my fingertips burn where they brush against the beginnings of an erection coiled at his crotch, and if I don't move quick then I'll linger, my sister doesn't need to see that. "We'll talk about it," I promise, not meeting Dan's eyes. "When we get a few moments alone —"

He catches my wrists in his hands and pulls me towards him. "We can be alone now," he says, taking a step back in the direction of our room. The door stands open behind him like temptation. It would be that easy. "If he's not expecting us to come out and help him ..."

"He's not." Dan takes another step and I follow. Wasn't this what I had in mind? I have a feeling that, despite the amount of work we still have left on that back room before it's cleaned out to Penny's specifications, we're going to get very little done once that door is shut. Not that I mind. Another step, another. I like the gleam in his eyes, the wicked little way his mouth turns up in one corner. With a shy smile of my own, I murmur, "We're supposed to be cleaning out that room."

He stops and I find myself in a sudden embrace. "We'll clean," he swears. "Eventually."

When he leans in for a kiss, though, Caitlin interrupts ... again. "What did I tell you they were?" she asks.

I turn towards her, about to ask what the hell she's talking about, but then Trevor speaks up. "Horny asses," he declares, so matter-of-factly that I just stare at him. He glances at us, gives me a tight, thin-lipped smile, then leans onto the table, dangerously close to the pumpkin and the knife in Caitlin's hand. With one small finger he shoves his glasses up the bridge of his nose and nods as if confirming it. Beneath his breath, he whispers it again, slowly, enunciating each syllable until the phrase sounds prim in his little boy voice. "Horny *asses*."

"What are you teaching him?" I want to know.

"He's getting a well rounded education," Caitlin points out.

At the counter, Aunt Bobbie has been wiping out the sink while we go back and forth, studiously neutral and out of our conversation. It's safer that way. But at my sister's remark, she looks over her shoulder with reproach. "One his mother won't appreciate, I'm sure," she says now.

Caitlin shrugs, it's no concern of hers. "I can't help it if he's a fast learner. It's *those* two giving him the edumacation," she announces, aiming the blade of the knife at us, at *me*, like I'm the one teaching the kid words like *shit* and *fuck* and *ass*.

Dan starts to laugh. His hands grapple at my waist, tickling, making me laugh, too, and I squirm in his arms. "You know you're just encouraging them, right?" I point out, but he nips at the hollow of my throat, growls when I pull back, holds me tighter even as I try to get away and how can I hope to fight him when he's playful like this?

"Cover your eyes, Trevor," Caitlin says, and the boy does as he's told, cupping both hands over his glasses, fingers splayed so he can still see. "I thought you guys were taking it somewhere else? If you're not going to talk about all the *good* stuff in front of us, move along." To our cousin, she says, "I'm holding out for what soldier boy is going to say when he hears what Ray —"

"Caitlin," I warn. Can't she drop it?

"Caitlin," she mocks in a high voice. She stabs at the pumpkin like she has a grudge against it and whines again. "Caitlin. Caitlin. That's my name, don't wear it out." To Trevor, she says, "You're peeking."

Our cousin shifts on the chair and closes his fingers tight over his face. "Am not," he breathes. "Can I look now?"

"They're not gone yet." With a closed look I can't read, my sister wants to know, "Well? Are you leaving, or what?"

Don't tell me she's mad at me again, I pray. I can't tell, there's something in her eyes that defies definition, is she pissed? Playing around? Mad as shit, what? *She has more mood swings than a playground,* as Stephen used to say when we were younger, talking about his own sister. *Maybe she's ovulating,* I think, it would explain her mercurial moods, but right on the heels of that thought comes another so swift, there's no doubt that it's the truth. *Ask her and you're dead.* I can just see it now. "Cat, you're not on the rag, are you?" A flash of fury in her eyes and then *bam!* Mike is out for the count.

So I concede, "We're leaving," and I push Dan back into the room we share, shutting the door behind us. I'm careful not to slam it because I don't want them talking about us or laughing the way I wanted to laugh after Ray about ripped the door upstairs off its hinges. Leaning against the door, I roll my eyes and sigh. "Damn, that girl."

Dan runs his fingers down my chest, the touch feathery through my sweater. "We're alone now," he says.

I laugh and catch his hand in mine. "So we are," I murmur, pulling him to me.

He grins — I love his smile, and the way he brushes back the hair from my face, the way his lips close over mine in a sweet kiss. "All alone," he whispers against my mouth. My arms find their way around his neck, holding him tight, and this close his eyes are the world, so dark, so beautiful, like the sea at night. He kisses me again, a second time, and just as I'm about to fall into him again, to give into his lips and his tongue and his hands, he asks, "So are you going to tell me?"

"Tell you what?" I ask, jarred from the edge of submission.

Dan gives me a look that says he knows that I know what he's talking about and he's not going to let me play dumb about it. "Ray?" he asks. "Your father?"

With a wink, I tell him, "He likes you. We're cool."

"And Ray?" Dan wants to know. He has me up against the door, pinned between his hard body and the hard wood, and I feel safe here with him, I like the thickness swollen into my crotch, the last thing I want to talk about at this exact moment is my damn brother. But Dan is persistent. "What did he call you?"

I turn away from his next kiss and his lips glance over my cheek. "It was just the heat of the moment," I say. His hands distract me, his arms, his chest, everything about him begs to be held and touched and loved, can't he let this go? "He didn't mean it, Dan. Caitlin's just trying to start something and you know it."

"So what did he say?" he asks again. When I shrug, he adds, "If it's not that big a deal —"

"It's not."

"Then why won't you tell me?" *Damn* his logic. He strokes my cheek and I lean into his palm, this time I let him kiss me, his hips press his arousal into mine. "Mike —"

Taking a deep breath, I say, "He called me a faggot, okay?" Dan's eyes harden instantly, just as I knew they would, and his lips flatten together into a stern, white line, the only external show of his anger. Even though he hasn't moved a muscle, I imagine that I feel him pulling away from me, pulling into himself, deep down wherever it is that he hides his soul when he lets the military part of his mind take over. The change is like a sheet draped over him, that sudden, that complete, and I can barely see the ghostly shape of the man I love beneath the anger. "Dan," I sigh. He just stares at me and I cradle his neck in both hands, rub my thumbs over his cheeks, anything to loosen this emotion that's managed to turn him into stone. "Dan, no, it's not like that. Listen to me, he didn't mean it that way."

"How did he mean it?" he asks. His voice is clipped, each word as precise and final as a surgeon's cut. "In a *nice* way?"

"Dan, please." I smooth down his t-shirt, erasing the wrinkles in the fabric with my hands. His muscles are clenched tight beneath my fingers and I can't seem to work them free. "Hon, listen to me. Don't be like this, he said he didn't mean it."

Incredulous, he asks, "And that makes it all right?" I shrug, I don't know, and something in my helpless gesture makes Dan snap. "He's a fucking moron," he spits, pulling back from me now. I hold onto his shirt, try to keep him close, but he's pissed and he pushes me away. "I don't care if he's your brother, Michael, I really don't. Not if he's going to be saying shit like that to you. I won't have it."

"Daniel," I sigh. My hands find his shoulders and rub at the anger coiled there, I dig into the tension, work my way over his shoulder blades and down his back, massaging. At his waist, I try to tickle him but it doesn't work — when he's mad or upset, he's not ticklish, as if it's a sensation he can turn on and off like a light switch. "Dan, listen to me. Let me handle this, okay? Don't get all bent out of shape, please. I'll take care of it."

I ease my arms around his waist and hug him against me. "Please," I murmur in his ear, kissing the soft place just behind the lobe. "He didn't mean it." Dan crosses his arms in front of his chest, defiant, and I rub his stomach, down an inch or two into the waistband of his pants, up again to his arms and over the tight muscles. He's like a statue, I can't seem to get my fingers into the crooks of his elbows, the folds where his wrists bend. "Baby, open up to me," I sigh, working to get into him. He stands steadfast against my efforts. "He just said it because he was mad —"

"That's no excuse," Dan says, and no, it's not, but the words are said, they can't be taken back now, there's no use getting this worked up over a bad turn of phrase or wrong slip of the tongue. "He's almost over the line, Michael, and you know it."

The line, an imaginary boundary of Dan's that, once crossed, marks a point of no return. Over the line and you get pulled aside, you get "talked to," like our neighbor back home or the drunken kid outside of Wal-Mart one night who thought me an easy target. He couldn't have been more than eighteen on a good day, and so shit-faced that when he called out to me, his voice was slurred and I couldn't make out what he said. My arms were full of those thin plastic shopping bags that the cashiers tend to fill to overflowing, and Dan was far enough behind me, shoving his wallet back into his pocket as he juggled his own bags, that we didn't appear to be together. This was sometime over the summer, when we were getting ready for the trip to Ocean City, and the shopping spree was one final stop to fill up on every-thing we needed before we left.

When I didn't respond to the kid's first shout, he called again. "Hey, you. Hey!" I could see him from the edge of my vision, overweight and dressed in a black t-shirt that threatened to split where it stretched across his belly. He leaned against the trunk of an old car and as I walked by, he detached himself from the vehicle to follow. "I'm talking to you," he said, weaving after me. When a hand touched my shoulder, I jerked it off, didn't look around, kept walking. "I said I'm talking to you."

"No, you're not." My lover's voice, quiet and sure like salvation. *Now* I turned, and Dan had a hand on the stranger's arm, stopping him. With a nod at me, he said, "Get to the car, Michael. I'll be right there."

I don't know what was said — he never tells me. But I have a feeling that if Dan talks to Ray, the rift it will open between my brother and me will make the one my aunts have with Jessie pale in comparison.

42: Good Clean Fun

SOMEHOW I MANAGE to keep Dan from tearing through the house in search of my brother like one of the four horsemen of the Apocalypse. Instead I guide him to the bed, lay him down on his stomach and straddle his hips, continuing my massage. He lets me work the muscles loose in his back and arms, though I don't for a moment believe he's forgotten what has him so angry in the first place. *Goddamn faggot* indeed. But he closes his eyes and gives into me, and when I slide off his back to lay beside him, he curls an arm around me, holds me close. He doesn't mention going after Ray — I know he will, the same irrefutable way I know the sun will rise in the morning and the stars come out at night. Even when clouds cover them, they're there. I know it, I *feel* it, he'll talk to Ray. If my brother's lucky, he won't say or do anything more to piss Dan off before their little chat. Otherwise I'm afraid that any future trip home will be strained, no matter what my dad thinks. Between my mom and Ray, both of them hating us, I don't think I can handle coming home again. Family dinners will have to be eaten out in public, where the presence of others will keep us somewhat civil, and if we have to stay the night, it will be in a room at a local hotel. Regardless, I know that it *won't* be fun — Ray gets his stubborn streak from my mother, we all do, but he has the added misfortune of not realizing when he's wrong. He'll think Dan's picking on him, he won't understand that anything my lover says later will be a direct result of the homophobic comments he's made this weekend. He just doesn't seem to comprehend that he might not be right, that something *he* says might offend someone. He forgets so easily that he thinks everyone else should, too.

Not Dan.

I know he's thinking about my brother — I can almost see the thoughts whirling behind his eyes and none of them are good. If I ask what's on his mind, he'll tell me, he doesn't like secrets between us. He'll say he's still going to talk to Ray, just to set things straight, and there's no stopping that. I could try to dissuade him and he'd hear me out, he's great at listening to me, but I can't hold him back for long. *Just let us get through the funeral tomorrow,* I think as I study my lover's face, his eyelashes, his skin. This close he's amazing and I want to breathe him in, fill my lungs and my soul with his presence, love him completely. *No more talk of Ray,* I want to tell him. *No more thoughts of him, only me. I'm here, Dan, not him. Only think of me.*

But I keep quiet, because there's a part of me that doesn't want to even mention Ray out loud. Then we'll *have* to talk about him, and I don't want him here between us. So I stare into Dan's eyes and he stares back into mine, the silence broken only by our breath, the rasp of his thumb along my cheek, the sigh of my hand strumming through his hair. Beyond the closed door muffled voices carry into us, Aunt Bobbie and Caitlin talking low enough that I can't make out what they say. Every now and then Trevor laughs, a boyish squeal like a splash of red paint across a white fence. Above us the house settles around footsteps, creaks and groans beneath the shuffling of boxes — doors open and close, heavy furniture is moved across the floors, windows that have been shut since the first frost now screech open to air out dusty rooms. When we're finished here, the house won't be recognizable anymore. It will simply be an empty shell, the memories inside scattered to all corners of the family, or sitting priced on a shelf in a thrift shop, or left at the curb for the trash pickup. All the summers we lived here, all the times we shared, all the laughter and the tears, *my* memories, tossed away like so much garbage. I'm glad we're leaving soon, hopefully before they finish cleaning. I don't want to see the place hollowed out.

We lie so close together that our foreheads touch, one pillow shared between us. When Dan speaks, his lips kiss mine. "Can we talk a bit?" he whispers.

Not about Ray, I think, studying him. *And not about my father, either.* Snuggling into him, I tease, "We've been talking all morning. There's other stuff we need to take care of now."

He misreads my meaning and suddenly his hand is between my thighs, rubbing at the spot where the seams of my jeans meet just behind my balls. With a gentle squeeze, his palm closes over my dick, hard in the instant he touched me *there.* "What other stuff do you have in mind?" he murmurs. His fingers knead in a slow, maddening rhythm and I shift against him, spreading my legs to drape one knee over his hip, anything to get him closer to me.

I wait for the first low moan I know is coming — when he gets turned on, he does it, a sort of lustful purr, desire mingled with need deep in his throat, a primal, possessive sound that tells me he's ready to rumble. When I hear it this time, I arch into his hand, my knee slipping off his hip to press into his own swelling erection. He starts to lay me back, his fingers working at me through my jeans, his lips insistent on mine. Then, somehow, between kisses I manage to tell him, "I meant we need to get this room cleaned out."

He stops with the finality of a vibrator that's been switched off and looks at me, looks *through* me, trying to see if I'm joking or not. I struggle to keep my face neutral. "You want to *clean?*" he asks with an incredulous laugh. "Right this second?"

"It needs to get done," I say, giggling at the expression on his face. I caught him completely off-guard and I love that — I love the silly look of disbelief in his eyes, the way his mouth opens and closes without anything to say, and when he opens it again, I put a finger under his chin. His mouth snaps shut. "Let me up, Danny-boy," I laugh.

He rolls away from me, still silent, in shock almost. I can practically hear his thoughts, they're broadcasting loud and clear like a strong radio signal. *But we were — no, wait ... weren't we just — ?* "Michael?" he asks, lost. I crawl over top of him to get out of the bed, but just as I'm about to stand, he grabs my waist and holds me down to him. "Okay, hold up a minute. What's going on here?"

"We need to get this room cleared out," I tell him. I try to sound earnest, but his confused look sets me giggling again. I hide my face beneath his arm, where he's warm and still smells of spicy deodorant. "Oh baby," I sigh, wrapping my arms around his chest. "I'm just playing around."

"I thought that's what we *were* doing," Dan says. I laugh and slide off him — my feet find the floor but he doesn't let go, just holds me so that I'm bent across his body on the bed. I hear the playful tone in his voice when he tells me, "You're going to have to finish what you started here."

"What *I* started?" I cry. I didn't start it, *he* did, pulling me to him in the bed and kissing on me, hand on my dick like that's *my* fault. When I try to stand, he holds me tight, but he's ticklish now and my fingers dance across his stomach, the muscles fluttering beneath my touch. "Lest you forget, you're the one all over me."

He lets me up but keeps a tight grip on my wrists so that as I stand, I pull him into a sitting position. "Can you blame me?" he asks. He nips at my fingers, which I curl into fists, but his teeth close over my knuckles in tiny, mock bites. "All I wanted to do was talk a bit but no, you had to get all freaky on me, can't get enough of your boy, can you?"

I laugh and try to twist out of his hands. "Dan," I giggle. His teeth leave little indentations where he bites at me and he licks them away, his tongue wet and deliciously warm on my skin. "This isn't talking."

"At least it's not cleaning, either," he jokes. He's impossibly strong, and when I try to wriggle away, I just end up all turned around, my back to him and my arms crossed in front of my stomach, his hands still clamped to my wrists. Both of us are laughing breathlessly now and he pulls me into his lap, hugs me tight. "You're not going anywhere," he growls, planting a sloppy kiss on my cheek.

"Dan!" I laugh, squirming away. Once I'm on my feet again, I wipe at the damp imprint of his lips on my face, still giggling. "Rubbing it in," I say before he can ask. He reaches for me but I skip back. "Later," I tell him.

"You don't want to?" he asks. This time he pushes up from the bed and swipes at me, almost catching the front of my sweater before I move out of reach. "You want to make me beg, is that it? You like to bring a soldier to his knees?"

"I'd like to get this room straight," I say, though every part of my body cries out for him. When he sits back down on the edge of the bed, I lean on his knees, my face right in front of his, and I kiss the tip of his nose. "Let's just get this out of the way first," I murmur. In an effort to quiet me, he covers my mouth with his, but I pull away. Doesn't he know how hard it is to resist him when he's like this? "Get this place straight and then I'm all yours, what do you say?"

"I say why not now?" At my laugh, he kisses me again. "Sorry," he sighs. "I'm just playing, you know it." Another kiss, this one lingering. "I'm glad everything's cool again."

For some reason I think he means with my dad. "Yeah," I say, standing. I turn away from the bed and almost groan at the boxes and bags I left piled up in the far corners of the room. Maybe cleaning wasn't such a good idea after all. "I'm just glad things worked out. You don't know how scared I was going out there —"

Dan's bare foot connects with my ass. "I'm talking about with *us*," he laughs.

Slapping at his ankle, I tell him, "I knew that."

"Yeah, right." He lies down on his back, stretching across the bed, arms folded behind his head as he watches me dig into the nearest bag. When I bend over to pull the bag towards me, he lets out a loud wolf whistle that I'm sure my sister heard through the closed door. This time his toes dig into my butt when he kicks out at me. "Damn, boy."

"Weren't you going to help me here?" I ask. I manage to grab his ankle and try to pull him off the bed. "Or did you just want to watch?"

He slides onto the floor with a *thump*, then scoots over to me, his foot still in my lap. "This wasn't *my* idea," he reminds me, but he takes the bag from me and starts to root through it. "I don't know what to keep and what to throw away."

I glance into the bag — it's full of clothes, the costumes that used to hang on the wardrobe rack until yesterday, when I took them down and folded them carefully away. The rack went out with the trash and the clothes

... to be honest, I don't know what to do with them, either. I just know I don't want them, and Penny doesn't, I can't believe anyone does. What are they doing with the clothes? "Just set that one aside," I tell him, shoving the clothes he's pulled out back into the bag. "As long as we get things organized a bit, you know? So when we leave, there's not too much left to do in here."

Dan ties the bag back up, then hefts it over his shoulder and chucks it onto the bed, out of our way. "When *are* we leaving?" he asks carefully.

I hand him a box filled with magazines, *Women's Day* and *National Geographic* and one or two issues of *Playboy* that we used to giggle over as kids. I'm sure Evie never knew they were back here. I think Doug bought them from Grosso's back in his teens, the summer he showed up with a few scraggly chin hairs he called a goatee. Seeing them again makes me think of the day Stephen first kissed me and that ad in the magazine that started it all — *HOT GAY SEX!!* and my heart hammering in my chest as we raced back to Evie's. When *are* we leaving? It's a good question. "I don't know."

"The funeral's tomorrow," Dan offers.

I don't want to think about that. "I know," I say. It's tomorrow, of course it is. She's been dead since Saturday, we'll bury her tomorrow. *That's crass,* a voice in my mind whispers, a voice that sound suspiciously like my mom's. *We say passed in this family. She passed on Saturday, and the service is tomorrow. Euphemisms to make dealing with death easier on a body.* Only it's easier for me if I think of it in crude, childish terms, it makes it somehow less real. You see death on the nightly news — people don't *pass* in car wrecks, they don't *pass* in drive-by shootings. Color over it all you like, the reality still shines through. Aunt Evie is gone, not here, *dead.* The funeral's tomorrow.

My lover touches my arm, rubs my elbow through the sleeve of my sweater. "I know you don't want to talk about this," he says quietly, and he's right, I don't. "But last night, after you laid down? I was in the living room with everyone else because I thought you just needed to be alone —"

"You're so good to me," I say, patting his knee.

With a quick smile, he continues. "Your aunts were making plans. About tomorrow. Who sits where and what time it starts, and what to do if Jessie shows up. Is she going to?"

"I don't know," I admit. Just thinking of tomorrow makes my stomach churn — adding Aunt Jessie into the picture is too much to bear. Hopefully she went straight to Morrison's after dropping me off this morning and made her peace with her sister, she won't have to come to the service. It occurs to me that I forgot to tell Caitlin about meeting her ... well, if she's still pissy with me later, I'll mention it, just sort of play it off. "Oh, you'll never guess who I ran into at Grosso's." If that doesn't get her talking to me again, I can pick at Ray. He's one common denominator we can always count on to rally together against. Whatever sympathy I felt for him earlier has evaporated, leaving behind a slimy residue that films over my emotions. I'm not mad at him anymore. Things aren't exactly *okay* between us yet, but I'm not where Dan is, I'm not angry. There's no use to it. Ray's probably already forgotten about the whole thing himself.

"Maybe could you call her?" Dan asks. I almost answer, *who?*, but he's still talking about Jessie. "Just tell her it's not a good idea to come by tomorrow. Or don't you know where she's staying?"

"I don't know," I say again. I sound like a broken record, but I really don't. I just met her today, the woman's still a mystery to me. I suspect it wouldn't be hard to find out where she's at — there are only a handful of places in Sugar Creek to stay at: an EconoLodge halfway between here and Union City, the Talley-Ho Inn on the other side of town, a bed and breakfast behind the new Wawa we passed coming into town, that's about it. As far as I know she has no friends here, no one she can stay with, and she's probably not even staying in town at all, if none of the others know she's here. With a confidence I don't feel, I tell Dan, "I'm sure it'll be okay, babe. Nobody's going to want to make a scene."

He's watching me, I can feel his gaze on my shoulders as I lean over a bag full of stuffed animals — prizes from the annual town fair, mostly, won at the Coin Toss or Ski-ball, teddy bears and kitty cats, puppy dogs with large plastic eyes, even a green alien or two, brought back to the house and proudly displayed but forgotten when we left for home. "We have to be at the funeral parlor tomorrow by eleven," Dan is saying, and I nod but don't look at him. Can't he see that I'm busy? That I don't want to talk about this right now? "I'm thinking it'll take most of the day, you know? When Ma died, I remember the service went on forever. *Everyone* had something to say, and I don't have half the relatives you do."

"Dan," I sigh. "I don't —"

"Want to think about it," he finishes for me, "I know. I'm just saying the whole thing will take awhile, that's all. I don't know when you're thinking we'll leave but I don't think it'll be tomorrow night." He lets this sink in. The service, then the drive to the cemetery, the graveside ceremony, a reception afterwards because my family is big on getting together to eat. Finally he adds, "You're due back at the office Thursday."

He's right. I haven't thought about work, or school — I missed two classes this week, I should've called my professors but I just forgot. We left my parents' house in such a rush and it's been nonstop ever since. Has it really only been a few days? Dan's on leave until next Monday but I only took off part of the week. No one knows I'm up here, I never called the law firm. Three days bereavement, isn't that what I get? Did it start Monday or the day I'm off vacation? What the hell kind of vacation is this?

"Shit," I murmur. My head hurts, my chest, my legs and arms and I just want to crawl into the bed now, is that too much to ask? Let someone else take care of everything for me. *That's what Dan is here for,* I think, and even though I know it's bad to pawn it all off on him, thank God he *is* here, that's all I can say. What would I do without him?

"I can call Debbie if you want," he says. My boss, yes, he should call her. "How about we leave first thing Thursday? And I'll tell her you're going to be out until next week." He doesn't say he thinks I'll need this coming weekend to recuperate — he doesn't have to, I already know that.

I nod. "Sure," I say, and when he stands, I tug at his pant leg until he leans down over me. "Thanks," I whisper, giving him a kiss. He'll call the office for me, he'll handle it all. Tomorrow, too, he'll get me through it. Let Jessie show up, if she has to. Dan's here for me, I'll survive.

43: Penny's Pills

TOGETHER WE FINISH the back room around the same time that the sunlight peeking in through the single window takes on a golden, end of the day hue. Shadows grow like cobwebs from the boxes and bags we've gone through and set aside — it seems like all we did was move the mess from one side of the room to the other. But the walls are bare now, only nails and a few stray flecks of tape left from the pictures that used to hang there, and you can see the floor, it's a light-colored, unstained wood that hid beneath a handmade rug for all these years. There's dust in the corners, a few paperclips, some tiny pieces of torn paper, shit that will be swept up soon enough. Looking around the room with my hands on my hips, I'm reminded of a scene from that cartoon special I watched as a kid, *How the Grinch Stole Christmas*. It's on every year. After the Grinch has been through the town, stealing the Christmas trees and presents and food, the homes he left behind looked like this — barren, picked over, dead. No more happiness in them. No memories left, no joy. I can't believe this is what we used to call the "junk room" growing up — I can't mesh the image in my head of a room overflowing with personality with this empty place. I can't believe this is the same room we slept in the first night here, the one we could barely walk around in because it was packed to the seams … surely all those knick-knacks and hand-me-down clothes can't be contained within a couple boxes, a few bags. All those memories can't be so neatly packed away.

A couple boxes, a few bags, and nothing I saw among them that I wanted to keep, nothing that would sit on my coffee table back home, or on a bookcase in my bedroom, and with just one look remind me of this place. Nothing at all.

Dan calls the office for me. The people there all know him — the few nights when a case I was working on kept me at the office late, he was there, six o'clock sharp with dinner in one hand, a book in the other. After eating, he would curl up in the chair beside my desk and read quietly while I poured over legal texts and files of past cases. Every so often he'd look up and give me a smile or blow me a kiss, and somewhere on the other side of the office, I would hear someone sigh, the way young girls sigh over love scenes in the movies. Once we hired a temp to help file some of the never-ending paperwork our place seems to create, and she took an instant liking to me. A crush, childish and cute, but after the first day of her constant smiles every time I walked by, it grew old. Then I overhear her tell my boss, Debbie, that she thought I was cute. "Too bad, honey," Debbie said, almost sympathetic.

The temp sighed. "I knew it," she said, shaking her head. Red curls bounced around her face like ribbons. "All the good ones are either gay or taken."

With a laugh, Debbie told her, "In his case, it's both."

It's Debbie who Dan manages to get on the phone now, and he tells her in quiet tones what happened. He sits on the bed while he makes the call on my cell phone because I have free long distance, and he half-turns away so I won't overhear. Some words come through, though, select phrases that still hurt my heart — *his great-aunt ... up here in Pennsylvania, the western part of the state ... used to spend the summer here when he was little ... not really doing too well right now.* That's the understatement of the year. I'm not doing too well at all. As I move around the room, he watches me, his gaze following like the eyes of a painting that seem to look at you no matter where you stand. "He'll be in on Monday," he says. Not *he'll be better Monday*, because in all honesty I probably won't. But I'll be back to work then, at least, I'll be back home, and I can force myself back into the regularity of my normal life, I can pretend things will be okay until they finally are. Isn't that the way we cope with death? Keep going like it didn't happen. Keep moving to prove to ourselves that *we're* still alive, even if we don't feel like living on.

I still don't want to believe that she's gone, or that this is the end of Sugar Creek for me.

Then he calls his superior, a man I'm almost ninety percent sure knows who I really am and why one of his enlisted boys lives off post with a "friend," but he adheres to the Army's *don't ask, don't tell* policy and because Dan's a good soldier, he's never been rude to me. I've run into him a few times on base while I waited for Dan after TDY, and he nodded curtly at me each time. Once he even came over to the car with Dan, leaned onto my open window as my lover stowed his bags in the trunk, and laughed. "What can I do to convince you to sign up for the service, kid?" he wanted to know. "If you're half the soldier Dan the Man is, I want you in my unit. You're more punctual than most of the boys I've got under me."

"He's joking," Dan told me later, as if afraid that I might actually rush to the nearest recruitment office and enlist. "It means he's cool with you."

"He knows?" I asked then, my heart quickening in my chest. I could just imagine a messy court-martial, Dan discharged, was sodomy still a viable reason to kick someone out of the Army? What would he possibly do then? The military is in his blood, he's always dreamed of being a decorated hero — what would happen if our relationship took that dream away from him? If he thought that somehow *I* took it away?

But Dan shook his head, easing my fears. "I wouldn't say *that*," he said, and his hand slipped across the space between our seats to find my knee. The weight was suddenly comforting, like a wet towel on sunburn. "I think he suspects something — he's not stupid. I live with you, he knows that, even though I keep a room in the barracks. And you're in the parking lot with the other guys' wives when I come in from the field." That made me smile, *other guys' wives*. Something about the image of me the anxious military spouse makes me giddy. "When we have anything going on," Dan continued, "ballgame, or cookout, or tickets to a show, you're at my side. He's not *blind*."

True. "Has he ever asked about me?" What would my lover say if he did?

"No," Dan said, squeezing my knee. "He's not going to, either. You're my roommate to him, that's all, so don't sweat it, Michael." By this time we were off post, the gate growing smaller and smaller in my rearview mirror, and he dared to lean over for a tender kiss. "Don't worry, hon. I'm not going to have to choose between you and the corps. I won't do it."

One of my hands dropped from the steering wheel to cover his, my fingers slipping easily into his palm. This time he had been gone two weeks, a short stint compared to some that I had to live through, but I was glad to have him home nonetheless. "Do they really call you Dan the Man?" I laughed. When he didn't answer, I glanced over and saw a faint blush in his cheeks. I liked that. *Dan the Man.* Later, after making love on the couch because neither of us could wait long enough to take it into the bedroom, and we were both exhausted from the depth of passion that shook us when we came, he cuddled up to me and I murmured it again. "Dan the Man," with one arm around his shoulders hugging him back to me, his head resting on my other arm, my fingers stroking through the tiny stubs of his hair. "Dan *my* man."

"You know the next time one of the guys calls me that," he said with a husky, satiated laugh, "all I'm going to be able to think about is you." I see nothing wrong with that.

Now I listen as he talks to his commander, whom he calls Tavitts at home but *sir, yes sir* over the phone. He speaks in clipped tones, much more professional than when he spoke with my supervisor, and he doesn't smile at all as he talks. This time he just sticks to the facts — Michael's great-aunt died, we're in Pennsylvania, we'll be back home Thursday night. After a few more *yes sir*'s, he recites my cell number, just in case someone needs to get in touch with him. "Yes sir," he says, nodding. I glance at him as I lift a few of the bags, full of old newspapers and torn clothing and some broken ceramics that I'm going to pitch. He gives me a tight smile and says it again, "Yes sir, I know sir, I should've called Monday, I'm sorry." A heartbeat later, again. "Sir, yes sir." He rolls his eyes and shakes his head, a grin threatening to break across the serious mask he's wearing for this call. "A nation at war, I know, sir. Yes, yes sir."

I grin and he waves at me to get out of here before I make him laugh. For as long as I've known Dan, his squad has been *on alert*, whatever that means. Ready to rush overseas at a moment's notice, I guess, and I'll admit I did have a few sleepless nights over that at first — imagining MPs banging down our door in the middle of the night, or a phone call during dinner, a call to arms he had to respond to, me bleary-eyed and half asleep kissing him at the door for what might be the last time. In every war film I saw, the soldier's lifeless eyes were Dan's, staring up at an unseen sky. Every man that fell beneath a bullet was my lover, every plane shot down, every ship up in flames. It got to where I wouldn't watch the History channel, I *couldn't*, because every death was *his* death, and I didn't want to deal with that. I didn't want to admit that I could lose someone so vibrant and alive, someone I loved so much, that easily.

Dan had no clue of what I was going through until the night we saw *Saving Private Ryan* — I didn't want to, tried to come up with anything else to do, anything at all, but it was on cable and Dan hadn't seen it yet, I couldn't find a good enough reason to say no. And I thought I did just fine, closing my eyes during most of it, cuddling into his chest when there was fighting onscreen, getting up for drinks if it got *too* bad. But that night I woke crying into my pillow, my lover's name over and over again, while he held me tight. "Michael, please," he sighed, rocking me in his arms, terrified by my sobs. "Baby, what is it? God, tell me what's wrong, please."

I didn't know how to put my fears into words. I didn't want to lose him, true. I didn't want to see him become just another casualty of war. I also didn't want him to go off and forget about me. I didn't want him to *die*, and most of all I sure as hell didn't want to learn to live without him. Oh God *Jesus* that scared me most of all — that he would leave me behind and somehow I'd have to find the strength on my own, I'd have to continue without him. Alone.

Somehow he pieced together my tear-chopped words and half-formed sentences. With tender kisses, he dried my eyes, my cheeks, cooled my fevered brow. "I'm not going anywhere," he promised, and although he doesn't know that for sure, he can't say with any certainty that he won't be shipped off to the Middle East, I believed him. At three in the morning, I guess I'll believe damn near anything. "I'm not leaving you, Mike. Those soldiers on TV, they're not *me*." *I know*, I thought, pouting like a petulant child. "I'm not front-line material, baby," he explained, "you know this. I'm supply. We stay back with the tents."

"Supply is the first thing they wipe out," I muttered. I'd seen the movies. Take out the supply line and you cut an army's legs right out from under it.

"Listen to you," he said with affection. His hands smoothed away the creases in my brow. "Mr. Military Expert, hmm?" I sort of smiled at that, and he laughed gently. "I'm not going anywhere," he told me again. Then he raised my hand to his lips and kissed my fingers. "I promise you."

I sighed, unconvinced. "Dan —"

"Baby, listen," he replied. Without another word, he placed my hand on his chest. I felt his heart beat against my knuckles, and when I looked into his dark eyes, they glistened like the reflection of the moon in a nighttime lake. Finally, in a voice so soft that I felt the words more than heard them, he whispered, "I love you."

As if that can make everything better, but somehow it does. It did then — it eased my troubled mind, calmed my fears, let me fall asleep in his embrace. How could someone like him ever die? *How could Evie?* I think, the smile freezing on my face as I watch him nod on the phone, a gesture Tavitts can't see on the other end of the line. "Be right back," I tell Dan, and he waves at me distractedly with another *yes sir* into the phone. Tossing one bag over my shoulder, I set a second one aside to open the door, then push it through into the kitchen with my foot and close the door behind me.

I smell the roasting pumpkin seeds now, a crisp, slightly burnt scent that tickles my nose like a sneeze. Caitlin is gone, Trevor too, but the pumpkin remains on its bed of newspaper in the middle of the table. Firelight flickers in its carved eyes, its wicked mouth, a candle already lit inside the hollowed-out gourd. *Not bad*, I think. I'll have to tell my sister she did a good job when I see her next.

Penny sits at the table now, in the same chair where Ray spilled his milk down the front of his shorts earlier. She has a dazed look in her eyes, one I've seen on the faces of people on TV who have survived natural disasters or horrible accidents, a disbelief that they can't be alive, they couldn't live through what just happened ... could they? What *did* just happen?

Also seated, Aunt Billie looks up as I close the door and gives me a weak smile. "Michael," she says sadly. "Hey." There's a cup of coffee in front of her, hands wrapped around it for warmth, but I get the impression that she isn't drinking from it. "Are you doing okay?"

"Fine," I assure her with a bright grin. She must mean with Dan, this morning on the porch. I look from her to Penny, to my mom rooting through a drawer full of aspirin and Band-Aids that we always called the *medicine drawer*, to Aunt Bobbie at the sink drying dishes that she packs away into a large cardboard box on the counter, and ask, "Did you guys just get in or something?"

"Or something," Penny murmurs. Her voice is ethereal, ghostlike. "Did you find my pills?"

My mom answers her. "I'm looking, sweetie." As if noticing me for the first time, she flicks her hair back from her face and sighs. "Hi Mike. Don't pick on Ray."

"Hi to you, too," I say coolly. I'm a little pissed at her, to be honest, for comparing my brother to me. A voice in my mind that sounds suspiciously like Dan's quips, *Not that there's any comparison there.* I busy myself with the trash bags in my hands so she won't see me grin.

Moving quick, I take the trash outside, where it's grown considerably colder — and darker — since my last trip to the shed. A motion sensitive light comes alive as I near the trashcans, which are sitting a little ways from the side of the shed and the bench my father made, the weatherproofing still drying. My bags go into the cans, even though there's nothing edible in them. Animals will tear them apart regardless. Then I hurry back to the house, where warm light spills from the windows like the heat from the oven that Aunt Bobbie has open as I step into the kitchen. "Where'd they go?" I ask, meaning Penny and Mom. They're gone.

"Penny's a little upset," Aunt Bobbie explains. She pulls a cookie sheet covered with pumpkin seeds out of the oven. When I reach for one, she slaps my hand away. "Watch it, Mike! They're hot."

"No shit," I laugh. I manage to snag one anyway, and the tiny kernel just about blisters my fingers — this is more than hot. This is scalding. I blow on it to cool it off, then test it with the tip of my tongue. I feel the skin deaden there instantly, *stupid move.* Now I won't be able to taste anything until that heals, I *hate* that. "Upset why?"

"We were at Morrison's all day," Aunt Billy says. She motions at an empty chair but I squat down beside her instead and drop the pumpkin seed onto the table. My aunt smoothes down my hair like I'm just eight years old again, and she gives me that sad smile of hers that makes my throat close up to see it. "Taking care of a few last minute details. Penny wanted to come but we really shouldn't have let her." With a sigh, she adds, "She has Valium but I don't know how we're going to get through tomorrow."

Me either, I think, but I don't dare say that out loud. Instead I tell her, "We'll just have to." Lowering my voice, I glance over at Bobbie scraping seeds into a bowl and ask, "What about Aunt Jessie?"

Aunt Billy looks at me sharply, her eyes narrowing behind her wire-frame glasses. "What about her?"

She doesn't know her sister's in town. Either Jessie didn't go to Morrison's after all, or the funeral home is better at keeping quiet about who visits the dead. What did Jessie say? *This is what they do. Families have these types of issues all the time.* With another glance at Bobbie, who either doesn't hear us whispering or pretends not to, I shrug and say, "I just wondered if she'd … if you thought she might —"

"She won't," Aunt Bobbie says suddenly. So she's listening after all. Shaking her head, she tells me, "Some things are better left alone, Michael. You're old enough to know that by now."

"I'm just —" I start.

She scrapes the last of the seeds into the bowl and sets the cookie sheet in the sink, where it sizzles in the sudsy dishwater. "You mean well, I know. Just …" She flounders for something to say, some task to give me to take my mind off my errant aunt, and comes up with nothing. "Are you done with that room yet?"

I stand and stretch, my muscles achy from cleaning all afternoon. "Almost." Before she says anything else, I pop the pumpkin seed into my mouth — much cooler now — and say, "I know when someone's trying to change the subject. I'm not going to mention her again, don't worry."

"At least not around your mom or Penny," Aunt Billy says. Sure, I can do that.

44: Dan's Little Talk with Ray

DINNER IS CHINESE — a few dozen little take-out containers scattered across the kitchen table like a buffet. A good foot taller than the hungry kids who clamor for the food, Dan stands at the edge of the crowd and simply reaches over the children's heads — he snags two closed boxes, starts to move back but thinks better of it and grabs a third, smaller container that can be nothing but rice. I stand by the back door with a beer in either hand. No soda for me — I suspect that a beer or two now might help me sleep through the night. The funeral's tomorrow. I'm going to need all the help I can get.

When Dan clears the table, I step out onto the porch and hold the screen door open for him, as well. It's cold out here but the wind has died down and by the house, there's barely even a breeze to lift the hair from my brow. The door slams shut behind us and Dan steps up to me, an arm easing around my waist, his chin resting on my shoulder. "Where do you want to sit, cutie?" he asks. His playful mood from earlier has lingered — everything he says to me sounds like a proposition, making me grin like a fool.

I look around the porch quickly, my hands numb from the icy cans. The heavenly smell of oyster sauce and garlic wafts through the screen door, startling my stomach into a hungry rumble beneath Dan's hand. I want to eat, I want to get a little buzzed, and I want some loving tonight, in that order. But first, a place to sit … "There?" I ask, nodding at the far end of the porch, where my father and a few of my uncles mill around a stone urn filled with sand. Evie always called them her *ashcans*, and they got dumped with the trash. My dad doesn't smoke, and I hate the smell of cigarettes, but after our little understanding this afternoon, I think maybe we should be over there, beer in hand, just one of the guys.

Dan takes a step in that direction, his fingers hooked around one belt loop on my jeans to lead me along, when I hear the unmistakable sound of a fork dropped to the wood behind me, followed by a soft curse. "Fuck."

"Hold up," I say, stopping Dan with a hand on his arm. Turning, I see

Ray bent to retrieve his fork from the porch where it's fallen. He scrambles for it with one hand, an open take-out container in the other, and I know two seconds before it happens that he's going to lose some of the food inside. A heartbeat later, *presto!* Large chunks of broccoli tumble out of the open top to plop wetly by his feet. He mutters something incoherent and spears them with the fork. Without realizing it, I close the distance between us, Dan right behind me. "You're not going to eat those," I say when Ray starts to stick the broccoli florets back into his container.

"I'm not," he grumbles without looking up. He stands and wipes his fork across the porch railing, knocking the pieces of broccoli to the ground below. "Go away."

"Ray —" I start.

"Just go away, Mike," my brother says. He throws himself down to the wooden bench that runs along the railing and pouts into the container, poking his food with his fork halfheartedly. "I'm not in the mood for your shit right now, okay?"

I sit down beside him. "I'm not in the mood to be shitty," I tell him, setting the beer between us. "Don't touch those. They're not for you."

"I don't want any," Ray mutters, but I can see the way he eyes the cold cans, as if tempted to snatch one when I'm not looking. Then he glances at Dan, who sits down facing me, one leg on the bench pressing into mine. With unmasked interest, Ray watches my lover open one of the take-out containers he carries and hand it to me before opening the other for himself. I have some kind of lo mein, dark noodles clogged with vegetables and what looks like beef. Ignoring Ray, I peer into Dan's container — he holds it out for me to see the thick, spicy clumps of General Tso's chicken that he's ended up with. "What did you get?" my brother wants to know.

"Food," I tell him. His pout hardens and I laugh. "Lighten up, Ray. I got lo mein. You want some?"

With a shake of his head, he practically glares at me as he shovels a forkful of fried rice into his mouth. When it becomes apparent that I'm not leaving any time soon — I pop open both cans of beer, hand one to Dan and take a deep sip from the other, the liquid sliding down my throat like foamy ice — Ray scoots a little ways away from me, like he's pulling into himself, he doesn't want to be near me. "You had to sit here," he mumbles.

I shrug. "It's a free country," I tell him. Another sip of beer, this one curling into my groin like a warm ember, and my laugh sounds slippery to my ears. Patting Dan's thigh, I point out, "My baby keeps it that way."

Ray gives me a sullen look over the top of his food, then his gaze shifts past me to Dan before dropping away. "Cut it with the lovey-dovey crap, will you?" he groans.

Well, excuse me, I think. A dull anger rises in my chest — I'm trying to be social here, can't he see that? I'm trying to be *nice,* despite what he called me this afternoon, and he's determined to get us fighting again, I just know it. "Jump down my throat already, will you?" I stab at the noodles in my little take-out box to release the tension building inside me. "Damn, Ray. What the hell's *your* problem tonight?"

"Nothing," comes the reply. *Nothing, nothing.* Always the same answer, *nothing,* like he doesn't trust me with the reasons why he's so upset. *Probably thinks I'm going to bust on him,* I tell myself, and yeah, I might, but he doesn't know that for certain. I could surprise him. I've grown now, I'm not the same little boy who laughed when his older brother would trip going up the steps (which he did quite frequently, still does). *Hell, give me something,* I pray silently, studying him. *I'm trying to meet you halfway here, numb nuts. I'm trying to make things right without either of us having to apologize, can't you see that?*

No, he can't, because he's too busy fucking around with his food to look up at me, to see the sincerity in my face, to see that I'm really very sorry for whatever it is he's going through right now even though I'm not sure what that is, exactly, but I know the symptoms all too well. The restlessness, the dropsies, the feeling that nothing is going your way, I've been there, done that. I suspect it has nothing much to do with me or Dan or our relationship — that's just the surface, a bruise that indicates a deeper wound, but he's not going to probe for it, he's not going to prod at the pain, it hurts too much and he doesn't have anyone like Dan who will *force* him to face up to it. I watch him helplessly, unable to think of a single thing to say to make him realize that I know, I *know.*

Suddenly someone kicks my shoe, and I look up to find my sister there, rummaging through another take-out container with a pair of chopsticks. Without greeting, she bends down and pokes her sticks into my container. "What do you have?"

I pull away from the inquisitive sticks. "Lo mein," I tell her. "Cat —"

"Triple phoenix delight," she says. Before I can stop her, she scoops out a huge helping of noodles from my container and drops them into hers. How can she be so dexterous with those chopsticks? As I watch, she replaces what she took of my food with some of hers, mixing the two dinners together. I look at her, incredulous, but she's already chowing down on my lo mein, *mine.* "You've still got plenty," she tells me, pointing at my container. Next she moves to Ray and does the same thing, rooting through his food before he can stop her. "What do you have?"

He shoves at her but she shoves back, as quick as a reflex. "You might as well give up," I say with a laugh. "She's tenacious."

"She's a pain in the ass," he mutters. Caitlin kicks his foot for that, and even though he tries to move away, she still gets a good handful of broccoli from him. "Caitlin!"

"Here, jeez." As she dumps some of her triple phoenix delight into his take-out container, he tries to move away, and clumps of sesame-seed chicken land on his legs, dark liquid staining his jeans. "Ray, dammit. Look what you're doing!"

"Me?" he cries, pushing her back. This time she slaps his arm, as if this is his fault … he mops at the mess on the front of his pants. "Get out of here," he tells her. When she starts to object, he shakes his head. He doesn't want to hear it. "Just go."

"Fuck you, too," Caitlin mutters. She kicks him once more for good measure and then stalks away.

As she passes by, one tiny foot strikes my shoe but I pull my leg in quickly — I don't want her mad at *me*. I glance at Dan, who's watching Ray with guarded eyes, a closed expression on his face, and I wonder what's on my lover's mind. Does he feel sorry for my brother? Maybe he wishes we sat with my dad instead? Nudging him with my elbow, I whisper, "Dan?"

The response is instantaneous. His gaze shifts to me, a smile already pulling at his lips, his eyes lit up like a holiday. Leaning closer, he presses his knee into my hip and raises an eyebrow, and for a moment I think he's going to say something low and sexy that my brother won't hear, but instead his gaze flicks past me. "We didn't sit here just to bother you, Ray," he says.

His voice *is* low, but Ray hears him just fine — he jumps as if goosed, and soy sauce dribbles through the folds in the bottom of his container to course down his arm, dark and thick as blood. Wiping at the sauce, my brother gathers all the courage he must possess and spits out, "Bullshit."

"Despite what you think," Dan continues in the same even tone, as if Ray didn't interrupt. There's an edge to his words, a sharpness that demands to be heard, not quite anger, not yet, but it could turn into anger. That's the promise in his voice — he *could* get mad, violent even, quite easily. I don't want to see that, and I'm quite sure my brother doesn't *dream* of it. Locking his steady gaze on Ray, Dan continues, "The past few days have been rough on you, I know. I've been there before myself."

"Yeah, right." Ray snorts into his food but won't look this way, not for long. When he glances over here, it's at me, not Dan. My lover scares him, I'm sure. I don't know where Ray's getting the balls to bite back like he is, unless he thinks I can hold my boy back. *How did you put it?* I think ruefully. *Yeah, right?*

"You're not making things any better here, Ray," Dan says. His words sound like a threat, serious. "Not with that attitude. Blaming everyone else for the way you're feeling inside isn't going to work, and I guarantee that blaming *Michael* isn't going to make you feel any better." *Don't bring me into it,* I pray, but it's too late. I frown into my food and realize that I'm hearing Dan's *little talk* for the first, and hopefully last, time. His voice is that of a god, carved in stone, displeasure held in check with the thinnest of threads. The wrong word, the wrong reaction, and his wrath will rain down, that's the promise I hear in that voice. Ray hears it, too, I know he does, because he looks at Dan now, flinching like he doesn't want to meet that terrible gaze but he's helpless against it. When he has my brother's full attention, Dan tells him, "I won't stand by and watch the man I love suffer because of you, Ray, I simply won't. You're going to stop harassing him, end of story. No more petty comments, no more bickering, no more crude remarks about our relationship. Do we understand each other?"

In a final, weak show of defiance, Ray mutters, "I'll do what I want to."

But there's no conviction in his voice, and he winces when Dan says, "That's just it, Ray. You don't want to. Trust me."

For a long moment, no one speaks. The world around us has stopped, a snapshot of this exact second, I see everything around me at once — the screen door half-open as Aunt Billy steps outside, Caitlin picking over the sweet and sour chicken on a plate our cousin Emily holds out to her like an offering, a flash of dusky ankle as Kenny's girlfriend starts down the porch steps. All sound has melded into a high-pitched cacophony, something you'd hear in a movie, a rustling of a crowd with no voices bright enough to stand out by themselves. *Ray's going to say something,* I think wildly, *he's going to be a smart-mouth and Dan won't put up with it, he'll lunge across me, he's a soldier, he can kill with his bare hands and I can't stop him, I can't, I love him to death and I can't stop him, I'm not that strong.*

Then Ray looks away, into the congealing mess in his take-out container, and the world rushes back into motion, double-time to make up for the lost moment and speed up to where we are. Noises deafen me — talk and laughter and the slap of the screen door, the creak of a step, they pound my brain and I swallow the rest of my beer to drown them out, I gulp down the second can, as well. I'll get Dan another one. I'll get it now.

As I start to stand, Ray sniffles a little and tells me, "I'm sorry."

I glance over at him but he's still glaring at his food, like it's to blame. "Me too," I say, and I am, God I am, so damn sorry, he just doesn't know.

The cooler's by the door. I dig two more cans out of the melting ice and shake the water from them as I walk back to where Dan waits for me. He and Ray don't look at each other, don't speak — all that needed to be said is out, isn't it? Nothing left to go on about. Sinking down between them, I hand my lover a beer and give him a tight grin. "I drank your other one."

"That's okay," he tells me. And suddenly it is. I feel loose and wobbly and frighteningly thrilled, the way I felt after the first time we ever had sex. *Mine*, I thought then, my mind racing with the possibilities that one word conjures up. He talked with Ray and things didn't go bad, my brother apologized, things are going to be okay. Why? Because of Dan. He says it's okay and it is.

I finish my third beer without realizing it. Still thirsty, I eye the half-empty can by Dan's knee. "Are you …?" I ask, pointing at the drink.

He looks up from his dinner to frown at me. "How many have you had?" he wants to know. Sheepishly, I spread three fingers across my thigh. "Don't you think that's enough?"

"One more," I say, nodding to get him to agree with me. My fingers walk from my leg onto his knee, up his thigh, to his crotch, and I manage to poke at the pillowy spread between his legs before he laughs and moves my hand away. Not very far, though, and his fingers hold tight to mine. "Half of one," I compromise.

That gets me the rest of his beer. Once it's gone, I'm thirsty *again*, and I start to stand but my legs don't want to cooperate, they feel like the noodles I've been eating, long, limp strands that threaten to spill me onto the floor. One step and the world spins around me like a child's toy. "Woah," I laugh, reaching out. I find Dan reaching back.

"You're a little bit lit," he tells me, easing a strong arm around my waist.

I raise my forefinger and thumb to my eye and squint through the inch between them. "Just a little bit," I agree. I let him lead me through the crowd — so many people! Shoving and bumping me, talk talk talk talk *talking* until their words buzz through my head like the beer. *Thirsty,* I think, watching the cooler come closer and closer as we near the door … but then we're inside, no more food, no more party, no more drink. "Dan?" I ask, confused. "I want …"

With a hand on the knob to our door, he stops. "What do you want, hon?" he asks. He waits patiently as I think this through.

"The bathroom," I announce. Yes, I definitely want to go to the bathroom. I *need* to, before we go to bed. Tenderly my lover takes my elbow, slips that iron-like arm around my waist, leads me through the kitchen and down the hall to the bathroom. "You wait here," I tell him at the door, pointing at the ground for emphasis.

That makes him laugh. "It's nothing I haven't seen before," he tells me. For some reason I find this funny, the funniest thing I've heard all night, I start giggling and can't stop. Take a piss, wash my hands, brush my teeth and almost choke on the toothpaste because I'm trying not to laugh. Nothing he hasn't seen before. I hear the words echo in my mind and my eyes water from holding in the fun.

He makes me sit on the closed lid of the toilet while he brushes his teeth and washes his face. Then he takes a damp cloth to *my* face, like a mother cleaning up a little boy. When we're ready to go, I stumble into the hall before he can catch me. "Watch your step," I tell him, and he laughs. My giggles come back, chased by hiccups that leave me breathless, even though I don't really see what's so funny about what *I* said.

Into our room. He strips me down, underwear and all, then pulls back the covers on the bed. I fall to the mattress gratefully, scooting up against the wall to make room for him. It's dark but I watch him undress anyway, a silhouette in the shape of a man. *Nothing I haven't seen before*, I think sleepily. Then he's in the bed with me, the covers pulled up to our chins, and his arms circle around me again. For a moment I think we should make love — I *need* him, the way I needed the beer earlier, I'm thirsty and this time he's what I want. But he pulls me to him, my back to his chest, my butt fitting into the hollow of his crotch perfectly. "Night, lover," he murmurs, kissing my cheek. When I grind back into him, his arms tighten around me. "You're not in the mood," he tells me.

My head spins, my eyes are heavy, I can't keep them open. "I'm not?" I whisper.

He shakes his head. I believe him. He kisses the back of my neck, and somewhere between his hands on my body and his breath on my skin, I fall asleep.

45: Seeing Things

I'M AWARE OF being awake. Not waking *up*, exactly, but a subtle shift in consciousness, almost like coming to my senses after fainting, one second nothing and then I'm simply here, eyes closed, alive.

With a piercing ache just above my right eye that feels like something pick pick picking away at my brain. *A headache,* I think, groaning as I roll onto my back. Just what I need. Four beers last night — three and a half, if you want to get technical about it — what was I *thinking*? *Thirsty,* my mind whispers, and at first I think that's a reply. But as I yawn and stretch in the narrow bed, careful not to disturb Dan, I realize that my throat is raw and scratchy, parched, not a memory but thirsty *now*. My tongue tastes of stale beer, my breath smells like a brewery, I must look real fine this morning. In rare form. Hung over for my aunt's funeral, it's like the punch line of a bad joke.

When I try to sit up, my head throbs and I fall back to the pillow, trembling. *Please no,* I pray as waves of nausea wash over me. *Please no, God, please.* I don't want to be sick. Beside me, Dan snuggles closer and snores softly, each breath a rumbling grumble, his arms folded across his chest and pressed into my side like he's trying to huddle up for warmth. Only it's hot in here, *too* hot, I kick the blankets away as I roll onto my side. My stomach churns in protest and I curl into myself, backing up against the wall so I can bring my knees to my chest, my arms wrapped around my waist, my head hunched down between my shoulders. My brow rests against Dan's forearm, which is cool and dry but warms quickly. I'm sick.

The pain behind my eye flares brightly then dips away, rushes at me again, dissolves, hurries back — moving slowly, I inch closer to Dan, and even though he's asleep, his arms unfurl as he feels me near him, they envelope me, draw me in, hold me against the heart beating in his chest. One rock-hard nipple pokes my closed eyelid as if pointing out where it hurts. Between us, my knees lean on his thighs, and his hands strum down over the nubs of my spine before his arms tighten, trapping me. I burrow closer.

It seems like I lay for hours before my stomach finally settles, but my headache doesn't want to fade away. I'm not sure of the time — early morning, most likely, since there's no sun coming through the window yet and Dan isn't awake. He's military, rolls out of bed at 0600 hours on the dot day in and day out, regardless of weekends or vacation or holidays. So it's predawn, then, the house quiet, everyone else still asleep, everyone but me. I *would* be asleep, if not for this pounding behind my eyes. It woke me up, I swear it's going to stab at me until I simply give in and die. Nothing can hurt this much and not kill you.

Aspirin.

The word floats through my subconscious, searching for something to connect with. An image surfaces — my mom bent over the medicine drawer yesterday, rummaging through bottles of pills and cough syrup for Penny's prescription. In my mind I see the drawer open before me, an apothecary overflowing with the promise of health. Smooth white pills to soothe the pain. That's what I need, something in *there*, something to make it all go away.

If I can stand. If I can walk that far — the idea roils my stomach and makes my head hurt worse. But I have the whole rest of the day to get through and if I can get started now, if I can get a handful of pills to calm this raging pain in my head, if I can just get out of *bed*, I should be able to make it, I should be okay. Here's hoping. *Please, God,* I pray, a litany that tumbles through my head over and over again, *please, please.*

Somehow I make it out of bed. Step one. When I first pull back from Dan, though, there are a few tense moments where I'm sure he won't let me go. "Baby," I whisper, the hoarse voice frightening me in the early darkness — is that mine? "Let me up. Dan ..." His arms are constricting bands around me that tighten the more I try to get away. I don't want to wake him up and I'm about ready to give in and call it quits — I'll get aspirin later, what's a few hours with pain like this? — but at that moment he relaxes and I slip from his embrace. As I climb over him, he rolls into the warmth I've left behind, burrowing into the pillow that still smells of my hair and hugging the blankets where I slept to his chest.

When I stand, my head clouds over in fast, sharp pain and I swoon, almost fall back to the bed, I'd surely wake Dan up *then*, but the sensation recedes like the tide and I'm okay, I tell myself this just to make sure, "I'm okay." Okay — cold, but okay. Freezing, in fact, naked and shivering, what happened to the heat in this place? *Turned down low for the night,* I think, that would be my dad's handiwork. Heaven forbid he sweat in his sheets. He sleeps in longjohns this time of the year and piles on the covers with no regard for guys like myself who like to sleep buck naked and curled up against a lover for warmth. Having the heat down is fine while I'm asleep but the minute I step out of bed, I'm an icicle. Add goose bumps to my list of ailments today.

Beneath my feet, the wooden floor is cold and hard. What was I thinking, getting out of bed at this hour? *Aspirin*, I remind myself, but now that I'm standing, the headache isn't as bad as I thought it was. In fact, it's almost bearable. Almost. But I'm up, I should at least take a look in the drawer — I know the second I lie back down, all the blood will rush into my head and it'll start to throb again. I don't need that. I don't *want* it. Without turning on the light, I shuffle around until I find the sweater I wore yesterday and dig my toes into it to warm them up. Then, bent at the waist, I let my hands drift over the wooden boards, so empty now that we cleaned this room out, so *bare*. Just crouching down like this brings the pain flaring back to life, as I knew it would, and where the hell is our suitcase? When the room was packed with shit, it sat open on the floor by the bedside table and now I can't find it, I'm going to have to turn the lamp on anyway, I don't want to wake Dan up, it's too damn *early* —

There. My hand closes over the handle and I pull the suitcase to me. It scratches over the hardwood floor but it's a small sound, Dan doesn't hear it in his sleep. Fumbling through our clothes, I find a pair of shorts. Dan's PT trunks, though I don't realize this until I pull them on and they mold to my ass and cock — *definitely* not mine. I'm not in the same shape he is, I have an *office* job, I don't get a week out in the field every month or so to work off the fat that settles in my hips and waist. "You're not fat," Dan tells me if I mention it, and to emphasis his point, he'll crawl between my legs and bite at the sensitive skin along my inner thighs. "This is all padding," he says with playful nips that drive me crazy. "I like you soft. If I wanted a hard, lean boy, I'd get with someone in my unit, but I don't like that kind of guy, Michael. I like you."

And admit it, I think as I pull a t-shirt down over my head, also his, *you love his teeth on you, his tongue, his strong hands*. If this headache goes away anytime soon, I could wake him up a *little* earlier, just for some quick loving. I seem to remember him telling me I wasn't in the mood last night but that's bullshit. When am I ever not in the mood for him?

When it's the day of your great-aunt's funeral, my mind whispers. Suddenly the air around me drops another ten degrees, the hair on my arms stands at attention, the skin on my ribs *shudders* with the chill. Whatever ardor I felt shrivels like my balls, tiny walnuts of ice, I rub at my crotch to warm them up again. I'm not going to think of the funeral just yet. Another few hours and the sun will rise, it'll be daylight officially, I'll have to focus on that but right this minute, when I'm the only one awake in this place? I'm not going

---

to let my mind drift in that direction. I'm going to get the aspirin and get back into bed. I won't think any further than that.

Moving quietly, I unlock the door and ease it open just wide enough to slip through. There's no one in the kitchen — at this hour, I didn't expect there would be — but the room is brightly lit from the backyard spotlight that shines in through the windows above the sink. My dad and his damn beacons, as if the mother ship has landed outside. I pull the door to our room shut behind me so the light won't shine in there and bother my lover. Something like *that* wakes him up, he's likely to think it's heaven's light shining down. Can't have a normal porch light like everybody else. I'm sure that says something about my family, something I don't even want to touch.

The kitchen table has been cleared of the take-out boxes and soy sauce packets, napkins, chopsticks, all the paraphernalia of dinner last night. A few crushed beer cans top an overflowing trashcan, set in front of the back door as a blatant reminder for whoever heads that way to take the garbage out with them. On the counter by the sink, still sitting on a bed of newsprint, is Caitlin's pumpkin, lit only with the light from the window behind it. Shadows inside the hollowed-out gourd seem to move as I walk by, making the chiseled leer appear to widen, the carved eyes follow my steps. *It doesn't know me* — the thought comes unbidden to my mind, drawn from some primal well deep inside. Something I read years ago comes back, one of the reasons for dressing up in costumes for Halloween, to confuse the spirits of the dead still wandering the earth. *I'm dressed in Dan's clothes right now, it won't know who I am, it can't get me, I'm safe.*

Another step and the wicked gleam in those dead eyes disappears. It's just a pumpkin, it can't get *anyone*, I know, I saw Aunt Bobbie clean it out this afternoon, I watched Caitlin cut into the hard flesh. What I thought was a treacherous snarl is nothing more than a jagged slit, scary eyes are just empty holes I could poke my fingers through if I wanted to. I don't want to. I'm not going to touch the damn thing. I don't like it.

A noise behind me makes me whirl around, on edge. *The house settling,* I tell myself, that's all it is, but for a moment I see something, some*one*, I see Evie as she was the last time I was down here, five years ago. She's sitting at the table with her large, tanned arms crossed in front of her, and I know who it is she's waiting for. It's me. I never came back here, I don't know why, I just couldn't seem to fit it into my schedule and now look at what's happened, she's died, I'll never see her again. *I'm sorry,* I think, watching her watch me. Or rather, stare *through* me, like she doesn't see me, I don't exist for her. As I think this, her clear brow furrows, her wide mouth pulls down into a caricature of sadness. "Michael?" she asks, her voice as hollow as the pumpkin on the counter.

My arms break out in fresh pimples of fear at the sound. It's the same voice that used to tell me everything would be alright when I was a little boy and fell down or broke something or got in trouble yet again with my mom. The same voice that laughed in delight when I called to tell her I would be going to college. The same voice that sympathized when I came home in tears that time Stephen left me at the playground, pissed because all I could talk about was Joe Kneesi. The last words I ever heard in this voice were, "I miss you, boy." And those big arms wrapped me in a strong hug — how could they be gone now? How could that voice be silenced? How could a heart like Evie's, so large that there was no end to her love — no matter how much she poured out on us, there was always more, *always* — how could a heart like that cease to beat? How could it *fail* and just give up? How could someone like her possibly die?

"Michael?" she says again in that eerie echo of her once vibrant voice. *Here*, I try to say, *I'm right here*, but the words won't come and she continues to look through me as if *I'm* the ghost. *It's the clothing*, I think, of *course* — I'm wearing Dan's shorts, his shirt, she doesn't recognize me. *Costumes to confuse spirits of the dead*, wasn't that what I read? She never met Dan. She doesn't know his clothing, she doesn't know *me*.

"Here," I whisper. She seems to turn her head like she heard me, but it might just be the light again, that infernal theft-deterrent bulb my dad thought necessary as if this were downtown Philly and not backwater Sugar Creek. "Right here, Aunt Evie." This time she *does* look at me, I can see the light shining in her eyes, I can see the faint smile toying with the corners of her mouth. On the table, her hands fold together as if in prayer, and my voice is as soft as the rustle of leaves outside when I tell her, "These are Dan's clothes but it's me, Evie, I promise. Dan's still asleep. You'd like him, I just know you would."

"Michael," she sighs.

My name sounds like forgiveness in the gray light. "I'm sorry," I tell her. *For not coming sooner*, I add silently. *For not telling you about who I was before, about Stephen or Matthew when I came last time, or Dan when I called you on the phone earlier this year. Of everyone in this house, I think you alone would've understood, Evie. You would've accepted me for who I am. You would've told my mom to grow the hell up, told Aunt Sarah to lay off me, told my brother to mind his own business. You would've been on my side, Evie, I just know it. So why aren't you here? Why the hell aren't you here?*

Tears blind me and I wipe them away with the back of my hand, upset that I'm crying again. Is this ever going to stop? And now my nose will stuff up, I'll lie back down and wake again with an even greater headache, my sinuses clogged with tears and what should have beens and why nots. Maybe if she accepts my apology, everything will be alright. If she'll just look at me the way she's always done in the past, without judgment, without regret, without pinning the crimes of the world and whatever she might feel inside on *me* like everyone else seems intent to do ... maybe that would be enough to let me move on. If I heard the words in her voice one more time, *don't worry about it, Michael, it's going to be alright* —

But when I lower my hand, she's gone. A trick of the light, then, and God knows there's so much of it. She was never there in the first place, she *couldn't* have been — she's dead, passed, gone, however you put it, she's not coming back. She didn't just say my name, she wasn't here. *I'm sorry, Aunt Evie*, I think again. *For everything.*

For a moment I'm not sure what I was doing. *Talking to Evie*, my mind replies, but why am I out here in the first place? Not because I heard her and came out to chat. My gaze wanders around the room but she doesn't appear again, she's gone back to wherever it is spirits go. I don't question if she was there or not — she was, I saw her, I *heard* her, she was as real as the pumpkin on the counter, the light in its eyes as bright as a headache.

Aspirin.

In response, the pain behind my eyes throbs once, a weak echo of what I felt when I first woke up. Still, I don't need it lingering like a bad memory. I think of Dan and the brief sexiness I felt when I slipped on his clothes. He's in that bed alone — I need to fix that. But first ...

There's a bottle of aspirin in the medicine drawer, just as I thought. Nearly full, too. My hands shake when I twist off the cap. Four pills — no, three. No, four, because I don't want that headache coming back. When I put the bottle back in the drawer, I notice another one, brown, obviously prescription, *Valium* written on the label. Without thinking I pick it up and shake it. The tiny sound of pills rattling together startles the silence of the house around me. Palming the aspirin, I open the Valium and dump a handful of the pills out. They're small and yellow, a hollow *V* in the center of each one. Penny's pills, prescribed to get her through today. I wonder how long she'll need them? *No refills*, the bottle says. I wonder if they work.

Before I can change my mind, I take two of them. *Mother's little helper*, I think, only it's not Mom they're for, it's her sister. And maybe me, if things get bad enough. Two should suffice.

At the fridge I stand in the cold glow of light and pop the aspirin in my mouth, then drink straight from the half-empty carton of milk to wash them down. *My* milk, I bought it. I consider tossing down the Valium, too, but I don't need them yet. The aspirin should be enough. *Please*, I pray. The pain is starting to come back, as if the sight of Evie sitting at the kitchen table had startled it into submission and now that she's gone again, it's remembered it has a job to do and hopes to make up for lost time by driving deep into my brain. It's the milk, spiking into my head like ice, so unbelievably cold that it's almost tasteless, and I squeeze my eyes shut against the light, the pain. All I can think of is Dan asleep in our warm bed. I can almost feel his arms around me.

I cross the kitchen, keeping away from the pumpkin and the emotions shifting through its hollow head, but at the door to our room I have to stop and look back at the table one last time. I guess I hope Evie will be there again, watching me, the smile in her eyes finally reaching her lips. *You're right,* she'll say, *I do like him,* and for a breathless moment I actually *hear* the words, though she doesn't materialize again. *I do like him, Michael. Everything's going to work out just fine, you'll see.*

"I hope so," I whisper to the empty kitchen.

Dan snores softly as I enter the room, closing the door behind me to cut out that light. I fumble for the suitcase again and find it in the darkness. The Valium get shoved into the pocket of what I hope are my pants, not his. Then it's off with the shorts, the shirt, and back into bed, beneath the covers, into my lover's arms where I belong. When Dan mumbles something incoherent, I whisper to him, "I saw Evie in the kitchen. She likes you, baby, just as I knew she would."

His arms tighten and he snuggles closer as if trying to warm me up. I'm so damn cold. I cuddle into him and try to think of nothing at all as I stare out the window, where the sky has begun to lighten with the coming dawn.

46: The Morning of the Funeral

I DON'T MANAGE to get back to sleep. Instead I wait until the watch on Dan's wrist reads quarter after five and then I get up, I just can't pretend anymore. I'm awake, that's all there is to it. The house is still quiet as I dress in his shorts and shirt again, and the kitchen is mercifully empty when I step out of our room. I hear a few muffled snores from the living room as I pass by the closed French doors on my way to the bathroom, but no one else seems to be up. I don't see Evie, either — it's just me this time.

I take a shower, making it quick because I don't want Dan to wake up alone, but also I can't afford a long, invigorating shower — I'll never hear the end of it if I use all the hot water. When I'm done, the mirror isn't even fogged, and I can hear footsteps above me, the others waking up, probably hoping to snag the bathroom first. I take my time, brushing my teeth, running a razor over my chin even though I don't really need a shave, moussing my hair into the middle part look that I think makes me look smarter than I really am. All I need is a blazer and khakis and I'm set for a day at the office, but I didn't think to pack anything remotely dressy. This was supposed to be a weekend at my parents', nothing more. No nights at the opera, no fancy dinners out on the town — they live in the heart of Virginia, twenty miles south of Richmond, in a small city where the streets roll up at dusk. Fortunately it's autumn and I have a few dark clothes tucked into the suitcase, or we would've had to stop by the house on the way up here after all. But brown should be okay, I hope, and I know Dan has a pair of black jeans he can wear. We'll make it work.

While I'm toweling off, the door knob starts to turn, first one way, then the other. It's locked, thank God, or whoever it is out in the hall would've busted in on me. "I'm in here," I call out, as if this isn't evident.

There's a light knock, and then my sister's voice comes in a harsh whisper, right up against the side of the door like she has her face pressed to the wood. "Michael. What the hell are you doing?"

I slap the door with the towel and laugh at her little yelp of surprise.

"What do you think I'm doing?" I ask as I wrap the towel around my waist. "Can't I take a shower in peace?"

The knob turns again, harder this time. "You're done," Caitlin says. She kicks the door for emphasis. "I heard the water turn off *hours* ago. So unless you're in there jerking off —"

Without warning, I unlock the door and yank it open so fast, she has to catch herself on the jamb to keep from falling into the tiny bathroom. "I am *not* jerking off," I tell her, indignant.

My sister stands there in a black t-shirt and faded boxers she obviously slept in, her hair a tangled mess and her eyes ringed with dark circles of makeup she forgot to wash off. "Not anymore," she mutters. Stepping aside, she motions impatiently. "Well? You just gonna stand there all day or what? Others need to shower, too."

A dozen retorts run through my head, but I discard them all. This is Caitlin, the queen of comebacks. So I just gather my clothes up from the floor — *Dan's* clothes, actually — and I push my way past her into the hall. At the last possible moment, I reach behind me and slap her butt, hard enough that my hand stings. An angry cry escapes her throat, but she's already in the bathroom and I'm dancing down the hall, laughing because I got her this time, I *got* her, with none of her reflexive retaliation. In the kitchen I see Ray, pouring milk into a bowl overflowing with cereal, and my laughter turns to unstoppable giggles. I have half a mind to tell him that I drank straight from that carton earlier, and I just got Caitlin good, and my headache's gone, thank God, and Evie told me she liked Dan … but I don't. My brother looks up at me with his bed-frazzled hair and bloodshot eyes, frowns at my bare chest and the towel draped around my waist, and has the audacity to mutter, "What?" as if I've lost my mind.

I can't tell him. I just shake my head and pat him on the back, fresh laughter bubbling up inside of me as he dumps the last of the milk into his bowl, the fucker. "That's my milk," I say.

When I pick off a few flakes of cereal from the top of the bowl, he slaps my hand away. "You want some, go buy more," Ray growls, covering the bowl protectively. "Don't eat mine."

"Don't worry," I laugh. Everything seems infinitely funny all of a sudden.

His eyes narrow in distrust. "What's with you today?" I shrug, I don't know. Just playing around, I reach for his bowl but he jerks it away, splashing milk and cereal on the counter. "If you're going to be like this later, you might want to take something now to calm your ass down. Mom'll shit."

I think of the yellow pills I swiped earlier — do I need them yet? I don't think so. This is just nervous energy setting me off. "Lighten up, Ray," I tell him. It seems like I'm *always* telling him that, *lighten up*, he's too damn serious for someone so lazy and unambitious.

"We're going to a funeral," he reminds me. With one hand he sweeps the cereal from the counter into the sink, leaving milk streaked behind. "Unless you forgot —"

"I didn't forget." I just don't want to think about it until I absolutely, positively have to. Before he can say another word, I duck into the back room and close the door on him and his *calm your ass down* bit. Jeez, try to be nice to him and he wants to know what's wrong with me. See if I goof with him again.

I'm well aware of the fact that in another five hours, I'll be sitting in one of Morrison's ostentatious viewing rooms, listening to an uncle ramble on about how wonderful Evelyn Mendelton was and how much she'll be missed while trying everything I can not to stare at the coffin. God, I hope it's not open. I've never seen a dead body before, except on TV and in the movies, and even on the nightly news, it doesn't seem real to me. If I walk into that funeral parlor and the coffin is open, I'm going to need more than two little pills to get through *that*, a hell of a lot more.

There's enough sunlight now to get dressed without turning on the light. Squatting by the open suitcase, I find the pants with the pills in the pocket — a pair of my dark brown khakis, just as I hoped, they'll be fine for the funeral. Beneath them is a sweater the color of freshly turned earth, Dan's black jeans, a gunmetal gray button-down shirt of his that will work. Evie was never one for extravagance — her idea of dressing up to eat out was cleaning the dirt off the kids' faces with a warm washcloth before we all piled into the car for McDonald's. I don't think she's going to be overly upset that we're not in suits to see her go.

As I stand, the towel falls to pool at my feet, the terry cloth warm and damp on my skin, a sharp contrast to the cold hardwood floor. Naked, I shuffle through the suitcase again in search of underwear and socks, riffling through handfuls of Army green briefs and the gray socks Dan favors, looking for something of mine. One tan sock is folded into a t-shirt of his, its mate blending in with his socks. He's become such a part of me in these past few months, hasn't he? Integrating himself into every aspect of my life until I'm not sure where I end and he begins. What would I do without him? I hope I never have to find out. *Love you*, I think, glancing over at the sleeping form on the bed.

Dan stares back.

He has the covers fisted to his mouth, and above the quilt, his eyes glisten in the meager sunlight. For a second we just stare at each other, him hidden beneath the blankets and me bare-ass in the middle of the room. Then his eyes crinkle in an unmistakable smile and I laugh. "How long have you been watching me?" I want to know.

"Long enough to be sporting wood," he replies.

I laugh again and pull a pair of my own underwear from the depths of the suitcase as if by magic. "I hope you're enjoying the show," I say, facing him so he can watch me dress. I put a little wiggle in my hips as I work the briefs up over my thighs, then turn about face and tease him by tugging the underwear up over my ass inch by excruciating inch. "Like what you see?"

An arm snakes out from beneath the covers, grabs the waistband of my briefs, pulls me back stumbling to the bed. I shriek with laughter as Dan grapples with me — his hands are everywhere, my stomach, my chest, my legs, my cock. With a sexy growl, he kisses my shoulders, the back of my neck, my cheek, anywhere his lips can touch. "Dan!" I cry, putting up a light resistance to his roaming hands. Everywhere he touches, I feel palm-shaped patches of lingering warmth stain my skin, and his kisses leave wet imprints all over my upper body. Like a trapdoor spider, he tries to pull me under the covers with him, but I kick and fight in defiance until my laughter turns breathless. "Baby —"

Pressing his lips to my ear, he tells me, "Stop."

The result is instantaneous — I stop thrashing and just lie in his arms like a rag doll, my head back on his shoulder, my heart beating wildly in my chest. "I love you," he whispers, kissing along my collarbone. "Don't fight me."

"I'm not." His hands stroke my stomach, my legs, soothing me. Maybe this is what Ray meant, something to calm me down. I close my eyes and never want to open them again, just lie here in this embrace and feel these hands petting me quiet. "I love you, too," I murmur. "I was just playing."

Dan's lips smile in the hollow of my throat. "I know." He works his way up my neck to my mouth, turning my face towards his as we kiss. "Are you ready for today?" he wants to know.

I shrug, an awkward movement lying like I am in his arms. "As ready as I can be," I reply. I realize that isn't quite an answer.

But Dan nods, as if he didn't expect anything more. He studies me for a moment, our faces merely an inch apart, and this close I can see the stubble growing in above his ears, thick wires of hair that he'll see in the mirror today after his shower and shave away to a dark smudge. "You saw your aunt last night," he says.

It's not a question. He means Evie, I know he does, and when I slip out of his arms, he lets me go. I slide off the bed, tugging my underwear up over my nakedness. The sound of the waistband snapping into place is loud between us. Kneeling on the floor, I turn and fold my arms on the bed, rest my chin on my wrists, look at him peeking out from the blankets like a little boy.

"I thought you were asleep," I tell him. Last night, after coming back from the kitchen, I was fairly certain Dan wasn't awake when I got back into bed.

He pushes the covers away enough so he can run a finger along an invisible line on the outside of my forearm where the hair seems to end. "Maybe I dreamed it then."

"No," I assure him, "you didn't." I bite at the back of my hand and stare into the promising shadows where the covers have pulled away from his body. There's a hint of muscle, one nipple dusky with darkness, then a tantalizing stretch of shade that runs the length of his chest to gather at his waist. When he pulled me onto the bed, I felt his *wood*, a hard shaft poking into my hip with an almost obscene insistence. I wonder if we have time to take care of that now. It'll turn the discussion away from the dead woman I spoke to last night, at any rate. "I thought you were asleep," I say again.

His response is simply, "Do you want to talk about it?"

Actually now, by the light of day, last night seems unreal to me — maybe *I* was the one dreaming, I don't know. But if I say no, Dan will think I'm shutting him out again and that's the last thing I want to do, especially at a time like this. "I had a headache," I start. Holding my eyelid shut, I tell him, "Here. It woke me up."

Even though the pain is gone, he leans forward and kisses the bridge of my nose by my right eye as if that alone would have been enough to make everything better. I close my other eye, too, and let him kiss me — I don't have the heart to tell him that the pain has gone away. "Thanks, baby," I whisper as he lies back. Jokingly, I ask, "Where were you at three o'clock this morning?"

"Right beside you," he says with a laugh. "You could've woken me up."

Something in my chest swells with sudden emotion. I love him, have I said that? I say it again just so he can hear the words, and they earn me another kiss, this one on my lips. "I didn't want to bother you," I murmur. He's about to say I'm not a bother — the words are on the tip of his tongue, I see them in his eyes — but before he can set them free, I hurry on. "I just got up to get some aspirin. They keep it in a drawer out in the kitchen? And that pumpkin Caitlin made was on the counter, all cut up and spooky and shit. Then I heard something behind me." I pause — it sounds silly now, did I really see Aunt Evie? It was just everything catching up with me, perhaps, the unspent emotions and the constant fighting, the headache, I'm sure that was a factor in it, too. "It wasn't a *ghost*. More like ... I don't know, like she was just *there*, sitting there like she came downstairs for a midnight snack or something. She wasn't ..." I trail off, I don't know how to explain it. "She wasn't all white or see-through or anything like that. I don't know, Dan, it was just her. She looked exactly the same way she did the last time I saw her, she looked *alive*, stupid as that sounds."

I wait for him to tell me it doesn't sound stupid but he says nothing. With a sigh, I rest my head on the backs of my hands and tell him, "It was like she wasn't dead at all. She was sitting there staring at me but I don't think she saw me. Or she didn't recognize me. I was wearing your shirt."

A gentle hand touches my hair, smoothes through the mousse and spray without disturbing a strand, he's very good at that. I'm funny about my hair, I don't like people touching it, I don't like it to move much on its own if I can help it. When I bought my car, the salesman tried so hard to sell me a convertible. "Young guy like you needs to go topless," he said with a wink — old enough to be my father and easily twice my weight, he kept his hands shoved into the pockets of his pants in an attempt to hide the erection he fingered every time I looked away. What a creep. "Go cruising downtown, hit the clubs, eh, eh?"

Not quite. A convertible would mean messy hair, and I don't go for that wind-blown look. I don't go for old fat guys, either, and when he acciden-tally brushed against my backside as I leaned over to look under the hood, I told him, "My boy's in the Army." I kept my voice amicable enough, didn't look at him, didn't have to — I felt him stiffen beside me, in fear or indigna-tion or both. "Touch me again, fuckhead, and *he'll* be the one to buy this car from you. I'm sure he'll want to come down here personally once he hears just how *attentive* you are to me." *That* made the bastard back up a bit.

As if he knows my mind is drifting, Dan asks, "Did she say anything to you?"

"My name," I whisper. My voice is muffled against my hands like a se-cret. "Like she was looking for me. Michael? Michael? And I go, right here, I'm right here, Aunt Evie. That's when she saw me, and she sort of sighed my name and disappeared." Taking a shuddery breath that frightens me, I tell him, "When I was coming back in the room, I thought I heard her say I was right, she does like you. I was right."

Dan doesn't speak. I look up at him and see something I don't recognize in his eyes, something sad, something old and distant like a memory. "You don't believe me?" I ask quietly. Of course he doesn't. Who would? "Maybe I was still half-asleep —"

He places his fingers against my lips to silence me. "Right after Ma died, I thought I'd see her again," he says, his voice quiet in the gray sunlight. "I was just a kid, you know. I watched all those shows about life after death and people coming back from the grave, all that crap. I was into ghosts and flying saucers and ESP — I was so sure that she would come back one final time to say goodbye to me. Because I was her only grandkid, right? And I hadn't had a chance to tell her how much I loved her before she was gone."

I nod, encouraging him to continue. He grins as he says, "A friend of mine even had a Ouija board — you know, that game where you all put your hands on the triangle piece and call on the ghost of Elvis to appear, and try to pretend that you're not the one making the thing move?" I laugh at that, imagining a much younger Daniel Biggs sitting in front of a Ouija board, *knock if you can hear me* ... I played those slumber party games, too, right here in this house, Stephen on one side and Ray on the other, spooking ourselves for fun. But Dan's smile fades with his memories. "Nothing."

"I'm sorry," I whisper, kissing the tips of his fingers. "Hon —"

He shakes his head, quieting me. "About a year after she passed away, I was sitting in the dining room at the house, thinking it was about when we normally took the trip out to see her, only there was no one to see out there anymore. Even Uncle Ernie had moved on. No reason to go any longer. And God, this sadness just descended on me, all of a sudden I wanted to break down and cry, I couldn't seem to shake it off." He takes my hands in his and presses them to his bare chest, where his skin is warm from the covers. "Then I felt someone come up behind me and hug me tight. I thought it was my mom but when I looked, no one was there. That's when I heard Ma, after all that time. *It's okay, Danny*, she told me." Squeezing my fingers, he says again, "It's okay."

"That's what Evie said," I sigh, relieved. What happened last night *was* real, then, and he believes me. *It's okay*, she said, so maybe it is, it really is. Or will soon be.

47: Comfortable Together

B Y EIGHT, THE whole house is awake and emotions are running high. There's a tension threaded through everyone, from Theresa's little Crystal to Aunt Bobbie, strung so tight that the slightest remark plucks our nerves and the simplest gesture creates a domino effect of unbridled anger that threatens to topple us all. Each passing moment brings us closer to eleven o'clock ... and closer to tearing each other apart. Even from the safe haven of the back room, I can hear the bickering — Ray hollers at someone for bumping into his chair, a child screams out *mine! mine!*, a door opens to angry shouts and then slams shut to trap them inside. *God*, I pray. I sit on our bed and watch Dan shovel oatmeal into his mouth. I'm too anxious to eat. He's still naked, but the covers are pulled discreetly over his crossed legs and up to his waist. In one hand he holds the bowl of Quaker Oats I made for him — using water to mix the instant oatmeal, since my thick-headed brother drank the last of the milk. Any other normal person and Dan's little talk last night would've been enough to frighten them off. Hell, anyone else would've gone out and bought milk just to make sure I had some in the fridge. Anyone but Ray. He probably thinks that being my brother makes him somehow immune to my lover's veiled temper. I might let something like emptying the milk two days in a row slide, but that sort of petty meanness sticks with Dan. He might not mention it today, or tomorrow, or even next week, but it's there just below the calm pool of his mind, taking on water, gathering weight, and heaven help you when it resurfaces.

If he notices that there isn't any milk in the oatmeal now, though, he doesn't mention it. He *shouldn't* notice, as I dumped a good two tablespoons of sugar into the bowl and stirred it up real good, because he has one hell of a sweet tooth. The first morning he ever woke up beside me, I made oatmeal for breakfast and watched, fascinated, as he just about upended the sugar bowl into it. "You know how sweet I like it," he said, giving me a saucy wink that made my cheeks flush. I feel my face heat up at the memory of that first night, still so bright after ten months together, and Dan nudges me with one foot. "You're thinking something nasty," he says. "It better be about me."

"Who else?" I reply, picking at his toes through the blanket.

They wiggle in my palm and my lover holds his bowl out towards me as an offering. "Have some," he says. When I shake my head, he admonishes, "You'll be hungry later."

"So I'll eat later." I'm just not hungry now. I don't think I'd be able to keep anything down if I was.

Dan frowns but doesn't answer. Instead, he finishes off the oatmeal himself, scraping the bowl to get every last drop. When he's done, he sets the bowl aside and motions me closer. I lean towards him. He takes hold of my upper arms, kneading the muscles in his hands, warm through the sweater I wear. "Listen to me, hon," he says. I nod, I'm listening. "Today is for you. Aunt Evie has passed on now — funerals are only for the living to say goodbye. I know it's going to be hard but that's what I'm here for, right?"

I cover one of his hands with my own. "Right."

"Listen," he says again, as if I might not be. I squeeze his hand to show that I'm hearing him. "You talk to me today, Michael, you hear me? Keep the channels open at all times —"

With a laugh, I tease, "I like it when you talk military to me."

A faint smile flickers across his face and is gone. "All I'm trying to say," he tells me, his voice gentle, "is keep me informed, Michael, please. If there's something that makes you uncomfortable, let me know. If you suddenly have to get the hell out of there, tell me, I'll lead the way. This won't be pleasant, I know that, but you're the only one I care about. If you need to leave, you say the words and I'm out the door with you. If you're going to be sick or you don't think you can make it or you don't want to do something, you don't have to, no matter what the rest of your family says."

I don't want to think things like that — it'll be fine. I assure him, "I'll be okay."

"If you aren't," he persists, "let me know, please." His gaze bores into me, holds me steady, won't let me look away. "I can't read your mind, hon, much as I'd like to sometimes, and you know it. So just think of me today, okay? Lean on me if you need to. That's why I'm here."

Tears choke my throat but I swallow them down, blink them away when they rise unbidden in my eyes. *Sure,* I think flippantly, *I can do that, I can let you be strong for me, no problem,* but when I try to speak, the words won't come and I don't like the tiny croak that is my voice. "Come here," Dan murmurs, pulling me to him. It's an awkward position, me lying across his lap, but we make it work. My arms wrap around his waist and he hugs me close, his hands smoothing down my sweater where it's bunched at my back. "It's going to be okay, Michael," he whispers. "We're going to get through this.

Trust me."

I do.

We lie together for long minutes that turn into half an hour or more. Finally Dan sighs, a signal that he's grown uncomfortable in this position, and I shift out of his arms to stretch beside him on the bed. "I should start getting ready," he tells me. He brushes a strand of wayward hair from my face and smiles sadly. "Are you going to be okay for a while?"

I roll onto my side and prop my head up with one hand. "While you're in the shower?" I pretend to think it over, savoring the look of consternation that crosses my lover's face. "Gee, I really don't know."

Punching my arm, he growls, "Just for that, you're not invited."

"I've already had my shower," I remind him. As he climbs out of bed, though, the covers fall away to reveal his smooth, naked flesh, and suddenly a second shower doesn't seem like a bad idea. He turns, allowing me a glimpse of his half-erect cock before he bends to pick up the shorts I wore earlier and left on the floor when I dressed. "Hey now," I tease, "I didn't say we couldn't negotiate …"

"Too late," he laughs. The shorts come up his muscled legs and over his taut buttocks to snap around his lean waist. "You missed your chance, babe. I'm going to have to take care of *this* —" he cups his sheathed crotch, the front of his shorts bulging in his hand — "by myself."

"Or I could do it right here," I say, reaching for him.

My fingers graze his ass before he moves away. "It's less messy in the tub," Dan tells me with another laugh. Slipping a t-shirt on over his head, he adds, "I'll think of you."

I lie back on the bed and pout, a trait I've picked up from my sister this past weekend. "You do that," I grumble. I hope he sees the wounded expression on my face. I hope it looks convincing enough.

Dan manages to look suitably sympathetic. "Aww, poor baby," he cajoles and I pout harder, until my lips hurt. He laughs as he scoops up his toiletries — toothbrush, razor, the soap and toothpaste we both share. Heading for the door, he throws a glance over his shoulder and says, "You'll get over it."

That surprises me. "Ha!" I cry, struggling to sit up amid the blankets. He stops in the open doorway and I can see that the kitchen is filled with children, little girls in black dresses, little boys in small suits that hurt the heart to see. They crowd around Aunt Sarah, who wears a very somber, very dark velvet pants suit that seems to absorb the light when she moves. She's dishing out frozen waffles as fast as the toaster can pop them up, and already her hair has started to curl in frazzled little ringlets that frame her face. On the cusp of that disorder, Dan stares at me, waiting, the ghost of a smile on his lips because he's sure whatever I have to say will amuse him to no end. "I'm going to keep that in mind the next time you want some loving," I threaten. "I won't put out, you'll see, and when you start to whine and cry and *beg*, I'll just be like you'll get over it."

His smile bursts forth in full bloom. "Yeah, right," he says, closing the door behind him. "Like you can hold out on me, Mike."

Sad thing is, he's right, I'm weak against him, and I laugh at the empty room, I know he's right. Our silly banter has me aroused now — I toy with the idea of following him to the bathroom anyway, what would he say? Nothing, really. We'd end up in the shower together, naked and wet and soapy ... *and the whole house will hear us,* I think. That puts a damper on my lust real quick. All those kids in the kitchen, countless relatives in the living room and hall? The last thing I need is someone picking on me at the funeral home because Dan and I got frisky in the shower. We'll wait until later, tonight maybe, or tomorrow after we're home and have the whole place to ourselves. It'll be so good to get our privacy back after this trip, to regain some semblance of normalcy and get our *lives* back. This weekend I've fallen into the image of who my parents think I am — like a spider spinning her web, my mother effectively trapped me into the middle child mold she has fashioned in her mind. It was a role I took on willingly enough the moment I stepped into her house, sleeping in my old bedroom, striving hard to be the boy she wanted me to be and not the man I've since become.

Then came my revelation at dinner Saturday night, and I tore away her dreams as easily as dusty gossamer threads wisp to nothingness when you knock down a cobweb. She hasn't had one civil word for me since. Is this the way it's going to be from now on? My father's silent acceptance, my sister's *so what?* attitude, my brother's grudging tolerance ... and her. I'm not asking for open arms here, I realize that would be pushing it, but it's almost like she's avoiding me, like I've done something so heinous and so deliberate to her that she might never, ever find it in herself to forgive me. Then what? That's one question I don't really know how to answer — and then what?

It occurs to me that maybe I should find out.

Getting out of the bed, I smooth the wrinkles out of my pants, tuck in my undershirt, pull my sweater down so I look alright. I slip into my loafers, dark enough to wear with this outfit, and run a nervous hand through my hair to make sure it's not sticking up at any odd angles. Then I yank the blankets up to the pillows, hastily making the bed, before I head out into the kitchen and allow myself to get sucked into the noisy morning chaos that is my family.

I get a few mumbled *hello*s but for the most part, the kids ignore me. They're too busy eating or shouting or kicking each other under the table, opening their mouths to display tongues full of half-chewed food, yelling

"I'm gonna tell!" and "Stop touching me! Aunt Sarah, make him stop it now!" It's worse than a preschool in here, and right in the center of it all, Ray and Kenny sit at the table punching each other and whoever gets in their way. I don't even want to know what that's all about, I don't have the energy to get caught up in this shit today, so I hurry through the kitchen and down the hall, past the bathroom where the sound of the shower through the closed door makes me picture Dan beneath the hot spray, *what* an image.

Up the stairs two at a time before my resolve crumbles and down the hall in search of the bedroom my parents are sharing. I'm not sure which one it is, but most of the doors are open, my aunts and uncles dodging around each other as they rush to the bathrooms or into other rooms, calling for their scarves or their ties or "Has anybody seen my shoes? The black wing-tips, does anyone know where I put them? Anyone?"

I keep against one wall, out of the way. At one point Ginger comes up to me and grabs my elbow, pinching me with blood-red fingernails, a dazed look on her face like that you'd see on someone who just walked away from a plane crash. "Mike?" she asks, unsure. One eye is made up perfectly, dusky blue eyeshadow above long lashes, eyeliner dark and unsmudged, but the other eye is wide and pale, as if she did one and forgot about the other. Self-consciously, she picks at the mascara clumped on the lashes of her good eye and sighs. Tiny flecks of black make-up fall to her cheek like soot. "Does this look alright?" she asks me, motioning at her navy dress. "It's not black, though. Do you think that's going to be a problem? I should've brought black. Closets *full* of black dresses back home. I thought this was darker."

"You look fine," I tell her, prying her fingers off my arm as I pat her hand. "I'm not wearing black, either."

"Closet full of black dresses," she says again, softly this time, like she's speaking to herself. Before I can point out that I'm in brown, she wanders away, picking at her lashes the way a small child would a healing scab.

I bump into the wall and hurry on, staring into the faces of the people that I pass in the hopes that one of them will look back at me. None of them do. We're all inside our own private pain, none of us want to open up and let another in. To do that would be to admit the hurt and it's still too tender to touch, we haven't healed yet, there's no closure. Somewhere someone cries quietly, someone else murmurs low, comforting words. I don't want to stop anyone and ask which room my mom is in. If I can't find her myself, I can always talk to her later. My sudden courage to face her and demand an answer to my questions, to find out *why* and *what now*, has faded like the washed out paint on the walls, and all I want to do is sneak back downstairs to my room before she knows I've been here. I can talk to her after the funeral. It doesn't have to be right this second.

I'm just about to turn around — Dan should be finished his shower by now, I don't *have* to talk to Mom — when I hear my sister's voice rise in anger from a room at the end of the hall. "What's wrong with this?" she cries, and without thinking, I pick up my pace, hurrying down to her. "You're always saying I'm too damn depressing and the first time I wear something *normal*, you have a shit fit."

My mom answers her, just as upset. "Caitlin! I don't have the time to go into this with you right now. You're *not* wearing that."

"It's my body," Caitlin replies. As I near the room, she steps out into the hall, and at first I don't realize what the problem is here. She wears a bright teal dress with tiny sleeves, a scalloped neckline, and princess seams that cause the skirt to twirl out around her knees when she turns. Her skin is deathly pale against the splash of color, her hair pulled into a severe ponytail, so dark it looks as if someone inked it in. But when she looks up at me, her makeup is still harsh and unforgiving, thick black lines like bruises rimming her eyes. "I'll wear whatever the hell I want to," she yells back into the room. "What do you care? It's not *your* funeral."

Mom sounds weary when she starts, "Caitlin —"

"I'm not changing!" My sister storms off down the hall, muttering, "Out of my way, Mike," as she pushes past me. "I'll wear whatever the fuck I *want*, see if you can tell me different. What do you care what I look like anyway?"

She directs the question at me, but I just shake my head and shrug, I don't know. "You look pretty," I tell her. It's the truth.

"Fuck off," she says. I move aside and let her go.

I watch her until she turns the corner, skirt billowing around her like the sea, and her black Mary Janes *clip clip clip* down the wooden steps, a sound that reminds me of an electric typewriter. *Well*, I think, straightening my sweater, *I found Mom's room.* Trouble is, I'm not sure I'm ready to go inside.

I don't have much choice — I'm already here. Might as well get it over with. Cautiously I lean into the open doorway, one foot angled after Caitlin in case I have to run for it, too. She'll be in a mood now, I remind myself. She lost the woman who practically raised her as her own, she lost the son she thought she knew, she probably thinks she has a very tenuous grip on what's left of her world, too. *Gently*, I think. *Gently* ... "Mom?"

"What?" She sits on the double bed, already neatly made, and stares at her reflection in a small mirror on the bedside table. One hand is raised to her face, an eyeliner pencil held between fingers that tremble slightly — she tries to steady them with the pinky against her cheek but it doesn't work, the sharpened tip of the pencil wavers as it nears her eye. With a dramatic sigh, she sets the pencil down and frowns into the mirror at me. In a peevish voice, she asks, "Michael, what is it? Can't you see I'm busy here?"

I take a step into the room. "Mom, I'm sorry —"

That's as far as I get before she buries her face in her hands and begins to weep.

48: My Mom

THE TEARS FRIGHTEN me — I'm not used to seeing my mother cry. For all her histrionic tendencies, she's not one to simply break down and *sob*. It's a sign of weakness to her, giving in, giving up, childish behavior that she will not accept. "What are you crying for?" she used to ask when we were younger — or rather, used to ask Ray, because I learned early on that crying wouldn't get me anywhere with her. "Tears ain't money, honey, they won't buy you squat."

Tears ain't money, honey, I think now, watching her shoulders shake as she huddles into herself on the edge of the bed. I'm almost afraid to speak, sure that the words will slip out and she'll descend on me like a bird of prey, tearing and biting and clawing me apart in her sorrow. But before I realize it, I'm kneeling in front of her, taking her into my arms as if she's the child. "Oh Michael," she sighs. Her anger surfaces through her tears and she punches at me with useless fists that flutter around my shoulders like crippled birds. I hold her closer, catch her hands between us and they clench in my sweater as she murmurs, "*Damn* you."

"It's not my fault," I remind her. I mean Aunt Evie's death, she knows that, she nods in agreement, not my fault. But that's not the only thing she's blaming on me, and I whisper into her hair, tacky with styling spray and smelling faintly of aerosol. "I know you think this is intentional, Momma, but it's not. Please believe me. Do you think I chose to be this way? To hurt you like this?" Her tears sting my neck, burn through my sweater to my skin below. "If there was anything I could have done to make it easier —"

"You didn't have to tell me," she cries.

Her words are muffled where her face is buried against my shoulder, but they sting as if she's shouted them for the whole house to hear. I rub her back and swear that I feel each tear brand my flesh. "Would you rather I lied to you about it?" I ask gently. "Sure Mom, I remember Mary Margaret what's-her-face. Pretty girl. Did she happen to leave her number?"

"Stop it." I hide my face in the dried ends of her over-processed hair and hate my mouth for the things it says sometimes. "That's not what I mean." Hugging me tighter, as if trying to imprint the memory of this moment into her bones, she whispers. "I had such high hopes for you, Michael."

"I'm gay," I tell her, "not dead. It's not the end of the world. I'm still here —"

But she doesn't hear me. If she does, she isn't listening. Instead, she talks over me in a teary voice that I have to fall silent to hear. "Such *high* hopes," she murmurs. "Such dreams. You could've had a family of your own — you'd make a wonderful father, I just know it. And now ... and now this."

"Those are your *dreams*, Mom, not mine." Though I keep my voice down, she shudders against me as if I've screamed at her, and her hands grip my sweater until I'm sure the knitting will unravel in her hard palms. "You never asked me what *I* wanted. It's my life, but you don't seem to care much about whatever dreams I might have."

She pulls away from me then, with a sigh that I feel deep in my own chest, it's that painful, that sad. Her eyes are puffy and red — even if she could steady her hands, there's no way she could outline her lids with the thin pencil on the table beside her mirror. Suddenly she looks too old to be my mother, she looks *ancient,* and I'm struck with an image years and years from now, this whole weekend played out all over again only at *her* house after she's gone. It's a never-ending cycle, isn't it? A constant struggle to survive that you can never, ever win. In the end, it always comes down to those we leave behind. "Mom," I sigh, brushing matted hair from her face.

She shoos my hand away and rubs at her eyes. "Tell me what your dreams are, then," she says as she blinks up at the ceiling to stop her tears. "Tell me where you see yourself going from here on out, Michael, because I surely don't know anymore."

"Same place I was always going," I assure her. She shakes her head like she can't believe it, and I rest my chin on her knees, hugging her legs through her black rayon pants the way I used to when I was a little boy. I would look up at her with what I hoped were large, sad eyes and plead with her, please Momma, *please* let me get this comic, or *please* let Stephen come over today, or *please* don't make me sit next to Ray in church. When she looks down at me now, I can see all those memories play out in her mind, though I'm the adult here, aren't I? I'm the one with the calm, reasoning voice, I'm the one trying to dry the tears, me. I'm not a child any longer. "I'm not headed to hell just because I love a boy," I say with a smile she won't or can't return. "I'm not going to suddenly become a stripper, or a porn star, or contract AIDS and die in a back alley somewhere."

Wiping her cheek, she mumbles, "Those things happen, you know."

I frown and imagine my eyes like a puppy's, pleading, begging. "I'm not saying they don't," I admit. "I'm just saying they won't happen to me." She shakes her head, she's not buying it, and my chest hurts to see fresh tears stand out like crystal beads in her eyes. "I have a lover, Mom, just one. I love Dan. The same way you felt for Dad when you promised to love and honor him for the rest of your life, no matter what. What I have with Dan is just like that."

"You're talking about marriage." My mother shakes her head again, clearing away thoughts I'm not privy to, and her face crumples in her hands like a used tissue. "Is that where this is going, Michael? You can't be *serious*."

"I'm in love," I tell her again. I don't know how many different ways I can say it, I don't know what to do to get it through to her. "I've never been more serious about anything in my whole life."

Her hands drop to her lap. Her fingers twist in the hem of her white blouse, which she'll tuck into her pants when she finishes getting ready to go. There's a black vest hanging on the door to her closet like a mantle of mourning — she'll shrug into that, button it up, and the only white showing then will be her starched collar, her billowy sleeves. How much longer before we have to tuck our grief into these dark clothes? Before we must stand in Morrison's and shake hands with the people of Sugar Creek, accepting their condolences with sad smiles and lowered heads? I can almost hear them now, the murmurs, the apologies, the reminiscences shuffling together like the whisper from a deck of cards worked between a dealer's hands. "You're still young," Mom says. "Who's to say this isn't just a phase —"

I cut her short. "It's not. This is *me*, Mom. It's who I am." The look she gives me says she's not convinced — I can see a hope deep inside her that refuses to die. Forcing a laugh, which comes out more bitter than I intended, I tell her, "I didn't *choose* to be this way. I didn't wake up one day and think you know, maybe I'm going to like guys for awhile. It didn't happen like that. I've just known it forever — other boys my age were looking at girls and me ..." I laugh again. "I was looking at them. You remember Stephen?"

Her hands stop their nervous twitching in her lap, and the corner of one reddened eye jumps with an unconscious tic. "Robichaud?" she whispers. When I nod, she closes her eyes and sighs. "Don't tell me he's ..."

"Gay." The word makes her cringe, and I say it again, not out of spite but because she's going to have to get used to it. "I guess you could say he was my first boyfriend, in a way. It wasn't actual intercourse, we were too young, and I wouldn't call it love. Experimentation, maybe, though he —"

"Michael." With a faint shake of her head, she presses her hand to her mouth, as if the thought of me and Stephen doing whatever it was we did together is too much for her to stomach.

Gently I say, "I'm twenty-five, Mom. I'm an adult now. I'm having sex."

"You don't have to *tell* me about it," she sighs. With one hand she touches the side of my face, her thumb tracing the curve of my jaw as she stares at me, *through* me, trying to see someone I no longer am. "You don't have to be so damn *proud.*"

Surprised, I laugh and cover her hand with mine, pressing her palm to my face. "What, would you rather I keep it to myself? Or deny who I am? Live in misery just because you don't want to deal with it? Happens to everyone else's sons, is that it? Not yours. *Never* yours." Before she can reply, I point out, "You raised me better than that."

Now she smiles, her fingers feathering through the ends of my hair as she studies me. I feel the beginnings of tears prick my own eyes and I blink them away, I don't need to cry again. It won't help me anyway, not with her. She's down to sniffling, once or twice dabbing at the corners of her eyes to smear away the tears that haven't fallen yet, but she isn't sobbing any longer. Whatever squall of emotions that rained in her heart when I first came in here has passed — she's gathering herself together again, and in another half hour or so, you would never know a storm came through. But I don't fool myself, I know this respite has nothing to do with our coming to a common ground. I can see it in the set of her jaw, feel it in the tremor of her hand on my face, as if she wants to curl those fingers into a fist and pound me back into the person she thinks I should be. *I'm not that boy anymore, Mom,* I think, leaning into her touch with an alert wariness that whispers this moment is slipping away and we'll be back at odds again soon enough. *I don't know if I ever really was. For eighteen years I lived in your house and managed to hide it from you, like a secret pet that I cared for and nurtured in the privacy of my own mind, taking it out only when I found someone — like Stephen — who I could trust not to come running back to you. I did lie to you, can't you see that? As long as I possibly could. And see where it's gotten us now? You wanted me to keep this up?* If not for Dan, I *might* have, too — why bother telling her until she absolutely needed to know?

But now it seems sudden to her, I've pulled back the curtain and shown her a glimpse of my *real* life, the secret I've harbored all these years, and she thinks this is just a passing phase. It's not. "I'm not going to grow out of this," I whisper, closing my eyes so I won't have to see the pain in hers anymore. Her gaze bores right through me like radiation, burning and searing and tearing everything in its path as she aims for my soul. I have to protect that at all costs. "I'm not gay to be spiteful, or to get attention, or to break your heart. I put up with too much to *want* to be this way, Mom, you just don't know. You've seen the news, heard the stories, I'm sure. You know it's hard —"

"Oh, honey," she sobs, and she pulls me to her, holds my face against her breasts the way she used to when I came to her as a child, bruised or bleeding or upset, *hurt*, and she couldn't take away the pain. I can smell her perfume, a heavy gardenia scent I've always associated with older women because it's a favorite of Aunt Bobby, too. Aunt Billie wears a warm musk, and Aunt Sarah likes those light florals that tickle your nose. Evie always wore a spicy blend of both, which smelled as wonderful as the ocean on summer nights. I wonder if there's still a bottle of that somewhere around here. I should take it home as my inheritance, keep it in the bathroom, spritz it on my shirt when I'm feeling sad or alone and need to know she's only a prayer away.

Stroking my smooth cheek, my mom kisses the top of my head and sighs. "As if I don't worry enough about you," she says. One tear slips down my face to the corner of my mouth, where it stings salty and hot. I stick out my tongue and lick it away. "Living so far from home, all by yourself, going to school, working full-time, on your own ..."

"I have Dan," I remind her. Taking her wrist in both hands, I look up and hope she doesn't see that I'm close to crying now, too. "He's such a good man, Mom. You couldn't ask for someone better, honest. Attentive and loving and strong. So strong. He's just what I've always wanted in a partner, what I *need* to survive. I can't imagine life without him. He'll keep me safe." At her wry attempt at a smile, I plead, "Give him a chance, please. Give us *both* a chance, that's all I'm asking for here. I'm still your son." Sitting back, I brush away an errant tear that trickles forgotten down the side of her nose and wait. When she looks at me, her smile softens into something almost familiar, almost forgiving. "I still love you."

Her chin trembles and I expect more sobs, maybe a teary apology, something sappy and sweet, straight off a Hallmark greeting card, blank verse in flowing script that tugs at the old heartstrings. But no — she's had time to compose herself, and the woman who sits before me drying her eyes is the same self-possessed mother I've always known, her emotions reined in as she struggles to get this situation — and me — under her control. "I'm not okay with it," she says. The look in her eyes demands a response so I nod, I know. Nothing has really changed between us, I know this. "Not by a long shot. Don't think for a moment that I condone this ... this *relationship* of yours, because I don't, not at all."

I nod again. "I know —"

"I don't like it," she interrupts, cutting me off. "I don't think it's right."

Exasperated, I sigh, "*Mom*. Right or not, he's a part of my life now. You have to realize this — you have to *respect* it, respect *me*, if I mean anything to you at all."

"You do," she says, touching my hair, my face, with a loving hand. "You know you mean the world to me, Michael, you and Caitlin and Ray ..."

She trails off as her fingers straighten my collar, an automatic gesture that is at once so absent and so poignant, so *real*, that my throat swells shut with unbidden emotion. I could press my point, but what's the use? We're at an impasse now, I know her feelings on the subject of my homosexuality, she knows exactly where I stand when it comes to Dan, and as the poet said, "Never the 'twain shall meet." We stand on two separate banks of a river of emotion that cuts between us, too deep to ford, too wide to cross — I can see where she's coming from as clearly as if she stood on an opposing shore, but I can't stretch over this divide that separates us, I can't just abandon my own feelings. One day we might manage to span this gap between us — this is just a foundation, a place to build upon, not necessarily an end but a means to one, and years from now maybe we will finally meet halfway across a bridge we started today. I can live with that hope. If she stays civil to Dan in the interim ... "Don't make me choose," I say softly. "Between him and you, Mom, don't, because I won't do it. He means the world to *me* and I don't want to have to stay away if it's going to be a problem with bringing him to the house."

My mother looks at her hands, in her lap again, and then at the clock beside the bed. It's getting late, the morning almost gone, and I can practically hear her counting down the time she has left to get ready. "Mom?" I prompt. This is one of her tricks, I know it too well — ignore the question instead of answering, see if it goes away. "If you're going to treat him like shit, I'd just as soon stay away. I'm not coming down to visit you guys without him, and I sure as hell ain't sleeping alone."

"I told you it's fine," she replies, though she said nothing of the sort. Perhaps she means Saturday night, when she said we could share my old room but imposed that *no sex* moratorium on us. Barking a short laugh, she mutters, "I guess it'll have to be."

I sit back on my knees and nod, glad she sees that much, at least. She looks at the clock again, then picks up the eyeliner pencil where she set it by the mirror as if noticing it for the first time. I try to think of something else to talk about, something to tell her, something to say, but all that comes to mind is Ray and his little snit yesterday and I don't want to bring that up now, not when we're finally getting somewhere. She can't *help* comparing him to me, it's her way of motivating him to do something with his life, and the less he tries, the more she's going to push him. He should know that by now. Once or twice when I fell short of her expectations, I got the same treatment. In fifth grade when I was sent to the principal's office for sticking markers in my glue to color it, for example, or when I refused to go to the prom, because at that time I wasn't comfortable enough with myself to ask out the one person I would have loved to go with, the captain of our soccer team, who was damn fine and straight as a ruler and didn't even know I existed. Both times she compared me to Ray, and not favorably. "Do you want to end up like your brother?" she asked — in fifth grade, this meant being suspended so often that the principal's secretary knew my mother by name; in high school, that I might remain dateless and alone and live above the garage simply because Ray didn't go to *his* prom, either. I'm surprised she hasn't remarked yet, "Look at your brother, *he's* not gay," it's something she would do.

But maybe she knows that my reply would be something along the lines of, "And he's not happy, Mom. Barely employed, alone, still living at home. Do you honestly want me to be like *that?*" No, better not to bring Ray up at all. That's an issue he has with her, I'm not going to allow myself to be dragged into the middle of it. I simply smile and ask, "So we're okay?"

That short laugh again, and a tight smile. "I'm okay, you're okay," she says, then pats my arm. "Go on, Mikey. Let me put my face on, will you?"

With a final hug, I rise to my feet and tuck a strand of hair behind her ear. "Caitlin looks pretty in that dress," I tell her, for no reason at all.

The sardonic look she gives me makes me grin. "She looks like she's going to a damn cocktail party," she mutters. "Wears black every day of the year except the one time she *needs* to. I swear that girl is so contrary." When I laugh, she frowns at me. "Why are you laughing, mister? You're just as bad."

And to be honest? That's exactly the reason why.

49: My Sister

FROM THE WAY Mom turns to frown into her mirror, eyeliner now in a steadier hand, I know our little heart-to-heart is over. There's no sense of resolution, no blinding flash of completeness, but I feel better anyway, and when I think of future visits home, I don't cringe with fear at what might happen. She's not about to rush out and start a local chapter of PFLAG by any stretch of the imagination, but maybe she'll open up a little to Dan, get to know him and see why I love him, surprise herself into liking or even loving him too. He's a good man, she has to see this. He's wonderful to me. Without him here this weekend, I would probably be lying on the floor curled into myself, trying to dull the pain that even now threatens to crack through my heart. Can't she see how well he's holding me together? Like a glass trinket that's been dropped to the floor and broken into several sharp, jagged pieces, I've picked them up and tried my best to glue them back together again, but Dan holds them while the glue sets, he holds *me*. Knowing my mother respects that I need someone like him in my life is enough for now. Acceptance will come later — it must.

"You go talk to her," my mom says suddenly, meaning Caitlin. "Let me get ready, Mikey. It's almost quarter after nine." She leans close to the mirror, eyes wide, and guides the pencil around the red rim of her eyelid effortlessly. Glancing sideways at me, she says, "We don't have much time. Is that what you're wearing?"

"What's wrong with it?" I want to know. I look down at my dark sweater still bunched in memory of her fists, my dark khakis wrinkled where I knelt on the floor. "It's all I brought with me. I didn't pack for a funeral when we came down to visit you guys, you know."

With a curt nod, she tells me, "It's fine." Then she starts around her other eye, pressing so hard that the soft pencil crumbles, leaving tiny little nuggets of brown eyeliner behind. These she wipes with one quick finger wrapped in a tissue, which comes away smeared with lines like tilled soil. "See if you can talk your sister into something else, will you? That dress ..."

I laugh at the thought of me talking Caitlin into anything she doesn't want to wear. "What makes you think she'll listen to me?" I ask. "You already tried —"

Mom holds her hand up, silencing me. "Michael, please," she warns. "I'm running a little behind here so work with me, will you?" I nod, chastised. "We're leaving in an hour or so. At least make an attempt, could you do that for me?"

"Sure." An attempt. That's all it *will* be, I already know.

But I go in search of my sister. On my way down the hall, I peer into every open door, smile at my relatives still getting dressed or ready to go. In one room Uncle Doug stands at attention while Kenny's girlfriend Neeshi ties a necktie on him like a hangman's noose, Kenny next in line, his own tie in hand. In another room, my cousin Emily jerks a comb through her blonde locks, tears on her face — from working through the tangles or the impending funeral, I'm not sure which. When she sees me, she shrieks in anger and tries to throw the comb, but it sticks in her hair so she chucks a shoe at me instead. It hits the door as I hurry down the hall.

Caitlin's obviously not still up here. I take the stairs two at a time, passing my dad on my way down. He looks stiff and uncomfortable in the freshly ironed shirt he wears, and the look he gives me discourages conversation. *Don't say a word,* his eyes caution. But I've never been one to heed such warnings, so as I stand aside to let him by, I wave. "Hey."

He grunts in reply, typical Dad. "Where's your mother?" he demands.

Pointing upstairs, I start, "In the room —"

"Is she ready yet?" Before I can answer, he's trooping the rest of the way up the steps, muttering to himself. "Rush to get *me* out of the damn house, will you."

I don't pursue that. Instead I turn away, let them argue it out, I've had enough confrontations for today. *And I'm heading right into another one,* I think ironically, but with any luck maybe I won't find Caitlin before we go. Then I won't have to fall victim to her biting anger. If she wants to wear teal, that's fine with me. It's not *my* funeral.

At the bottom of the steps, the front door stands open. Cold wind skitters through the screen door into the house, bringing with it the rustle of leaves raking over the yard and the distant smell of burning wood. In front of the door, tiny hands clutching the screen as if the spaces in the mesh were as big as links in a chain fence, stands little Trevor, dressed in a maroon V-neck sweater, ready to go. His face is pressed to the screen and when I come up behind him, I can see the front yard in miniscule through his large glasses. Hunkering down to his level, I rest my chin on the top of his head and ask, "What 'cha looking at, buckaroo?"

With a childish giggle, he squirms away from me and turns, smiling. "I'm not a buckaroo," he tells me.

I ruffle his hair. "Have you seen Cat?" If anyone knows where my sister is, it's Trevor, who has eagerly taken on the role of her unofficial sidekick since we arrived. But he just shakes his head and looks back out the door as if afraid he'll miss something. Smoothing down the short, thick hair I mussed, I ask, "What are you looking at out there?"

"I'm waiting for the car," he says.

The car. The front yard is filled with them, pickup trucks and SUVs and sedans — everyone staying in this house has a vehicle parked down by the street. My own Lumina is on the outside of the impromptu car lot, I can barely see the roof and part of the rear bumper from here. "Which car?" I want to know.

He probably means he's waiting to get *into* the car, he's ready to saddle up and ride into town, and I don't want to have to be the one to break it to him that we're not going to be leaving for another hour or so. I'm just about to ask if he still uses a car seat — if not, maybe he can ride with us, he's a good kid — when he hushes me and points outside. "Here it comes again," he whispers dramatically. In the distance I can hear the low purr of an engine coming closer. "This one."

The sound slowly grows louder — the car must be cruising at a good ten, fifteen miles an hour, tops. Someone out for a morning drive, or someone lost, though how anyone could get lost in Sugar Creek is beyond me. The town is little more than three miles in any direction. Only one street leads straight through and that's State Route 17. West leads to Franklin and east is Union City, just past the turnoff for 322, the highway we took coming up here. All the residential streets that wind through Sugar Creek circle back to the main strip because the creek runs on one side and there are woods all around. It's damn near impossible to get lost here, and it's not exactly a place teeming with tourists. Before the car comes into view, I think I know who it will be. "How many times has it driven by?" I ask Trevor.

The little boy holds up two fingers, then changes his mind and goes for three. "This makes three?" I clarify.

He nods. "Three now," he says, leaning into the screen to try and see as far as he possibly can down the road. "Here it is. This is three times."

My stomach roils beneath sudden anxiety and when the car coasts into view, I'm right, God, I *hate* it when I'm right. It's the same mauve Saturn I saw parked outside of Grosso's yesterday — *Aunt Jessie.* So she hasn't left town yet. As she drives in front of the house, she slows down to almost a crawl, her engine growling like an animal held in check. I can see her clearly enough, though her window is rolled up and the morning sun winks off the glass like a spotlight — her face is pinched with sadness, her eyes haunting, her mouth drawn down in an exaggerated frown. "It's Aunt Evie," Trevor whispers in awe.

"No, it's not." *It's Jessie,* I correct silently, but I don't tell him that. He's heard the speculation, even at his age — what he knows of our curiously absent aunt is incongruous with this silent, heartbroken woman inside that car. He's too young to understand what really happened to keep her away from us all these years. Hell, I've just barely begun to understand it myself. There's no way I could possibly explain it in terms that he could swallow.

"It looks like her," he says with child-like aplomb. Together we watch the car pass out of sight and then I stand. Taking his hand, I lead him away from the screen and start to close the door. "No!" he cries. He catches the door in his small hands and tries to hold it open, but I'm stronger than he is and it's a battle he doesn't win. As I lock the door to keep it shut, he punches me in the thigh. "I was *standing* there, horny butt."

With a hand on the top of his head, I tilt his face up and tell him, "Watch it, kid." I stare at him, hard and long, until finally he drops his gaze. He punches me again but it's weak and unpersuasive. Turning him away from the door, I give him a gentle push down the hall, towards the kitchen where everyone who has already dressed has gathered, from the sound of it. "Go on," I say, guiding him. "Finish getting ready."

"I am ready," he pouts. When he tries to skirt around me, I hold onto his shoulders and steer him down the hall. "Let me go. I'm ready."

As we pass the first of the two French doors that lead into the living room, he tries to duck inside but I won't let him. "Maybe she's just lost, Trevor," I reason. "Leave her alone, will you? She's not bothering anyone. She's probably not even coming back."

But he's five years old, there's no reasoning here. "You don't know that."

I don't reply. What happened to my *not going to argue* resolution, hmm? He lets me lead him down the hall, past the telephone table, past the bathroom, and we're just a few steps from the kitchen when he twists out of grip. For a moment he stares up at me, shocked that he's free. Then he punches me once in the groin, dangerously close to my crotch — another five inches and he'd see just how fast my reflexes work, and we'd both be in a world of hurt. But he settles for that final jab before he takes off, through the second French door and into the living room, out of reach. Laughter bubbles out to me, my name giggled in a little boy voice that expects me to give chase. He's heading for the windows, I know it, or the door once I'm gone, though I don't think he'll be able to open it alone. *Clomp clomp clomp,* his shoes over the hard carpet, and then, when I don't follow, a few steps head back in my direction. "Michael?" he calls out, breathless.

Raising my voice, I tell him, "I'm not running after you. I have to find Caitlin. Come on, Trev —"

He peeks around the corner of the doorway. "Catch me," he laughs, and he's off again. *If he's like this at the funeral,* I think, but I don't finish that thought. Maybe I should slip the Valium I'm carrying to *him. Here, Trevor, have some candy* ... "Michael, you can't catch me."

That trick was old when *I* was a kid. "I can't play right now," I tell him, hating the way that sounds, like I'm too grown up to fool around. *Different games,* I muse, thinking of Dan, and I can't keep the smile from my face. I don't hear anyone in the bathroom, maybe he's back in the room by now. If I can just get that far without running into Caitlin, I can tell my mom I at least *tried* to look for her. *I saw Jessie, though, does that count?* Somehow I don't think so.

In the kitchen, I'm just as invisible as I was the first time I passed through. Ray's gone, and Kenny's upstairs, but Aunt Sarah's still here, at the sink rinsing dishes. A boy around eight or nine years old stands to her left, scrubbing the plates before handing them over, and a girl around the same age dries the dishes as Sarah finishes each one. Those are my Uncle Tommy's children, I think, or maybe Lenore's, I've forgotten how they're related to me. Cousins, that's all I know. Younger than me, so I didn't play with them when I used to come here for the summer. They look at me as I go by but don't say anything, as if I'm a ghost here, not Evie but me, some-one they can't see or touch but whose presence they feel all the same, like a sudden chill on a warm day, a cloud over the sun. "Any of you guys seen Caitlin?" I ask no one in particular.

I'm not surprised when no one answers.

The door to the back room is closed, just as I left it. Thinking Dan's in-side, probably getting dressed, I knock as I turn the knob and step inside. "Hey, babe —"

My sister replies, "Hey."

I look up and see her sitting at the foot of the bed, back against the wall, her knees drawn up to her chest and her skirt pulled down to cover her legs. Only the toes of her shoes can be seen beneath the billows of that dress. Closing the door behind me, I tell her, "Get your shoes off my bed."

She does so without a word. I look around the room as if Dan could possibly be hiding somewhere, but he's not. It's just me and Caitlin. "If you're looking for lover boy," she says, "he's back in the bathroom. Came in wearing nothing but a grin —"

"Cat," I warn, jealousy rising in me at the thought of my sister checking out my man.

With a wave of her hand, she brushes it away. "And a *towel,*" she amends.

"You didn't let me finish. He was wearing a *towel*. Calm the fuck down already, I didn't see his *balls*, or anything like that. Unfortunately."

Cautiously I sit on the edge of the bed, far enough away from her that if she gets it in her head to start a fight, I'll be out of hitting distance, at least. "He just left," she says, kicking out one foot. When it swings back, her heel rings off the post beneath the bed and she does this over and over again — I'm not sure if it's to annoy me or because she likes the sound it makes. "I told him I'd go but he said no, don't bother, he'd dress in the bathroom and be right back. You know he's sweet as hell, right?"

"I know," I assure her. Smoothing down the quilt I'm sitting on just for something to do, I ask, "So you chased him away?"

"I didn't *chase* him," she sighs. "Jesus, Mike. He could've kicked me out, it's his room, too." At the word *kick*, her shoe hits the bedpost so hard that I can feel the frame vibrate under me.

She resumes her previous rhythm, her shoe scraping across the hardwood floor as she swings her foot back and forth. I open my mouth to say something — ask her why she's in here, for starters, or what's up with the party dress for Evie's burial — when she cuts me off. "Do I really look pretty in this?" she asks.

There's an uncertainty in her voice that sounds so unlike my self-assured sister that I'm taken aback. "Very pretty," I tell her, my hand reaching out to touch the hem of the skirt. It's made of a rayon blend, so soft it almost feels like satin beneath my fingers. Tenderly, I stroke the material one way, then switch directions — there's a very faint nap that makes the fabric look darker if I brush it upwards. Maybe if she rubbed it all the wrong way, the dress would be dark enough for our mother. Has Caitlin worn anything dressy this weekend she could change into? All that I've seen her in are black t-shirts, black jeans. Choosing my words carefully, I point out, "It's very … teal. Very pretty. But don't you have anything … hmm, in black? Maybe?"

Caitlin looks at me and I'm surprised to see tears in her eyes. She bites her lower lip to keep it from trembling, blinks rapidly to keep the eyeliner circled around her eyes from smearing, and I'm struck with a feeling of *déjà vu* so poignant, I almost choke. She looks like my mother, the same sadness in her eyes, the same struggle not to cry, years younger but identical in her grief. "Cat, what —"

"Aunt Evie bought me this dress," she says. Her gaze drops to her lap, where her hands twist in the fabric, darkening it. "This past summer, when she let me get my tongue done?" In case I could've forgotten, she sticks out her tongue, exposing the silver rod through the center of it. "She said this was my color. I told her I liked the black one better but she insisted on this. It was her money, what could I do?"

Definitely not say no — that was a foreign concept to Evie, a word that held little meaning for her. When she had her wallet out ready to spend, you best just step aside and let her go. All you had to do was cooperate, tell her your sizes, try on the clothes, let her do the rest. Every year without fail, just before we left Sugar Creek for the summer, we were piled into a car or two or three, however many it took to hold us all, and driven to Union City or Franklin or Pittsburgh, wherever Evie felt like shopping. She paraded us through the malls and department stores, snatching up sweaters and under-wear and jeans, anything she thought we'd need for school. There was no use telling her we didn't need new clothes — we got them anyway. So I can easily imagine the resolute look in my aunt's eyes when she saw the dress Caitlin wears now and knew she had to get it for her niece. "Did you tell Mom that?" I ask, my voice soft.

She shakes her head. "She didn't give me a chance," she whispers. "I walk in and she's all like you're not wearing *that*, and what am I supposed to say?" One corner of her mouth twitches in an attempt to smile. "Gee, Mom, what was I thinking? Let me go change."

"Tell her Evie bought it for you," I suggest. She'll see why Caitlin wants to wear it, then, and any protest will dissolve in guilt.

But Caitlin wipes her face, smudging eyeliner into two lines that give her cat's eyes, and declares, "I ain't telling her shit! This is my fucking dress, I'll wear it if I want to."

Somehow I don't think I will be able to convince her otherwise. Lower-ing her voice, she mumbles, "Evie said she liked this color on me."

"It's very pretty," I agree. I can't think of anything else to say.

50: Getting Ready to Go

A FTER OUR LITTLE talk, Caitlin curls up at the foot of my bed, her shoes kicked to the floor and her dress fanned out around her legs, which are pulled in close to her body so the skirt covers them. "Wake me up when it's time to leave," she mumbles, burying her face in the crook of her arm pillowed beneath her head.

I stretch out on the opposite end of the bed, careful not to wrinkle my clothes. For long moments we lie quietly, the only sound in the room our shallow breathing. Caitlin's eyes are closed and mine keep drooping shut — the patterns on the ceiling, cast from the trees outside the window, aren't interesting enough to hold my attention, and the tension eating away at the edges of the day is already gnawing at me, as well. Suddenly I'm well aware of the fact that I got up before dawn and didn't get back to sleep. What would a few minutes now hurt? The thought of giving into the luxury of a quick snooze is almost too much to resist.

The opening of the door jars me awake. I raise my head off the mattress — when did it grow so heavy? — only to find my lover above me, fully dressed and smiling faintly. Relieved, I sink back to the bed and murmur, "Dan." A few feet away, Caitlin sighs in her sleep. "Lay down with me a minute."

Laughing, he stretches out beside me. He smells wonderful, clean and slightly damp like he just stepped out of the shower, and when he nuzzles into my neck, his freshly buzzed hair scratches my cheek. "You're going back to bed already?" he asks softly so he won't disturb my sister.

"Just resting my eyes," I tell him. I turn towards his warmth and find myself in his embrace, one strong arm wrapped around my waist, the other easing beneath my shoulders. I kiss his chin, the only part of him I can reach without stretching, and I want to know, "What time is it?"

"You've got about a half hour left to go," he replies. With his lips against my ear, his breath hot on my neck, he whispers, "I know better ways to pass the time."

Desire snaps me awake, his closeness like a shotgun beside me. Whatever drowsiness clings to me is gone in the instant I raise my head to see the lust in his eyes staring back. "A half hour?" I sit up, interested, and trail a hand down the buttons of his gray shirt. "We've managed that before."

He laughs again and catches my hand just as it begins to trace the outside of his dick through his jeans. "Your sister," he cautions.

"What about her?" I twist free from his grasp and reach for him again, this time getting a good handful of his hardening cock before he stops me. Laying down to cuddle up to him, I unbutton his collar, the next button down, the next, then kiss the hollow of his throat, my tongue licking his smooth skin. My second kiss is more ardent, insistent, and the next button on his shirt gives way to me, exposing the low-cut neck of his undershirt and the faint smattering of freckles across his upper chest. I'm working my way down to his nipple, hard beneath my palm and straining at his shirt — I'll push the material aside and bite at the tender bud through his thin undershirt, I can almost feel it between my teeth. My sister is the last thing on my mind. Another button comes undone, I'm that much closer to taking him into my mouth. "She's asleep," I assure him.

A foot connects with my lower back. "I am not," Caitlin grumbles behind me.

Without raising my lips from my lover's neck, I slap her leg away. "If you're up, you can leave," I tell her, though I don't know if she hears me or not — my words are muffled against Dan's skin. He holds me at bay but just barely, his hands in my sweater as if he's not sure whether to pull me to him or push me away. When she kicks me again, I pinch her ankle, squeezing until she yelps. "Why don't you just go?"

"No." Now both feet strike my buttocks, first one, then the other, rapidly, as if she's peddling a bicycle. "You're disgusting, Mike. We're about to go to a *funeral* and all you can think about is getting off."

"What's wrong with that?" I ask.

Rebuttoning his shirt, Dan admits, "I see nothing *wrong* with it."

I stop him before he can get to his collar and hide everything from me again. "What do you think you're doing?" I laugh. "Caitlin, aren't you leaving?" No reply, just her feet in my ass, she's starting to piss me off. "Stop it already, will you?"

"Take it somewhere else," she says, as if this isn't *my* room. "I don't want to watch you two making out."

"Then don't look." I swat her legs but she manages to avoid my hand, and her next kick lands the heel of her foot into my kidney. Pain erupts across my abdomen and I howl, turning on her like a loosened animal, suddenly all anger and swinging fists. "Get the *fuck* out of here!" I shout, getting in one good hit before she pulls her legs back beneath her skirt, out of sight. Dan holds onto my arms, his grip unforgiving, and I struggle to break free. "Get out, Caitlin. Don't make me say it again. Get out or I'll —"

"Shh, Michael," Dan murmurs. He hugs me to him but I'm more than a little mad, I'm fucking *livid* now, my side is on fire where she kicked me and she's going to pay for that, I'm going to see to it. But when I struggle against him, he rises from the bed, pulls me to my feet, guides me to the door. "Come on, hon. Calm down."

"That *hurt*," I growl, glaring over his shoulder at my sister. She's curled into a tight ball at the end of the bed and watches me with frightened eyes, an unspoken apology written all over her face. "Caitlin!"

"I didn't mean it," she mumbles.

Dan has the door open and blocks my way to the bed, so I can't just duck around him and go after her. "She didn't mean it," he repeats, his voice low. "Come on, Michael, let it go."

"It hurt," I pout. At his concerned look I rub my side, where her foot dug into my kidney. Before he can ask, I tell him, "Right here."

His hands cover mine, his fingers slipping beneath my sweater, lifting it up out of the way. Leaning down, he kisses my bare skin, his lips warm on my flesh. I hold my breath and meet his gaze when he looks up, smiling. "That better?" he asks.

"A little," I concede. Actually, his mouth leaves a wet imprint that I feel long after he's smoothed my sweater back down and rubbed his hands over the spot. I look around — the kitchen has cleared out and we're alone, except for Caitlin in the other room. Trying hard to hold onto my anger, I fumble with the front of my pants and say, "She kicked my butt, too. If you could just —"

From behind Dan, my sister lets out a surprised laugh, and my lover grins as he slaps my backside. "I'm not kissing your ass," he tells me.

"But it hurts, too."

"It's going to hurt a lot worse," he starts, but he glances around the empty kitchen and sighs. I can hear voices from the living room, children chattering from the open door beside us that leads to the basement, footsteps upstairs rushing around to get ready. Partially because we're alone — and partially because he wants to show off for my sister, I know him all too well — he sinks to his knees and gives my left buttock a quick peck through my pants. Not quite what I had in mind, but the sight of him squatting beside me, the feel of his hands on my hips, makes the blood pound through my groin and suddenly I can feel each heartbeat pulse in the tip of my dick. "How's that?" he asks.

My voice is husky and thick. "Better," I manage. *A hell of a lot better if we could get that half hour alone,* I think, and I'm wondering if I could actually physically *drag* Caitlin from the room when Dan sinks his teeth into me. I can feel the bite through the pants I wear, a huge, healthy chomp that almost makes me come. "Hey!"

With a laugh, he stands and kisses my neck, one hand rubbing away the mark his mouth made on my butt. "Just playing," he murmurs, his eyes dancing with mirth. "Maybe later ..."

Fuck that. "Maybe now," I declare. Stepping around him, I give my sister what I hope looks like a sincere smile and practically beg, "Caitlin, come on, give us five minutes, that's all I'm asking for here, okay? Please?"

She's about to protest — I can tell from that smirk on her face — when my mom comes into the kitchen, her heels clicking importantly on the tiled floor. "Mike, where's your sister?" she asks, distracted, as she fiddles with the cuffs of her shirt. Seeing Dan, she gives him a tight smile that's as warm as snow before her gaze slips almost gratefully past us into the back room. The halfhearted smile dies. "You didn't talk her out of that damn dress," she says. She speaks of Caitlin in the third person as if my sister can't hear her, a tactic she uses when she's close to furious. At least her tears have dried up and she's regained some semblance of control over her grief — my mother crying is not a sight I want to see again any time soon. "I thought you said you would."

"I said I'd talk to her," I amend, taking a step closer to Dan. His hands still rest on my hips, a comforting touch. Mom sees it and looks away. "I never swore she'd actually *listen* to me."

Her fingers pick at the cuff of her sleeves, first one, then the other, tweaking the fabric nervously until the satin is smooth around her wrists. I wait — when she doesn't reply immediately, I dare to glance in at Caitlin, who's watching her closely. She sees me turn and sticks her tongue out at me, exposing that metal rod rammed down the center. Suddenly I can hear my own voice in my mind, years younger, a memory bubbling to the surface of my soul — Ray and I in the back seat of the car on the way here years ago, the two of us sharing a bag of potato chips, and whenever he shoved a handful into his mouth, he'd open wide to show me the chewed up mess. "Mom," I whined, every single time. "Ray's sticking his tongue out at me."

I had to be seven or eight then, Ray three years older, and we were only halfway through the bag of chips before Mom snatched it from us. Balling it up into her lap, she cried, "Raymond! Michael! Stop it right this instant. If I hear one more sound out of either one of you before we get to Aunt Evie's, I'm going to have your father turn this car around and go back home."

"I wasn't —" I started.

"Michael, I'm not playing," she warned. She turned around in the front seat so we could see she meant business, but I sat behind her and all I saw was half of her face, one angry eye, one corner of her mouth drawn down in a wicked frown, and I threw myself against the side of the car to be as far away from her as I could without getting out. "I don't want to hear *anything* else, got that?" I nodded quickly. Ray, not realizing she was talking to him, too, had to be prompted. "Both of you. Or we're going home."

A common threat, but one serious enough not to be taken lightly. We waited all year for the morning when my father shook us both awake before the first light of dawn. We would dress quickly, wolf down bowls of cereal with a nervous energy that buzzed and crackled between us like the excitement of Christmas Eve, then take our pillows and blankets into the back seat of the car, kicking and hitting as we settled in for the long ride. By the time we reached DC, our differences would be forgotten, our anxiety worn down like batteries until we both fell asleep propped together like dolls tucked away on a shelf.

Even now I can feel that same euphoria and it's hard to keep an adult's mind in this house that held so much for me as a child.

"Fine," my mother sighs. Satisfied with her cuffs, she smoothes them down, then smoothes down her vest, tugging at the points by her waist to make sure the fabric is as taut as it's going to get. Without looking at Caitlin, she says, "It's time to go."

"Already?" I ask. I hate the trepidation I hear in my own voice, but what happened to the half hour we had? I frown at Dan's watch and see it's already five after ten. "I thought you said we had a few minutes."

His smile is apologetic. "I guess we used them up."

No … "Already?" I ask again, doubtful. Now that the time has come to leave, I don't want to — the lethargic morning has disappeared, time rushes by, I feel it slipping away from me like water tumbling over rocks in the creek, and no matter how tight I clench my fists, I can't seem to hold onto it. "Morrison's is just in town," I protest, haggling for more time. "When do we *need* to be there? It doesn't start until eleven —"

"We need to be there now," my mom declares. "Caitlin, get a move on."

"We've got a whole hour," I try.

"Mike." There's a warning in my mom's voice that silences me. "Don't push me, mister, not today. The service is at eleven but we have to be there early and you know it. Caitlin." From the other room I hear the creak of bed springs as my sister sits up. "So are you kids coming, or what?"

Kids, like I'm not out of my teens. I wonder if she's conscious of doing that, pegging Dan and me as children, de-sexing us in her mind as if that somehow negates our relationship. It's okay if he has his arms around my waist or if his chin rests on my shoulder, as long as it's nothing overt, nothing that hints at more between us. "We're coming," I mutter.

Dan slips his hand into mine and I lead him across the kitchen, my mind in the past. Morrison's is just a few blocks beyond Grosso's, back off the main street that leads out of Sugar Creek. I haven't actually been in there before, not *really* — this is my first funeral, no one I've known has ever died, though once Stephen and Ray talked me into sneaking up to the basement window one summer day before my freshman year of high school. It was sweltering outside, as I recall. The three of us were half-naked in the unself-conscious way that young boys have in the heat, dressed in only swimming trunks and nothing else. Sweat dripped down our bare, suntanned backs and though we rode our bikes, we dropped them at the curb to get a closer look at the quiet funeral parlor. The parking lot's black tarmac simmered beneath our feet. "You go look," I told Ray, who shook his head and stopped in the grass, afraid to move any closer. Morrison's is an old converted house, much like Aunt Evie's, with a wraparound porch and a bay window on one side that gives it a lopsided, old fashioned appearance. When Ray chickened out, I turned to Stephen. "It's not like they keep dead people in there, right?"

Stephen shook his head and pushed his glasses up on his nose with one finger. "You go then," he told me. He followed me a few more feet, just until my brother was out of hearing distance, and lowered his voice to a hot whisper. "Do it," he hissed. "All you have to do is look in and tell us what you see." I glanced at him dubiously, but he smiled like the sun above us, bolstering my courage. "Come on, Mikey. Do it and I'll make it worth your while later."

Later meant after we had ditched Ray and it was just the two of us. At that time, anything Stephen did with his tongue and mouth and hands on my body was worth my while, worth *anything* to be honest, and my dick stiffened at the promise in his words. Before I could lose my nerve, I hurried to the house, running hunched over like I'd seen soldiers do in war movies, as if anyone inside who looked out couldn't possibly see me weaving through the trim grass. At the porch I threw myself to the ground, landing hard on my knees. As I crawled forward, my dick poked beneath me like a stick jammed down the front of my shorts, each movement sending shivers of pleasure and fear mingling through me, until I almost came from sheer anticipation alone. Just a quick look, I probably wouldn't see anything anyway, and then Stephen could take me into the woods and work his hands into my pants and get me off. I'd even think of this, I told myself, as his fingers squeezed and pinched, his tongue licked, his lips sucked, this dread moment, excitement and apprehension and the hard, hard ground pushing my balls into my dick. I just wanted to lie there and hump the earth, get myself off in the cool shade of the funeral parlor, smear myself with my own juices and shiver in decadence and sin.

By the time I got to the first window, I had one hand fisting in the front of my shorts, but whether it was to rub at my erection or hold in my orgasm, I wasn't sure. When I sat up and squatted to see inside, my genitals seemed to hang between my legs like a savage's, bloated, pulsating, begging for release. The front of my shorts tented obscenely, my dick rock solid and *throbbing*, I swore I could see it through the material, veins standing out thick with blood. Holding my breath, I moved tall weeds aside and peered into the window.

I was right. Nothing.

A storage room of sorts, unlit and dusty. Unable to contain myself any longer, I hiked down the front of my shorts and came right there, a thin discharge like skim milk that beaded in the grass. Relief coursed through me like a sigh. "Well?" Stephen and Ray asked when I finally got myself together again and raced out to where they waited.

I laughed, delighted. "Not a damn thing, like I said." I feigned a punch at Ray and hit his upper arm hard enough to redden the skin when he flinched. Then, climbing onto my bike, I shouted out, "Race you guys home!"

That day comes back now as bright as the summer sun and I almost stagger beneath the weight of sudden shame at jerking off by the basement window. It's Dan who keeps me from stumbling, his hand strong in mine, his presence a promise that I'll make it through today with him by my side.

51: My Brother

OUTSIDE, THE FRONT lawn looks more like a parking lot than ever — people mill around the cars trying to figure out who's driving what and who's riding where. Everyone's dressed nicely, from the youngest child to the oldest adult, sweaters and dresses and suits and slacks replacing the easy attire of the weekend, the t-shirts and jeans I've grown used to seeing these past few days. A couple boys toss around a football until they're scolded, and a handful of girls in long, dark dresses stand clumped together with plastic purses hanging from their shoulders, giggling when their brothers and cousins get yelled at. Doug pulls at his tie, uncomfortable, but when Dan and I step out onto the porch, he says something to Kenny that causes them both to look at our car and laugh. "Hey Mike!" Kenny calls out — he starts to mime a blowjob, his tongue poking out one cheek comically, until Neeshi tugs hard on the collar of his ironed shirt and he mumbles an insincere, "Sorry." Behind me, Caitlin laughs, and I'm struck with a sense of a carnival atmosphere, a gathering at a tailgate party or barbeque, not a group of relatives off to a funeral for one of their own. *Nervous energy*, I tell myself. We're just coping any way we can.

I start down the steps and Dan falls in behind me, his feet an eerie echo of my own as we come down off the porch. "Where is this place again?" he asks, taking my elbow.

"Not far," I tell him. "I can drive, if you want."

As he digs in his front pocket for the keys, he frowns at me, concerned. "You sure?"

"Dan, I can drive." His frown deepens and instantly I regret my tone. Softening my voice, I assure him, "I'm fine, babe. Keys?"

Almost reluctantly, he hands them over. I close my fingers around his and don't let go when he tries to pull away. For a moment longer his frown lingers. Then he sees my smile and laughs. "I guess I can let you drive just this once," he teases.

"You're too kind," I say, grinning, "since it *is* my car."

His arm slips around my waist and his next step presses him against me, his body settling into mine with an easy familiarity that's developed between us over the past ten months we've been lovers. It's a feeling I don't ever want to lose, it strengthens me, keeps me putting one foot in front of the other, wakes me up in the morning and drifts me off to sleep at night. It's the only thing I really need to help me get through this thing called life.

At the car, I unlock the passenger side door and hold it open so Dan can slip inside, but Caitlin gets there first. "If I call shotgun, do I get it?" she asks, though she must know the answer — she moves the seat forward to climb into the back without waiting for a reply.

The minute she sits down, a half dozen kids rush the car, vying for the coveted spot beside her. Emily, the oldest, knocks another girl aside and flips her hair over her shoulder, out of her face. "*I'm* riding with them," she declares. Inside the car, Caitlin glares at me balefully. I can't help but grin.

Once Emily's inside, Dan starts to move his seat back into position when Trevor pushes between us. "Me too," he says, jumping onto the seat. Emily sticks her foot up to keep him from crawling into the back, and he shrieks in childish anger. "Me *too*," he insists. "Michael, tell her —"

"Emily," I sigh. I'm already wondering if I can possibly take someone else's car instead. Maybe Dan and I could ride with one of my aunts? Hell, even my parents are preferable to *this*.

Before I can suggest it, though, Uncle Tommy's wife Debbie is there, smiling apologetically as she slips by me to catch Trevor around the waist. "Come on, big boy," she coos, plucking him from the car. He kicks and grabs at the door, screams in protest, suddenly violent in his anger. "He has a car seat," Debbie explains with a wan smile. I pry Trevor's tiny hands from where they've latched onto the door frame and he snaps at me, his eyes wide and uncompromising behind his glasses. "Trevor, you have to ride with Mommy. You have your own seat —"

"I want to ride with Caitlin!" he shouts. From the back seat, my sister cringes and Emily wears a smug look that reads, *I'm riding with her and you're not, so there. Are we this bad?* I wonder. I don't have to look around to know that everyone has stopped whatever it was they were doing just to watch us. Oblivious to the scene he's causing, Trevor continues to shriek, "No! No no no!"

His mother sighs. "Trevor, please —"

Ducking beneath the child's kicking feet, I lean into the car, exasperated and more than a little embarrassed. Over his cries, I ask Caitlin, "Can you ride with him, or something?" I just want his tantrum to end, is that asking too much here? And my mother is upset because I'm *not* having children? Who the hell could put up with one of *these*?

Caitlin huffs and punches the back of the seat as I pull it forward again to give her room to get out. "I'm already strapped in," she starts.

Trevor howls in my ear, his hands in my sweater to keep his mom from moving too far away — each step she takes pulls me with them, and I feel like I'm struggling to hold my ground as I cling to the seat. With great, hiccupping breaths, the boy cries out, "Cat! Wanna ride, Cat!" Over and over and *over*, this kid's all worked up now and won't — or *can't* — stop. "Cat!"

"Je-*sus*," she mutters, fumbling with the buckle of her seat belt. Before I can ask her again, she surges forward and pushes her way out of the car. "Quit your bitching, kid. I'm gonna sit with you, just shut the hell up already, will you?"

Despite the bitterness in her voice, Trevor listens. He draws in a deep breath and holds it, his eyes watery prisms behind his glasses as he stares at Caitlin. "Ride with me?" he asks, not daring to hope.

When she nods, disgusted, he wriggles in his mother's arms until she puts him down. Then he takes my sister's hand and tries to get into my car again. "Not this one," she sighs. I have a feeling that after today, my mom's only chance for grandkids will be Ray, heaven forbid. "We'll ride in yours, how's that?"

Ignoring her, Trevor climbs halfway onto the passenger seat and smacks Emily's foot, still between the seats. "I've got her now," he taunts.

"Cause you're a crappy crybaby," Emily replies. She kicks his arm, setting him off again. "Mom! Tell him to leave me alone!"

As Debbie and Caitlin drag the screeching boy from the car, Dan turns his back on them, brushing my arm with his elbow to get my attention. In a low, intimate voice, he murmurs, "Is it too late to call this whole thing off?"

I laugh and touch his stomach, my hand flat against his silky shirt, the hint of muscle beneath my palm. "I know, right?"

"I'm riding with you, Trevor!" Caitlin yells, shaking our cousin's arm in an attempt to quiet him. "Shit, stop crying, will you? I'm riding in your goddamn car already so just shut the hell up."

Beside her, Debbie frowns at my sister's language, but when Trevor listens, she grins, relieved. "Caitlin, thank you," she says. "You don't know how much this means to him. He's really taken with you."

"Yeah, yeah." The complement is waved aside as Caitlin starts forward, jerking Trevor so he'll follow. He trails behind, hitching his breath with each step like an oversized pair of pants that won't stay up around his waist. "Which car is yours again?"

I look over the remaining children — some have trailed off after Caitlin, a tiny entourage of groupies all hoping to squeeze into the other car with her, and who am I kidding? When I was that age, I would've loved a back-talking, gum-smacking, quick cussing cousin like Cat, full of attitude, the epitome of *cool* in a child's eyes. Someone they secretly envied, someone they would never dare to be. Even now I can see the conflict in Emily's eyes, the desire to tag along behind my sister warring with the reluctance to share her with her little brother. Twice she starts to get out of the car, and twice she throws herself back against the seat, unsure. "We can take what, two more?" I ask Dan. "Three? We should get going."

Dan takes control of the situation, just as I hoped he would. Clapping his hands, he shouts out, in a voice that would make any commanding officer proud, "Are we leaving here sometime today or not?" The half-dozen kids still lingering by the car snap to attention, nodding eagerly, and a few of the boys who left return — they like Dan. Who doesn't? *My mother*, I think to myself, but maybe that will change. At least she's giving him a chance, so there *is* hope. When each small face is turned to him, Dan holds up three fingers and says, "We can take two more. Pick —"

One of the little girls giggles, a cutie with dark red hair and thick freckles covering her face. "That's three," she points out.

Dan frowns and tries again. Two fingers this time, and he tells them, "Okay, so we can take three of you?"

My heart swells with their laughter — I never imagined he'd be this play-ful around kids. While he negotiates the seating arrangements, I cross in front of the car, already lost in thought. My mom should see him like this, *then* she'll fall for him. Further proof that Evie would've loved him, I *know* it. And who's to say maybe there *won't* be grandkids down the road? Years from now, of course, after I'm through with school and he's out of the mili-tary, when we've been together for so long that every breath I take without him by my side just doesn't seem right, when we're *married*, maybe then we can discuss something like adoption. True, I could do without the screaming and carrying on, but the easy way he teases my young cousins brings out a whole new side to him, another facet beyond the soldier, a hint at the man inside whom I so dearly love —

"What's the problem here?" Ray asks, cutting into my daydream.

I stop at the side-view mirror on the driver's side and look up to find my brother leaning against the door, arms folded defiantly in front of his chest. "You're late," I tell him. With one hand, I try to shoo him aside so I can get into the car, but he ignores the gesture. "Show's over, Ray. The problem's solved. Move along."

"What happened?" he persists. Caitlin's already gone, Trevor's crying has stopped, the car shakes as four kids climb into the back seat, *four*, even though I know we can't safely fit more than two but it appears that Dan's a sucker for a child's smile, same as Evie was — none in the front seat, though, I'm drawing the line there. I don't want any of them in his lap when I'm trying to drive, and I sure as hell don't want to reach over for his hand and find little fingers in its place. I don't have to look at the time to know that we're already running behind, and now Ray wants to know what was holding us up. As if he didn't hear Trevor throwing a fit. As if he couldn't look over here and *see* what the fuck was going on in the first place.

"It's over with, okay?" I tell him, my voice terse, my words short. This time I don't wave him aside, this time I place a hand on his arm and try to pull him off the door but he doesn't budge. "Ray, it was nothing. Come on, we're going to be late."

"Mom wanted to know," he mutters, as if that's going to make me change my mind. "I personally don't give a shit what the kid was screeching about. All I know is we're already late and it's your fault. Stop pushing me."

"It's not —" I sigh. There's no use arguing with someone like him. Rubbing at my temples, which have begun to hurt again as if haunted by the ghost of my early morning headache, I take a deep breath and, with deliberate care, ask, "Can you move already?"

"Can you answer my question?" Ray retorts.

What question would that be? I almost ask, but I bite the smart-ass comment back. "I *told* you, it's over. There's nothing to see." When he doesn't move, I push his shoulder gently and joke, "If we're late now, it'll be *your* fault."

He jerks away from me and, with a quickness that he must've learned from our sister, shoves me hard into the side of the car. "Ray," I start, barely getting my arms up in front of me before he does it a second time. The side-view mirror slams into my hip, snapping on its spring as I'm pushed back against the car. "What the fuck's *your* problem?" I want to know.

Without a reply, he hits me again, his palms flat against my chest. I push him away, a move that surprises him, and he staggers back a step before he snarls at me. "I'm not fighting with you," I say, smoothing down my sweater. Remembering his earlier comment, I suggest, "Maybe you should be the one to take something to calm your ass down. What the hell's gotten into you?"

"Michael," he growls, and he hunkers into himself like a quarterback about to rush the line. I have a brief second of bright clarity where I think about stepping aside to let him ram his fool head into the side of my car, even though I know I could grapple with him, bring him to the ground, I'm stronger than he is, I *know* it —

And then Dan is there, in front of me like a shield, one staying hand on Ray's shoulder, keeping him at bay. I have to reach out to touch my lover's back just to assure myself that he's real. "What's going on here?" he asks, his voice dangerously low.

Ray looks past him at me, still bristling. "Babe," I sigh, relieved. Part of me would love to see Dan kick my brother's sorry ass, just because he's pulling something at a time like this. But I know that if anything happens out here under the watchful eyes of my relatives, it will just be ammunition for my mom against my lover, she'll never let him live it down. And it wouldn't even be his fault, but that hasn't stopped her blind anger before. So I tug at his shirt to pull him to me, putting much needed distance between him and Ray, and I murmur, "Everything's cool. He was just leaving —"

I don't have to see Dan's face to know he doesn't believe that one. "You must have a death wish," he purrs, his voice deceptively soft, "or you're incredibly stupid, one of the two. I'm not sure which yet." I close my eyes, I don't want to see this — my body hums with sudden fear as Dan continues. "But I know you couldn't have possibly forgotten what we talked about last night. Do you want to push me, Ray? Is that it? Do you want to see just how far I let it go before pushing back?"

"Dan," I whisper. *Please,* I beg silently. *Not here, please God, not here.*

He ignores me. "I don't talk to hear my own voice," Dan says, speaking so no one will overhear. When I open my eyes, he has the collar of Ray's shirt fisted in his hand, and my brother has been dragged close to us, his face next to Dan's as if they're gossiping like housewives. Over my lover's shoulder, Ray glares at me, anger and embarrassment mingled together in one hateful gaze. "I don't make promises I can't keep," Dan assures him. A tug on his collar shifts Ray's eyes to him. "I will hurt you, Ray, if I have to. Being his brother doesn't mean shit to me. Michael's all I care about here, got that? And I'm going to do everything I can to make sure nothing happens to him. Nothing hurts him, nothing bothers him, nothing at all." My lover turns as if to whisper in my brother's ear, and I catch a glimpse of a chilling smile that doesn't quite reach his eyes. "I'm a soldier, Ray. Trained to protect those I love. To fight for what's mine. You might want to keep that in mind, next time you're looking for trouble."

I rub my hand up his back, hoping to diffuse the tension coiled between his shoulders. "Dan," I whisper again. Ray's eyes flicker but don't manage to break free from the prison of my lover's gaze, he can't look away, he doesn't dare. "Please."

At first I'm not sure if he'll listen. He just stares at my brother, willing him to keep going, practically *begging* for a fight. But then I feel tight muscles relax beneath my hand and the fingers curled in Ray's collar loosen. Almost tenderly, Dan smoothes down the bunched fabric. "Are we clear on this?" he asks. He speaks quietly, the way he always does. Someone who didn't know him better might miss the implied threat that runs under his words like an electric current through water — you can't see it but it's there, deadly and just *waiting* for you to make the mistake of stepping into the stream. And like electricity, there are no second chances. Dan only tells you once. For most people, that's enough.

Ray's slower than most, though — he always has been. But this close he can see Dan isn't kidding. It's in the set of his jaw, the gleam in his eyes. These aren't idle threats but sure bets of what *will* happen if he crosses Dan again, he can read that guarantee in the soldier's mask that stares him down. Finally he drops his gaze and takes a step back. Beneath his breath, he mumbles, "Sir, yes sir."

Dan tenses at the slight, but Ray turns and stalks off. When my lover starts after him, I hold him back. "That was rude," he declares, loud enough for Ray to overhear.

Rubbing his arm, I admit, "I know." With a faint smile, I add, "Ray isn't the sharpest tool in the shed."

The sardonic look Dan gives me makes me laugh. "Oh really? I hadn't noticed."

52: The Funeral Procession

I SHOULD HAVE ridden with Caitlin," Emily mutters for the hundredth time since getting into the car — we're not even halfway to Grosso's yet and she won't let up. It's *I should ride with Cat* and *Trevor's such a wuss* and *if I had known I'd be stuck here with you guys*, as if we're all that bad. She sits behind me and kicks the back of my seat, her small shoes hitting just above my kidney, still sore from Caitlin's attack. Two inches lower and I'd have to turn around, hands slapping into the back seat the way my dad used to do when we were fighting in the car, hitting anyone within reach just to shut us up. "Trevor *always* gets anything he wants. It's not fair. I should be with her —"

Annoyed, I hit the brakes and glare at her in the rear-view mirror. "You want to get out now?" I ask. Behind her reflection I can see a row of cars, headlights on despite the bright sun — next in line is Aunt Sarah with that perpetual frown on her face, hands up above the steering wheel as if to ask, *now what?* "It's not far, Emily, if you want to walk. Or hey, wait on the curb, I'm sure your mom will stop and pick you up when she drives by."

My cousin just stares at me with a sullen expression that only a budding teenager can pull off, and she kicks at my seat, hard enough to jar my teeth. "Knock that shit off," I growl. She sulks, her eyes hateful in the mirror. Someone beeps behind us, and ahead a gap has opened in our procession, a good two or three yards between my car and my parents' in front of us. "You want to get out?" I ask again. "Make up your mind, girlfriend, 'cause we don't have all day —"

"Just go," she says. When I don't let up off the brake right away, she kicks the back of my seat. "I said *go* already."

Dan turns and gives her a withering look. "And he said stop kicking the seat," he tells her, his voice quiet. One of the other kids back there coughs but no one speaks, no one dares break the sudden silence that's enveloped us. Emily tries to stare Dan down and can't — she barely meets his gaze before she looks away. I hear her shoes scrape down the back of my seat and then the pressure from her feet is gone. "Thank you."

"You don't scare me," she mumbles, half to herself. My lover chooses to ignore this and turns away. In the mirror Emily's lower lip starts to tremble — she crosses her arms and pouts out the window, her pride wounded. "Just go," she says again, her voice thick with tears.

This time I listen, and the car surges forward to catch up with the others. A glance in the side-view mirror shows a line of cars stretching back for as far as I can see — I wouldn't be surprised if some still sit in front of Aunt Evie's house, lights on, waiting for their chance to pull out. Silence hangs like a pall over us, and with the windows rolled up, it's even more stifling in here — the only sounds are the radio playing low and the rustle of a dress from the back seat, the scrape of shoes as my cousins try to get comfortable. Then the road curves and Grosso's comes into view, squalid and rundown and so damn *old* in the unforgiving sun that I have to blink back tears that blur my vision. Without looking away from the road, I fumble blindly into the seat next to me, reaching, searching ...

Dan is already reaching back.

His fingers close over mine, both hands taking me into the safety of his palms, and his strength floods through me like adrenaline. "Almost there," I say, though I'm not quite sure who I'm talking to, myself or him.

My car follows the others down the street with little help from me — I feel like just one more car in a roller coaster ride, all of us chained together, I can almost hear the steady *chink chink chink* of a crane pulling us along. We're driving so slow that I don't have to brake when we take the turn right past the market, which I notice with proud satisfaction is closed. Mr. Grosso shuts down only twice a year, Christmas Day and Easter Sunday, that's it, no exceptions ... except today. In the summertime, he opens six in the morning, a little later in the winter months, and has always said he doesn't close until the last customer leaves the store. I think this is the first time I've ever seen a *Closed* sign hanging in that window, *ever* — it hangs there silently, a testament to the type of woman Evie was, what she meant to this town, what she meant to *me*.

Closed, like the sign says. I can still see the exact shape of my mother's mouth when she announced over dinner that Evie was gone, I remember the way my dad's jaw stopped in mid-chew, the way Dan's hand stiffened in mine before he even knew who we were talking about, he just sensed the shock and knew he had to hold onto me, he knew the sign was going up, *closed*. With the clarity of a photograph, that moment is frozen in time, filed away with the precious few earth-shattering memories I've gathered in my life. Among them is the wonder and trepidation that flashed through me the first time my mother let me hold Caitlin almost a full week after she came home from the hospital. Before then it was always, "Watch the baby," and

"Keep it down, the baby's sleeping," and "You can't play with her, Mike, she's too little." I thought she might be made of porcelain or glass, the way my mother carried on, and one afternoon when I was supposed to be watching cartoons, I snuck upstairs to the crib to see what the fuss was all about.

She lay curled up like a doll, tiny hands fisted at her cheeks, tiny eyes scrunched shut, tiny legs pulled up to her belly. I had never been so close to a baby before — I was nine, that galooting age when boys weren't allowed near babies, or kittens, or anything delicate like that. Still, she looked so *perfect*, a miniature human, I just had to touch her. When I reached into the crib, though, I heard my mom's voice in quiet warning, "Michael."

I turned. Mom was right behind me — I hadn't heard her come into the room. "She's so small," I whispered. I tried to take a step back but my mom was so close that I bumped into her and stopped where I was. "I wasn't going to hurt her," I promised, looking up into my mother's face. "Honest, Momma. I just wanted to see ..."

With a sigh, Mom reached over me into the crib and lifted Caitlin into her arms. For a moment I craned my neck back as she cradled the baby to her, and then she knelt down and lowered her arms, draping them over me so Caitlin was in front of us both. "You want to hold her?" she asked softly.

"You sure?" I asked, scared. When my mom nodded, I started to ease my arms around my mother's own, around the baby, who felt so small and fragile in my embrace. Pulling back, I shook my head. I didn't want to break her, I didn't want to be held accountable if something happened, I was too big and clumsy and I was going to hurt her, I just *knew* it —

But Mom murmured, "It's okay. I've got her." So I tried again, carefully wrapping my arms around the baby. When my mom didn't move away, I grew bold and stepped closer, mimicking my mother's stance until it seemed like the baby was in *my* arms. As I stared down at Caitlin's tiny, precious face, scarcely able to breathe for fear of waking her, my sister felt the warmth of a body beside her and turned into me, cheeks nuzzling my chest, mouth open in a tiny, tiny sigh.

The memory hits me hard — despite how far along she was in the pregnancy that year, Mom still insisted on visiting Evie. Everyone laughed when we arrived, joked that they didn't think we'd make it, and with a rare smile, my dad admitted that there was a time or two driving down those back country roads when he thought the baby was going to come no matter what. That first night here, after the traditional welcoming dinner over the grill, Mom complained of gas. Two hours later, it was labor. The next morning, Evie woke Ray and me and Stephen, spending the night, to drive us into Franklin to see the new baby. In that pre-dawn world, as we sped down the road, Grosso's had been open. Now it's closed.

The sign moves out of sight as we take the turn and Morrison's looms into view, as nondescript as any other house in town. The only suggestion that it's something more is the discreet sign in the front yard, wooden, that hangs between fat, rounded posts, black letters scripted ornately across the white paint. *Est. 1923*, it reads, *Morrison's Funeral Home,* and beneath that the address, a phone number, and in tiny print that seems to grow as we get closer, *Proudly Serving the Fine People of Sugar Creek.*

Pavement stretches back down the street towards Grosso's — the parking lot. As I pull in, I notice a long, black car parked at the far end of the lot, closest to the house. Curtains obscure the interior of the vehicle, and a silver curlicue decorates the raised roof. The black surface gleams like obsidian, polished and waxed and still damp with morning dew. Without looking at the license plate, I know it reads *MRRSN 1.* They've had that same plate on that hearse for as long as I can remember. There aren't any others, just this one, they don't *need* any others in a town of this size, but that *1* is there nonetheless, hopeful. I don't want to park near that car. I try not to even look at it, my gaze roaming the parking lot instead, as if I have to search for a spot. "Any one will do," Dan tells me.

But someone directs traffic — one of the funeral home employees, an elderly man whose dark suit and tie is so incongruous with the day around him that he looks like a bruise against the clear blue sky. He stands in the middle of the first aisle of the lot and uses both hands to direct us into the parking spots. The first car turns left, pulling into a space right beside the hearse, thank *God* that's not me. Next car turns right, parking behind the hearse. Who's idea again was it for us to be so close to the front of the line? *You had to get out first,* I tell myself, waiting for my turn to park. *You were on the street, Michael, what were you going to do? Pull over and wait until all the other cars left?* Right now, with the hearse at the edge of my vision like a blind spot, that doesn't seem like it would've been a bad idea.

Then it's our turn. I'm motioned into a spot on the right, in the row behind the hearse. Three or four cars stretch between us and the end of the lot, a small buffer of space but a comfort nonetheless — at least the damn coffin-carrier isn't right behind us or directly on either side. I can't even see it in any of my mirrors, though when I get out of the car it's there, insidious, malignant, waiting with the unflappable calm of a bully in the schoolyard after the last bell rings. I keep my head down, my eyes averted — it still seems to appear in the corners of my vision, haunting, dark like the shadowy image that lingers after a burst of bright light. When I close the door, it's there, I can feel it behind me, I can see it even though I try desperately *not* to. I don't know how I'll make it past that damn car and into the funeral parlor without losing my mind.

A hand on my arm startles me, and when I turn, I find myself in a sudden, soft embrace. "Michael," my Aunt Billy sighs, her perfume a comforting rush that envelopes me like nostalgia. Beneath her quiet words, I can hear a faint tremor, and she shivers in my arms, her strength a mirage that threatens to dissipate like fog in the sun. "How are you holding up?" she wants to know.

"Carefully," I tell her. It brings an absent smile to her face and she hugs me tighter, as if she hopes that I'll be able to stop the trembling that runs through her tall, thin frame. "What about you?" I ask. "Are you doing okay?"

"I'll be fine," she assures me. Pulling back, she smoothes a hand through my hair, down the side of my face, to the collar of my sweater. She watches her fingers as they straighten the knit with a maternal touch. "A few more hours, honey, and all this will finally be over. We'll make it, you'll see. We're all going to be fine."

I'm not sure what to say to that, but as I start to reply, she turns away, already talking to Emily. "And how are you doing today, sweetheart?" she asks, taking the young girl's hand.

My cousin buries her face in Aunt Billy's chest to block out the nightmarish vision just a few cars away. "I want to go home," she whispers. Our aunt pets the girl's hair with long, soothing strokes and murmurs that she knows, she knows.

"Well?" Dan asks, coming around the front of the car to where I stand. He eases a comforting arm around my shoulders, pulls me close and gratefully I lean into him, let him take control. Concern laces his features, giving him an almost angry appearance with furrowed brow, mouth drawn down, eyes flashing in the sunlight. "Are you sure you're up for this?"

I force a laugh that sounds fake to my own ears. "I have to be," I tell him. "Too late to turn back now."

Aunt Billy leads Emily to the house and I start to follow, but Dan doesn't budge, just catches my hand and I turn to find him staring at me with such intensity that I have to ask, "What?"

Taking a step to close the distance between us, he lowers his voice and reminds me, "I'm here for you, Michael. Remember that. If you need to get out at any time, you let me know and I'll lead the way. If it's too much for you in there, if you can't handle it, don't start worrying what your family's going to say if you leave. I'm with you no matter what, you know that. I'll stand beside you throughout the whole service, but if you need to go, then I'll be right behind you on the way out."

His words fill my heart with an emotion I don't think I can contain. "I love you," I sigh, and I press my lips to his in a hungry kiss, despite the crowd that's growing in the parking lot — relatives, mostly, though I see a few residents of Sugar Creek have already made it out to pay their last respects to one of their own. Let them say what they will, I need this, I need *him* to make it through today. With my forehead resting against his, I meet his steady gaze and smile sadly. One hand cups the back of his neck, my fingers rubbing over the bristly hairs that he trimmed short this morning, and the other is splayed across the front of his shirt as if drawing strength from his muscled chest, his warmth.

I stare at him and can hardly imagine our roles reversed, me the strong one, him weak and vulnerable and on the verge of tears. There are moments, but not many — the time Dan cut off the tip of his finger one night while cooking dinner, for instance. His eyes filled with pain and his face blanched, he just stared as dark blood welled up beneath his nail. I was at the sink, rinsing vegetables, talking about something or other, and didn't even notice that he had stopped what he was doing. "Mike," he had said then, his voice gravelly, almost in awe. He cleared his throat, tried again, and when I looked up, I saw one single red rivulet winding down his finger like a stray tear. As I watched, it hung suspended from the base of his thumb and for a breathless moment, neither of us said a word. Then it dripped to the floor.

Spurred into motion, I grabbed his wrist and forced his hand beneath the rushing water in the sink. "Hold it here," I instructed, squeezing the first knuckle of his finger hard to stop the bleeding. I was running on pure instinct alone. Pulled out a drawer, grabbed a handful of towels, shook them out onto the floor even as I assured him, "It's just a little cut, baby, you're going to be okay. Just rinse it off and I'll get the car, can you do that for me? Just rinse it off."

By the time we reached the emergency room, he had bled through one towel and I simply wrapped another around his whole hand, I didn't know what else to do. He held his arm against his chest and I held him as tight as I dared, regardless of the other people in the emergency room, fuck them. This was D.C., they had seen gay men before and he *needed* me. I hugged him to me, his head buried in my shoulder as I kept up the litany, *shh baby, you're going to be fine, it's okay.* I trembled inside, terrified. My courage was wearing thin and I didn't know how much longer I could keep it up — I wanted to yell at the unfairness of my lover's hurt, I wanted to barge through the swinging doors that led to the rest of the hospital and *demand* that someone care for him *now*, I wanted to make the bleeding stop and the pain go away and I couldn't. All I *could* do was let him cling to me, hide his face against my chest and let *me* take care of things for a little while, until he was ready to go on again.

Here, in the shadow of Morrison's, a house we used to think was haunted simply because it was a funeral home, I realize he's doing the same for me now — giving me a sanctuary, a place to hide until I'm ready to move on. In the meantime, he'll keep this show going, he'll take care of everything, he'll take care of *me*. Until I can start taking care of myself again. "What would I do without you?" I ask, hypothetical. I don't want to know the answer to that. I hope I never have to find out.

With a self-depreciating smile, Dan ducks his head, a thin color flooding his cheeks. I laugh and raise his chin so he'll look at me — he's a little boy again, how adorable he must have been at eight or ten, when he was so easily embarrassed. "What's wrong?" I want to know. My smile slips a notch but doesn't disappear entirely. He's so cute like this, I'm going to have to try harder from now on to get him to blush.

He kisses my thumb and admits, "I was just thinking the same thing."

Casually, I tease, "You're wondering what I'd do without you, too?"

That makes him grin. "Michael!" He laughs and slips a hand into mine as I lead him from the car. Suddenly I'm all too aware of the parking lot filling up around us, the somber clothes, the dark moods, the tears. I can almost imagine my mom at the house already, probably standing at one end of the porch and glaring across the yard at us, misreading this tender moment. But as we fall in with the stream of people heading inside, I don't see her, thank God. The last thing I need right now are her judgmental eyes trying to lay the blame on me.

53: Morrison's Funeral Home

STEPPING INTO THE funeral home is disconcerting at first — it's unlike anything I could have expected and for some reason that throws me off. There are no black drapes on the walls, no dark burgundy chairs, no flickering candles leading the way to some back room where the coffin is propped open on a raised bier. Nothing like that at *all*. If anything, I'm struck more by the normalcy of the house, the polished walnut-stained floors, the Queen Anne furniture, the nature prints and family photographs that decorate the off-white walls. Just like any other home. There's nothing macabre, nothing *sacred*, not here.

Just inside the front door, there's an airy, formal sitting room to my left, where the rest of the family is gathering. It's well-lit by morning sunlight streaming through bay windows, no flickering candlelight here, and at the far end of the room, a fireplace hints at cooler weather to come. Next to the doorway, a weathered staircase leads up along the wall much like the stairs at Aunt Evie's. A narrow hallway beside the stairs heads off into the back of the house, a kitchen perhaps, or maybe a common area where services are held. We'll be guided back there soon enough, I suppose. For now, a couple of men in dark suits casually bar the path, and another blocks the stairs, Morrison's employees who nod and look at us with just enough sympathy in their faces to be polite.

Off to my right is a single, inconspicuous door, partially shut against the crowd and the muted sounds of soft voices and thin tears. Even though this is the first time I've been in here, I know *that* has to be where they keep the black curtains, the lamps turned down low, the coffin my aunts so painstakingly picked out ... I don't want to go in there. Like a stubborn child, I press back against Dan, my hand finding his and squeezing it tight. "Are you alright?" he wants to know.

Numbly I nod — I'll be fine. "Okay," I whisper. He touches my arm to reassure me and I lean into him gratefully. "Just ... let's not stand right *here*, please?" We're in the path of the front door, anyway, we need to move.

"Somewhere else, maybe," I murmur, though I don't know where.

We look around. Most of my relatives have already retreated to the sitting room, where they exchange hugs and sad smiles. In quiet tones they talk of Evie as if she's still alive, repeating the same phrases, the same stories, over and over again. *So good with the kids,* someone says, and another, *It's a shame she has none of her own.* "We're her children, all of us," my mother declares, her voice standing out from the others, I'd recognize it anywhere. I catch a glimpse of her, arms around Penny's shoulders as silent tears course down my aunt's slack cheeks. Thinking of the Valium in my pocket, I wonder how many of those little yellow pills are already in her system this morning.

When Dan tries to lead me that way, I resist. "No," I say simply — I don't want to immerse myself in that communal grief. I have nothing to add to it, nothing to contribute. The whole scene looks fake to me somehow, a tableau on stage, a part in a play, the sorrow contrived and the actors just hoping to make it through their lines until the curtain falls. Those who cry are trying too hard; those that don't, not hard enough. And then there's me, somewhere in the middle, with private memories I don't want to share. As long as I keep them inside, there's a part of Evie still alive in my heart, I can feel her essence flicker like a tiny flame that no one can ever extinguish.

Anticipating my response, Dan turns in midstep and leads me a little ways down the hall, away from the crowded front room. He flashes a stilted grin at one of the funeral home employees nearby, then stops a few feet from the closed door and whatever darkness lies in the room beyond. Leaning back against the wall, Dan pulls me to him and we stand together side by side, out of the flow of traffic. From here we can see the front door, held open by another ubiquitous employee. *The men in black,* I think, stifling a dangerous giggle that rises in me at the thought. Dan gives me a curious glance, half-smiling because he sees the mirth in my eyes and wants in on the joke. Before he can ask, though, I shake my head and frown against a grin that wants to spread across my face. "It's nothing," I whisper.

"Will you tell me later?" he asks, shifting so his arm rests against mine.

"Sure." I kiss his cheek and am just about to tell him now anyway — whenever I look at one of the suited morticians, I almost hear the opening theme from *The X-Files* and I know he'd find that funny, no matter how morbid it sounds — but I catch my mom watching us, disapproval written clearly in the set of her lips, and I don't say a word. Instead, I just clear my throat and turn away, feeling chastised the way I used to when I was younger and she caught me goofing off in church. "Later," I mumble.

Dan slips his hand into mine and we stand there like two boys at our first high school dance, too afraid to step out onto the gym floor and mingle. Personally, I'm hoping against hope that the wall will simply swallow us whole, or maybe the floor beneath our feet will open up, drop us down into someplace quiet where we can be alone. With longing I think of the back room off Aunt Evie's kitchen and the roughly-made bed, the pillows waiting, the blankets turned down at one corner. When this is all over, I'm going to get out of these sad, depressing clothes and curl up beneath those covers and sleep the rest of the day away, tomorrow too, until it's time for us to leave Sugar Creek behind. Part of me wishes we were heading out tonight, even though I know we'll both be too tired to drive. I just don't want to stay longer than necessary.

"Michael," Dan murmurs, and I look up as my mom starts towards us, an arm around Penny's shoulders to drag my complacent aunt along behind her. I can imagine what she has to say about impropriety, it was just a quick *peck*, for Christ's sake, this isn't the place to go off on me about it, talk about your damn discretion —

Suddenly one of the men in black steps out from the crowd and takes her arm. "Mrs. Knapp," he purrs, snagging her attention. She turns towards him, irritated, but his hand covers hers and he's good at what he does, didn't Aunt Jessie say that? His soft voice is almost hypnotic when he leans close to tell her, "We're ready for the viewing."

The viewing. The words have the same effect on my mother as they do on me — she opens her mouth to say something sharp enough to shake him off but stops, her argument gone. With an almost Herculean effort, she pulls herself together and tries again. Nothing. Instead of a cutting remark, all she manages is a weak echo of his own words. "Ready?"

The man nods. "Yes, ma'am," he says, courteous and so damn efficient that she doesn't even realize he's leading her towards the partially closed door. "We'll start seating the family first," he tells her, nodding until she starts to nod, too. "If you'll spread the word among your aunts? Quietly, of course."

"Of course." She throws me one final, reproachful look, then spots Aunt Bobbie near the staircase. "Bob, can you help me with Penny? They're letting the family in …"

Slowly, as if they've been roused from sleep, my relatives begin to shuffle into some semblance of a line, Mom and Penny in front of them all, just outside the door. They're close enough to us now that if she wanted to, Mom could simply lean over and say something to me, mention the quick kiss in public perhaps, or point out our laced hands. But she's busy with her sister, whose dazed look is beginning to wear off with the pills — it's gotten through to her what's happening now, she knows what lies behind that door, and Penny shakes her head, canceling out the idea of stepping into the room beyond. "No," she says, without conviction. "Laura, no. I can't —"

"You can," Mom assures her and then, in the same encouraging tone, she says to no one in particular, "I can't handle her like this alone. A little help here would be nice."

My aunts appear as if by magic, fairy godmothers conjured into being at the distress in my mother's voice. Aunt Billy takes Penny's arm and looks over her shoulders at us, a sad smile marring her delicate features. Aunt Bobbie steps up to my mother's side, hemming her in, and Aunt Sarah squeezes in behind her sisters. "Excuse me, sorry," she murmurs as everyone moves back to make room for her. "Penny, doll, I'm here for you. I'm here, Laura. Right here."

"Are we ready then?" Bobbie asks. She nods to show she's ready and looks at her sisters each in turn — Billy smiles, her eyes widening behind her glasses, and Sarah fluffs her hair, distracted. My mom takes a deep, steadying breath, spears me with one last look that promises we'll talk when this is all over, and then she nods, too. *Ready.* The only one who doesn't respond is Penny. Her eyes have glossed over like an animal caught in headlights and her gaze slides right by me, unseeing. A pang of sympathy stabs through my chest, a mortal wound, what's going to happen to her now? They'll get the house cleaned out, everything inside sold or given away, and we'll all go back to our respective lives, but what about her? What will *she* do? For me, Sugar Creek was a summer vacation, a winter holiday, a place where I could retreat when life grew too hectic or too routine. But much as I love this place, there was always an undeniable sense of homecoming when we left, and the times spent here, my family and friends, they all faded into bittersweet memories that still shine golden in my mind. Sugar Creek was a refuge for me, a haven, a place where I could hide away from my "real" life of school and parents for the length of a summer or a few weeks at Christmastime.

So where will Penny go to find sanctuary? This has never been a vacation for *her*, she lives here, it's *her* reality. Aunt Evie's presence is stamped into every street, every house, every tree and rock, how can Penny escape that? Maybe someone will take her, *hopefully* they will, one of our aunts or my mother even, someone who lives far enough away from the tiny town and its incessant creek bubbling down through the years. She can't stay here. I see it in her dull eyes, her trembling chin. She simply can't stay.

Somehow the four women manage to move her forward a step or two. An undertaker eases the door open, speaking soft words that I can't hear. *They're good at what they do,* I think as Penny struggles not to cry. Her face scrunches up like a napkin balled in a fist and for a moment I don't think she'll make it — two fat tears course down either cheek to catch in the corners of her mouth ... she wipes at one, then the other, then surprises me with an almost imperceptible nod. As if that's all they've been waiting for, my aunts surge ahead, guiding Penny and my mom through the door, into the viewing room and out of my sight.

The undertaker steps aside as others in line follow. "Family first," he says quietly, though there are only a handful of people here so far that I'm not related to in one way or another. I recognize the Grossos near the back of the line, speaking with my father — as if he feels my gaze, my dad turns and rolls his eyes like this is the absolute *last* place he wants to be. *Don't blame you*, I think. At least Aunt Jessie isn't here. What kind of scene would that make? If the front door swung open and she stood there on the porch? Or smiled at me, called my name, said *oh Michael, hey, it's good to see you again*, what could I say to that? *Hi Jessie, fancy meeting you here, how's it hanging?*

"Michael?" Dan asks, concerned. His hand tightens around mine and my smile feels like plastic on my face. The hallway has cleared out a bit, though my dad still stands in the doorway to the sitting room, frowning at the molding like he thinks it needs a good coat of paint. "Maybe we should head inside now? If you want?" *What if I don't want?* I think. But just how long can I stay out here with no one noticing? Is it really so bad in the other room? Nobody else is lingering behind … "Mikey?" Dan prompts, my childhood nickname cute in his voice. "What do you want to do, babe?"

I'm not sure. "I want —" I start, but whatever I'm about to say is lost when the front door *does* open, inch by excruciating inch, the way closet doors do in nightmares just before monsters attack. *It's Jessie*, I think wildly, I don't know what made her think it'd be okay to come here, I don't know what she expects to find —

Only the woman who enters isn't her. She's taller than my aunt and years younger, with dark, wispy hair that I recognize all too well. Last time I saw it, she had it pulled back in braids but it's short now, cut to her chin in a look beauticians call *feathered*. That square jaw, those flashing eyes, the straight nose that I always thought looked better on her brother — Stephanie Robichaud. True, she's almost Ray's age now, no longer a little girl with scabby knees and quick fists, but I can't help cringing behind Dan as she scans the room. *Please don't see me*, I pray. My heart thuds in my chest, I know she didn't come alone, and as she holds the door open, I press against my lover's side, my knees weak. Sensing my fear, Dan fists a hand into my pants, pulling the material taut across the back of my thigh. "Who's she?" he wants to know.

Her name is on the tip of my tongue when *he* comes in. *Jesus help me.* Stephen, dressed in black jeans and a faded denim jacket, he pushes the dark hair out of his eyes with one nervous hand but doesn't look around like his twin. Instead he looks at me as if he knew before he even came in where I stood, and his eyes are large and so sad, I can't bear to stare into them for long. That black isn't for Evie — it's for his heart. I held it in my hands and never realized … no, I knew. Somehow I always knew. And I took it for granted because we were friends and he never actually came out and *said* the words until the other day. Until it was too late.

He sees Dan, he *has* to. "I'll be right in," he tells his sister, in words I read on his lips more than hear spoken aloud. A hand on her back points her towards the viewing room, but not before she sees me. Doubt crosses her face, a foreign look for Stephanie Robichaud, the legendary bully of Sugar Creek, and she almost says something to him — she never liked me, and her gaze rakes over Dan like hot coals, she knows who he must be. *The boyfriend,* the man who came between her brother and the one love of his life. *No, Steph,* I think humorlessly. *That man was me. I'm the one who tore him up inside, I'm the one who misused him all those years. I didn't need any help, I seem to be good at shit like that all by myself.*

"Go on," Stephen says again. His sister says something low and biting, something I can't hear, but the way she storms past us after the others makes me think I don't really need to know what it was. As Stephen crosses the hall, heading this way, the room seems to shrink. Suddenly I can't breathe, and where Dan touches me, his body burns like hellfire against mine.

Stephen stops in front of us and, with deliberate care, pushes his glasses up the bridge of his nose. A shy smile toys with one corner of his mouth, then the other, but never seems to pull both sides up at the same time. "Michael," he sighs, shoving his hands deep into his pockets. As if remembering his manners, he pulls them out again, sticks one towards us woodenly, and attempts another smile. "You must be Dan."

"I'm guessing you're Stephen," my lover says, taking the offered hand in a firm shake. "Michael's told me a lot about you."

That's putting it mildly, but if Stephen wonders just what was said, he doesn't ask. Instead he shoves his hands into his pockets again and rocks back on his heels, staring at a spot on the floor between our feet. "I'm sure he has," he murmurs. My heart twists in my chest. *Oh Stephen, I'm so sorry …* an awkward moment later, he adds, "You're not quite what I expected."

Dan laughs, surprised. "Neither are you," he admits.

That gets a wan grin from my old friend and I see myself in his shoes, the outsider, meeting an old flame's new love — would I be as self-possessed? As civil? I only hope so. "Thanks for coming out, Steve," I tell him. There's something in my throat that wants to choke me quiet but I swallow it back. "I really appreciate it."

He gives me one of his *aw shucks* shrugs, the kind that make his face flush self-consciously. "It's nothing," he says, though I suspect it's a hell of a lot more than that. I can almost see the anxiety eating into him, it's in the tremor of his voice, his unsteady hands, the way he shifts from foot to foot like he's waiting to use the bathroom or something. When he looks at me, he sort of looks *around* me, his eyes flickering like butterflies, afraid to rest in any one spot for too long. Maybe he thinks Dan will say something, or I will. I can't imagine there's anything left to say. With another shrug, Stephen whispers, "She was practically my aunt, too. Not so much now but when we were little, you know."

"Yeah."

Beside me, my lover shifts uncomfortably and I want to thank him for staying here with me, as unnecessary as it might be. The man in front of us is nothing to be afraid of anymore — it's just Stephen, same as always. Despite whatever's happened in our lives, whatever's come between us, we're still friends. Deep down where it matters, there's a feeling between us stronger than any sexual tie, any confession of love, any passage of time. There's still a place inside of me where I'm six years old again and squatting beside a hole in the backyard, just as there's a place in him where he's eight and watching me, waiting for the moment I notice him standing in the shadows.

In that place, our heart of hearts, where time and sex and even *life* have no meaning, I know without a doubt that if I hold out a shovel and ask him to play, despite whatever he feels for me, whatever I can't feel in return, he will always, *always*, say yes.

And I know that I love him for that.

54: Saying Goodbye

S O," STEPHEN SAYS, searching for something to say, something to keep him here beside me despite my lover at my side. He seems more at ease when he looks at Dan than when he looks my way, which makes me sad because he was *my* friend, once, and there was never any awkwardness between us before. When I didn't know how he felt about me, when I could pretend his attentions weren't more than I wanted them to be. I wonder if it's going to be like this from now on, this halting conversation, this uneasy company. An uncomfortable fear spins out from him like a spider web, ensnaring the three of us in its grip, a fear of showing anything more than the most elementary of emotions. More might be misread, misinterpreted, leaving us all hurt and upset. Better to keep it like this, with our banal small talk, than to delve deeper and invite trouble. The thought depresses me. Stephen was always the one person I could confide in, the one friend I could tell anything to and now I can't, because his reasons for opening up to me were as selfish as mine are where Dan is concerned. He did it because he loved me, *loves*, and if I continue to take advantage of that, if I try to act as if nothing has happened and we're still where we were in the past, he'll confuse my attempts at friendship for love. Because I know that's what he's offering me, and I can't take it. I'm with Dan. Stephen deserves so much more out of life than simply longing for a boy like me.

Still, he puts up a good front, smiling as if he's not torn up inside. "You're in the military?" he asks, just to fill the silence around us.

With a nod, Dan confirms, "Army."

Memories like an incoming tide surge over me, drowning me in the past. "Stephen used to want to join the military," I offer. He gives me a shy smile and I prod his foot gently with the tip of my shoe. "Remember? You always said you wanted to sign up with the Air Force. Whatever became of that?"

"That was just dreaming out loud," he laughs. I grin at the sound, so carefree, so sudden, so much the old Stephen that I feel the years disappear and the discomfort between us fade. "I did talk to a recruiter once. You know, those college day things they make you do in high school?" When I nod, he sighs. "He told me sure, sign up, even gave me a pen and a huge packet of stuff to read through, said he'd have his officer call me later on to schedule a physical and all that."

"What happened?" I want to know. Maybe it's not too late for him, I'm thinking. Get out of this dead-end town, move on without me, find someone else —

But he taps the frames of his thick glasses with one slender finger and explains, "These. He took one look at my eyes and said they have plenty of positions. You know, ground control, engineers, shit like that. I told him I wanted to fly, and he almost laughed at me. Not with those specs, he said. Pilots have to have 20/20 and I sure as hell don't." His smile slips, and with a rueful laugh, he adds, "So there went that."

The silence returns, just as stifling as before. Dan takes my hand in his, squeezes my fingers reassuringly, as if to remind me that he's still here. More people have shuffled into the hall — they speak quietly to the employees they know, asking after children or mentioning the weather, adding almost as an afterthought a comment or two about Evie's passing. That's what they call it here, as if death is just a graded performance one can pass or fail. With low voices and sad smiles our way, they head into the viewing room. Most of them probably don't know my name, just that I'm one of Evie's kids — they probably think Dan is, too, and even though Stephen is from Sugar Creek, he's one of us by association. He belonged to Evie, too.

"All these people," I murmur, impressed. Family's one thing but this is the whole *town* we're talking about now. The front door barely closes before it's opened again … this place can't possibly hold everyone. I wonder if there are any seats left inside, or if Dan and I will have to stand during the service. I'm sure my mother didn't save us a place, she has her hands full with Penny and it's something that would never cross her mind, holding two seats. Maybe one for me, that would be it, and afterwards she'd want to know why I didn't sit with the family. I'm just about to suggest that we follow everyone inside — much as I don't want to see the reality of a coffin or my dead aunt's sad, closed face — when Stephen, in an attempt to keep me talking, says, "I ran into Ray at the store yesterday."

"Grosso's?" I ask, distracted. "You guys, maybe we should go on in."

But Stephen shakes his head. "The Wawa. You saw it on your way in, didn't you? It's been open a few years now." With an embarrassed grin, he looks at his shoes and tells us, "I'm sort of the manager there."

I stop, impressed. "Hey, that's great. You own the whole store?"

"Not *really*," he says, but from the way he's grinning, it's obvious that he's only being modest. "It's a franchise, I guess you could say. I've been taking business courses forever, you know, and I just thought I'd put them to use. It's just a *store*."

"It's a pretty big store," I point out. Before I can think better of it, I clap him on the back, a gesture that pinks his cheeks. "I'm proud of you, man."

His face flushes a deep red, the way it used to when we were younger and I'd fake a grab at his crotch or ass in front of someone else. I did it once at his house — we were in the kitchen, his mother at the sink cleaning his glasses because he fell of his bike and they landed in the mud. I was on the floor, rubbing a hot, wet washcloth over Stephen's scraped knees as he stood beside her, hitching his breath and struggling not to cry. He was a teenager, he *couldn't* cry, but his bike had jumped the curb going too damn fast and he pitched over the handlebars, hitting the ground like a runner sliding into base. His legs were a mess of thin bloody lines, his shirt torn, one of the nose pads on his glasses broken off, and I did the only thing I could think of to do to cheer him up. There in the kitchen, squatting in front of him, I looked up and stared until I had his full attention, and then I lunged forward, pretending to bite at the front of his shorts.

His mother didn't see me — she had her back to us, trying to fix his glasses, but he *thought* she did, and he turned the darkest shade of purple I've ever seen, *ever*. Later, when his glasses were wobbly but useable, and the torn shirt and muddy shorts lay discarded on the floor of his bedroom, I remember kissing every single scratch, every scrape, as he lay on his bed in his underwear, staring down at me over a tenting erection. No wonder things are awkward between us now — every moment brings back another memory like that one, another time he mistook my curious friendship for true love. *Why did you let me go on like that, Stephen?* I want to ask, but I don't dare. *Why didn't you tell me sooner, look Mike, this is what I feel when we're together, I just want to make sure we're on the same page?* And what would I have said? No, but if given enough time, if I lived *here* instead of a thousand miles away, if I had never met Dan and never knew just what real love *felt* like, then maybe, just maybe, I could've said yes.

But it's too late for that. I know it, Stephen *must* know it — it's in the clasp of Dan's hand in mine. Whatever friendship we had is shattered, and we step through the jagged shards, careful not to cut ourselves on *what might have been* and *how we once were*. With a lonely sigh that makes my heart ache to hear it, Stephen tells us, "Old man Grosso isn't all that pleased with it, you can be sure."

It takes me a second to realize that he's still talking of the store, his life without me, his *real* life, where I'm just a melancholy memory. As much as it hurts to know he's regaled me to the past, maybe that's where I belong to him. My present is here, beside me, *Dan*. "Yeah," I admit. "I'm sure he's not too thrilled with the competition. So you saw Ray there?"

Stephen nods. "Buying milk —"

"That *bastard!*" I laugh, incredulous. When Dan smirks, I slap his arm but that just makes him snicker. "He drank all my damn milk and had the *audacity* to go buy more without sharing it. You know he drank the rest of mine this morning, right?" At my lover's amused grin, I shake my head, amazed. "He's *such* an ass."

"He's never been quite right," Stephen admits. *That's* putting it mildly. Then he laughs and takes a step closer, so no one passing will overhear. "He stops me, right? And goes, hey Steve, did you know Mikey's *gay*?" The last word is barely audible, a hissed whisper that must be exactly the way my brother gasped it in the store. I have to laugh again. "I was like, oh wait, you didn't know?"

"I just came out to them Saturday." Was it really just a few days ago? It feels like months, years even. "At dinner. We rehearsed it the whole way to my parents' house and as soon as I get up the courage to tell them, Penny calls about Evie. So there went my plan, you know? The whole script, right out the window."

One corner of Stephen's mouth twists in sympathy but I shrug, nonchalant. When I think about the anger I housed earlier, I'm almost surprised that I could have been so damn childish. Aunt Evie isn't to blame for the way my mother reacted to my news, or the way my dad didn't. And neither am I. Under different circumstances, given who they are, who *I* am, I realize that nothing would change. My father would still be distant and uncaring on the surface, a mask he's hidden behind my whole life, and my mom would still try to pin the weight of her own anger and fears on me, it's what she does best. Evie's passing just added fuel to fires that would have burned without her death, I know that now. I can't blame her for the way things happened, no more than I can blame myself.

"It's okay," I tell Stephen, and it is. For the first time all weekend, I can see what everyone meant when they told me over and over again that things would work themselves out, everything would be fine, we'd get by. If nothing else, we'll get by. This funeral will end in a few hours, we'll be okay. Tomorrow the sun will rise, we'll pack the car and say our goodbyes, we'll leave Sugar Creek behind. I'm going to make it, I always have before. Someone once said, "What doesn't kill you makes you stronger." And with a family like mine? I must be strong as hell to have survived this long. I'll make it a little further along down this road called life.

"You're a braver man than me," Stephen says, that shy smile back on his face again. I used to love the way he would smile at me, slowly, like he wasn't sure I would smile back. "My sister knows — how could she not?"

"Because you're twins?" I ask. I never understood how that could be — Stephen's everything his sister isn't, two sides of one coin, everything good in him and everything spiteful and mean in her. Beauty and the beast, I said once ... *only* once, because Stephanie was *fast* and she bruised my arm with her knuckles for that comment. I wonder if she still hits as hard, and to be honest, I really don't care to find out.

But Stephen laughs. "Because she's so damn nosy," he replies. "Being twins has nothing to do with it. She *still* wants to know where I'm going and who I'm on the phone with, jeez." Lowering his voice, he adds softly, "She didn't know about you, though. About what we ..." He sighs, looks at Dan, looks away. "What we used to do."

"It's okay," I whisper. Easing an arm around my lover, I give him a quick wink and say, "He knows."

"Well, she didn't," Stephen says. "After I got back from Evie's the other day, she wanted to know where I went so I told her, to see you. Somehow we got to talking and I guess I let it slip, I don't know, but she's pissed to all hell now."

I rub Dan's back and laugh. "Because she hates me," I say. Then I lean against Dan's arm and murmur, "Thank you for staying with me here."

My lover's reply is a smoldering gaze, a faint smile. "Where else would I want to be?" he asks. "And who could possibly hate you?"

"Steph hates *everyone*," Stephen tells us. "But I think what really has her so upset is that she didn't figure it out herself, you know? All those years we were friends and she never clued in. Like Ray."

"Oh God," I groan. "If she ever heard you comparing her to him ..."

Stephen laughs. "You'd be coming to *my* funeral," he teases. Then, realizing just where we are, he runs a hand through his hair to push it from his face and shakes his head. "That was bad taste, I'm sorry. I didn't mean —"

I hold up a hand to stop him. "It's okay." Unconsciously, my hand drifts to his arm. "Thanks for coming, Steve. I really appreciate it."

That bashful smile again, and he looks up at Dan. "Can I ... would a hug be okay?" he wants to know. His eyes shift to me, full of something I can no longer read. "If not, I understand. I mean, if I were you, I might not —"

I don't let him get any farther. Extracting my hand from my lover's, I pull Stephen into a tight embrace, hugging him hard as if to prove to myself that things are okay between us. With my lips against his ear, I whisper, "I love you, man. Maybe not the way you want me to, but it's there all the same. We've been too much to each other, you know? You're in me, no matter what. You always will be."

He stiffens against me. "I meant what I said," he breathes. He smells like he does in my memory, a mix of the wintergreen mints he favors and Ivory soap, which he's used to wash his hair with for as long as I've known him. "It floats," he told me once, when I asked why. "When you drop it in the tub, you don't have to go searching for it. It just bobs right up to the surface, here I am. And it's easy, just one bar for your whole body, your hair, everything. No farting around with a half million different bottles and tubes and shit like Stephanie has. One bar, that's it. Life can't get much simpler than that."

Now that same scent fills me with a nostalgia so poignant, it brings tears to my eyes and I blink them away. I feel like I'm clinging to him as the memories wash over me. "If you ever find yourself alone," he's saying quietly so Dan won't hear his words, "remember me. I'm here for you, Michael. I always will be. Promise to keep that in mind. Promise you'll think of me."

"I will," I promise, pulling away.

Reluctantly he lets me go. "Thanks," he sighs, but I'm not sure who he's thanking or why. To Dan, he holds out a hand that my lover shakes readily enough, and he says, "You're a lucky guy, but I'm sure I don't need to tell you that."

"No, you don't," Dan admits. One arm finds its way around my waist almost possessively — I'll have to thank him later for standing so stoic through that hug. "It was nice meeting you, Stephen. I'm sorry it couldn't have been under better circumstances but ..." He smiles, pinning my old friend with that look of his that dares anyone to disagree. "I don't think any time is a good one when it comes to something like this."

"Yeah," Stephen sighs. "I almost didn't want to come. I told myself you'd be the jealous type, or ugly, or mean." Looking at me, he admits, "I was sort of hoping for that, I guess, after your sister mentioned a boyfriend. Part of me wants to rescue you, Mike. Even if you don't want me to."

I start to apologize but he shakes his head, cutting me off. "No, it's alright," he tells me. Almost pleading, he asks, "Just keep in mind what I told you? If things don't work out?"

"Sure." Dan's fingers entwine through mine and I hope that Stephen doesn't hold out much hope on that happening in this lifetime. But if it eases his mind to know that I still think of him now and then, I see nothing wrong with that. After everything we were to each other, the least I can do is promise to remember him. He's too much a part of my past, of everything that made me who I am today, to think that somehow this is it. I'll think of him from time to time, I'll send him a card at Christmas, and when things get rough day in and day out, when living falls into a routine, I might close my eyes and he'll be there, laughing on his bike or splashing into the creek, kissing me behind the shed or just lying beside me in the grass, he'll be there. A child again, waiting to play with the child in me. Friends, nothing more.

Nothing less.

From the open doorway, my sister peeks out at the three of us. Her eyes are red-rimmed and raw from crying and when she sees Stephen, she runs a finger along her lower lashes to wipe away smudged eyeliner. "You know there's a funeral today, right?" she asks, her voice thick with tears and just as sarcastic as ever. "Or hey, did you guys forget? Because Ray and I can give your seats up, if you're not planning to attend."

"And you think your sister's bad," I mutter. Stephen laughs, and before Caitlin can speak, I tell her, "We're coming already. You saved us seats?"

"What," she asks, surprised, "you think Mom did? Get in here before she gives them away and you have to stand. This thing's going to take all *day*."

She disappears into the room again and Stephen follows her. "Take care, Mike," he says. "You too, Dan. Take care of him."

"I'll do my best," my lover says.

Dan starts after them but I hold him back. "Wait a minute," I say. The hall has emptied out now, the service about to start, but I wrap my arms around his neck and pull him to me for a sweet kiss. "Thank you," I sigh against his mouth. When he starts to speak, I kiss him again. "Don't ask for what. You already know. For everything."

A third kiss and I let him lead the way, his hand strong and sure in mine.

THE END

About the Author

J. M. SNYDER is a self-published author of gay erotic fiction who lives in Virginia. Always writing, Snyder plans to publish another novel and possibly a short story collection in 2005.

Visit www.jmsnyder.net for excerpts from the author's other published works as well as exclusive fiction, upcoming titles, and purchasing information. Positive feedback, as well as infrequent hate mail, can be sent to the author at jms@jmsnyder.net.

Printed in the United States
96488LV00005B/205-207/A

9 781411 615137

SNMP Application
Developer's Guide

Other VNR Business Technology/Communications Books...

Designing TCP/IP Internetworks
by Geoff Bennett

Information Proficiency: The Key To The
Information Age
by Thomas J. Buckholtz

Doing More Business on the Internet
by Mary J. Cronin

Networking Device Drivers
by Sanjay Dhawan

Routing in Today's Internetworks
by Mark Dickie

Spinning the Web: How To Provide Information
On The Internet
by Andrew Ford

Digital Signal Processing in Communications
by Marvin E. Frerking

The Complete Cyberspace Reference and
Directory
by Gilbert Held

Working With NetWare: For Network
Supervisors and Users
by Gilbert Held

Global Expansion In The Information Age: Big
Planet, Small World
by Thomas J. Howard

Online Marketing Handbook: How To Sell,
Advertise, Publicize, and Promote Your
Products and Services On the Information
Superhighway
by Daniel S. Janal

Digital Telephony and Network Integration,
2nd Edition
by Bernhard E. Keiser and Eugene Strange

Low-Cost E-Mail With UUCP: Integrating
UNIX, DOS, Windows and MAC
by Thomas Wm. Madron

The Illustrated Network Book: A Graphic
Guide to Understanding Computer Networks
by Matthew G. Naugle

Making Telecommuting Happen: A Guide for
Telemanagers and Telecommuters
by Jack M. Nilles

JPEG Still Image Data Compression Standard
by William B. Pennebaker and Joan L. Mitchell

Successful Reengineering: An Implementation
Guide To Using Information Technology
by Daniel Petrozzo and John C. Stepper

Using Wireless Communications in Business
by Andrew M. Seybold

Fax Power: High Leverage Business
Communications
by Philip C. W. Sih

Applications for Distributed Systems and
Network Management
by Kornel Terplan and Jill Huntington-Lee

SNMP Application Developer's Guide
by Robert L. Townsend

A Network of Objects: How To Lower Your
Computing Cost and Improve Your Applications
Delivery
by Thomas C. Tsai

Communications Standard Dictionary,
2nd Edition
by Martin H. Weik, DSc.

SNMP Application Developer's Guide

Robert L. Townsend

VAN NOSTRAND REINHOLD

I(T)P™ A Division of International Thomson Publishing Inc.

New York • Albany • Bonn • Boston • Detroit • London • Madrid • Melbourne
Mexico City • Paris • San Francisco • Singapore • Tokyo • Toronto

Copyright © 1995 by Van Nostrand Reinhold

 Published by Van Nostrand Reinhold, a division of
International Thomson Publishing Inc.
The ITP logo is a trademark under license.

Printed in the United States of America.
For more information, contact:

Van Nostrand Reinhold
115 Fifth Avenue
New York, NY 10003

International Thomson Publishing GmbH
Königswinterer Strasse 418
53227 Bonn
Germany

International Thomson Publishing Europe
Berkshire House 168-173
High Holborn
London WCIV 7AA
England

International Thomson Publishing Asia
221 Henderson Road #05-10
Henderson Building
Singapore 0315

Thomas Nelson Australia
102 Dodds Street
South Melbourne, 3205
Victoria, Australia

International Thomson Publishing Japan
Hirakawacho Kyowa Building, 3F
2-2-1 Hirakawacho
Chiyoda-ku, 102 Tokyo
Japan

Nelson Canada
1120 Birchmount Road
Scarborough, Ontario
Canada M1K 5G4

International Thomson Editores
Campos Eliseos 385, Piso 7
Col. Polanco
11560 Mexico D.F. Mexico

1 2 3 4 5 6 7 8 9 10 QEBFF 01 00 99 98 97 96 95

Library of Congress Cataloging-in-Publication Data

Townsend, R. L. (Robert L.)
  SNMP application developer's guide / R.L. Townsend
      p.   cm.
  Includes index.
  ISBN 0-442-01874-6
  1. Simple Network Management Protocol (Computer network protocol)
I. Title.
  TK5105.5.T69 1995
  005.7'1—dc20
                                                    95-2739
                                                    CIP

Project Management: Jo-Ann Campbell • Production: mle design • 562 Milford Point Rd. • Milford, CT 06460 • 203•878•3793

*To those in my family who gave me the strength
and to those who have written a book before—
they will understand.*

Contents

Introduction

When I was in my teens, my grandmother would tell me about having walked behind a wagon from Missouri to Minnesota; they didn't ride, because they wanted to keep the horses from tiring. She would tell me about the first time she saw a n automobile, and the first airplanes. Now we are in the midst of a technological revolution that is sure to bring as much change for us as the car and airplane did for my grandmother.

Technology is now overwhelming us: it is critical that we get a handle on it. We must manage technology so that it does not manage us. That implies that network management is very important. This book is dedicated to conquering the technology of network management. It will provide all the information required to understand the basics of network management using SNMP, or simple network management protocol. It will also provide significant detail relating to overall network management.

This book provides a comprehensive look at the issues surrounding network management. The focus is on SNMP, but there is much material relating to network management in general.

The material is presented so that no previous knowledge of SNMP is required. You will, however, require some background in computer networking, computer science, or some related understanding. To be able to make use of and understand the C code, the reader should be familiar with the C programming language. I have tried to take a lighthearted approach to the material, but SNMP isn't the most humorous subject in the world.

Throughout the book I have stressed the issues found in the real world. If you are looking for a protocol specification, you will find the book off base; if you are interested in developing an SNMP agent or application, you will find it very useful. Some parts of the book may be dated by the time you read it; the field changes quickly and there is some delay in the publishing process. However, I have done my best to help the practitioner rather than the theorist.

To increase the clarity of the issues, source code has been used throughout the book. A complete listing of the presented code is available on the included diskette. The book also includes a bit of background material, particularly relating to the Internet, which was the birthplace for many of the network protocols.

USING THE SOURCE CODE

About the Source Code

Included with this book is one of the most complete sets of SNMP source code available, from both the Massachusetts Institute of Technology (MIT) and Carnegie-Mellon University (CMU).

The source code was selected from a number of public domain versions. The selection criteria were portability, functionality, and appropriate comments, which were particularly important because documentation of public domain code is generally limited.

The MIT code represents an early effort. This code was called SNMP; its name was later changed to version 2, or SNMPv2. The CMU code was selected to represent SNMP version 1, since it is the basis of many of the commercial products in use today. The disk contains source for data encryption standard (DES) and serial communications as well.

The last directory on the diskette contains the requests for comments, or RFCs, that relate to SNMP, some of which are also available in a more complete form on the Internet.

Loading the Source Code

You should load the source code onto your system now, so you have access to the examples and RFCs. To load the material, simply place the disk in the appropriate drive, change your directory to that drive, and type install. Should something go wrong and the automatic installation does not work, copy the files onto your hard disk, uncompress them using—pkunzip, which is included on diskette, then untar them using the tar utility, also included.

The pkunzip command format is:

```
pkunzip <source file name>
```

The tar command format is:

```
tar-xvf <file name>
```

The source code requires a great deal of hard disk space. The install menu provides for a partial load of the source code. It may be wise to load one part at a time to assure sufficient disk space.

Internet Access

Anyone who is active in any area of computer science, especially those involved in the development of software, should have Internet access. Whether you are developing software or just hacking, the Internet is as important as any other development tool you use.

Along with public domain source code, you gain access to newsgroups and a world of information. No matter what the question, you can find some newsgroups somewhere whose members are ready to show just how much they know by answering your question. There are even newsgroups to tell you how to gain access to the Internet, on alt.internet.services.

One word of caution is in order regarding newsgroups subscription. There are hundreds of megabytes of information posted each week. You may want to subscribe to a limited number of groups until you see just how much information is downloaded; otherwise the phone line charges will be excessive unless you live in an area with local access.

If you are doing SNMP development there are three newsgroups that you will want to join as soon as you can:

- comp.protocols.snmp

- info.nysersnmp

- info.snmp

Many of the protocols related to SNMP have newsgroups also, such as the TCP/IP (transmission control protocol/internet protocol) group, SLIP (serial line over IP), and PPP (point-to-point protocol).

Some of the better known companies that provide access to the Internet are:

Performance Systems International, Inc.
PO. Box 2986
Reston, VA 22090-9862
(703) 620-6651

CompuServe
5000 Arlington Centre Boulevard
Columbus, OH 43220
(800) 848-8990

Prodigy
445 Hamilton Avenue
White Plains, NY 10601
(800) 284-5933

America Online
8619 Westwood Center Drive
Vienna, VA
(800) 227-6364

Delphi
3 Blackstone Street
Cambridge, MA
(800) 544-4005

Dialog
3460 Hillview Avenue
Palo Alto, CA
(800) 334-2564

GEnie
401 N. Washington Street
Rockville, MD 20850
(800) 638-9636

Organization

The book is organized in a manner that reflects the steps that must be taken to implement SNMP. It starts with basic information in Chapters 1 and 2 relating to how to get started. Chapter 3 lays the groundwork for SNMP development, giving you a basic understanding of network management and the protocol. Chapter 4 takes you into the supporting protocols. It provides an overview of the transport protocols and some of the issues relating to SNMP communications. Chapter 5 goes into the SNMP internals and lays the basis for Chapter 6, which deals with the management information base, or MIB. Chapter 7 provides MIB tool information and information about standard MIBs. Chapters 8 through 12 take up issues of the SNMP protocol itself. Chapter 13 describes an agent implementation based on the MIB code included on the diskettes.

As you can see, this book is not intended to provide the details of the protocol. It is intended to help get the protocol up and operational. All too often, people believe the problem is getting the protocol functional, when the real issue is the peripheral material. Most public domain agents function just fine; what you need to do is get them compiled on a target system, and correct any problems they have. But what about a MIB, what about traps, what about a protocol stack? Those are the issues addressed here. Most programmers can take the source code from the diskettes and have the agent up and operational in a week.

I hope that everyone will find this book useful and readable. Let's cut to the chase: Welcome to the world of SNMP and network management.

1

Overview

BACKGROUND

Computer networks are everywhere, in various sizes and architectures. The largest of them is the national network, commonly referred to as the Internet. It crosses the country as a highway of high speed communications circuits operating at 45 megabytes per second. The original network had thirteen hubs with primary connections to the backbone. The National Science Foundation (NSF), IBM and the University of Michigan (MERIT) founded the current Internet in the mid-80s under the name NFSNET. The NSF provided funding, IBM provided research and equipment, and Merit provided operations. Today, the NSFNET connects to many other networks, such as the NASA Science Internet, and links hundreds of universities, researchers, several super computers, and many individuals.

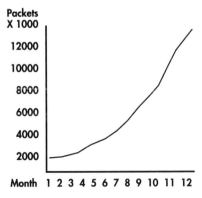

Figure 1.1. The first year traffic on the NSFNET.

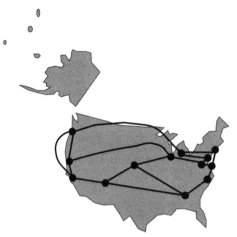

Figure 1.2. The Original NSFNET Configuration.

I had the opportunity to work with Paul Bosco, IBM and one of the original Internet promoters. Bosco consulted with me regarding performance issues; he was sure from the start that the Internet would grow so rapidly that performance would be a major issue, and his assumption proved to be correct. Within two years the network had outgrown the T1 lines (U.S. standard line speed, primarily for phone lines) and the older IBM RTs. RTs were IBM's original AIX workstations.

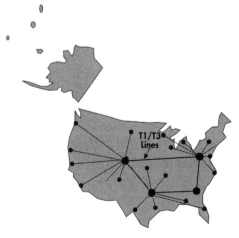

Figure 1.3 The current Internet Configuration.

When the Internet picked up the traffic from a couple of older networks, a desperate need for more bandwidth was created. I developed and deployed a number of performance enhancements that helped the network continue until the new RS6000 machines and T3 lines (U.S. standard line speed primarily for phone lines) could be deployed. The performance of the RS6000s relieved the strain at the time, but even that technology would soon be outgrown.

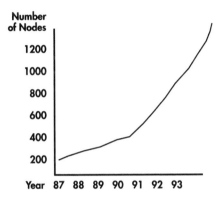

Figure 1.4 Worldwide growth.

Shortly after the cut over to T3, the planners began to work on fiber-distributed data interface (FDDI) speed equipment. Bosco believed that even FDDI would not provide all the bandwidth needed and went off to do some research with MIT on SONET (Synchronous Optical NETwork) speed equipment. I saw a need for network management and stayed on to help with that. It was then that I became involved with SNMP. It was clear that the network would need some sort of management. After all, there were sites located out in the middle of nowhere, and when something went wrong someone would have to visit the site. This was not a task that anyone wanted. Given the topology, some form of network management would help.

As I became involved with network management I also became involved with the request for comments (RFC) process and stayed with this effort for almost two years. After working on the theoretical aspects of network management, I wanted to really utilize this knowledge doing commercial implementations.

Network management became my main focus for a number of years. I worked with several proprietary network management systems as well as SNMP. I spent most of my time in the real world, working with more than a dozen clients to help them implement SNMP. It became clear that many people misunderstood SNMP, and few understood the difficulty of implementing it correctly.

SCOPE

The simple network management protocol has been well received by the industry. Virtually every vendor of network equipment must offer SNMP to be a player in the marketplace. After all, 911 emergency phone systems, cellular phone systems, and lottery systems have been using SNMP for management and control for years. SNMP is growing at a rate of 100 percent a year, and this growth rate has made knowledge of SNMP and TCP/IP necessary for every computer science professional.

SNMP is growing so quickly that it is being used over various transport protocols that do not support it as well as user datagram protocol (UDP). When SNMP was developed, only limited thought went into utilizing it with other transport protocols. SNMP was considered to be a short-term fix, while other standards were formalized. In reality it has done much the same thing that TCP has done, gained a large base that will be difficult to displace. This leads me to believe that SNMP will be with us for a long while.

Additionally, I feel that SNMPv2 will not be as forthcoming as its designers would believe. The designers may have spent too much time on theory and not enough time with the end user/implementor. The security and complexity have made it difficult to implement and there is not enough motivation to make the leap. The time spent on V2 may have actually taken some of the fire out of SNMP as a whole. Only time will tell, but if we look at OSI we might realize that if it is to complex or takes to long to implement it will lose market share. The best widget in the world isn't worth doing if it can not be sold.

Since SNMP continues to penetrate other transport protocols, there is a complete chapter dedicated to utilizing SNMP with other transport layers. It is not as extensive as it could be but it does give sufficient detail to begin an implementation with other protocols.

The first part of the book will take you through an orderly progression of SNMP, such that the reader will be able to handle any implementation of SNMP. You should come away with enough knowledge of network management to deal with most issues that come along. Yet you will not find a rehash of the protocol, you can get that from the RFCs. The book focuses on what it takes to get SNMP up and operating. The protocol has been designed by others and now it is ours to use. If what you want is to recreate the wheel and build another SNMP package you will find this lacking. If you have a package, even if it is public domain, this material will be just what you need to get it operational.

SNMP OVERVIEW

It is often thought that SNMP is a map of some network with a full color user interface. Nothing could be farther from the truth. SNMP is a protocol that runs under all of those colorful user interfaces. SNMP itself is content to operate in the background on a system and the casual observer would not realize that SNMP was even functioning. SNMP provides hand shaking between two systems. The systems will communicate information that relates to conditions of equipment or even intangibles. Intangibles being such things as general system condition, which is intangible in that you really cannot touch it. This may come from some calculation that is done on the server (agent) side of the handshaking. This information is generally requested by the client (management) side. This request comes in the form of a Protocol Data Unit (PDU). This request will traverse a network using the normal network facilities. The transport protocol and manner by which the network does its job is of no consequence to SNMP. The management station just sends out an SNMP PDU with the intent of using the information that is returned. The information that is returned may be applied to a sophisticated program that analysis the data or simply displayed on the screen for a person to evaluate. This book will deal only with the agent (server) side of the handshaking equation. The management side will be left for another day and other work. Generally the management side will consist of a product such as HP OpenView or some other management platform. Those platforms will then be expanded to cover the specifics of the network they are to be used in. Although they can provide some of the basics as soon as they are installed they cannot have the kind of intelligence needed without a great deal of software development.

Recognizing this fact, many vendors have added additional applications on top of management software. HP has added an Operations Center and is soon to announce other applications that will provide a degree of knowledge on the management station. Many vendors are adding capabilities such as "trouble ticket" generation, dispatching and other functionality that brings them closer to really managing a network.

Since the focus here is on the agent (server) side of the equation we should understand what the agent is. To better understand what it is we can look at what it is not. What it is not means what it does not do. It does not:

- function as a communications protocol
- provide a graphics interface
- inherently know about your hardware or software
- know about errors or other problems
- know about the management environment

So the next question is what does it do? Well SNMP will do a great deal but it does not have that knowledge inherently. That knowledge comes in the form of a Management Information Base (MIB). This MIB as it is called has values contained in it, much as a data base would. That is probably why it is often referred to as a database. It is actually much like a database. The dot notation used to refer to the MIB values actually provides a reference into the data. The agent will parse this dot notation, using it to get to the value that is to be returned to the management side. This value can be calculated, static or could have been updated by another application. This MIB and how it is constructed is a key element of SNMP and it will be covered in detail in this work.

A number of network products are discussed along with several new technologies. A number of the products discussed are offered on the HP OpenView platform and by a number of other vendors that remarket OpenView under their label.

FURTHER STUDY

For more information regarding topics introduced in this chapter, see *Your LAN and the Internet*, by Mark Gibbs, Network World Magazine (November 8, 1993).

REFERENCES

Fisher, Sharon. *Communications Week*, "Secure SNMP, Anyone?" April 4, 1994.

Telecommunications Magazine, Cover Story. May 1993.

An Executive Introduction to HP OpenView, Developer NSM Platform Products.

2

Vital Data

INTRODUCTION

There is a good deal of generalized information that is important to those trying to develop an agent or any other product relating to SNMP. This chapter
covers that information. It has everything from data relating to classes, vendors, and more. It is a smorgasbord that should prove to be of value to everyone. It is being presented early on so you can get in touch with the people or
companies needed to get the wheels turning. It will not require a detailed reading, but you will want to know what material it contains. Much of the material
here has been gathered directly from material presented on the Internet in the
SNMP news group forum.

THE DATA

The Simple Network Management Protocol is a protocol for Internet network
management. Formally specified in a number of RFCs, all of the material is
openly available. These RFCs are all contained on the disk that comes with
this work. Many of the early RFCs are of little value and are probably not
worth obtaining, while others are very useful.

Below is a break out of the more important RFCs.

- RFC 1155—Structure and Identification of Management Information for
  TCP/IP-based internets

- RFC 1156—Management Information Base Network Management of
  TCP/IP-based internets

- RFC 1157—A Simple Network Management Protocol
- RFC 1158—Management Information Base Network Management of TCP/IP based internets: MIB
- RFC 1212—Concise MIB Definitions
- RFC 1213—Management Information Base for Network Management of TCP/IP-based internets: MIB
- RFC 1215—A Convention for Defining Traps for use with the SNMP
- RFC 1442—Structure of Management Information for Version 2 of SNMP
- RFC 1444—Conformance Statements for Version 2 of SNMP
- RFC 1445—Administrative Model for Version 2 of SNMP
- RFC 1446—Security Protocols for Version 2 of SNMP
- RFC 1447—Party MIB for Version 2 of SNMP
- RFC 1448—Protocol Operations for Version 2 of SNMP

WHERE TO FIND MATERIAL

As mentioned, there are a number of RFCs contained on the diskettes, but you may find that there is other material that is not available. You can get any or all RFCs in a number of different ways. You can get them from the Internet, CD-ROM, and via Hard Copy.

You can get access to the Internet via a number of providers. A number of them are presented in the table below. The list is not complete, nor does inclusion of a provider make a statement of the quality of that provider.

Network	Service Area	
ANS	U.S. and International	(800) 456-8267
CERFNet	Northern CA	(415) 723-7520
CICnet	Midwest	(313) 998-6102
INet	Indiana	(812) 855-4240
JVNCNet	U.S.	(800)35TIGER
MIDnet	MID U.S.	(402) 472-5032
MSEN	Michigan	(313) 554-8649
NevadaNet	Nevada	(702) 784-6133
NovX	North West	(206) 447-0800
NYSERnet	NY, NY	(212) 443-4120
PREPnet	Pennsylvania	(412) 268-7870
PSCNET	Eastern U.S.	(412) 268-4960
PSInet	U.S.	(800) 82PSI82
SDSCnet	San Diego	(619) 534-5043
SURAnet	South West	(301) 982-4600
THEnet	Texas	(512) 471-3241
UUNET/Alternet	U.S.	(800) 4UUNET3
WiscNet	Wisconsin	(608) 262-8874
WVNET	Pacific	(206) 262-8874

Table 2.1 Network Access

Through the Internet

RFCs can be obtained from a service provided by RFC-INFO@ISI.EDU. You can use this service in several ways. You can ask for a list of RFCs or request them by RFC number. The lists can be searched by key such as author's name, title, date, etc. To use the service you must log into RFC-INFO@ISI.EDU with your requests in the body of the message. The request is not case sensitive.

To start you may want to request the manual. That is done by using the request:

```
help:manual
```

If you use the Internet to gather the RFCs you are cautioned to check everything along the way. Many things change daily on the Internet, and by the time this work makes it to print, the material may be dated.

You can also get RFCs at various sites through out the United States by logging in as:

```
name = anonymous
password = guest
```

Some of the locations that contain RFCs are:

- ftp.internic.net

- ftp.uu.net

- merit.edu

- nis.nsf.net

- src.doc.ic.ac.uk

- animal-farm.nevada.edu

- cs.columbia.edu

- world.std.com

A word of caution is due here. If you download all the RFCs, and you are being billed for the network time, you may want to consider what RFCs are important to you. If you download them all, make sure your bank will give you the loan you will need to pay for the service.

If you use any of these sites you can use remote printing sites as well. These sites can be used for any remote printing but we present them in the context of requesting RFCs.

Country	Code	Area Code	Location
U.S.	+1	408, 415, 510	Bay Area
U.S.	+1	317	Michigan
U.S.	+1	313	U of Mich.
U.S.	+1	301	So. Maryland
U.S.	+1	212	Staten Is.
U.S.	+1	202	Washington, DC
Netherlands	+31		Amsterdam
U.S.	+1	617	O'Reill & Assoc
U.S.	+1	718	Queens, Bronx
U.S.	+1	818	Riverside, CA
U.S.	+1	909	Chino, CA
U.S.	+1	917	NY, NY
Australia	+61		Melbourne

Table 2.2 Remote Printer Sites.

The table depicts only the area that has remote printer sites. You can find these sites in your area, through the phone directory, listed under printers.

Hardcopy

There are a number of sites from which hardcopy can be obtained, they are:

- DDN Network Information Center
  Government Systems, Inc.
  14200 Park Meadow Drive, Suite 200
  Chantilly, VA   22021
  Ph. (703) 802-4535; Fax (703) 802-8376

- SRI International
  Network Information Systems Center
  333 Ravenwood Avenue, Room EJ291
  Menlo Park, CA 94025
  Ph. (415) 859-6387; Fax (415) 859-6028
  E-mail: nisc@nisc.sri.com
  2.3.3 Via CD-Rom

You can get a CD Rom with all the RFCs from:

- Info Magic
  P.O. Box 708
  Rock Hill, NJ 08553-0708
  Ph. (800) 800-6613
  Ph. (609) 683-5501
  Various titles and pricing

- Walnut Creek CDROM
  1547 Palos Verdes Mall, Suite 260
  Walnut Creek, CA 94596
  Ph. (800) 786-9907
  Ph. (510) 947-5996
  Various titles and pricing

- In Europe, contact:
  CDROM Versand
  Helga Seyb
  Fuchsweg 86
  Tel: +49-8106-302210

ADDITIONAL INFORMATION

With the growing popularity of the Internet, the ways to access information have grown at the same rate. The type of information you want access to can also dictate the way it is accessed. For example, if there is a mailing list for the information you want, you need only subscribe; the systems will do the rest. Some of the mailing lists that are important to the SNMP community are presented below. It is a great way to keep up with what is going on. No matter how shy you may be, you need only read; no response or comment is required. It will only take a short period of time before you know the names of all the regulars. You may even wonder if some of the people do any work or just read and send mail.

Mailing Lists

- SNMP mailing list—SNMP@psi.net
  A discussion of the current hot topics in the SNMP community.

- ISO mailing list—iso@nic.ddn.mil
  Discussion of ISO standards, in some cases related to SNMP.

Each mailing list has its own benefit. There are other mailing lists relating to protocols and general discussions that may be of value as well. They can be found and checked out by cruising the Internet with any of the various packages available.

User Groups

- ISO news group—comp.protocols.iso
  Relating to ISO standards, in some cases relative to SNMP

- SNMP news group—comp.protocols.snmp
  Relating to SNMP
  SRI International
  Network Information Systems Center
  333 Ravenwood Avenue, Rm EJ291
  Menlo Park, CA 94025
  Ph. (415) 859-6387
  Fax (415) 859-6028
  E-mail nisc@nisc.sri.com [2]

BOOKS AND RELATED WRITING

There are a number of good works and each offers something different. Some are reworks of the protocol; others offer insight that is only available from those who have been in the trenches. I have added some commentary that is relevant to each work.

- *The Simple Book: An Introduction to Management*
  of TCP/IP-based Internets
  by: Marshall T. Rose
  ISBN 0-13-812611-9
  © 1991 Prentice-Hall, Inc.

This book was one of the first SNMP works and still serves as a primary reference for many people. It has a good deal of insight into the protocol.

- *The Simple Book: (Second Edition)*
  by: Marshall T. Rose
  ISBN 0-13-177254-6
  © 1994 Prentice-Hall, Inc.

This is the second edition of this work. It takes into account the changes that have taken place but it still focuses on the protocol and that may be what you are looking for. If you are using someone else's agent, you may not want so much of the protocol and more of how it works.

- *SNMP, SNMP V2 and CMIP:*
  The Practical Guide to Network Management Standards
  by: William Stallings
  ISBN 0-201-63331-0
  © 1993 Addison-Wesley Publishing Co, Inc.

A second printing of *SNMP, SNMPv2, and CMIP: The Practical Guide to Network Management* (Addison-Wesley, 1993) is now in bookstores. For anyone with a first printing, an errata sheet is available via anonymous ftp in the file SNMP.errata in directory ftp/pub on aw.com.

This work has a good deal of information in all areas. It tends to cover just about everything you could want as far as the protocol and the world of SNMP. Initially it received some unfair criticism. In some chapters you can tell what the issues of the moment were by the writing.

NOTE: Everyone should understand that books take months to get in print and can easily appear somewhat behind in a field that changes as fast as this. (I suppose it could be that I am just getting slow in my old age and the information is not really coming that fast. Where did I leave that crutch?)

- *Network Management: A Practical Perspective*
  by: Allan Leinwand and Karen Fang
  ISBN 0-201-52771-5
  © 1993 Addison-Wesley Publishing Co, Inc.

This is more directed at network management in general than SNMP specifically.

- *Internetworking with TCP/IP (3 Volumes)*
  Volume 1: Principles, Protocols, and Architecture
  by: Douglas E. Comer
  ISBN 0-13-468505-9 (Note: 2nd Edition)
  © 1991 Prentice-Hall, Inc.

This work has a good deal of information related to TCP/IP with chapters 25, 26 and 27 devoted to SNMP. This is early SNMP yet still very good background information.

- *Volume 2: Design, Implementation, and Internals*
  by: Douglas E. Comer and David Stevens
  ISBN 0-13-472242-6
  © 1992 Prentice-Hall, Inc.

This work has a lot of TCP/IP information with chapters 18, 19 and 20 relating to SNMP. It provides a good deal of code for study and some excellent concepts. The whole book starts to take on the feel of object-oriented coding and design that is beneficial when dealing with ASN.1 and many of the OO (Object Oriented) languages.

- *Volume 3: Client-Server Programming and Applications*
  by: Douglas E. Comer and David Stevens
  ISBN 0-13-474222-2 (Note: BSD Socket Version)
  © 1993 Prentice-Hall, Inc

This book is included primarily for its completeness.

- *Open Systems Networking: OSI & TCP/IP*
  by: David Piscitello and A. L. Chapin
  ISBN 0-201-56334-7
  © 1993 Addison-Wesley

Primarily relating to OSI, this book also contains material about TCP/IP and SNMP.

- *Managing Internetworks with SNMP*
  by: Mark A. Miller, P.E.
  ISBN 1-55851-304-3
  © 1993 M&T Books, New York, NY

The title is somewhat deceptive, since it would lead you to believe that the work was from a management perspective. It actually relates heavily to the understanding of SNMP. It is a good work for understanding the protocol through case studies.

- *Understanding SNMP MIBs*
  by David Perkins
  © 1992 David Perkins

This work is published by David Perkins and can be obtained via E-mail at dperkins@synoptics.com. It isn't clear what the cost is but it is worth what ever the cost.

- *Network Management Tools Catalog*
  by R. Stine
  NOC Tools Working Group

This work is available on the Internet at noctools@merit.edu. This work contains a number of tools that are worth knowing about. Specific to SNMP it has information related to an SNMP library and an SNMP Trap Deamon. Many of the products listed are commercial products.

- *There's Gold in them thar Networks!*
  by J. Martin
  Ohio State University
  RFC 1402

A good deal of information related to the Internet. How to get source code, books, etc.

- *A Laymans Guide to a Subset of ASN.1, BER and DER*
  by Burton Kaliski Jr.
  RSA Data Security, Inc.
  Redwood, CA

A good deal of information relating to encoding and decoding rules.

TRAINING, SEMINARS, AND MORE...

This is not intended to be an extensive list. It is merely a selective list of companies that will be around by the time this work gets out. The companies listed here have a long history of quality and reliability.

- Interop Company
  480 San Antonio Road
  Mountain View, CA 94040
  Ph. (415) 962-2522
  Fax (415) 966-5010
  E-Mail: onsite@interop.com

- Network World Technical Seminars
  Ph. (800) 643-4668 (direct: 508-820-7493)
  Fax (800) 756-9430
  [Fax back line, ask for document 55]

- Technology Conversion, Inc.
  3326 Transit Avenue
  Sioux City, IA 51106
  Ph. (712) 276-4024

One of the newest commercial products for the Internet is a product called Mosaic. It has been around in a number of forms for some time and is now commercially available from:

- Mosaic Communications Corp.
  650 Castro St. #500
  Mountain View, CA 94041
  Ph. (415) 254-1900

This is one of the best ways to navigate the Internet when looking for information.

PERIODICALS ORIENTED TO SNMP AND NETWORKING

There are more periodicals for the computer industry than any other. A complete list is outside the scope of this book, but I have listed some that seem to be more relevant than the rest.

- One bi-monthly newsletter is "SIMPLE TIMES"
  You can subscribe via email at st-subscriptions@simple-times.org
  ConneXions, The Interoperability Report
  480 San Antonio Road, Suite 100
  Mountain View, CA 94040
  Ph. (415) 941-3399
  Fax (415) 949-1779

- IBM Internet Journal
  12225 Greenville Ave., Suite 700
  Dallas, Texas 75243
  Ph. (214) 669-9000

- Network World
  161 Worcester Rd.
  Framingham, MA 01701
  Ph. (508) 820-3467

- Network Computing
  600 Community Drive
  Manhasset, NY 11030
  Ph. (708) 647-6834

STANDARDS ORGANIZATIONS

- ISO Standards
  1, Rue de varembe
  CH-1211
  Geneva 20
  Switzerland
  41 22 749-0111

- National Institute of Standards and Technology
  Rm B-64
  Technology Building 225
  Gaithersburg, MD 20899
  Ph. (301) 975-2816

- DDN Network Information Center
  Government Systems, Inc.
  14200 Park Meadow Drive, Suite 200
  Chantilly, VA 22021
  Ph. (703) 802-4535; Fax (703) 802-8376

- ISO and ANSI Standards
  American National Standards Institute
  11 West 42nd. Street; 13th floor
  New York, NY 10036
  Ph. (212) 642-4900

SNMP AGENT VENDORS

- Paul Freeman and Associates
  14 Pleasant Street; PO BOX 2067
  Westford, MA 01886-5067
  pwilson@world.std.com

- Performance Systems International, Inc.
  11800 Sunrise Valley Drive; Suite 1100
  Reston, VA 22091
  Ph. (703) 620-6651

- SNMP Research, Inc.
  3001 Kimberlin Heights Rd.
  Knoxville, TN 37920
  Ph. (615) 573-1434

- Epilogue Technology Corp.
  P.O. Box 217
  Capitola, CA 95010-0217
  Ph. (408) 426-8786

- Hewlett-Packard
  Network & System Management Division
  3404 East Harmony Road
  Fort Collins, CO 80525
  Ph. (303) 229-3800

- Technology Conversion, Inc.
  3326 Transit Avenue
  Sioux City, IA 51106
  Ph. (712) 276-4024

FOR FURTHER STUDY

The following document contains useful information that is beyond the scope of this chapter:

Krol, Ed. *The Whole Internet User's Guide and Catalog.* ISBN 1-56592-025-2. November, 1992. (Informative—relating to Internet access and usage.)

REFERENCES

Baker, Steven. *UNIX Review*, "The Evolving Internet Backbone." September, 1993.

Cikoski, Tom. *FAQ (Frequently Asked Questions)*. Newsletter on newsgroup.

3

Network Management

INTRODUCTION

Network management at first glance appears to be a clear-cut issue of monitoring and control. Yet a closer look makes it clear that perspective plays an important role. Examine what network management means to the average corporation. The management perspective can be broken down to multiple perspectives, none of which would be at a low component level. The network support personnel may never relate to any perspective other than the component level, having no knowledge of the management view.

The problem becomes even worse for network equipment manufacturers. Let's consider network management from a hub manufacturer's point of view. It is easy for that vendor to see network management from the hub looking out.

All too often the communications manufacturers are driven by this one-sided perspective which is held by their technical staff. It is their perspective, but it may not be a marketable perspective. The developer must consider what the end user wants and is willing to pay a premium for. As in the computer industry, the networking area is full of better ideas that do not have a market, while the customer longs for solutions.

This book takes the perspective of its user, the SNMP developer. It does not go into the theory or the debates that surround network management. The academic types can do that.

NETWORK MANAGEMENT CONSIDERED

Network management has two main requirements, monitoring, and control. Both have various levels—physical, logical, and topology. The two requirements apply to each of the five types of management.

- Fault Management
- Accounting Management
- Configuration Management
- Performance Management
- Security Management

Network management has taken many approaches to providing network management. Some were proprietary, while others have been open protocols. Some of the protocols used include:

- HEMS—High level Entity Management
- SGMP—Simple Gateway Monitoring Protocol
- SNMP—Simple Network Management Protocol
- CMIP—Common Management Information Protocol

All of these management protocols have made an effort to manage all or a portion of a network, each gaining its own degree of success and acceptance. Each has addressed different problems of network management in different ways, some times similar and some times very different. None has gained the popular support that SNMP has. Part of that popularity is simple timing. With the expansion of the Internet and technology, SNMP was at the right place at the right time and had many of the characteristics needed. Yet it was far from an ideal solution, and there is an ever growing use of CMIP and CMIP over TCP. CMIP over TCP is often referred to as CMOT, but the CMOT RFC is outdated and the reference incorrect.

SNMP has at times received some bad press. On occasion people have been critical of its short comings, without having an alternative. No matter how SNMP is viewed, it solves some of the problems and fills a need. Whether it evolves to be the ultimate solution to network management only time will tell. Surely network management as well as SNMP will continue to evolve.

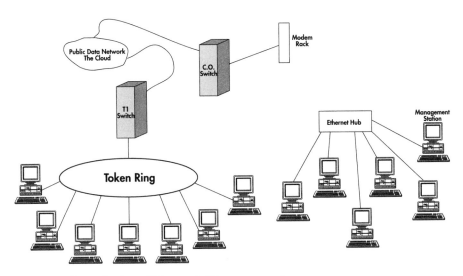

Figure 3.1 Complexity of Network Management.

Figure 3.1 shows just how complex a network can be. This growing complexity would be difficult for any network management system. SNMP was not meant to be the end. It was designed and developed to be an interim solution. Even if it had been intended to be a long-lived solution, the complexity of networks could become impossible to deal with. For example, contemplate the possibility of a network that bridged several states via leased lines and interconnected 100 sites with 2000 nodes. This is an actual implementation for which SNMP is used. The 2000 nodes are POS (Point of Sale) registers and the goal is to keep a hundred stores on-line. The network complexity exceeds anything that could be designed on a network map or even on a layered map, yet SNMP is expected to deal with such a net. SNMP actually does a reasonable job. How to represent the network graphically presents more problems. Another problem is that there are so many TRAPS (SNMP Error Notifications) at times that the network monitoring stations are overwhelmed.

As network management has evolved, there has been the perception that it is a new technology. In reality, network management has been around since the early days of computing in various forms. The early mainframes developed sophisticated networks and learned to manage them. The mainframe environments can require the management of thousands of devices. SNMP implementations, on the other hand, have trouble supporting several hundred devices. One could ask why, if we have progressed, we can not deal with the number of elements that the early mainframes could? The answer is in the complexity of the networks. The number of elements that a mainframe would manage could be quite large but they were all of a set number of types. A mainframe may manage hundreds of 3270 pieces of equipment. With limited types of equipment, using few protocols, network management is not a problem. Networks managed by SNMP may have those same 3270s talking SNA (System Network Architecture) over SDLC (Synchronous Data Link Control) through an IP network across X.25 (CCITT Standard Protocol for Transport Level) into a router on to a FDDI ring back out to a token ring back to a mainframe. This example makes it clear that the complexity of such networks far exceeds the mainframe network.

Because of this growth and expansion, many of the old ideas of network management become outdated. Protocols such as SNMP are replacing the proprietary management systems. SNMP can be used to manage complex networks thanks to the Management Information Base (MIB) concept. The MIB can be expanded to include information about all of the equipment on the network. The MIB creates the feel of an "open" architecture because the key elements of the equipment must be part of the MIB.

This requirement that the elements of the managed equipment be known to SNMP, and the MIB can, at times, create problems. As the network grows, so must the understanding and information relating to the network. The information contained in the MIB can grow very large. As the network grows, it can become very difficult to represent all of the MIB data in a reasonable manner for viewing.

Additionally the growth of information consumes more and more Network Management Station (NMS) resources. The growth comes mostly in the form of data structures used to hold MIB information. The actual data should be dynamic, since an intelligent cache scheme is impossible to build, yet the data structures are required to provide a memory location for data manipulation. In some cases this memory can be reduced through dynamic allocation, but that requires extra CPU cycles and the agent can possibly run out of memory at runtime, causing other problems.

Most of the commercial management systems address those problems in one way or another, yet no one seems to really have the answer. Companies, such as HP, have taken the approach of Distributed Management. Still others suggest layering the components of the network, while others use multiple NMSs and manage a limited number of components with each station.

SNMP Network Management

The Internet community has adopted Simple Network Management Protocol as the standard for network management. The SNMP protocol uses a query-response model, also viewed as a client/server. The client/manager end generates the queries. The server/agent generates the response. SNMP gives a management station the ability to query a piece of equipment for parameters relating to that device. The client can also generate a command to change a parameter on the agent. In addition, SNMP gives the agent the ability to notify the management station when events happen.

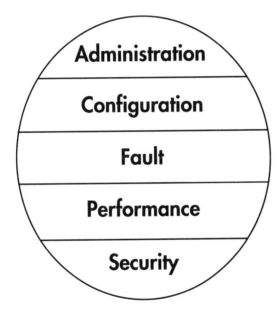

Figure 3.2 Management Functionality.

The whole SNMP environment has evolved in part with the IEEE network management mentality and in part with the OSI mentality. This combination of thinking formed a protocol that is functional while having a growth path as well as a degree of compatibility. (I am using the term compatibility very loosely in this case.)

The SNMP model and the OSI (CMIP) model do not map directly to each other. The OSI model utilizes the commands:

- get   retrieve information
- set   change values

- action   performs a command

- create   forms a new instance of the object

- delete   removes a specified object instance

- event-report   signals that an event of importance has taken place

The SNMP model uses the command set:

- get   retrieve information

- set   change values

- getnext used to retrieve the next value in a table or row

- trap   signals that an event of importance has taken place

Some SNMP agents and managers have expanded functionality that comes close to a direct map between the two. Packages such as PEER and HP OpenView have expanded the templates to accommodate a near-direct mapping. Others have made no attempt at mapping. The industry trend is moving towards a one-to-one mapping or complete replacement of SNMP with the CMIP model. This trend is in part being driven by the telephone companies (telecos). Many have gone directly to a CMIP implementation using such products as the Redix CMIP/OSI stack. The current CMIP implementations are few and far between, but their numbers are growing every day. The problem is the same as with TCP/IP vs. the OSI Stack, the current product base. Can those using SNMP be converted to CMIP?

CMIP is gaining popularity in many circles. Such prominent vendors as HP, IBM, and AT&T offer CMIP implementations. HP and IBM both utilize the same ISO stack while AT&T utilizes the USL (UNIX Software Labs) ISO stack. The functionality available through the use of CMIP suggests that it may be utilized more and more in the future. CMIP is discussed throughout this book.

IEEE Network Management Model

Many of the works that have come from the IEEE have come under the 802 project heading. This project comes as a series of documents titled 802.X. This framework did not even begin to deal with the need for network management. Because of this the nature of network management under 802 is to provide some services at the lower layer while allocating the majority of the responsibility to the upper layers. The 802 projects were all started long before the network management issues came to the forefront.

The 802 concept of network management comes in the form of CMIP. There are a number of elements involved in this architecture, they are:

- LAN MANAGEMENT SERVICE (LMMS) which defines the services available to the user of LMMS.

- LAN MANAGEMENT PROTOCOL ENTITY (LMMPE) defines the element that is actually responsible for communicating the management information through data exchanges.

- CONVERGENCE PROTOCOL ENTITY (CPE) defines reliability and other protocol characteristics of the transport.

This provides a minimal framework for network management. It is not nearly strong enough to deal with all of the network management issues of today's vast networks. It does provide potential for the lower transport layers.

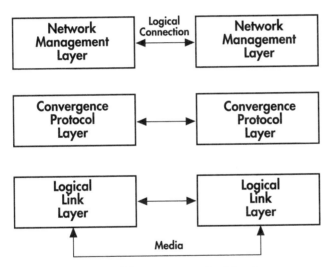

Figure 3.3 IEEE Management Architecture.

OSI Network Management Model

The OSI model, developed much later than the 802 model, provides more support for current notion of network management. It provides for network management by category. That is to say, network management is a given, and it is simply divided into categories. Those categories are:

- Fault management that defines the detection, isolation, and correction of abnormal operations.

- Accounting management that defines the ability to establish charges and identify costs.

- Configuration management that defines control of equipment and the collection of data relating to the equipment.

- Performance management that defines the performance related behaviors.

- Security management that provides for establishing and reporting security mechanisms.

These categories cover the various elements network management, but do not provide for a comprehensive approach to network management.

SNMP Network Management Model

SNMP was developed initially with thinking from both of the architectures outlined above. SNMPv2 has moved more in the direction of the OSI model. This move has also resolved some of the complaints about V1 while creating others. The evolution of SNMP will make an evolution to an OSI environment easier when and if the time came. Although many would say that SNMP is here to stay and OSIs network management will fall by the wayside, the development of SNMPv2 did help to achieve an environment that is more compatible with that of OSI. The problem is that the cost is complex, and, as could be expected, the marketplace has not accepted those changes well. To date, few vendors have chosen to implement SNMPv2. Some major organizations, such as Lawrence Livermore Labs, have chosen other alternatives that are easier.

Although it must be said that recent improvements from the user community may correct some of the over-kill of V2 Security, some of the proposals would reduce the security requirements of SNMPv2. This has been the major issue. The use of Data Encryption Standard (DES) has made V2 implementation complex, and since DES cannot be exported, it has also created a number of marketing issues. There are internationalized versions of DES available that meet all the requirements and can be exported. There is an international version on the accompanying diskettes.

MANAGEMENT VIA SNMP

SNMP uses a subset of ASN.1 (Abstract Syntax Notation) as input. The ASN input provides a method by which the data can traverse various architectures without a problem. This allows machines using an 8-bit architecture to use the same data abstraction as a 64-bit machine, or a machine that uses BIG ENDIAN architecture to utilize the same data as one using LITTLE ENDIAN.

SNMP has made networks somewhat manageable, has allowed fast implementation and deployment to become the de facto standard. Virtually every network vendor has deployed products using SNMP. IANA (Internet Assigned Numbers Authority) currently has over 1000 enterprise ids on file, and it grows larger every day. The enterprise number is required for a vendor to develop a MIB specific to their equipment. It is conceivable that a vendor could implement around the standard MIBs, although normally there are equipment specifics that are more important for the network management. For example, a packet in count may not be as important to a network manager as a MIB variable that reflects the percent of system utilization. A network manager may not care about packets if the system is 100 percent busy and dropping packets anyway. In which case the packet count may consist of retransmissions, providing a distorted count.

As the acceptance of SNMP grows, it becomes important for all computer professionals to understand the SNMP philosophy. We need to know what the limitations are, and what part SNMP really plays in network management. This is as important to the developer as the code, since without that understanding it would be difficult to appreciate or do justice to an SNMP development.

Limitations of SNMP

Probably one of the best points for SNMP is that there are few limitations. In the creation of the SNMP protocol there was a good deal of thought given to making it expandable. Even though the name Simple Network Management Protocol conjures up thoughts of a limited protocol, that is not the case. The use of the MIB approach allowed for expansion of the information base and created a protocol that could change and grow with little difficulty. The use of SMI (Standard Management Information) to allow for MIBs that could be transported between hardware platforms made for a knowledge base that could be utilized on most any hardware.

The MIB has also created a problem that should be understood. All too often people will believe that SNMP, when added to a platform, is ready to go. They give little, if any, thought to the fact that SNMP doesn't know about their hardware. That knowledge comes from the MIB. The company implementing the SNMP agent must develop the MIB and the code to support it. This is not a factor for the end user, since end users reap the benefits of the vendor developing the MIB. They simply compile the MIB on their NMS, load it, and they are ready to go. It is the vendor of the networking equipment that must develop access routines that will fill the SNMP variable from internal equipment variables. The vendor must build the hooks to the system. For example, the vendor may want to provide port status. They must provide a means by which SNMP can "get" that data. SNMP receives an SNMP "GET REQUEST," parses the request to see if it is a valid MIB element, and then returns the value of that element. Returning that value may mean that some function call calculates the value or gets it in some other way but that is NOT a function of SNMP. That functionality must come from the system itself, as it interacts with SNMP.

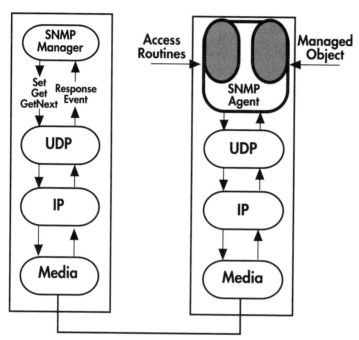

Figure 3.4 Relation of Manager and Agent.

Figure 3.4, above, shows the basic relationship of the manager and agent. All too often this relationship is not clearly understood. It is often assumed that the manager inherently knows about the equipment to be managed. Many vendors do not initially realize that they must produce SMI code (a MIB) to provide to their customer. The vendor will need to provide a MIB for every management station that is to manage the equipment. The management station must have the vendors MIB to be able to manage the equipment. The customer will compile the SMI on his or her machine, load it, and only then will the management station know about the equipment to be managed.

Often times the customer will hit some glitch when compiling the MIB, and that customer will soon be on the phone for support. This happens because all MIB compilers are not created equal. Many vendors have used one compiler to test their SMI code only to find it will not compile at the customer's site. SNMPv2 makes no difference in this area since Standard Management

Information is defined outside of the SNMP protocol. It is true that management stations, using only standard MIBs, can find many of the objects on the network but they have no management capability at that point.

Issues

Although SNMP has aged somewhat, there are still unresolved issues that need to be addressed. Some issues have to do with the overall nature of network management. The networks approach the complexity of a living organism. This complexity makes it clear that network management overall is in an embryonic state.

Another tough issue is that of applying network management across administrative boundaries. This issue is very complex and far outside the scope of this work. Suffice it to say that end-to-end management is impossible in large networks without this issue being resolved.

Still another issue is that of archival and retrieval of historic data. The current technology relates mainly to real time data. Often times a network manager needs historic data to analyze what the events were that led up to a problem. This issue requires additional work before an approach can even be developed. The issues of what data and how much data are to be archived needs consideration. An understanding of what is important data is also required. If these issues are not analyzed, there is the real possibility that storage capabilities will be quickly exhausted.

What Part Does SNMP Play?

Many end users will look at a Network Management Station (NMS) with the icons and alarms and call it SNMP. What they are actually looking at is the GUI (Graphic User Interface) front end of the SNMP protocol. It is not SNMP, and the GUI could be from any of a number of vendors. SNMP is the protocol that manages and knows about the network equipment. By having the same MIB on the management station as on the managed equipment it is able to provide lists of variables at the NMS that can be queried (get) or set on the managed equipment. SNMP will, through the use of MIB variables, allow the network manager to configure, view, and change variables on the managed equipment. In reality the network manager does little of that. The network manager will spend most of his or her time watching for alarms from the managed equipment. These alarms come to the NMS in the form of traps. The traps can cause icons to turn red or flash, and the network manager will respond to that. After receiving an alarm, the network manager may use the SNMP "GET" to retrieve variables that will help determine what has happened.

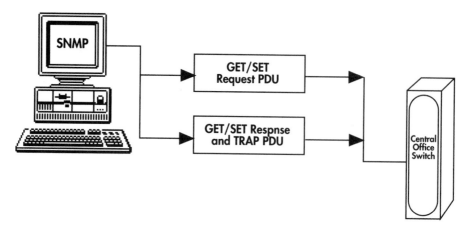

Figure 3.5 SNMP Command Exchange.

The network manager may perform any of a number of tasks using WNMP. The manager may want to balance the network load and would use SNMP to retrieve the variables that would allow him or her to determine what the through put has been. Any number of management and control type issues can be dealt with, provided the agent in the managed equipment has the required functionality. It is the conversation that takes place between the NMS and the managed equipment that is SNMP.

Much of the discussion around SNMP seems to be on the nuances of the agent workings, but I have not yet seen anyone develop an agent from square one. Most of the clients I work with start with a commercial agent or the public domain code. There are those who will say that the process should not be more complicated than this. Those who have implemented around the agent code will understand that after the agent is going, the fun is just starting. It is then that all the little routines that access values, calculate the machine uptime, and all the other variables that SNMP gets credit for are implemented. We must not forget that SNMP does not define where the data comes from, or how. Such definition is outside the scope of SNMP. Remember that SNMP is a framework that does not know about any equipment. The MIB provides that knowledge, and how all that data gets gathered. It is easy to understand that the authors could not define how to get variables on every piece of equipment and every OS ever used. Nor could they know what variables would be important on a piece of equipment, so they wisely left the how to get the variables to the vendors of the equipment.

This point is important to vendors for several reasons. First, the vendor will need to understand that every significant hardware change may require changes to the MIB. Second, the vendor must realize that if it publishes its MIB, and changes hardware, or has versions that do not support the MIB, there may be support issues that are hard to resolve. Last, but not least, is the problem of maintaining and documenting the MIB. Just to maintain the MIB for one major router vendor has required three full-time clerical personnel.

MYTHS, MAGIC, AND FOLKLORE

No writing relating to network management would be complete without a section relating to some of the myths, magic, and folklore that surrounds network management. The primary reason for such a section is to try to bring some semblance of sanity to the picture. It is common for various groups to have mistaken ideas about network management. How did they come up with such incorrect information? It is actually easy given the amount of information that flows from day to day. All too often the developers of SNMP agents have had nothing more than a few books to use for guidance, and even the best works will leave questions. Often the material will not cover the "how to" aspect of a protocol.

One myth that has gone on for some time is the idea that a PC can do all the network management. Even the Pentium chip cannot handle the load of a large network. Even if a single machine could handle the load, it would soon become I/O-bound, trying to deal with hundreds of managed pieces of equipment.

Another myth that often seems to surface is the idea that a vendor needs to support every standard MIB ever created. Vendors need to look at the cost of such thinking, as well as looking at the logic behind it. Does the material in any particular MIB have an relation to their equipment? That is to say, does a network manager really need the material from MIB II to manage the equipment, or would some other values be better?

The myths go on and on, giving the casual observer the feeling that it is all magic.

The MIB Compiler

Many development compilers will generate "STUB" function calls that can be used to help the developer. These stubs are the hooks into the system. They are the functions that are called when the SNMP agent does a "GET" or a "SET" function. These functions must be coded by the developer. The code generally requires access to variables that may only be known to the hardware developers.

These compilers will also generate the test functions used for SNMP set operations. Test functions allow the agent to "test" for the setability of a variable. These compilers generally come with commercial SNMP packages, but they cannot be found for public domain software. Many groups suggest that such compilers not be used. Many groups would rather not use a MIB compiler to help with the development effort. They feel that tighter or faster code can be achieved without using them. If a compiler is not used to generate the stub functions, the SMI encoding can only serve as a way to convey the data structures of the managed entity.

MIB compilers can relieve some of the "brute force" mentality of simply coding all of the agent interface. The tighter and faster code may be required on occasion, but for the most part, a few lines of code will not matter on a processor like the Intel 960 CA or any of the faster CPUs of today. The stubs generated by a compiler tend to help to assure that the programmer covers all of the needed stubs. The stubs also help to pinpoint errors in the SMI encoding.

Rumors

Network management can be very difficult. Much of a network manager's day is spent dealing with little issues, but when the time comes to deal with major network problems, the administrator will earn every penny of their pay. The SNMP application that a network manager is using to try to fix the problem must not be limiting. To keep the network manager from being limited, the MIB must have useful objects. A well-documented, functional, and intelligent MIB makes all the difference. The agent and MIB must provide factual data. Many agents are way off in things as simple as variable counts. Unfortunately there is a movement to simplify the MIB and agent, primarily to make the agent implementation easier. The agent and MIB should be simple in order to make the implementation manageable, but the MIB must contain enough detail for the network manager to do the job. In trying to achieve this balance some of the push for the buzz word implementations must go away. For example, the implementations that claim RMON and MIB II support may be doing more harm than good. If these MIBs have little or no relevance to the equipment to be managed, why should they be supported? For example, MIB II has no meaning at all on equipment that uses a proprietary protocol.

There has been and will be many complains about SNMPs lack of capability. It is often stated that SNMP will not provide knowledge of the status of the equipment or it won't provide usable information. There is even a debate about where the knowledge should live, on the management station, or with the agent. The management station could "GET" data and calculate a condition based upon that data, or the agent could have a variable that reflects a specific condition. Given a correctly constructed MIB, the agent can provide such information with no problem. For example, the agent could have a variable that generated an access routine that checked out several elements of the managed equipment and calculated the status of the equipment. This is not at all an unusual procedure. For example, if you study the mib2.c code you will see that the MIB compiler used, generated a function call to calculate system uptime.

```
extern int          SNMP_GET_sysUpTime();
extern void         *calc_system_uptime();
static struct attribute ATTR_sysUpTime =
{
      &ATTR_ID_sysUpTime,
      SNMP_GET_sysUpTime,
      NULL,
      NULL,
      calc_system_uptime,
      NULL,
      7,                /* TimeTicks */
      0,
      -1,
};
```

NOTE: Throughout this work the compiler output will be that of the **PEER GDMOC SMI** compiler.

By viewing the code structure (above) that came from a MIB compiler, it can be understood that the SNMP agent that uses this structure makes references through pointers. It must be understood that this output will not necessarily work with any other agent code. Generally the compiler output is tuned to interface in a specific way with a specific agent. The structure indicates that it expects a function called SNMP_GET_sysUpTime to live outside this file. It expects that function to do some calculation and to return the system up time as an integer.

NOTE: In the SNMP world, system up time is a calculation reflecting how long the SNMP system has been operational, not how long the system itself has been up. This indicates that the "startup" of SNMP must save the system time in a variable to be used later to calculate SystemUpTime. The calculation would go something like:

current time - saved time = uptime

This same MIB stubs could be used to provide MIB variables that have a good deal of intelligence and meaning to the management station. For example the agent MIB could have a variable that reflects overall condition of the system. This could be a calculated value using several factors to indicate the overall system condition.

FOR FURTHER STUDY

The following documents contain useful information that is beyond the scope of this chapter.

HP OpenView Distributed Management
Communications Infrastructure Programmers Guide
Part No. J2319-90003, © July, 1992
Peer SNMP Programmers Guide
Peer Networks Inc.
3375 Scott Boulevard
Santa Clara, CA 95054 (SNMP programming information.)

HP OpenView SNMP Agent Administrator's Reference
Hewlett-Packard Company
3404 East Harmony Road
Fort Collins, CO 80525-9599
Ph. (303) 229-2321 (SNMP Agent information.)

REFERENCES

Duffy, Jim. *Network World*, "User helps vendors bring v2 to the market." January, 1994.

Fisher, Sharon. *Communications Week*, "Secure SNMP, Anyone." April 4, 1994.

Gaskin, James. *Network Computing*, "UNIX Network Management is Surely in Your Future." January 15, 1994.

Stallings, W. *STACKS: The Network Journal*, "New Life for SNMP." June, 1993.

4

SNMP Transport

INTRODUCTION

Having looked at the basics of networking and SNMP, we will now look at the protocol that carries the SNMP message. The transport protocol is not part of SNMP, but SNMP was designed with the Internet in mind and has close ties to User Datagram Protocol (UDP). SNMP can be used with any of a number of transport protocols if they provide the required support. The demands placed on the transport protocol are few, making it easy to use SNMP with various protocols. One problem that SNMP does pose for a number of transports is the connectionless mentality. For example, the trap mechanism can send a trap given a specific condition. The condition can happen at any time. This creates real problems for connection-oriented protocols, dial-up protocols, and most Wide Area Network (WAN) environments. That is not to say that it cannot be done, but it does mean that the SNMP agent should use a good deal of sanity in developing a strategy for sending TRAP Protocol Data Units (PDUs).

THE LAYERING

UDP is the transport of choice for SNMP, although it can be used with any transport that will support its requirements. Since SNMP was intended as an interim solution, other transport protocols did not get a lot of consideration. During the original design it was thought that OSI could deal with the other protocols, and SNMP need only to provide an interim solution for the Internet and a TCP/IP environment. Even with this limited scope, SNMP took the approach of layering. This layering of SNMP over UDP over IP is the norm for the Internet world. Unfortunately many do not hold to the layered module as much as one would like. Many agents can be found that embed the transport in the SNMP agent. This is often seen in PC environments. Often the PC SNMP agents will work through socket drivers that are layered over media drivers. Many will simply throw out any layering in between SNMP and the socket layer. This approach somewhat destroys the protocol stack, yet at times it is the only way to squeeze SNMP into a system. In cases such as embedded systems there often is not enough memory available to do anything else. In reality if the SNMP agent works correctly, how the layering is done becomes a moot point.

Figure 4.1 below shows how SNMP is positioned on UDP/IP stack in the normal implementation.

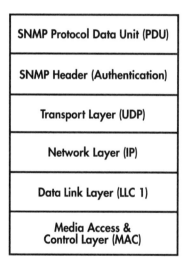

| SNMP Protocol Data Unit (PDU) |
| SNMP Header (Authentication) |
| Transport Layer (UDP) |
| Network Layer (IP) |
| Data Link Layer (LLC 1) |
| Media Access & Control Layer (MAC) |

Figure 4.1 SNMP—UDP Layering.

THE COMMON TRANSPORT

No matter which side, manager, or agent the SNMP PDU comes from, the transfer takes place in the same manner. That is, the data is formulated into an SNMP packet. After the data is placed in the buffer it is ASN.1 encoded. UDP then takes the hand off of the packet. This hand off comes only when the packet is ready to be sent. UDP gets the port number that it is to use with the packet.

NOTE: The port abstraction is an old and well-worn method of associating a structure definition with an application. The structure will contain data that allows the operating system to figure out where to send the data. It should be understood that there are two ports involved, the source and the destination. The destination port can be on the same machine as the source.

The UDP port number also provides a reference to the protocol that is the Upcall (the protocol that is above UDP) associated with this packet. The port numbers used by SNMP are "well known" ports. That means that the port numbers are set aside for the use of SNMP. The port numbers 161 and 162 are for SNMP usage. With 161 for normal SNMP exchanges and 162 for trap messages. These port numbers need to be set up somewhere for SNMP to access. In a UNIX environment the ports get set up in "/etc/services." On an embedded system, generally there will not be a file structure and the port number gets hard wired into the code.

NOTE: For SNMP implementations using SMUX the port 199 has been set aside for SMUX use.

The UDP port is mapped to a socket. The socket abstraction is also associated with a structure that is used to provide additional information to the operating system about the actual "place" to send the data.

NOTE: Place as used above may mean an interrupt vector, a memory address, or any of a number of other methods used to direct the operating system.

Many operating systems and protocol stacks are moving away from the socket abstraction to the file descriptor abstraction. That is to say, rather than opening a socket, the protocol stack would open a file descriptor that just happened to be a network device. When the protocol stack opened the file descriptor it would actually be setting up all the structures and memory required for the media adapter.

Application Layer
Presentation Layer
Session Layer
Transport Layer
Network Layer
Data Link Layer
Physical Layer

Figure 4.2 ISO Model Stack.

It must be noted that below that session layer it is acceptable for the OSI stack to utilize the IP protocol. This is a common approach in the U.S. but much less acceptable in Europe.

Services Required

SNMP places a number of requirements on the transport protocols that support it. In comparison to other applications, the requirements are few. SNMP assumes a Transport and Network protocol stack is present. Without the protocol stack, the SNMP PDU will not be sent.

NOTE: In reality the SNMP agent will not build without the transport being resolved.

The layers used by SNMP should be able to provide at least five functions. They are:

- **End-to-End Checksum**: Greatly enhances the reliability of the data transfer.

- **Multiplexing/Demultiplexing**: Provide multiplexing and demultiplexing services.

- **Routing**: Routing improves the overall utility of network management by being able to re-route packets around failed areas. This allows network management to continue operating during localized loss of service.

- **Media Independence**: This capability allows many different types of network elements to be managed. Tying SNMP to a particular data link protocol limits the ability of SNMP to manage a variety of network equipment.

- **Fragmentation and Reassembly**: This is related to media independence.

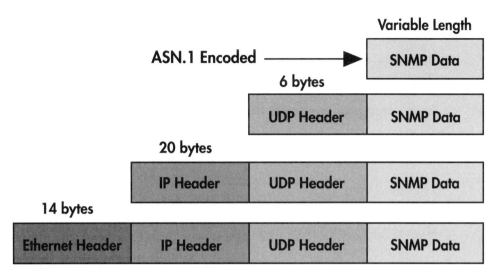

Figure 4.3 SNMP—Transport Layers.

The requirements are not absolute and they can often be worked around. For example, on a dedicated secure network such as a financial network, routing may not be required. Fragmentation and reassembly may not be required if the media does not fragment, and some protocols do not support or require checksums. The requirements are based upon the ideal environment, and they are not always essential for SNMP as for reliable communications.

NOTE: There are a number of RFCs that address SNMP utilizing transports other than SNMP, and the reader should refer to the RFCs for detail of that particular transport.

SNMP PDU (PROTOCOL DATA UNIT)

The SNMP PDU is first formulated using ASN encoding. It is then placed in a buffer, and UDP is told to "do its thing." SNMP calls the UDP service to carry the PDU using the UDP API.

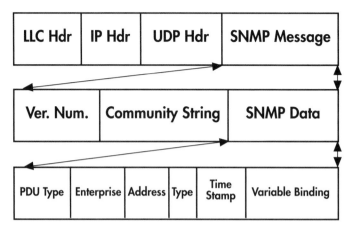

Figure 4.4 SNMP PDU.

The SNMP PDU consists of a number of fields.

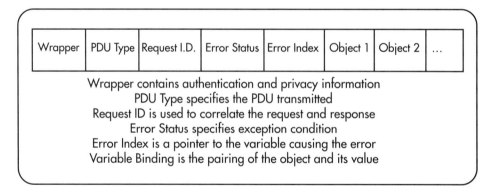

Figure 4.5 SNMP PDU with Detail.

The SNMP PDU is placed in the data area of a UDP datagram. The **data** area of a single UDP datagram is usually sufficient for an SNMP PDU, **even** when the SNMP PDU has multiple variables bound to it. (More on **multiple** bindings later.)

UDP DATAGRAMS

The SNMP PDU is handed off to the UDP protocol or whatever other protocol may be used for transport. UDP provides a connectionless architecture that can make using SNMP difficult at times. For example, during a series of sets, one may fall through the "cracks" and not be delivered. The network manager will not know this has happened. It would be difficult at best to generate a MIB that would be able to determine that it had received all the rules in the form of SNMP SET commands. Therefore, the manager will need to do a number of SNMP GET commands to assure that all the SETs got through given the unreliable UDP protocol. Even when a reliable transport protocol is used, it is wise to follow a SNMP SET with a GET to assure that the variable was set. It is true that there is an SNMP response generated by the agent for every message it receives, but over an unreliable protocol, you cannot be sure that the response is going to get to you. That means that the manager will need to provide a good deal of intelligence relating to how the agent should perform. Many SNMP MIBs do not provide sufficient descriptions (information) to understand the relation of one piece of data to another. Often times this aspect of the MIB data is not even considered.

NOTE: In the scenario above it was assumed that the variables were sent with separate PDUs. In some cases it is possible to use multiple variables bound to one PDU.

The Datagram

The SNMP PDU described above is encapsulated in the UDP datagram. Figure 4.6 depicts this encapsulation technique.

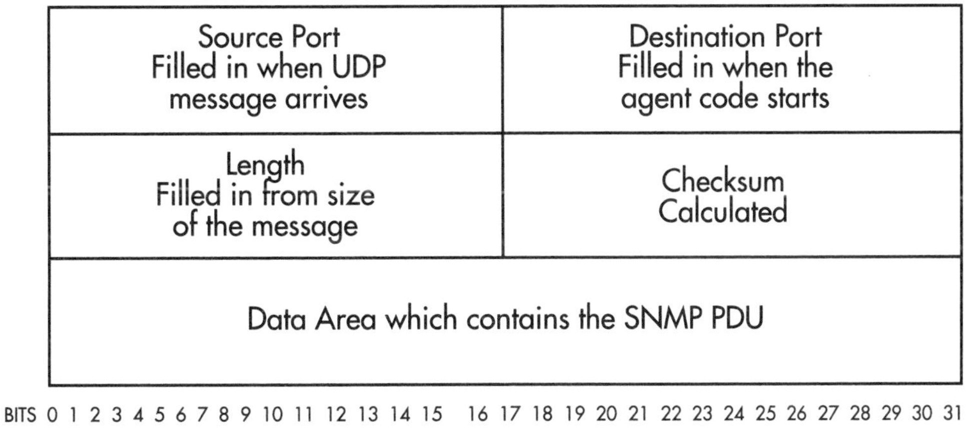

Source Port Filled in when UDP message arrives	Destination Port Filled in when the agent code starts
Length Filled in from size of the message	Checksum Calculated
Data Area which contains the SNMP PDU	

BITS 0 1 2 3 4 5 6 7 8 9 10 11 12 13 14 15   16 17 18 19 20 21 22 23 24 25 26 27 28 29 30 31

Figure 4.6 SNMP—UDP Datagram.

As can be seen in the drawing, the fact the UDP Datagram contains an SNMP PDU is of no real concern to UDP. It is simply going to hand off to IP without regard to what it is carrying for data. When it hands off to IP, we get one more layer of encapsulation, and we are that much closer to the data being put on the wire.

Below is an example of UDP code that utilizes the socket abstraction and therefore does not call IP directly. The calls to IP are made by the socket layer.

```
/*****************************************************************************
The include files assume the Berkeley UNIX environment.
*****************************************************************************/


#include      <sys/types.h>
#include      <sys/socket.h>
#include      <netinet/in.h>
#include      <ctypes.h>
#include      <debug.h>
#include      <local.h>
#include      <udp.h>

typedef struct UdpTag {
                    int     udpSocket;
                    struct  sockaddr        udpSockAddr;
                    CIntfType       udpRefCnt;
                    }UdpType;

typedef UdpType *UdpPtrType;
SmpStatusType udpSend (udp, bp, n)
SmpSocketType udp;
CBytePtrType bp;
CIntfType n;


{
UdpPtrType     tp;
int    result;

/*****************************************************************************
 * Check that there is a valid socket

*****************************************************************************/
if (udp == (SmpSocketType) 0)
      {
      return (errBad);
      }

tp = (UdpPtrType) udp;
/*****************************************************************************
```

```
* Set up a do loop to assure that all of the data is sent.
* Call protocol stack to send the data - function call sendto

**************************************************************************/
      do {
            result = sendto (tp->udpSocket, (char *) bp, (int) n, (int) 0,
                    & (tp->udpSockAddr), sizeof (struct sockaddr_in));
            n -= result;
            bp += result;
            } while ((result > 0) && (n > 0));
/*************************************************************************
 * This error can never happen theoretically but it has.

**************************************************************************/
      if (result < 0) {
            perror ("udpSend");
            return (errBad);
                       }
      else
                       {
                       return (errOk);
                       }
}
```

THE IP PACKET

IP provides more to the transfer than another layer of code involved in the transport of the data. It provides the ability to fragment the packet and do the routing to get it to the other end. The IP interface and a short segment of code are presented below to aid the understanding.

```
/*************************************************************************
The include files assume the Berkeley UNIX environment.
**************************************************************************/
extern struct mib_ip ip_mib;
extern struct mib_icmp icmp_mib;

static int    err_cksum = 0;        /* checksum error                   */
static int    err_small = 0;        /* packets smaller than minimum     */
static int    err_header = 0;       /* packets smaller than length field */

int ip_output(mp, src_netp)
register mblk_t *mp;
NET_ENTRY *src_netp;
{
int    bcast;
int route_opt = 0;
unsigned char *optptr;
```

```
int optlen;

uph = &((S_IP_TX *)mp->b_rptr)->uph;
/****************************************************************************
 * Validate that there is a new packet.

 ****************************************************************************/
if (!src_netp) {                    /* NEW! packet from UDP */
            uph->ps_offset = 0;
            uph->ps_pkt_type = PS_FROM_ME;
            if (uph->ps_ttl == 0)
                    uph->ps_ttl = ip_mib.ipDefaultTTL;
/****************************************************************************
 * If SNMP stats are defined we will help to keep the stats. This is where the
 * SNMP variable is updated. The variables can be updated by the code as is
 * done here or the SNMP agent can extract the values in some way. Although
 * when it comes to counting packets and the like it is difficult at best
 * trying to do the counting outside of the transport protocol. This segment
 * supports SNMP.

 ****************************************************************************/
#ifdef SNMP_STATS
            ip_mib.ipOutRequests++;
#endif
      }

optptr = (unsigned char *)(uph->ps_options);
optlen = uph->ps_optlen;
/****************************************************************************
 * Check to see if we are dealing with a broadcast  packet.

 ****************************************************************************/
if (bcast = is_nw_bdcst(uph->ps_dst.typec))
    {
    if (!gwy_lookup(uph->ps_dst.typec, &first_hop, -1) ||
          first_hop == BDCST_PKT)
          {
          for (snp=net_entry; snp < NetNum; snp++)
              {
```

As can be seen from the IP code segment, SNMP variables get updated in the code. You will need to add such counters to your IP, UDP, and ICMP code to support the various MIB variables should you use those MIB groups. Your existing IP code may already support such counters. However, some protocol stacks do not provide SNMP support in the IP code. When SNMP is not supported by the protocol, it can be simulated elsewhere, but it is never as accurate as when it is done in the transport layer. In some cases the vendor of the transport will provide a stack that does support SNMP. In other cases, the vendor will not support SNMP, and you cannot get the source. In those cases the only alternative is to simulate the counters as accurately as possible.

Version	IHL	Type of Service	Total Length	
Identifier			Flags	Fragment Offset
Time to Live		Protocol	Header Checksum	
Source Address				
Destination Address				
Options and Padding				

Figure 4.7 IP Header.

The UDP code would need to call the function "ip_output(mp, src_netp)" to send the packet. You will note that in the code itself there is reference to UDP showing clearly the interrelationship of UDP and IP.

SNMP INPUT

The segments above deal with the out bound packets. This section describes the steps taken to receive a packet. For the most part it is the reverse of the packet send.

It is important to understand that when the packet is received, the first step is for IP to strip off the IP header. IP will check the validity of the packet and then hand off to UDP if UDP is the protocol referenced in the header data. In the case of SNMP, the upper protocol will probably be UDP. UDP will strip off the UDP header after validating the packet.

NOTE: Both IP and UDP are clearly defined in RFCs, and a very simple view is being presented here. It should also be understood that a media header would actually precede the IP header. The media header may be token ring, ethernet, or any of a number of other media types.

UDP will note the "PORT" identifier and associate that port with SNMP. Recall that the SNMP port number is 161, and no other protocol is to use that number. UDP then knows that it is to schedule an interrupt and call SNMP. If someone sends garbage to your IP address with the SNMP port set in the UDP header, that garbage could get to the SNMP agent. Many agents have some routine that attempts to recover a bad PDU. If the packet is completely garbage it gets discarded. Many garbled PDUs can be recovered to some degree. In the case of a PDU with multiple variables bound to it the error status becomes important because of the all or none approach to variable bindings used in SNMPv1.

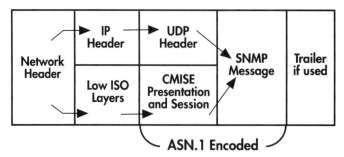

Figure 4.8 SNMP Message.

TLV (TYPE, LENGTH, VALUE)

The external representation of SNMP data is much different from the internal representation. External meaning when the PDU is outside of the hardware on the wire. Externally an SNMP PDU is represented as TLV (Type, Length, Value). The three fields break out as follows:

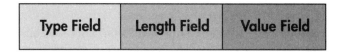

Figure 4.9 TLV Format.

Type Field Encoding

Look at the TLV Format in Figure 4.9. Note that the Type Field is the first field. The type field can be any of the fields represented in Tables 4.1-4.3. Each of the types, known as a TAG, is represented as a HEX value. The TAG is used in various ways in different agents. Some agents will take advantage of the TAG field information while others will make less use of the implications of the field. The agent can make a fast determination relating to the PDU based on the TAG.

UNIVERSAL CLASS	Type Field Value
INTEGER	00000010 = 02H
OCTET STRING	00000100 = 04H
NULL	00000101 = 05H
OBJECT IDENTIFIER	00000110 = 06H
SEQUENCE	00110000 = 30H
SEQUENCE OF	00110000 = 30H

Table 4.1 Universal Class.

APPLICATION CLASS	Type Field Value
IpAddress	01000000 = 40H
Counter	01000001 = 41H
Gauge	01000010 = 42H
TimeTicks	01000011 = 43H
Opaque	01000100 = 44H

Table 4.2 Application Class.

CONTEXT-SPECIFIC CLASS	Type Filed Value
GetRequest	10100000 = A0H
GetNextRequest	10100001 = A1H
GetResponse	10100010 = A2H
SetRequest	10100011 = A3H
TRAP	10100100 = A4H

Table 4.3 Context-Specific Class.

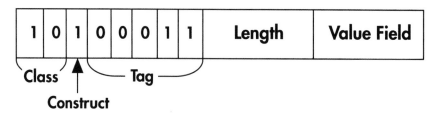

Figure 4.10 Type Field Encoding.

The agent can make determinations of the validity of the entire PDU using the type field.

Length Field Encoding

The length field contains, in octets, the length of the contents in one of three forms. The forms are:

- definite short (0)
- definite long (128)
- indefinite

SNMP prohibits the use of indefinite.

Bits	8	7	6	5	4	3	2	1
Number of Octets in Value Field	0	1	2	3	4	5	6	7
Short Definition Form - Length = 0 - 127 Octets								

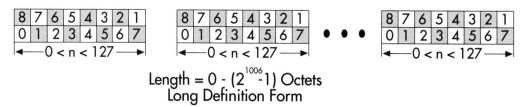

Figure 4.11 Length Field Encoding.

The encoding being described relates to the ASN encoding. This encoding and decoding is provided by a BEDL (Basic Encoding and Decoding Library). The purpose of encoding and decoding is to allow communications between architecturally different systems. Consider the case where a management station using a 32-bit Big Endian architecture wanted to communicate with an 8-bit Little Endian architecture. There would need to be a conversion on the sender side and then again on the receiver side. Such conversions can eat up CPU time as well as being difficult to code. By using ASN encoding we remove such problems. By studying the debug output in the appendix the reader can see the lengthy steps that the BEDL goes through to encode or decode the data.

Value Field Encoding

The value field contains zero or more octets and conveys the value of the data. Each octet contains a digit or character of information. Should it be that the value is a term like "foo" it would be represented in the value field as three octets (see Figure 4.12).

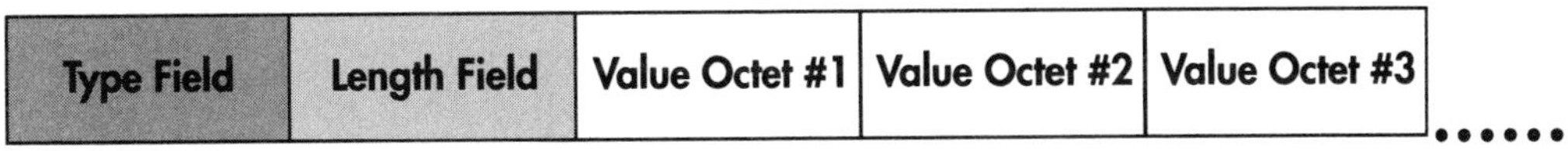

Figure 4.12 Value Field Encoding.

The PRIMITIVE types that can be contained in this field are:

- NULL
- INTEGER
- OCTET STRING
- OBJECT IDENTIFIER

The UNIVERSAL aggregate types (specific to SNMP) are:

- SEQUENCE
- SEQUENCE OF

The NULL primitive shall not contain any octets, and the length octet must be set to zero. The INTEGER value must be a primitive consisting of one or more octets. The smallest number of octets possible shall be used. The OCTET STRING, UNIVERSAL type 4, contains from zero to many octets related to the data value. The OBJECT IDENTIFIER contains octets of an ordered list of sub-identifiers concatenated together. Each sub-identifier is represented by one or more octets. If the sub-identifier is 128, it is split into a series of 7-bit pieces, each in its own octet. The last of the series is identified by the MSB (most significant bit). Zero representing the last octet, while all other octets contain a one. The first octet must not equal 80H, since that is used to compress out leading zeros.

This may seem to be of little significance to the implementor and of more use to an SNMP developer. In fact, this is relatively important. In cases where the SNMP application is in question you may find it useful to look at the data going over the wire. A network analyzer would present the data such that you would need to understand how the octets should be laid out. It is just as important when dealing with the agent itself, since many agents will display the octets for debug purposes.

CMIP

Several of the major SNMP Management Software vendors base their products on the HP OpenView software. IBM, DEC and AT&T/NCR all utilize the HP code to develop their management station software. Thus, it is likely they all have some elements in common. One thing that they all have in common is that they offer an OSI/CMISE stack. The native stack offered by HP OpenView is based upon the ISODE (International Standards Organization Decode/Encode) releases. The interface complies with ROSE (Remote Operations Service Element) standard. This layers over the LPP (Lightweight Presentation Protocol) which is layered over UDP/IP. The CMISE (Common Management Information Services Element) complies with ISO DIS 9595/9596 standard. This layering complies with the ISO standard and delivers the CMOT implementation. Several of the vendors using the OpenView code have replaced these layers with their own stack. One of those vendors, AT&T, utilized the UNIX Software Labs (USL) ISO stack.

There are several good works relating to the ISO stack, and they should be consulted for a better understanding of the ISO stack. It is also helpful to review the ISODE code available on the accompanying diskettes.

The ISO stack can be taken to mean many layers. All of the upper layers of the ISO stack use BEDL's to encode and decode packets above and beyond the data encoding and decoding. When the upper layers of the ISO stack are used with UDP/IP it is commonly referred to as CMIP over TCP/IP.

The upper layers provide all of the Presentation Layer primitives and are interfaced to the lower layers through some abstraction. In System V the abstraction is the TLI (Transport Layer Interface) while in other operating systems the file abstraction is used.

FOR FURTHER STUDY

The following documents contain useful information that is beyond the scope of this chapter.

Comer, Douglas E. *Internetworking with TCP/IP (3 Volumes)*. Prentice-Hall, Inc. 1991. (All three volumes have much to offer.)

Henshall, John and Sandy Shaw. *OSI Explained*. Ellis Horwood Publishing. (Good introduction to OSI.)

OVWindows and SNMP Platform, Hewlett-Packard, 3404 East Harmony Road Fort Collins, CO 80525-9599. (General SNMP information HP University)

REFERENCES

Comer, Douglas E. *Internetworking with TCP/IP* (3 Volumes). Prentice-Hall, Inc. 1991.

5

SNMP Internals

INTRODUCTION

Every agent ever written has some differing approach to handling the internal workings of the agent. The code and how it works, provided it works, is not as important as the Application Programming Interface (API). Some of the agents have chosen to publish this interface. One that has published its interface comes from Paul Freeman and Associates. The document is included on the accompanying disk. More vendors should publish their interface, or adhere to a currently published one, thereby creating some type of standard. Publishing the interface makes the utilization of the agent much easier. Unfortunately in a world of trade secrets and proprietary information, this is not likely to happen.

Many of the currently available agents are targeted at UNIX, or MS-DOS. Because of this, there is often an issue with the porting of the agent to an embedded system. Many embedded systems run on a real time OS such as PSOS or VRTX. These operating systems have their own compilers as well as a specific way of processing. There must be more agents developed for real time environments or agents that are more portable. The problem is made even worse when a MIB compiler is used. The MIB compilers generally utilize the host compiler to compile the MIB. The MIB compiler will run in several passes. The first pass handles the Standard Management Information (SMI) code, converting it to code acceptable to a "C" compiler. This first pass is generally done utilizing the host compiler. Even though the executable that runs may be called something entirely different it is actually utilizing the host compiler. On a UNIX system the process will fork and exec the "cc" compiler. The developer must be sure that, in the case of a cross compile the correct compiler is used.

Often times this will not be the same compiler found in /usr/bin. The MIB compiler then runs the "C" compiler and leaves the output of the token pass (first pass). This leaves "C" code that can be compiled at a later time when combined with the agent code.

Regardless of the agent's nature, target environment, or logic, there are a number of constants that all agents must adhere to. It is those constants that we will address here. The method of coding or logic that could be used is beyond the scope of this book.

THE MIB

A number of SNMP agents are available, both commercially and as public domain. Some of the commercial agents carry price tags in the thousands of dollars. That price includes source code that you compile on your platform. No matter how you get your agent—commercial or public domain—a large portion of the work is in creating the MIB and its data relations.

Many will say that doing the agent code is the majority of the work. There may in fact be a good deal of work there, even if you start with a commercial agent, but the MIB and its support logic will prove to take the most time. No agent can possibly know about the hardware unless someone has done a MIB for that exact platform and is willing to provide it. This is one of the most misunderstood areas for SNMP implementations, since many believe that all the user needs to do is get the agent on the hardware and SNMP is ready to go, not so.

There is much hoopla about MIB II and the other MIBs that are currently defined, but I have found very few clients who can gain complete benefit from the standard MIBs unless they are building a router or bridge. There are a number of MIBs for the standard technologies, but in many cases they have taken the approach of trying to cover every possible variable that could exist for the protocol or platform. An approach that would make things a bit easier would be to define the very minimal basics and let each vendor expand with the specifics of its equipment. A company doing a proprietary piece of equipment probably will not care if it can provide the user with the number of packets dropped. In some cases it is in the vendors best interests if the number of packets dropped is not known. For that matter the equipment may not even keep such a count and may have to do a great deal of work to provide such a count.

There is an RFC that covers MIB II so it will not be presented here. Instead we focus on the creation of an MIB that relates to the proprietary equipment and protocols.

Hundreds of issues can arise in the creation of an MIB. In all cases, the creation of the MIB must start with data gathering. Data gathering relates to determining what must be represented and what the network manager can really use. This information may be expanded with variables that will be of benefit to the testing or service groups. The point to be made is that every variable that can be represented need not be included. Often the size of the MIB is almost viewed as a statement about the quality of the equipment. Nothing could be further from the truth. In most cases a large MIB ends up containing excess baggage that will at some point be dropped anyway.

As the data is gathered, you must also develop the data relations. For example, the relations of the data for a phone switch can determine how the communications cards get represented in the MIB. To determine whether the cards are an element of a row in a card rack or whether they are an element related to a product you must have some notion of the data relations. Some slots in the rack may be empty or use different cards that are not network cards; how should this be represented in the MIB? This interrelation between rack, card, and slot must be depicted in the MIB. Remember, the way this information is represented in the MIB as DOT notation must make some kind of sense. This becomes much like normalizing a database. Many times a database person can be of real assistance in creating these relations.

In a real world case, a client built its MIB such that it represented the slot in a rack by the card in the slot. The client had forgotten that a slot could be empty so the configuration would not continue until a card type was entered. The configuration would then force the user to enter configuration data. The system would hang when it tried to apply the configuration to a card slot that was empty.

The MIB structure and relations can be very complex. An example of when detailed information should be utilized in a MIB would be with a phone switch. Many phone switches want to provide the ability to set up rules for the phone lines. The rules are information telling the phone switch to do things like gather touch tones or generate a dial tone. The rules can be complex, and no set number of rules is required. Nor is there a set pattern used with the rules. Developers should remember that the MIB includes TRAP information. The MIB may also include what management stations are to receive TRAPs. Traps seem to be an area that does not get enough up-front thought. At first it may seem to be simple but let's consider a case in which the equipment has a temperature setting kept in the MIB, the agent may be structured to send alarms if the temperature is out of range. So what happens when the equipment gets a cold boot? You may see a flurry of alarms, which is not exactly what was intended. The MIB should be constructed with range and initialization values. That will do a great deal to reduce the TRAP problem, but there must also be logic that regulates the number of TRAPs sent. The logic might be constructed such that the agent will only repeat a TRAP every so many seconds. This logic has to be analyzed giving thought to the connectionless nature of the protocol. If the period between sending TRAPs is too long and the TRAPs are not getting through, a serious problem may go unattended.

Extensible MIB/Agent

All the vendors made a good effort to ensure that the agent MIB could be extended (extensible) and that information could be conveyed to the management station. Extensibility has merit in a world of embedded systems, such extensibility may be of little value. After all, how many routers will ever extend the MIB. Such extensibility is far more important on the management platform. In the management environment the agent MIB extensions are placed in a file structure. That can be impossible on an embedded system that does not have a file system. The extensibility is much more appropriate on the management station.

MIB History

The first MIB, called MIB I, was described in RFC 1156 and published in 1990. This MIB got divided into 8 groups—System, Interfaces, Address Translation, IP, ICMP, TCP, UDP, and EGP. MIB I has been replaced by elements of the Concise MIB. Proprietary MIBs have been forthcoming, but they are not at all of the quality that one would hope for. Most of them seem to be very simple and often they do not even cover the elements that would be important to a network manager. Very few MIB developers ever ask themselves "what does a network manager need to be able to manage this equipment?" All too often they will provide meaningless counters and other things that the network manager probably will never look at and does not care about.

THE ENTERPRISE MIB

As pointed out earlier, the MIB development is the heart of an SNMP implementation. The MIB must be consistent with both the objects and format of the MIB standards.

Hundreds of vendors have implemented MIBs yet only some are published. Vendors generally provide an MIB to their clients only. This selective distribution of a MIB can end in some strange scenarios. While it can limit the chances that changes will take place without the end user/client receiving the changes, often there is a request on the Internet for a MIB. This is a real problem since simply acquiring an MIB that is made by the vendor for a particular piece of equipment does not guarantee that it will work. For example, if the vendor has updated the platform to support SNMP and there is just a different revision level for the SNMP version, the person who acquired an MIB via the Internet may call the vendor and asks "why doesn't the SNMP work on my system?" The vendor then has to jump through hoops to determine what is going on. Users should always go to the vendor for the correct MIB, but there is no way to enforce such a policy so the problem is sure to continue.

Below is a small section of an MIB that has had the names changed to protect the innocent. It provides a small look at a client's MIB. This MIB was based upon TEMPLATES that readily compile on HP OpenView. There are many differences between compilers, and you should develop your MIB/SMI coding so that it can be used by as many compilers as possible. Although this MIB will compiler on HP OpenView, PEER, and others, it will not compile on SNMPc which is a very popular product. This can become an issue for vendors if it is not addressed with some consistent policy. If you are using an agent that provides a compiler with extensions to help development, you will probably want to utilize those extensions, provided your MIB can also be delivered without the extensions for your clients. An example of this is the case of the HP compiler which will allow you to define ACCESS functions that will provide stub call lines to assist the programmer. These extensions, on some compilers, will cause real problems in the form of compiler errors.

A real-world example of SMI code is presented below.

```
- Card summary (ref: 2.2.1)
- ==========================
- Create a table of slots for the equipment rack
- The table is created under "system 1" - this allows
- the vendor to develop multiple pieces of equipment
- using different MIB's all under the vendor's id.

xyzSlotTable  OBJECT-TYPE
     SYNTAX  SEQUENCE OF XyzSlotEntry
     ACCESS  not-accessible
     STATUS  mandatory
     DESCRIPTION
             "This table contains an entry for each slot on the XYZ
             system. Each entry uniquely identifies the physical
             position of a card."
     ::= {systems 1}

- Below we expand the table to further identify the card, rack and slot

xyzSlotEntry  OBJECT-TYPE
     SYNTAX  XyzSlotEntry
     ACCESS  not-accessible
```

```
            STATUS  mandatory
            DESCRIPTION
                    "Each entry contains the rack (R), level (L)
                    and the slot# (S) identifier which uniquely
                    identifies the position of the card."
            INDEX   { xyzSlotIndex }
            ::= { xyzSlotTable 1 }

    XyzSlotEntry ::=
        SEQUENCE {
                xyzSlotIndex    INTEGER,
                xyzSlotRack     INTEGER,
                xyzSlotLevel    INTEGER,
                xyzSlotNumber   INTEGER
                }


    xyzSlotIndex  OBJECT-TYPE
        SYNTAX  INTEGER
        ACCESS  read-only
                C_STRUCT row, FIELD description
        STATUS  mandatory
        DESCRIPTION
                "This is the key to the accompany XyzSlotTable,
                identifies the card for which a entry exists."
        ::= { xyzSlotEntry 1 }

    xyzSlotRack   OBJECT-TYPE
        SYNTAX  INTEGER
        ACCESS  read-only
                C_STRUCT row, FIELD description
        STATUS  mandatory
        DESCRIPTION
                "Identifies the rack."
        ::= { xyzSlotEntry 2 }

    xyzSlotLevel  OBJECT-TYPE
        SYNTAX  INTEGER
        ACCESS  read-only
                C_STRUCT row, FIELD description
        STATUS  mandatory
        ::= { xyzSlotEntry 3 }

    xyzSlotNumber OBJECT-TYPE
        SYNTAX  INTEGER
        ACCESS  read-only
                C_STRUCT row, FIELD description
        STATUS  mandatory
        ::= { xyzSlotEntry 4 }
```

```
xyzCardType    OBJECT-TYPE
       SYNTAX INTEGER
       ACCESS  read-only
               C_VARIABLE atype
       STATUS  mandatory
       DESCRIPTION
               "Identifies the slot number."
       ::= { xyzSlotEntry 4 }
```

All of the definitions above provide information relating to the contents of a card cage. It allows, through the use of a table, the structuring of data into rows and columns—a table.

MIB Definition

For a MIB to be of value to various management platforms there needed to be a consistent method for definition of objects. The consistency of the MIB module is addressed in RFC 1212. Prior to RFC 1212 there were two methods of defining objects: a textural definition and using ASN.1 OBJECT-TYPE macros.

The OBJECT-TYPE Macro is constructed of several elements:

- SYNTAX—defines the data structure of an object.

- ACCESS—defines the access of the object—for example: read-only, read-write or not-accessible.

- STATUS—defines the implementation requirements of the object. It may be optional, obsolete, etc.

- DESCRIPTION—may or may not be present. Provides a textural definition.

- INDEX—used with the row objects only.

- DEFVAL—optional, is used to populate values of column objects.

RFC 1212 provides for a textural definition within the OBJECT-TYPE macro, thus reducing the amount of documentation required internally. Unfortunately this does not resolve the issue of user documentation. The user is the client who will eventually get your MIB. The user will generally need a hardcopy that gives him or her a good deal more information than will be contained in the documentation area of the MIB. The hardcopy should provide the user with some understanding of the MIB as a whole as well as information about how the data interrelates. For example, if SNMP Variable X should never be set without SNMP variable Y being set first, this protocol must be conveyed to the user/client. All too often, vendors will not provide sufficient detail for the MIB variables to be of value. If the name of the MIB variable does not sufficiently explain the variable and the documentation is lacking, the variable has no value to the user.

Even the standards leave ambiguity, such as "uptime." What is uptime, how long the system has been up? No, it is how long SNMP has been active. Nothing specifically to do with the system.

The OBJECT-TYPE macro utilized in a MIB would take the form shown in the example below.

The example is taken from the compilation of MIB.

```
— the System group
— Implementation of the System group is mandatory for all
— systems.  If an agent is not configured to have a value
— for any of these variables, a string of length 0 is
— returned.

  sysDescr OBJECT-TYPE
      SYNTAX  DisplayString (SIZE (0..255))
      ACCESS  read-only
      STATUS  mandatory
      DESCRIPTION
          "A textual description of the entity.  This value
          should include the full name and version
          identification of the system's hardware type,
          software operating-system, and networking
          software.  It is mandatory that this only contain
          printable ASCII characters."
      ::= { system 1 }


  sysObjectID OBJECT-TYPE
      SYNTAX  OBJECT IDENTIFIER
      PROMPT "network management subsystem id"
      ACCESS  read-only
      STATUS  mandatory
      DESCRIPTION
          "The vendor's authoritative identification of the
          network management subsystem contained in the
          entity.  This value is allocated within the SMI
          enterprises subtree (1.3.6.1.4.1) and provides an
          easy and unambiguous means for determining `what
          kind of box' is being managed.
      ::= { system 2 }

  sysUpTime OBJECT-TYPE
      SYNTAX  TimeTicks
      PROMPT "System Up time"
      ACCESS  read-only
      STATUS  mandatory
      DESCRIPTION
          "The time (in hundredths of a second) since the
          network management portion of the system was last
          re-initialized."
      ::= { system 3 }
```

These elements of the SMI are elements contained in the standard MIB and are variables that should be contained in every MIB at some level. Often it is sufficient for a MIB to import this information. That is done through the use of an IMPORT statement in the MIB.

An example of using IMPORT with a MIB is presented below.

```
RFC1213-MIB DEFINITIONS ::= BEGIN

IMPORTS
        mgmt, NetworkAddress, IpAddress, Counter, Gauge, TimeTicks
                FROM RFC1155-SMI
        OBJECT-TYPE
                FROM RFC-1212;

—  This MIB module uses the extended OBJECT-TYPE macro as
—  defined in [14];


—  MIB-II (same prefix as MIB-I)

mib-2     OBJECT IDENTIFIER ::= { mgmt 1 }

Taken from MIB II  SMI.
```

The OID (Object ID)

The private MIB gets implemented on a branch of the Object IDentifier (OID) tree. If the developer intends to utilize any proprietary data in the MIB he or she will need to have a branch on the MIB tree that defines the enterprise. The enterprise can gain a number specific to his or her organization by contacting:

IANA (Internet Assigned Numbers Authority)
Joe Kemp USC/ISI
Voice 310-822-1511 ext. 171
Fax 310-823-6714
E-mail: IANA-MIB @ isi.EDU

Every organization that intends to develop in the SNMP world will probably want its own number. The assigned number will be in the 1200 range by the time this is published. This number provides a location on a search tree that is unique to a specific organization. A developer may want to apply for a number while he or she begins the MIB data collection process. The number only takes a few days to get and requires only a minimal amount of information about the organization.

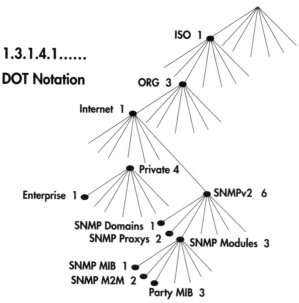

1.3.1.4.1......
DOT Notation

Figure 5.1 The OID Tree.

Additional information about existing private MIBs can be acquired, on the Internet, from Venera.isi.edu, directory MIB. A file of special interest is snmp-vendors-contacts, which lists currently-assigned private enterprise codes. Many private MIBs are included in this directory. The information in this file and directory can also provide insight about the various organizations that provide some type of SNMP product or support.

At this point, the reader should be looking into the data required to create a MIB, thinking about the organization of the data, and have at least applied for an ID number. Having all of that in place, the work of creating the SMI code should begin. Do not go into this thinking that the first cut will be the last. The effort of organizing the SMI and the data relations can become an ongoing effort. It may be that you will begin your SMI encoding and continue with your agent development. As the agent progresses, it will be easier to determine what changes would be important to the SMI code.

ASN.1, BER, AND DER (ABSTRACT SYNTAX NOTATION ONE, BASIC ENCODING RULES, AND DISTINGUISHED ENCODING RULES)

As one might believe, ASN.1, BER, and DER are all related to a degree. ASN.1 defines an abstract notation that allows data to be described without concern for how it is actually implemented. This allows each hardware platform to use the most appropriate technique to implement the rules. ASN.1 uses types to describe the data, and BER describes how to represent those types. DER is a subset of BER that gives a unique encoding to each ASN.1 value.

ASN.1 Terminology and Notation

ASN.1 uses octets as a descriptor. An octet being 8-bits with bit 8 the most significant bit and bit 1 is the least significant. ASN.1 uses the following meta syntax:

- BIT   monospace denotes literal characters
- n1   italics denotes variables
- []   brackets indicate that a term is optional
- {}   braces group related terms
- | bar delimits alternatives
- ...   ellipsis indicate repeated occurrences
- =   equals sign expresses terms as sub-terms

ASN.1 uses type fields with some fields using tags. The fields CHOICE and ANY do not use tags while all others do. The four tag classes are:

- universal—used for types whose meaning is the same in all applications
- application—for types specific to an application
- private—for types specific to an enterprise
- context-specific—for types specific to their usage

ASN.1 encoding could be made into a book of its own, and further study should be given to the encoding rules. Much material is available on the subject including several International Standards Organization (ISO) documents.

BER Terminology and Notation

BER provides three ways to describe ASN.1 values as octet strings. The three methods are:

- primitive—definite length encoding
- constructed—definite length encoding and constructed
- constructed—indefinite length

An explanation of the workings of BER is beyond the scope of this book. Any number of documents which do that are available. The important factor is to have a definition of the terms, since they are often used without explanation.

Each of the BER encoding methods has three or four parts:

- **Identifier octets**—these identify the class and tag number

- **Length octets**—for definite length methods these define the number of octets contained. For constructed these indicate the length of indefinite.

- **Contents octets**—for primitive these provide a representation of the value. For constructed these provide a concatenation of the BER encoding of the component value.

- **End-of-contents octets**—for constructed methods these denote the end of contents. For other methods these are absent.

DER Terminology and Notation

DER encoding provides for a subset of the BER encoding. It is not utilized or discussed to the degree that BER encoding is, and it will not be reviewed here. The specific rules of DER encoding are available in many documents and are available from many sources.

The encoding rules become more important for those attempting to debug the protocol than for those trying to use an existing package. Any package worth having will have all of those issues resolved. Of course if you are developing an agent from scratch, you will want to understand the DER encoding.

INTERNALS

Some of the issues that are touched on in this section greatly differ between V1 and V2. The reader is cautioned to refer to the latest appropriate RFC for clarification as well as for specific requirements. The reader should monitor the discussions on the Internet. A good deal of knowledge can be gained from these discussions. You need not comment, but most readers will have questions that can be answered by those who monitor these groups.

Internal Data Representation

In the last chapter we looked at the SMI data representation. Here we take a look at the agents view of the data. It must be understood that the data can be represented differently from one SNMP agent to the next, but the most common representation is the use of a balanced tree structure. The B-Tree is a common data processing methodology that is well documented elsewhere, and we will not go into it in detail here.

NOTE: BTree software is included on the accompanying diskette.

It should be noted that some compilers and agents will allow various data bases to be interfaced via the MIB and MIB compiler. Those that allow the MIB compiler to interact with a database will provide calls directly to the data base Standard Query Language (SQL). A number of agents will use a simple B-Tree to contain the MIB elements. The OIDs will be stored in the tree. When the agent needs to find an OID, it will search the nodes on the tree using the OID for the search criteria. If the node is found, the OID is valid, and so on. There is generally logic in the agent to convert OID to a type or a textural name to OID. These conversions will allow the B-Tree to store the values in various ways. Each tree node will contain a structure that will utilize a structure to hold the type, value and length fields. There may be additional material contained in these structures. Generally, agents are created such that the structure can be modified (enlarged) without changes to the agent code. Such changes can be done to allow the structures to contain pointers to functions and other material. The function pointers can be utilized to access functions that do calculations, gather data, or do any of a number of other things that may become important for providing good quality data. CMIP provides the capability for such functions. They are called ACTIONS, and it is clear that such action capability can greatly enhance network management capability. SNMP did not provide as elegant an operation as ACTIONS, yet with a little creativity and understanding the same effect can be had.

Many vendors currently offer an interface to at least one commercial database. HP plans to offer a generic database interface this year. This allows the use of a database to store the MIB data doing data retrievals by normal database calls. Unfortunately, an intelligent data cache is impossible to build and most of the data must be retrieved or calculated each time it is accessed.

Table Access

Another element that is internal to the agent is table access. SNMP requires that a table mechanism be available. Most commercial agents will have the objects for a table created and ready to go. Developers creating SNMP agents from scratch or using one of the public domain agents may have to create the table mechanism.

SNMP also requires that the agent be able to add and delete rows from the table. The agent must be able to add a row with a SET operation. It must also be able to delete a row with a SET operation. The exact mechanics of how the agent does this is a matter for the implementor, and generally the mechanics are specific to a given agent. Often an agent will simply mark a row as not valid and not delete the row and that is acceptable, since the RFCs do not specify the mechanism for doing the deletion. Many agents and most management stations will utilize the MIB to provide the OBJECTs for table rows. The structures for a table are presented below. Another interesting element of the compiler output shown below is that it comes from the SMI encoding above (see the Enterprise MIB section previously described in this chapter).

```
/****************************************************************************
 * The OID (DOT NOTATION) is carried in the ubyte below. A ubyte is simply a
 * common name that is a type specific to the hardware it is utilized on.
 ****************************************************************************/

static ubyte  ATTR_ID_ASN_xyzCardType [] =
     {
     0x80, 0x0d, 0x2b, 0x06, 0x01, 0x04, 0x01, 0x86, 0x76, 0x01, 0x01, 0x01,
     0x04, 0x01, 0x00,
     };

static struct object_id     ATTR_ID_xyzCardType = {
     15,
     ATTR_ID_ASN_xyzCardType,
};

/****************************************************************************
 * The function below is generated by the MIB compiler as a stub. This
 * particular stub will provide all the material needed. Most stubs will need
 * to be fleshed out by the programmer.
 *
 * This stub returns the card type from a type field contained in the
 * structure. The type must have been filled in elsewhere, possibility during
 * an initialization or by another piece of code in the host application.
 *
 ****************************************************************************/
static int
SNMP_GET_xyzCardType(ctxt, indices, attr)
void               *ctxt;
void               **indices;
INTEGER            *attr;
     {
     *attr = ((struct if_row_context *)ctxt)->type;
     return(SNMP_ERR_NO_ERROR);
     }


extern int          SNMP_GET_xyzCardType();
static struct attribute ATTR_xyzCardType =
     {
     &ATTR_ID_xyzCardType,
```

```
      SNMP_GET_xyzCardType,
      NULL,
      NULL,
      NULL,
      NULL,
      NULL,
      3,              /* INTEGER */
      -2147483648,
      2147483647,
      };
/*****************************************************************************
 * Card status is a reply of card type above. It can be noted that the code
 * generated for the status is not correct. This would indicate that the SMI
 * used to generate the code was not correct. Just as with any code the
 * compiler will generate code that is worthless if it gets bad input.

 *****************************************************************************/
static ubyte  ATTR_ID_ASN_xyzCardStatus [] =
      {
      0x80, 0x0d, 0x2b, 0x06, 0x01, 0x04, 0x01, 0x86, 0x76, 0x01, 0x01, 0x01,
      0x04, 0x01, 0x00,
      };

static struct object_id       ATTR_ID_xyzCardStatus = {
      15,
      ATTR_ID_ASN_xyzCardStatus,
};


static int
SNMP_GET_xyzCardStatus(ctxt, indices, attr)
void                 *ctxt;
void                 **indices;
INTEGER              *attr;
      {
      *attr = ((struct if_row_context *)ctxt)->type;
      return(SNMP_ERR_NO_ERROR);
      }

/*ARGSUSED*/
static int
SNMP_SET_xyzCardStatus(ctxt, indices, attr)
void                 *ctxt;
void                 **indices;
INTEGER              *attr;
      {
      ((struct if_row_context *)ctxt)->type = *attr;
      return(SNMP_ERR_NO_ERROR);
      }

extern int           SNMP_GET_xyzCardStatus();
```

```
extern int              SNMP_SET_xyzCardStatus();
static struct attribute ATTR_xyzCardStatus =
        {
        &ATTR_ID_xyzCardStatus,
        SNMP_GET_xyzCardStatus,
        SNMP_SET_xyzCardStatus,
        NULL,
        NULL,
        NULL,
        NULL,
        3,              /* INTEGER */
        -2147483648,
        2147483647,
        };

static ubyte  ATTR_ID_ASN_xyzUnusedPorts [] =
        {
        0x80, 0x0d, 0x2b, 0x06, 0x01, 0x04, 0x01, 0x86, 0x76, 0x01, 0x01, 0x01,
        0x04, 0x02, 0x00,
        };

static struct object_id      ATTR_ID_xyzUnusedPorts = {
        15,
        ATTR_ID_ASN_xyzUnusedPorts,
};

/*ARGSUSED*/
static int
SNMP_GET_xyzUnusedPorts(ctxt, indices, attr)
void                *ctxt;
void                **indices;
INTEGER             *attr;
        {
        *attr = ((struct ports *)ctxt)->portNum;
        return(SNMP_ERR_NO_ERROR);
        }

/*ARGSUSED*/
static int
SNMP_SET_xyzUnusedPorts(ctxt, indices, attr)
void                *ctxt;
void                **indices;
INTEGER             *attr;
        {
        ((struct ports *)ctxt)->portNum = *attr;
        return(SNMP_ERR_NO_ERROR);
        }
```

```
/***************************************************************************
 * The code also keeps track of the ports, both used and unused. Note that
 * the code uses a call to an external function to provide this information.
 * The external calls return an integer which is the number of ports.

 ***************************************************************************/
extern int          SNMP_GET_xyzUnusedPorts();
extern int          SNMP_SET_xyzUnusedPorts();
extern void         *xyzUnusedPorts();
static struct attribute ATTR_xyzUnusedPorts =
      {
      &ATTR_ID_xyzUnusedPorts,
      SNMP_GET_xyzUnusedPorts,
      SNMP_SET_xyzUnusedPorts,
      NULL,
      NULL,
      xyzUnusedPorts,
      NULL,
      3,              /* INTEGER */
      -2147483648,
      2147483647,
      };
/***************************************************************************
 * Here is an array of structures (a table) that  contains the card type,
 * status and number of unused ports. The function above that returned status
 * should have referenced the status field. It should also be noted that used
 * ports are not kept. Used ports can be calculated given unused ports.

 ***************************************************************************/
static struct attribute *ATTRS_xyzSlotNumber [] =
      {
      &ATTR_xyzCardType,
      &ATTR_xyzCardStatus,
      &ATTR_xyzUnusedPorts,
      NULL
      };

static ubyte  GROUP_ID_ASN_xyzSlotNumber [] =
      {
      0x80, 0x0b, 0x2b, 0x06, 0x01, 0x04, 0x01, 0x86, 0x76, 0x01, 0x01, 0x01,
      0x04,
      };

static struct object_id      GROUP_ID_xyzSlotNumber = {
      13,
      GROUP_ID_ASN_xyzSlotNumber,
};

struct class_definition      SMI_GROUP_xyzSlotNumber =
      {
      SNMP_CLASS,
```

```
            &GROUP_ID_xyzSlotNumber,
            ATTRS_xyzSlotNumber,
            NULL,
            NULL,
            NULL,
            NULL,
            NULL,
            NULL,
            NULL,
            NULL,
            NULL,
            };

    struct contained_obj CONT_GROUP_xyzSlotNumber = {
            &SMI_GROUP_xyzSlotNumber,
            NULL
    };

    static ubyte  ATTR_ID_ASN_lcPortIndex [] =
            {
            0x80, 0x0e, 0x2b, 0x06, 0x01, 0x04, 0x01, 0x86, 0x76, 0x01, 0x01, 0x01,
            0x01, 0x01, 0x01, 0x01,
            };

    static struct object_id       ATTR_ID_lcPortIndex = {
            16,
            ATTR_ID_ASN_lcPortIndex,
    }


    /****************************************************************************
     * Below we have a port index used. The port index can be used as a reference
     * into the port table.

     ****************************************************************************/
    static int
    SNMP_GET_lcPortIndex(ctxt, indices, attr)
    void                *ctxt;
    void                **indices;
    INTEGER             *attr;
            {
            *attr = ((struct system_context *)ctxt)->description;
            return (SNMP_ERR_NO_ERROR);
            }

    extern int          SNMP_GET_lcPortIndex();
    extern struct attribute *INDEXES_lcPortEntry[];
    static struct attribute ATTR_lcPortIndex =
            {
            &ATTR_ID_lcPortIndex,
            SNMP_GET_lcPortIndex,
```

```
        NULL,
        NULL,
        NULL,
        NULL,
        &INDEXES_lcPortEntry[0],
        3,              /* INTEGER */
#define MIN_lcPortIndex        1
        MIN_lcPortIndex,

#define MAX_lcPortIndex        8
        MAX_lcPortIndex,
        };

static ubyte  ATTR_ID_ASN_lcPortName [] =
        {
        0x80, 0x0e, 0x2b, 0x06, 0x01, 0x04, 0x01, 0x86, 0x76, 0x01, 0x01, 0x01,
        0x01, 0x01, 0x01, 0x02,
        };

static struct object_id        ATTR_ID_lcPortName = {
        16,
        ATTR_ID_ASN_lcPortName,
};

/*ARGSUSED*/
static int
SNMP_GET_lcPortName(ctxt, indices, attr)
void                   *ctxt;
void                   **indices;
OCTETSTRING            *attr;
        {
        *attr = ((struct system_context *)ctxt)->uptime;
        return(SNMP_ERR_NO_ERROR);
        }

/*ARGSUSED*/
static int
SNMP_SET_lcPortName(ctxt, indices, attr)
void                   *ctxt;
void                   **indices;
OCTETSTRING            *attr;
        {
        ((struct system_context *)ctxt)->uptime.len = attr->len;
        bcopy(attr->val, ((struct system_context *)ctxt)->uptime.val,
                       attr->len);
        return(SNMP_ERR_NO_ERROR);
        }

extern int             SNMP_GET_lcPortName();
extern int             SNMP_SET_lcPortName();
extern void            *calc_system_uptime();
```

```
extern struct attribute *INDEXES_lcPortEntry[];
static struct attribute ATTR_lcPortName =
        {
        &ATTR_ID_lcPortName,
        SNMP_GET_lcPortName,
        SNMP_SET_lcPortName,
        NULL,
        NULL,
        calc_system_uptime,
        &INDEXES_lcPortEntry[0],
        1,              /* OCTETSTRING */
#define MIN_lcPortName          0
        MIN_lcPortName,
#define MAX_lcPortName          8
        MAX_lcPortName,
        };
```

In the compiler output above, the references to indices relates to the table indexing. This particular compiler output was part of a step-wise refinement of the SMI/MIB. To take full advantage of the material an understanding of "C," structures and pointers will be required. The output above has taken several pages for a small example; a large MIB can take hundreds of pages and thousands of lines of code. The example above was limited to the most relevant parts. It should be examined carefully since the interrelations are subtle.

FOR FURTHER STUDY

The following documents contain useful information that is beyond the scope of this chapter.

Kaliski, Jr. Burton. *A Layman's Guide to a Subset of ASN.1*, "White Paper—RSA Data Security," Inc., Redwood, CA. (A must BER, and DER.)

Perkins, David. *Understanding SNMP MIBs White Paper*. July 7, 1992. (A MUST!)

REFERENCES

Galvin, J. and McCloghrie, K. *Internet request for comment Security Protocols for version 2 of the Simple Network Management V2*. RFC 1446, April 1993.

Perkins, David. *Understanding SNMP MIBs White Paper*. July 7, 1992.

6

The MIB

INTRODUCTION

We have talked about the need to gather the data to create the SMI and the MIB but we have avoided the detail of how to create the SMI/MIB. Reading the RFCs relating to the MIB and SMI coding can be somewhat intimidating. At best, it is difficult to understand. I will try to provide some simple explanation of the how and why of creating SMI/MIB in this chapter. Some of the material will not get the coverage it deserves. To provide that level of detail would require a book, not a chapter. A more complete presentation of SMI usage and MIB creation can be gained from the booklet done by David Perkins entitled *Understanding SNMP MIBs*. It is an excellent work by any standard.

MIB GROUPINGS

By this time you have heard the term MIB, but what does it really refer to? Well, it can refer to different things depending on the context. When reading this material, the context should be considered in evaluating the term MIB. SNMP utilizes the managed data in somewhat a conventional database mentality. Some wrongfully refer to the MIB as a "database" although for all intent and purpose it is a database. When in machine memory, the MIB variables can be dynamically allocated only as needed. The dynamic allocation helps to conserve memory. This model goes against the conventional database model so it is not considered to be a database.

Many MIBs include (IMPORT) standard MIBs to have access to the standard groups. When a standard group contains some objects that are applicable to your implementation you IMPORT that MIB. When using a standard MIB not all groups of the MIB need be implemented; but all objects of the groups used must be implemented to claim compliance. This can become an issue for equipment that does not support some of the MIB elements.

MIB II provides six basic groups, they are:

1. SNMPv2 Statistics Group

    Objects that provide basic instruction of the SNMPv2 entity. An example is packets received, authentication errors, etc.

2. SNMPv1 Statistics Group

    Objects that provide basic instrumentation of the SNMPv2 entity that also implements SNMPv1; for example, community name.

3. Object Resource Group

    Objects that allow an SNMPv2 entity acting in an agent role to describe its dynamically-configurable objects.

4. Trap Group

    Objects that allow the SNMPv2 entity, when acting in an agent role to be configured to generate TRAP PDUs.

5. Well-Known Traps Group

    Objects that describe the six well-known traps from SNMPv1:

    - coldStart
    - warmStart
    - linkDown
    - linkUp
    - authenticationFailure
    - egpNeighborLoss

6. The Set Group

    Objects that allow several, cooperating, SNMPv2 entities all acting in a manager role to coordinate their use with the SNMPv2 Set operation. Functioning similar to a "locking" mechanism.

OBJECT IDS

The objects in the MIB get assigned an object id (OID), unique to that object. OIDs are non negative integers that get organized in a hierarchical ordering. The OID is assigned a textural name to help the human interpretation. The DOT notation (Figure 6.1) positions the object in the object tree. OIDs are written in the following formats:

```
SYNTAX
"{"  {{<name>["("<number>")"]} | <number>} ..... "}"
                    or
<number> ["."<number>].....
Where
<name> is a component name;
                    and
<number> is a component value.
```

MIB Definitions ::=Begin

DisplayString ::=
  OCTETSTRING

iso	OBJECT IDENTIFIER ::= { (1) }
mgmt	OBJECT IDENTIFIER ::= {iso org(3) dod(6) internet(1) mgmt(2) }
mib	OBJECT IDENTIFIER ::= {mgmt(1) }
directory	OBJECT IDENTIFIER ::= { internet(1) }
experimental	OBJECT IDENTIFIER ::= { internet(3) }
private	OBJECT IDENTIFIER ::= { internet(4) }
enterprises	OBJECT IDENTIFIER ::= { private(1) }
system	OBJECT IDENTIFIER ::= { mib(1) }
interfaces	OBJECT IDENTIFIER ::= { mib(2) }
at	OBJECT IDENTIFIER ::= { mib(3) }
ip	OBJECT IDENTIFIER ::= { mib(4) }
icmp	OBJECT IDENTIFIER ::= { mib(5) }
tcp	OBJECT IDENTIFIER ::= { mib(6) }
udp	OBJECT IDENTIFIER ::= { mib(7) }
egp	OBJECT IDENTIFIER ::= { mib(8) }

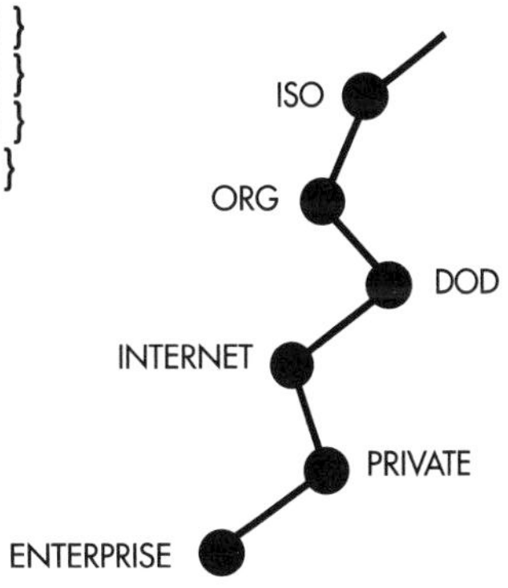

Figure 6.1 OID Tree.

Along with the tree, above it is important to see that translated into the actual SMI implementation presented on the following page.

```
system         OBJECT IDENTIFIER ::= { mib-2 1 }
interfaces     OBJECT IDENTIFIER ::= { mib-2 2 }
at             OBJECT IDENTIFIER ::= { mib-2 3 }
ip             OBJECT IDENTIFIER ::= { mib-2 4 }
icmp           OBJECT IDENTIFIER ::= { mib-2 5 }
tcp            OBJECT IDENTIFIER ::= { mib-2 6 }
udp            OBJECT IDENTIFIER ::= { mib-2 7 }
egp            OBJECT IDENTIFIER ::= { mib-2 8 }
```

The lines above define an object identifier for each of the elements in the left hand column. It provides a relation of the OBJECT with its parent, the object on the right—in this case mib-2.

```
- historical (some say hysterical)
- cmot       OBJECT IDENTIFIER ::= { mib-2 9 }
transmission OBJECT IDENTIFIER ::= { mib-2 10 }
snmp OBJECT IDENTIFIER ::= { mib-2 11 }
```

As this step-by-step relation gets down to the portion of the MIB that relates to the specific equipment to be managed, the objects at the level of the specific vendor equipment are said to be "ENTERPRISE"-specific. The ENTERPRISE-particular dot (node) on the tree references the specific number assigned to the vendor organization by IANA. The accepted approach is to have additional nodes under the enterprise node. These additional nodes provide for areas that can be used for individual products, test areas, and so on.

The naming convention used in this enterprise MIB is that, if the development is intended to become IEFT () standard MIB, the names must be unique. For experimental and proprietary MIBs this requirement is not and could not be enforced.

STRUCTURED MANAGEMENT INFORMATION (SMI)

SMI describes how to use a subset of ASN.1 to define an information module. Other restrictions are placed on "standard" information modules as well. It is strongly recommended that "enterprise-specific" information modules also adhere to these restrictions, although it cannot be enforced.

SMI is a set of conventions that are set out in the Internet documents and elsewhere. The types, allowed within the guidelines set forth by SMI are:

```
Primitive Types
- INTEGER
- OCTET STRING
- OBJECT IDENTIFIER
- NULL
Constructor Types
```

```
- SEQUENCE
- SEQUENCE of
```

(The SMI templates used in this book comply with "Draft Proposal of SMI Part 4—Guidelines for the Definition of Managed Object" ISO/IEC 10165-4.)

Defined Types

Only the ASN.1 primitive types are permitted. These are referred to as non-aggregate types. Enumerated INTEGERS can be utilized, but when they are, a named number with a value of 0 must not be present in the list of enumerations.

Constructor Types

Sequence constructor type is permitted, providing that it is used to generate either lists or tables.

For lists, the syntax takes the form:

```
SEQUENCE { <type1>, ..., <type N> >
```

where each <type> resolves to one of the primitive types listed. DEFAULT and OPTIONAL types can not appear in the sequence definition.

For tables, the syntax takes the form:

```
SEQUENCE OF <entry>
```

where <entry> resolves to a list constructor.

Lists and tables are often known as aggregate types.

Defined Types

In addition, new application-wide types may be defined, so long as they resolve into implicitly defined ASN.1 primitive types. There are few defined types at this time. Most of the implementations are content to utilize MIB II and RMON, the buzz words. Yet some vendors wish to supply additional types to make for a more intelligent MIB. After all the MIB is the definition of the data within the system. If that data is to represent some complex knowledge, it may require more than the basic types.

It is important to understand that there are also ASN.1 compilers available. These compilers deal with straight ASN.1 code without the conversion to the SMI format. These compilers tend to be utilized with ISO software more than with the SNMP software.

A strict ASN.1 compiler may be used with an ISO protocol stack to generate code for a user application. It would provide all the calls required to interface with the host BEDL (Basic Encoding/Decoding Libraries).

Using SMI to Create the MIB

At this point you may find yourself thoroughly confused. Don't feel bad; SMI ASN.1, BER and DER can all start to run together. We will make an effort to put it together in a manner that is easier to deal with. While the exact specifications can be found in the following documents.

- *Concise MIB format*—RFC1212: by M. Rose and S. McCloghrie
- *Structure of Management Information*—RFC1442: by J. Case, K. McCloghrie, M. Rose, and S. Waldbusser
- *Trap format*—RFC1215; by M. Rose

SMI Encoding Components

Standard Management Information is a subset of ASN.1 and observes the related keywords. Some of them are:

- BEGIN
- DEFINED
- DEFINITIONS
- END
- EXPORTS
- IDENTIFIER
- IMPORTS
- INTEGER
- NULL
- OBJECT
- OCTET
- OF
- SEQUENCE
- STRING

SMI is divided into three parts: module definitions, object definitions, and trap definitions.

(1)   Module definitions are used when describing the semantics of an information module.

(2)   Object definitions are used when describing the syntax and semantics of a managed object.

(3)   Notification definitions are used when describing unsolicited management information.

These parts are used to create the SMI encoding. A short example is presented below. The example is the TCP portion of the a standard MIB. It represents the use of the various components of SMI encoding.

```
— the TCP group

tcpRtoAlgorithm OBJECT-TYPE
        SYNTAX  INTEGER {
        other(1),    — none of the following
        constant(2), — a constant rte
        rsre(3),     — MIL-STD-1778, Appendix B
        vanj(4)      — Van Jacobson's algorithm [11]
                }
        ACCESS  read-only
        STATUS  mandatory
        ::= { tcp 1 }

tcpRtoMin OBJECT-TYPE
        SYNTAX  INTEGER
        ACCESS  read-only
        STATUS  mandatory
        ::= { tcp 2 }

tcpRtoMax OBJECT-TYPE
        SYNTAX  INTEGER
        ACCESS  read-only
        STATUS  mandatory
        ::= { tcp 3 }

tcpMaxConn OBJECT-TYPE
        SYNTAX  INTEGER
        ACCESS  read-only
        STATUS  mandatory
        ::= { tcp 4 }

tcpActiveOpens OBJECT-TYPE
        SYNTAX  Counter
        ACCESS  read-only
        STATUS  mandatory
        ::= { tcp 5 }
```

```
tcpPassiveOpens OBJECT-TYPE
        SYNTAX  Counter
        ACCESS  read-only
        STATUS  mandatory
        ::= { tcp 6 }

tcpAttemptFails OBJECT-TYPE
        SYNTAX  Counter
        ACCESS  read-only
        STATUS  mandatory
        ::= { tcp 7 }

tcpEstabResets OBJECT-TYPE
        SYNTAX  Counter
        ACCESS  read-only
        STATUS  mandatory
        ::= { tcp 8 }

tcpCurrEstab OBJECT-TYPE
        SYNTAX  Gauge
        ACCESS  read-only
        STATUS  mandatory
        ::= { tcp 9 }

tcpInSegs OBJECT-TYPE
        SYNTAX  Counter
        ACCESS  read-only
        STATUS  mandatory
        ::= { tcp 10 }

tcpOutSegs OBJECT-TYPE
        SYNTAX  Counter
        ACCESS  read-only
        STATUS  mandatory
        ::= { tcp 11 }

tcpRetransSegs OBJECT-TYPE
        SYNTAX  Counter
        ACCESS  read-only
        STATUS  mandatory
        ::= { tcp 12 }

- the TCP connections table

tcpConnTable OBJECT-TYPE
        SYNTAX  SEQUENCE OF TcpConnEntry
        ACCESS  read-only
        STATUS  mandatory
        ::= { tcp 13 }
```

```
tcpConnEntry OBJECT-TYPE
        SYNTAX   TcpConnEntry
        ACCESS   read-only
        STATUS   mandatory
        ::= { tcpConnTable 1 }

TcpConnEntry ::= SEQUENCE {
    tcpConnState
        INTEGER,
    tcpConnLocalAddress
        IpAddress,
    tcpConnLocalPort
        INTEGER (0..65535),
    tcpConnRemAddress
        IpAddress,
    tcpConnRemPort
        INTEGER (0..65535)
}

tcpConnState OBJECT-TYPE
        SYNTAX   INTEGER {
                    closed(1),
                    listen(2),
                    synSent(3),
                    synReceived(4),
                    established(5),
                    finWait1(6),
                    finWait2(7),
                    closeWait(8),
                    lastAck(9),
                    closing(10),
                    timeWait(11)
                 }
        ACCESS   read-only
        STATUS   mandatory
        ::= { tcpConnEntry 1 }

tcpConnLocalAddress OBJECT-TYPE
        SYNTAX   IpAddress
        ACCESS   read-only
        STATUS   mandatory
        ::= { tcpConnEntry 2 }

tcpConnLocalPort OBJECT-TYPE
        SYNTAX   INTEGER (0..65535)
        ACCESS   read-only
        STATUS   mandatory
        ::= { tcpConnEntry 3 }
```

```
tcpConnRemAddress OBJECT-TYPE
        SYNTAX  IpAddress
        ACCESS  read-only
        STATUS  mandatory
        ::= { tcpConnEntry 4 }

tcpConnRemPort OBJECT-TYPE
        SYNTAX  INTEGER (0..65535)
        ACCESS  read-only
        STATUS  mandatory
        ::= { tcpConnEntry 5 }
```

Several complete MIBs are included on the diskettes. Many of the MIBs provided with popular vendor equipment.

Steps to MIB Creation

The steps used in creating a MIB are few but specific. This is a very large part of getting an agent up and functional. The MIB creation should take the steps:

- Gather the variables relevant to the target system.
  (discussed in earlier chapters)

- The first step is to construct a skeletal MIB module.

- Categorize the objects into groups.

- For each managed object class, determine whether there can exist multiple instances of that managed object class. If not, then for each of its attributes, use the OBJECT-TYPE macro to make an equivalent definition. Multiple instances are defined as a conceptual table.

- Begin compiling MIB.

- Refine MIB observing compiler output for correct data relations.

The detail of this process is available in the RFC. As indicated in the RFC, objects are created based on the OBJECT TEMPLATE.

Each entry (object) in the MIB relates to a number in the dot notation. That is to say, the dot notation 1.3.1.6...would be represented by a node with at least three branches, with the third branch having at least six branches and so on. In DOT notation, a scalar object has a 0 (zero) added to the end of the OID. In the case of a columnar entry an index plus a non-zero suffix is added to identify a specific object within a table. For example, to identify the first row, second column we would end the OID with 1.2. The 1 (one) represents the index indicating the first row, and the 2 (two) specifies the second column.

In the case of a table with no rows, the columnar variable in the table is without instance. This means an empty table.

aTable (OID X.X.X.X.X.3.6)						
Row 1	1.1	1.2	1.3	1.4	1.5	1.6
Row 2	2.1	2.2	2.3	2.4	2.5	2.6
Row 3	3.1	3.2	3.3	3.4	3.5	3.6

Figure 6.2 Columnar Example.

Templates

The syntax of SMI can be somewhat complex, and for the complete explanation you should refer to the RFC1212, RFC1442 and ISO/IEC 10165. Below is an example of the template set used by a major SNMP vendor. This particular vendor provides templates that contain enhancements. Such enhancements may not work with other vendors. A developer should utilize templates that are compatible with their agent. The developer should also consider the clients MIB compiler which may not be compatible. It is always safe to utilize a basic template with no enhancements. A study of the MIBs on the accompanying diskettes will provide an understanding of the basic structures.

```
class_label  MANAGED OBJECT CLASS
    [DERIVED FROM   <immediate-superclass-label>
                    [,<immediate-superclass-label>]* ;
    ]
    [ALLOMORPHIC SET <class-label> [, <class-label>]* ;
    ]
    [CHARACTERIZED BY:
            [BEHAVIOR DEFINITIONS <behavior-def-label>
                            [,<behavior-def-label>]* ;
            ]
            [FWSTRUCT TYPE        "<struct xyz>";
            ]
            [ATTRIBUTES <attribute-label><propertylist>
                                [FIELD   "<C-struct-field>"]
                                [FUNCTION <change-func>]
                                [SPECIAL  <special-type>]*
                                [DBACCESS <group> <access>]*
                                [<specific-error-label>]
                        [,<attribute-label><propertylist>
                                [FIELD   "<C-struct-field>"]
                                [FUNCTION <change-func>]
```

```
                                    [SPECIAL  <special-type>]*
                                    [DBACCESS <group> <access>]*
                                    [<specific-error-label>]]* ;
                ]
                [GROUP ATTRIBUTES <group-label>[<attribute-label>]*
                            [,<group-label>[<attribute-label>]*]* ;
                ]
                [OPERATIONS
                        [PROVISION  [DBACCESS <group> [,<group>]*];
                        ]
                        [CREATE    [FUNCTION <create-func>]
                                   [DBACCESS <group> [,<group>]*];
                        ]
                        [DEFAULT CREATE FUNCTION <def-create-func>;
                        ]
                        [DELETE    <delete-modifier>
                                   [FUNCTION <create-func>]
                                   [DBACCESS <group> [,<group>]*];
                        ]
                        [ACTIONS <action-label>
                                    [<specific-error-label>]
                                [,<action-label>
                                    [<specific-error-label>]]* ;
                        ]
                ]
                [NOTIFICATIONS <notification-label>
                                    [<specific-error-label>]
                                [,<notification-label>
                                    [<specific-error-label>]]* ;
                ]
                [PACKAGE <package-label>
                                PRESENT IF <condition-definition> ;
                ]*
                [PROMPT "<user-friendly-prompt>" ;
                ]
                [IMAGES:
                        [CHILD  <image_label> ;]
                        [PARENT <image_label> ;]
                ]
        ]
        [CONDITIONAL PACKAGES <package-label> PRESENT IF <condition>
                        [,<package-label> PRESENT IF <condition>]*;
        ]
        [PARAMETERS <parameter-label> [,parameter-label]* ;
        ]
REGISTERED AS <object-identifier> ;

supporting productions:
```

```
   propertylist ->      [GET | REPLACE | GET-REPLACE]

 delete-modifier ->    only-if-no-contained-object
                       | deletes-contained-objects

access ->             READ | WRITE | READWRITE
*****************************************************************************
*****************************************************************************
 <attribute_label>    ATTRIBUTE
      [DERIVED FROM           <attribute-label> ;]
      [WITH ATTRIBUTE SYNTAX  <syntax-label> ;]
      [MATCHES FOR            <qualifier>[,<qualifier>]* ;]
      [PERMITTED VALUES
              [RANGE          <low-number> TO <high-number>;
              ]
      ]
      [BEHAVIOR               <behavior-definition-label> ;]
      [DEFAULT                ["] <default-value> ["];]
      [PROMPT                 "<user-friendly-prompt>" ;]
      [DBACCESS               <dbgroup><access>[,<dbgroup><access>]*;]
      [ANNOTATIONAL;]
 REGISTERED AS <object-identifier> ;

 syntax-label ->      INTEGER | OCTETSTRING | NetAddr | PrintableString

 qualifier -> Equality | Ordering | Substrings | Set Comparison
            | Set Intersection

 special-type -> OP_STATUS | ADMIN_STATUS | RDN
              | SERVICE_USER | SERVICE_PROVIDER

 access ->    READ | WRITE | READWRITE

*****************************************************************************
*****************************************************************************
  name definition (defines containment tree)
 <name-binding-label> NAME BINDING
      SUBORDINATE OBJECT CLASS    <class-label>;
      NAMED BY
      SUPERIOR OBJECT CLASS       <class-label>;
              [WITHIN ANCHOR      <anchor-label>
                                         [,<anchor-label>]* ;]
      [WITH ATTRIBUTE             <attribute-label>;
      ]
 REGISTERED AS <object-identifier>;
*****************************************************************************
*****************************************************************************
 <anchor_label>       ANCHOR POINT
```

```
                              X               Constant;
                              Y               Constant;
                              PROMPT          "<user-friendly-string>";
                              EMPTY IMAGE     <image_label>;

******************************************************************************
******************************************************************************
  <syntax-label> ::= SEQUENCE
        SPECIAL <special_identifier>
        {
        <name>  <syntax>
                [ DEFAULT       <default_value> ]
                [ PROMPT        "<display-str>" ]
                [ PERMITTED VALUES
                        [RANGE          <low-number> TO <high-number>
                        ]
                ] ;
        [ <name>        <syntax>
                [ DEFAULT       <default_value> ]
                [ PROMPT        "<display-str>" ]
                [ PERMITTED VALUES
                        [RANGE          <low-number> TO <high-number>
                        ]
                ] ;
        ]
  }


******************************************************************************
******************************************************************************
    <label>NOTIFICATION
        BEHAVIOUR <label> [, <label>]* ;
        MODE confirmation-mode;
        [ PARAMETERS <label> [, <label>]*;]
 [WITH INFORMATION SYNTAX <syntax-label>
  [AND ATTRIBUTE IDS <field-name> <attr-label>
                                        [FIELD "<C-struct>"]
                    [, <field-name> <attr-label>
                                        [FIELD "<C-struct>"]
                                                        ]* ;]
      [ WITH REPLY SYNTAX <syntax-label>; ]
 REGISTERED AS <object-identifier> ;

 confirmation-mode -> CONFIRMED | NON-CONFIRMED |
                    CONFIRMED AND NON-CONFIRMED

******************************************************************************
******************************************************************************
 <label> BEHAVIOUR
        DEFINED AS <text> ;
[REGISTERED AS <object-identifier>;]
```

```
****************************************************************************
****************************************************************************
<label> ATTRIBUTE GROUP
      [ GROUP ELEMENTS <label> [, <label>]* ; ]
      [ DESCRIPTION <descriptive-text> ]
REGISTERED AS <object-identifier>;


****************************************************************************
****************************************************************************
<action-label> ACTION
      [
      BEHAVIOUR <label> [, <label>]* ;
      ]
      [
      MODE confirmation-mode ;
      ]
      [PARAMETERS <label> [, <label>]*;]
      [WITH INFORMATION SYNTAX <label>;]
      [WITH REPLY SYNTAX <label>;]

  REGISTERED AS <object-identifier> ;



****************************************************************************
****************************************************************************
<label> PARAMETER
      CONTEXT <context-type>;
      [ WITH SYNTAX <syntax-label> ; ]
      [ BEHAVIOUR <label> [, <label>]* ; ]
[ REGISTERED AS <object-identifier> ] ;

context-type -> ACTION-INFO | ACTION-REPLY | EVENT-INFO | EVENT-REPLY |
                SPECIFIC-ERROR | COMMON-ERROR | label
```

As mentioned earlier, this is an expanded template set and the developer should consult the template set that comes with their MIB compiler. Of course if you are not using a MIB compiler, you should stick with the very basic templates in the development of your MIB.

It should be observed that there are references to a database in the template above. Those references relate to the use of a conventional database. HP supports several databases. IBM and AT&T support only Ingress at this time. PEER and some of the agent packages also support databases of one kind or another.

Template Usage

There is good deal of confusion that comes from templates, their role, and how they are used. A TEMPLATE really is a guide nothing more, and nothing less. It instructs the user about what fields are available and what can be applied to the field. The TEMPLATE maps to a structure, the fields of which are filled by the information provided in the SMI encoding. Note that a number of vendors have expanded on this TEMPLATE, and those vendors require compliance with their TEMPLATE as well as with the Standard TEMPLATE.

The TEMPLATE forms the basis for a formal definition of whatever that TEMPLATE may relate to. There are a number of TEMPLATEs for example NOTIFICATION presented below. Some vendors expand their compilers to be able to deal with other templates. One of the best examples of this is the HP Metadata compiler. Their Metadata compiler is documented to "support any MIB definition (Internet)." Although the next line of the documentation states "the Metadata compiler has some specific rules and interpretations of the SMI."

From the HP TEMPLATE you may get a feeling of object orientation, and your feeling would be correct. The OpenView platform is object-oriented and supports such concepts as classes and inheritance.

How does the expanded HP TEMPLATE affect you? Well, in reality it doesn't—unless you are building a management application to run there. What it does do is point out that one of the biggest players in the network management area is not limited by Internet SMI rules but they are compatible with all the rules. There is a difference...

```
OBJECT-TYPE MACRO ::=
BEGIN
    TYPE NOTATION ::=
                    "SYNTAX" type(Syntax)
                    UnitsPart
                    "MAX-ACCESS" Access
                    "STATUS" Status
                    "DESCRIPTION" Text
                    ReferPart
                    IndexPart
                    DefValPart

    VALUE NOTATION ::=
                    value(VALUE ObjectName)

    UnitsPart ::=
                    "UNITS" Text
                  | empty
```

```
        Access ::=
                    "not-accessible"
                  | "read-only"
                  | "read-write"
                  | "read-create"

        Status ::=

                    "current"
                  | "deprecated"
                  | "obsolete"

     ReferPart ::=

                    "REFERENCE" Text
                  | empty

     IndexPart ::=
                    "INDEX"     "{" IndexTypes "}"
                  | "AUGMENTS" "{" Entry        "}"
                  | empty
    IndexTypes ::=
                    IndexType
                  | IndexTypes "," IndexType

     IndexType ::=
                    "IMPLIED" Index
                  | Index
         Index ::=
                      - use the SYNTAX value of the
                      - correspondent OBJECT-TYPE invocation
                    value(Indexobject ObjectName)
         Entry ::=
                      - use the INDEX value of the
                      - correspondent OBJECT-TYPE invocation
                    value(Entryobject ObjectName)

    DefValPart ::=
                    "DEFVAL" "{" value(Defval Syntax) "}"
                  | empty

         Text ::= """" string """"
END
```

It is important to look at what functionality is provided by the various fields. All of the fields are discussed in detail in the RFC, and only high points are presented here.

The ACCESS clause must be present, and it must provide the definition for the minimum support required by this object. Many MIB compilers will reject the field if an ACCESS is not defined for any OBJECT that has a read-write access.

The STATUS clause, which must be present, defines the implementation support required for that object type.

The DESCRIPTION clause need not be present, but when it is, it contains a textual definition of that object type which provides all semantic definitions necessary for implementation.

Note that, in order to conform to the ASN.1 syntax, the entire value of this clause must be enclosed in double quotation marks.

The REFERENCE clause, need not be present, contains a textual cross-reference.

The INDEX clause, which may be present only if that object type corresponds to a conceptual row, defines instance identification information for that object type.

The DEFVAL clause, need not be present but if used, it defines an acceptable default value that may be used with an object instance.

Notification

The Internet TEMPLATE for NOTIFICATION (TRAPS) is readily available through the Internet and RFCs. This template, as with all the others, is simply a guide to the format. There are hundreds of templates available through the Internet, some for SNMP, some for CMIP, and some for compilers that will process various combinations. Compatibility with the standards and usability by the compiler you use are the important factors to remember.

```
The NOTIFICATION TEMPLATE

    <label>   NOTIFICATION
            BEHAVIOR <label> [, <label>]* ;
            MODE confirmation-mode;
            [ PARAMETERS <label> [, <label>]*;]
      [WITH INFORMATION SYNTAX <syntax-label>
      [AND ATTRIBUTE IDS <field-name> <attr-label>
                    [, <field-name> <attr-label>
                                 ]* ;]
            [ WITH REPLY SYNTAX <syntax-label>; ]
      REGISTERED AS <object-identifier> ;

    confirmation-mode -> CONFIRMED | NON-CONFIRMED |
                    CONFIRMED AND NON-CONFIRMED
```

USING SMI ENCODING

The SMI compiler input file (MIB) used to generate the "C" code, has the nature of many programming languages. For example, "ifdef" is used as in "C." Below we look at an example to depict the use of the templates covered earlier. It is important to understand that this file is the input to a compiler. Even when SMI code complies with the basic specifications it may not compile. Many compilers have their own quirks to contend with. Several MIB definitions are IMPORTed by this code. These IMPORTs provide a way for the compiler to resolve the various types.

```
#ifndef DDUCK_MIB_SMI
#define DDUCK_MIB_SMI

#include "snmptypes.h"
#include "dduck.h"

DDUCK-MIB DEFINITIONS ::= BEGIN

IMPORTS
        mgmt, NetworkAddress, IpAddress, Counter, Gauge, TimeTicks
                FROM RFC1442-SMI
        OBJECT-TYPE
                FROM RFC-1212;

NOTE: Basic SMI OBJECT IDENTIFIERS are left out for simplicity.

dduck4          OBJECT IDENTIFIER ::= { enterprises xyz }
systems         OBJECT IDENTIFIER ::= { dduck4 1 }

— The following variables are in the order required
— to support MIB II. The MIB II variables are then
— followed by the enterprises variables. The MIB
— could be separated to allow only the enterprise
— variables to be used.

— object types

— the System group
sysDescr OBJECT-TYPE
        SYNTAX  DisplayString (SIZE (0..255))
        ACCESS  read-only
        STATUS  mandatory
        DESCRIPTION
        "A textual description of the entity.  This value
        should include the full name and version
        identification of the system's hardware type,
        software operating-system, and networking
        software.  It is mandatory that this only contain
        printable ASCII characters."
        ::= { system 1 }
```

It is easy to see that the SMI/MIB is created using the various templates and laid out in a relational, ordered fashion.

(Lines which start with a dash (-) are comment lines.)

ENTERPRISE MIB CREATION

The purpose of creating your own MIB is to define your data. To do, that you will need to know about the elements that make up a MIB. We have already covered the creation of a standard MIB, the Enterprise MIB is an expansion of the same concepts. Through the study of this material, looking at existing MIBs and further study, you should be able to construct an intelligent MIB.

As the data related to the equipment is gathered, the vendor will come to the realization that there is a good deal of work both in the gathering and formulation of the data. The vendor should always be cautious in that the MIB can grow to be unmanageable very quickly. In the creation of the MIB, the vendor should consider what management of the equipment really means. For example, does managing the equipment include knowing what is in every register or about every insignificant variable?

The developer must also take into consideration the various quirks related to MIB compilers. The developer will want to concentrate on the MIB compiler it selects for use. Some of the commercial agents come with compilers, while the public domain agents generally do not. Although there is a general MIB compiler with ISODE that can be used, the developer should also compile the MIB using the commercial management compilers.

Publicly Available MIB Compilers (copyrighted)

- SMIC (SNMP MIB Compiler)
  Available at:
  Host: ftp.synoptics.com
  Area: /eng/mibcompiler

- MOSY (Managed Object Syntax-compiler Yacc-based)
  Available at:
  Host: ftp.uu.net
  Area: /networking/iso/isode

Commercial Compilers

- MIB 2 Schema (SunNet Manager)
  Sun Microsystems Corp.
  2550 Garcia Avenue
  Mountain View, CA 94043

- Open View Network Node Manager
  Hewlett-Packard Co.
  3404 E. Harmony Road
  Ft. Collins, CO 80525

- GDMOC
  PEER Networks, Inc.
  3375 Scott Boulevard
  Santa Clara, CA 95054

- Technology Conversion, Inc.
  3326 Transit Avenue
  Sioux City, IA 51106
  Ph: (712) 276-4024

This is not intended to be a complete list or a representation of quality.

FOR FURTHER STUDY

The following documents contain useful information that is beyond the scope of this chapter.

Perkins, David. *Understanding SNMP MIBs*, "White Paper." July 7, 1992.

Recommendation X.200, "Reference Model of Open Systems Interconnection for CCITT Applications." (See also ISO 7498.)

Recommendation X.208, Specification of Abstract Syntax Notation One (ASN.1) (See also ISO 8824.)

RSA PKCS #s (6-7-8-9) White papers relating to RSA Data Security, Inc. various parts of MIBs Redwood City, CA and encoding.

Extensible SNMP Agent Administrator's Reference, "Tech Manual." Hewlett-Packard Company, 3404 East Harmony Road, Fort Collins, CO 80525-9599.

REFERENCES

Galvin, J. and K. McCloghrie. *Security Protocols for version 2 of the Simple Network Management Protocol (SNMPv2)*, "RFC 1446." Internet request for comment. April 1993.

Galvin, J. and K. McCloghrie. *Party MIB for version 2 of the Simple Network Management Protocol*, "RFC 1447." Internet request for comment. April 1993.

7

Issues and Problems

INTRODUCTION

Given that SNMP was created to fill the gap until the OSI management protocols were completed, it has actually shown few problems. The public domain software from MIT and CMU has been ported to various platforms with few problems. A few problems do exist. Most of the real, significant problems, relate to the overall Internet mentality. That mentality evolves around the UNIX environment and the related network protocols, TCP/IP. With UNIX being a time sharing system and TCP/IP being the preferred networking the move to other architectures can be interesting. Many of the advances in technology, both hardware and software, have remedied some of the problems. For example Microsoft Windows and Windows NT lend themselves to SNMP nicely. Unfortunately, not to many companies want to have to run such a large operating system on an embedded system just to have SNMP.

Additionally, there is a movement among PC vendors to implement management standards that do not fit the SNMP mold. Companies working on DMI (Desktop Management Interface) have gone away from the SNMP trend. They have made accommodations for SNMP, but they are only accommodations and do not fit well or work well when interfaced to SNMP. The Desktop Management Task Force (DMTF) has chosen to try a different approach that will require a good deal of work before it is usable for a commercial environment.

Microsoft, a major industry force, seems to be leaning towards SNMP and away from DMTF, slowing the interest in DMTF.

THE MIB COMPILER

In the process of compiling an agent, there may be several compilers involved. The first compiler will generally be the hosts MIB compiler. In reality, the MIB compiler will utilize the first pass of the host compiler. This compiler processes the MIBs SMI coding into another programming language. That language will generally be "C" code. That code is then compiled along with the agent code. This step will utilize the target compiler, which in most cases will be a compiler targeted at an embedded system operating for a real time OS. Care must be exercised to assure that the compilers used are compatible with the target environment.

Since the MIB compiler uses the hosts own compiler, it is easy to generate structures that will not compile on the target system. The target systems compiler should be used to compile the MIB. This is done by setting the variable CC to the path of the target compiler, not the host compiler.

After the SMI encoding has been compiled and "C" code generated, the output will also contain function stubs that reflect the calls required by the variables. It must be noted that all MIB compilers do not generate these stubs. In some cases the access stubs will have to be generated by hand.

Not all agents expect MIB compiler output, nor will they utilize it. To make matters worse some agents do not work with the output off some compilers since there is no real standard in this area. This only becomes an issue in the cases in which a public domain or commercial agent/compiler is being used. If you are doing either part of the equation yourself, it is easy to adjust the input or output to accommodate the other.

Most commercial compilers provide the complete source code for the compiler. In the source code there is a number of output routines which can be tuned to the agent that is being used.

Below are examples of the output routines used by a standard GDMO compiler.

```
/* function to print NotifObj */
void
pNotifObj (FILE *stream, NotifObj *p, int32 ilev)
{
    ilev++;
    if (stream == NULL)
      stream = stdout;
    if (p) {
#ifdef PRINT_DOC_NAME
      if (p->documentName)
          fprintf(stream, "%s\tNOTIF DOC\n",p->documentName);
#endif
    if (p->templateName)
```

```
                fprintf(stream, "%s\tNOTIFICATION\n",p->templateName);
        /* print behaviours */
        if (p->behaviours) {
                indent(stream, ilev);
                fprintf(stream, "BEHAVIOUR\t");
                pTemplateLabelList (stream, p->behaviours, ilev);
                fprintf(stream, ";\n");
}
/* print parameters */
if (p->parameters) {
        indent(stream, ilev);
        fprintf(stream, "PARAMETERS\t");
        pTemplateLabelList (stream, p->parameters, ilev);
}

/* print withInfoSyntax */
if ((p->withInfoSyntax) && (p->withInfoSyntax->T==presentTag)) {
        indent(stream, ilev);
        fprintf(stream, "WITH INFORMATION SYNTAX\t");
        pWithSyntax (stream, p->withInfoSyntax, ilev);
}

/* print andAttrIds */
if (p->andAttrIds) {
        indent(stream, ilev);
        fprintf(stream, "AND ATTRIBUTE IDS\n");
        pAndAttributeIds (stream, p->and AttrIds, ilev);
        fprintf(stream, ";\n");
} else
        fprintf(stream, ";\n");

/* print withReplySyntax */
if ((p->withReplySyntax) && (p->withReplySyntax->t==presentTag)) {
        indent(stream, ilev);
        fprint(stream, "WITH REPLY SYNTAX\t");
    fprintf(stream, "%s\tNOTIFICATION\n",p->templateName);

/* print behaviours */
if (p->behaviours) {
        indent(stream, ilev);
        fprintf(stream, "BEHAVIOUR\t");
        pTemplateLabelList (stream, p->behaviours, ilev);
        fprintf(stream, ";\n");
    if (stream == NULL)
        stream = stdout;

    if (p) {
#ifdef PRINT_DOC_NAME
        if (p->documentName)
            fprintf(stream, "%s\tNOTIF DOC\n",p->documentName);
#endif
```

```
    if (p->templateName)
        fprintf(stream, "%s\tNOTIFICATION\n",p->templateName);

/* print behaviours */
if (p->behaviours) {
    indent(stream, ilev);
    fprintf(stream, "BEHAVIOUR\t");
    pTemplateLabelList (stream, p->behaviours, ilev);
    fprintf(stream, ";\n");
}
/* print parameters */
if (p->parameters) {
    indent(stream, ilev);
    fprintf(stream, "PARAMETERS\t");
    pTemplateLabelList (stream, p->parameters, ilev);
    fprintf(stream, ";\n");
}
/* print withInfoSyntax */
if ((p->withInfoSyntax) && (p->withInfoSyntax->t == presentTag)) {
    indent(stream, ilev);
    fprintf(stream, "WITH INFORMATION SYNTAX\t");
    pWithSyntax (stream, p->withInfoSyntax, ilev);
}

/* print andAttrIds */
if (p->andAttrIds) {
    indent(stream, ilev);
    fprintf(stream, "AND ATTRIBUTE IDS\n");
    pAndAttributeIds (stream, p->and AttrIds, ilev);
    fprintf(stream, ";\n");
} else
    fprintf(stream, ";\n");

/* print withReplySyntax */
if ((p->withReplySyntax) && (p->withReplySyntax->t == presentTag)) {
    indent(stream, ilev);
    fprintf(stream, "WITH REPLY SYNTAX\t");
    fprintf(stream, "%s\tNOTIFICATION\n",p->templateName);

/* print behaviours */
if (p->behaviours) {
    indent(stream, ilev);
    fprintf(stream, "BEHAVIOUR\t");
    pTemplateLabelList (stream, p->behaviours, ilev);
    fprintf(stream, ";\n");

/* print parameters */
if (p->parameters ) {
    indent(stream, ilev);
    fprintf(stream, "PARAMETERS\t");
    pTemplateLabelList (stream, p->parameters, ilev);
```

```
            fprintf(stream, ";\n");
    }

    /* print withInfoSyntax */
    if ((p->withInfoSyntax) && (p->withInfoSyntax->t == presentTag)) {
            indent(stream, ilev);
            fprintf(stream, "WITH INFORMATION SYNTAX\t");
            pWithSyntax (stream, p->withInfoSyntax, ilev);
    }

    /* print andAttrIds */
    if (p->andAttrIds) {
            indent(stream, ilev);
            fprintf(stream, "AND ATTRIBUTE IDS\n");
            pAndAttributeIds (stream, p->andAttrIds, ilev);
            fprintf(stream, ";\n");
    } else
            fprintf(stream, ";\n");

    /* print withReplySyntax */
    if ((p->withReplySyntax) && (p->withReplySyntax->t == presentTag)) {
            indent(stream, ilev);
            fprintf(stream, "WITH REPLY SYNTAX\t");
            pWithSyntax (stream, p->withReplySyntax, ilev);
            fprintf(stream, ";\n");
    }

    /* print registeredAs */
    if (p->registeredAs) {
            indent(stream, ilev-1); /* indent (ilev); */
            fprintf(stream, "REGISTERED AS { ");
            pRegisteredAs (stream, p->registeredAs, ilev);
            fprintf(stream, ");\n");
    }
  }
}


/* function to print ActionObj */
voic
pActionObj (FILE *stream, ActionObj *p, int32 ilev)
{
  ilev++;

  if (stream == NULL)
      stream = stdout;
    if(p->documentName)
          fprintf(stream, "%s\tACTION DOC\n", p->documentName);
```

```
#endif
    /* print templateName */
    if (p->templateName)
        fprintf(stream, "%s\t ACTION\n", p->templateName);

    /* print behaviours */
    if (p->behaviours) {
        indent(stream, ilev);
        fprintf(stream, "BEHAVIOUR\t");
        pTemplateLabelList (stream, p->behaviours, ilev);
     fprintf(stream, ";\n");
    }
    /* print modeConfirmed */
    if (p->modeConfirmed) {
        indent(stream, ilev);
        fprintf(stream, "MODE\tCONFIRMED;\n");
    }
    /* print parameters */
    if (p->parameters) {
        indent(stream, ilev);
        fprintf(stream, "PARAMETERS\t");
        pTemplateLabelList (stream, p->parameters, ilev);
        fprintf(stream, ";\n");
    }

    /* print withInfoSyntax */
    if ((p->withInfoSyntax) && (p->withInfoSyntax->t == presentTag)) {
        indent(stream, ilev);
        fprintf(stream, "WITH INFORMATION SYNTAX\t");
        pWithSyntax (stream, p->withInfoSyntax, ilev);
        fprintf(stream, ";\n");
    }
    /* print withgReplySyntax */
    if ((p->withReplySyntax) && (p->withReplySyntax->t == presentTag)) {
        indent(stream, ilev);
        fprintf(stream, "WITH REPLY SYNTAX\t");
        pWithSyntax (stream, p->withReplySyntax, ilev);
        fprintf(stream, ";\n");
    }

    /* print registeredAs */
    if (p->registeredAs) {
        indent(stream, ilev-I); /* indent (ilev); */
        fprintf(stream, "REGISTERED AS\t{ ");
        pRegisteredAs (stream, p->registeredAs, ilev);
        fprintf(stream, " };\n");
    }
}
```

Some of the do-it-yourself agents can take their own form of input, making a MIB compiler worthless. Some agents actually read up the MIB at run time. It has been suggested that this makes them more flexible. That is not necessarily true; some agents, as well as management systems, can read and use the SMI file as input and compile and link at run time. Still other agents utilize MIB libraries via a UNIX concept of shared libraries. Most real time OSs running on embedded systems can better utilize compiler output that can be compiled into their source. The other concepts are somewhat out of place on most embedded systems since most don't have file systems. Therefore, they can not utilize a shared library, and they have no need to bind to a new MIB at runtime.

Various compilers have differing output, but it must be clear that the compiler output is very important to the overall implementation. Compiler output has been presented elsewhere and will not be presented again here. A good deal of work is involved even after the compiler is done. For example, many stub functions are generated that must be filled in by the implementors. The compiler output can in some cases become overbearing. When compiled, some MIBs will exceed 9,000 lines with over 600 function stubs. That was just the private MIB portion, the complete MIB can be much larger. When a number of MIBs are coupled together on a management station, the MIB grew to well over 25,000 lines (several megabytes). Most of the lines are structures and other such elements that are not a great deal of trouble for the implementors. However, the volume alone can become troublesome when limited memory is available. It should also be considered that the MIB will be placed with your clients, and they will need to compile the MIB into their management station. A huge MIB may be more than any client wants to bear, or worse, their system may not be able to handle it because of memory limitations.

It must be understood that no matter how the MIB is done, with a compiler or by hand, the access routines must be developed. The MIB compiler can ease some of the burden, but nothing will relieve the developer of that task. The task of developing these routines can become very large, depending upon the size of the MIB.

Anyone implementing SNMP should be cautious of MIB compilers that utilize proprietary formats, although a proprietary compiler is better than the brute force, hard-code-it-in approach. Any compiler will give some assurance of portability. It will also help you to find problems before the end user.

It has been stated that brute force coding of the agent code is the best approach. Personally, if I have tools that will ease my life, I use them. In these days where time to market is tight and all of us are being overloaded, I would be hard pressed to believe that the cost of a compiler could not be justified. I cannot believe that the code could be that much tighter or better when done by hand. I would believe that with the new processors running at 60 or more MHz and doing multiple instruction per clock cycle, we would have difficulty making a case that a few lines of code could matter. Yes, I know there will be those who say that a few lines of code can kill you, but in reality, if your code is that bad, or your project is that tight, this book probably is not the answer to your problem.

COMPILER OUTPUT

Although the MIB may have run through the compiler it is not necessarily correct. Even worse, it may not run through the compiler. Some times the base problem will be complex, while other times, it will be a simple issue of compiler quirks and every compiler has at least one. The real key to a quality compiler is that they comply with the GDMO standard. Unfortunately, even the compilers that do comply with the GDMO standard can operate differently, since the standard leaves room for interpretation.

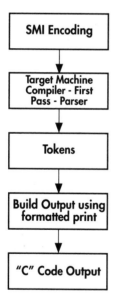

Figure 7.1 Compiler Operation.

Many compilers offer lists of options such as the ability to count the objects in the MIB. Some have options to create skeletons and various other types of output. The single most important output is the creation of procedure skeletons, and this should be a requirement of whatever compiler is used.

Another valuable characteristic of some compilers is the ability to list important statistics about the MIB. These statistics can include the number of

Traps, the total imports, the total exports, etc. Not all compilers will generate such detail, but it is clearly an advantage if they do, since the implementation of the MIB can be difficult.

INTERFACE ERRORS

Since the MIB interface really is responsible for the values contained in the variables, the interface logic, the stubs, and the related code must be correct. Yet in all too many cases it is not. This is best depicted by the fact that in a study done by a trade journal most agents did not return correct values. Some were off by rather large amounts in some very basic areas. Unfortunately, the agent was blamed for the problems when in most cases the problem was probably with the MIB or the ACCESS stubs. Other issues, such as what is a packet, also come into play. At first glance one would say a packet is a packet is a packet. But what about the case in which a number of fragments are sent, and some are dropped and retransmitted and dropped again and once again retransmitted. Which part of that constitutes a packet, and how is it calculated? What if the network is 100% busy, and 60% of it is retransmissions? How is that represented to the network manager?

Some agents actually returned 0 (zero) for a number of the variables they claim to support. This in fact, is probably due to a lack of interface logic or worse yet the implementor believed that the variable would somehow just get filled in by magic. Many times it ends up being a variable that did not get an access routine coded correctly.

OPERATING SYSTEM ISSUES

SNMP was originally targeted at the UNIX environment. This may have not been done intentionally, but the intent was for a time sharing system. In the MS-DOS (Microsoft Disk Operating System) used on most PCs there is no easy way to time slice between applications. That is the primary reason that most of the network management work is done under MS Windows. Windows provides the time slice capability so the networking application need not. This does not mean that SNMP cannot be done under DOS, but it does mean it will take more work. There are a number of methods by which SNMP can be made to work with DOS. It is not clear that one has an advantage over the other, but one of the best ways to do it is through the use of the MIT IP stack. This source code is available from MIT and other locations. It provides a time share system for a DOS environment. The code is mature and stable. It is so mature that references to the original PC can be found. By using the tasking functionality, all of the same capabilities of a time share system can be obtained.

Another approach to the PC environment is to use one of the public domain IP stacks that have capability of being interrupt driven. Then the whole process can be embedded within the application. However, this creates other issues that need to be dealt with, such as re-entrancy problems.

One other issue that plagues the PC environment is the overall architecture. The overwhelming power of the CPU chips leads many to believe that they can handle whatever comes their way, but this is not the case. The processor may be able to handle the work load, but the architecture will tend to become I/O bound in many instances. This is not completely the fault of the architecture and more an issue of the various vendors implementations of I/O cards and the never ending quest to keep the price down.

CONFIGURATION

SNMP utilizes the support of the network that it lives on. For example, SNMP will use the routing capabilities of the network. The network configuration must be set up correctly. The protocol stack must be able to get the data to SNMP. This may include handling fragments and other issues relating to networks. The configuration may be required to provide some basic parameters for SNMP as well. For example if the management station routes are kept in the MIB, with the MIB being dynamic, it will need to gather this information from some configuration file somewhere.

MEMORY ISSUES

With many SNMP agents the old line of "memory is cheap, just use more" is not always true. Many embedded systems do not have any additional memory available. In some cases memory is available, but the size of the MIB may over run what ever memory is available. In either of these cases, there is not a great deal that can be done. The best approach that has been found up to now is to utilize a conservative agent and MIB. The agent contained on the diskettes is the base code used by many vendors such as HP, IBM, and AT&T. It is a relatively small agent, and with a reasonably sized MIB, the size of the agent can be kept to under 40K. Other reductions can be made in the overall size by utilizing the right compiler, stripping the code at compile time, and using other tricks known to most code developers.

PORTABILITY ISSUES

There are a number of areas in which any of the agents can have problems when porting. Whether it is a commercial agent or a public domain version, the code can cause problems in areas, such as the ASN.1 ENCODING routines and the header files. In some cases, the ENCODE and DECODE routines will not assign types or sizes correctly. Some of the agents come with their own header files to try to assure portability. Unfortunately, the use of their own header files can create other issues when there are conflicts between headers that are included from some other file. The whole issue requires some additional work in most cases. Often the protocol structures defined in the headers will not match, creating even more problems. There can be issues of incompatible port and socket structures, primarily in the address fields. Some agents still use the old style Internet addressing while the system may use the newer addressing. In all cases the include files should be checked and double checked. Developers should also work to assure that when cross compiling code for another machine, the correct headers are included and not the host system headers. Often, the environment may be set up such that the path of the local includes will be used when there is an include nested in another include. Developers will some times hard code the source code and then the nested includes will still grab the wrong include. When this happens without the developer being aware of it, the outcome can be code that will execute somewhat and take forever to debug.

Most of these issues are known to all developers, but they are often overlooked. If you build either a commercial or public domain agent, you will more likely encounter these types of problems.

FOR FURTHER STUDY

The following documents contain useful information that is beyond the scope of this chapter.

Case, Jeff. *RFC1157*. (A Simple Network Management Protocol.)

Krol, Ed. *The Whole Internet User's Guide and Catalog*. ISBN 1-56592-025-2. November 1992. (Informative—relating to Internet access and usage.)

McCloghrie, K. and M.T. Rose. *RFC1155*. (Structure and Identification of Management Information for TCP/IP-based Internets.)

HP OpenView SNMP Agent Administrator's Guide. Hewlett-Packard, 3404 East Harmony Road, Fort Collins, CO 80525. (Good general information.)

8

TRAPs

INTRODUCTION

Many of the writings on SNMP have not emphasized TRAPs and their usage. I find that surprising, given the importance of letting the management station know what is taking place on the managed equipment. I have also seen clients get excessively excited about traps. One client spent over a million dollars to have the Icon flash red when a trap arrived. The icon would change colors, but not flash and to the client it was worth the money to assure that the icon flashed to draw the attention of the person monitoring the network.

Experiences with clients that made me aware of what importance TRAPs really had to the end user. Unfortunately TRAPs leave much to be desired for providing the support that most end users desire. For example, what happens to a trap when a system is already in trouble? If the managed equipment is dropping packets because the interface cannot handle the load, does the TRAP ever get out? If trap does get out, has the agent been constructed with some type of threshold so that a flood of TRAPs does not merely add to the already overloaded network? The issues relating to traps can go on and on. Some say that the logic of what happens with the TRAP is outside the scope of the SNMP agent, while others say TRAPs are the agents' responsibility. No matter which way it is viewed, it will not matter if the overall mechanism does not work.

In this chapter I address only the protocol of the trap. The actual implementation will take a good deal of thinking about the specifics of the system being developed. As an SNMP development takes place, the developer must keep the trap-directed polling approach of SNMP in mind. That approach, being a compromise between polling and the interrupt-driven mentality, requires a good deal of architecting in advance. Architecting is what we used to do before we had tight time-to-market developments.

PURPOSE

The purpose of the TRAP mechanism is very clear. It is to notify the management station of some event that has taken place that probably was not intended. That event can be something fairly simple, or it can be a major catastrophe. I have seen a number of examples here and there that use "myLinkDown" as a trap. I have always wondered how that trap got to the management platform if it was in-band service...just a thought.

Version	Community	Trap PDU

Figure 8.1 SNMP V1 TRAP.

The SNMPv1 TRAP was a separate form of PDU, while in V2 it has been modified to be consistent with other PDUs. This allows Manager-to-Manger communications. In V2 the capability for "InformRequest," manager-to-manager communication exists. This change has made the SNMPv1 obsolete in a V2 environment. Therefore, a developer must define the intended version early on. The V2 Trap is controlled by the access control list (ACL). This mechanism is defined in the Party MIB. This mechanism can be used to control what entity the TRAP is addressed to.

NOTE: The included source code (MIT version) has the ACL mechanics in place. This makes it an excellent study vehicle for development of the Party MIB.

USAGE

Enterprise-specific Trap

Consider a simple example of an enterprise-specific trap that is sent when a communication link failure is encountered:

```
myEnterprise OBJECT IDENTIFIER ::= { enterprises 9999 }

myLinkDown TRAP-TYPE
    ENTERPRISE  myEnterprise
    VARIABLES   { ifIndex }
    DESCRIPTION
            "A myLinkDown trap signifies that the sending
            SNMP application entity recognizes a failure in
```

```
                    one of the communications links represented
                    in the agent's configuration."
        ::= 6
```

CONSTRUCTS

The TRAP mechanism, initially defined in the RFC 1215, is outlined below.

```
<trap-name>           TYPE TYPE
      ENTERPRISE      <object-identifier>)
      [VARIABLES      {<snmp-var> [, <snmp-var>] *}]
      [DESCRIPTION    "<description>"]
      [REFERENCE      "<reference-text>"]
      ::= <trap-number>
```

An example of the usage of a trap:

```
overTemp    TRAP-TYPR
            ENTERPRISE          thisEnterprise
            VARIABLES           { ifIndex }
            DESCRIPTION         " The box is over temperature. Please
                                consult the temperature variable to
                                determine the current temperature."
            ::= 9
```

The exact TRAP-TYPE macro could use a bit more explanation, which follows.

```
        TRAP-TYPE MACRO ::=
        BEGIN
            TYPE NOTATION ::= "ENTERPRISE" value
                        (enterprise OBJECT IDENTIFIER)
                    VarPart
                    DescrPart
                    ReferPart
            VALUE NOTATION ::= value (VALUE INTEGER)

            VarPart ::=
                "VARIABLES" "{" VarTypes "}"
                    | empty
            VarTypes ::=
                VarType | VarTypes "," VarType
            VarType ::=
                value (vartype ObjectName)

            DescrPart ::=
                "DESCRIPTION" value (description DisplayString)
                    | empty
```

```
ReferPart ::=
        "REFERENCE" value (reference DisplayString)
        | empty

END
```

V2 Traps

If a Trap-PDU is received, it is mapped into a SNMPv2-Trap-PDU. This is done by prepending onto the variable-bindings field two new bindings: sysUpTime.0, which takes its value from the timestamp field of the Trap-PDU; and snmpTrapOID.0, which is calculated thus: if the value of generic-trap field is 'enterpriseSpecificc,' then the value used is the concatenation of the enterprise field from the Trap-PDU with two additional sub-identifiers, '0,' and the value of the specific-trap field; otherwise, the value of the corresponding trap defined is used. (For example, if the value of the generic-trap field is 'coldStart,' then the coldStart trap is used.) Then, one new binding is appended onto the variable-binding's field: snmpTrapEnterpriseOID.0, which takes its value from the enterprise field of the Trap-PDU.

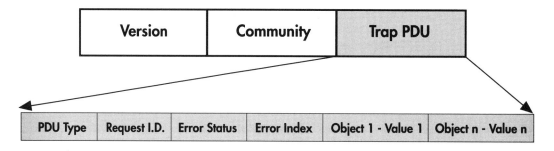

Figure 8.2 TRAP Message.

The TRAP PDU

The format for a TRAP PDU takes the form:

Enterprise field—which identifies the type of equipment generating the trap.

Agent address—is the address of the equipment generating the trap.

Trap type field—which tells the nature of the event.

Time Stamp—tells when the trap was generated.

Variable bindings—provides useful information that was selected via the MIB implementation.

The TRAP PDU format within an IP packet format is presented below.

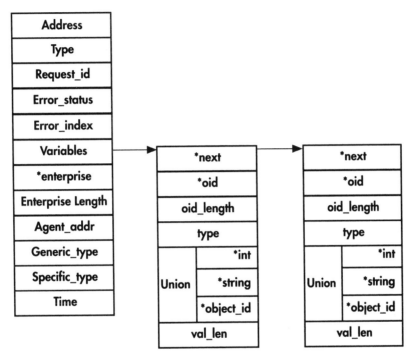

Figure 8.3 SNMP TRAP PDU.

* Also identifies duplicate traps.

STANDARD TRAPS

It was viewed that keeping the number of standard traps to a minimum was important. Therefore only six standard traps have been incorporated into the RFCs. They are:

```
coldStart TRAP-TYPE
      ENTERPRISE  snmp
      DESCRIPTION
                 "A coldStart trap signifies that the sending
                 protocol entity is reinitializing itself such
                 that the agent's configuration or the protocol
                 entity implementation may be altered."
```

```
        ::= 0

warmStart TRAP-TYPE
    ENTERPRISE  snmp
    DESCRIPTION
            "A warmStart trap signifies that the sending
            protocol entity is reinitializing itself such
            that neither the agent configuration nor the
            protocol entity implementation is altered."
    ::= 1

linkDown TRAP-TYPE
    ENTERPRISE  snmp
    VARIABLES   { ifIndex }
    DESCRIPTION
            "A linkDown trap signifies that the sending
            protocol entity recognizes a failure in one of
            the communication links represented in the
            agent's configuration."
    ::= 2

linkUp TRAP-TYPE
    ENTERPRISE  snmp
    VARIABLES   { ifIndex }
    DESCRIPTION
            "A linkUp trap signifies that the sending
            protocol entity recognizes that one of the
            communication links represented in the agent's
            configuration has come up."
    ::= 3

authenticationFailure TRAP-TYPE
    ENTERPRISE  snmp
    DESCRIPTION
            "An authenticationFailure trap signifies that
            the sending protocol entity is the addressee
            of a protocol message that is not properly
            authenticated.  While implementations of the
            SNMP must be capable of generating this trap,
            they must also be capable of suppressing the
            emission of such traps via an implementation-
            specific mechanism."
    ::= 4

egpNeighborLoss TRAP-TYPE
    ENTERPRISE  snmp
    VARIABLES   { egpNeighAddr }
    DESCRIPTION
            "An egpNeighborLoss trap signifies that an EGP
            neighbor for whom the sending protocol entity
            was an EGP peer has been marked down and the
            peer relationship no longer obtains."
    ::= 5
```

The traps themselves are fairly explanatory, so I will only make a few small points about them. One is that the numbering sequence starts at 0 (zero) ending at 5, with enterprise specific traps starting at 6 and going up. The second point is the fact that a minimum number of defined traps was probably a wise direction since they can become dated. Consider, example "egpNeighborLoss." How many pieces of network equipment really utilize this trap?

MISCELLANEOUS

Traps seem to create more than their fair share of confusion for many developers. For reasons that are not clear to me, traps are often viewed as something that needs to be dealt with in some special manner. Traps are as any other element of the MIB, although there is a special arrangement for sending a trap PDU. Only some of the better developers will include information in the MIB that can be used to determine what traps are sent to what managers. All of this can easily be built into a table.

Another issue that seems to confuse many developers is the question of how to send a trap. There are many different methods used for the various agents but in most implementations the developer will find a "RAW" mode and a "COOKED" mode. The RAW mode will allow code to develop an SNMP trap and use the transport in a "RAW" mode to send the PDU. That is a very crude way and should probably be avoided if possible. The better choice is to utilize the internal functionality to build the PDU, the "COOKED" mode. In the example MIT code included on the diskettes, a programmer would need only call the functional trapCreate() to create the PDU and send it. The parameters used with the function call provide all the required information for the trap message to be created and sent. Most reasonable agents will have an interface that allows the trap to be created and sent without a great deal of additional work.

Another problem that seems to arise with traps is the question of "how does SNMP know to send a trap?" The answer is simply, SNMP does not know when. Your code must call the appropriate trap functionality at the appropriate time. For example, if you were building a network hub, every time there was an error condition that the network manager should know about, you would call the functionality to send a trap. That could require a lot of calls to be added to existing systems if a centralized error messaging approach was not implemented during the original design.

The developer will usually not realize all of the times that a trap must be sent from the agent. For example, the "Cold Start" trap is often overlooked. This trap should be sent as soon as the agent is started, yet caution must be used to assure that the MIB is loaded and available, or that any other initialization that may be required has been started. Many agents that are licensed and have an internal way to check the license will do so before they send a cold start trap. This approach is used so that the management station does not get notification from an agent that will exit because of an invalid license.

The addition of trap logic can be one place that requires a great deal of time for people adding SNMP to an existing system. Much thought should be given to exactly how this will be approached before the development begins.

An example of using the MIB/SMI to handle the TRAP information is presented below. It is lengthy to allow the required detail, yet it is far from complete, a creative developer could enhance it a great deal. Yet it provides some interesting ideas for those creating their first MIB.

```
xyzSpecificAlarmState OBJECT-TYPE
  SYNTAX INTEGER {
    disarmed(1),
    armed(2)
  }
  ACCESS read-write
  STATUS mandatory
  DESCRIPTION
    "This indicates whether the repeater is allowed to send specific
     alerts (traps). 1 means disabled, 2 means enabled to send alerts."
  ::= {xyzSpecificGroup 3}

xyzSpecificTrapDestEntry OBJECT-TYPE
  SYNTAX      XyzSpecificTrapDestEntry
  ACCESS      not-accessible
  STATUS      mandatory
  DESCRIPTION
        "Status information and control variables for a
         particular repeater in the system."
  INDEX    { xyzSpecificTrapId }
  ::= { xyzSpecificTrapDestTable 1 }

XyzSpecificTrapDestEntry ::= SEQUENCE {
  xyzSpecificTrapId            INTEGER,
  xyzSpecificTrapDstAdr  IpAddress,
  xyzSpecificTrapDstPro  INTEGER
}

xyzSpecificTrapId OBJECT-TYPE
  SYNTAX      INTEGER (1..127)
  ACCESS      read-only
  STATUS      mandatory
  DESCRIPTION
    "Number of Trap Destination entry. 1 for first entry, 2 for second
     entry, etc."
  ::= { xyzSpecificTrapDestEntry 1 }
```

```
xyzSpecificTrapDstAdr OBJECT-TYPE
  SYNTAX    IpAddress
  ACCESS    read-write
  STATUS    mandatory
  DESCRIPTION
  "This is an IP address to which alerts (traps) should be sent when
  significant events occur."
   ::= { xyzSpecificTrapDestEntry 2 }
xyzSpecificTrapDstPro OBJECT-TYPE
  SYNTAX    INTEGER {
    none(1),      — Disabled
    ip(2),        — TCP/IP
    ipxII(3),     — IPX Ethernet II
    ipx8022(4),   — IPX 802.2 RAW
    ipx8022SNAP(5), — IPX 802.2 SNAP
    ipx8023(6)    — IPX 802.3 Physical Layer
  }
  ACCESS    read-write
  STATUS    mandatory
  DESCRIPTION
    "This is a code indicating the protocol to use when sending alerts.
    1 means disabled, i.e. the corresponding xyzSpecificTrapDstAdr
    variable is not really intended to receive traps.  2 = TCP/IP protocol,
    3 = IPX protocol using Ethernet II, 4 = IPX protocol using RAW 802.2,
    5 = IPX protocol using 802.2 SNAP, 6 = IPX protocol using 802.3 physical
                                        layer."
   ::= { xyzSpecificTrapDestEntry 3 }


— Traps for use by Repeaters

— Traps are defined using the conventions in RFC 1215 [10].
  XyzExtPortEntry ::= SEQUENCE {
    xyzBasPortRptrId               INTEGER,
    xyzBasPortGroupId                   INTEGER,
    xyzBasPortId                   INTEGER,
    xyzBasPortAdminState           INTEGER,
    xyzBasPortAutoPartitionState   INTEGER,
    xyzBasPortLinkState            INTEGER,
    xyzAddrLastSourceAddress       MacAddress,
    xyzAddrSourceAddrChanges       Counter,
    xyzMonPortReadableFrames            Counter,
    xyzMonPortReadableOctets            Counter,
    xyzMonPortFrameCheckSequenceErrs    Counter,
    xyzMonPortAlignmentErrors           Counter,
    xyzMonPortFrameTooLongs             Counter,
    xyzMonPortShortEvents               Counter,
    xyzMonPortRunts                     Counter,
    xyzMonPortCollisions                Counter,
    xyzMonPortLateCollisions            Counter,
    xyzMonPortDataRateMismatches        Counter,
    xyzMonPortAutoPartitions            Counter
```

```
        }


    xyzDosWsTrapId OBJECT-TYPE
    SYNTAX      INTEGER (1..127)
    ACCESS      read-only
    STATUS      mandatory
    DESCRIPTION
    "Number of Trap Destination entry. 1 for first entry, 2 for second
    entry, etc."
    ::= { xyzDosWsTrapDestEntry 1 }

    xyzDosWsTrapDstAdr OBJECT-TYPE
    SYNTAX      IpAddress
    ACCESS      read-write
    STATUS      mandatory
    DESCRIPTION
    "This is an IP address to which alerts (traps) should be sent when
    significant events occur."
    ::= { xyzDosWsTrapDestEntry 2 }

    xyzDosWsTrapDstPro OBJECT-TYPE
    SYNTAX      INTEGER
    ACCESS      read-write
    STATUS      mandatory
    DESCRIPTION
    "This is a code indicating the protocol to use when sending alerts.
    1 means disabled, i.e. the corresponding xyzDosWsTrapDstAdr
    variable is not really intended to receive traps.  2 means use
    TCP/IP protocol.  3,4,5,6 mean use IPX protocol using Ethernet II,
    RAW 802.2, 802.2 SNAP or 802.3 physical layer."
    ::= { xyzDosWsTrapDestEntry 3 }

  xyzDosWsApiTrap OBJECT-TYPE
    SYNTAX      DisplayString
    ACCESS      read-only
    STATUS      mandatory
    DESCRIPTION
    "This is a string set by external applications
    which use the PC Agent API to send an SNMP trap "

    ::= { xyzDosWs 24 }

  xyzDiscover OBJECT-TYPE
    SYNTAX      INTEGER
    ACCESS      read-only
    STATUS      mandatory
    DESCRIPTION
    "This is used in agent discovery by EliteView "

    ::= { xyz 127 }
END
```

FOR FURTHER STUDY

The following documents contain useful information that is beyond the scope of this chapter.

RFC 1052, NRI. Cerf, V., "IAB Recommendations for the Development of Internet Network Management Standards." April 1988.

Rose, M. and K. McCloghrie. *RFC 1065, TWG* "Structure and Identification of Management Information, for TCP/IP-based internets." August 1988.

REFERENCES

Rose, M. *A Request for Comments: 1215.* "Convention for Defining Traps for use with the SNMP." March, 1991.

9

SNMP Commands

OVERVIEW

The SNMP command set is well-known, and readers may wonder why devote a chapter to the commands. I would suggest that it is important to take at least a small look at each command with comment as to their usage and error conditions.

As we look at the SNMP command set, it is important to realize that most will not see the command set directly. On the accompanying diskettes, there is a set of SNMP commands for testing and that may be the only time you will see them. The norm is to have a management station that translates higher level abstracts to the lower level GET/SET scenario, and by doing so, they often hide small issues that one needs to understand. To be able to understand those issues, the GET/SET commands must be understood.

An example of why such understanding may be important here. Let's say that a management station sends and SNMP GET Request to an agent. Suppose the packet is delayed on its arrival at the agent. During that time the management station, not getting a response, sends another GET and then receives the response from the first. In the meantime, the second GET response is dropped on the network. What does the NMS know at that time? Is the first GET used, or is another GET issued because a response from the second did not arrive?

NOTE: Only some management stations will generate another GET if the response is not forthcoming. Those that do generally have a time-out value that can be set for networks with slow response times.

To aid understanding Table 9.1 presents the command set for both V1 and V2.

COMMAND	DESCRIPTION	FROM - TO	V1	V2
Set	Assigns a value to a variable	NMS to Agent	YES	YES
Get	Returns value of variable(s)	NMS to Agent	YES	YES
GetNext	Returns value of list of variables	NMS to Agent	YES	YES
GetBulk	Returns a number of variables	NMS to Agent	NO	YES
Inform	Transmits unsolicited information	NMS to NMS	NO	YES
TRAP	Transmits unsolicited information	Agent to NMS	YES	YES
Responses	Responses to commands	Agent to NMS	YES	YES

Table 9.1 Command Set Comparison.

SNMP GET

The SNMP GET Command initiates a network management query to remote agent and causes a response to be transmitted by the agent. The SNMP GET command attempts to retrieve the items of management information.

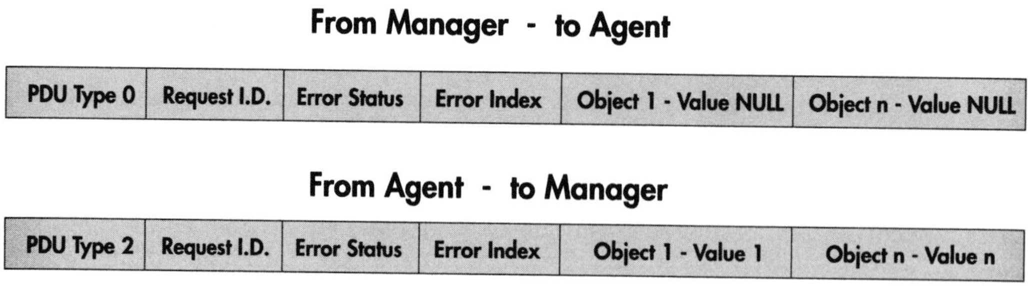

From Manager - to Agent

PDU Type 0	Request I.D.	Error Status	Error Index	Object 1 - Value NULL	Object n - Value NULL

From Agent - to Manager

PDU Type 2	Request I.D.	Error Status	Error Index	Object 1 - Value 1	Object n - Value n

Figure 9.1 SNMP GET Request / Response.

The GET request can generate a number of errors that are returned from the agent. Those errors include noSuchName, tooBig, and genErr. The small set is expanded through the use of error index numbering. The common errors that arise from the agent are presented below.

- **Aggregate error**—this error arises when the management station has mistakenly tried to retrieve a row object. The error returned is "noSuchName" with an error index that indicates the variable.

- **Variable error**—this error is an indication of an attempt to retrieve a variable that cannot be retrieved. The error returned is "genErr" with the error index set.

- **Set error**—this error indicates that the response PDU would exceed some limitation known to the agent. The error returned is "tooBig" with the error index set.

- **Binding error**—this error is returned when a variable does not exactly match. The returned error is "noSuchName" with the appropriate index.

The error status/return has received a good deal of comment. It has been stated that they are not as clear as they could be. Also there is the thinking that someone trying to get information can extract some information, given the SNMP error returned. Both of these issues still receive a good deal of debate within the community.

SNMP GETNEXT

The SNMP GETNEXT command attempts to retrieve the specified subtrees of the MIB. The approach to the SNMP GETNEXT command may vary from agent to agent and NMS to NMS. The GETNEXT command can do what is called "run off." Run off is a condition in which the agent will pass or stick at the end of a table causing masses of worthless data. This behavior can be seen in the MIT agent included in the sample code. When a getnext is done on the route table the agent will often return routes infinitely.

From Manager - to Agent

PDU Type 1	Request I.D.	Error Status	Error Index	Object 1 - NULL	Object n - NULL

From Agent - to Manager

PDU Type 2	Request I.D.	Error Status	Error Index	Object 1 - Value 1	Object n - Value n

Figure 9.2 SNMP GETNEXT Request/Response.

The GETNEXT request can generate a number of errors that are returned from the agent. Those errors are the same as those from SNMP GET with slightly different causes. The set is expanded through the use of error index numbering. The common errors that arise from the agent are presented below.

- **Size error**—this error indicates that the response PDU would exceed some limitation known to the agent. The error returned is "tooBig" with the error index set.

- **Binding error**—this error is returned when a variable does not exactly match. The returned error is noSuchName with the appropriate index.

- **Lexicographical error**—this condition arises when the successor to a requested variable in the binding field can not be retrieved. The error status returned is genErr with the appropriate index.

The fact that many GETNEXT Implementations are lacking became apparent with the introduction of GETBULK. In particular, when a get-next request contains an operand with an arbitrarily generated suffix, some agent implementations will handle this improperly and return a result that is lexicographically less than the operand!

(In most agents getnext and getbulk use the same logic.)

SNMP GETBULK

The management station can repeatedly invoke the get-next operator, using the results of the previous operation as the operands to the next operation. This approach can be laborious. The approach of SNMP GETBULK was developed to alleviate the burden of repeated GETNEXT commands. GETBULK has a complete RFC dedicated to its implementation (RFC 1187). Although the RFC has been around for some time, there has not been a great deal of interest in GETBULK.

From Manager - to Agent

PDU Type 4	Request I.D.	Error Status	Error Index	Object n - Number

From Agent - to Manager

PDU Type 2	Request I.D.	Error Status	Error Index	Object 1 - Value 1	Object n - Value n

Figure 9.3 SNMP GETBULK Request/Response.

GETBULK returns the same types of errors as GETNEXT.

The GetBulkRequest operates essentially by executing multiple GetNext requests. The GetBulkRequest PDU is similar to other PDUs, except that the syntax of two fields changes. The fields Error Status is replaced by Non-Repeaters, and Error Index is replaced by Max-Repetitions. The values of these fields indicate the processing that is to take place. The Non-Repeaters field defines how many of the requested variables will not be processed repeatedly. This field is used when some of the variables are scalar objects, that is, objects having one instance.

The retrieved variables are returned in a Response PDU, according to the manner in which those variables were requested. The total number of variables can be calculated by:

```
    = MIN-OF + (MAX-REPS * MAX-NUM)
    Where
    MIN-OF = minimum value of Non-Repeaters field and number of variable
bindings
    MAX-REPS = Max-Repetitions field in request
    MAX-NUM = minimum of number of variable bindings and zero
```

SNMP SET

The SNMP SET command initiates a network management request to remote management agent to change the value of an SNMP Variable. The SET command, when used on a table row that contains multiple variables, will have multiple variables, one for each object, all with the same instance identifier.

In SNMP, at the protocol level, a management station issues an SNMP set operation containing an arbitrary set of variable bindings. In the case where an agent detects that one or more of those variable bindings refer to an object instance not currently available in that agent, it may, according to the rules of the SNMP, behave according to any of the following paradigms:

(1)   It may reject the SNMP set operation as referring to non-existent object instances by returning a response with the error-status field set to "noSuchName" and the error-index field set to refer to the first vacuous reference.

(2)   It may accept the SNMP set operation as requesting the creation of new object instances corresponding to each of the object instances named in the variable bindings. The value of each (potentially) newly created object instance is specified by the "value" component of the relevant variable binding. In this case, if the request specifies a value for a newly (or previously) created object that it deems inappropriate by reason of value or syntax, then it rejects the SNMP set operation by responding with the error-status field set to badValue and the error-index field set to refer to the first offending variable binding.

(3)   It may accept the SNMP set operation and create new object instances as described in (2) above and, in addition, at its discretion, create supplemental object instances to complete a row in a conceptual table of which the new object instances specified in the request may be a part.

From Manager - to Agent

PDU Type 3	Request I.D.	Error Status	Error Index	Object 1 - Value 1	Object n - Value n

From Agent - to Manager

PDU Type 2	Request I.D.	Error Status	Error Index	Object 1 - Value 1	Object n - Value n

Figure 9.4 SNMP SET Request / Response.

The SET command is one of the most difficult to implement within the agent. It is also the most frustrating from the user perspective. It can (and will) return a number of errors to the NMS. Although the errors are similar to the other SNMP commands, they differ enough that they are presented below.

- **Variable Binding error**—this error arises when the variable binding's field is not available for Set operations. The error returned is "noSuchName" with an error index that indicates the variable.

- **Variable Field error**—this error is an indication that the variable binding field does not conform to the TLV requirements. The error returned is "badValue" with the error index set.

- **Size error**—this error indicates that the response PDU would exceed some limitation known to the agent. The error returned is "tooBig" with the error index set to 0 (zero).

- **General Set error**—this error is returned when a variable cannot be altered for whatever reason. The returned error is "genErr" with the appropriate index.

SNMP INFORMREQUEST

InformRequest is used for manager-to-manager communications. This capability could readily be utilized for distributive management as well as providing redundant management. This functionality was introduced for V2 but several vendors are retrofitting V1 with similar functionality.

RESPONSES

One factor not clearly understood is that there is an SNMP Response to every SNMP command. Some believe that commands, such as the SET, do not have a response. It is also thought, by some, that the set should return some indication that the set took place. Neither is correct. A management application should routinely follow a SET with a GET to assure that the value in question was set.

V2 Responses

SNMPv2 agent will not generate a Response-PDU with an error-status field having a value of "noSuchName," "badValue," or "readOnly." These error status were dropped in V2. All of these subtle differences must be addressed by implementors attempting the development of a bilingual agent.

FOR FURTHER STUDY

The following documents contain useful information that is beyond the scope of this chapter.

RFC 1052, NRI. Cerf, V. April 1988. (IAB Recommendations for the Development of Internet Network Management Standards.)

REFERENCES

Case, J., M. Fedor, M. Schoffstall, and J. Davin. *RFC 1157.* (Simple Network Management Protocol.)

10

V1—V2 Coexistence

INTRODUCTION

For the most part I intermingle material from V1 and V2, and up to this point, I have stayed away from many references to SNMPv2 specifics. That was due in part to the fact that there is a general uneasiness with V2. Few vendors and users have shown interest in V2. This is due primarily to the security features that were part of V2. I have always believed that when a piece of software becomes more trouble than it is worth, it will not find the market share it had hoped for. There will be those who will say I am wrong and that the complexity is required, but I will let the sales and implementation numbers speak for me.

The single biggest issue for V2 is the encryption (DES). Not only is it very slow—having been created for hardware implementations—it is also banned from export to many countries. This makes for a sales and marketing nightmare. There are, however, a number of people working on simplified security with several proposals already out. Surely one will provide a workable solution. With that said, I would still be negligent if I did not spend some time talking about V1 to V2 conversion.

There are at least two approaches to dealing with V2, without moving away from V1 completely. These are favorable to the complete conversion because of the need to stay compatible with everybody.

The two approaches that seem to be receiving favor are Bilingual Managers and using Proxy Agents. To fully explore the subject the RFC 1452 that covers the coexistence of V1 and V2, each is presented briefly on the following page.

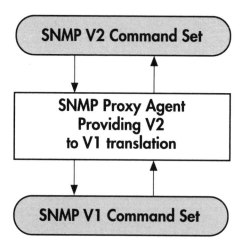

Figure 10.1 Command Mapping

The major enhancements/changes of SNMPv2 are:

• New Macros

• New Data Types

• Textual Conventions

• Manager-to-Manager

• Bulk Transfer

• More Error Codes

• Enhanced Security

Each of these elements is discussed in the text. Most are familiar with the enhanced security and the requirements it places on the development. Many implementations have developed only limited security. Many of the V2 enhancements add complexity. For example, an SNMPv2 entity must be capable of acting as either an agent or manager. This characteristic provides the Manager-to-Manager capability. Other enhancements include the improvements to the SNMP PDUs and additional error codes. The additional error codes allow the NMS to more readily determine why an operation may have failed.

PROXY AGENTS

Proxy agents are described in the RFC 1452 as the approach to the coexistence of V1 and V2. Coexistence is the term used in the RFC, and I love it. It brings to mind two parties that cannot tolerate each other, but somehow manage to coexist. That is, in fact, the case with V1 and V2: they do not communicate with each other without an intermediary (a proxy).

The required characteristics of a proxy agent are covered in the RFC and will not be detailed here. I will, however, touch on some of the high points.

To perform as a proxy agent, the SNMP code must be configured as an agent. Recall the SNMPv2 requires that the code be able to perform as either the agent or manager. In this case, it is performing as an agent that will convert requests from one version to the other. In order to do this correctly, a number of criteria must be met.

- When translating from SNMPv2 to SNMPv2 the agent must:

  (1) If a GetRequest-PDU, GetNextRequest-PDU, or SetRequest-PDU is received, then it is passed unaltered.

  (2) If a GetBulkRequest-PDU is received, the proxy agent sets the non-repeater and max-repetitions fields to zero, and sets the tag of the PDU to GetNextRequest-PDU.

- When translating from SNMPv1 acting as an agent to SNMPv2 acting as a manager, the agent must:

  (1) If a GetResponse-PDU is received, then it is passed unaltered.

  (2) If a Trap-PDU is received, then it is mapped into a SNMPv2-Trap-PDU. This mapping is done via specific rules that are outlined in the RFC. Make sure you have some spare time when you read this part of the RFC; you'll need it.

A number of other considerations are also necessary when constructing a proxy agent. It is a complex effort and should not be taken lightly. The complete details are far outside the scope of this work.

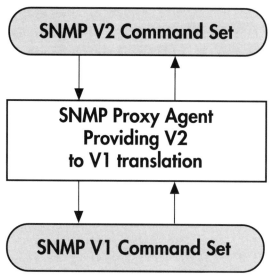

Figure 10.2 Proxy Agent.

Additional Uses for Proxy Agents

Another capability of proxy agents is that they can be developed to talk to non-SNMP management agents. Just as they are used to convert V1 to V2 or vise versa, they can be developed to translate to any management protocol.

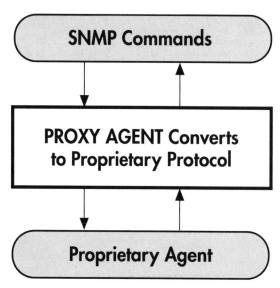

Figure 10.3 Additional Use of Proxy Agent.

Another capability of a proxy is to be able to shield an SNMP agent from access control policies. For example, the proxy could shield the NMS from the complexity of MIB views. Interestingly enough, this has not been implemented to any great extent. The proxy could also shield the agent from redundant requests.

Proxy Agents—Problems

One of the issues that has arisen from the introduction of proxy agents is open access. Through the use of a proxy agent, a vendor can hide the true protocol being used. This allows flexibility, but it also creates a situation in which vendors are more prone to develop a proxy agent than to completely embrace the SNMP environment. At some point this could create a troubling situation, since the protocol will have a number of problems, none of which will have a clear source for solution. One party will point the finger at the next, and the end user will be left with no solutions.

BILINGUAL MANAGERS

Another approach to coexistence of the two versions is the use of a bilingual manager. When a bilingual manager is used, it communicates with an SNMPv1 agent using a V1 protocol. When communicating with an SNMPv2 agent, it will switch to a V2 protocol. When functioning as a V2 manager, the InformRequest can be used. In the administration process of the manager, it is instructed what protocol to use with a given agent. This approach is very flexible, given that it can manage any agent used by any vendor. In this case, the manager accepts the burden of using the correct protocol.

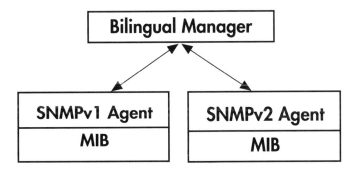

Figure 10.4 Bilingual Manager.

The bilingual manager does not inherently know what command set it should use to communicate with a given agent. They make the determination which version to use for a given agent based upon information contained in the MIB. For example, when communicating with a V2 agent, the InformRequest can be used. When communicating in a V1, mode the InformRequest would not be available.

CONVERSION

If a complete conversion to V2 is required, a good deal of work will be required for the MIB. Much of the early text of this book is related to the SMI/MIB creation. This is due to the fact that it tends to be one of those areas that is often overlooked until someone realizes the magnitude of the effort required. That same level of effort is required for conversion to V2. Below I touch on some of the issues of the conversion.

MIB Conversion

As with everything else relating to SNMP, MIB Conversion is presented in an RFC somewhere, and the RFC is the best source for the complete detail. What is presented here are the key points.

In general, conversion of a MIB module does not require the deprecation of the objects contained therein. Only if the semantics of an object truly change should deprecation be performed.

- The IMPORTS statement must reference SNMPv2-SMI. Many of the V1 implementations referenced RFC1155-SMI and RFC-1212. Just adding SNMPv2-SMI IMPORTs while leaving the other two does not work.

- The MODULE-IDENTITY macro must be invoked immediately after any IMPORTs or exports' statement.

- Hyphen characters must be removed.

- Various SYNTAX clauses must be changed.

- For all objects, the ACCESS clause must be replaced by a MAX-ACCESS clause.

- For any columnar object which is used solely for instance identification in a conceptual row, the object must have the value of its MAX-ACCESS clause set to "not- accessible."

- For all objects, if the value of the STATUS clause is "mandatory," the value must be replaced with "current."

- For all objects, if the value of the STATUS clause is "optional," the value must be replaced with "obsolete."

- For any object not containing a DESCRIPTION clause, the object must have a DESCRIPTION clause defined.

- For any object corresponding to a conceptual row that does not have an INDEX clause, the object must have either an INDEX clause or an AUGMENTS clause defined.

This is not intended to be complete; it does however, give some idea of the requirements and will get you started. Along with the changes listed, there are a number of changes that are recommended. It has been my experience that when the protocol authors make a recommendation, it should be given due consideration. As with the initial MIB creation, the conversion will require time and effort. Every object in the MIB will need to be reviewed. MIBs containing thousands of objects can require many hours.

FOR FURTHER STUDY

The following documents contain useful information that is beyond the scope of this chapter.

Recommendation X.208. Specification of Abstract Syntax Notation One. (See also ISO 8824.)

REFERENCES

Case, J., K. McCloghrie, M. Rose, and S. Waldbusser. *RFC 1444*. "Conformance Statements for version 2 of the Simple Network Management Protocol (SNMPv2)."

Chen, Tai. *Data Communications*, "Proxy Agents Block SNMP's Open Promise." November 1993.

Fisher, Sharon. *Communications Week*, "Secure SNMP, Anyone." April 4, 1994.

11

V2 Modifications

INTRODUCTION

One of the major changes of V2 is the addition of new data types. V2 has added support for types that were not supported in V1. The ASN.1 types from RFC 1155 that have not changed are INTEGER, OCTET STRING and OBJECT IDENTIFIER. The defined data types from RFC 1155 that have not changed include IpAddress, TimeTicks and Opaque. The data types that are new with SNMPv2 include BIT STRING, Integer32, Counter32, Gauge32, NsapAddress, Counter64 and UIntger32.

Error Codes

Another major change was the addition of more expanative error codes. The changes in the error codes are reflected in Table 11.1.

V2 Error	GET	GETNEXT	GETBULK	SET	INFORM
noErro	✗	✗	✗	✗	✗
tooBig	✗	✗		✗	✗
getErr	✗	✗	✗	✗	
noAcces				✗	
wrongType				✗	
wrongLength				✗	
wrongEncoding				✗	
wrongValue				✗	
noCreation				✗	
inconsistentValue				✗	
resourceUnavailable				✗	
commitFailed				✗	
undoFailed				✗	
authorizationError	✗	✗	✗	✗	✗
notWriteable				✗	
inconsistentName				✗	

Table 11.1 Error Codes

There are three error codes that are never generated in V2, they are:

- noSuchName
- badValue
- readOnly

These error codes were dropped in part for security reasons.

M2M (MANAGER TO MANAGER)

One of the more significant enhancements provided by SNMP v2 is the ability for entities to be configured as either managers or agents. It also implies that two managers can communicate. This manager to manager (M2M) communications can be significant for implementations that want one central manager to communicate to distributed subnets. Such an architecture could be developed utilizing a central manager that talked to distributed managers, each on a subnet. The accompanying software has the MIT agent which can be configured as a manager or agent or both, dependent on the compile flags.

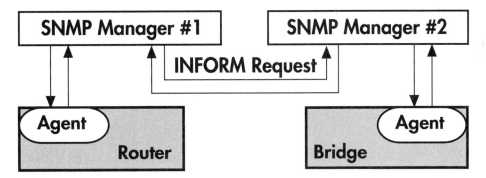

Figure 11.1 Manager to Manager Communication.

The M2M capability is supported by the M2M MIB. The M2M MIB defines procedures for one manager to talk to another manager. To support these procedures, three new concepts were used. They are:

- alarms
- events
- notifications

The alarm is used to trigger an event. The event may cause notifications to be reported to any number of management stations. The information PDU is used for this purpose.

The M2M MIB is divided into groups as we saw with the SNMP–V2 MIB. The groups represent each of the procedures listed above. The groups are:

- **ALARM GROUP**—this group contains information related to configuration threshold alarms for entities acting in a dual, manager/agent, role.

- **EVENT GROUP**—this group provides an event table that associates an event type with a notification.

- **NOTIFICATION GROUP**—provides information related to the notifications.

M2M introduces the ability to provide distributed management. Distributed network managemant is needed and will enhance network management. Most vendors including IBM, HP and AT&T are working on this type of functionality.

V2 SECURITY

The issue of security for V2 is truely a sore spot for many. To implement the complete security requirements for V2 would require a good deal of time and effort. It has been said that an interim step may be forthcoming because of the complexity of V2 security. The reader should consult the latest information on the Internet before going too far with V2 security. I ended up getting one of those little, frustration-relieving, punching dolls when I first started dealing with V2 security.

The Authentication Protocol provides a mechanism by which SNMPv2 management communications transmitted by the party may be reliably identified as having originated from that party. The authentication protocol reliably determines that the message received is the message that was sent.

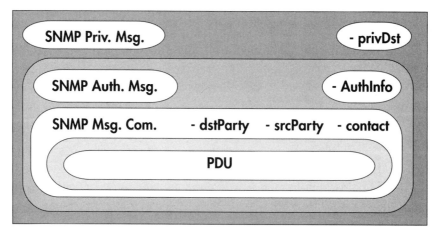

Figure 11.2   V2 Security Envelope.

The Symmetric Privacy Protocol protects messages from disclosure by encrypting their contents according to a secret cryptographic key known only to the originator and recipient. The additional functionality afforded by this protocol is assumed to justify its additional computational cost.

The Digest Authentication Protocol depends on the existence of loosely synchronized clocks between the originator and recipient of a message. The protocol specification makes no assumptions about the strategy by which such clocks are synchronized.

The three paragraphs above are excerpts from the RFC 1446. They provide a bit of the flavor of V2 security. They also start to give the reader an idea of the pain involved with V2 security. That pain grows when the implementor realizes that there are export rules that come into play with the use of the encryption algorithm (DES) outlined in V2. To add to the problem, the CPU cycles required to utilize DES are extreme for an embedded real time system. The CPU requirements became clear to me in a recent implementation. When the system was at 75 percent of capacity and it received an SNMPv2 PDU, it would immediately go 100 percent busy and begin to drop the network traffic. This was not exactly what the client wanted to see. It didn't do much for my day, either.

DES is Data Encryption Standard and the specifications for it are published by at least two sources:

- National Institute of Standards and Technology

- American National Standards Institute

A working version of DES code is included on the accompanying source diskettes.

When Privacy is used, the entire PDU, except for the 'priv Dst' field is ASN.1 encoded. The Privacy Protocol will utilize three variables, 'party Priv Protocol,' 'party Priv Private' and 'party Priv Public.' These variables are kept in the Party Database. The database contains information about each 'Party' in the form of five authentication variables. The variables, 'party Auth Protocol,' 'party Auth Lifetime.' The authentication mechanism, MD5, utilizes these variables. MD5 provides for the verification of the integrity of the message.

The Access Control has four components, 'Destination Party,' 'Source Party,' 'Resources' and 'Privileges.' The access control is provided through the use of these elements and there may be multiple access control policies. through the four tables in the Party MIB access privileges can be determined. The four MIB control tables are, 'party table,' 'context table,' 'access control table' and the 'MIB view tables.'

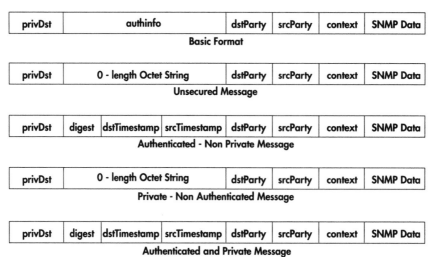

Figure 11.3 SNMPv2 Message Security Formats

FOR FURTHER STUDY

The following documents contain useful information that is beyond the scope of this chapter.

Document	Description
ISO 3307, Information interchange	Representations of time of the day.
ISO 4031, Information interchange	Representation of local time differentials.
ISO 6523, Data interchange	Structure for identification of organizations.

Data Encryption Standard, National Institute of Standards and Technology. Federal Information Processing Standard (FIPS) Publication 46-1.

ANSI X3.92-1981, (December, 1980)	Data Encryption Algorithm, American National Standards Institute
(FIPS) Publication 81, December, 1980)	DES Modes of Operation, National Institute of Standards and Technology. Federal Information Processing Standard
ANSI X3.106-1983 (May 1983)	Data Encryption Algorithm Modes of Operation, American

12

Other Transport Protocols

INTRODUCTION

SNMP was originally developed to utilize UDP, although some consideration was given to the possibility that it might be used with other transport protocols. Remember that SNMP was only intended to be an interim solution so other transports did not appear to be a main concern. As SNMP has taken more and more of a foothold, the need for the comparability with other transport protocols has grown and grown. A number of RFCs being generated that outlines the use of SNMP with other transports. Currently there are RFCs for SNMP over OSI, SNMP over AppleTalk, SNMP over IPX, with others proposed. One of the original SNMP RFCs, RFC 1089 (SNMP over Ethernet) provides insight to the requirements of SNMP.

Many of the SNMP agents do not have the hooks for utilizing transports other than UDP, and they are not very amenable to any attempt to change that. Others have most of the interface isolated and can be easily adapted to other transports. No matter what transport protocol is utilized the key factor is the support of the five properties listed in Chapter 4. Again they are:

- End-to-End Checksum

- Multiplexing/Demultiplexing

- Routing

- Media Independence

- Fragmentation and Reassembly

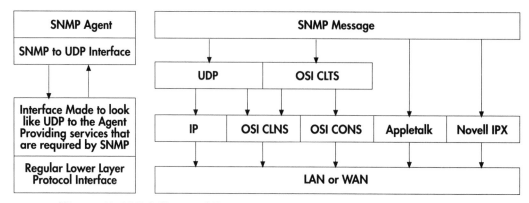

Figure 12.1 MultiProtocol Layering.

One example of an agent that can be adapted to other protocols is the MIT version included on the accompanying diskette. The interface (below) is easily modified to make a call to other transports without changing the agent or the transport.

```
SmpStatusType udpSend (udp, bp, n)

SmpSocketType          udp;
CBytePtrType           bp;
CIntfType              n;

{
        UdpPtrType              tp;
        int                     result;

        if (udp == (SmpSocketType) 0) {
                return (errBad);
        }

        tp = (UdpPtrType) udp;
        do {
                result = sendto (tp->udpSocket, (char *) bp,
                        (int) n, (int) 0,
                        & (tp->udpSockAddr), sizeof (struct sockaddr_in));
                n -= result;
                bp += result;

        } while ((result > 0) && (n > 0));

        if (result < 0) {
                perror ("udpSend");
                return (errBad);
        }
```

```
        else {
                return (errOk);
        }
}
```

A quick and dirty implementation would be to replace the area in bold type with some other protocol or possibly a subroutine that handled the new protocol gracefully. True, this is a fairly "dirty" approach that should only be utilized for prototyping, but it demonstrates the area where the developer could attack.

Using Multiple Protocols

Often the SNMP agent is required to be able to use multiple protocols. This happens when there is a need to have an out-of-band channel for communications. There will generally be an in-band and out-of-band, both, with SNMP communications required. This is a challenge for all but the best commercial SNMP agents. It can become very complex if the agent is on an embedded system and must be able to route the SNMP response back on any available route. That is to say, the original in path may have hung, and the routing needs to take a different route and protocol back to the initiator.

Many problems can arise when utilizing multiple protocols. Multiple protocol stacks within the same environment tend to cause memory issue, buffer conflicts, duplicate infrastructures and transport bound applications. The co-residence of multiple protocols also tends to eat CPU cycles and cause still other problems. From a development perspective multiple protocols require additional support as well as the additional burden of version and release control. Even with all of these issues, many vendors find it to be worthwhile to enhance SNMP with added transport protocols. In some cases it can and should be done, but the cost must be understood.

Other transports that have gained a great deal of interest for use with SNMP are SLIP and PPP. This allows vendors to dial up their clients around the world to assist with management of unruly systems. These protocols will be covered in some detail later in this chapter.

X.25

A native X.25 implementation of SNMP would be extremely difficult, requiring a great deal of code and work. It would require the understanding and implementation of X.121, the X.25 addressing scheme. All of this is outside the scope of this work, however, there is an approach to utilizing X.25, to utilize "tunneling."

Tunneling

Tunneling is the use of X.25 simply as a delivery vehicle. It is done by making an X.25 connection and then sending the UDP/IP packets across as though they were a form of data. The down side of this approach is that some type of equipment must be used to make the X.25 connect with and host the UDP/IP data. This approach is in popular demand for SNMP because of the wide coverage and availability of X.25.

LLC and LLC2

The developer should not need to know what the second layer protocol is. That should be the case when LLC is utilized, but on occasion LLC will create some difficulty. SNMP should not tie itself to any Layer Two protocol, and LLC is no exception. The primary reason for their inclusion here is to consider LLC2 which does "spoofing" of the various end point equipment.

LLC and LLC2 are protocol layers that are clearly defined by the IEEE 802 project. LLC defines a connectionless protocol, while LLC2 defines the same protocol with enhancements to support the connection oriented model. LLC lives and breathes under many versions of token-ring but is seldom utilized with Ethernet or 802.3. (Ethernet is the DIX base of 802.3). LLC2 is not often implemented because of the complexity involved with "spoofing" on when an unreliable media is used.

Developers should consult the appropriate RFC related to using SNMP with the transport protocol they intend to use. It is also appropriate to refer to any documents relating to that specific transport. The developer should also consider the use of encapsulation. That is the process of placing the entire SNMP PDU in the data segment of a transport, and letting the transport carry the SNMP data without further knowledge of the fact that it is carrying a complete PDU. This method is often used for ISO implementations and can just as easily be utilized with SNMP. It provides a fast method for development, and in cases where the transport source is not available, it is the only way to achieve an implementation.

SLIP and PPP

SLIP (Serial Line /IP) and PPP (Point to Point Protocol) are very popular protocols that are utilized a great deal in the embedded systems world. PPP tends to be used with local consoles while SLIP primarily serves as a means by which a dial up connection can be made. The dial up connection can serve as a means for a vendor to trouble shoot networking equipment without being on site or as an out-of-band connection.

To implement SLIP or PPP in an SNMP agent the methodology is similar. Either protocol must be mapped into the UDP mentality of SNMP. Depending on how far the developer wants to go for a clean implementation the size of the task will vary. In those cases where the implementor needs a fast turn, the same approach that was outlined in the beginning of this chapter could be used. In those cases where the implementation needs to be pristine the developer may need to add some type of logic to support a type of addressing algorithm.

VARIOUS TRANSPORT PROTOCOL

Some of the transport protocols we have mentioned were given no more than a single paragraph. That really was all that was required since the data is merely the cargo for most transport layers. The transport protocol itself has little or no knowledge of the cargo.

SNMP provides the ASN.1 encoding before the data is passed to the transport. Various layers of the transport may do further encoding of headers into ASN.1 yet that has no affect on SNMP.

When utilizing other transport layers, the main concern should be adapting the API (Application Programming Interface) from SNMP to the transport interface. If the transport happens to utilize ASN.1 encoding, the developer will need to assure that BEDLs (Basic Encoding and Decoding Library) is compatible across the transport interface.

The developer will also need to recognize the type of transport interface that is native to the target system. For example, an agent being developed for System V UNIX would probably utilize the TLI (Transport Layer Interface) rather then Berkeley Sockets. In other cases the use of the file abstraction may be most appropriate. The exact interface is dependent on the target system.

FOR FURTHER STUDY

The following documents contain useful information that is beyond the scope of this chapter.

Document	Description
Data Communications Computer Networks and Open Systems	Third Addition by F. Halsall
"Connectionless Network Protocol (ISO 8473)	by Satz, G

"SNMP over Ethernet," RFC 1089
February 1989

by Schoffstall, M.,
Davin, C.,Fedor, M., and
J. Case

RFC 793
September 1981

by Postel, J.,
"Transmission Control Protocol"

RFC 768

by Postel, J.,   [5] "User
Datagram Protocol"

RFC 1449

"Transport Mappings for version
2 of the Simple Network
Management Protocol (SNMPv2)"
Case, J., McCloghrie, K., Rose,
M., and Waldbusser, S.,

Principles of Communication and
Networking Protocols ©Computer Society
Press 1984

by Simon Lam

SNA Perspective
August 1992 ©CSI

IBM

REFERENCES

Stallings, W. *Handbook of Computer Communications* (Three Volumes).
Macmillan Publishing, 1987.

13

An Agent

Other chapters have focused on developing the periphery of an agent. The point being that the knowledge simply is not there yet. The thinking seems to be to focus on the detail of the SNMP protocol rather than delivering functionality that utilized with the SNMP protocol. Every single agent could easily do a warm boot of a piece of equipment. Looking at the code, below:

```
#define MAGIC          0              /* for cold restart */
/* #define MAGIC        0x1234        /* for warm restart */

#define BOOT_SEG       0xffffL
#define BOOT_OFF       0x0000L
#define BOOT_ADR       ((BOOT_SEG << 16) | BOOT_OFF)

#define DOS_SEG              0x0040L
#define RESET_FLAG     0x0072L
#define RESET_ADR      ((DOS_SEG << 16) | RESET_FLAG)

static MixStatusType    sysBootSet (cookie, name, namelen, asn)

MixCookieType           cookie;
MixNamePtrType          name;
MixLengthType           namelen;
AsnIdType               asn;

{
     cookie = cookie;
     name = name;
     namelen = namelen;
     asn = asn;
     void ((far *fp)()) = (void (far *)()) BOOT_ADR;
```

```
/*
            Could add a great deal to make the
            system happy before the boot is done.
*/

*(int far *)RESET_ADR = MAGIC;
(*fp)();
return 0;        /* never gets here, but keeps compiler happy */
}
```

It can be seen that a developer could readily do a warm boot. Such functionality would be exercised by doing an SNMP Set of the variable by the NMS. The set would transcend the network and trigger the code to do the warm boot.

Let's now look at the flow of the set through the agent. We will utilize the flow of the MIT agent code included on the diskette. That code is an excellent example since it is the base code utilized by HP, AT&T and IBM in their agent products.

Note: All three of these vendors have multiple agents to analyze an agent problem without being sure that the agent uses this code base.

We will begin analyzing the agent with the receipt of the PDU. Ethernet, IP, UDP are assumed.

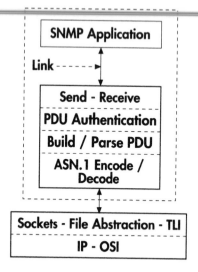

Figure 13.1 Architecture.

The SNMP agent at start up will bind to the appropriate port filling a socket structure with the appropriate information. This socket abstraction is often an area for problems. Many have utilized differing socket structures and often the fields simply do not match. In other cases there will be discrepancies in network address field of this structure. The return address is taken from the incoming packet. This allows the SNMP response to get back to the correct manager. This can be utilized for dealing with multiple managers.

After the agent stores off this information it will begin the process of decoding the SNMP PDU. In the debug code presented in the appendix it can be seen that the agent will go through many cycles to decode the PDU. The agent will evaluate the data as the decoding takes place. The agent walks the OID tree as the decoding happens. Should the agent find that the OID does not exist in the MIB the agent will stop decoding and return the appropriate message. If the decoding completes the agent will know exactly what MIB element is the target of the PDU.

With the agent now having a handle on the MIB element it will exercise logic to determine what can be done with this element. The element may be READ ONLY and the PDU was a set.

The agent would reject the set returning the appropriate message to the NMS. The information relating to the MIB element is contained in the MIB structure. Every element of the MIB will consist of a structure with the basic information relating to that element.

```
typedef struct MibStrTag{
                    CUnsfType    mibStrMaxLen;
                    CUnsfType    mibStrLen;
                    CBytePtr     mibStrData;
                    } MibStrType;
typedef MibStrType *MibStrPtrType;


MibStatusType   mibIntlRW();
MibStatusType   mib;ntlRO();
```

Figure 13.2 Internal MIB Structure.

Every agent will utilize some different structure to maintain MIB information. Some agents provide the ability to extend the MIB. The MIT agent does not since it is intended to be an embedded agent and not expanded when in use.

At this point the agent knows what can be done with the target MIB element. If the SNMP PDU is a GET REQUEST the MIB structure will be accessed via a pointer. That pointer in the MIT MIB can be a pointer to a function. That function would execute and return the appropriate value. Since the MIT agent uses an assignment of the pointer value, the return of the function is assigned as well. That return value, after being assigned, is the actual MIB variable. Generally this variable is named by the MIB element name. In some cases the MIB pointer will be a pointer to a value that is to be updated by other parts of the system. Generally such updates will be outside the scope of the agent. Bad values in these elements are often attributed to the agent. Many will observe values that are not correct and make a statement about the quality of the agent when it is actually the surrounding system at fault.

Now that the agent has the value for the MIB element it begins the process of encoding the value. The first step associated with encoding is to add a type field. Then to begin the encoding. Upon completion of the encoding the value is placed in a buffer. A pointer to the buffer is then given to the appropriate transport protocol. The transport protocol was stored during the receipt of the SNMP PDU. Since the MIT code functions in this manner, there may be multiple transport protocols utilized at the same time. This is ideal for providing out-of-band backup or dial up management.

The MIT agent is structured to run to completion. That is, the PDUs are serialized. Most agents function in this manner to assure that conflicting requests are not processed out of the sequence received.

Some functionality that is not available in the MIT agent includes the ability to unwind variables or do a test of a variable. Both of these relate to SNMPv1's requirement that all variables of a SET multiple binding be set or none are set.

The main objection to the MIT code is its complexity. It is highly portable taking less than a week to port to PSOS and Vertex. It ports to DOS as a TSR and with a little care it can be built in to an executable that is only 32K. This small size and great portability make it an excellent starting point for an agent implementation. Documentation is a bit slim but can be found in a commercial form.

Although there is no compiler with the MIT agent there are several GDMO compilers available.

The code is structured into directories as seen below:

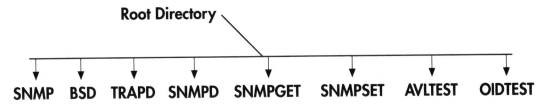

Figure 13.3 Directory Structure.

Each directory is specific to the functionality. The SNMP directory builds all of the encoding and decoding logic into a library. The BSD directory provides all the logic to link with Berkeley Sockets. SNMPD will link with SNMP and BSD to provide an agent to run on a Berkeley type system. TRAPD will link with SNMP and BSD to provide a TRAP demon. SNMPGET and SNMPSET will link with SNMP GET and SET functions. There are also test directories (not listed) that can be used to test the builds and the functionality.

The MIT agent can readily be coupled to the BTREE software included on the diskette. The BTREE software can be coupled to a GDMO compiler output to provide an agent and compiler package equal to the $30,000.00 commercial packages. Utilizing this code, an intelligent MIB based on information in this book, a completed agent can be done for under $5000.00. It will function better than the commercial versions and it will be your own.

FOR FURTHER STUDY

The following documents contain useful information that is beyond the scope of this chapter.

Document	Description
MIT Documentation	On Diskette

REFERENCES

Case, J., M. Fedor, M. Schoffstall, and J. Davin. *RFC 1157* "Simple Network Management Protocol."

APPENDIX A

NSFNET—Information

The day-to-day operations of NSFNET are done by MERIT at Ann Arbor, Michigan. A new Network Operations Center (NOC) in the University of Michigan's Computing Center Building is the focus of the daily operations. Under the supervision of engineers, technicians and operators the hardware and software of the NSFNET is monitored and maintained. The NOC provides round the clock operations and control.

Merit produces and delivers on-line information about the network and assists technical personnel at the middle level sites. Information files are available for anonymous FTP from Merit/NSFNET Information Services machine. An electronic newsletter, The Link Letter, is published monthly with technical articles and features about the NSFNET.

You can reach the Merit/NSFNET Information services at:

Phone: (800) 66-MERIT
Electronic Mail: NSFNET-Info@merit.edu
U.S. Mail: Merit/NSFNET Information Services
                    1075 Beal Avenue
                    Ann Arbor, Michigan 48109-2112

APPENDIX B

SNMP Implementations of Note

This appendix relates to the various SNMP implementations. It is not intended to cover every one, just some of the more successful ones. "Successful" here means market share and does not relate to quality; that evaluation will have to come from the long-term users of these implementations.

MACSNMP

The implementation of SNMP for the Macintosh computer is called MacSNMP and consists of a number of components. It is capable of dealing with its own MIB and third-party MIBs. The manager operates over both AppleTalk and straight TCP/IP.

NOTE: AppleTalk is an off shoot of TCP/IP.

MacSNMP is also supported by Apple Internet Router.

CABLETRON SYSTEMS INC.

Cabletron Spectrum, Remote LANview Windows, and MIB Navigator are all available from Cabletron, and they allow managers to work with the MIB and various configuration information. Primarily targeted at the Cabletron platforms, the tools are available for use with third-party equipment.

DEC POLYCENTER

Digital Equipment has been known for distributed interconnect. In years past the standing line was "if you want to connect two different systems, do it through a DEC system." The DEC SNMP implementation is no different in that it operates under the EMA (Enterprise Management Architecture). PolyCenter runs on virtually all of the DEC platforms. The manager supports a number of the OSI management components. The EMA operates as an environment that allows a number of "presentation" modules to operate.

HEWLETT-PACKARD CO.

Hewlett-Packard has taken the lead in UNIX, quietly selling more UNIX products than any other vendor. HP is showing the same competitiveness in the SNMP management arena. Every development lab that I go to seems to have at least one HP OpenView platform. HP has taken several different approaches to SNMP management. It offers the base product as well as a distributed OpenView product. The API (Application Programmers Interface) is very complete and the overall system is very good. This has led to HP's product being relabeled and sold by a number of other vendors. OpenView is based upon an object-oriented approach with the various objects registering through an Object Registration Service. This service provides such things as mapping the names to network addresses. HP also provides a MIB browser that is a very useful tool.

IBM

IBM System Monitor/6000 runs on AIX, providing a user interface to various agents and network components. This product has some capabilities that many of the other implementations simply do not support. That is due to the fact that it utilizes three types of interfaces. One interface provides a centralized mentality. This interface has lent itself to integration into the SNA world. The SNMP Traps can be converted to SNA alerts and vise versa. The system also has strong device discovery capability. It also provides network monitoring for fault and performance measurements. This product will probably remain one of the only manager in the SNA arena for some time because of the difficulty relating to LLC2.

AT&T/NCR ONEVISION

One Vision is a port of HP OpenView, as is the IBM implementation. It offers a few enhancements, but for the most part IBM, AT&T, and HP are all the same. HP is clearly in the lead since it has the development before the IBM and AT&T, but it is quickly ported and the three stay fairly consistent.

NOVELL NETWARE MANAGER

Novell's NetWare Management System provides integrated network management for NetWare LANs. Support for some third-party hubs and routers is also available. The MIBs are loaded as NLMs (Network Loadable Modules) on the server.

SUNCONNECT SUNNET MANAGER

SunNet Manager comes from SunConnect, a division of Sun Microsystems, Inc. It is that separation that has driven the product to be developed to deal with any agent, regardless of the vendor. SunNet has strict adherence to the Internet standards which helps it to achieve this compatibility. SunNet Manager will operate across various protocols. It was developed around an object-oriented philosophy that provides a good deal of functionality. It allows the user to define macros and has such tools as a MIB browser and 3-dimensional graphics for presentation.

CASTLE ROCK SNMPc

SNMPc is a PC-based management application that has gained a lot of popularity because of its price. It is not only inexpensive, but offers a great deal of functionality. It is somewhat simpler to setup than some of the larger network management applications while having all the functionality of a larger network. The maps and services are every bit that of any of the larger applications.

APPENDIX C

SNMPv2 Related RFCs

Introduction to version 2 of the
Internet-standard Network Management Framework

Request for Comments: 1441 April 1993

Authors:

J. Case	SNMP Research, Inc.
K. McCloghrie	Hughes LAN Systems
M. Rose	Dover Beach Consulting, Inc.
S. Waldbusser	Carnegie Mellon University

Structure of Management Information
for version 2 of the Simple Network Management Protocol (SNMPv2)

Request for Comments: 1442 April 1993

Authors:

J. Case	SNMP Research, Inc.
K. McCloghrie	Hughes LAN Systems
M. Rose	Dover Beach Consulting, Inc.
S. Waldbusser	Carnegie Mellon University

Textual Conventions for version 2 of the
Simple Network Management Protocol (SNMPv2)

Request for Comments: 1443 April 1993

Authors:

J. Case	SNMP Research, Inc.
K. McCloghrie	Hughes LAN Systems
M. Rose	Dover Beach Consulting, Inc.
S. Waldbusser	Carnegie Mellon University

Conformance Statements for version 2 of the
Simple Network Management Protocol (SNMPv2)

Request for Comments: 1444 April 1993

Authors:

J. Case	SNMP Research, Inc.
K. McCloghrie	Hughes LAN Systems
M. Rose	Dover Beach Consulting, Inc.
S. Waldbusser	Carnegie Mellon University

Administrative Model for version 2 of the
Simple Network Management Protocol (SNMPv2)

Request for Comments: 1445 April 1993

Authors:

J. Galvin	Trusted Information Systems
K. McCloghrie	Hughes LAN Systems

Security Protocols for version 2 of the
Simple Network Management Protocol (SNMPv2)

Request for Comments: 1446 April 1993

Authors:

J. Galvin   Trusted Information Systems

K. McCloghrie   Hughes LAN Systems

Party MIB for version 2 of the
Simple Network Management Protocol (SNMPv2)

Request for Comments: 1447 April 1993

Authors:

J. Galvin   Trusted Information Systems

K. McCloghrie   Hughes LAN Systems

Protocol Operations for version 2 of the
Simple Network Management Protocol (SNMPv2)

Request for Comments: 1448 April 1993

Authors:

J. Case   SNMP Research, Inc.

K. McCloghrie   Hughes LAN Systems

M. Rose   Dover Beach Consulting, Inc.

S. Waldbusser   Carnegie Mellon University

Transport Mappings for version 2 of the
Simple Network Management Protocol (SNMPv2)

Request for Comments: 1449 April 1993
Authors:

J. Case	SNMP Research, Inc.
K. McCloghrie	Hughes LAN Systems
M. Rose	Dover Beach Consulting, Inc.
S. Waldbusser	Carnegie Mellon University

Management Information Base for version 2 of the
Simple Network Management Protocol (SNMPv2)

Request for Comments: 1450 April 1993
Authors:

J. Case	SNMP Research, Inc.
K. McCloghrie	Hughes LAN Systems
M. Rose	Dover Beach Consulting, Inc.
S. Waldbusser	Carnegie Mellon University

APPENDIX D

DEBUG Output From NMS

Below is the output from the debug of an SNMP SET operation.

```
smpRequest:
asnAppend:
head:
[ C 3 ] SEQUENCE {
}
item:
[ U 2 ] INTEGER {
      00
}
result:
[ C 3 ] SEQUENCE {
      [ U 2 ] INTEGER {
            00
      }
}
asnAppend:
head:
[ C 3 ] SEQUENCE {
      [ U 2 ] INTEGER {
            00
      }
}
item:
[ U 2 ] INTEGER {
      00
}
result:
[ C 3 ] SEQUENCE {
      [ U 2 ] INTEGER {
            00
```

```
        }
        [ U 2 ] INTEGER {
                00
        }
}
asnAppend:
head:
[ C 3 ] SEQUENCE {
        [ U 2 ] INTEGER {
                00
        }
        [ U 2 ] INTEGER {
                00
        }
}
item:
[ U 2 ] INTEGER {
        00
}
result:
[ C 3 ] SEQUENCE {
        [ U 2 ] INTEGER {
                00
        }
        [ U 2 ] INTEGER {
                00
        }
        [ U 2 ] INTEGER {
                00
        }
}
asnAppend:
head:
[ C 3 ] SEQUENCE {
        [ U 2 ] INTEGER {
                00
        }
        [ U 2 ] INTEGER {
                00
        }
        [ U 2 ] INTEGER {
                00
        }
}
item:
[ U 16 ] SEQUENCE {
}
result:
[ C 3 ] SEQUENCE {
        [ U 2 ] INTEGER {
                00
```

```
        }
        [ U 2 ] INTEGER {
                00
        }
        [ U 2 ] INTEGER {
                00
        }
        [ U 16 ] SEQUENCE {
        }
}
result: 00011748
smpSend:
asnAppend:
head:
[ U 16 ] SEQUENCE {
}
item:
[ U 2 ] INTEGER {
        00
}
result:
[ U 16 ] SEQUENCE {
        [ U 2 ] INTEGER {
                00
        }
}
asnAppend:
head:
[ U 16 ] SEQUENCE {
        [ U 2 ] INTEGER {
                00
        }
}
item:
[ U 4 ] OCTETSTRING {
        70 75 62 6C 69 63
}
result:
[ U 16 ] SEQUENCE {
        [ U 2 ] INTEGER {
                00
        }
        [ U 4 ] OCTETSTRING {
                70 75 62 6C 69 63
        }
}
asnAppend:
head:
[ U 16 ] SEQUENCE {
        [ U 2 ] INTEGER {
                00
```

```
        }
        [ U 4 ] OCTETSTRING {
                70 75 62 6C 69 63
        }
}
item:
[ C 3 ] SEQUENCE {
        [ U 2 ] INTEGER {
                00
        }
        [ U 2 ] INTEGER {
                00
        }
        [ U 2 ] INTEGER {
                00
        }
        [ U 16 ] SEQUENCE {
        }
}
result:
[ U 16 ] SEQUENCE {
        [ U 2 ] INTEGER {
                00
        }
        [ U 4 ] OCTETSTRING {
                70 75 62 6C 69 63
        }
        [ C 3 ] SEQUENCE {
                [ U 2 ] INTEGER {
                        00
                }
                [ U 2 ] INTEGER {
                        00
                }
                [ U 2 ] INTEGER {
                        00
                }
                [ U 16 ] SEQUENCE {
                }
        }
}
[ U 16 ] SEQUENCE {
        [ U 2 ] INTEGER {
                00
        }
        [ U 4 ] OCTETSTRING {
                70 75 62 6C 69 63
        }
        [ C 3 ] SEQUENCE {
                [ U 2 ] INTEGER {
                        00
```

```
                }
                [ U 2 ] INTEGER {
                        00
                }
                [ U 2 ] INTEGER {
                        00
                }
                [ U 16 ] SEQUENCE {
                }
        }
}
```

```
30 18 02 01 00 04 06 70 75 62 6C 69 63 A3 0B 02 01 00 02 01 00 02 01 00 30 00
udpSend:
30 18 02 01 00 04 06 70 75 62 6C 69 63 A3 0B 02 01 00 02 01 00 02 01 00 30 00
30 18 02 01 00 04 06 70 75 62 6C 69 63 A2 0B 02 01 00 02 01 00 02 01 00 30 00
asnNew dp 106B0
asnType0
asnType0 dp 106B0 np A718
aslChoice 1
asnLen0 asnLenVerify Max -1 Tot 2 Len 24 Min 20 4 4
asnSeq 4
asnPush
asnType0
asnType0 dp 10688 np A738
aslChoice 1
asnLen0 asnLenVerify Max 24 Tot 2 Len 1 Min 1 4 4
asnInteger0: 00
asnInteger1: 00
asnInteger0: 4
asnInteger0: 00010688
asnInteger1: 00
asnInteger0: 2
asnInteger1: 100
asnInteger1: 00
asnInteger1: 4
asnInteger1: 00010688
asnInteger1: 1
asnPop
asnSeq 4
asnPush
asnType0
asnType0 dp 10660 np A758
aslChoice 1
asnLen0 asnLenVerify Max 21 Tot 2 Len 6 Min 0 4 4
asnInteger2: 2
asnInteger2: 2
asnInteger2: 2
asnInteger2: 2
asnInteger2: 2
asnInteger2: 1
```

```
asnPop
asnSeq 4
asnPush
asnType0
asnType0 dp 10638 np A778
aslChoice 1
asnLen0 asnLenVerify Max 13 Tot 2 Len 11 Min 12 4 4
asnSeq 4
asnPush
asnType0
asnType0 dp 10610 np A7D8
aslChoice 1
asnLen0 asnLenVerify Max 11 Tot 2 Len 1 Min 1 4 4
asnInteger0: 00
asnInteger1: 00
asnInteger0: 17
asnInteger0: 00010610
asnInteger1: 00
asnInteger0: 2
asnInteger1: 100
asnInteger1: 00
asnInteger1: 17
asnInteger1: 00010610
asnInteger1: 1
asnPop
asnSeq 4
asnPush
asnType0
asnType0 dp 105E8 np A7F8
aslChoice 1
asnLen0 asnLenVerify Max 8 Tot 2 Len 1 Min 1 4 4
asnInteger0: 00
asnInteger1: 00
asnInteger0: 20
asnInteger0: 000105E8
asnInteger1: 00
asnInteger0: 2
asnInteger1: 100
asnInteger1: 00
asnInteger1: 20
asnInteger1: 000105E8
asnInteger1: 1
asnPop
asnSeq 4
asnPush
asnType0
asnType0 dp 105C0 np A818
aslChoice 1
asnLen0 asnLenVerify Max 5 Tot 2 Len 1 Min 1 4 4
asnInteger0: 00
asnInteger1: 00
```

```
asnInteger0: 23
asnInteger0: 000105C0
asnInteger1: 00
asnInteger0: 2
asnInteger1: 100
asnInteger1: 00
asnInteger1: 23
asnInteger1: 000105C0
asnInteger1: 1
asnPop
asnSeq 4
asnPush
asnType0
asnType0 dp 10598 np A838
aslChoice 1
asnLen0 asnLenVerify Max 2 Tot 2 Len 0 Min 0 4 4
asnSeqOf
asnPop
asnSeq 2
asnPop
asnSeq 2
asnPop
asnDecode bytesLeft 3814
smpInputEvent [ C 2 ] SEQUENCE {
        [ U 2 ] INTEGER {
                00
        }
        [ U 2 ] INTEGER {
                00
        }
        [ U 2 ] INTEGER {
                00
        }
        [ U 16 ] SEQUENCE OF {
        }
}
Request Id: 0
Error: noError
Index: 0
Count: 0

4
result: 0
```

Below is the output from the debug of an SNMP GET of a nonexistent OID.

```
smpRequest:
asnAppend:
head:
[ U 16 ] SEQUENCE {
}
item:
[ U 6 ] OBJECTIDENTIFIER {
        90 49
}
result:
[ U 16 ] SEQUENCE {
        [ U 6 ] OBJECTIDENTIFIER {
                90 49
        }
}
asnAppend:
head:
[ U 16 ] SEQUENCE {
        [ U 6 ] OBJECTIDENTIFIER {
                90 49
        }
}
item:
[ U 4 ] OCTETSTRING {

}
result:
[ U 16 ] SEQUENCE {
        [ U 6 ] OBJECTIDENTIFIER {
                90 49
        }
        [ U 4 ] OCTETSTRING {

        }
}
asnAppend:
head:
[ U 16 ] SEQUENCE {
}
item:
[ U 16 ] SEQUENCE {
        [ U 6 ] OBJECTIDENTIFIER {
                90 49
        }
        [ U 4 ] OCTETSTRING {

        }
}
result:
```

```
[ U 16 ] SEQUENCE {
    [ U 16 ] SEQUENCE {
        [ U 6 ] OBJECTIDENTIFIER {
                90 49
        }
        [ U 4 ] OCTETSTRING {

        }
    }
}
asnAppend:
head:
[ C 0 ] SEQUENCE {
}
item:
[ U 2 ] INTEGER {
      00
}
result:
[ C 0 ] SEQUENCE {
    [ U 2 ] INTEGER {
            00
    }
}
asnAppend:
head:
[ C 0 ] SEQUENCE {
    [ U 2 ] INTEGER {
            00
    }
}
item:
[ U 2 ] INTEGER {
      00
}
result:
[ C 0 ] SEQUENCE {
    [ U 2 ] INTEGER {
            00
    }
    [ U 2 ] INTEGER {
            00
    }
}
asnAppend:
head:
[ C 0 ] SEQUENCE {
    [ U 2 ] INTEGER {
            00
    }
    [ U 2 ] INTEGER {
```

```
                    00
            }
    }
    item:
    [ U 2 ] INTEGER {
            00
    }
    result:
    [ C 0 ] SEQUENCE {
            [ U 2 ] INTEGER {
                    00
            }
            [ U 2 ] INTEGER {
                    00
            }
            [ U 2 ] INTEGER {
                    00
            }
    }
    asnAppend:
    head:
    [ C 0 ] SEQUENCE {
            [ U 2 ] INTEGER {
                    00
            }
            [ U 2 ] INTEGER {
                    00
            }
            [ U 2 ] INTEGER {
                    00
            }
    }
    item:
    [ U 16 ] SEQUENCE {
            [ U 16 ] SEQUENCE {
                    [ U 6 ] OBJECTIDENTIFIER {
                            90 49
                    }
                    [ U 4 ] OCTETSTRING {

                    }
            }
    }
    result:
    [ C 0 ] SEQUENCE {
            [ U 2 ] INTEGER {
                    00
            }
            [ U 2 ] INTEGER {
                    00
            }
```

```
        [ U 2 ] INTEGER {
                00
        }
        [ U 16 ] SEQUENCE {
                [ U 16 ] SEQUENCE {
                        [ U 6 ] OBJECTIDENTIFIER {
                                90 49
                        }
                        [ U 4 ] OCTETSTRING {

                        }
                }
        }
}
result: 00011738
smpSend:
asnAppend:
head:
[ U 16 ] SEQUENCE {
}
item:
[ U 2 ] INTEGER {
        00
}
result:
[ U 16 ] SEQUENCE {
        [ U 2 ] INTEGER {
                00
        }
}
asnAppend:
head:
[ U 16 ] SEQUENCE {
        [ U 2 ] INTEGER {
                00
        }
}
item:
[ U 4 ] OCTETSTRING {
        70 75 62 6C 69 63
}
result:
[ U 16 ] SEQUENCE {
        [ U 2 ] INTEGER {
                00
        }
        [ U 4 ] OCTETSTRING {
                70 75 62 6C 69 63
        }
}
asnAppend:
```

```
head:
[ U 16 ] SEQUENCE {
        [ U 2 ] INTEGER {
                00
        }
        [ U 4 ] OCTETSTRING {
                70 75 62 6C 69 63
        }
}
item:
[ C 0 ] SEQUENCE {
        [ U 2 ] INTEGER {
                00
        }
        [ U 2 ] INTEGER {
                00
        }
        [ U 2 ] INTEGER {
                00
        }
        [ U 16 ] SEQUENCE {
                [ U 16 ] SEQUENCE {
                        [ U 6 ] OBJECTIDENTIFIER {
                                90 49
                        }
                        [ U 4 ] OCTETSTRING {

                        }
                }
        }
}
result:
[ U 16 ] SEQUENCE {
        [ U 2 ] INTEGER {
                00
        }
        [ U 4 ] OCTETSTRING {
                70 75 62 6C 69 63
        }
        [ C 0 ] SEQUENCE {
                [ U 2 ] INTEGER {
                        00
                }
                [ U 2 ] INTEGER {
                        00
                }
                [ U 2 ] INTEGER {
                        00
                }
                [ U 16 ] SEQUENCE {
                        [ U 16 ] SEQUENCE {
```

```
                                    [ U 6 ] OBJECTIDENTIFIER {
                                            90 49
                                    }
                                    [ U 4 ] OCTETSTRING {

                                    }
                            }
                    }
            }
    }
[ U 16 ] SEQUENCE {
        [ U 2 ] INTEGER {
                00
        }
        [ U 4 ] OCTETSTRING {
                70 75 62 6C 69 63
        }
        [ C 0 ] SEQUENCE {
                [ U 2 ] INTEGER {
                        00
                }
                [ U 2 ] INTEGER {
                        00
                }
                [ U 2 ] INTEGER {
                        00
                }
                [ U 16 ] SEQUENCE {
                        [ U 16 ] SEQUENCE {
                                [ U 6 ] OBJECTIDENTIFIER {
                                        90 49
                                }
                                [ U 4 ] OCTETSTRING {

                                }
                        }
                }
        }
}
```

```
30 20 02 01 00 04 06 70 75 62 6C 69 63 A0 13 02 01 00 02 01 00 02 01 00 30 08
30 06 06 02 90 49 04 00
udpSend:
30 20 02 01 00 04 06 70 75 62 6C 69 63 A0 13 02 01 00 02 01 00 02 01 00 30 08
30 06 06 02 90 49 04 00
30 20 02 01 00 04 06 70 75 62 6C 69 63 A2 13 02 01 00 02 01 02 02 01 01 30 08
30 06 06 02 90 49 04 00
asnNew dp 106A0
asnType0
asnType0 dp 106A0 np A708
aslChoice 1
```

```
asnLen0 asnLenVerify Max -1 Tot 2 Len 32 Min 20 4 4
asnSeq 4
asnPush
asnType0
asnType0 dp 10678 np A728
aslChoice 1
asnLen0 asnLenVerify Max 32 Tot 2 Len 1 Min 1 4 4
asnInteger0: 00
asnInteger1: 00
asnInteger0: 4
asnInteger0: 00010678
asnInteger1: 00
asnInteger0: 2
asnInteger1: 100
asnInteger1: 00
asnInteger1: 4
asnInteger1: 00010678
asnInteger1: 1
asnPop
asnSeq 4
asnPush
asnType0
asnType0 dp 10650 np A748
aslChoice 1
asnLen0 asnLenVerify Max 29 Tot 2 Len 6 Min 0 4 4
asnInteger2: 2
asnInteger2: 2
asnInteger2: 2
asnInteger2: 2
asnInteger2: 2
asnInteger2: 1
asnPop
asnSeq 4
asnPush
asnType0
asnType0 dp 10628 np A768
aslChoice 1
asnLen0 asnLenVerify Max 21 Tot 2 Len 19 Min 12 4 4
asnSeq 4
asnPush
asnType0
asnType0 dp 10600 np A7C8
aslChoice 1
asnLen0 asnLenVerify Max 19 Tot 2 Len 1 Min 1 4 4
asnInteger0: 00
asnInteger1: 00
asnInteger0: 17
asnInteger0: 00010600
asnInteger1: 00
asnInteger0: 2
asnInteger1: 100
```

```
asnInteger1: 00
asnInteger1: 17
asnInteger1: 00010600
asnInteger1: 1
asnPop
asnSeq 4
asnPush
asnType0
asnType0 dp 105D8 np A7E8
aslChoice 1
asnLen0 asnLenVerify Max 16 Tot 2 Len 1 Min 1 4 4
asnInteger0: 02
asnInteger1: 02
asnInteger0: 20
asnInteger0: 000105D8
asnInteger1: 02
asnInteger0: 2
asnInteger1: 100
asnInteger1: 02
asnInteger1: 20
asnInteger1: 000105D8
asnInteger1: 1
asnPop
asnSeq 4
asnPush
asnType0
asnType0 dp 105B0 np A808
aslChoice 1
asnLen0 asnLenVerify Max 13 Tot 2 Len 1 Min 1 4 4
asnInteger0: 01
asnInteger1: 01
asnInteger0: 23
asnInteger0: 000105B0
asnInteger1: 01
asnInteger0: 2
asnInteger1: 100
asnInteger1: 01
asnInteger1: 23
asnInteger1: 000105B0
asnInteger1: 1
asnPop
asnSeq 4
asnPush
asnType0
asnType0 dp 10588 np A828
aslChoice 1
asnLen0 asnLenVerify Max 10 Tot 2 Len 8 Min 0 4 4
asnSeqOf
asnPush
asnType0
asnType0 dp 10560 np A848
```

```
aslChoice 1
asnLen0 asnLenVerify Max 8 Tot 2 Len 6 Min 4 4 4
asnSeq 4
asnPush
asnType0
asnType0 dp 10538 np A868
aslChoice 1
asnLen0 asnLenVerify Max 6 Tot 2 Len 2 Min 0 4 4
asnObjectId0 1
asnObjectId1 2
asnObjectId1 49 1
asnPop
asnSeq 4
asnPush
asnType0
asnType0 dp 10510 np A888
aslChoice 1
asnLen0 asnLenVerify Max 2 Tot 2 Len 0 Min 0 4 4
asnPop
asnSeq 2
asnPop
asnSeqOf
asnPop
asnSeq 2
asnPop
asnSeq 2
asnPop
asnDecode bytesLeft 3686
smpInputEvent [ C 2 ] SEQUENCE {
      [ U 2 ] INTEGER {
             00
      }
      [ U 2 ] INTEGER {
             02
      }
      [ U 2 ] INTEGER {
             01
      }
      [ U 16 ] SEQUENCE OF {
             [ U 16 ] SEQUENCE {
                    [ U 6 ] OBJECTIDENTIFIER {
                           90 49
                    }
                    [ U 4 ] OCTETSTRING {

                    }
             }
      }
}
Request Id: 0
Error: noSuchName
```

```
Index: 1
Count: 1

Name: 53.1
Kind: OctetString
smxValueToText: Kind 2 Len 0
Value: ""

4
result: 0
```

APPENDIX E

DEBUG Output From Agent

```
NIL
systmInit: Hostid 1426085885
rteInit: rteHashSize 8
asnNew dp 12728
asnType0
asnType0 dp 12728 np C7F8
aslChoice 1
asnLen0 asnLenVerify Max -1 Tot 2 Len 33 Min 20 4 4
asnSeq 4
asnPush
asnType0
asnType0 dp 12700 np C818
aslChoice 1
asnLen0 asnLenVerify Max 33 Tot 2 Len 1 Min 1 4 4
asnInteger0: 00
asnInteger1: 00
asnInteger0: 4
asnInteger0: 00012700
asnInteger1: 00
asnInteger0: 2
asnInteger1: 100
asnInteger1: 00
asnInteger1: 4
asnInteger1: 00012700
asnInteger1: 1
asnPop
asnSeq 4
asnPush
asnType0
asnType0 dp 126D8 np C838
aslChoice 1
asnLen0 asnLenVerify Max 30 Tot 2 Len 6 Min 0 4 4
```

```
asnInteger2: 2
asnInteger2: 2
asnInteger2: 2
asnInteger2: 2
asnInteger2: 2
asnInteger2: 1
asnPop
asnSeq 4
asnPush
asnType0
asnType0 dp 126B0 np C858
aslChoice 1
asnLen0 asnLenVerify Max 22 Tot 2 Len 20 Min 12 4 4
asnSeq 4
asnPush
asnType0
asnType0 dp 12688 np C8B8
aslChoice 1
asnLen0 asnLenVerify Max 20 Tot 2 Len 1 Min 1 4 4
asnInteger0: 00
asnInteger1: 00
asnInteger0: 17
asnInteger0: 00012688
asnInteger1: 00
asnInteger0: 2
asnInteger1: 100
asnInteger1: 00
asnInteger1: 17
asnInteger1: 00012688
asnInteger1: 1
asnPop
asnSeq 4
asnPush
asnType0
asnType0 dp 12660 np C8D8
aslChoice 1
asnLen0 asnLenVerify Max 17 Tot 2 Len 1 Min 1 4 4
asnInteger0: 00
asnInteger1: 00
asnInteger0: 20
asnInteger0: 00012660
asnInteger1: 00
asnInteger0: 2
asnInteger1: 100
asnInteger1: 00
asnInteger1: 20
asnInteger1: 00012660
asnInteger1: 1
asnPop
asnSeq 4
asnPush
```

```
asnType0
asnType0 dp 12638 np C8F8
aslChoice 1
asnLen0 asnLenVerify Max 14 Tot 2 Len 1 Min 1 4 4
asnInteger0: 00
asnInteger1: 00
asnInteger0: 23
asnInteger0: 00012638
asnInteger1: 00
asnInteger0: 2
asnInteger1: 100
asnInteger1: 00
asnInteger1: 23
asnInteger1: 00012638
asnInteger1: 1
asnPop
asnSeq 4
asnPush
asnType0
asnType0 dp 12610 np C918
aslChoice 1
asnLen0 asnLenVerify Max 11 Tot 2 Len 9 Min 0 4 4
asnSeqOf
asnPush
asnType0
asnType0 dp 125E8 np C938
aslChoice 1
asnLen0 asnLenVerify Max 9 Tot 2 Len 7 Min 4 4 4
asnSeq 4
asnPush
asnType0
asnType0 dp 125C0 np C958
aslChoice 1
asnLen0 asnLenVerify Max 7 Tot 2 Len 3 Min 0 4 4
asnObjectId0 1
asnObjectId1 2
asnObjectId1 2
asnObjectId1 02 1
asnPop
asnSeq 4
asnPush
asnType0
asnType0 dp 12598 np C978
aslChoice 1
asnLen0 asnLenVerify Max 2 Tot 2 Len 0 Min 0 4 4
asnPop
asnSeq 2
asnPop
asnSeqOf
asnPop
asnSeq 2
```

```
asnPop
asnSeq 2
asnPop
asnDecode bytesLeft 3685
smpInputEvent [ C 0 ] SEQUENCE {
        [ U 2 ] INTEGER {
                00
        }
        [ U 2 ] INTEGER {
                00
        }
        [ U 2 ] INTEGER {
                00
        }
        [ U 16 ] SEQUENCE OF {
                [ U 16 ] SEQUENCE {
                        [ U 6 ] OBJECTIDENTIFIER {
                                93 59 02
                        }
                        [ U 4 ] OCTETSTRING {

                        }
                }
        }
}
smpGetOp
smpGetOp: asn:
[ C 0 ] SEQUENCE {
        [ U 2 ] INTEGER {
                00
        }
        [ U 2 ] INTEGER {
                00
        }
        [ U 2 ] INTEGER {
                00
        }
        [ U 16 ] SEQUENCE OF {
                [ U 16 ] SEQUENCE {
                        [ U 6 ] OBJECTIDENTIFIER {
                                93 59 02
                        }
                        [ U 4 ] OCTETSTRING {

                        }
                }
        }
}
smpGetOp: seq:
[ U 16 ] SEQUENCE OF {
        [ U 16 ] SEQUENCE {
```

```
                     [ U 6 ] OBJECTIDENTIFIER {
                             93 59 02
                     }
                     [ U 4 ] OCTETSTRING {

                     }
             }
     }
smpGetOp: bind:
[ U 16 ] SEQUENCE {
       [ U 6 ] OBJECTIDENTIFIER {
                93 59 02
       }
       [ U 4 ] OCTETSTRING {


       }
}
smpGetOp: name:
[ U 6 ] OBJECTIDENTIFIER {
        93 59 02
}
smpGetOp 1
smpGetOp: error 2
smpGetOp: rseq:
[ U 16 ] SEQUENCE OF {
}
smpReply:
asnAppend:
head:
[ C 2 ] SEQUENCE {
}
item:
[ U 2 ] INTEGER {
        00
}
result:
[ C 2 ] SEQUENCE {
       [ U 2 ] INTEGER {
               00
       }
}
asnAppend:
head:
[ C 2 ] SEQUENCE {
       [ U 2 ] INTEGER {
               00
       }
}
item:
[ U 2 ] INTEGER {
        02
```

```
}
result:
[ C 2 ] SEQUENCE {
        [ U 2 ] INTEGER {
                00
        }
        [ U 2 ] INTEGER {
                02
        }
}
asnAppend:
head:
[ C 2 ] SEQUENCE {
        [ U 2 ] INTEGER {
                00
        }
        [ U 2 ] INTEGER {
                02
        }
}
item:
[ U 2 ] INTEGER {
        01
}
result:
[ C 2 ] SEQUENCE {
        [ U 2 ] INTEGER {
                00
        }
        [ U 2 ] INTEGER {
                02
        }
        [ U 2 ] INTEGER {
                01
        }
}
asnAppend:
head:
[ C 2 ] SEQUENCE {
        [ U 2 ] INTEGER {
                00
        }
        [ U 2 ] INTEGER {
                02
        }
        [ U 2 ] INTEGER {
                01
        }
}
item:
[ U 16 ] SEQUENCE OF {
```

```
         [ U 16 ] SEQUENCE {
              [ U 6 ] OBJECTIDENTIFIER {
                    93 59 02
              }
              [ U 4 ] OCTETSTRING {

              }
         }
    }
result:
[ C 2 ] SEQUENCE {
     [ U 2 ] INTEGER {
          00
     }
     [ U 2 ] INTEGER {
          02
     }
     [ U 2 ] INTEGER {
          01
     }
     [ U 16 ] SEQUENCE OF {
          [ U 16 ] SEQUENCE {
               [ U 6 ] OBJECTIDENTIFIER {
                    93 59 02
               }
               [ U 4 ] OCTETSTRING {

               }
          }
     }
}
smpSend:
asnAppend:
head:
[ U 16 ] SEQUENCE {
}
item:
[ U 2 ] INTEGER {
     00
}
result:
[ U 16 ] SEQUENCE {
     [ U 2 ] INTEGER {
          00
     }
}
asnAppend:
head:
[ U 16 ] SEQUENCE {
     [ U 2 ] INTEGER {
          00
```

```
            }
        }
    item:
    [ U 4 ] OCTETSTRING {
            70 75 62 6C 69 63
        }
    result:
    [ U 16 ] SEQUENCE {
            [ U 2 ] INTEGER {
                    00
            }
            [ U 4 ] OCTETSTRING {
                    70 75 62 6C 69 63
            }
        }
    asnAppend:
    head:
    [ U 16 ] SEQUENCE {
            [ U 2 ] INTEGER {
                    00
            }
            [ U 4 ] OCTETSTRING {
                    70 75 62 6C 69 63
            }
        }
    item:
    [ C 2 ] SEQUENCE {
            [ U 2 ] INTEGER {
                    00
            }
            [ U 2 ] INTEGER {
                    02
            }
            [ U 2 ] INTEGER {
                    01
            }
            [ U 16 ] SEQUENCE OF {
                    [ U 16 ] SEQUENCE {
                            [ U 6 ] OBJECTIDENTIFIER {
                                    93 59 02
                            }
                            [ U 4 ] OCTETSTRING {

                            }
                    }
            }
        }
    result:
    [ U 16 ] SEQUENCE {
            [ U 2 ] INTEGER {
                    00
```

```
        }
        [ U 4 ] OCTETSTRING {
               70 75 62 6C 69 63
        }
        [ C 2 ] SEQUENCE {
               [ U 2 ] INTEGER {
                      00
               }
               [ U 2 ] INTEGER {
                      02
               }
               [ U 2 ] INTEGER {
                      01
               }
               [ U 16 ] SEQUENCE OF {
                      [ U 16 ] SEQUENCE {
                             [ U 6 ] OBJECTIDENTIFIER {
                                    93 59 02
                             }
                             [ U 4 ] OCTETSTRING {

                             }
                      }
               }
        }
}
[ U 16 ] SEQUENCE {
        [ U 2 ] INTEGER {
               00
        }
        [ U 4 ] OCTETSTRING {
               70 75 62 6C 69 63
        }
        [ C 2 ] SEQUENCE {
               [ U 2 ] INTEGER {
                      00
               }
               [ U 2 ] INTEGER {
                      02
               }
               [ U 2 ] INTEGER {
                      01
               }
               [ U 16 ] SEQUENCE OF {
                      [ U 16 ] SEQUENCE {
                             [ U 6 ] OBJECTIDENTIFIER {
                                    93 59 02
                             }
                             [ U 4 ] OCTETSTRING {

                             }
```

```
                        }
                    }
                }
            }
```

```
30 21 02 01 00 04 06 70 75 62 6C 69 63 A2 14 02 01 00 02 01 02 02 01 01 30 09
30 07 06 03 93 59 02 04 00
udpSend:
30 21 02 01 00 04 06 70 75 62 6C 69 63 A2 14 02 01 00 02 01 02 02 01 01 30 09
30 07 06 03 93 59 02 04 00
4
```

APPENDIX F

Basic SMI/MIB Example

```
mgmt          OBJECT IDENTIFIER ::= { iso org(3) dod(6) internet(1) mgmt(2) }
mib           OBJECT IDENTIFIER ::= { mgmt 1 }
directory     OBJECT IDENTIFIER ::= { internet 1 }
experimental  OBJECT IDENTIFIER ::= { internet 3 }
private       OBJECT IDENTIFIER ::= { internet 4 }
enterprises   OBJECT IDENTIFIER ::= { private 1 }

system        OBJECT IDENTIFIER ::= { mib 1 }
interfaces    OBJECT IDENTIFIER ::= { mib 2 }
at            OBJECT IDENTIFIER ::= { mib 3 }
ip            OBJECT IDENTIFIER ::= { mib 4 }
icmp          OBJECT IDENTIFIER ::= { mib 5 }
tcp           OBJECT IDENTIFIER ::= { mib 6 }
udp           OBJECT IDENTIFIER ::= { mib 7 }
egp           OBJECT IDENTIFIER ::= { mib 8 }

- object types

- the System group

sysDescr OBJECT-TYPE
    SYNTAX  OCTET STRING
    ACCESS  read-only
    STATUS  mandatory
    ::= { system 1 }

sysObjectID OBJECT-TYPE
    SYNTAX  OBJECT IDENTIFIER
    ACCESS  read-only
    STATUS  mandatory
    ::= { system 2 }
```

```
sysUpTime OBJECT-TYPE
    SYNTAX  TimeTicks
    ACCESS  read-only
    STATUS  mandatory
    ::= { system 3 }

- the Interfaces group

ifNumber OBJECT-TYPE
    SYNTAX  INTEGER
    ACCESS  read-only
    STATUS  mandatory
    ::= { interfaces 1 }

- the Interfaces table

ifTable OBJECT-TYPE
    SYNTAX  SEQUENCE OF IfEntry
    ACCESS  read-write
    STATUS  mandatory
    ::= { interfaces 2 }

ifEntry OBJECT-TYPE
    SYNTAX  IfEntry
    ACCESS  read-write
    STATUS  mandatory
    ::= { ifTable 1 }

IfEntry ::= SEQUENCE {
    ifIndex
        INTEGER,
    ifDescr
        OCTET STRING,
    ifType
        INTEGER,
    ifMtu
        INTEGER,
    ifSpeed
        Gauge,
    ifPhysAddress
        OCTET STRING,
    ifAdminStatus
        INTEGER,
    ifOperStatus
        INTEGER,
    ifLastChange
        TimeTicks,
    ifInOctets
        Counter,
    ifInUcastPkts
        Counter,
```

```
        ifInNUcastPkts
          Counter,
        ifInDiscards
          Counter,
        ifInErrors
          Counter,
        ifInUnknownProtos
          Counter,
        ifOutOctets
          Counter,
        ifOutUcastPkts
          Counter,
        ifOutNUcastPkts
          Counter,
        ifOutDiscards
          Counter,
        ifOutErrors
          Counter,
        ifOutQLen
          Gauge
}

ifIndex OBJECT-TYPE
    SYNTAX  INTEGER
    ACCESS  read-only
    STATUS  mandatory
    ::= { ifEntry 1 }

ifDescr OBJECT-TYPE
    SYNTAX  OCTET STRING
    ACCESS  read-only
    STATUS  mandatory
    ::= { ifEntry 2 }

ifType OBJECT-TYPE
    SYNTAX  INTEGER {
        other(1),      − none of the following
        regular1822(2),
        hdh1822(3),
        ddn-x25(4),
        rfc877-x25(5),
        ethernet-csmacd(6),
        iso88023-csmacd(7),
        iso88024-tokenBus(8),
        iso88025-tokenRing(9),
        iso88026-man(10),
        starLan(11),
        proteon-10MBit(12),
        proteon-80MBit(13),
        hyperchannel(14),
        fddi(15),
```

```
            lapb(16),
            sdlc(17),
            t1-carrier(18),
            cept(19),
            basicIsdn(20),
            primaryIsdn(21),
                      - proprietary serial
            propPointToPointSerial(22)
        }
    ACCESS   read-only
    STATUS   mandatory
    ::= { ifEntry 3 }

ifMtu OBJECT-TYPE
    SYNTAX   INTEGER
    ACCESS   read-only
    STATUS   mandatory
    ::= { ifEntry 4 }

    ifSpeed OBJECT-TYPE
      SYNTAX   Gauge
      ACCESS   read-only
      STATUS   mandatory
      ::= { ifEntry 5 }

    ifPhysAddress OBJECT-TYPE
      SYNTAX   OCTET STRING
      ACCESS   read-only
      STATUS   mandatory
      ::= { ifEntry 6 }

    ifAdminStatus OBJECT-TYPE
      SYNTAX   INTEGER {
         up(1),        - ready to pass packets
         down(2),
         testing(3)    - in some test mode
                              }
      ACCESS   read-write
      STATUS   mandatory
      ::= { ifEntry 7 }

    ifOperStatus OBJECT-TYPE
      SYNTAX   INTEGER {
         up(1),        - ready to pass packets
         down(2),
         testing(3)    - in some test mode
         }
      ACCESS   read-only
      STATUS   mandatory
      ::= { ifEntry 8 }
```

```
ifLastChange OBJECT-TYPE
  SYNTAX  TimeTicks
  ACCESS  read-only
  STATUS  mandatory
  ::= { ifEntry 9 }

ifInOctets OBJECT-TYPE
  SYNTAX  Counter
  ACCESS  read-only
  STATUS  mandatory
  ::= { ifEntry 10 }

ifInUcastPkts OBJECT-TYPE
  SYNTAX  Counter
  ACCESS  read-only
  STATUS  mandatory
  ::=  { ifEntry 11 }

ifInNUcastPkts OBJECT-TYPE
  SYNTAX  Counter
  ACCESS  read-only
  STATUS  mandatory
  ::= { ifEntry 12 }

ifInDiscards OBJECT-TYPE
  SYNTAX  Counter
  ACCESS  read-only
  STATUS  mandatory
  ::= { ifEntry 13 }

ifInErrors OBJECT-TYPE
  SYNTAX  Counter
  ACCESS  read-only
  STATUS  mandatory
  ::= { ifEntry 14 }

ifInUnknownProtos OBJECT-TYPE
  SYNTAX  Counter
  ACCESS  read-only
  STATUS  mandatory
  ::= { ifEntry 15 }

ifOutOctets OBJECT-TYPE
  SYNTAX  Counter
  ACCESS  read-only
  STATUS  mandatory
  ::= { ifEntry 16 }

ifOutUcastPkts OBJECT-TYPE
  SYNTAX  Counter
  ACCESS  read-only
```

```
          STATUS  mandatory
          ::= { ifEntry 17 }

      ifOutNUcastPkts OBJECT-TYPE
          SYNTAX  Counter
          ACCESS  read-only
          STATUS  mandatory
          ::= { ifEntry 18 }

      ifOutDiscards OBJECT-TYPE
          SYNTAX  Counter
          ACCESS  read-only
          STATUS  mandatory
          ::= { ifEntry 19 }

          ifOutErrors OBJECT-TYPE
          SYNTAX  Counter
          ACCESS  read-only
          STATUS  mandatory
          ::= { ifEntry 20 }

      ifOutQLen OBJECT-TYPE
          SYNTAX  Gauge
          ACCESS  read-only
          STATUS  mandatory
          ::= { ifEntry 21 }

      — the Address Translation group

      atTable OBJECT-TYPE
          SYNTAX  SEQUENCE OF AtEntry
          ACCESS  read-write
          STATUS  mandatory
          ::= { at 1 }

      atEntry OBJECT-TYPE
          SYNTAX  AtEntry
          ACCESS  read-write
          STATUS  mandatory
          ::= { atTable 1 }

      AtEntry ::= SEQUENCE {
          atIfIndex
              INTEGER,
          atPhysAddress
              OCTET STRING,
          atNetAddress
              NetworkAddress
      }
```

```
atIfIndex OBJECT-TYPE
  SYNTAX  INTEGER
  ACCESS  read-write
  STATUS  mandatory
  ::= { atEntry 1 }

atPhysAddress OBJECT-TYPE
  SYNTAX  OCTET STRING
  ACCESS  read-write
  STATUS  mandatory
  ::= { atEntry 2 }

atNetAddress OBJECT-TYPE
  SYNTAX  NetworkAddress
  ACCESS  read-write
  STATUS  mandatory
  ::= { atEntry 3 }

— the IP group

ipForwarding OBJECT-TYPE
  SYNTAX  INTEGER {
  gateway(1), — entity forwards datagrams
  host(2)     — entity does NOT forward datagrams
     }
  ACCESS  read-only
  STATUS  mandatory
  ::= { ip 1 }

ipDefaultTTL OBJECT-TYPE
  SYNTAX  INTEGER
  ACCESS  read-write
  STATUS  mandatory
  ::= { ip 2 }

ipInReceives OBJECT-TYPE
  SYNTAX  Counter
  ACCESS  read-only
  STATUS  mandatory
  ::= { ip 3 }

ipInHdrErrors OBJECT-TYPE
  SYNTAX  Counter
  ACCESS  read-only
  STATUS  mandatory
  ::= { ip 4 }

ipInAddrErrors OBJECT-TYPE
  SYNTAX  Counter
  ACCESS  read-only
  STATUS  mandatory
```

```
        ::= { ip 5 }

ipForwDatagrams OBJECT-TYPE
  SYNTAX  Counter
  ACCESS  read-only
  STATUS  mandatory
  ::= { ip 6 }

ipInUnknownProtos OBJECT-TYPE
  SYNTAX  Counter
  ACCESS  read-only
  STATUS  mandatory
  ::= { ip 7 }

ipInDiscards OBJECT-TYPE
  SYNTAX  Counter
  ACCESS  read-only
  STATUS  mandatory
  ::= { ip 8 }

ipInDelivers OBJECT-TYPE
  SYNTAX  Counter
  ACCESS  read-only
  STATUS  mandatory
  ::= { ip 9 }

ipOutRequests OBJECT-TYPE
  SYNTAX  Counter
  ACCESS  read-only
  STATUS  mandatory
  ::= { ip 10 }

ipOutDiscards OBJECT-TYPE
  SYNTAX  Counter
  ACCESS  read-only
  STATUS  mandatory
  ::= { ip 11 }

ipOutNoRoutes OBJECT-TYPE
  SYNTAX  Counter
  ACCESS  read-only
  STATUS  mandatory
  ::= { ip 12 }

ipReasmTimeout OBJECT-TYPE
  SYNTAX  INTEGER
  ACCESS  read-only
  STATUS  mandatory
  ::= { ip 13 }
```

```
ipReasmReqds OBJECT-TYPE
  SYNTAX  Counter
  ACCESS  read-only
  STATUS  mandatory
  ::= { ip 14 }

ipReasmOKs OBJECT-TYPE
  SYNTAX  Counter
  ACCESS  read-only
  STATUS  mandatory
  ::= { ip 15 }

ipReasmFails OBJECT-TYPE
  SYNTAX  Counter
  ACCESS  read-only
  STATUS  mandatory
  ::= { ip 16 }

ipFragOKs OBJECT-TYPE
  SYNTAX  Counter
  ACCESS  read-only
  STATUS  mandatory
  ::= { ip 17 }

ipFragFails OBJECT-TYPE
  SYNTAX  Counter
  ACCESS  read-only
  STATUS  mandatory
  ::= { ip 18 }

ipFragCreates OBJECT-TYPE
  SYNTAX  Counter
  ACCESS  read-only
  STATUS  mandatory
  ::= { ip 19 }

— the IP Interface table

ipAddrTable OBJECT-TYPE
  SYNTAX  SEQUENCE OF IpAddrEntry
  ACCESS  read-only
  STATUS  mandatory
  ::= { ip 20 }

ipAddrEntry OBJECT-TYPE
  SYNTAX  IpAddrEntry
  ACCESS  read-only
  STATUS  mandatory
  ::= { ipAddrTable 1 }
```

```
IpAddrEntry ::= SEQUENCE {
  ipAdEntAddr
    IpAddress,
  ipAdEntIfIndex
    INTEGER,
  ipAdEntNetMask
    IpAddress,
  ipAdEntBcastAddr
    INTEGER
}

ipAdEntAddr OBJECT-TYPE
  SYNTAX  IpAddress
  ACCESS  read-only
  STATUS  mandatory
  ::=  { ipAddrEntry 1 }

ipAdEntIfIndex OBJECT-TYPE
  SYNTAX  INTEGER
  ACCESS  read-only
  STATUS  mandatory
  ::=  { ipAddrEntry 2 }

ipAdEntNetMask OBJECT-TYPE
  SYNTAX  IpAddress
  ACCESS  read-only
  STATUS  mandatory
  ::=  { ipAddrEntry 3 }

ipAdEntBcastAddr OBJECT-TYPE
  SYNTAX  INTEGER
  ACCESS  read-only
  STATUS  mandatory
  ::= { ipAddrEntry 4 }


- the IP Routing table

ipRoutingTable OBJECT-TYPE
  SYNTAX  SEQUENCE OF IpRouteEntry
  ACCESS  read-write
  STATUS  mandatory
  ::= { ip 21 }

ipRouteEntry OBJECT-TYPE
  SYNTAX  IpRouteEntry
  ACCESS  read-write
  STATUS  mandatory
  ::= { ipRoutingTable 1 }
```

```
IpRouteEntry ::= SEQUENCE {
   ipRouteDest
      IpAddress,
   ipRouteIfIndex
      INTEGER,
   ipRouteMetric1
      INTEGER,
   ipRouteMetric2
      INTEGER,
   ipRouteMetric3
      INTEGER,
   ipRouteMetric4
      INTEGER,
   ipRouteNextHop
      IpAddress,
   ipRouteType
      INTEGER,
   ipRouteProto
      INTEGER,
   ipRouteAge
      INTEGER
}

ipRouteDest OBJECT-TYPE
   SYNTAX   IpAddress
   ACCESS   read-write
   STATUS   mandatory
   ::= { ipRouteEntry 1 }

ipRouteIfIndex  OBJECT-TYPE
   SYNTAX   INTEGER
   ACCESS   read-write
   STATUS   mandatory
   ::= { ipRouteEntry 2 }

ipRouteMetric1 OBJECT-TYPE
   SYNTAX   INTEGER
   ACCESS   read-write
   STATUS   mandatory
   ::= { ipRouteEntry 3 }

ipRouteMetric2 OBJECT-TYPE
   SYNTAX   INTEGER
   ACCESS   read-write
   STATUS   mandatory
   ::= { ipRouteEntry 4 }

ipRouteMetric3 OBJECT-TYPE
   SYNTAX   INTEGER
   ACCESS   read-write
   STATUS   mandatory
   ::= { ipRouteEntry 5 }
```

```
ipRouteMetric4 OBJECT-TYPE
  SYNTAX  INTEGER
  ACCESS  read-write
  STATUS  mandatory
  ::= { ipRouteEntry 6 }

ipRouteNextHop OBJECT-TYPE
  SYNTAX  IpAddress
  ACCESS  read-write
  STATUS  mandatory
  ::= { ipRouteEntry 7 }

ipRouteType OBJECT-TYPE
  SYNTAX  INTEGER {
  other(1),      — none of the following

  invalid(2),    — an invalidated route

                 — route to directly
  direct(3),     — connected (sub-)network

                 — route to a non-local
  remote(4),     — host/network/sub-network
    }
  ACCESS  read-write
  STATUS  mandatory
  ::= { ipRouteEntry 8 }

ipRouteProto OBJECT-TYPE
  SYNTAX  INTEGER {
   other(1),     — none of the following

                 — non-protocol information
                 —   e.g., manually
   local(2),     —   configured entries

                 — set via a network
   netmgmt(3),   —   management protocol

                 — obtained via ICMP,
   icmp(4),      —   e.g., Redirect

                 — the following are
                 — gateway routing protocols
   egp(5),
   ggp(6),
   hello(7),
   rip(8),
   is-is(9),
   es-is(10),
```

```
        ciscoIgrp(11),
        bbnSpfIgp(12),
        oigp(13)
          }
      ACCESS  read-only
      STATUS  mandatory
      ::= { ipRouteEntry 9 }


ipRouteAge OBJECT-TYPE
    SYNTAX  INTEGER
    ACCESS  read-write
    STATUS  mandatory
    ::= { ipRouteEntry 10 }


— the ICMP group

icmpInMsgs OBJECT-TYPE
    SYNTAX  Counter
    ACCESS  read-only
    STATUS  mandatory
    ::= { icmp 1 }


icmpInErrors OBJECT-TYPE
    SYNTAX  Counter
    ACCESS  read-only
    STATUS  mandatory
    ::= { icmp 2 }


icmpInDestUnreachs OBJECT-TYPE
    SYNTAX  Counter

    ACCESS  read-only
    STATUS  mandatory
    ::= { icmp 3 }


icmpInTimeExcds OBJECT-TYPE
    SYNTAX  Counter
    ACCESS  read-only
    STATUS  mandatory
    ::= { icmp 4 }


icmpInParmProbs OBJECT-TYPE
    SYNTAX  Counter
    ACCESS  read-only
    STATUS  mandatory
    ::= { icmp 5 }


icmpInSrcQuenchs OBJECT-TYPE
    SYNTAX  Counter
    ACCESS  read-only
    STATUS  mandatory
    ::= { icmp 6 }
```

```
icmpInRedirects OBJECT-TYPE
  SYNTAX  Counter
  ACCESS  read-only
  STATUS  mandatory
  ::= { icmp 7 }

icmpInEchos OBJECT-TYPE
  SYNTAX  Counter
  ACCESS  read-only
  STATUS  mandatory
  ::= { icmp 8 }

icmpInEchoReps OBJECT-TYPE
  SYNTAX  Counter
  ACCESS  read-only
  STATUS  mandatory
  ::= { icmp 9 }

icmpInTimestamps OBJECT-TYPE
  SYNTAX  Counter
  ACCESS  read-only
  STATUS  mandatory
  ::= { icmp 10 }

icmpInTimestampReps OBJECT-TYPE
  SYNTAX  Counter
  ACCESS  read-only
  STATUS  mandatory
  ::= { icmp 11 }

icmpInAddrMasks OBJECT-TYPE
  SYNTAX  Counter
  ACCESS  read-only
  STATUS  mandatory
  ::= { icmp 12 }

icmpInAddrMaskReps OBJECT-TYPE
  SYNTAX  Counter
  ACCESS  read-only
  STATUS  mandatory
  ::= { icmp 13 }

icmpOutMsgs OBJECT-TYPE
  SYNTAX  Counter
  ACCESS  read-only
  STATUS  mandatory
  ::= { icmp 14 }

icmpOutErrors OBJECT-TYPE
```

```
   SYNTAX  Counter
   ACCESS  read-only
   STATUS  mandatory
   ::= { icmp 15 }

icmpOutDestUnreachs OBJECT-TYPE
   SYNTAX  Counter
   ACCESS  read-only
   STATUS  mandatory
   ::= { icmp 16 }

icmpOutTimeExcds OBJECT-TYPE
   SYNTAX  Counter
   ACCESS  read-only
   STATUS  mandatory
   ::= { icmp 17 }

icmpOutParmProbs OBJECT-TYPE
   SYNTAX  Counter
   ACCESS  read-only
   STATUS  mandatory
   ::= { icmp 18 }

icmpOutSrcQuenchs OBJECT-TYPE
   SYNTAX  Counter
   ACCESS  read-only
   STATUS  mandatory
   ::= { icmp 19 }

icmpOutRedirects OBJECT-TYPE
   SYNTAX  Counter
   ACCESS  read-only
   STATUS  mandatory
   ::= { icmp 20 }

icmpOutEchos OBJECT-TYPE
   SYNTAX  Counter
   ACCESS  read-only
   STATUS  mandatory
   ::= { icmp 21 }

icmpOutEchoReps OBJECT-TYPE
   SYNTAX  Counter
   ACCESS  read-only
   STATUS  mandatory
   ::= { icmp 22 }

icmpOutTimestamps OBJECT-TYPE
   SYNTAX  Counter
   ACCESS  read-only
   STATUS  mandatory
```

```
      ::= { icmp 23 }

icmpOutTimestampReps OBJECT-TYPE
  SYNTAX  Counter
  ACCESS  read-only
  STATUS  mandatory
  ::= { icmp 24 }

icmpOutAddrMasks OBJECT-TYPE
  SYNTAX  Counter
  ACCESS  read-only
  STATUS  mandatory
  ::= { icmp 25 }

icmpOutAddrMaskReps OBJECT-TYPE
  SYNTAX  Counter
  ACCESS  read-only
  STATUS  mandatory
  ::= { icmp 26 }

— the TCP group

tcpRtoAlgorithm OBJECT-TYPE
  SYNTAX  INTEGER {
  other(1),    — none of the following
  constant(2), — a constant rto
  rsre(3),     — MIL-STD-1778, Appendix B
  vanj(4)      — Van Jacobson's algorithm [11]
    }
  ACCESS  read-only
  STATUS  mandatory
  ::= { tcp 1 }

tcpRtoMin OBJECT-TYPE
  SYNTAX  INTEGER
  ACCESS  read-only
  STATUS  mandatory
  ::= { tcp 2 }

tcpRtoMax OBJECT-TYPE
  SYNTAX  INTEGER
  ACCESS  read-only
  STATUS  mandatory
  ::= { tcp 3 }

tcpMaxConn OBJECT-TYPE
  SYNTAX  INTEGER
  ACCESS  read-only
  STATUS  mandatory
  ::= { tcp 4 }
tcpActiveOpens OBJECT-TYPE
```

```
   SYNTAX   Counter
   ACCESS   read-only
   STATUS   mandatory
   ::= { tcp 5 }

tcpPassiveOpens OBJECT-TYPE
   SYNTAX   Counter
   ACCESS   read-only
   STATUS   mandatory
   ::= { tcp 6 }

tcpAttemptFails OBJECT-TYPE
   SYNTAX   Counter
   ACCESS   read-only
   STATUS   mandatory
   ::= { tcp 7 }

tcpEstabResets OBJECT-TYPE
   SYNTAX   Counter
   ACCESS   read-only
   STATUS   mandatory
   ::= { tcp 8 }

tcpCurrEstab OBJECT-TYPE
   SYNTAX   Gauge
   ACCESS   read-only
   STATUS   mandatory
   ::= { tcp 9 }

tcpInSegs OBJECT-TYPE
   SYNTAX   Counter
   ACCESS   read-only
   STATUS   mandatory
   ::= { tcp 10 }

tcpOutSegs OBJECT-TYPE
   SYNTAX   Counter
   ACCESS   read-only
   STATUS   mandatory
   ::= { tcp 11 }

tcpRetransSegs OBJECT-TYPE
   SYNTAX   Counter
   ACCESS   read-only
   STATUS   mandatory
   ::= { tcp 12 }

- the TCP connections table
```

```
tcpConnTable OBJECT-TYPE
  SYNTAX   SEQUENCE OF TcpConnEntry
  ACCESS   read-only
  STATUS   mandatory
  ::= { tcp 13 }

tcpConnEntry OBJECT-TYPE
  SYNTAX   TcpConnEntry
  ACCESS   read-only
  STATUS   mandatory
  ::= { tcpConnTable 1 }

TcpConnEntry ::= SEQUENCE {
  tcpConnState
      INTEGER,
  tcpConnLocalAddress
      IpAddress,
  tcpConnLocalPort
      INTEGER (0..65535),
  tcpConnRemAddress
      IpAddress,
  tcpConnRemPort
      INTEGER (0..65535)
}

tcpConnState OBJECT-TYPE
  SYNTAX   INTEGER {
      closed(1),
      listen(2),
      synSent(3),
      synReceived(4),
      established(5),
      finWait1(6),
      finWait2(7),
      closeWait(8),
      lastAck(9),
      closing(10),
      timeWait(11)
    }
  ACCESS   read-only
  STATUS   mandatory
  ::= { tcpConnEntry 1 }

tcpConnLocalAddress OBJECT-TYPE
  SYNTAX   IpAddress
  ACCESS   read-only
  STATUS   mandatory
  ::= { tcpConnEntry 2 }

tcpConnLocalPort OBJECT-TYPE
  SYNTAX   INTEGER (0..65535)
  ACCESS   read-only
```

```
     STATUS  mandatory
     ::= { tcpConnEntry 3 }

tcpConnRemAddress OBJECT-TYPE
     SYNTAX  IpAddress
     ACCESS  read-only
     STATUS  mandatory
     ::= { tcpConnEntry 4 }

tcpConnRemPort OBJECT-TYPE
     SYNTAX  INTEGER (0..65535)
     ACCESS  read-only
     STATUS  mandatory
     ::= { tcpConnEntry 5 }

- the UDP group

udpInDatagrams OBJECT-TYPE
     SYNTAX  Counter
     ACCESS  read-only
     STATUS  mandatory
     ::= { udp 1 }

udpNoPorts OBJECT-TYPE
     SYNTAX  Counter
     ACCESS  read-only
     STATUS  mandatory
     ::= { udp 2 }

udpInErrors OBJECT-TYPE
     SYNTAX  Counter
     ACCESS  read-only
     STATUS  mandatory
     ::= { udp 3 }

udpOutDatagrams OBJECT-TYPE
     SYNTAX  Counter
     ACCESS  read-only
     STATUS  mandatory
     ::= { udp 4 }

- the EGP group

egpInMsgs OBJECT-TYPE
     SYNTAX  Counter
     ACCESS  read-only
     STATUS  mandatory
     ::= { egp 1 }

egpInErrors OBJECT-TYPE
     SYNTAX  Counter
     ACCESS  read-only
```

```
     STATUS  mandatory
     ::= { egp 2 }

  egpOutMsgs OBJECT-TYPE
     SYNTAX  Counter
     ACCESS  read-only
     STATUS  mandatory
     ::= { egp 3 }

  egpOutErrors OBJECT-TYPE
     SYNTAX  Counter
     ACCESS  read-only
     STATUS  mandatory
     ::= { egp 4 }

  — the EGP Neighbor table

  egpNeighTable OBJECT-TYPE
     SYNTAX   SEQUENCE OF EgpNeighEntry
     ACCESS  read-only
     STATUS  mandatory
     ::= { egp 5 }

  egpNeighEntry OBJECT-TYPE
     SYNTAX  EgpNeighEntry
     ACCESS  read-only
     STATUS  mandatory
     ::= { egpNeighTable 1 }

  EgpNeighEntry ::= SEQUENCE {
     egpNeighState
        INTEGER,
     egpNeighAddr
        IpAddress
  }

  egpNeighState OBJECT-TYPE
     SYNTAX   INTEGER {
         idle(1),
         acquisition(2),
         down(3),
         up(4),
         cease(5)
       }
     ACCESS  read-only
     STATUS  mandatory
     ::= { egpNeighEntry 1 }

  egpNeighAddr OBJECT-TYPE
     SYNTAX  IpAddress
     ACCESS  read-only
     STATUS  mandatory
     ::= { egpNeighEntry 2 }
```

Glossary

A

abstract syntax: a description of a data type that is independent of machine-oriented structures and restrictions.

Abstract Syntax Notation One: the OSI language for describing abstract syntax.

access mode: the level of authorization implied by an SNMP community.

ACK: short for acknowledgment.

acknowledgment: a response sent by a receiver to indicate successful reception of information.

active open: the sequence events that occur when an application entity directs the TCP software to establish a connection.

address class: a method used to determine the boundary between the network and host portions of an IP address.

address mask: a 32-bit quantity indicating which bits in an IP address refer to the network portion.

address resolution: a means for mapping network-layer addresses onto media-specific addresses.

Address Resolution Protocol: the protocol in the Internet suite of protocols used to map IP addresses onto the media address.

administrative framework: a scheme for defining a policy of authentication and authorization.

agent: the SNMP process running on the server end of the exchange. Serving variables to the client Network Management System.

American National Standards Institute: the U.S. national standards body. ANSI is a member of ISO.

ANSI: *see American National Standards Institute.*

AP: *see application process.*

API: *see Application Programmer's Interface.*

application layer: that portion of an OSI system ultimately responsible for managing communication between application processes (APs).

Applications Programmer Interface: a set of calling conventions defining how a service is called by a program or programmer.

ARP: *see Address Resolution Protocol.*

ARPA: Advanced Research Projects Agency now known as DARPA.

authentication entity: that portion of an SNMP agent responsible for verifying that an SNMP entity is a member of the community it claims to be in. This entity is also responsible for encoding/decoding SNMP messages according to the authentication algorithm of a given community.

ARPA: *see Defense Advanced Research Projects Agency.*

ASN.1: *see Abstract Syntax Notation One.*

B

baseband: network technology that uses a single carrier frequency and requires all stations attached to the network to participate.

baud: the number of times per second a signal can change on a transmission line. Transmission lines use two signals so baud rate equals the number of bits per second that can be transferred.

BER: *see Basic Encoding Rules.*

big endian: format with most-significant byte (bit) comes first.

BISYNC: BInary SYNchronous Communication—an early low-level protocol developed by IBM.

broadband: network technology that multiplexes multiple, independent network carriers on a single cable.

broadcast address: a media-specific or IP address referring to all stations on a media.

broadcasting: the act of sending to the broadcast address.

bps: bits per second.

bridge: a computer that connects two or more networks.

C

C: the "C" programming language.

Case Diagram: a pictorial representation of the relationship between counter objects in a MIB.

CCITT: *see International Telephone and Telegraph Consultative Committee.*

checksum: an arithmetic sum used to verify data integrity.

CL-mode: *see connectionless-mode network service.*

CLTS: connectionless-mode transport service.

CMIP: *see Common Management Information Protocol.*

CMIP over TCP: a mapping of the OSI network management framework to management of networks based on the Internet suite of protocols.

CMIS: Common Management Information Service.

CMISE: *see Common Management Information Service Element.*

CMOT: *see CMIP over TCP.*

CO-mode: *see connection-oriented mode.*

Common Management Information Protocol: the OSI protocol for network management.

Common Management Information Service: the service offered by CMIP.

Common Management Information Service Element: the application service element responsible for exchanging network management information.

community: an administrative relationship between SNMP entities.

community name: an opaque string of octets identifying a community.

community profile: that portion of the managed objects on an agent that a member of the community is allowed to manipulate.

connection-less mode: a service that does not provide a handshaking such as to guarantee delivery of data.

connection-oriented mode: a service that has handshaking such that data delivery is guaranteed.

CONS: connection-oriented network service.

COTS: connection-oriented transport service.

D

DARPA: *see Defense Advanced Research Projects Agency.*

DARPA Internet: *see Internet.*

data: the user information.

data link layer: that portion of an OSI system responsible for transmission, framing, and error control over control over a single communications link.

datagram: a self-contained unit of data transmitted independently of other datagrams.

default route: when sending an IP datagram, an entry in the routing table which will be used if no other route is appropriate.

default route: when sending an IP datagram, an entry in the routing table which will be used if no route is appropriate.

Defense Advanced Research Projects Agency: an agency of the U.S. Department of Defense that sponsors high-risk, high-payoff research. The Internet suite of protocols was developed under DARPA auspices. DARPA was previously known as ARPA, the Advanced Research Projects Agency, when the ARPANET was built.

device: a network element of some kind.

direct routing: the process of sending an IP datagram when the destination resides on the same IP network (or IP subnet) as the sender.

dotted quad notation: a convention for writing IP addresses in textual format.

E

EGP: *see Exterior Gateway Protocol.*

end-system: a network device performing functions from all layers of the OSI model. End-systems are commonly thought of as hosting applications.

End-System to Intermediate-System Protocol: the ISO protocol used for gateway detection and address resolution.

end-to-end services: the services collectively offered by the lower three layers of the OSI model.

ES: *see end-system.*

ES-IS: *see End-System to Intermediate-System Protocol.*

experimental MIB: a MIB module defined in the experimental portion of the Internet management space.

Exterior Gateway Protocol: a protocol used by gateways in a multinet network environment to determine that a piece of equipment can be reached.

External Data Representation: a transfer syntax defined by Sun Microsystems, Inc.

F

Federal Research Internet: *see Internet.*

File Transfer Protocol: the application protocol offering file service in the Internet suite of protocols.

FIN: the finish bit in a TCP segment.

flow control: the mechanism whereby a receiver informs a sender how much data it is willing to accept.

fragment: an IP datagram containing only a portion of the user-data from a larger IP datagram.

fragmentation: the process of breaking an IP datagram into smaller parts, such that each fragment can be transmitted in whole on a given physical medium.

frame: packet transmitted across a media.

FTP: *see File Transfer Protocol.*

G

gateway: a router connecting two or more networks.

GOSIP: Government Open Systems Interconnection Profile.

H

hardware address: *see media address.*

header: *see protocol control information.*

HEMS: *see High-level Entity Management System.*

High-level Entity Management System: an early internetwork management experiment.

host: an end-system.

host-identifier: that portion of an IP address corresponding to the host on the IP network.

host-number: that portion of a sub-networked IP address corresponding to the host-number on the subnet.

I

IAB: *see Internet Activities Board.*

IANA: *see Internet Assigned Numbers Authority.*

ICMP: *see Internet Control Message Protocol.*

IEEE: *see Institute of Electrical and Electronics Engineers.*

IESG: *see Internet Engineer Steering Group.*

IETF: *see Internet Engineering Task Force.*

indirect routing: the process of sending an IP datagram to a gateway for forwarding to the final destination.

instance: *see object instance.*

instance-identifier: a means of identifying an instance of a particular object type.

Institute of Electrical and Electronics Engineers: a professional organization, which as a part of its duties to the community, performs some pre-standardization work for OSI.

interface layer: the layer in the Internet suite of protocols responsible for transmission on a single physical network.

intermediate-system: a network device performing functions from the three lower-layers of the OSI model. Intermediate-systems are commonly thought of as routing data for end-systems.

International Organization for Standardization: the organization that produces many of the world's standards. OSI is only one of many areas standardized by the ISO/IEC.

International Telephone and Telegraph Consultative Committee: a body comprising the national Post, Telephone, and Telegraph (PTT) administrations.

Internet: a collection of connected networks, primarily in the United States, running the Internet suite of protocols. Sometimes referred to as the DARPA Internet, NSF/DARPA Internet, or the Federal Research Internet.

Internet Activities Board: the technical body overseeing the development of the Internet suite of protocols.

Internet Assigned Numbers Authority: the entity responsible for assigning numbers in the Internet suite of protocols.

Internet Community: anyone, anywhere, who uses the Internet suite of protocols.

Internet Control Message Protocol: a simple reporting protocol for IP networks.

Internet Drafts: a means of documenting the work in progress of the IETF.

Internet Engineering Steering Group: the group coordinating the activities of the IETF.

Internet Engineering Task Force: a task force of the Internet Activities Board charged with resolving the short-term needs of the Internet.

internet layer: the layer in the Internet suite of protocols responsible for providing transparency over both the topology of the internet and the transmission media used in each physical network.

Internet Protocol: the network protocol offering a connectionless-mode network service in the Internet suite of protocols.

Internet suite of protocols: a collection of computer-communications protocols, originally developed under DARPA sponsorship. The Internet suite of protocols is currently the de facto answer to open systems.

internet: a network—with the Internet being the largest internet in existence.

Internet—standards Network Management Framework: RFC's 1155, 1156, and 1157.

Internet-standard MIB: RFC 1156.

Internet-standard SMI: RFC 1155.

IP address: a 32-bit quantity used to represent a point of attachment to the internet.

ISO Development Environment: a research tool developed to study the upper-layers of OSI.

ISO/IEC: *see International Organization for Standardization.*

ISODE: *see ISO Development Environment.*

K

kernel dive: the process of reading information out of the kernel.

L

LAN: *see local area network.*

LAP/LAPB: modified form of HDLC used as link level protocol for X.25.

layer management entity: in OSI, the instrumentation within a layer which talks to the SMAE.

leaf object: an object type defined in a MIB module which has no child nodes. In particular, tables and rows are not leaf objects.

lexicographic ordering: an ordering methodology.

lightweight presentation protocol: a protocol implementing a minimal OSI presentation service, but doing so using a special-purpose protocol.

LME: *see layer management entity.*

local area network: any one of a number of technologies providing high speed, short delay, with limited geographical size.

LPP: *see lightweight presentation protocol.*

M

managed node: a network device containing a network management agent implementation.

management framework: *see Internet-standard Network Management.*

Management Information Base: a collection of objects that can be accessed via a network management protocol. See Structure of Management Information.

management protocol: *see network management protocol.*

management station: *see network management station.*

maximum transmission unit: the largest amount of user-data that can be sent in a single frame on a particular media.

media address: the address of the physical interface.

media device: a low-level device which does not use a protocol at the internet layer as its primary function.

MIB: *see Management Information Base.*

MIB Module: a collection of managed objects.

MIB view: *see view.*

MIB-I: *see the Internet-standard MIB.*

MIB-II: currently RFC 1158 and RFCs.

MTU: *see maximum transmission unit.*

multi-homed: a host or gateway with more than one attachment to an IP network.

N

National Bureau of Standards: *see National Institute of Standards and Technology.*

National Institute of Standards and Technology: the branch of the U.S. Department of Commerce charged with keeping track of standardization. Previously known as the National Bureau of Standards.

NBS: *see National Institute of Standards and Technology.*

network: a collection of sub-networks connected by intermediate-systems and populated by end-systems.

network byte order: the Internet-standard ordering of the bytes corresponding to numeric values.

network layer: that portion of an OSI system responsible for data transfer across the network, independent of both the media comprising the underlying sub-networks and the topology of those sub-networks.

network management: the technology used to manage an internet.

network management agent: the implementation of a network management protocol which exchanges network management information with a network management station.

network management protocol: the protocol used to convey management information.

network management station: the system responsible for managing a network.

network-identifier: that portion of an IP address corresponding to a network in an Internet.

NIST: *see National Institute of Standards and Technology.*

NMS: *see network management station.*

NSF: National Science Foundation.

NSF/DARPA Internet: *see Internet.*

O

OSI: *see Open Systems Interconnection.*

Open Systems Interconnection: an international effort to facilitate communications among computers of different manufacture and technology.

P

---

passive open: the sequence of events occurring when an application entity informs the TCP that it is willing to accept connections.

PDU: *see protocol data unit.*

PE: *see presentation element.*

physical layer: that portion of an OSI system responsible for the electro-mechanical interface to the communications media.

ping: a program used to used to test IP-level connectivity from one IP address to another.

port number: identifies an application entity to a transport service in the Internet suite of protocols.

presentation element: in the ISODE, a "C" data structure capable of representing any ASN.1 object in a machine independent form.

presentation stream: a set of routines providing an abstraction of elements.

protocol control information: a data object exchanged by machines. It usually contains protocol information as well as data.

protocol data unit: a data object exchanged by machines, containing both protocol and user data.

protocol machine: a finite state machine, that is used to implement a particular protocol.

prototype: object type corresponding to an instance.

PTT: the post, telephone, and telegraph authority.

R

---

reassembly: the process of recombining fragments, at the final destination, into the original protocol packet.

Request for Comments: the document series describing the Internet suite of protocols and related experiments.

RFC: *see Request for Comments*.

router: a piece of software or hardware that directs packets through a network.

RS232: a standard of EIA for serial communications.

S

---

segment: a unit of used in network exchanges.

selector: a portion of an address identifying a particular entity at an address.

service primitive: a method of modeling how a service is requested or accepted by a user.

session layer: that portion of an layered system responsible for adding control mechanisms to a data exchange.

SGMP: *see Simple Gateway Monitoring Protocol*.

Simple Gateway Monitoring Protocol: the predecessor of SNMP.

Simple Gateway Transfer Protocol: the application protocol offering message handling.

Simple Gateway Management Protocol: the application protocol offering network management in the Internet suite of Protocols.

SMAE: *see System Management Application-Entity*.

SMI: *see Structure of Management Information*.

SMTP: *see Simple Mail Transfer Protocol*.

SMUX: *see SNMP Multiplexing Protocol*.

SMUX peer: an application entity which has formed a SMUX association with an SNMP agent.

SNMP: *see Simple Network Management Protocol*.

SNMP Multiplexing Protocol: a local-mechanism used for communication between an SNMP agent and an arbitrary user-process.

SNMP Working Group: the working group of the IETF which standardized the technology used for network management.

SNPA: sub-network point of attachment.

socket: a pairing of an IP address and a port number.

Structure of Management Information: the rules used to define the objects that can be accessed via a network management protocol. see Management Information Base.

subnet: a physical network within an IP network.

subnet mask: a 32-bit quantity indicating which bits in an IP address that particular physical network within an IP network.

sub-network: a single network connecting several nodes on a single transmission media.

SYN: the synchronize bit in a TCP segment.

system management: the OSI name for network management.

system management application-entity: in an OSI system, the process responsible for coordinating between the LMEs and the management protocol.

T

TCP: *see Transmission Control Protocol.*

TCP/IP: *see Internet suite of protocols.*

TELNET: the application protocol offering virtual terminal service.

three-way handshake: a process whereby two protocol entities synchronize during connection establishment.

TLV: tag, length and value.

traceroute: a program used to determine the route taken by a packet across a network.

Transmission Control Protocol: a transport protocol offering a connection oriented transport service.

transport layer: that portion of a layered protocol responsible for reliability and multiplexing of data transfer across a network.

transport-stack: the combination of protocols, at the transport layer and below.

trivial authentication: password-based.

U

UDP: *see User Datagram Protocol.*

upper-layer protocol number: identifies a transport entity to the IP.

URG: the urgent bit in a TCP segment.

urgent data: user-data delivered in sequence but somehow more interesting to the receiving application entity.

User Datagram Protocol: the transport protocol offering a connectionless-mode transport service in the Internet suite of protocols.

user-data: conceptually, the part of a protocol data unit used to transparently communicate information between the users of the protocol.

V

variable: a pairing of an object instance name and associated value.

view: the collection of managed objects realized by an agent which is visible to a community.

W

WAN: *see wide area network.*

well-known port: a transport endpoint which is documented by the IANA.

wide area network: any one of a number of technologies providing geographically distant transfer.

X

X.121: the addressing format used by X.25 based networks.

X.25: a connection-oriented network facility.

X.409: the predecessor to Abstract Syntax Notation One.

XDR: *see External Data Representation.*

Y

yacc: yet another compiler compiler.

Acronyms

AARP—AppleTalk address resolution protocol

ACK—Acknowledgement

ACS—Asynchronous communication server

ACSE—association control service element

AIX—Advanced interactive executive (IBM's UNIX look a like)

ANSI—American National Standards Institute

ARE—All routes explorer

ARP—Address resolution protocol

ARPA—Advanced Research Project Agency

ARPANET—Advanced Research Project Agency Network

ARQ—Automatic Repeat Request

ASE—application-service element

ASN.1—Abstract Syntax Notation One

ATM—Asynchronous transfer mode

BBN—Bolt, Beranek and Newman

BER—basic encoding rules

BNF—Backus - Naur Form

bps—Bits per second

BSC—Binary synchronous communications

BSD—Berkley Software Distribution

BTU—Basic transmission unit

CCITT—International Consultative Committee on Telegraphy and Telephony

CLNP—Connectionless network protocol

CMIP—Common management information protocol

CMIS—Common management information service

CMISE—Common management information service element

CMIP—Common Management Information Protocol

CMIPDU—Common management information protocol data unit

CMOL—CMIP on IEEE 802.2 Logical Link Control

CMOT—Common management information protocol over TCP/IP

CMU—Carnegie-Mellon University

CRC—cyclic-redundancy check

CREN—The Corporation for Research and Educational Networking

DARPA—Defense Advanced Research Projects Agency

DCA—Defense Communication Agency

DCE—Data Communications Equipment

DDN—Defense data network

DDP—Datagram delivery Protocol

DES—data-encryption standard

DIX—Digital , Intel and Xerox

DLC—Data link control

DNS—Domain name server

DSU/CSU—Data service unit/channel service unit

DTE—Data Terminal Equipment

DTR—Data terminal ready

EBCDIC—Extended binary coded decimal interchange code

EGP—external gateway protocol

EIA—Electronic Industry Association

EMA—Enterprise management architecture

ES-IS—end system to intermediate system

FDDI—fiber-distributed data interface

FTP—file-transfer protocol

GOSIP—Government Open Systems Interconnection Profile

HEMS—high-level entity-management system

HDLC—high-level data-link control

HMP—host-monitoring protocol

IAB—Internet Activities Board

ICMP—internet-control message protocol

IEN—Internet Engineering Notes

IETF—Internet Engineering Task Force

IP—internet protocol

IS-IS—intermediate system to intermediate system

ISO—International Organization for Standardization

kbps—Kilo Bits Per Second

LAN—local area network

LLC—Logical link control

LMMS—LAN/MAN management services

LMMU—LAN/MAN management user

LMMPE—LAN/MAN management protocol entity

MAN—metropolitan area network

MD5—Message Digest 5

MIB—management information base

MIT—Massachusetts Institute of Technology

NME—network-management entity

NFS—Network File System

NSAP—network service-access point

NAK—Negative Acknowledgement

NSFNET—National Science Foundation Network

NOC—Network operations center

OO—Object-Oriented

OSI—Open systems interconnection

OSPF—Open shortest path first

PAD—Packet Assembler Disassembler

PDU—Protocol data unit

PING—Packet InterNet Groper

PPP—Point to Point Protocol

RFC—Request for comments

RIP—Routing Information Protocol

RMON—Remote network monitoring

ROSE—Remote-operations-service element

SAP—Service-access point

SDLC—Synchronous Data Link Control

SDU—Service data unit

SGMP—Simple gateway-monitoring protocol

SLIP—Serial Line/IP

SMAE—Systems-management application entity

SMAP—Systems-management application process

SMASE—Systems-management application-service element

SMF—Systems-management function

SMFA—Systems-management functional area

SMI—Structure of management information

SMP—Simple management protocol

SMTP—Simple mail-transfer protocol

SNA—System Network Architecture

SNMP—simple network-management protocol

SNMPv2—simple network-management protocol version 2

TCP—transmission-control protocol

UDP—user datagram protocol

WAN—wide area network

Index

802 model of network management, 26–27

A

ACCESS clause, 91
accounting management, 27
ACTIONS, 67
agents, 25, 26, 32, 34, 55, 56, 66, 149–53
    interface errors and, 105
    proxy, 131–33
    relationship of managers and, 30
agent vendors, 18–19
aggregate error, 123
American National Standards Institute, 18
ANS, 9
API (Application Programming Interface), 147
archival and retrieval of historic data, 31
ASN (Abstract Syntax Notation), 28
ASN.1 (Abstract Syntax Notation One), 64
    terminology and notation, 65
ASN.1 compilers, 79

B

BEDLs (Basic Encoding and Decoding Library), 147
BER (Basic Encoding Rules), 64, 65–66
bilingual managers, 133–34
binding error, 123, 124
books and related writing on SNMP, 13–15
Bosco, Paul, 2, 3
B-Tree (balanced tree structure), 66–67

C

Case, J., 80
CERFNet, 9
Chapin, A. L., 14
CICnet, 9
CMIP (Common Management Information Protocol), 22, 52
    model, 25–27